West's Law School
Advisory Board

PRINCIPLES OF COUNTER–TERRORISM LAW

By

Jimmy Gurulé
Professor of Law,
University of Notre Dame

Geoffrey S. Corn
Associate Professor of Law,
South Texas College of Law

CONCISE HORNBOOK SERIES®

WEST®
A Thomson Reuters business

Mat #40832280

Concise Hornbook Series and Westlaw are trademarks registered in the U.S. Patent and Trademark Office.

© 2011 Thomson Reuters

> 610 Opperman Drive
> St. Paul, MN 55123
> 1–800–313–9378

Printed in the United States of America

ISBN: 978–0–314–20544–5

Preface

Master Sergeant Horvath: "Sir, what are your orders?"

Captain Miller: "We have crossed some strange boundary here; the world has taken a turn to the surreal."

Master Sergeant Horvath: "Clearly, but the question still stands."[1]

In the film *Saving Private Ryan*, this exchange takes place on a bridge in Normandy between Captain Miller (the character played by Tom Hanks who was charged with the mission of finding Private Ryan and bringing him out of hostilities), and Miller's senior non-commissioned officer Master Sergeant Horvath. Miller is trying to decide how to deal with something he never expected: Private Ryan, having been informed of the death of his three brothers, refuses to obey Miller's order to get to the rear and return home and demands to remain in combat to fight alongside his beleaguered and outnumbered comrades as they struggle to hold the critical bridge and protect the allied beachhead. Miller is confronted with the dilemma of how to respond to Ryan's determination *not* to save himself and spare his mother the anguish of possibly losing her fourth son in combat—a situation that no one in the chain of command that ordered the rescue—including General Marshall—had even contemplated.

The sentiment expressed by Captain Miller in the face of a wholly unexpected turn of events is in many ways a parable for the dilemma confronted by the United States following the terrorist attacks of September 11th, 2001. The nation, and in particular the political leadership of the nation, was confronted with the dilemma of how to respond to a threat that had manifested itself in a manner and magnitude that had not been effectively contemplated.[2] On that day, the world indeed did seem to have taken a turn for the surreal, but as Master Sergeant Horvath emphasized to Captain Miller, this in no way obviated the necessity for decisive action. How the United States would respond to the threat of future attacks from international terrorists, and more specifically how domestic and international law influenced that response, is the focus of this text.

1. Saving Private Ryan, (October 8, 1998), http://www.imdb.com/title/tt0120815/.
2. It is of course true that substantial criticism has been leveled at the government for failing to adequately anticipate and prepare for the type of terrorist attacks that occurred on September 11th. Indeed, substantial controversy surrounds the failure to do so. However, this in no way alters the reality that the nation was not prepared for the level of magnitude of these attacks, nor that these attacks came as a tremendous shock to the people and the leaders of the United States and many other countries around the world.

The terror attacks of September 11, 2001 were unquestionably the most effective, destructive, and terrifying in modern history. Although the threat of terrorism was nothing new, never before had a terrorist group inflicted such widespread and catastrophic damage on its selected victim. What made the attacks seem even more remarkable and the day even more surreal was the selected victim—the United States. To the shock and dismay of almost the entire world, the most powerful nation in the world had fallen into the crosshairs of a terrorist plot of unprecedented scope and ferocity.

On September 21, 2001, ten days after the most destructive terrorist attack in United States history, President Bush addressed a Joint Session of Congress. The President placed the American people on notice that the United States would employ every element of national power, including military power, to detect, disable, and defeat the threat of international terrorism:

> On September the 11th, enemies of freedom committed an act of war against our country. Americans have known wars, but for the past 136 years they have been wars on foreign soil, except for one Sunday in 1941. Americans have known the casualties of war, but not at the center of a great city on a peaceful morning. . . .
>
> Americans have known surprise attacks, but never before on thousands of civilians. All of this was brought upon us in a single day, and night fell on a different world, a world where freedom itself is under attack.
>
> Americans have many questions tonight. Americans are asking, "Who attacked our country?"
>
> The evidence we have gathered all points to a collection of loosely affiliated terrorist organizations known as al Qaeda . . .
>
> There are thousands of these terrorists in more than 60 countries.
>
> *Our war on terror begins with al Qaeda, but it does not end there.*
>
> It will not end until every terrorist group of global reach has been found, stopped and defeated.[3]

No other event since the fall of the Berlin Wall and the end of the Cold War has shaped the national security policy of the United States

---

3. *See* Transcript of President Bush's address to a joint session of Congress on Thursday night, September 20, 2001 (emphasis added), *available at:* http://archives.cnn.com/2001/US/09/20/gen.bush.transcript/.

more profoundly than the terror attacks of that tragic day. Almost immediately following these attacks, it became clear that the United States would leverage every instrument of national power to detect, disrupt, and when possible destroy international terrorists and the resources necessary for their operations. This represented a profound philosophical shift in national security policy. On September 10, 2001, the threat of terrorism, while undoubtedly understood as genuine and significant, was viewed almost exclusively through the lens of law enforcement. Criminal investigation and prosecution were the predominant tools in the arsenal of counter-terrorism. Even that term—counter-terrorism—reflected a mentality that terrorism was a reality that had to be managed. By September 12, 2001, that philosophy changed dramatically. Literally overnight terrorism, and in particular international or "transnational" terrorism, had manifested an order of magnitude that justified and necessitated a more proactive and aggressive response—a response intended to not merely counter terrorism, but defeat it. The most significant aspect of this reaction would be the invocation of wartime legal authority to achieve this critical national security objective.

But the attacks of September 11th also revealed two fundamental dilemmas that have and will likely continue to generate legal uncertainty and debate for years to come. First, where does terrorism fit within the continuum of international threats? Second, if certain terrorist threats necessitate the invocation of war powers, where is the line between the law enforcement and the wartime components of this struggle to be properly drawn? The two distinct responses to this threat that defined the pre and post September 11th U.S. policy in many ways reveal an unavoidable reality: transnational terrorism straddles a line between the threat posed by traditional organized criminal activity and that posed by armed, organized, and committed military forces. It is therefore unsurprising that both the law enforcement and military responses to terrorism are almost inevitably doomed to be both under-inclusive and over-broad.

National security involves leveraging every possible component of national power in order to achieve the security objective. The mnemonic DIMEC represents the components of national power that the government seeks to leverage in this process. Each of these letters represents an important source of that power: D for diplomacy; I for intelligence; M for military; E for economic, and C for criminal. Using each of these sources of national power in the effort to disrupt or defeat the terrorist threat is a complex and challenging process. One factor that adds to this complexity is that the use of these components of national power implicates both domestic and international law. The study of terrorism law is therefore the study of how these sources of law authorize or constrain the leveraging of these components of national power, and how policies for the purpose of achieving the objective of protecting the nation from this threat have evolved within this legal framework.

The purpose of this book is to explore the relationship between law and national security policy as it relates to responding to the threat of transnational terrorism. This requires analyzing the U.S. response to this threat through three primary modalities: first, military response; second, criminal law enforcement response; and finally, economic response. Each of these response modalities offers certain advantages and disadvantages in this struggle. More importantly for purposes of this text, each of these modalities implicates a fundamentally different legal framework. How each of these legal frameworks has been understood and applied by the United States to date will be the primary emphasis in the chapters that follow.

Understanding the impact of the law related to the response to terrorism must begin with an understanding of the fundamental difference between a peacetime and wartime exercise of national power.[4] In many ways, these differences came to define both the post September 11th U.S. response to transnational terrorism and the criticisms that response triggered—criticisms that continue to this day.

These two broad legal frameworks involve distinct authorities and obligations. At the most fundamental level, the peacetime legal framework is based on an assumption that respect for the law is the norm, and violation the exception. This assumption drives the entire criminal law model, which is focused on deterring and when necessary punishing the wrongdoer. Deprivations of life and liberty pursuant to this model are therefore always based on individualized justifications. While criminal law has been used to deal with the threat of terrorism since that threat became a reality of the modern strategic environment, its effectiveness has always been stressed by two realities. First, criminal law is fundamentally responsive or reactionary. After the commission of a crime, the alleged offender is apprehended, charged with the relevant criminal offense or offenses, prosecuted, and punished. Second, the ability to prevent terrorism through criminal investigation and prosecution has always been limited to its deterrent effect. Deterrence, however, in relation to terrorism has proven to be of limited effectiveness. In fact, the entire concept of terrorism is often defined by a quite rational decision by terrorist operatives to engage in activities with full knowledge of the risk of criminal sanction or, in the case of suicide bombers, the intention to die for the terrorist cause. Of course, in the latter scenario the threat of criminal punishment has no deterrent value whatsoever. In short, the effectiveness of criminal law as a response to terrorism has been perceived as increasingly strained,

---

4. *See generally* Geoffrey S. Corn, *Mixing Apples and Hand Grenades: The Logical Limit of Applying Human Rights Norms to Armed Conflict* (forthcoming in the Journal of International Legal Studies), *available at*: http://papers.ssrn.com/sol3/papers.cfm?abstract_id=1511954.

particularly by highly organized and well armed terrorist groups like al Qaeda.

The limited effectiveness of normal criminal sanction vis-à-vis terrorists has produced a trend in the United States to adjust criminal laws to be more preventive than responsive. The primary tool in the contemporary criminal law arsenal for dealing with terrorism, the federal offense of providing material support to terrorism, is the principal manifestation of this adjustment. But this has also generated significant questions as to the legitimacy of this law and whether it infringes on fundamental constitutional values including First Amendment freedom of association and Fifth Amendment due process protections. Irrespective of these questions, the increasing reliance on the material support statutes indicates the perceived limits of the traditional crimes for punishing the actual perpetrators of terrorist acts as an effective tool to deal with the terrorist threat.

This offense also reveals another fundamental tenet in the U.S. struggle against terrorism: the recognition that depriving terrorists of resources is essential for success. To that end, another front has gained increasing significance in this battle: the freezing and seizing of financial assets.[5] A robust body of U.S. law now enables the federal government to investigate, track, and freeze or seize assets connected with terrorist organizations. These laws, which will be discussed in detail, involve the coordinated leverage of intelligence, economic, diplomatic, and criminal components of national power. Perhaps the most complex and least understood front in this struggle, any genuine understanding of terrorism law necessitates understanding how the United States uses this power to deny terrorists the resources needed to execute their agenda.

Further, Congress has enacted several important statutes authorizing civil liability for personal injury or death caused by acts of international terrorism. Civil causes of action benefit the victims of terrorism by affording them the remedies of American tort law against the actual perpetrators of terrorist acts as well as their financial sponsors and facilitators. While the prospect of large civil monetary judgments may arguably have minimal or no deterrent value for the actual perpetrators of terrorist attacks, such causes of action may deter secondary actors such as corrupt charities and banks from providing and collecting funds or providing financial services to foreign terrorist organizations. However, as will be discussed in later chapters, plaintiffs face enormous legal obstacles to the enforcement of civil monetary judgments against the aiders and abettors of terrorist acts.

These components of national power were, however, all operative leading up to the terror attacks of September 11th. In spite of this,

---

5. *See* Jimmy Gurulé, Unfunding Terror: The Legal Response to the Financing of Global Terrorism (Edward Elgar 2008).

those attacks led to the almost immediate conclusion that the nation had not fully leveraged its power to protect itself from a terrorist threat of unprecedented proportions. In the weeks and months following September 11th, the United States adopted a radically new approach to dealing with this threat: Terrorism was classified as an "armed attack" triggering the inherent right of self-defense as defined by the Charter of the United Nations. The significance of this classification soon became clear as the United States launched Operation Enduring Freedom, a large-scale military assault on the Taliban forces in control of Afghanistan and the al Qaeda operatives that were using Afghanistan as their safe haven and base of operations.

It soon became apparent that the primary responsibility for dealing with this terrorist threat had shifted from law enforcement agencies to the Department of Defense, and that shift ushered in an entirely new paradigm for defending the nation against the threat of transnational terrorism. Although the military had been used previously in very limited engagements against terrorist base camps, and more commonly in a support role for law enforcement agencies, the United States had never characterized the struggle against terrorism as an armed conflict with all the rights associated with successfully waging war. But when President Bush, followed in close order by Congress, decided to treat this threat as an armed attack and to employ "all necessary force" to respond to this threat, the role of the military ceased to be supportive of law enforcement activities; primacy had clearly shifted to the military response, a response that became an armed conflict in its own right.

The significance of this characterization was profound: the United States had invoked an entirely new legal framework for dealing with the threat of transnational terrorism. By treating the response as an armed conflict, the United States signaled an invocation of the international law of armed conflict (LOAC) as a source of authority to target, detain, and punish the terrorist enemy. Because, however, this body of law had neither contemplated nor accounted for treating a transnational non-state entity as an enemy within an armed conflict framework, the characterization would spawn an avalanche of criticism based on the legal uncertainty associated with trying to fit the proverbial square peg of terrorism into the round LOAC hole. When the United States announced that it was establishing a long-term preventive detention facility in Guantánamo Bay Cuba, it became abundantly clear that the characterization of the struggle against terrorism was in fact directly related to an invocation of legal authority that would enable the United States to take a far more aggressive and preventive approach to the threat.

One of the primary objectives of this book is to expose the reader to the legal issues associated with this characterization, and why these issues produced such controversy. However, it is initially important to

understand the fundamental distinction in the authority available for
the United States to respond to the threat of terrorism implicit in the
characterization of this struggle as an armed conflict. Unlike the
peacetime legal framework, the armed conflict/wartime framework is
based on a different foundation which triggers a package of authorities
related to achieving a fundamentally different effect. The law related to
the regulation of armed conflict is premised on the assumption that an
armed opposition group intends to cause violent harm to a State's
military forces. This in turn produces a presumption of hostility that
justifies resort to force-often times deadly force-as a measure of first
resort. As a result, resort to force during armed conflict is not based on
assessment of whether the object of that force represents an actual
threat, but is instead based on a determination that an individual falls
within the status of enemy belligerent. This presumptive authority to
employ force against individuals determined to be part of armed
opposition groups continues until the individual effectively disasso-
ciates himself from that group, normally through surrender (how this
can be achieved by a terrorist operative remains an elusive question to
this day).

Once opposition personnel are captured, their treatment reveals
another critical distinction between the peacetime legal framework and
the armed conflict legal framework. It is a fundamental tenet of
criminal law that individuals are presumed innocent until proven
guilty beyond a reasonable doubt, and accordingly are presumptively
entitled to liberty unless and until their guilt has been established to
that legal standard. Furthermore both due process and fundamental
human rights law require that individuals alleged to have engaged in
criminal misconduct be promptly charged and that the charges be
adjudicated in a prompt timeframe before an impartial and independent judicial tribunal.

In contrast, individuals captured in the context of an armed
conflict are treated according to a different presumption. Their association with armed opposition groups triggers a presumption of threat
that justifies their preventive detention until hostilities have terminated, or in certain situations until the detaining power is satisfied that
the individual no longer poses a threat of returning to hostilities. In
certain types of armed conflict this presumptive authority to preventively detain is implemented through the concept of prisoner of war
status. But as will be explained in later chapters, this status is reserved
by international law to only certain individuals engaged in certain
types of armed conflicts. The most fundamental requirement of entitlement to prisoner of war status is association with state authority.
Accordingly, individuals detained pursuant to a determination that
they are sufficiently associated with non-state hostile groups are conclusively excluded from prisoner of war status. The question that arose
when U.S. forces began to capture alleged al Qaeda operatives was

whether these individuals could nonetheless be subjected to a LOAC preventive detention regime. For the United States, the answer to this question was never seriously in doubt. What became far more complex however, was whether these non-POW detainees (originally designated unlawful enemy combatants and subsequently re-designated unprivileged belligerents) were entitled to any substantive or procedural protections in relation to their detention, and if so the content of these protections.

In many ways this is a narrative that continues and will continue to be written. Contrary to the hopes of many of the supporters of candidate Obama, President Obama does not appear to be willing to abandon the wartime model for dealing with transnational terrorism. Instead, like his predecessor President Bush, he has continued to invoke all components of national power, including the military component, to deal with differing aspects of the struggle against transnational terrorism. It is therefore apparent that anybody who seeks to gain a genuine understanding of the law related to the struggle against terrorism, and in particular how the United States has and ostensibly will execute operations pursuant to that law, must gain an appreciation of the law that guides the invocation of the four core components of a national power related to this struggle: military, criminal, economic, as well as civil causes of action.

JIMMY GURULÉ
GEOFFREY S. CORN

November 2010

Acknowledgments

Professor Jimmy Gurulé

I would like to compliment an outstanding group of Notre Dame Law students who contributed to the PRINCIPLES OF COUNTER-TERRORISM LAW. I am enormously grateful to Kaitlin Dow (Class of 2011), Jessika Osorio (Class of 2010) and Jennifer Minich (Class of 2010) for their hard work, invaluable research assistance and careful proofreading of book chapters and sections. These students made important contributions to the book. However, special recognition is reserved for Kareem Salem (Class of 2012). Kareem Salem provided tireless technical and research assistance, researching both domestic and international legal sources. He edited and cite-checked footnotes, proofread chapters, and assisted in preparing the Index and Bibliography, always with a positive attitude and professional demeanor. I would also like to thank Chris O'Byrne, Notre Dame Law School research librarian, for his valuable efforts. Chris O'Byrne is amazing, responding to every research request in a highly competent and timely manner. His research is always extensive, thorough and complete. He is a tremendous asset to the Law School. Finally, special thanks and appreciation are extended to my co-author Professor Corn, an expert on the law of armed conflict. He was a pleasure to work with throughout the entire project. This was truly a team effort.

Professor Geoffrey S. Corn

First, I would like to acknowledge the support provided by my co-author. I am immensely indebted to Professor Gurulé for conceiving of this project, inviting me to participate, and offering consistently timely and salient comments on my drafts. Like my co-author, I too owe an enormous debt of gratitude to the tremendous contributions of my research assistants, all students at South Texas College of Law. Without their collective efforts, this project simply would not have come to fruition. Kareem Salem's South Texas counterpart equally entitled to special praise is Jessica Poarch (Class of 2012). Her tireless commitment to supporting this effort was in many ways decisive. However, she was not alone in her efforts, and I simply could not have completed this project without the contributions of Lorne Brook (Class of 2012), Thomas Kelley (Class of 2012), and Nalaka Senaratne (Class 2012). Finally, I would like to especially thank all the outstanding mentors from my days in uniform as an officer in the United States Army. The foundation of knowledge and experience laid during my military career has been by far the most important contributor to my scholarly efforts, and without the challenge form and support of these mentors I know I would not be where I am today.

Summary of Contents

Table of Contents

PART III.   ECONOMIC SANCTIONS

PRINCIPLES OF COUNTER–TERRORISM LAW

Part I
THE MILITARY RESPONSE*

* Portions of this Part are based on the War on Terror and The Law of War: A Military Perspective (Geoffrey S. Corn, ed., Oxford Univ. Press, 2009).

1

Chapter 1

THE LEGAL BASIS FOR THE USE OF FORCE

A. TRANSNATIONAL TERRORISM AS AN "ARMED ATTACK" TRIGGERING THE INHERENT RIGHT OF SELF-DEFENSE

The treatment of terrorism as a threat justifying resort to military force involves application of international law norms regulating both the authority of a state to use military force (the international law concept of *jus ad bellum*), and the manner in which that force may be legally employed (the international law concept of the *jus in bello*).[1] Most of the public debate surrounding the treatment of terrorism as an armed conflict has focused on the latter, which has been particularly stressed by policies related to targeting, detention, and trial of terrorist operatives. An important predicate issue however, is the law related to the treatment of terrorism as an event that justifies use of military force by a state.

The branch of international law defining the authority of states to use military force to achieve national security objectives is known as the *jus ad bellum*.[2] Loosely translated this term refers to the legality of war. In response to the general failure of international law to prevent the outbreak of World War II, the victorious Allies set about to close perceived gaps in the pre-World War II treaty regime created to prohibit the use of aggressive force (the Kellogg–Briand Pact and the League of Nations). These efforts resulted in the use of force framework enshrined in the Charter of the United Nations. Since the creation of the United Nations, this framework has evolved to become a universally accepted standard for legitimate resort to military force by states.[3]

The hallmark of this framework is a prohibition against the aggressive use of military force under all circumstances.[4] But this same prohibition existed prior to the outbreak of World War II and

---

1. Peter Haggenmacher, Grotius et la doctrine de la guerre juste, 250, 597 (Paris, 1983).

2. Giuliano Enriques, *Considerazioni sulla teoria della guerra nel diritto internazionale* [Considerations on the Theory of War in International Law], 7 Rivista di diritto internazionale [Journal

of International Law] 172 (1928) (this was the first use of the words *jus ad bellum*).

3. *See generally* Yoram Dinstein, War, Aggression, and Self-Defense (3d ed. 2001).

4. U.N. Charter art. 2, para. 4.

the drafters of the U.N. Charter clearly understood that the efficacy of any future prohibition would turn on effective enforcement. In addition, they understood that the law must provide authority for states committed to responding to acts of aggression to come to the aid of victim states.[5] Achieving these two objectives came to define the use of force framework that the drafters created. First, the aggressive use of force was explicitly prohibited in article 2 (4) of the Charter.[6] Second, the U.N. Security Council was vested with the authority to authorize use of military force in response to a breach of the peace, an act of aggression, or a threat to international peace and security.[7] Such uses of force would be lawful precisely because they would be conducted for the purpose of restoring international peace and security pursuant to the authority granted by the community of nations through the Security Council. Finally, all states were granted the right to act in individual and collective self-defense in response to an act of aggression committed by a member of the community of nations.[8] This right, enshrined in article 51 of the Charter, has been interpreted to apply not only to actual acts of aggression, but also to imminent threats of aggressive attack.

Determining what constitutes an act of aggression or a threat to international peace and security triggering the individual and collective right of self-defense has always been complex.[9] In 1974, the United Nations General Assembly sought to provide greater clarity on the trigger for acts of individual and collective self-defense by adopting General Assembly Resolution 3314[10] defining aggression. Although General Assembly Resolutions do not bind member states, this definition has been regarded favorably by distinguished *jus belli* scholars[11] and relied on by the International Court of Justice.[12]

Resolution 3314 lists six situations that qualify as aggression:

> (a) The invasion or attack by the armed forces of a State of the territory of another State, or any military occupation, however temporary, resulting from such invasion or

---

5. U.N. Charter arts. 42, 51 (stating that the use of force is only authorized for the purposes of collective or individual self-defense or pursuant to a resolution by the Security Council).

6. *See* U.N. Charter art. 2, para. 4, *supra* note 3.

7. U.N. Charter art. 39.

8. *See* U.N. Charter arts. 42, 51, *supra* note 4.

9. *See generally* YORAM DINSTEIN, WAR, AGGRESSION, AND SELF-DEFENSE (4th ed. 2005).

10. G.A. Res. 3314 (XXIX), annex, U.N. Doc. A/9631 (Dec. 14, 1974).

11. *See, e.g.*, YORAM DINSTEIN, WAR, AGGRESSION, AND SELF-DEFENSE (4th ed. 2005).

12. *See* Case Concerning Military and Paramilitary Activities in and Against Nicaragua, (Nicaragua v. United States of America), 1986 I.C.J. 14, at para. 195 (indicating that the definition of aggression annexed to the Resolution "may be taken to reflect customary international law.").

attack, or any annexation by the use of force of the territory of another State or part thereof,

(b) Bombardment by the armed forces of a State against the territory of another State or the use of any weapons by a State against the territory of another State;

(c) The blockade of the ports or coasts of a State by the armed forces of another State;

(d) An attack by the armed forces of a State on the land, sea or air forces, or marine and air fleets of another State;

(e) The use of armed forces of one State which are within the territory of another State with the agreement of the receiving State, in contravention of the conditions provided for in the agreement or any extension of their presence in such territory beyond the termination of the agreement;

(f) The action of a State in allowing its territory, which it has placed at the disposal of another State, to be used by that other State for perpetrating an act of aggression against a third State;

(g) The sending by or on behalf of a State of armed bands, groups, irregulars or mercenaries, which carry out acts of armed force against another State of such gravity as to amount to the acts listed above, or its substantial involvement therein.[13]

How, if at all, this definition impacts the invocation of individual or collective military action in response to threats or acts of terrorism is a complex question with no simple answers.[14] First, it is

---

13. G.A. Res. 3314 (XXIX), annex, U.N. Doc. A/9631 (Dec. 14, 1974).

14. The recent adoption of a definition of aggression by the Review Conference of the Rome Statute of the International Criminal Court (held in Kampala, Uganda between May 31 and June 11, 2010) adds a potentially new dimension to this analysis. The amendment to Article 8 of the Rome Statute defines aggression as follows:

1. For the purpose of this Statute, "crime of aggression" means the planning, preparation, initiation or execution, by a person in a position effectively to exercise control over or to direct the political or military action of a State, of an act of aggression which, by its character, gravity and scale, constitutes a manifest violation of the Charter of the United Nations.

2. For the purpose of paragraph 1, "act of aggression" means the use of armed force by a State against the sovereignty, territorial integrity or political independence of another State, or in any other manner inconsistent with the Charter of the United Nations. Any of the following acts, regardless of a declaration of war, shall, in accordance with United Nations General Assembly resolution 3314 (XXIX) of 14December 1974...

The Resolution then incorporates the list of acts constituting aggression contained in General Assembly Resolution 3341. *See* Resolution RC/Res.6, *Adopted at the 13th plenary meeting, on 11 June 2010, by consensus (28 June 2010), available at* http://www.icc-cpi.int/

clear that the primary focus of the Resolution is state action, and not the actions of transnational non-state terrorist groups. In fact, it is highly unlikely that the drafters of the Resolution (or more precisely the definition of aggression annexed to the Resolution) seriously contemplated individual or collective response to such a threat. Second, the Resolution itself indicates that the list is non-exhaustive, and that the Security Council may determine other acts constitute aggression (how this impacts the right of individual states to also make such determinations is unclear). Third, the acts listed *presumptively,* but not *conclusively* qualify as aggression. None of these acts fall into that definition when committed pursuant to the inherent right of individual or collective self-defense or pursuant to Security Council authorization. Because, as will be explained below, the United States engages in such conduct only pursuant to an assertion of such authority, determining whether such conduct is *in fact* aggression is contingent on the validity of these assertions.

Adding to this complexity is the simple reality that the terrorist attacks of September 11, 2001 created an entirely new category of controversy surrounding the definition of aggression, the exercise of individual and collective self-defense, and the authority of the Security Council to invoke the collective security authority of the U.N. to respond to the threat of transnational terrorism. How this

iccdocs/asp_docs/Resolutions/RC–Res.6–ENG.pdf.

Assuming the amendment is ratified by the member states, it will not take effect until 2017. Furthermore, the Security Council will play a significant role in any prosecutorial effort. First, the Security Council retains primacy in determining when a state has been the victim of aggression, and may (as in the case of any other crime defined by the Statute) refer the matter to the ICC. However, the ICC prosecutor is vested with authority to initiate an investigation into an allegation of aggression either on her own initiative of in response to a request by a state party. In such situations, if the Security Council has not determined that the alleged incident qualifies as an act of aggression in a period of six months from the time of the request to initiate an investigation, the Prosecutor must obtain authorization from the Court to proceed. The Security Council is authorized to block such an investigation, but doing so requires a Resolution (and therefore the agreement of all permanent members) which must be renewed annually. *Personam* jurisdiction extends only to na-

tionals of a state part that has not opted out of the aggression amendment. *See* Julia Martínez Vivancos, *QUESTIONS & ANSWERS ON THE CRIME OF AGGRESSION AMENDMENT ADOPTED AT THE ICC REVIEW CONFERENCE IN KAMPALA, UGANDA,* The American Non–Governmental Organizations Coalition for the International Criminal Court, (July 22, 2010), *available at* http://www.amicc.org/docs/Aggression QA.pdf.

The potential impact of this amendment on U.S. officials responsible for ordering the execution of counter-terror military operations in the future seems too speculative to really assess at this point. Even assuming the United States accedes to the treaty and therefore becomes subject to the jurisdiction of the Court, how the Security Council and/or prosecutor would interpret such operations is impossible to predict. Nonetheless, the incorporation by the amendment of the Resolution 3314 definition is an important endorsement of the significance of that definition.

controversy is impacted by the *jus ad bellum* is critical to the legitimacy and efficacy of the struggle against terrorism.

B. THE UN CHARTER AND THE RIGHT OF SELF DEFENSE[15]

The international legal regulation of the use of military force by states is founded on a per se prohibition against use of force as a means of achieving a national objective. Article 2 (4) of the Charter of the United Nations provides that "All Members shall refrain in their international relations from the threat or use of force against the territorial integrity or political independence of any state, or in any other manner inconsistent with the purposes of the United Nations."[16] This does not, however, mean that all uses of force are illegal. Instead, the U.N. Charter paradigm is best understood as establishing a presumptive prohibition against the use of force by states against other states. This presumption may be rebutted— that is the use of force is lawful—by two justifications established by the Charter itself. The first justification is when such use is a collective security action authorized by the Security Council pursuant to Chapter VII of the Charter.[17] The second justification is when such use is for the purpose of individual or collective self-defense as recognized in Article 51 of the Charter.[18]

The relationship between these two justifications indicates that while the use of military force is presumptively prohibited, states are entitled to resort to such use for the limited purposes of collective action in response to an act of aggression, breach of the

15. For an excellent summary of the U.N. Charter's use of force legal framework, *see* The Judge Advocate General's Operational Law Handbook, 2007, at Ch. 1 (Legal Basis for the Use of Force). *See also* YORAM DINSTEIN, WAR, AGGRESSION, AND SELF-DEFENSE (3d. ed. 2001).

16. *See* U.N Charter art. 2, para. 4.

17. Article 42 provides:

Should the Security Council consider that measures provided for in Article 41 would be inadequate or have proved to be inadequate, it may take such action by air, sea, or land forces as may be necessary to maintain or restore international peace and security. Such action may include demonstrations, blockade, and other operations by air, sea, or land forces of Members of the United Nations.

U.N. Charter art. 42.

18. Article 51 provides:

Nothing in the present Charter shall impair the inherent right of individual or collective self-defence if an armed attack occurs against a Member of the United Nations, until the Security Council has taken measures necessary to maintain international peace and security. Measures taken by Members in the exercise of this right of self-defence shall be immediately reported to the Security Council and shall not in any way affect the authority and responsibility of the Security Council under the present Charter to take at any time such action as it deems necessary in order to maintain or restore international peace and security.

U.N. Charter art. 51.

peace, or threat to international peace and security; or when defending themselves or other member states against acts of unlawful aggression. The drafters of the United Nations Charter were clearly focused on interstate relationships and the threats to international peace and security resulting from acts of aggression by one state against other states. However, over time the scope of activities determined by the Security Council to qualify as such threats, thereby triggering the Council's collective security authority, have expanded beyond interstate disputes. Mass exodus of refugees across borders, internal armed conflicts, internal acts of genocide, crimes against humanity, and even impunity for violations of international law have provided the basis for the invocation of this collective security authority. This trend reflects the responsiveness of the collective security mechanism to the evolution of the nature of the threats faced by states and the broader international community. In the view of many experts, this collective security authority now extends to the threat to international peace and security resulting from transnational non-state entities such as organized terrorist groups.[19]

Invoking the collective security justification for the use of military force in response to a terrorist attack requires an affirmative determination by the Security Council that the terrorist attack qualifies as a defined trigger for collective action. Article 41 of the U.N. Charter establishes a prerequisite for the authorization of collective action: a Security Council determination that there has been a breach of the peace, act of aggression, or threat to international peace and security.[20] Prior to 9/11, although the Security Council had expanded the range of international crises that fell within the scope of Article 41 and therefore provided justification for collective action (for example humanitarian crises such as those that occurred in Kosovo and Somalia, or mass migrations such as was ongoing in Haiti in 1992), it had never determined that terrorism fell within that category. It was therefore unclear in the wake of those attacks whether the collective security exception to the presumptive prohibition against use of military force could provide a valid legal basis to respond.

That uncertainty was ostensibly eliminated soon after the September 11th terrorist attacks. On September 12, 2001 the Security Council passed Resolution 1368. That Resolution appeared to classify the threat of international terrorism as a threat to international peace and security.[21] Accordingly, the Security Council

19. *See* JEREMY M. SHARP, CONG. RESEARCH SERV., Order Code RS21324, CONGRESSIONAL ACTION ON IRAQ 1990–2002: A COMPILATION OF LEGISLATION (2002).

20. U.N. Charter art. 41.

21. *See generally* S.C. Res. 1368, U.N. Doc. S/RES/1368 (Sept. 12, 2001).

indicated its determination "to combat by all means threats to international peace and security caused by terrorist acts."[22] That same resolution recognized the right of individual and collective self-defense in response to acts of international terrorism, and expressed on behalf of the Security Council "its readiness to take all necessary steps to respond to the terrorist attacks of 11 September 2001, and to combat all forms of terrorism."[23]

While there is some scholarly debate as to whether Resolution 1368 should be properly interpreted as authorizing a military response to international terrorism,[24] the general consensus is that the Resolution was a clear indication that the Security Council considered the threat of international terrorism to trigger one of the exceptions to the presumptive prohibitions against use of military force. Even assuming there is uncertainty as to the overall import of this Resolution, there is virtually no uncertainty as to the interpretation of the United Nations Charter adopted by the United States in the wake of the terrorist attacks. First, the United States was obviously instrumental in bringing Resolution 1368 before the Security Council and in securing its adoption. More importantly, however, was the official notice provided to the Security Council by Ambassador John Negroponte, the US Permanent Representative to the Security Council.

On October 7, 2001 Ambassador Negroponte submitted a letter to the President of the Security Council.[25] In that letter Negroponte noted that:

> In accordance with <u>Article 51 of the Charter of the United Nations</u>, I wish, on behalf of my Government, to report that the United States of America, together with other States, has initiated actions in the exercise of its inherent right of individual and collective self-defense following armed attacks that were carried out against the United States on September 11, 2001.[26]

Negroponte also placed the Security Council on notice as to the scope of the use of force being invoked by the United States pursuant to the Article 51 right of individual and collective self-defense:

> In response to these attacks, and in accordance with the inherent right of individual and collective self-defense, United States armed forces have initiated actions designed to prevent

22. *Id.*

23. *Id.* at ¶ 5.

24. *See* William Michael Reisman, *In Defense of World Public Order*, 95 Am. J. Int'l. L. 833 (2001).

25. *See* Letter from John D. Negroponte to UN Security Council President (Oct. 7, 2001), *available at* http://www.bits.de/public/documents/US_Terrorist_Attacks/negroponte.htm.

26. *Id.*

and deter further attacks on the United States. These actions include measures against Al–Qaeda terrorist training camps and military installations of the Taliban regime in Afghanistan.[27]

This notice was provided in accordance with Article 51 of the Charter which requires member states that invoke the inherent right of self-defense to inform the Security Council of their action and the justification so that the Security Council is afforded the opportunity to effectively assume responsibility for the situation in an effort to restore international peace and security.[28] It is noteworthy that no such assumption of responsibility followed this notification by the United States. Accordingly, not only does this letter clearly manifest interpretation of the inherent right of self-defense invoked by the United States in response to the terror attacks of September 11th, it also suggests that this interpretation was ultimately accepted, at least by acquiescence, by the Security Council.

This is not to suggest that invoking the right of self-defense in response to international terrorism is without controversy. There are many experts who argue that the threat of international terrorism is insufficient to trigger a use of force pursuant to Article 51,[29] or that this threat justifies collective security use of force by the Security Council. These experts focus on the traditional definition of self-defense, which itself focused on traditional military threats, primarily those resulting from state action. Because international terrorist groups do not take the form of traditional military threats, these experts question the legality of an individual or collective military response to terrorism.[30] For them, international terrorism has been and remains a form of international criminal activity to be addressed through cooperative law enforcement.

The nature of the threat, however, has not been the primary focus of controversy in relation to invocation of the right of self-defense to the threat of terrorism. A far more controversial aspect of this invocation has been determining when the threat has reached the requisite self-defense trigger point. Article 51 of the Charter of the United Nations never defined exactly when the right of self-defense could legitimately be invoked by a state. Although the language of the article indicates that the right is triggered in response to an "armed attack," that term has never been interpreted by the international community as to require a state to wait until it has become an actual victim of an attack in order to act in

---

27. *Id.*
28. U.N Charter art. 51.
29. Mary Ellen O'Connell, *The Myth of Preemptive Self–Defense,* The

American Society of International Law Task Force on Terrorism (Aug. 2002).
30. *Id.*

self-defense. Of course, if the state is attacked, that is the clearest case of a legitimate invocation of the article 51 right of self-defense. But what has always been more difficult is determining at what point a State may act to preempt an imminent attack before it occurs.

The controversy surrounding the invocation of the inherent right of self-defense as a preemptive measure certainly predates the threat of international terrorism. Scholars have long debated the triggering criteria for this right. As a general proposition, a requirement of imminence has always been the accepted standard for the legitimate use of force in self-defense.[31] This imminence requirement is directly related to the fact that the authority to act in self-defense is an exception to the presumptive prohibition against use of force. It therefore requires a narrow interpretation of the self-defense exception in order to operate consistently with the overall framework for the use of force established by the U.N. Charter. Accordingly, while preemptive self-defense has and remains an accepted principle in the use of force equation, preventive self-defense has always been perceived as legally invalid.

It was this line between preemption and prevention that proved controversial in the wake of the September 11th terrorist attacks. Responding to an asserted new type of threat to the nation, President Bush began to articulate what later came to be characterized as the Bush doctrine of preemption.[32] According to the President, as reflected in the U.S. National Security Strategy published in 2002, the combination of terrorist capability and access to weapons of mass destruction necessitated a much more aggressive use of military force to eliminate such threats even when they might be in their nascent stage.[33] Accordingly, the inherent right of self-defense was invoked to justify resort to military force to disable terrorist capabilities even before those capabilities manifested themselves in the form of an imminent threat.[34]

This apparent modification of the triggering criteria for the use of military force pursuant to the right of self-defense was widely condemned as invalid. Critics asserted that expanding the scope of self-defense to include preemptive action would open the door to

31. *See generally* Mark L. Rockefeller, *The "Imminent Threat" Requirement for the Use of Preemptive Military Force: is it Time for a Non-temporal Standard?*, DENV. J. INT'L. L. & POL'Y (2004); Anthony C. Arend, *International Law and the Preemptive Use of Military Force*, 26 WASH. Q. 89 (2003).

32. President Bush spoke of "preemption" in a speech on combating terrorism at West Point in May 2002. Mike Allen & Karen DeYoung, *Bush: U.S.*

Will Strike First at Enemies; In West Point Speech, President Lays Out Broader U.S. Policy, WASH. POST, June 2, 2002, at A01.

33. *See, The National Security Strategy of the United States*, (Sept., 2002), *available at* http://georgewbush-whitehouse.archives.gov/nsc/nss/2002/nss3.html

34. *Id.*

acts of aggression cloaked in a disingenuous legal characterization.[35] The degree of criticism generated by the Bush doctrine calls into question whether it significantly altered the traditional imminence requirement for resort to military force in self-defense or whether it will be treated as an aberration and not influence the evolution of this law.

There does, however, seem to be increasing support for the legitimacy of invoking that inherent right in response to an act of terrorism or a threat of a large-scale terrorist attack. A particularly significant indication of this support is provided by NATO's collective response to the September 11th attacks. On September 12, 2001, NATO (for the first time in its history) invoked Article 5 of the NATO treaty authorizing member states to act in the collective self-defense of the United States.[36] There can be no doubt that this invocation was based on a consensus among the alliance partners that the terror attacks qualified as an act of aggression, as Article 5 makes such aggression the *sine qua non* for its invocation:

Article 5

"The Parties agree that an armed attack against one or more of them in Europe or North America shall be considered an attack against them all and consequently they agree that, if such an armed attack occurs, each of them, in exercise of the right of individual or collective self-defence recognized by Article 51 of the Charter of the United Nations, will assist the Party or Parties so attacked by taking forthwith, individually and in concert with the other Parties, such action as it deems necessary, including the use of armed force, to restore and maintain the security of the North Atlantic area.

Any such armed attack and all measures taken as a result thereof shall immediately be reported to the Security Council. Such measures shall be terminated when the Security Council has taken the measures necessary to restore and maintain international peace and security."[37]

It is possible that at the time of this invocation the NATO member states assumed the attacks were executed by a state, thereby diluting the significance of this action in terms of the relationship between terrorism, aggression, and self-defense. This, however,

---

35. *See generally* O'Connell, *The Myth of Preemptive Self–Defense, supra* note 22; Lawrence J. Lee, Mark R. Shulman et al., *The Legality and Constitutionality of the President's Authority to Initiate an Invasion of Iraq,* 41 Colum. J. Transnat'l L. 15 (2002).

36. *See Collective Defence,* NATO, http://www.nato.int/cps/en/SID–85648058–8934EDC9/natolive/topics_59378.htm (last visited Aug. 12, 2010).

37. The North Atlantic Treaty, art. 5, Apr.4, 1949, *available at http://www.nato.int/cps/en/natolive/official_texts_17120.htm.*

seems unlikely. Even on that early date, it was generally assumed the United States had been the victim of terrorist attacks. Even assuming, however, that such uncertainty existed, NATO made no effort to repeal or modify its invocation as responsibility for the attacks became clear in the days and weeks that followed. Accordingly, NATO's action stands as an important milestone not only in the history of the alliance, but also in the understanding of the nature of terrorist violence.

Indeed, this understanding, and the justification for the use of military force derived from it, has been central to the ongoing efforts of the United States to disable or destroy Al Qaeda terrorist networks not only in Afghanistan but in other locations such as Pakistan, Yemen, and Somalia. These ongoing efforts also suggest that even if response to such threats is not characterized as an act of preemption, the very nature of terrorism requires a contextual modification to the concept of imminence. The long-term consequences of the efforts of the United States and other countries, like Israel and Turkey, to defend themselves against the ongoing threat of transnational terrorism through an invocation of the inherent right of self-defense are still evolving. It does seem clear that as states continue to invoke this right to respond to transnational terrorism that it will be increasingly difficult to assert no such right exists in international law.

It is also likely that certain established interpretations of international law and the authority to use force in self-defense will continue to serve as guideposts for states invoking this right in response to the threat of terrorism. The concept of imminence is generally understood to be derived from a centuries-old incident that involved a response by Canadian forces loyal to the Crown against dissident forces seeking to achieve independence.[38] In 1837, the dissident forces took refuge on an island in the Niagara River straddling the border between the United States and Canada. Canadian forces loyal to the Crown launched a raid against the dissident forces, captured a ship called the Caroline from them, and towed it back to a Canadian port where it was burned. The incident triggered a diplomatic dispute between United States and the United Kingdom over the legitimacy of the action directed against the dissident forces in US territory.

The significance of the Caroline incident lies in the principles that provided the foundation for the resolution of the dispute. A series of elements justifying resort to self-defense was enunciated by US Secretary of State Daniel Webster.[39] According to Webster,

---

38. *See* Terence Taylor, *The End of Imminence?*, 27 WASH. Q. 57 (2004).

39. Christopher Greenwood, *International Law and the Pre-emptive Use of Force: Afghanistan, Al–Qaeda, and Iraq,*

employing force for the purpose of self-defense in anticipation of an act of aggression is only justified when the threat is considered instant, overwhelming, and leaving no choice of means, and no moment for deliberation.[40] This definition of imminence has been almost universally accepted as the appropriate criteria for determining when the use of force in self-defense is legally permissible as an anticipatory action.

It is clear that the response to the terror attacks of September 11th, and what came to be known as the Bush doctrine of preemption, went beyond the Caroline imminence principles and called into question the U.S. commitment to those principles. Many critics of the Bush doctrine challenged the assertion that use of force could be justified in self-defense as a preemptive measure. They argued that this was nothing more than a subterfuge to provide legal sanction for preventive military action, an exercise of authority unjustified by the inherent right of self-defense and inconsistent with the U.N. Charter.[41] Others, including the Bush administration, took the position that the nature of the threat of terrorism required a more expansive interpretation of the concept of imminence.

The new administration of President Barak Obama has apparently abandoned the theory of preventive self-defense. However, President Obama has not abandoned the use of military force to attack terrorist operatives outside of the theater of active combat operations in Afghanistan and Iraq. In fact, it is well documented that his administration has significantly increased the number of such attacks, relying on unmanned aerial vehicles (Predator drones) to execute these missions, and the inherent right of self-defense to legally justify them.[42] Whether characterized as preemption or prevention, the outcome seems consistent with the policies of President Bush: the United States will continue to invoke the right of self-defense to justify resort to military force to attack transnational terrorist targets.

The two post September 11th Presidents have not been solely responsible for this invocation of the inherent right of self-defense. Following those attacks, Congress also invoked this right as a legal basis for authorizing the President to use the armed forces of the United States to seek out and destroy or disable transnational terrorist capabilities. In the 2001 Authorization for the Use of

SAN DIEGO INT'L L. J. 7, 12–13 (2003) (quoting letter from Daniel Webster to Henry S. Fox [British ambassador] of April 24, 1842).

40. *Id.*

41. *See The Legality and Constitutionality of the President's Authority to Initiate an Invasion of Iraq, Report*, 41 COLUM. J. TRANSNAT'L L. 15, 21–22 (2002–2003).

42. *See* Kenneth Anderson, *Predators over Pakistan*, THE WEEKLY STANDARD, Mar. 8, 2010, *available at* http://www.weeklystandard.com/print/articles/predators-over-pakistan; *see also* Jane Mayer, *The Predator War*, THE NEW YORKER, Oct. 26, 2009.

Military Force, a Joint Resolution overwhelmingly passed by Congress and a law that remains in effect to this day, Congress noted that the terrorist attacks of September 11th "render it both necessary and appropriate that the United States exercise its rights to self-defense . . . "[43] The Resolution also provides:

> That the President is authorized to use all necessary and appropriate force against those nations, organizations, or persons he determines planned, authorized, committed, or aided the terrorist attacks that occurred on September 11, 2001, or harbored such organizations or persons, in order to prevent any future acts of international terrorism against the United States by such nations, organizations or persons.[44]

This Resolution (which for purposes of the use of military force is essentially synonymous with a declaration of war) leaves absolutely no doubt about the interpretation of international law at the core of the U.S. struggle against transnational terrorism. Congress, the President who signed the Resolution into law, and his successor who continues to rely on it to justify targeting, detaining, and trying terrorist operatives, all believe transnational terrorism justifies a legal right to use military force in self-defense.

C.   WHAT TYPE OF RESPONSE IS PROPORTIONAL?

Another accepted element of the legitimate invocation of the inherent right of self-defense is proportionality.[45] States resorting to military force in response to an actual or imminent threat are obligated to use only the amount of force required to restore the status quo of peace and security.[46] The purpose of this proportionality requirement is clear: to prevent states from exploiting the right of self-defense to transform their response to an act of aggression by exceeding the objective of self-protection.

Like the imminence requirement, there has never been a clear consensus on how to define the proportionality element of a valid exercise of self-defense. The responding state or states are responsible for balancing their legitimate self-defense need with the requirement to minimize the risk of further conflagration. If the use of force system operates ideally, the U.N. Security Council will intervene promptly to assume responsibility for restoring international peace and security. However, this has rarely been the case in practice. Instead, each exercise of self-defense since 1945 has contributed to a body of practice that adds substance to the parameters of the proportionality element.

---

43. Authorization for the Use of Military Force, Pub. L. 107–40, 115 Stat. 224 (2001) [hereinafter AUMF].

44. *Id.*

45. *See* YORAM DISNTEIN, WAR, AGGRESSION, AND SELF-DEFENSE, 192–208 (3d ed. 2001).

46. *Id.* at 208–12.

The response to transnational terrorism adds a new layer of complexity to the analysis of this element. Some experts question the proportionality of the invasion of Afghanistan to oust the Taliban regime in response to the September 11th attacks. However, the fact that a substantial number of nations committed forces in support of this objective—to include non-NATO nations such as Sweden—provides significant evidence in support of the conclusion that this military response was widely considered to be consistent with the requirements of Article 51.[47] The use of military strikes against terrorist operatives outside of Afghanistan (drone attacks) raises a far more complicated issue of proportionality. However, the primary debate surrounding these attacks relates to the predicate issue of whether invocation of the right of self-defense can even extend to such operatives (as discussed above).

D. WHEN IS THE RIGHT TO SELF-DEFENSE EXHAUSTED?

Even assuming that the inherent right of self-defense justifies resort to military force to destroy, disable, or disrupt transnational terrorist networks, another particularly difficult issue is determining when that authority terminates. Article 51 of the United Nations Charter suggests that resort to self-defense, either individual or collective, should be understood as a temporary expedient pending intervention of the Security Council exercising its primary responsibility to maintain international peace and security.[48] Unfortunately practice is rarely consistent with this distribution of authority over the use of military force. Instead, exercises of the right of self-defense has often been met by Security Council inaction, leaving the responding state or states to make their own determination of when the status quo ante has been restored and the authority of self-defense has terminated.

While such determinations have never been simple, determining the point at which an aggressive threat has been neutralized has always been easier when dealing with the conventional state threat then when dealing with unconventional non-state threats. Characterizing transnational terror networks as armed groups triggering the inherent right of self-defense has made this determination even more complicated. The self-proclaimed war on terrorism being conducted by the United States is now the longest war in the nation's history, with no clear end in sight. Indeed, the Supreme Court of the United States in its *Boumediene* decision suggested that individuals captured during the course of this conflict face a genuine prospect of 'generational' detention.[49]

---

47. *See* U.N Charter art. 51; *See also* YORAM DISNTEIN, WAR, AGGRESSION, AND SELF-DEFENSE, 192–208 (3d ed. 2001).

48. *See* U.N Charter art. 51.

49. Boumediene v. Bush, 553 U.S. 723 (2008).

Identifying the point in time when the authority to take military action based on the inherent right of self-defense terminates is obviously critical in relation to the legal rights and obligations triggered by that authority. In the absence of Security Council action to assume responsibility for responding to the threat that triggered the individual or collective self-defense response, it seems difficult to avoid the reality that the responding state is ultimately entrusted with the responsibility to determine when that authority terminates. This in fact may be one of the reasons why there is such widespread hostility to the notion of treating transnational terrorism as a threat justifying resort to self-defense; unlike more traditional military threats, the difficulty in determining when the threat has been neutralized produces an almost inevitable indefinite source of authority to use military force.

The right of self-defense is not, however, an indefinite source of authority. The underlying premise justifying resort to military force as a measure of self-defense is that a state is entitled to defend itself from actual or imminent threat.[50] Doing so operates to restore an environment of international peace and security. Accordingly, the use of force employed pursuant to this authority is justified only so long as it is necessary to protect the state from the triggering threat.

Of course, this raises the most troubling question in relation to determining the endpoint of such justification: how is a state to judge when the threat of a highly dispersed non-state transnational terrorist group has been defeated or degraded sufficiently so that the threat no longer exists at a level justifying resort to military force? There is no clear answer to this question. To date, states like the United States and Israel appear to be treating the threat of transnational terrorism as a threat with no viable end-state or termination point. Indeed, the inability of the state to determine when its actions have eliminated the threat of terrorism is a significant factor relied on by critics of the characterization of terrorism as a military threat triggering the right of self-defense.[51] For these critics the very nature of terrorism falls outside the category of threats triggering the right of self-defense precisely because terrorism defies the traditional methods by which armed opponents are brought to submission. Nonetheless, so long as states continue to invoke the inherent right of self-defense in response to the threat of terrorism, the question of when action in self-defense is no longer justified by virtue of the disabling effect of their military response will remain critical.

---

50. U.N. Charter art. 51.

51. *See* O'Connell, *The Myth of Preemptive Self–Defense, supra* note 29.

E. THE IRAQ WAR AND INTERNATIONAL TERRORISM

The 2003 invasion of Iraq by the U.S. designated 'Coalition of the Willing' raised even more complex imminence and proportionality issues. Although the United States never officially invoked the Article 51 right of self-defense as the exclusive legal basis for the invasion (instead asserting that Security Council resolutions from the first Gulf War of 1991 provided legal authorization), self-defense was always an implicit aspect of the legality equation. In fact, the Authorization for the Use of Force against Iraq enacted by Congress in October of 2002 explicitly included Article 51 as one of a number of asserted sources of legality for the attack.[52]

In the lead up for the invasion, the administration of President Bush continuously emphasized the need to prevent the transfer of weapons of mass destruction from Iraq to al Qaeda.[53] This emphasis clearly exposed the policy—if not legal—invocation of the right of self-defense as a basis for the invasion. This interpretation of Article 51 was at the time and has since been widely condemned as invalid.[54] This condemnation included a statement by then Secretary General of the United Nations Kofi Annan indicating the invasion violated international law.[55] While an extensive discussion of the legality debate is well beyond the scope of this chapter, it does highlight the continuing significance of the imminence and proportionality elements of self-defense.

With regard to the imminence element, most critics of the United States emphasized the fact that the possible threat from the Saddam Hussein regime was too speculative to come close to the type of overwhelming threat necessary to trigger the right of self-defense. The mere fact that the United States was able to seek a Chapter VII authorization from the Security Council for the invasion was seen to corroborate this conclusion. Of course, the Bush Administration adopted a much more expansive interpretation of imminence, one that justified preventive military action. Ultimately, the fact that the Department of State persisted in relying upon the 1991 Gulf War Resolutions as a source of legal authority for the invasion suggests that self-defense was never understood as providing a solid legal basis for the invasion.

52. *See* H.R.J. Res. 114, 107th Cong. (2002).

53. George W. Bush, President of the United States addresses the Nation (Mar. 19, 2003) (transcript available at: http://www.cnn.com/2003/US/03/19/sprj.irq.war.bush.transcript/index.html); *See also* George W. Bush, President of the United States addresses the Nation, "*A Grave and Gathering Danger*" (Sept. 12, 2002) (transcript available at: http://old.nationalreview.com/document/document091202.asp).

54. *See* O'Connell, *The Myth of Preemptive Self–Defense, supra* note 29 at 6.

55. Ewen MacAskill & Julian Borger, *Iraq war was illegal and breached UN charter, says Annan,* THE GUARDIAN, (Sept. 16, 2004),*available at* http://www.guardian.co.uk/world/2004/sep/16/iraq.iraq.

The proportionality element was also problematic for the United States. Many critics, including some traditional military allies, objected to the invasion of a country and the ouster of a regime in response to a threat that they believed could be managed with a far more judicious use of non-military and if necessary military measures. Sanctions, and perhaps even narrowly tailored military strikes were seen as more consistent with the nature of the threat represented by Saddam Hussein's intransigence on the issue of disarmament.

Like so many legal issues related to the military component of the struggle against terrorism, the issue of Iraq is a story that continues to be written. For example, at the date of this writing a formal inquiry into the legality of the invasion is ongoing in the United Kingdom, with many observers anticipating a conclusion at odds with the Bush and Blair interpretations of international law.

F. COLLECTIVE SECURITY IN RESPONSE TO THE THREAT OF TRANSNATIONAL TERRORISM

An alternate potential source of authority to engage in military action against transnational terrorism would be authorization pursuant to Chapter VII of the United Nations Charter.[56] Should the Security Council determine that a terrorist entity constituted a threat to international peace and security, and that peaceful measures would be ineffective in responding to such threat, the Council could authorize member states to employ military force for the purpose of defeating the threat for the purpose of restoring international peace and security.[57] Although the collective security mechanism of the UN Charter was originally conceived to respond to threats to international peace and security resulting from the actions of states, it seems clear that incidents involving non-state entities have also been understood by the Security Council to fall into the category of threats justifying collective action to protect international peace and security.

To date, the Security Council has not acted pursuant to Chapter VII to authorize collective military action in response to a threat created by a terrorist network or terrorist entity. The Security Council Resolution passed immediately following the terrorist attacks of September 11, 2001, while acknowledging the inherent right of self-defense in response to those attacks, did not authorize collective action against Al Qaeda or any other terrorist entity.[58] In fact, at least one distinguished scholar has challenged the interpretation that this Resolution authorized any type of military response

---

56. *See* U.N. Charter art. 39.

57. *Id*. at arts. 40–41.

58. *See* S.C. Res.1368, U.N. Doc. S/RES/1368 (Sept. 12, 2001).

to terrorism.[59] Indeed, it is difficult to conclude with certainty that even the acknowledgment of the Article 51 right of self-defense contained within that Resolution was an acknowledgment that the right of self-defense could be invoked in response to a terrorist network. Instead, it is plausible that the reference to the inherent right of self-defense was focused not exclusively on Al Qaeda, but instead on the state that harbored and sponsored this terrorist threat, namely Afghanistan.[60]

Limiting either collective action or the entire right of self-defense to states determined to provide safe haven or sponsorship for transnational terrorist organizations is certainly less controversial than applying both of those authorities to the terrorist organizations themselves. Consistent with well-established principles of state responsibility, responsibility for terrorist attacks emanating from the state of sponsorship can appropriately be attributed to the sponsoring state for purposes of both collective security and inherent self-defense. Clearly, this is not the interpretation of the Security Council response to the terror attacks of September 11 adopted by the United States. Nonetheless, even an expansive or liberal reading of that resolution does not support the conclusion that it

59. *See, e.g.*, William Michael Reisman, *International Legal Responses to Terrorism*, 22 HOUSTON J. INT'L L. 3, 51–54 (1999).

60. *The Security Council,*

Reaffirming the principles and purposes of the Charter of the United Nations,

Determined to combat by all means threats to international peace and security caused by terrorist acts,

Recognizing the inherent right of individual or collective self-defence in accordance with the Charter,

1. *Unequivocally condemns* in the strongest terms the horrifying terrorist attacks which took place on 11 September 2001 in New York, Washington, D.C. and Pennsylvania and *regards* such acts, like any act of international terrorism, as a threat to international peace and security;

2. *Expresses* its deepest sympathy and condolences to the victims and their families and to the people and Government of the United States of America;

3. *Calls* on all States to work together urgently to bring to justice the perpetrators, organizers and sponsors of these terrorist attacks and *stresses* that those responsible for aiding, supporting or harbouring the perpetrators, organizers and sponsors of these acts will be held accountable;

4. *Calls also* on the international community to redouble their efforts to prevent and suppress terrorist acts including by increased cooperation and full implementation of the relevant international anti-terrorist conventions and Security Council resolutions, in particular resolution 1269 (1999) of 19 October 1999;

5. *Expresses* its readiness to take all necessary steps to respond to the terrorist attacks of 11 September 2001, and to combat all forms of terrorism, in accordance with its responsibilities under the Charter of the United Nations;

6. *Decides* to remain seized of the matter.

S.C. Res.1368, U.N. Doc. S/RES/1368 (Sept. 12, 2001).

represented a Chapter VII authorization for collective security action by the community of nations.

Although the Security Council has yet to invoke the collective security mechanism of the Charter in response to transnational terrorism, such action might offer certain advantages over simply acknowledging the right of member states to act in self-defense in response to terrorist threats. By submitting the response authority to the judgment of the Security Council, the members of the Council would be in a position not only to determine when the terrorist threat justified resort to military action, but also the legitimate scope of such action, and the duration of the authority for military action.

Action by the Security Council in response to a request by a member state or states for authorization to use force in response to a breach of the peace or act of aggression would undoubtedly also implicate existing standards for assessing aggression. Two sources of authority are particularly relevant to such assessment: the decision by the International Court of Justice in the case of *Nicaragua v. United States*,[61] and the U.N. General Assembly Resolution defining aggression. While neither of these sources are binding on the Security Council, they are both widely regarded as articulating accepted principles of law related to aggression and self-defense, and therefore important guideposts.

The ICJ's *Nicaragua* opinion arose out of Nicaragua's allegation that the United States had, *inter alia,* engaged in illegal aggression by mining Nicaraguan harbors, conducting sabotage missions against Nicaraguan ports, oil installations, and a naval base; and provided ongoing support to the *contras,* and internal dissident group challenging the Sandanista government.[62] The United States challenged the jurisdiction of the Court and terminated participation in the proceedings when the Court rejected that challenge. Prior to withdrawing, however, the United States proffered collective self-defense as a theory of legality for the activities directed against Nicaragua.[63] This theory was premised on an assertion that Nicaragua's support for the leftist insurgents in El Salvador amounted to unlawful aggression against that neighboring state, and therefore the United States was legally permitted to engage in conduct in defense of El Salvador.

The Court first concluded that the United States was responsible for laying mines and the alleged acts of sabotage.[64] Accordingly,

61. Case concerning Military and Paramilitary Activities in and Against Nicaragua, (Nicar v. U.S.), 1986 I.C.J. 14 (June 27).

62. Case concerning Military and Paramilitary Activities in and Against Nicaragua, (Nicar v. U.S.), 1986 I.C.J. 14, 22 (June 27).

63. *Id.* at 34.

64. *Id.* at 147.

the Court ruled that these actions did constitute acts of aggression in violation of customary international law.[65] However, the far more significant aspect of the decision relates to the Court's analysis of the relationship between the conduct and sponsorship of non-state dissident forces and the definition of aggression triggering the right of individual and collective self-defense. First, the Court concluded that:

> [i]t may be considered to be agreed that an armed attack must be understood as including not merely action by regular armed forces across an international border, but also "sending by or on behalf of a State of armed bands, groups, irregulars or mercenaries, which carry out acts of armed force against another State of such gravity as to amount to (*inter alia*) an actual armed attack conducted by regular forces, "or substantial involvement therein."[66]

Accordingly, the decision supports the invocation of the inherent right of self-defense in response to an act of aggression by both regular armed forces of another state *and* paramilitary forces acting as an agent or on behalf of a state. This therefore supported individual and collective action against Afghanistan based on a legitimated determination Afghanistan bore state responsibility for the conduct of the al Qaeda terrorists who committed the September 11th attacks. Furthermore, although the decision did not address the relationship between non-state paramilitary activities and the inherent right of self-defense, the fact that the Court concluded military action by paramilitary forces can qualify as aggression bolsters the U.S. theory of self-defense in response to the attacks of September 11th.

The Court also addressed the level of state sponsorship of paramilitary activities necessary for the attribution of those activities to the state.[67] This issue was relevant to both the assertion that the United States had committed acts of aggression against Nicaragua (by supporting the *contras*), and the assertion that armed activities against Nicaragua directed or supported by the United States were justified as collective self-defense in response to Nicaraguan aggression towards El Salvador (by supporting the FMLN leftist insurgents in El Salvador). The Court concluded that it

> . . . does not believe that the concept of 'armed attack' includes not only acts by armed bands where such acts occur on a significant scale but also assistance to rebels in the form of the provision of weapons or logistical or other

65. *Id.* at 103.
66. *Id.* at 195.
67. *Id.* at 104.

support. Such assistance may be regarded as a threat or use of force, or amount to intervention in the internal or external affairs of other States.[68]

Thus, the Court drew a demarcation line between the use of paramilitary (or irregular) forces as a state proxy, with their hostilities effectively directed by the state and logistical provision (including military logistics such as weapons and ammunition) to such forces.[69] According to the Court, only the former category qualified as aggression triggering the inherent right of individual and collective self-defense.

Based on this demarcation, the Court concluded that U.S. support for the *contras* rose to the level of aggression, because this support included "organizing or encouraging the organization of irregular forces or armed bands . . . for incursion into the territory of another state".[70] In contrast, the Court rejected the assertion that Nicaraguan support for the FMLN in El Salvador qualified as an act of aggression. Specifically, the Court found that:

> . . . between July 1979 and the early months of 1981, an intermittent flow of arms was routed via the territory of Nicaragua to the armed opposition in that country. The Court was not however satisfied that assistance has reached the Salvadorian armed opposition, on a scale of any significance, since the early months of 1981, or that the Government of Nicaragua was responsible for any flow of arms at either period. Even assuming that the supply of arms to the opposition in El Salvador could be treated as imputable to the Government of Nicaragua, to justify invocation of the right of collective self-defence in customary international law, it would have to be equated with an armed attack by Nicaragua on El Salvador.[71]

Although the ICJ's analysis focused exclusively on state sponsorship of paramilitary or irregular forces and how that sponsorship triggers the right of self-defense, it must be considered instructive on the response to acts of violence by transnational terrorist groups. The Court's decision arguably establishes a criterion for determining what level of state sponsorship and support justifies attribution of terrorist violence to the state. If this is true, any state invoking the inherent right of self-defense to use force against another state based on a sponsorship theory—such as the international use of force against Afghanistan based on al Qaeda sponsorship—must establish support more analogous to command and control than simply logistics. This is obviously a significant consid-

---

68. *Id.* at 106.

69. *Id.* at 106–7.

70. *Id.* at para. 228.

71. *Id.* at para. 230.

eration for states such as Israel that face a continuing threat of terrorist violence facilitated by support from other states. It is unclear, however, whether the nature of the military logistics support might have produced a different outcome from the ICJ. Specifically, would the provision of such support qualify as aggression if the weapons provided the capability to inflict mass destruction? While the ICJ's opinion did not include any such qualifier because those facts were not before the Court, this factor might lead states to assert a different interpretation of aggression.

The decision also has potential significance in relation to the contemporary U.S. practice of drone attacks directed against suspected terrorist operatives outside of an area of traditional combat operations. Such attacks implicate a combination of *jus ad bellum* and *jus in bello* issues. It arguably provides a framework for defining what activities should properly be considered belligerent in nature and therefore provide a basis for the invocation of the inherent right of self-defense to engage in such attacks. By distinguishing logistics support from operational control of irregular forces, the decision provides potential support for the use of such attacks against individuals exercising operational command and control over transnational terrorist operatives. However, it also calls into serious question the legality of directing such attacks against individuals providing logistical support to terrorist operatives, such as financiers and terrorist recruiters.

Another aspect of the Court's decision that may become significant in future U.S. efforts to disable terrorist operatives with military force, was the Court's response to the U.S. invocation of the right of collective self-defense. While the Court acknowledged that customary international law recognizes the right of states to respond to acts of aggression collectively, it rejected the U.S. invocation of that right. This rejection was based not only on the determination that Nicaraguan support for the FMLN did not rise to the level of aggression, but also on the conclusion that El Salvador had not reacted to the Nicaraguan activity by invoking its inherent right of individual self-defense. In essence, the Court concluded that state cannot act in collective self-defense unless and until the protected victim invokes that right.[72]

Should the U.S. determine in the future that a terrorist group is threatening the stability of another state, it would be difficult to sustain a claim of collective self-defense to use force against that group unless the state being assisted treated the terrorist activity as an act of aggression. This may be irrelevant in response to a purely internal threat, in which case U.S. intervention would require consent of the state, or perhaps a sufficient showing that the

---

72. *Id.* at para. 222–23.

terrorist group posed an imminent threat to the United States. However, by treating the conduct of transnational terrorist groups as triggers for the right of self-defense, the United States has opened this proverbial Pandora's box of applying use of force doctrines developed with a focus on state responsibility to threats that act independently of the type of state sponsorship so central to the ICJ's decision.

G. CONCLUSION

Characterizing terrorism as an armed attack has profound legal consequences. The first of these consequences is that the victim state may consider the act of terrorism as an event triggering the inherent right of individual or collective self-defense. State action pursuant to this authority will itself trigger a legal framework fundamentally distinct from the normal law enforcement framework historically relied on to deal with terrorism. As a result, use of military power will likely follow such a characterization, and that use will involve an exercise of state power that would be considered legally prohibited pursuant to a law enforcement legal framework, allowing for deprivations of life, liberty, and property in a manner inconsistent with peacetime legal authorities. The U.S. response to the terror attacks of September 11th provide the quintessential example of how characterizing terrorism as a threat justifying resort to the use of force in self-defense produces significant second and third order legal consequences for both the state actors engaged in response and the individuals they encounter during their counter terror operations. It is therefore unsurprising that such an approach to the threat of terrorism has and will continue to generate substantial criticism and legal opposition. Nonetheless, it seems impossible to ignore the reality that for some states and the international community invoking the right of self-defense in response to the threat of transnational terrorism will remain an important option for protecting national security.

Chapter 2

TRIGGERING THE LAW OF ARMED CONFLICT

A. THE PRE 9/11 PERCEPTION OF MILITARY COUNTER–TERROR OPERATIONS

Prior to the terrorist attacks of September 11, 2001, response to international terrorism was viewed almost exclusively as an exercise of law enforcement authority. A number of terrorist attacks had been directed against U.S. military targets (for example, the U.S.S. Cole in Yemen), and the U.S. had employed military assets to strike at terrorist capabilities on at least one occasion (a missile attack against al Qaeda base camps in Afghanistan and suspected chemical weapons facility in Sudan). Nonetheless, the use of military combat power to destroy or disable terrorist capabilities was an exceptional event as law enforcement efforts to apprehend and try alleged terrorists remained the primary tool in the U.S. counter-terrorism arsenal.[1]

This did not mean the military played no role in U.S. counter-terrorism efforts. The military took substantial steps to protect itself from the threat of terrorism, actions that fell collectively under the category of force protection.[2] But these actions did not involve offensive efforts to locate and destroy or disable terrorist capabilities. Instead, they were (and remain) better understood as defensive measures implemented to reduce the vulnerability of U.S. forces.[3] The military also routinely conducted missions in support of law enforcement efforts. Such missions, characterized as military support to law enforcement, involve provision of logistics, intelligence, training, communication, transport, and other support to civilian law enforcement agencies. Unlike traditional combat opera-

---

1. *See* RAPHAEL PERL, CONG. RESEARCH SERV., Order Code IB10119, TERRORISM AND NATIONAL SECURITY: ISSUES AND TRENDS (2004), *available at www.fas.org/ irp/*crs/IB10119.pdf.

2. The Department of Defense Dictionary defines force protection as:

> Preventive measures taken to mitigate hostile actions against Department of Defense personnel (to include family members), resources, facilities, and critical information. Force pro-

tection does not include actions to defeat the enemy or protect against accidents, weather, or disease.

See Chairman of the Joint Chiefs of Staff Joint Publication 1–02, Department of Defense Dictionary of Military and Associated Terms, (12 April 2001(As Amended Through April 2010)) *available at* http://www.dtic.mil/doctrine/ new_pubs/jp1_02.pdf.

3. *Id.*

tions, these missions do not involve a lead role or responsibility for the military.[4]

Although this support role generally defined the use of national military capabilities to respond to the threat of terrorism, there were exceptions involving direct military action against terrorist capability even before September 11th.[5] The U.S. response to the attack on the United States embassies in Kenya and Tanzania is the most significant example that is publically known. Based on a determination of al Qaeda responsibility for these bombings, President Clinton ordered a cruise missile attack against suspected training facilities in Afghanistan and a suspected chemical weapons plant in Sudan, Operation Infinite Reach.[6] The United States invoked the inherent right of self-defense as a legal justification for this action, signaling a potential shift in paradigm from the traditional law enforcement approach to military counter-terror efforts.[7] However, there was no significant follow on operations of similar character that were made known to the public. Even assuming other covert military operations were directed against terrorist capabilities during this same time period, the use of the military in direct action as a primary response to terrorism certainly remained the exception and not the rule.

B. THE POST 9/11 RESPONSE AND THE INVOCATION OF THE LAW OF ARMED CONFLICT

The U.S. approach to the military role in counter-terrorism changed radically in the days and weeks following September 11th, 2001. The scale, intensity, and destructive effect of those attacks led the President,[8] followed soon thereafter by Congress,[9] to invoke the war powers of the nation as the primary modality for protecting the nation against future attacks. Almost immediately following the

---

4. *See* Operational Law Handbook 426–434, (John Rawcliffe ed. The Judge Advocate General's Legal Center & School, U.S. Army) (2007) *available at* http://www.fas.org/irp/doddir/army/law 2007.pdf; *see also* The Judge Advocate General's Domestic Operational Law Handbook (DOPLAW) for Judge Advocates (Volume I), 2006, at Ch. 2.

5. *See, e.g.* William S. Cohen, Statement to The National Commission On Terrorist Attacks Upon the United States, (Mar. 23, 2004), *available at* http://www.9–11commission.gov/ hearings/hearing8/cohen_statement.pdf.

6. Jan Kittrich, *Can Self–Defense Serve as an Appropriate Tool Against International Terrorism?*, 61 Me. L. Rev. 133, 162–63 (2009); *see also* National Commission on Terrorist Attacks upon the United States. (Philip Zelikow, Exec-

utive Director; Bonnie D. Jenkins, Counsel; Ernest R. May, Senior Advisor). *The 9/11 Commission Report.* New York: W.W. Norton & Company, 2004.

7. *See* William J. Clinton, U.S. President, Address to the Nation by the President, (Aug. 20, 1998), *available at* http://clinton6.nara.gov/1998/08/1998– 08–20–president-address-to-the-nation. html.

8. *See Transcript of President Bush's address to a joint session of Congress on Thursday night, September 20, 2001*, (Sept. 21, 2001, 2:27AM), http:// archives.cnn.com/2001/US/09/20/gen. bush.transcript/.

9. *See* Authorization for Use of Military Force, Pub. L. No. 107–40, 115 Stat. 224 (2001).

attacks, the Secretary of Defense began to articulate to the public the far more robust role that would be assumed by the armed forces in this effort. These statements, along with those of the President and other high level government officials indicated that the military response would not be subordinate to a primary law enforcement effort. Nor would the military response be limited to striking al Qaida's state sponsor in Afghanistan. Instead, the nation would embark upon a military campaign of global reach, the scope of which was defined by the newly coined designation of a Global War on Terrorism.[10] This new approach to protecting national security and disrupting and defeating the threat of transnational terrorism was articulated in the National Security Strategy of 2002:

> The struggle against global terrorism is different from any other war in our history. It will be fought on many fronts against a particularly elusive enemy over an extended period of time. Progress will come through the persistent accumulation of successes—some seen, some unseen.

> Today our enemies have seen the results of what civilized nations can, and will, do against regimes that harbor, support, and use terrorism to achieve their political goals. Afghanistan has been liberated; coalition forces continue to hunt down the Taliban and al-Qaida. But it is not only this battlefield on which we will engage terrorists. Thousands of trained terrorists remain at large with cells in North America, South America, Europe, Africa, the Middle East, and across Asia.

> *Our priority will be first to disrupt and destroy terrorist organizations of global reach* and attack their leadership; command, control, and communications; material support; and finances. This will have a disabling effect upon the terrorists' ability to plan and operate.[11]

Any doubt about the transformation in the U.S. approach to defending itself against transnational terrorism was eliminated when the President issued his order establishing the military commissions. On November 13, 2001, President Bush issued Military Order #1 titled "Detention, Treatment and Trial of Certain Non–Citizens in the War Against Terrorism." In that Order, the President determined that:

10. *See generally The National Security Strategy*, WHITEHOUSE.GOV (Sept. 2002), http://georgewbush-whitehouse.archives.gov/nsc/nss/2002/; *see also Establishing the Global War on Terrorism Medals*, WHITEHOUSE.GOV (Mar. 20, 2003), http://georgewbush-whitehouse.archives.gov/news/releases/2003/03/20030312–6.html.

11. *The National Security Strategy: III. Strengthen Alliances to Defeat Global Terrorism and Work to Prevent Attacks Against Us and Our Friends*, WHITEHOUSE.GOV (Sept. 2002), http://georgewbush-whitehouse.archives.gov/nsc/nss/2002/nss3.html.(emphasis added).

> International terrorists, including members of al Qaida, have carried out attacks on United States diplomatic and military personnel and facilities abroad and on citizens and property within the United States on a scale that has created a state of armed conflict that requires the use of the United States Armed Forces.[12]

With this determination, the President indicated that the United States would invoke the law of armed conflict as the source of authority to detain and punish (and by implication attack and kill) terrorist operatives and protect the nation from the continuing and global threat of international terrorism. By that time, the U.S. was engaged is a large scale military campaign in Afghanistan directed against both al Qaeda capabilities and the Taliban government that provided the safe haven and support for those forces. These operations reflected a fundamentally different role for the military than the support to law enforcement that defined its pre-September 11th participation in counter-terror efforts: terrorism was no longer to be regarded as a law enforcement challenge requiring periodic military support; terrorism was an armed hostile threat to the nation requiring the employment of the full spectrum of combat capability.

The President's decision to characterize the struggle against terrorism as an armed conflict and invoke the war powers of the nation in response was endorsed by Congress. In fact, this endorsement occurred even before the President's explicit enunciation of the existence of an armed conflict in Military Order #1. On September 18, 2001, Congress passed a Joint Resolution titled "An Authorization of the Use of Military Force" (AUMF) and authorizing "the use of United States Armed Forces against those responsible for the recent attacks launched against the United States."[13] This Resolution explicitly authorized the President to "use all necessary and appropriate force against those nations, organizations, or persons he determines planned, authorized, committed, or aided the terrorist attacks that occurred on September 11, 2001, or harbored such organizations or persons, in order to prevent any future acts of international terrorism against the United States by such nations, organizations or persons."[14] The only limitation in scope of the authority granted to the President to respond to the threat of international terrorism with the full military force of the nation was that the response be limited to individuals, organiza-

---

12. Detention, Treatment, and Trial of Certain Non–Citizens in the War Against Terrorism, 60 Fed. Reg. 57833, 57833 (Nov. 16, 2001).

13. Authorization for Use of Military Force, Pub. L. No. 107–40, 115 Stat. 224, 224 (2001).

14. *Id.*

tions, and states determined by the President to be responsible for the September 11th attacks.[15]

This Resolution, which as of the date of publication of this text remains in force, serves as an explicit invocation of the war powers vested by the Constitution in the Congress. Although Article I, Section 8 of the Constitution vests Congress with the power to declare war and grant letters of Marque and Reprisal, joint resolutions authorizing the use of military forces have become the contemporary method used by Congress to exercise its war authorization power.[16] Since the end of the Second World War, similar join resolutions have been used by Congress to provide express legislative support for the conflict in Vietnam, both conflicts in Iraq, and even contentious peacekeeping missions in Lebanon and Somalia.[17] Furthermore, Congress is fully aware that these joint resolutions authorizing the use of military force are considered "functional equivalents" of declarations of war for purposes of determining the constitutional authority of the President to wage war. In fact, even the War Powers Act, a law passed at the height of congressional assertiveness of its war authorizations role, explicitly provides that a joint resolution fully satisfies the constitutional requirement of legislative authorization for the President to wage war.[18] This has also been an interpretation of the constitutional effect of statutory authorizations to wage war that has been consistently embraced by the judiciary.[19]

The AUMF enacted by Congress following the September 11th attacks reflects the congressional decision to invoke the broadest possible legal basis for military action directed against al Qaeda and its state sponsors. Within the AUMF Congress indicated that a military response to the terrorist attacks was justified both as an act of self-defense and pursuant to the authorization itself. This was somewhat confusing because, assuming a military response was a legitimate act of self-defense, no express statutory authorization would be necessary to conduct a response from a constitutional perspective. In the *Prize Cases*, the Supreme Court established what has become a well accepted precedent that when war is thrust upon the nation the president is not only authorized but obligated to meet force with force.[20] In light of this, it is likely Congress sought to indicate in the strongest terms its express support for the

---

15. *Id.*

16. *See* DAVID ACKERMAN, CONG. RESEARCH SERV., Order Code RS21009, RESPONSE TO TERRORISM: LEGAL ASPECTS OF THE USE OF MILITARY FORCE(2001), *available at* http://www.au.af.mil/au/awc/awcgate/crs/rs21009.pdf.

17. *Id.* at 1–2.

18. *See* War Powers Resolution, 50 U.S.C. §§ 1541–1548 (2).

19. *See* Orlando v. Laird, 443 F.2d 1039 (1971); Holtzman v. Schlesinger, 484 F.2d 1307 (1973)

20. The Brig Amy Warwick (The Prize Cases), 67 U.S. (2 Black) 635, 668 (1863).

continuing prosecution of a war initiated pursuant to the president's inherent defense of authority, with the full employment of military capability to achieve the national security objectives defined by the President.[21] Two things are certain: first, there can be no doubt that since the date of enactment of the AUMF, both President Bush and President Obama have exercised war powers pursuant to the collective war-making authority vested in the two political branches of the national government. Second, this collective war-making effort was and remains in direct response to the perceived ongoing threat presented to the nation by transnational terrorism.

During the initial phases of the military operation launched against the terrorist threat in Afghanistan, there was some uncertainty as to whether the United States considered itself in an armed conflict with the terrorist entity al Qaeda or in the alternative the state of Afghanistan with operations directed against al Qaeda merely subsidiary. In fact, since the inception of these military operations many experts have taken the position that it is impossible for the United States to be engaged in armed conflict with the transnational non-state entity, and that the struggle against al Qaeda was in fact and must be subordinated to the broader armed conflict in Afghanistan (initially between United States and the government of Afghanistan, and subsequently between United States forces operating in support of the legitimate Afghan government against a variety of dissident forces in that country).[22]

From an international law perspective it was almost inevitable that the U.S. theory of a global armed conflict against terrorism would be rejected in light of the prevailing restrictive interpretation of the scope of the armed conflict. As will be explained in more detail below, international law—and specifically the law of armed conflict (LOAC)—had not contemplated the possibility of what the United States characterizes a global war on terror, or non-interna-

---

21. Indicating that the military response was a justified act of self-defense seems to have also been intended by Congress to link this statutory authorization for the conduct of hostilities against al Qaeda to the international legal framework for the use of force. By invoking the right of self-defense and referencing article 51 of the United Nations charter, Congress was signaling its belief that military action directed against transnational terrorism was a proper exercise of the inherent right of self-defense enshrined in the United Nations charter.

22. *See* International Law Association, Use of Force Committee, Final Report on the Meaning of Armed Conflict in International Law, 25–28 (2010), *available at* http://www.ila-hq.org/en/committees/index.cfm/cid/1022; *See, e.g.,* Mary Ellen O'Connell, *Defining Armed Conflict*, 13 J. CONFLICT & SEC. L. 393 (Winter 2008); Gabor Rona, *Interesting Times for International Humanitarian Law: Challenges from the "War on Terror"*,Fletcher Forum of World Affairs, vol. 27:2, (Summer/Fall 2003) *available at* http://www.icrc.org/Web/eng/siteeng0.nsf/htmlall/5PWELF/$File/Rona_terror.pdf.

tional armed conflict of global scope. Accordingly, in an effort to characterize the nature of the military operations launched by the United States in a manner that was consistent with the then existing understandings of international law related to the use of force, many experts rejected the suggestion that the United States was engaged in a distinct, global armed conflict with al Qaeda, concluding that the use of LOAC authority against al Qaeda must be confined to armed conflicts in Afghanistan and Iraq.[23]

It seems clear, however, that the United States viewed its post September 11th military response to terrorism as involving two distinct armed conflicts: one against the Taliban regime of Afghanistan in response to its support for Al Qaeda, and the other against Al Qaeda itself. This bifurcated conflict policy was implicit in the global war terminology consistently invoked by the Bush administration.[24] It was also implicit in the AUMF which, while certainly authorizing military action against the Taliban regime, did not limit the scope of the authorization to that objective. It has also been manifested in the scope of counter-terror military attacks conducted by the United States since September 11th, many of which have been conducted outside Afghanistan.

One such attack—conducted against suspected al Qaeda operatives in Yemen[25]—generated an exchange between the United Nations Human Rights Commission and the U.S. representative to the Commission that led to an explicit enunciation of the U.S. view of the struggle against al Qaeda. In response to the drone attack, the Commission queried the United States on how the killing could be justified pursuant to international human rights law. In response, the U.S. representative indicated that the Commission lacked jurisdiction over the matter because the action fell under the regulatory framework of the law of armed conflict, and not human rights law. According to the response:

> [i]nternational terrorists, including members of Al Qaida [sic], have carried out attacks on United States diplomatic

23. Gabor Rona, *When is a war not a war?—The proper role of the law of armed conflict in the "global war on terror"*, "International Action to Prevent and Combat Terrorism"—Workshop on the Protection of Human Rights While Countering Terrorism, Copenhagen, 15–16 March 2004—Presentation given by Gabor Rona, Legal Adviser at the ICRC's Legal Division, *available at* http://www.icrc.org/Web/Eng/siteeng0.nsf/iwpList575/3C2914F52152E565C1256E60005C84C0 (last accessed 10 August, 2010).

24. *See* Geoffrey S. Corn, *Making the Case for Conflict Bifurcation in Afghanistan: Transnational Armed Conflict, Al Qaida, and the Limits of the Associated Militia Concept, International Law Studies (U.S. Naval War College), Vol. 85, 2009* (republished in the Israeli Yearbook of Human Rights).

25. *See* Dana Priest, CIA Killed U.S. Citizen In Yemen Missile Strike: Action's Legality, Effectiveness Questioned, Washington Post, (Nov. 8, 2002), *available at:* http://www.commondreams.org/headlines02/1108–05.htm

and military personnel and facilities abroad and on citizens and property within the United States on a scale that has created a state of armed conflict that requires the use of the United States Armed Forces.[26]

The notable absence of any linkage to the armed conflict with Afghanistan in this response is an early and explicit indication that the United States considered itself engaged in an armed conflict of potential global scope with Al Qaeda. A more recent indication of this position is contained in the Obama Administration's reply brief to the ongoing Guantanamo litigation it inherited from the Bush Administration. In support of its position that preventive detention of terrorist operatives at Guantanamo remains justified pursuant to the law of armed conflict, the government noted: that "The laws of war have evolved primarily in the context of international armed conflicts between the armed forces of nation states. This body of law, however, is less well-codified with respect to our current, novel type of armed conflict against armed groups such as al-Qaida and the Taliban."[27]

It is therefore difficult to dispute the conclusion that both the President and the Congress adopted a fundamentally different approach to the use of military power to defend the nation against transnational terrorism in the wake of the September 11th attacks. Subsequent decisions by the Supreme Court would complete the trilogy of tri-branch endorsement of an armed conflict characterization of this struggle.

C. UNDERSTANDING THE TRIGGERING MECHANISM FOR APPLICATION OF THE LAW OF ARMED CONFLICT[28]

To understand why characterizing the struggle against al Qaeda as an armed conflict sparked such controversy requires an understanding of the generally accepted Geneva Convention based law triggering standard. This standard is based on Common Articles 2 and 3 of these four treaties to the Geneva Convention. Common Article 2 defines the triggering event for application of the full corpus of the LOAC: international armed conflict.[29] Common

26. UN Econ. & Soc. Council, Comm'n on Human Rights, *Civil and Political Rights, Including the Questions of: Disappearances and Summary Executions,* 3, U.N. Doc. E/CN.4/2003/G/80 (Apr. 22, 2003).

27. Respondent's Memorandum Regarding the Government's Detention Authority Relative to Detainees Held at Guantanamo Bay, *In Re Guantanamo Bay Detainee Litigation,* Misc. No. 08–442 (TFH), 1 (D.D.C.), *available at*

http://www.wcl.american.edu/nimj/documents/BatesRevisedDetAuthFINAL.pdf?rd=1

28. This section, with light edits, is based on Geoffrey S. Corn, *Hamdan, Lebanon, and the Regulation of Armed Conflict: The Need to Recognize a Hybrid Category of Armed Conflict,* 40 VAND. J. TRANSNAT'L L 295 (2007).

29. *See* Geneva Convention for the Amelioration of the Condition of the Wounded and Sick in Armed Forces in

Article 3, in contrast, provides that the basic principle of humane treatment is applicable in non-international armed conflicts occurring in the territory of a signatory state.[30] Although neither of these treaty provisions explicitly indicates that they serve as the exclusive trigger for LOAC applicability, they rapidly evolved to have such an effect.[31] As a result, these two treaty provisions have been long

the Field, Aug. 12, 1949, T.I.A.S. 3362, art. 2; Geneva Convention for the Amelioration of the Condition of Wounded, Sick, and Shipwrecked Members at Sea, Aug. 12, 1949, T.I.A.S. 3363, art. 2; Geneva Convention Relative to the Treatment of Prisoners of War, Aug. 12, 1949, T.I.A.S. 3364 art. 2; Geneva Convention Relative to the Treatment of Civilian Persons in Time of War, August 12, 1949, T.I.A.S. 3365, art. 2 Each of these Conventions includes the following identical article In addition to the provisions which shall be implemented in peacetime, the present Convention shall apply to all cases of declared war or of any other armed conflict which may arise between two or more of the High Contracting Parties, even if the state of war is not recognized by one of them. The Convention shall also apply to all cases of partial or total occupation of the territory of a High Contracting Party, even if the said occupation meets with no armed resistance.

30. *See* Geneva Convention for the Amelioration of the Condition of the Wounded and Sick in Armed Forces in the Field, Aug. 12, 1949, T.I.A.S. 3362, art. 3; Geneva Convention for the Amelioration of the Condition of Wounded, Sick, and Shipwrecked Members at Sea, Aug. 12, 1949, T.I.A.S. 3363, art. 3; Geneva Convention Relative to the Treatment of Prisoners of War, Aug. 12, 1949, T.I.A.S. 3364 art. 3; Geneva Convention Relative to the Treatment of Civilian Persons in Time of War, Aug. 12, 1949, T.I.A.S. 3365, art. 3. Each of these Conventions includes the following identical article:

In the case of armed conflict not of an international character occurring in the territory of one of the High Contracting Parties, each Party to the conflict shall be bound to apply, as a minimum, the following provisions:

(1) Persons taking no active part in the hostilities, including members of armed forces who

have laid down their arms and those placed 'hors de combat' by sickness, wounds, detention, or any other cause, shall in all circumstances be treated humanely, without any adverse distinction founded on race, colour, religion or faith, sex, birth or wealth, or any other similar criteria.

31. *See* INT'L & OPERATIONAL LAW DEP'T, THE JUDGE ADVOCATE GENERAL'S LEGAL CENTER & SCHOOL, THE LAW OF WAR DESKBOOK, at Chapter 3 (2000); *see also* UK Ministry of Defense, *The Manual for the Law of Armed Conflict,* Oxford University Press (2004), at Para. 3.1; International Committee of the Red Cross, *What is International Humanitarian Law,* Advisory Service on International Humanitarian Law, (07/2004), *available at http://www. icrc.org/Web/eng/siteeng0.nsf/iwpList104/ 707D6551B17F0910C1256B66005B30B 3.* This fact sheet clearly reflects the international/internal evolution of the triggering paradigm:

International humanitarian law distinguishes between international and non-international armed conflict.

International armed conflicts are those in which at least two States are involved. They are subject to a wide range of rules, including those set out in the four Geneva Conventions and Additional Protocol I.

Non-international armed conflicts are those restricted to the territory of a single State, involving either regular armed forces fighting groups of armed dissidents, or armed groups fighting each other. A more limited range of rules apply to internal armed conflicts and are laid down in Article 3

3a3

understood as establishing the definitive LOAC triggering paradigm. In accordance with this paradigm, application of the LOAC has always been contingent on two fundamental factors: first, the existence of armed conflict; second, the nature of the armed conflict.[32]

The first of these triggering requirements is the existence of armed conflict. Although this is the most fundamental requirement for application of the LOAC, there is no definitive test for assessing when a situation amounts to armed conflict (a term undefined by the express language of either Common Articles 2 or 3). However, the International Committee of the Red Cross (ICRC) Commentary to these articles, widely considered as an authoritative interpretation of the Conventions, has traditionally been relied on to illuminate the meaning of armed conflict.[33] This Commentary provides several factors for assessing the existence of armed conflict, today widely regarded as the most authoritative and effective criteria for making such a determination.[34]

In relation to the existence of armed conflict between the armed forces of two or more states, the use of force by opposing regular armed forces makes the determination fairly straightforward. The Commentary indicates that the two principle concerns that motivated the adoption of the armed conflict trigger *vis a vis* inter-state conflict were concerns of law avoidance by refusal to acknowledge a state of war, and a concern that brevity/lack of intensity of such hostilities would lead to denial of the existence of a situation triggering LOAC humanitarian protections.[35] Both of

common to the four Geneva Conventions as well as in Additional Protocol II.

Id.

32. *See* Jeff A. Bovarnick, Law of War Deskbook, 39–40, 69–71 (Int'l and Operational Law Dep't, The U.S. Army Judge Advocate General's Legal Center and School Charlottesville, VA 2010), *available at* http://www.fas.org/irp/doddir/army/deskbook.pdf.

33. *See* Commentary, Convention (I) for the Amelioration of the Condition of the Wounded and Sick in Armed Forces in the Field. Geneva, 12 August 1949 (Jean S. Pictet ed., 1960), at 19–23. A similar Commentary was published for each of the four Geneva Conventions. However, because Articles 2 and 3—or *common*—to each Convention, the Commentary for these articles is also identical in each of the four Commentaries.

34. *See* INT'L & OPERATIONAL LAW DEP'T, THE JUDGE ADVOCATE

GENERAL'S LEGAL CENTER & SCHOOL, THE LAW OF WAR DESKBOOK, at Chapter 3 (2000). The International Criminal Tribunal for the Former Yugoslavia, while not explicitly relying on these criteria, nonetheless followed the general logic reflected therein when it determined in the first opinion addressing the jurisdiction of the Tribunal that "an armed conflict exists whenever there is a resort to armed force between States or protracted armed violence between governmental authorities and organized armed groups or between such groups within a State." *See also* Prosecutor v. Tadic, Case No. IT–94–1–AR72, Appeal on Jurisdiction (Oct. 2, 1995), at para. 70, *reprinted in* 35 I.L.M. 32 (1996).

35. *See* Commentary, Convention (I) for the Amelioration of the Condition of the Wounded and Sick in Armed Forces in the Field. Geneva, 12 August 1949 (Jean S. Pictet ed., 1960), at 32 ("It makes no difference how long the

these concerns grew out of the pre–1949 experience. With regard to the first concern, the very term "armed conflict" was adopted as a trigger for LOAC applicability for the specific purpose of emphasizing that such application must be triggered by *de facto* hostilities and not *de jure* war.[36] As for the second concern, the Commentary emphasizes that the existence of international armed conflict is in no way effected by the scope, duration, or intensity of hostilities. Instead, the term armed conflict was intended to apply to *de facto* hostilities no matter how brief or non-destructive they might be.[37] When such hostilities occurred between the regular armed forces of two states, the armed conflict prong of the triggering test for LOAC application would be satisfied.[38]

Determining the meaning of armed conflict in the non-international context has been more difficult. The key concern addressed by the ICRC Commentary in relation to this context was identifying the line between internal civil disturbances—situations subject to domestic legal regimes—and internal armed conflicts—situations triggering application of the humane treatment obligation of common article 3 to the four Geneva Conventions.[39] As the Commentary emphasizes, there is no single factor that establishes this demarcation line. Instead, a number of factors, when considered in any combination or even individually, were proposed to assess when a situation rises above the level of internal disturbance and moves into the realm of armed conflict.[40] Of the numerous factors offered by the Commentary, perhaps the most instructive was the focus on the state response to the threat: when a state resorts to the use of regular (and by regular it is fair to presume that the Commentary refers to combat) armed forces, the situation has most likely crossed the threshold into the realm of armed conflict.[41]

---

conflict lasts, or how much slaughter takes place. The respect due to human personality is not measured by the number of victims.").

36. *Id.*

37. *Id.*

38. An example of this application concept was the capture of U.S. Army personnel by Serbia after they had strayed across the Macedonia/Serbia border while participating in a United Nations authorized peacekeeping mission in Macedonia. Although neither the U.S. nor Serbia asserted a state of war existed, and although the confrontation between the U.S. forces and Serbian armed forces was brief and involved very little violence, the U.S. asserted the three soldiers were Prisoners of War by operation of the Geneva Convention Relative to the Protection of Prisoners of War because the confrontation in which they were captured qualified as an international armed conflict. *See* Geoffrey S. Corn, *To Be or Not To Be, That is the Question: Contemporary Military Operations and the Status of Captured Personnel,* 1999 Army Law. 1, 17 (1999); (cited in. Jennifer K. Elsea, Cong. Research Serv., Order Code PL31367, Treatment of "Battlefield Detainees" in the War on Terrorism (2007)).

39. *See* Commentary, Convention (I) for the Amelioration of the Condition of the Wounded and Sick in Armed Forces in the Field. Geneva, 12 August 1949 (Jean S. Pictet ed., 1960), at 49–50.

40. *Id.*

41. *Id.*

Although applying this armed conflict prong of the Common Article 2/3 conflict classification paradigm has not been without controversy, the ICRC Commentary criteria have proved remarkably effective in practice. For example, short duration/small scale hostilities between states have been treated as falling into the category of armed conflict, such as when the U.S. Naval pilot Lieutenant Bobby Goodman was shot down by Syrian forces while flying a mission in relation to the U.S. peacekeeping presence in Lebanon in 1982.[42] Even in the non-international context, resort to the use of regular armed forces for sustained operations against internal dissident groups that cannot be suppressed with only law enforcement capabilities makes it difficult for a state to credibly disavow the existence of armed conflict.

This is not, however, the exclusive analytical aspect of the Common Article 2/3 law triggering standard. It is the second consideration of this standard—the nature of the armed conflict—that links the extent of LOAC application to the character—international or non-international—of a given armed conflict. As noted above, pursuant to the structure of the Geneva Conventions, international armed conflicts within the meaning of common article 2 trigger the full corpus of LOAC regulation.[43] In contrast, non-international armed conflicts trigger a less comprehensive body of regulation: the humane treatment mandate of common article 3, in certain situations the rules of Additional Protocol II to the Geneva Conventions, and customary LOAC norms applicable to all armed conflicts.[44]

Because there is no defined meaning of "international" or "non-international" in articles 2 or 3, uncertainty continues in relation to application of this prong of the LOAC trigger.[45] As a

---

42. Interview Mr. W. Hays Parks, a senior attorney for the Defense Department and recognized expert on the law of armed conflict. Mr. Parks was personally involved in developing the United States position on the status of Lieutenant Goodman and indicated during the interview that the United States asserted prisoner of war status for Goodman as a matter of law due to the existence of an "armed conflict" between the United States and Syria within the meaning of Common Article 2.

43. *See, e.g.* U.K. Ministry of Defense, *The Manual for the Law of Armed Conflict,* Oxford University Press (2004), at para. 2.1; *see also* Int'l & Operational Law Dept, The Judge Advocate General's Legal Center & School, The Law of War Deskbook, at Ch. 3 (2000).

44. *See* Leslie C. Green, THE CONTEMPORARY LAW OF ARMED CONFLICT, at 59–61 (2d Ed.) (2000); *see also* INT'L & OPERATIONAL LAW DEP'T, Int'l & Operational Law Dept, The Judge Advocate General's Legal Center & School, The Law of War Deskbook, at Ch. 3 (2007).

45. *See generally* Adam Roberts, *Counter Terrorism, Armed Forces and the Laws of War,* Survival (quarterly journal of IISS, London), vol.44, no.1, (Spring 2002); *see also* JENNIFER ELSEA, CONG. RESEARCH SERV., Order Code RL31191, TERRORISM AND THE LAWS OF WAR: TRYING TERRORISTS AS WAR CRIMINALS BEFORE MILITARY COMMISSIONS (2001) (analyzing whether the attacks of September 11, 2001 triggered the law of war).

result, reliance on the ICRC Commentary is common when seeking to provide meaning to these terms. With regard to international armed conflict, the Commentary makes the existence of a dispute between states the dispositive consideration.[46] While this has been a generally effective *de facto* criterion, it has not eliminated all uncertainty related to when the use of armed force by one state in the territory of another state is the product of such a dispute, thereby triggering the law applicable to international armed conflicts. Such uncertainty emerges when the intervening state disavows the existence of a "dispute" as the predicate for the intervention.[47]

This "hostilities without dispute" theory was clearly manifest in the 2006 armed conflict in Lebanon, where neither Israel nor Lebanon took the position that the hostilities fell into the category of international armed conflict.[48] However, this was not the first example of use of such a theory to avoid the acknowledgement of an international armed conflict. In fact, the United States intervention in Panama in 1989 represents perhaps the quintessential example of this theory of 'applicability avoidance' due to the absence of the requisite dispute between nations. Executed to remove General Manuel Noriega from power in Panama and destroy the Panamanian Defense Force—the regular armed forces of Panama,[49] "Operation Just Cause" involved the use of more than twenty thousand U.S. forces who engaged in intense combat with the Panamanian Defense Forces.[50] Nonetheless, the United States asserted that the conflict did not qualify as an international armed conflict within the meaning of common article 2. The basis for this assertion was that General Noriega was not the legitimate leader of Panama, therefore the U.S. dispute with him did not qualify as a dispute with Panama.[51] Although the U.S. Federal District Court that adjudicated Noriega's claim to prisoner of war status ultimately

46. *See* Commentary, Convention (I) for the Amelioration of the Condition of the Wounded and Sick in Armed Forces in the Field. Geneva, 12 August 1949 (Jean S. Pictet ed., 1960), at 32.

47. *See, e.g.* United States v. Noriega, 808 F.Supp. 791, 794 (S. D. Fla.1992) (addressing and rejecting the U.S. assertion that the intervention in Panama to topple General Noriega did not qualify as an international armed conflict because the United States had been invited to intervene by Guillermo Endara, the democratically elected President of Panama).

48. *See* Pierre Tristam, *The 2006 Lebanon War: Israel and Hezbollah Square Off*, ABOUT.COM, http://middleeast. about.com/od/lebanon/a/me070918.htm (lasted cisited Aug. 11, 2010); *see also Security Council Calls for and End to Hostilities Between Hizbollah, Israel, Unanimously Adoption Resolution 1701*, U.N. Security Council, (Aug. 11, 2006), http://www.un.org/News/Press/docs/2006/sc8808.doc.htm (indicating that Hizbollah and not Lebanon was responsible for the attacks).

49. Thomas Donnelly, Margaret Roth, Caleb Baker, Operation Just Cause: The Storming of Panama (1991).

50. *Id.*

51. *See* United States v. Noriega, 808 F.Supp. 791, 794 (S. D. Fla.1992).

rejected this assertion,[52] it is not the only example of the emphasis of a lack of a dispute between states as a basis for denying the existence of a common article 2 conflict.[53]

Thus, despite the best efforts of the drafters of the Geneva Conventions to prevent law avoidance by adopting a *de facto* standard for determining the existence of international armed conflicts, uncertainty in coverage has remained problematic. This aspect of determining LOAC applicability has, however, had virtually no impact on analysis of conflicts like that between states and non-state groups (such as terrorist organizations). This is because there is no plausible basis to conclude that such combat operations, although manifesting all the classic indicia of armed conflicts, involve disputes between states. Instead, it is the uncertainty related to whether the transnational geographic scope of operations excludes them from the definition of non-international—with the accordant uncertainty as to what law such combat operations trigger—that has generated the greatest regulatory challenge in relation to combat operations against terrorist operatives.

The inclusion of common article 3 in the revision of the Geneva Conventions in 1949 represented the first interjection by treaty of international humanitarian regulation into the realm of non-international armed conflicts.[54] This was without question a landmark development in the regulation of hostilities. It is undeniable that the scope of the obligation imposed by common article 3 was minimal, and in fact regarded by the ICRC Commentary as essen-

---

52. *Id.*

53. A similar rationale was relied upon to conclude that combat operations conducted by U.S. forces in Somalia during Operation Provide Comfort did not result in an international armed conflict. *See generally* Ctr. for Law & Military Operations (CLAMO) & The Judge Advocate Gen.'s Sch., CLAMO Report: The Marines Have Landed at CLAMO (1998).

54. *See* Commentary, Convention (I) for the Amelioration of the Condition of the Wounded and Sick in Armed Forces in the Field. Geneva, 12 August 1949 (Jean S. Pictet ed., 1960), at 38. According to the Commentary:

> This Article is common to all four of the Geneva Conventions of 1949, and is one of their most important Articles. It marks a new step forward in the unceasing development of the idea on which the Red

Cross is based, and in the embodiment of that idea in the form of international obligations. It is an almost unhoped for extension of Article 2 above. Born on the battlefield, the Red Cross called into being the First Geneva Convention to protect wounded or sick military personnel. Extending its solicitude little by little to other categories of war victims, in logical application of its fundamental principle, it pointed the way, first to the revision of the original Convention, and then to the extension of legal protection in turn to prisoners of war and civilians. The same logical process could not fail to lead to the idea of applying the principle to all cases of armed conflicts, including those of an internal character.

Id.

tially redundant with peacetime human rights principles.[55] None-theless, because the conflicts subject to this provision of international law fell within what was at that time regarded as the exclusive realm of state sovereignty, the development was regarded as a major step forward in humanitarian regulation of conflict.[56]

The first step in understanding this component of the LOAC application equation is to understand the origins of common article 3. Responsive primarily to the brutal civil wars that ravaged Spain, Russia, and other states during the years between the two world wars, this trigger for application of this baseline humanitarian provision has historically been understood to include only one type of non-international armed conflict: internal (or intra-state).[57] Accordingly, during the five plus decades between 1949 and 2001, the term non-international evolved to become synonymous with internal. This most likely can be attributed to a combination of two factors: the original motivation leading to the development of common article 3 (the concern over civil wars); and the qualifying language indicating that common article 3 applies only to non-international armed conflicts occurring within the territory of a High Contracting Party.[58] Although this 'within the territory' qualifier became increasingly less meaningful as the Geneva Conventions progressed rapidly towards their current status of universal participation, it is difficult to ignore the logical impact of this term in the context of 1949: that it limited the scope of application of this "mini convention" to true intra-state conflicts.[59] However,

55. *Id.*

56. *See* COMMENTARY ON THE ADDITIONAL PROTOCOLS OF 8 JUNE 1977 TO THE GENEVA CONVENTIONS OF 12 AUGUST 1949, (Yves Sandoz et al. eds., 1987).

57. *See, e.g.* U.K. Ministry of Defense, *The Manual for the Law of Armed Conflict,* Oxford University Press (2004), at Para. 2.1; *see also* Int'l & Operational Law Dept, The Judge Advocate General's Legal Center & School, The Law of War Deskbook, at Ch. 3 (2000).

58. *Id.*

59. This point was relied upon by the Department of Justice Office of Legal Counsel in the first law of war applicability analysis provided to the President after the attacks of September 11, 2001:

Common article 3 compliments Common Article 2. Article 2 applies to cases of declared war or of any other armed conflict that may arise between two or more of the High Contracting Parties, even if the state of war is not recognized by one

of them. Common article 3, however, covers "armed conflict not of an international character"—a war that does not involve cross-border attacks—that occurs within the territory of one of the High Contracting Parties.

Common article 3's text provides substantial reason to think that it refers specifically to a condition of civil war, or a large-scale armed conflict between a State and an armed movement within its own territory. First, the test of the provision refers specifically to an armed conflict that a) is not of an international character, and b) occurs in the territory of a state party to the Convention. It does not sweep in all armed conflicts, nor does it address a gap left by Common Article 2 for international armed conflicts that involve non-state entities (such as an international terrorist organization) as parties to the conflict. Further, Common Article 3 addresses

nowhere does the article expressly use 'internal' as the indicator of the type of armed conflict triggering its humanitarian mandate. Instead, common article 3 expressly indicates that its substantive protections are applicable to all conflicts "not of an international character".[60]

This original understanding of common article 3, coupled with the reality that the vast majority of non-international armed conflicts between 1949 and 2001 were predominantly intra-state, resulted in an "either/or" LOAC triggering paradigm: armed conflicts falling under the definition of international within the meaning of common article 2 of the Geneva Conventions would trigger the entire corpus of the LOAC. In contrast, intra-state, or internal armed conflicts—those between a state and internal dissident forces—would trigger the far more limited corpus of LOAC regulation, including common article 3.[61] This paradigm is reflected in the following excerpt from a presentation by the ICRC Legal Adviser:

> Humanitarian law recognizes two categories of armed conflict—international and non-international. Generally, when a State resorts to force against another State (for example, when the "war on terror" involves such use of force, as in the recent U.S. and allied invasion of Afghanistan) the international law of international armed conflict applies. When the "war on terror" amounts to the use of armed force within a State, between that State and a rebel group, or between rebel groups within the State, the situation may amount to non-international armed conflict [62]
> . . .

only non-international armed conflicts that occur within the territory of a single state party, again, like a civil war. This provision would not reach an armed conflict in which one of the parties operated from multiple bases in several different states.

Jay S. Bybee, Memorandum for Alberto R. Gonzales, Counsel to the President, and William J. Haynes II, General Counsel of the DoD Re: Application of Treaties and Laws to al Qaeda and Taliban Detainees (Jan. 22, 2002). *available at* http://www.washingtonpost.com/wp-srv/nation/documents/012202bybee.pdf.

60. *See* Geneva Convention for the Amelioration of the Condition of the Wounded and Sick in Armed Forces in the Field, Aug. 12, 1949, T.I.A.S. 3362, art. 3; Geneva Convention for the Amelioration of the Condition of Wounded, Sick, and Shipwrecked Members at Sea,

Aug. 12, 1949, T.I.A.S. 3363, art. 3; Geneva Convention Relative to the Treatment of Prisoners of War, Aug. 12, 1949, T.I.A.S. 3364 art. 3; Geneva Convention Relative to the Treatment of Civilian Persons in Time of War, Aug. 12, 1949, T.I.A.S. 3365, art. 3.

61. *See, e.g.* U.K. Ministry of Defense, *The Manual for the Law of Armed Conflict,* Oxford University Press (2004), at Para. 2.1; *see also* Int'l & Operational Law Dept, The Judge Advocate General's Legal Center & School, The Law of War Deskbook, at Ch. 3 (2000).

62. *See* Gabor Rona, *When is a war not a war?—The proper role of the law of armed conflict in the "global war on terror",* "International Action to Prevent and Combat Terrorism"—Workshop on the Protection of Human Rights While Countering Terrorism, Copenhagen, 15–16 March 2004—Presentation given by Gabor Rona, Legal Adviser at

This excerpt illustrates the traditional interpretation of the situations that trigger LOAC application. According to this interpretation, there are only two possible characterizations for military activities conducted against transnational terrorist groups: international armed conflict (when the operations are conducted outside the territory of the state) or non-international armed conflict (limited to operations conducted within the territory of the state).

Unfortunately, this "either/or" triggering paradigm failed to account for the possibility that an extraterritorial non inter-state combat operation launched by a state using regular armed forces could qualify as an armed conflict triggering LOAC regulation. Such an operation would fail to satisfy the requisite dispute between states necessary to qualify as an international armed conflict within the meaning of common article 2. However, based on the traditional understanding of non-international armed conflict—an understanding shared by virtually all scholars and practitioners prior to o the U.S. military response to the terrorist attacks of September 11th—the possibility that an armed conflict falling somewhere between an internal armed conflict and an inter-state armed conflict could theoretically be subject to LOAC applicability was necessarily excluded. Accordingly, these "transnational" armed conflicts fell into a regulatory gap—a gap necessitating application of regulation by way of policy mandate.

Both the military component of the U.S. fight against al Qaeda and the 2006 conflict between Israel and Hezbollah have strained the "either/or" LOAC application paradigm.[63] While this strain has produced international and national uncertainty as to the law that applies to such conflicts, it has also provided what may actually come to be appreciated as a beneficial reassessment of the trigger for application of the fundamental LOAC principles.[64] In the lower

the ICRC's Legal Division, *available at* http://www.icrc.org/Web/Eng/siteeng0. nsf/iwpList575/3C2914F52152E565C125 6E60005C84C0 (last accessed 10 August, 2010).

63. *See* Kenneth Watkin, *Controlling the Use of Force: A Role for Human Rights Norms in Contemporary Armed Conflict,* 98 AM.J.INT'L.L. 1, 2–8 (2004) (discussing the complex challenge of conflict categorization related military operations conducted against highly organized non-state groups with trans-national reach); *see also* Kirby Abott, *Terrorists: Combatants, Criminals, or . . .?,* published in THE MEASURES OF INTERNATIONAL LAW: EFFECTIVENESS, FAIRNESS, AND VALIDITY, Proceedings of the 31st Annual

Conference of the Canadian Council on International Law, Ottawa, October 24–26, 2002; JENNIFER ELSEA, CONG. RESEARCH SERV., Order Code RL31191, TERRORISM AND THE LAWS OF WAR: TRYING TERRORISTS AS WAR CRIMINALS BEFORE MILITARY COMMISSIONS (2001) (analyzing whether the attacks of September 11, 2001 triggered the law of war).

64. *See generally Human Rights Council, Report of the Commission of Inquiry on Lebanon,* U.N. Doc. A/HRC/ 3/2 (Nov. 23, 2006), *available at* http:// www.ohchr.org/english/bodies/hrcouncil/ docs/specialsession/A.HRC.3.2.pdf.; *Text of Order Signed by President Bush on Feb. 7, 2002, outlining treatment of al-Qaida and Taliban detainees,* LAWOF-

court judgment in *Hamdan v. Rumsfeld*,[65] Judge Williams, in his concurring opinion, articulated the logic motivating this reassessment. In that opinion, he responded to the majority conclusion that common article 3 did not apply to armed conflict with al Qaeda because the President has determined that this conflict is one of international scope:

> Non–State actors cannot sign an international treaty. Nor is such an actor even a "Power" that would be eligible under Article 2 (¶ 3) to secure protection by complying with the Convention's requirements. Common Article 3 fills the gap, providing some minimal protection for such non-eligibles in an "armed conflict not of an international character occurring in the territory of one of the High Contracting Parties." The gap being filled is the non-eligible party's failure to be a nation. Thus the words "not of an international character" are sensibly understood to refer to a conflict between a signatory nation and a non-State actor. The most obvious form of such a conflict is a civil war. But given the Convention's structure, the logical reading of "international character" is one that matches the basic derivation of the word "international," i.e., *between nations*. Thus, I think the context compels the view that a conflict between a signatory and a non-State actor is a conflict "not of an international character." In such a conflict, the signatory is bound to Common Article 3's modest requirements of "humane" treatment and "the judicial guarantees which are recognized as indispensable by civilized peoples."[66]

Although the logic expressed by Judge Williams seemed pragmatically compelling, the fact remains that he was unable to convince his peers to adopt this interpretation. This reflected the pervasive impact of common article 2 and 3—and the legal paradigm they spawned—on conflict regulation analysis. But, as Judge Williams recognized, it is fundamentally inconsistent with the logic of the LOAC to detach the applicability of regulation from the necessity for regulation. What was needed was a pragmatic reconciliation of these two considerations.

WAR.ORG http://www.lawofwar.org/Bush_torture_memo.htm.

65. 415 F.3d 33, 44 (D.C. Cir. 2005).

66. *Id.* (Williams, Sr. Judge, concurring).

D. EMPLOYING NATIONAL COMBAT POWER TO EN-GAGE TRANSNATIONAL NON–STATE ACTORS: EX-POSING THE LIMITS OF POLICY BASED REGULAtion of Armed Conflict

Ironically, despite the effort to reject a hyper-technical LOAC application trigger,[67] the "international/internal" focus, the common article 2/3 LOAC triggering paradigm that evolved after 1949 did not eliminate this handicap. Nonetheless, prior to 9/11, few scholars or practitioners questioned this paradigm.[68] Instead, it was almost universally regarded as the definitive standard for determining LOAC applicability.[69] The large scale combat operations the United States conducted with "global scope" to engage and destroy al Qaeda military capabilities following September 11th stressed this paradigm as never before,[70] and exposed that it was too restrictive to cover this new category of armed conflict between state armed forces and transnational non-state military entities.[71]

67. *See* Commentary, Convention (I) for the Amelioration of the Condition of the Wounded and Sick in Armed Forces in the Field. Geneva, 12 August 1949 (Jean S. Pictet ed., 1960), at 32–33.

68. *See generally* Adam Roberts, *Counter–Terrorism, Armed Force and the Laws of War,* Survival (quarterly journal of IISS, London), vol. 44, no. 1, (Spring 2002), at 7; *also available at* http://www.ssrc.org/sept11/essays/roberts.htm.

69. *See* Int'l & Operational Law Dept, The Judge Advocate General's Legal Center & School, The Law of War Deskbook, at Ch. 3 (2000); *see also* LESLIE C. GREEN, THE CONTEMPORARY LAW OF ARMED CONFLICT, at 54–61 (2d Ed.) (2000).

70. *See* Kenneth Watkin, *Controlling the Use of Force: A Role for Human Rights Norms in Contemporary Armed Conflict,* 98 AM.J.INT'L.L. 1, 3–4 (2004) (discussing the complex challenge of conflict categorization related military operations conducted against highly organized non-state groups with trans-national reach); *see also* Kirby Abbott, *Terrorists: Combatants, Criminals, or . . .?,* published in THE MEASURES OF INTERNATIONAL LAW: EFFECTIVENESS, FAIRNESS, AND VALIDITY, Proceedings of the 31st Annual Conference of the Canadian Council on International Law, Ottowa, October 24–26, 2002; *see also* JENNIFER ELSEA, CONG. RESEARCH SERV., Order Code RL31191, TERRORISM AND THE LAWS OF WAR: TRYING TERRORISTS AS WAR CRIMINALS BEFORE MILITARY COMMISSIONS, 10–14 (2001) (analyzing whether the attacks of September 11, 2001 triggered the law of war).

71. *See* Rosa Brooks, *War Everywhere: Human Rights, National Security, and the Law of Armed Conflict in the Age of Terrorism,* 153 U. PA. L. REV. 675, 715–20 (2004–2005). Professor Brooks proposes an alternate response to this gap in legal regulation: reliance on international human rights law as a regulatory framework:

As traditional categories lose their logical underpinnings, we are entering a new era: the era of War Everywhere. It is an era in which the legal rules that were designed to protect basic rights and vulnerable groups have lost their analytical force, and thus, too often, their practical force.

* * *

In the long run, the old categories and rules need to be replaced by a radically different system that better reflects the changed nature of twenty-first century conflict and threat. What such a radically different system would look like is difficult to say, and the world community is unlikely to develop a consensus around such a new system anytime soon. This Article suggest, nonetheless, that international human rights law provides some benchmarks for evaluating U.S. government actions in the war on terror[. . .]

Unlike domestic U.S. law and the law of armed conflict, international human rights law ap-

Like an operational commander exploiting a seam between the defensive positions of enemy units, during the five years following September 11th, the Bush administration persistently exploited the seam in the triggering paradigm to justify denying legal applicability of LOAC humanitarian protections to captured and detained al Qaeda operatives.[72] While never abandoning the policy commitment

plies to all people at all times, regardless of citizenship, location, and status. Although human rights law permits limited derogation in times of emergency, it also outlines core rights that cannot be eliminated regardless of the nature of the threat or the existence or non-existence of an armed conflict. Applying standards of international human rights law in both domestic and international contexts would not solve all the problems created by the increasing irrelevance of other legal frameworks, but it would provide at least a basic floor, a minimum set of standards by which international and domestic governmental actions could be evaluated.

Id. at 681–82, 684–85. While such a concept of conflict regulation might indeed be effective to achieve the concurrent humanitarian objectives of both the law of armed conflict and human rights law, in the opinion of this author the traditional culture among professional armed forces linking regulation to the laws of war makes this a less feasible response than expanding the triggering criteria for principles of the laws of war. Indeed, the reliance by many armed forces over the past two decades on a policy based application of these principles (instead of reliance on human rights norms as a source of operational regulation) in situations of legal uncertainty corroborates the significance of this cultural dynamic, a consideration that seems to be ignored by proponents of a human rights military regulatory framework. Nonetheless, the mere fact that such an alternate regulatory approach is offered supports both the conclusion that the traditional regulatory paradigm is insufficient to meet the requirements of the contemporary battlefield and that some legally based regulatory framework is essential on that battlefield.

72. *See generally* Jay S. Bybee, Memorandum for Alberto R. Gonzales, Counsel to the President, and William J. Haynes II, General Counsel of the DoD Re: Application of Treaties and Laws to al Qaeda and Taliban Detainees (Jan. 22, 2002). *available at* http://www.washingtonpost.com/wp-srv/nation/documents/012202bybee.pdf.; *see also* Alberto R. Gonzales, Memorandum for the President, Subject: Decision re Application of the Geneva Convention on Prisoners of War to the Conflict with Al Qaeda and the Taliban (Jan. 25, 2002); Donald Rumsfeld, Memorandum for the Chairman of the Joint Chiefs of Staff, Subject: Status of the Taliban and Al Qaida,[sic] (Jan. 19, 2002), *available at* http://news.findlaw.-com/hdocs/docs/dod/11902mem.pdf.

In a message dated January 21, 2002, the Chairman notified combatant commanders of the Secretary of Defense's determination. Message from the Chairman of the Joint Chiefs of Staff, Subject: SECDEF Memo to CJCS Regarding the Status of Taliban and Al Qaida [sic] (Jan. 22, 2002), *available at*: http://news.findlaw.com/hdocs/docs/dod/12202mem.pdf; *see also Text of Order Signed by President Bush on Feb. 7, 2002, outlining treatment of al-Qaida and Talliban detainees,* LAWOFWAR.ORG http://www.lawofwar.org/Bush_torture_memo.htm. (announcing the President's determination that although the conflict against Afghanistan triggered the Geneva Conventions, captured Taliban forces were not entitled to prisoner of war status because they failed to meet the implied requirements imposed by the Convention on members of the regular armed forces).

This determination endorsed the analysis provided by the Office of Legal Counsel of the Department of Justice to the General Counsel of the Department of Defense that reflected a restrictive interpretation of legal applicability of the laws of war. *See* Department of Justice Office of Legal Counsel to the President and the General Counsel for the Department of Defense on the applicability of the Geneva Conventions to individuals detained by U.S. forces during military operations. *See* United States Depart-

to apply LOAC principles at the operational level of command,[73] deviation from these principles in relation to al Qaeda detainees became a focal point for criticism of U.S. policy.[74] This theory that a seam existed in the applicability of LOAC principles in the extraterritorial non-state context exposed the limits of the common article 2/3 "either/or" paradigm. The Bush administration's LOAC interpretation that generated this critical reaction focused on two principle factors: the non-state nature of al Qaeda and the global nature of the conflict.[75] Al Qaeda's non-state character resulted in the legitimate conclusion that the Global War on Terror could not properly be classified as a common article 2 conflict.[76] The second factor led to the more controversial conclusion that the global scope of the conflict excluded it from classification as a common article 3 non-international armed conflict. According to the President:

> Common Article 3 of Geneva does not apply to either al Qaeda or Taliban detainees, because, among other reasons, the relevant conflicts are international in scope and common Article 3 applies only to "armed conflict not of an international character."[77]

ment of Justice Office of Legal Counsel Memorandum of January 22, 2002, Memorandum for Alberto R. Gonzales, Counsel to the President, and William J. Haynes II, General Counsel for the Department of Defense, *Re: Application of Treaties and Laws to al Qaeda and Taliban Detainees.*

73. *See Text of Order Signed by President Bush on Feb. 7, 2002, outlining treatment of al-Qaida and Taliban detainees,* LAWOFWAR.ORG http://www.lawofwar.org/Bush_torture_memo.htm. According to that directive:

> Of course, our values as a nation, values that we share with many nations in the world, call for us to treat detainees humanely, including those who are not legally entitled to such treatment. Our nation has been and will continue to be a strong supporter of Geneva and its principles. As a matter of policy, the United States Armed Forces shall continue to treat detainees humanely and, to the extent appropriate and consistent with military necessity, in a manner consistent with the principles of Geneva.

Id. at para. 3.

74. *See, e.g* JENNIFER ELSEA, CONG. RESEARCH SERV., Order Code RL31191,

TERRORISM AND THE LAWS OF WAR: TRYING TERRORISTS AS WAR CRIMINALS BEFORE MILITARY COMMISSIONS, (2001) (analyzing whether the attacks of September 11, 2001 triggered the law of war); *See also U.S. Officials Misstate Geneva Convention Requirements,* HUMAN RIGHTS WATCH (Jan. 28, 2002), http://www.hrw.org/en/ news/2002/01/28/us-officials-misstate-geneva-convention-requirements (last visited Aug. 11, 2010); *United Nations Finds that U.S. Has Failed to Comply with International Obligations at Guantanamo Detention Center,* HUMAN RIGHTS WATCH (Feb. 15, 2006), http://hrw.org/ english/docs/2006/02/16/usdom12833. htm(last accessed Aug. 11, 2010).

75. Alberto R. Gonzales, Memorandum for the President, Subject: Decision re Application of the Geneva Convention on Prisoners of War to the Conflict with Al Qaeda and the Taliban (Jan. 25, 2002) (articulating the basis for the conclusion that al Qaeda detainees did not fall under either the law triggered by Common Article 2 nor the humane treatment obligation of Common Article 3).

76. *Id.*

77. *See Text of Order Signed by President Bush on Feb. 7, 2002, outlining treatment of al-Qaida and Taliban detainees,* at Par. 2.c. LAWOFWAR.ORG

This interpretation is also reflected in the following language from the Department of Justice analysis of LOAC applicability to al Qaeda and Taliban detainees:

> Analysis of the background to the adoption of the Geneva Conventions in 1949 confirms our understanding of Common Article 3. It appears that the drafters of the Conventions had in mind only the two forms of armed conflict that were regarded as a matter of general *international* concern at the time: armed conflict between nation-States (subject to article 2), and large-scale civil war within a nation-State (subject to article 3).
>
> . . .
>
> If the state parties had intended the Conventions to apply to all forms of armed conflict, they could have used broader, clearer language. To interpret Common Article 3 by expanding its scope well beyond the meaning borne by its text is effectively to amend the Geneva Conventions without the approval of the State parties to the treaties . . . [G]iving due weight to the state practice and doctrinal understanding of the time, the idea of an armed conflict between a nation-State and a transnational terrorist organization . . . could not have been within the contemplation of the drafters of Common Article 3.[78]

The accordant denial of the substantive humanitarian protections of common article 3 to detainees subject to trial by military commission led ultimately to the Supreme Court's decision in *Hamdan v. Rumsfeld*.[79] Because Hamdan asserted the procedures for the military commission established by order of President Bush violated the humane treatment mandate of common article 3, it was necessary for the Court to determine whether armed conflict between the United States and al Qaeda fell within the scope of non-international armed conflict within the meaning of that article.[80]

The Supreme Court rejected the Bush administration interpretation of non-international armed conflict and held that the substantive protections of common article 3 applied to individuals detained during the course of the non-international armed conflict in which Hamdan participated.[81] The Court interpreted common

---

http://www.lawofwar.org/Bush_torture_memo.htm.

78. *See* Jay S. Bybee, Memorandum for Alberto R. Gonzales, Counsel to the President, and William J. Haynes II, General Counsel of the DoD Re: Application of Treaties and Laws to al Qaeda and Taliban Detainees (Jan. 22, 2002). *available at* http://www.washingtonpost.

com/wp-srv/nation/documents/012202 bybee.pdf.

79. 548 U.S. 557 (2006).

80. *See* Hamdan v. Rumsfeld, 548 U.S. 557, 629-31 (2006).

81. *See* Hamdan v. Rumsfeld, 548 U.S. 557, 629-31 (2006). It is likely the Court understood this armed conflict as

article 3 as occupying the field of conflict regulation for any armed conflict not qualifying as an international armed conflict in accordance with common article 2. Thus, the Court endorsed the exact "residual conflict" concept explicitly rejected in the Department of Justice analysis of this treaty provision.[82] According to Justice Stevens' majority opinion:

> The Court of Appeals thought, and the Government asserts, that Common Article 3 does not apply to Hamdan because the conflict with al Qaeda, being " 'international in scope,' " does not qualify as a " 'conflict not of an international character.' " That reasoning is erroneous. The term "conflict not of an international character" is used here in contradistinction to a conflict between nations.[83]

Ironically, this analysis mirrors the logic that animated Department of Defense policy for decades. However, this was no statement of policy, but instead an enunciation of a legal obligation derived by the Supreme Court's controlling interpretation of a binding treaty.[84] Hailed as "landmark" by some and criticized as invalid by others, the decision resulted in an immediate 'about face' by the Department of Defense.[85] On the day of the decision, Under Secretary of Defense Gordon England issued a directive to all branches

to be one between the United States and al Qaeda. However, the Court never explicitly endorsed the theory that Hamdan had been captured in the context of a distinct armed conflict between the U.S. and al Qaeda. This has led some scholars to assert that the decision merely recognized that a non-international armed conflict occurred in Afghanistan after the fall of the Taliban regime, and that Hamdan had been captured in the context of that armed conflict. However, considering the Court's reliance of the AUMF, a statute that authorized the use of all necessary force against *inter alia* al Qaeda, coupled with the fact that the government argued common article 3 was inapplicable to Hamdan because of his involvement in a distinct armed conflict between the U.S. and al Qaeda, it is more likely the Court effectively acknowledged the existence of that distinct armed conflict.

82. *See* Jay S. Bybee, Memorandum for Alberto R. Gonzales, Counsel to the President, and William J. Haynes II, General Counsel of the DoD Re: Application of Treaties and Laws to al Qaeda and Taliban Detainees (Jan. 22, 2002),

available at http://www.washingtonpost.com/wp-srv/nation/documents/012202 bybee.pdf.

83. Hamdan v. Rumsfeld, 548 U.S. 557, 630 (2006) (citations omitted).

84. *See* Sanchez–Llamas v. Oregon, 548 U.S. 331 (2006). According to Chief Justice Roberts:

> If treaties are to be given effect as federal law, determining their meaning as a matter of federal law "is emphatically the province and duty of the judicial department," headed by the "one supreme Court."

Id. at 2684 (citations omitted).

85. *See* Marc Goldman, *What the Hamdan Ruling Really Meant,* THE WASHINGTON POST, July 26, 2006, at A16.; *see also* Jess Bravin, *Trial and Error: Justices Bar Guantanamo Tribunals— High Court Says President Exceeded War Powers; He May Turn to Congress—Ruling Won't Free Prisoners,* THE WALL STREET JOURNAL, June 30, 2006, at A1.

of the armed forces requiring the humane treatment of all detainees as a matter of legal obligation pursuant to common article 3.[86]

Almost immediately following this decision, the world witnessed five weeks of intense combat operations between the Israeli Defense Forces and the armed component of Hezbollah.[87] The intensity of this conflict, and especially the resulting collateral damage inflicted on civilians and civilian property, immediately shifted the international focus of LOAC applicability from the humane treatment principle implicated in the *Hamdan* decision to other core LOAC principles, including distinction, proportionality, and necessity.[88] This conflict and the international response it evoked indicate an obvious reality: that the international community expected compliance with these principles during all armed conflicts not merely as a matter of policy but as a matter of legal obligation. In essence, the international reaction to this conflict implicated the same rationale relied on by the Supreme Court in *Hamdan*—that all armed conflicts are subject to legal regulation and therefore any conflict not qualified as an international armed conflict is *ipso facto* a non-international armed conflict. However, the issues of concern related to that conflict indicate that such *ipso facto* armed conflicts not falling within the scope of common article 2 must trigger not only the humane treatment obligation, but *all* foundational LOAC principles.

The combination of these two events—the *Hamdan* decision and the armed conflict in Lebanon—initiated a critical evolution of the legal trigger for application of core LOAC principles. This evolution may indicate an emerging legalization of the policy approach adopted by the United States armed forces more than two decades ago and relied upon since then to provide a pragmatic response to the stoic legal paradigms that grew out of the Geneva Conventions. Like the common article 2/3 triggers, the key factor related to the LOAC applicability concept reflected in both the *Hamdan* decision and the reaction to the armed conflict in Lebanon is the *de facto* existence of armed hostilities. Unlike the common article 2/3 trigger, this new approach is not limited by either the non-state status of a party to the conflict or the geographic scope of the conflict. Instead, it represents an *ipso facto* application of core

---

86. Donna Miles, *England Memo Underscores Policy on Humane Treatment of* Detainees, GLOBALSECURITY.ORG (July 11, 2006), http://www.globalsecurity.org/security/library/news/2006/07/sec–060711–afps01.htm.

87. *See* John Ward Anderson & Edward Cody, *Israel Fights To Secure Key Region In Lebanon,* THE WASHINGTON POST, July 23, 2006, at A01.

88. *See* Richard Cohen, *No, It's Survival*, THE WASHINGTON POST, July 25, 2006, at A15. For a discussion of core LOAC principles, *see* A.P.V. ROGERS, LAW ON THE BATTLEFIELD (2d ed. 2004), at 1–29.

LOAC principles to any situation involving *de facto* hostilities where at least one of the parties to the conflict is a state.[89]

Although it is reasonable to assert that the common article 3's plain meaning indicates it has always served as a trigger for such an expansive scope of LOAC application, as noted above the "international/internal" armed conflict paradigm that evolved after 1949 became the definitive standard for determining such applicability. This paradigm did not contemplate the modern problem of transnational armed conflicts, and created the perceived necessity of establishing national policies to extend application of core LOAC principles to "all" military operations, no matter how characterized. Because this paradigm made conflict characterization the *sine qua non* of LOAC applicability, only such a policy extension could satisfy the military need to ensure all operations were subject to this regulatory framework. Absent such a policy, uncertainty as to the nature of a conflict operation would produce uncertainty as to "what rules should apply"—an uncertainty unacceptable from a military efficiency and discipline perspective. Thus, the policy extension is a powerful indication that *ipso facto* application of these principles to any armed conflict is in fact consistent with the purposes of the LOAC,[90] the needs of military discipline and efficiency, the humanitarian objective of these treaties (which emphasizes the significance of underlying principles)[91] and the historical internal disciplinary codes of regular armed forces.[92]

89. *See* Geoffrey S. Corn & Eric Tablot Jensen, *Transnational Armed Conflict: A 'Principled' Approach to the Regulation of Counter–Terror Combat Operations,* 42 Israel L. Rev. 45, 53–54 (2009).

90. *See* U. S. Dep't of Army, Field Manual 27–10, The Law of Land Warfare (July 1956), para. 3. According to this authoritative Department of the Army statement:

> The conduct of armed hostilities on land is regulated by the law of land warfare which is both written and unwritten. It is inspired by the desire to diminish the evils of war by:
>
> *a.* Protecting both combatants and noncombatants from unnecessary suffering;
>
> *b.* Safeguarding certain fundamental human rights of persons who fall into the hands of the enemy, particularly prisoners of war, the wounded and sick, and civilians; and
>
> *c.* Facilitating the restoration of peace.

Id. at par. 2.

91. Commentary, Convention (I) for the Amelioration of the Condition of the Wounded and Sick in Armed Forces in the Field. Geneva, 12 August 1949 (Jean S. Pictet ed., 1960), at 19–23:

> However carefully the texts were drawn up, and however clearly they were worded, it would not have been possible to expect every soldier and every civilian to know the details of the odd four hundred Articles of the Conventions, and to be able to understand and apply them. Such knowledge as that can be expected only of jurists and military and civilian authorities with special qualifications. But anyone of good faith is capable of applying with approximate accuracy what he is called upon to apply under one or other of the Conventions, provided he is acquainted with the basic principle involved.

Id. at 21.

92. *See* Leslie C. Green, The Contemporary Law of Armed Conflict, 20–33

The "either/or" law triggering paradigm may have proved generally sufficient to address the types of armed conflicts occur-

(2d Ed.) (2000); *see also* Leslie Green *What is—Why is There—the Law of War,* THE LAW OF ARMED CONFLICT: INTO THE NEXT MILLENNIUM Vol. 71, 176 U.S. Naval War College International Studies, Naval War College, Newport, Rhode Island (1998).

This conclusion is not just reflected in the extension of this regulatory framework by military policy. It is also reflected in the history from which these principles evolved. Throughout the post-Westphalian history of warfare, armed forces complied with such codes. *See* Leslie C. Green, THE CONTEMPORARY LAW OF ARMED CONFLICT, 20–33 (2d Ed.) (2000). Because such codes took the form of internal disciplinary mandates, little attention was given to the question of whether they were derived from legal obligation. However, the content of these internal military codes of conduct provided the seeds from which grew the contemporary international legal principles regulating armed conflicts. *See generally* Leslie Green *What is—Why is There—the Law of War,* THE LAW OF ARMED CONFLICT: INTO THE NEXT MILLENNIUM Vol. 71, 176 U.S. Naval War College International Studies, Naval War College, Newport, Rhode Island (1998); *see also* Thomas C. Wingfield, *Chivalry in the Use of Force,* 32 U. TOL. L. REV. 111, 114 (2001). Thus, while treating application of these principles to any armed conflict as a matter of legal obligation is a significant shift from the pre–2001 legal paradigm, the substantive impact of such application is not only consistent with the practices of many professional armed forces, but also with the historic understanding by armed forces that a battlefield without rules was an anathema to a disciplined force.

Several prominent law of war scholars who have written on this subject begin with a discussion of these historical roots to the contemporary legal regime for the regulation of armed conflict. For example, A.P.V. Rogers begins his book *Law on the Battlefield (See* A.P.V. Rogers, LAW ON THE BATTLEFIELD (1996)) with the following introduction:

Writers delve back through the history of centuries to the ancient civilizations of India and Egypt to find in their writings evidence of the practices intended to alleviate the sufferings of war. This evidence is to be found in agreements and treaties, in the works of religious leaders and philosophers, in regulations and articles of war issued by military leaders, and in the rules of chivalry. It is said that the first systematic code of war was that of the Saracens and was based on the Koran. The writers of the Age of Enlightenment, notably Grotious and Vattel, were especially influential. It has been suggested that more humane rules were able to flourish in the period of limited wars from 1648 to 1792 but that they then came under pressure in the drift towards continental warfare, the concept of the nation in arms and the increasing destructiveness of weapons from 1792 to 1914. *So efforts had to be made in the middle of the last century to reimpose on war limits which up to that time had been based on custom and usage.*

Id. at 1 (emphasis added) (internal citations omitted).

Professor Leslie Green has also written extensively on the historical underpinnings of the laws of war, highlighting the fact that throughout history, military leaders from a wide array of cultures have always imposed limits on the conduct of hostilities by their own forces. *See* Leslie C. Green, THE CONTEMPORARY LAW OF ARMED CONFLICT, 20–33 (2d Ed.) (2000); *see also* Leslie Green *What is—Why is There—the Law of War,* THE LAW OF ARMED CONFLICT: INTO THE NEXT MILLENNIUM Vol. 71, 176 U.S. Naval War College International Studies, Naval War College, Newport, Rhode Island (1998).In so doing, Professors Rogers and Green remind readers not only that the regulation of warfare is as ancient as organized warfare itself, but that the logic of such regulation transcends hyper-technical legal paradigms defining what is "war" and when such rules should apply.

ring up until 9/11. However, this fact no longer justifies the conclusion that no other triggering standard should be recognized. Instead, as the events since 9/11 have illustrated so convincingly, such recognition is essential in order to keep pace with the evolving nature of armed conflicts themselves. The prospect of an unregulated battlefield is simply unacceptable in the international community, a fact demonstrated by the response to the conflict in Lebanon.[93]

E. THE SUPREME COURT ENDORSES ARMED CONFLICT AGAINST TERRORISM?

The Supreme Court decision in *Hamdan v. Rumsfeld* was not the only indication that the Court recognizes the existence of an armed conflict between the United States and al Qaeda. Both LOAC based preventive detention and trial by military commission of captured terrorist operatives generated several critical Supreme Court decisions between 2005 and 2009. Subsequent chapters will address in more detail the impact of these decisions on the authority of the government to engage in such practices. What is significant in relation to the foregoing discussion is how these decisions effectively endorsed the armed conflict characterization of the government's counter-terrorism efforts.

The first decision to scrutinize the invocation of wartime authority in relation to the use of military force against al Qaeda and Taliban enemies was *Hamdi v. Rumsfeld*[94]. Hamdi, a U.S. citizen, had been captured in Afghanistan by the Northern Alliance (the anti-Taliban Afghan forces supported by the U.S. and other Coalition forces) and turned over the U.S. forces. Based on a determination by the U.S. military that he had been a member of Taliban and/or Al Qaeda forces fighting against Coalition forces, Hamdi was detained and transferred to the recently established detention facility at the U.S. Naval Station in Guantanamo Bay, Cuba. When it was subsequently determined that Hamdi had been born in the United States and was a U.S. citizen, therefore not subject to the Military Order issued by the President authorizing detention of alien enemy combatants at Guantanamo, he was transferred to the U.S. Naval Brig in Charleston, S.C. However, the government continued to treat him as an enemy combatant subject to preventive detention for the duration of hostilities.[95]

The legality of Hamdi's detention reached the Supreme Court on a writ of habeas corpus filed by his father on his behalf.[96] The

---

93. *See Lebanon/Israel: U.N. Rights Body Squanders Chance to Help Civilians*, HUMAN RIGHTS WATCH, Aug. 11, 2006, http://hrw.org/english/docs/2006/08/11/lebano13969_txt.htm, statements by Louise Arbour; *see also U.N.: Open Independent Inquiry into Civilian Deaths*, HUMAN RIGHTS WATCH, Aug. 7, 2006, http://hrw.org/english/docs/2006/08/08/lebano13939.htm, statements by Kofi Annan.

94. 542 U.S. 507 (2004).

95. *Id.* at 510.

96. *Id.*

Court concluded that once Hamdi was properly determined to be an enemy belligerent who had engaged in hostilities against U.S. forces in an area of active combat operations his detention was permitted pursuant to the laws and customs of war.[97] According to the Court, the AUMF enacted by Congress implicitly authorized preventive detention of such enemy belligerents as a necessary incident of successfully waging war.[98] Although the Court did not explicitly invoke the LOAC principle of military necessity, the link between the customary necessities of war and the AUMF indicate that it was the LOAC that led the Court to conclude Hamdi's detention was lawful.[99] Furthermore, although Hamdi had been a member of the Taliban, that fact did not seem particularly significant to the Court. Instead, it was his participation in belligerent conduct against U.S. and Coalition forces that justified his detention pursuant to the LOAC.[100]

The impact of this decision on the development of procedures for determining enemy belligerent status will be addressed in more detail in a subsequent chapter. What is important here is that the Court's opinion was implicitly predicated upon the conclusion that military operations conducted against the individuals, organizations, and states included within the AUMF triggered LOAC rights and obligations. Even Justice Scalia, whose dissenting opinion asserted that as a citizen Hamdi could not be preventively detained as an enemy belligerent but was instead entitled to criminal process, did not question the validity of invoking an armed conflict paradigm in the struggle against transnational terrorism. Instead, he took the position that citizens associated with enemy forces during periods of armed conflict should be tried for treason or some other offense of disloyalty[101]. However, while the Court did not challenge the invocation of wartime legal authority *vis a vis* Hamdi, the opinion cannot be read as an broad endorsement of a "global" war on terror. Unfortunately, the Court left to the lower courts the task of defining the permissible scope of application of this LOAC based preventive detention authority. Nonetheless, *Hamdi* served as an important first salvo in a line of decisions that would implicitly endorse LOAC invocation as a source of legal authority to prosecute the struggle against terrorism.

Rasul v. Bush,[102] decided the same day as *Hamdi,* bolstered the endorsement of the government's invocation of wartime authority in relation to counter-terror operations. Like Hamdi, the Petition-

97. *See Id.* at 519.
98. *Id.* at 517.
99. *See Id.* at 517.
100. *Id.*

101. *See generally Id.* at 553–578 (2004) (Scalia, J., dissenting).
102. 542 U.S. 466 (2004).

ers in Rasul (2 Austalian Citizens and 12 Kuwait citizens) had been captured in Afghanistan, detained by the U.S. military, and transported to Guantanamo.[103] Unlike Hamdi, the Rasul Petitioners were not U.S. citizens and were therefore retained in Guantanamo. Rasul filed a writ of habeas corpus challenging the legal authority for his preventive detention which ultimately reached the Supreme Court on the question of whether the Federal habeas corpus statute applied to the Naval Base at Guantanamo.[104]

The Supreme Court rejected the lower courts determination that the habeas statute did not run to Guantanamo.[105] In doing so, it also rejected the government's invocation of the holding in *Johnson v. Eisentrager,* a World War II era opinion that denied the writ of habeas corpus to enemy nationals tried by a military tribunal within the context of a declared war.[106] While the opinion dealt primarily with interpretation of the federal habeas statue, the centrality of *Eisentrager* to the opinion indicates that like *Hamdi, Rasul* reflected the Court's acknowledgment that it was addressing a wartime invocation of Executive authority.

The Court's next foray into the war on terror issue was its decision in *Hamdan v. Rumsfeld.*[107] As noted above, that case involved a challenge by Osama Bin Laden's driver to the legality of trial by the military commission established pursuant to a military order issued by President Bush in November, 2001 directing the Secretary of Defense to try captured unlawful alien enemy combatants for violations of the laws and customs of war. Although the Supreme Court invalidated the Commission established pursuant to that order by the Secretary of Defense, the opinion in no way questioned the validity of invoking the LOAC as a source of authority to deal with captured al Qaeda operatives. On the contrary, by relying on the LOAC—or more specifically concluding that common article 3 applied to the armed conflict in which Hamdan was captured—as a basis to conclude the Commission was invalid, the Court implicitly endorsed LOAC applicability to the military operations directed against transnational terrorism by treating that struggle as a non-international armed conflict.

Two aspects of the *Hamdan* decision are particularly significant in relation to this endorsement. First, unlike Hamidi, Hamdan was unquestionably a member of al Qaeda, not the Taliban. As a result of the fact that Hamdan's detention and trial resulted from his association with al Qaeda, the decision directly implicated the characterization of the struggle against that transnational terrorist group as an armed conflict. Second, accepting the premise that the

---

103. *Id.* at 469.

104. *Id.* at 471.

105. *Id.* at 485.

106. *Id.* at 483.

107. Hamdan v. Rumsfeld, 548 U.S. 557 (2006).

struggle against al Qaeda qualified as an armed conflict was the critical predicate to the Court's invocation of the LOAC as a source of legal obligations on the United States *vis a vis* its treatment of Hamdan. This may have resulted from the failure of the Petitioner to challenge the armed conflict characterization in his appeal. Nonetheless, *Hamdan* must be understood as having that validating effect, an understanding bolstered by the subsequent response by both the President and Congress.[108]

Another intriguing indication that the *Hamdan* Court understood that it was addressing LOAC applicability to the distinct transnational armed conflict between the United States and al Qaeda came in the context of the recent efforts by General Manuel Noriega to resist his extradition to France. After being captured by the United States during Operation Just Cause in 1989, the U.S. invasion of Panama to oust Noriega and install the democratically elected government, Noriega was transported to the U.S. to stand trial in federal court for pre-conflict narcotics offenses. Noriega claimed prisoner of war status because he was a member of the Panamanian armed forces captured in the context of an international armed conflict. The United States actually contested his entitlement to that status, arguing that the intervention had been in response to a request for the democratically elected President of Panama, Guillermo Endara. Relying heavily on the ICRC Commentary to common article 2, that trial court concluded that the armed conflict in Panama had been international and accordingly granted Noriega's request to be designated a prisoner of war.[109]

Unfortunately for Noriega, this in no way undermined the government's ability to prosecute him for his pre-capture criminal activities. Noriega was ultimately convicted and sentenced to a long term of incarceration in federal prison. However, as the result of his POW status, he was afforded certain treaty mandated privileges, such as the right to wear his uniform, annual visits from the ICRC, access to care packages, and segregation from the general population.[110]

As Noriega's term of incarceration approached, France requested that he be extradited to stand trial for money laundering offenses he had been convicted of in abstentia (France would set aside that conviction and re-try Noriega). Noriega challenged the extradition, invoking his status as a POW.[111] Noriega asserted that

---

108. *See* Donna Miles, *England Memo Underscores Policy on Humane Treatment of* Detainees, GLOBALSECURI-TY.ORG (July 11, 2006), http://www.globalsecurity.org/security/library/news/2006/07/sec–060711–afps01.htm; *see generally* Military Commissions Act of 2006, Pub. L. No. 109–366, 120 Stat. 2600.

109. *See* United States v. Noriega, 808 F.Supp. 791, 793–96 (S. D. Fla. 1992).

110. *See Id.* at 796.

111. *See U.S. judge OKs Noriega extradition to France*, CNN.COM, (Aug.

because France had not indicated a commitment to acknowledge his POW status and comply with the Geneva Convention Relative to the Treatment of Prisoner of War, his transfer to France would violate article 12 of the Convention, which indicates "Prisoners of war may only be transferred by the Detaining Power to a Power which is a party to the Convention and after the retaining Power has satisfied itself of the willingness and ability of such transferee Power to apply the Convention."[112]

The government challenged Noriega's ability to invoke article 12 to resist extradition. Ironically, it was the Military Commission Act of 2006 (MCA) (as amended in 2009) that provided the basis for this challenge, specifically Section 5 (a), which provides that:

> No person may invoke the Geneva Conventions or any protocols thereto in any habeas corpus or other civil action or proceeding to which the United States, or a current or former officer, employee, member of the Armed Forces, or other agent of the United States is a party as a source of rights in any court of the United States or its States or territories.[113]

It is unlikely Congress contemplated that this provision, included in the MCA in an effort to limit the judiciary to domestic law when addressing issues of terrorist detainee treatment, would provide the basis to contest Noriega's challenge to extradition. Nonetheless, the challenge placed before the courts the ability of Congress to place such limits on judicial review.

Both the trial court and the 11th Circuit Court of Appeals ruled in favor of the government and rejected Noriega's effort to block extradition.[114] Both courts relied on the MCA to conclude that Noriega could not invoke the POW Convention in support of his challenge. Noriega then petitioned the Supreme Court on a writ of certiorari. Although the petition was denied, the following excerpt from Justice Thomas' dissenting opinion indicates quite clearly that the Court considers the armed conflict with al Qaeda to be a distinct non-international armed conflict, and not one subordinated to the ongoing armed conflict with the Taliban:

> As the Eleventh Circuit's opinion makes clear, the threshold question in this case is whether MCA § 5(a) is valid. Answering that question this Term would provide courts and the political branches with much needed guidance on

---

28, 2007) http://www.cnn.com/2007/US/ law/08/28/noriega/index.html.

112. Convention Relative to the Treatment of Prisoners of War, Aug. 12, 1949, T.I.A.S. 3364 art. 12.

113. Military Commissions Act of 2006, Pub. L. No. 109–366, 120 Stat. 2600 (2006).

114. *See generally* United States v. Noriega, 808 F.Supp. 791 (S. D. Fla. 1992).

issues we left open in *Boumediene*. See *Boumediene*, 553 U. S, at ___, ___ (slip op. at 64–66, 68–70). Providing that guidance in this case would allow us to say what the law is without the unnecessary delay and other complications that could burden a decision on these questions in Guantanamo or other detainee litigation *arising out of the conflict with Al Qaeda.*[115]

These three seminal opinions collectively indicate that the decision by the two political branches of government to redefine the nature of the struggle against transnational terrorism following the September 11th attacks has enjoyed the implicit if not explicit support of the Supreme Court. The interesting illumination provided by the Noriega litigation only serves to confirm that these decisions should not be read narrowly as recognizing only an armed conflict in Afghanistan. Instead, they reflect a recognition that at least certain aspects of the struggle against al Qaeda qualify as an armed conflict triggering LOAC rights and obligations. Accordingly, there is little doubt related to the legitimacy of this redefinition—at least from the perspective of the United States. This does not, however, reflect a broader international consensus on the legitimacy of characterizing counter-terror efforts as an armed conflict invoking the LOAC authorities as a legal framework to support the prosecution of that struggle. On the contrary, the U.S. position on this issue remains the subject of substantial criticism in the broader international legal community.

F. AN ALTERNATIVE VIEW: REJECTING THE DESIGNATION OF COUNTER–TERROR OPERATIONS AS ARMED CONFLICT

As noted previously, prior to 1949, there was no defined criterion to determine when the LOAC (at that time called the law of war) came into force. As a general proposition, it was understood that it would apply to any war. However, uncertainty as to the international legal definition of war resulted in the existence of hostilities with an accordant disavowal by states that they were bound by the law of war.[116] Providing the law applicability trigger in terms other than "war" was a deliberate effort to maximize the humanitarian protections imposed by these treaties and to minimize the opportunity for the type of definitional law avoidance that defined the era between 1918 and 1945. The term "armed conflict" was intended to link applicability of the law with the pragmatic realities of military operations, not to be a complex legal term.[117]

---

115. Noriega v. Pastrana, 130 S.Ct. 1002 (2010) (Thomas, J. dissenting) (emphasis added).

116. *See* Commentary, Convention (I) for the Amelioration of the Condition of the Wounded and Sick in Armed Forces in the Field. Geneva, 12 August 1949 (Jean S. Pictet ed., 1960).

117. *Id.*

Events following September 11th fundamentally transformed the focus of the LOAC applicability debate. Suddenly, international law experts were presented with the invocation of LOAC based authority to attack, detain, and try transnational terrorist operatives. Lodging these operations under the broader umbrella of the conflict against the Taliban in Afghanistan presented little analytical difficulty: the conflict was international within the meaning of the LOAC and al Qaeda operatives were part of volunteer forces operating on behalf of the Taliban.[118] However, as noted above, the U.S. adopted a different interpretation of its relationship with al Qaeda. Not only would it consider operations in Afghanistan to include two distinct armed conflicts: one against the Taliban and one against al Qaeda; it viewed the latter conflict as one extending well beyond Afghanistan to any location where al Qaeda planned or executed its operations. Hence the term Global War on Terror.[119]

International law experts, and even many U.S. allies, challenged the validity of this theory of LOAC applicability.[120] Opponents of the interpretation emphasized the LOAC triggering paradigm that evolved prior to September 11th. For them, the notion that an armed conflict can exist between a state and a loosely organized non-state entity that operates transnationally is a legal fiction.[121] Instead, only two types of situations may properly trigger LOAC applicability. First, an armed conflict between two states—known in international law as an international armed conflict; second, an armed conflict between a state and an armed and organized non-state group or between two or more such groups of significant intensity and duration—known in international law as a non-international armed conflict.[122] Because al Qaeda (like virtually all international terrorist organizations) lacks the requisite level of organization and the operations conducted against such groups lack the requisite intensity and duration necessary to satisfy the definition of non-international armed conflict, such operations simply remain in the realm of law enforcement.[123]

118. *See* International Law Association, Use of Force Committee, Final Report on the Meaning of Armed Conflict in International Law, 3 (2010), *available at* http://www.ila-hq.org/en/committees/index.cfm/cid/1022.

119. *See National Security Strategy: III. Strengthen Alliances to Defeat Global Terrorism and Work to Prevent Attacks Against Us and Our Friends,* (Sept. 2002), http://georgewbush-whitehouse.archives.gov/nsc/nss/2002/nss3.html.

120. *See, e.g.,* Mary Ellen O'Connell, *Defining Armed Conflict* 13 J. Conflict & Sec. L. 393 (Winter 2008).

121. *See* International Law Association, Use of Force Committee, Final Report on the Meaning of Armed Conflict in International Law, 10–18 (2010), *available at* http://www.ila-hq.org/en/committees/index.cfm/cid/1022.

122. *Id.*

123. International Law Association, Use of Force Committee, Final Report on the Meaning of Armed Conflict

This LOAC interpretation is based on two primary sources of authority. First, the Geneva Conventions and their associated International Committee of the Red Cross Commentaries; second, the jurisprudence of the International Criminal Tribunal for the Former Yugoslavia (ICTY) analyzing the meaning of non-international armed conflict. It is the definition of this latter category of armed conflict where a significant divide has developed between the United States and these experts; a divide attributable primarily to the diverging assessment of the authority of the ICTY's jurisprudence.[124]

A recent report by a committee established by the International Law Association to analyze the meaning of the term armed conflict provides perhaps the clearest manifestation of this alternate LOAC interpretation.[125] That report, issued August of 2010, rejects the validity of a "Global War on Terror" as an armed conflict. Accordingly, it concludes that the LOAC cannot be invoked as a source of either authority or obligation in the context of counter-terror operations defined by U.S. operations directed against al Qaeda unless those operations are subordinate to a broader armed conflict involving another state or an armed and organized dissident group within a state.[126] According to the report:

> In May 2005, the Executive Committee of the International Law Association (ILA) approved a mandate for the Use of Force Committee to produce a report on the meaning of war or armed conflict in international law. The report was motivated by the United States' position following the attacks of 11 September 2001 that it was involved in a "global war on terror". In other words, the U.S. has claimed the right to exercise belligerent privileges applicable only during armed conflict anywhere in the world where members of terrorist groups are found. The U.S. position was contrary to a trend by states attempting to avoid acknowledging involvement in wars or armed conflicts.
>
> . . .
>
> . . . Plainly, the existence of armed conflict is a significant fact in the international legal system, and, yet, the Committee found no widely accepted definition of armed con-

in International Law, 26, 29 (2010), *available at* http://www.ila-hq.org/en/committees/index.cfm/cid/1022.

124. *See* Prosecutor v. Tadic, Case No. IT–94–1–AR72, Appeal on Jurisdiction (Oct. 2, 1995), at para. 70, *reprinted in* 35 I.L.M. 32 (1996).

125. *See generally* International Law Association, Use of Force Commit-

tee, Final Report on the Meaning of Armed Conflict in International Law, 10–18 (2010), *available at* http://www.ila-hq.org/en/committees/index.cfm/cid/1022.

126. *Id.*

flict in any treaty. It did, however, discover significant evidence in the sources of international law that the international community embraces a common understanding of armed conflict. All armed conflict has certain minimal, defining characteristics that distinguish it from situations of non-armed conflict or peace. In the absence of these characteristics, states may not, consistently with international law, simply declare that a situation is or is not armed conflict based on policy preferences. The Committee confirmed that at least two characteristics are found with respect to all armed conflict:

1.) The existence of organized armed groups

2.) Engaged in fighting of some intensity

In addition to these minimum criteria respecting all armed conflict, IHL includes additional criteria so as to classify conflicts as either international or non-international in nature.

. . .

. . . The Committee, however, found little evidence to support the view that the Conventions apply in the absence of fighting of some intensity. For non-state actors to move from chaotic violence to being able to challenge the armed forces of a state requires organization, meaning a command structure, training, recruiting ability, communications, and logistical capacity. Such organized forces are only recognized as engaged in armed conflict when fighting between them is more than a minimal engagement or incident.[127]

The report indicates substantial reliance on the seminal decision by the International Criminal Tribunal for the Former Yugoslavia (ICTY) in the case of *Prosecutor v. Tadic.*[128] That case involved the first war crimes trial at the ICTY related to the conflict in the former Yugoslavia. In order to respond to the defendant's jurisdictional challenge, the Tribunal was required to determine whether and what type of armed conflict existed in Bosnia at the time of the alleged war crimes. The Tribunal concluded that the conflict was non-international within the meaning of the Geneva Conventions, thereby falling within its jurisdiction. In reaching this conclusion, the Tribunal identified what might best be characterized as the 'Tadic factors' or the 'organizational test' to

---

127. International Law Association, Use of Force Committee, Final Report on the Meaning of Armed Conflict in International Law, 1–2 (2010), *available* *at* http://www.ila-hq.org/en/committees/index.cfm/cid/1022.

128. Case No. IT–94–1–A, Judgment (Appeals Chamber), 15 July 1999.

determine when a situation evolves from a response to internal civil unrest involving the exercise of peacetime law enforcement to that of armed conflict triggering LOAC authority.[129]

According to the Tribunal, in order for an armed conflict to exist outside the context of interstate hostilities, the dissident forces engaged in the struggle must operate pursuant to military organization, must conduct sustained operations, and must operate with military capability.[130] The International Law Association committee relied on these factors to conclude that transnational terrorist groups do not qualify as the type of dissident group required to trigger the LOAC in relation to a state response to that threat.[131] Accordingly, such operations are not armed conflicts. This interpretation of the LOAC triggering requirements is generally representative of a majority of states, international law experts, and international non-government organizations with competence in humanitarian law.[132]

At the current time, there is no indication the United States will modify its position that the struggle against al Qaeda qualifies as an armed conflict in response to this report, or to any other external criticism. President Obama has continued to assert authorities implicitly derived from the LOAC to justify his administration's efforts to destroy, disable, and degrade the threat of transnational terrorism. In his Nobel Prize acceptance speech, the new President specifically characterized the struggle against transnational terrorism as a war:

> But perhaps the most profound issue surrounding my receipt of this prize is the fact that I am the Commander-in-Chief of the military of a nation in the midst of two wars. One of these wars is winding down. The other is a conflict that America did not seek; one in which we are joined by forty two other countries—including Norway—in an effort to defend ourselves and all nations from further attacks.

> Still, we are at war, and I am responsible for the deployment of thousands of young Americans to battle in a distant land. Some will kill, and some will be killed. And so I come here with an acute sense of the cost of armed conflict—filled with difficult questions about the relation-

129. *Id.*
130. *Id.*
131. *See* International Law Association, Use of Force Committee, Final Report on the Meaning of Armed Conflict in International Law, 14–15 (2010), *available at* http://www.ila-hq.org/en/committees/index.cfm/cid/1022.

132. *See generally* International Law Association, Use of Force Committee, Final Report on the Meaning of Armed Conflict in International Law, (2010), *available at*: http://www.ila-hq.org/en/committees/index.cfm/cid/1022.

ship between war and peace, and our effort to replace one with the other.

. . .

A decade into a new century, this old architecture is buckling under the weight of new threats. The world may no longer shudder at the prospect of war between two nuclear superpowers, but proliferation may increase the risk of catastrophe. Terrorism has long been a tactic, but modern technology allows a few small men with outsized rage to murder innocents on a horrific scale.[133]

There is however one important difference between President Obama's LOAC interpretation in relation to this armed conflict and that of his predecessor: unlike President Bush, President Obama has not only invoked LOAC authority, but has emphasized the U.S. commitment to comply with the humanitarian constraints of the law:

Let me make one final point about the use of force. Even as we make difficult decisions about going to war, we must also think clearly about how we fight it. The Nobel Committee recognized this truth in awarding its first prize for peace to Henry Dunant—the founder of the Red Cross, and a driving force behind the Geneva Conventions.

Where force is necessary, we have a moral and strategic interest in binding ourselves to certain rules of conduct. And even as we confront a vicious adversary that abides by no rules, I believe that the United States of America must remain a standard bearer in the conduct of war. That is what makes us different from those whom we fight. That is a source of our strength. That is why I prohibited torture. That is why I ordered the prison at Guantanamo Bay closed. And that is why I have reaffirmed America's commitment to abide by the Geneva Conventions. We lose ourselves when we compromise the very ideals that we fight to defend. And we honor those ideals by upholding them not just when it is easy, but when it is hard.[134]

This is indeed an important step forward in the regulation of hostilities between the United States and al Qaeda. Nonetheless, characterizing this struggle as an armed conflict remains highly controversial and invalid in the view of many international legal

133. *Remarks by the President at the Acceptance of the Nobel Peace Prize,* WHITEHOUSE.GOV (Dec. 10, 2009) http:// www.whitehouse.gov/the-press-office/ remarks-president-acceptance-nobel-peace-prize.

134. *Id.*

experts. It is therefore essential that any scholar engaged in the study of this issue recognize the controversy related to this interpretation of the law and the source of that controversy. How these competing views will evolve over time and whether the U.S. interpretation will influence a more widespread evolution of LOAC understanding remains to be seen.

Chapter 3
TARGETING TERRORISTS WITH MILITARY FORCE

A. THE LAW OF ARMED CONFLICT AND TERRORIST TARGETING

The authority to employ deadly force as a measure of first resort is the fundamental defining aspect of armed conflict. Unlike peacetime situations, armed conflict involves the use of deadly force based not on individualized assessments of the threat, but instead on determinations that the object of violence falls within the category of "enemy." Once this determination is made, the law of armed conflict (LOAC) authorizes opposing forces to take all measures that are necessary to bring about the enemy's submission in the most efficient manner, so long as those measures are not otherwise prohibited by international law.[1] In stark contrast, when government actors operate pursuant to peacetime law enforcement authority, use of deadly force is reserved as a measure of last resort.[2] In that context, police officers are required to make individualized assessments that the individual they are considering using force against has acted in a manner that justifies resort to that level of force and that no lesser degree of force will adequately address the threat.

It should therefore be immediately apparent why characterizing the struggle against transnational terrorism as an armed conflict is profoundly significant in relation to the ability of the United States to attack and disable suspected terrorists. Invoking the LOAC authority to use deadly force—known in military parlance as

---

1. The principle of military necessity establishes the authority of armed forces engaged in hostilities to take those measures not otherwise forbidden by international law to bring about the prompt submission of an opponent. *See* US DEPARTMENT OF ARMY, FIELD MANUAL 6–20–10, TACTICS, TECHNIQUES AND PROCEDURES FOR THE TARGETING PROCESS, ch. 2 (8 May 1996). *See generally* Protocol Additional to the Geneva Conventions of 12 August 1949, and relating to the Protection of Victims of International Armed Conflicts (1977), 1125 UNTS 3 (entered into force 7 December 1978) [hereinafter AP I] and Protocol Additional to the Geneva Conventions of 12 August 1949,

and relating to the Protection of Victims of Non–International Armed Conflicts (1977), 1125 UNTS 609 (entered into force 7 December 1978) [hereinafter AP II].

2. Code of Conduct for Law Enforcement Officials, GA Res. 34/169 of 17 December 1979 (Code of Conduct), art. 1, commentary (a) and (b); Basic Principles on the Use of Force and Firearms by Law Enforcement Officials, Eighth U.N. Congress on Prevention of Crime and Treatment of Offenders, Havana, Cuba, Aug. 27–Sept. 7, 1990, (Basic Principles), preamble, note.

targeting authority—against such operatives within the context of a broader and geographically limited armed conflict such as that ongoing in Afghanistan (al Qaeda operatives associated with Taliban militants) is a common practice. While such targeting might implicate issues related to the sufficiency of the identification of the target, invocation of LOAC targeting authority in this context is not particularly controversial. However, as the geographic scope of operations targeting suspected terrorists expands beyond the boundaries of Afghanistan into not only the border regions of Pakistan, but also other countries such as Yemen and Somalia, the legitimacy of invoking LOAC based targeting authority triggers significant controversy.[3]

In response to the terror attacks of September 11th, the United States began targeting terrorist operatives with deadly military force in numerous locations around the world. In January 2010 alone, twelve predator drone strikes were conducted just in Pakistan.[4] As the scope of U.S. targeting operations against suspected terrorists became public knowledge, many observers surmised that these "targeted killings" of terrorist operatives reflected an invocation by the United States of this fundamental LOAC authority. In fact, as far back as 2003 the United States enunciated the theory of legality upon which it based subsequent drone attacks. This theory is reflected in a United States response to a United Nations Human Rights Committee query into the legal authority for these targeted killings. The query was triggered by a U.S. predator drone attack against a group of individuals in a civilian vehicle driving on a road in Yemen.[5] The Commission requested that the United States government explain how what the Commission characterized as a summary execution could be justified pursuant to international human rights law (which prohibits such summary process). In response, the United States representative to the human rights commission, without conceding that the United States had in fact conducted the predator strike, asserted the Commission had invoked the wrong source of international law in its query. Contrary to the assumption that international human rights law controlled U.S. strikes against terrorist operatives, the U.S. response emphasized that because it was engaged in a worldwide armed conflict with al Qaeda, the legality of such strikes could only properly be assessed pursuant to the LOAC.[6]

3. Report of the Special Rapporteur on extrajudicial, summary or arbitrary executions, Philip Alston, Study on Targeted Killings, 28 May 2010, A/HRC/14/24/Add.6 General Assembly, para.52–3 (hereinafter Study on Targeted Killings).

4. *See* Kenneth Anderson, *Predators over Pakistan*, THE WEEKLY STAN-

DARD, Mar. 8, 2010, *available at* http://www.weeklystandard.com/print/articles/predators-over-pakistan.

5. Jane Mayer, *The Predator War*, THE NEW YORKER, Oct. 26, 2009.

6. *See* Letter dated 14 April 2003 from the Chief of Section, Political and Specialized Agencies, of the Permanent

In essence, this response indicated that al Qaeda operatives qualified as lawful military objectives in accordance with the LOAC, and therefore the United States was acting with lawful international legal authority by engaging them with deadly force as a measure of first resort whenever and wherever they could be located.[7] In further support of the legality of such attacks, the U.S. has emphasized its authority to take necessary measures to ensure the nations self-defense and protection of national security.[8]

This assertion of global wartime targeting authority by the United States was and remains widely condemned as legally invalid. Like the asserted authority to preventively detain individuals associated with al Qaeda pursuant to the LOAC even when they are not captured in proximity to an area of ongoing combat operations (like Afghanistan or Iraq), the assertion of LOAC based targeting authority to kill these terrorist operatives based on an armed conflict that allegedly knows no geographical boundaries is perceived by many critics as fundamentally invalid.[9] Nonetheless, the United States continues to engage in such targeting operations, and to insist that international law provides the authority to do so.[10] This interpretation of international law was forcefully articulated by Harold Koh, the Legal Advisor to the Department of State, in an appearance before the American Society of International Law on March 25, 2010.

> As I have explained, as a matter of international law, the United States is in an armed conflict with al-Qaeda, as well as the Taliban and associated forces, in response to the horrific 9/11 attacks, and may use force consistent with its inherent right to self-defense under international law. As a matter of domestic law, Congress authorized the use of all necessary and appropriate force through the 2001 Authorization for Use of Military Force (AUMF). These domestic and international legal authorities continue to this day.

> As recent events have shown, al-Qaeda has not abandoned its intent to attack the United States, and indeed continues to attack us. Thus, in this ongoing armed con-

Mission of the United States of America to the United Nations Office at Geneva addressed to the secretariat of the Commission on Human Rights, UN Doc. E/CN.4/2003/G/80, at 2–3 (22 April 2003).

7. *Id.*

8. *Id.*

9. *See* Study on Targeted Killings, *supra* note 3, para. 34–36.

10. *See* Kenneth Anderson, *Predators over Pakistan, supra* note 4 (stating that the principle of self defense, according to international customary law, while not invoking the technicalities of the LOAC, must still adhere to the fundamental standards of necessity and proportionality and that the US currently adheres to LOAC and its standards).

flict, the United States has the authority under international law, and the responsibility to its citizens, to use force, including lethal force, to defend itself, including by targeting persons such as high-level al-Qaeda leaders who are planning attacks . . .

[S]ome have argued that the use of lethal force against specific individuals fails to provide adequate process and thus constitutes *unlawful extrajudicial killing*. But a state that is engaged in an armed conflict or in legitimate self-defense is not required to provide targets with legal process before the state may use lethal force. Our procedures and practices for identifying lawful targets are extremely robust, and advanced technologies have helped to make our targeting even more precise. In my experience, the principles of distinction and proportionality that the United States applies are not just recited at meetings. They are implemented rigorously throughout the planning and execution of lethal operations to ensure that such operations are conducted in accordance with all applicable law.[11]

Koh's comments on the international legal basis to attack al Qaeda operatives pursuant to the LOAC has not, of course, eliminated criticisms of this legal interpretation. However, it unequivocally identified the law relied on by the United States to justify these attacks, or targeted killings. How the LOAC informs the use of force against terrorist operatives is therefore a critical aspect to the execution of the effort to defeat, disable, or degrade the terrorist threat.

B. MILITARY NECESSITY: THE FIRST PRINCIPLE OF AUTHORITY

Targeting is the process whereby participants in armed conflict identify and engage people, places, or things that are determined to be lawful objects of attack. Accordingly, the targeting process involves two critical components. First, a military operational decision-maker determines that the attack against a person, place, or thing contributes to the efficient defeat of an enemy. This determination could be as simple as an infantry soldier deciding that the person he observes through his rifle sight is an enemy operative and therefore must be shot, or a complex as a high level commander approving a list of prioritized targets for attack by air and missile assets during the opening phase of a major armed conflict. Second, the decision-maker must determine that pursuant to the LOAC the proposed object of attack qualifies as a lawful object of attack.[12]

11. Annual Meeting of the American Society of International Law Washington, DC, March 25, 2010, Harold Hongju Koh, *available at* http://www.state.gov/s/l/releases/remarks/139119.htm.

The targeting process is therefore perhaps the most fundamental manifestation of the LOAC principle of military necessity, a principle considered by most LOAC experts as a core principle of the *jus in bello*.[13] This conclusion is bolstered by the fact that military necessity is a principle derived from some of the original sources of the LOAC.[14] Furthermore, because the authority to detect, destroy, or disable terrorist capabilities is the essential byproduct of invoking the principle of military necessity, it is equally unsurprising that the invocation of this principle (explicitly or implicitly through the exercise of authority historically reserved for situations of armed conflict), is a significant motivation for why the United States would choose to characterize the struggle against transnational terror as an armed conflict.

This principle, however, is not only a source of authority. Because the principle of military necessity implicitly incorporates limitations on the use of military power—limitations derived from the fact that only those measures that are *necessary* for the defeat of an enemy are justified by the principle—its invocation also requires adherence to the LOACs regulatory constraints.[15] This authority/constraint balance is reflected in both conventional and customary international law and lies at the very core of conflict regulation. The concept of imposing limitations on combatants is arguably as ancient as organized warfare itself, and is reflected in Napoleon's great maxim that "[I]n politics and war alike, every injury done to the enemy, even though permitted by the rules, is excusable only so far as it is absolutely necessary; everything beyond that is criminal."[16]

This balance between necessity and humanity is reflected in the definition of military necessity in U.S. Army Field Manual 27–10, *The Law of Land Warfare:*

> The law of war . . . requires that belligerents refrain from employing any kind or degree of violence which is not

12. *See* API, *supra* note 1, art. 52.

13. A.P.V. ROGERS, LAW ON THE BATTLEFIELD 3 (2d ed. 2004); Michael J. Davidson, *War and the Doubtful Soldier*, 19 NOTRE DAME J.L. ETHICS & PUB. POL'Y 91, 153 (2005); Olugbenga Shoyele, *Armed Conflicts and Canadian Refugee and Law Policy*, 16 INT'L J. REFUGEE L. 547, 555 (2004).

14. *See* A.P.V. ROGERS, LAW ON THE BATTLEFIELD at 4–5 (2d ed. 2004).

15. *See* Geoffrey S. Corn, *Hamdan, Lebanon, and the Regulation of Armed Conflict: The Need to Recognize a Hybrid Category of Armed Conflict*, 40 VAND. J. TRANSNAT'L L. 295 (2007); *see also* Geoffrey S. Corn & Eric Talbot Jensen, *Transnational Armed Conflict: A 'Principled' Approach to the Regulation of Counter–Terror Combat Operations*, 42 ISRAEL L. REV. 45 (2009).

16. *See* GEOFFREY BEST, LAW & WAR SINCE 1945, 244 (Oxford University Press, 1994) (quoting Max Huber in 'Die kriegsrechtlichen Vertage und die Kriegsraison' in Zeitschrift fur Volkerrecht, 7 (1913), 351–374, at 353).

actually necessary for military purposes and that they conduct hostilities with regard for the principles of humanity and chivalry. The prohibitory effect of the law of war is not minimized by "military necessity" which has been defined as that principle which justifies those measures not forbidden by international law which are indispensable for securing the complete submission of the enemy as soon as possible.[17]

Military necessity is therefore the international legal link between a desired military effect and the legally permissible actions taken to achieve that effect. Accordingly, the principle is intended to balance the legitimate needs of parties engaged in armed conflict to destroy, disable, and ultimately defeat an enemy, with a humanity derived imperative to limit the harmful effects of military action to only those that are justified by the necessity to achieve this military purpose.

C. TARGETING OF PERSONS AND PROPERTY IN ARMED CONFLICT

The destruction of enemy capability through the application of combat power is perhaps the most fundamental incident of waging war. It is therefore axiomatic that armed conflict involves the attacking the enemy's combat forces, equipment, and facilities. Military operators call the process of enemy target selection and engagement "targeting." During the targeting process—a process that is constantly ongoing—the military commander (supported by her staff) identifies military objectives; selects the most appropriate capability[18] to achieve the desired operational effect (often referred to as weaponeering),[19] executes military operations to employ the combat capability; and assesses the effects achieved. Compliance with the rules of targeting established by the conventional and customary LOAC is always complex. However, this complexity is substantially enhanced in the context of operations directed against terrorist enemy operatives. The uncertainity regarding the boundaries of how to define a lawful military objective and the unconventional nature of the non-state enemy has and will continue to exacerbate the challenge of achieving desired operational effects while complying with this law.

---

17. U.S. DEP'T OF ARMY, FIELD MANUAL 27-10, THE LAW OF LAND WARFARE 3-4 (July 1956) [hereinafter FM 27-10].

18. This includes kinetic or non-kinetic capability. For example, a commander may employ conventional kinetic munitions to target an enemy capability, or may choose to employ a non-kinetic capability, such as information, to achieve the desired effect.

19. This concept is referred to as "effects based targeting." It involves tailoring the application of combat power to the stated operational effect desired, which could include destroying, disabling, disrupting, or harassing an enemy.

The LOAC provides a framework for determining the legality of an intended object of attack, or target. The primary focus of this framework is the protection of civilians and civilian property. This protection is based on the international legal axiom that deliberately attacking civilians or property used exclusively for civilian purposes is never justified by military necessity. Accordingly, the LOAC mandates that attacks be limited to those persons, places, or things that qualify as lawful military objectives.[20] This requirement to distinguish between lawful military objectives and all other persons, places, and things is a fundamental LOAC principle known as the principle of distinction (also referred to as discrimination).[21] For purposes of determining what people may be lawfully attacked, the LOAC eventually established three categories of persons in an area of armed conflict: combatants, non-combatants, and civilians.[22] The principle of distinction establishes a presumptive protection for civilians: so long as they refrain from taking a direct part in hostilities they may not be made the deliberate object of attack.[23] However, distinction becomes much more difficult when civilians engaged in conduct considered by an armed force dangerous. If that conduct crosses the line to direct participation in hostilities, the civilian loses the protection from attack[24] for such time as the participation continues.[25] This principle is codified in treaties regulating both international and non-international armed conflicts, and has been interpreted by the International Court of Justice as a customary norm of international law applicable at all times to all armed conflicts.[26]

In order to facilitate compliance with the principle of distinction, the LOAC defines lawful objects of attacks as 'military objectives.' The definition of military objectives is found in The 1977 Protocol Additional to the Geneva Conventions of 1949 (AP I):

> Attacks shall be limited strictly to military objectives. In so far as objects are concerned, military objectives are limited to those objects which by their nature, location, purpose, or use make an effective contribution to military action and whose total or partial destruction, capture, or neutralization, in the circumstances ruling at the time, offers a definite military advantage.[27]

20. See AP I, *supra* note 1, art. 48.

21. See ROGERS, *supra* note 13 at 3 ("The great principles of customary law, from which all else stems, are those of military necessity, humanity, distinction and proportionality.").

22. See Eric T. Jensen, THE WAR ON TERROR AND THE LAWS OF WAR: A MILITARY PERSPECTIVE 44–45 (2009).

23. *Id.*

24. *Id.* at 46; see also AP I, *supra* note 1, art. 51(4).

25. AP I, *supra* note 1, art. 51(4).

26. Advisory Opinion, *Legality of the Threat or Use of Nuclear Weapons*, ICJ, 8 July 1996.

27. See AP I, *supra* note 1, art. 52(2).

In the classic inter-state armed conflict situation, determining which persons qualify as lawful military objectives has always been facilitated by the intersection with other LOAC provisions that dictate the requirements for qualification as a lawful combatant. These provisions first appeared in the 1899 Hague Convention and Annexed Regulations (revised without modification in 1907[28]) which established the rule that only certain individuals fighting on behalf of a state were privileged to engage in hostilities. These included primarily members of the armed forces and other militia or volunteer forces associated with the armed forces that complied with certain requirements.[29] This definition of "privileged combatant" was subsequently incorporated into the Geneva Convention Relative to the Treatment of Prisoners of War (GPW) as the core of the POW status qualification criteria.[30]

Compliance with these treaty provisions has therefore resulted in a simple reality of inter-state armed conflict: combatants have

28. Hague Convention No. IV Respecting the Laws and Customs of War on Land, Oct. 18, 1907, Stat. 2277, T.S. 539, *reprinted in* U.S. DEP'T OF ARMY, PAM. 27–1, TREATIES GOVERNING LAND WARFARE, (Dec. 1956).

29. *See* ROGERS, *supra* note 13, 30–34. Members of a *levee en masse* were also included. A *levee en masse* is an extremely unlikely event in contemporary military operations. *See* Nils Melzer, Legal Adviser, International Committee of the Red Cross, INTERPRETIVE GUIDANCE ON THE NOTION OF DIRECT PARTICIPATION IN HOSTILITIES UNDER INT'L HUMANITARIAN LAW (May 2009), *available at* http://www.icrc.org/Web/Eng/siteeng0.nsf/htmlall/p0990/$File/ICRC_002_0990.pdf [hereinafter IG] at 25.

30. *See* Convention (III) Relative to the Treatment of Prisoners of War, Aug. 12, 1949, 6 U.S.T. 3316, 75 U.N.T.S. 135, *reprinted in* DIETRICH SCHINDLER & JIRI TOMAN, THE LAWS OF ARMED CONFLICTS 430–31 (2d ed. 1981) which requires:

A. Prisoners of War, in the sense of the present Convention, are persons belonging to one of the following categories, who have fallen into the power of the enemy:

(1) Members of the armed forces of a Party to the conflict as well as members of militias or volunteer corps forming part of such armed forces.

(2) Members of other militias and members of other volunteer corps, including those of organized resistance movements, belonging to a Party to the conflict and operating in or outside their own territory, even if this territory is occupied, provided that such militias or volunteer corps, including such organized resistance movements, fulfill the following conditions:

(a) that of being commanded by a person responsible for his subordinates;

(b) that of having a fixed distinctive sign recognizable at a distance;

(c) that of carrying arms openly;

(d) that of conducting their operations in accordance with the laws and customs of war.

(3) Members of regular armed forces who profess allegiance to a government or an authority not recognized by the Detaining Power.

. . .

(6) Inhabitants of a non-occupied territory, who on the approach of the enemy spontaneously take up arms to resist the invading forces, without having had time to form themselves into regular armed units, provided they carry arms openly and respect the laws and customs of war.

historically distinguished themselves from the civilian population by wearing uniforms and operating in organized units subject to responsible military command. Accordingly, in the context of international armed conflict, members of the enemy armed forces—individuals normally distinguishable from the civilian population as a result of their compliance with the POW qualification criteria of the GPW—are lawful objects of attack until they have surrendered or been rendered combat ineffective by wounds or sickness. In contrast, all other individuals are presumptively protected from deliberate attack.[31]

The situation in non-international armed conflicts is, however, far more complicated. Unlike the law of international armed conflict, there is no definition of "lawful combatant" or "privileged belligerent" in the context of NIAC.[32] As a result, international law establishes no requirement and provides no incentive for non-state belligerent personnel to wear uniforms or otherwise distinguish themselves from the civilian population. This has created a dilemma for states engaged in armed hostilities against such forces: can there be enemy "combatants" in NIAC without an international legal definition of such a status?[33]

There are two evolving responses to this question. First, some experts assert that there are no non-state combatants in NIAC, only civilians who lose their presumptive protection by taking part in hostilities. The second response, which appears to be at the core of the U.S. approach to targeting non-state opposition personnel, is that although the LOAC lacks a definition for combatants in the context of NIAC, the conclusion that all opposition belligerent personnel are presumptively civilians is unjustified. Instead, members of armed organized non-state belligerent groups are properly characterized as unprivileged belligerents, and therefore may be treated for purposes of targeting no differently than members of regular armed forces of an enemy state in the context of international armed conflict.[34]

The difference between these two approaches may seem insignificant. Under either interpretation, state armed forces would be

31. Protocol Additional to the Geneva Conventions of 12 August 1949, and relating to the Protection of Victims of International Armed Conflicts (Protocol I), 8 June 1977, art. 50.

32. *See* Nils Melzer, Legal Adviser, International Committee of the Red Cross, INTERPRETIVE GUIDANCE ON THE NOTION OF DIRECT PARTICIPATION IN HOSTILITIES (May 2009), at 25–33 [hereinafter IG].

33. *See generally The Public Committee Against Torture et al. v. The Gov-*ernment of Israel, et al., HCJ 769/02, (Dec. 14, 2006) [hereinafter, Public Committee] (the Court rejected the government's assertion that terrorists are 'unlawful combatants' subject to attack at any time).

34. Memorandum from Office of the Assistant Att'y Gen. to Alberto Gonzales, Counsel to the President (Aug. 1 2002).

justified in targeting a terrorist operative engaged in conduct that is fundamentally inconsistent with the presumptive inoffensive character of civilians, or directly participating in hostilities. However, the difference is profound. Under the presumptive civilian approach, targeting such operatives is limited to situations when any civilian could be made the deliberate object of attack: in response to conduct by the individual that qualifies as direct participation in hostilities. While the meaning of this term is the subject of substantial contemporary debate, the underlying principle is clear: civilians are presumed inoffensive, and therefore are presumptively immune from being made the deliberate object of attack.[35] Accordingly, the burden is placed on the attacking armed force to validate on a case-by-case basis that the intended object of attack engaged in individual conduct that justifies rebutting the presumption of protection and subjecting the individual to deliberate attack. Thus, the determination of justified attack is dictated by the individual conduct of the object of attack, much like the decision-making process of a law enforcement officer in peacetime.

In contrast, the legality of targeting a member of a belligerent group, or 'combatant' is based on the determination that the individual is in fact a member of the enemy belligerent force.[36] Once this link between the intended object of attack and the enemy belligerent force is established, it is the status of the individual, and not the individual's offensive conduct, that justifies the use of force. Known in military terminology as status based targeting, the scope of this type of targeting authority is substantially more expansive. Unlike the civilian who is presumed inoffensive and therefore vested with an accordant presumptive protection from attack, a member of an enemy force—or combatant in the pragmatic meaning of that term—is presumed hostile and therefore presumptively subject to attack. Furthermore, the burden is shifted from the attacking forces to the object of potential attack to rebut this presumption by surrender. Accordingly, so long as the individual remains a viable operative for the will of the enemy leadership, an opposing force is authorized to target that individual with no obligation to first assess the individual's actual offensive behavior immediately preceding the attack.[37]

It seems relatively clear that U.S. targeting practice since it initiated the military response to the terror attacks of September 11th has been based on the assumption that there is indeed a

35. *See generally* IG *supra* note 32.
36. *See* Convention (III) Relative to the Treatment of Prisoners of War, *supra* note 30.
37. *See generally* Geoffrey S. Corn, *Mixing Apples and Hand Grenades: The* *Logical Limit of Applying Human Rights Norms to Armed Conflict,* forthcoming in The Journal of International Humanitarian Legal Studies, *available at:* http://papers.ssrn.com/sol3/papers.cfm?abstract_id=1511954.

category of terrorist "forces" subject to military attack pursuant to LOAC status based targeting authority. Whether called unlawful combatants, unprivileged belligerents, enemy operatives, or some other term, the import is the same: these individuals become lawful objects of attack as the result of their membership in or connection to a terrorist organization.[38] This practice reflects an extension of the concept of targetable combatant in international armed conflict to the realm of military operations directed against transnational terrorists.

Subjecting members of organized belligerent groups to status based targeting pursuant to the LOAC as opposed to civilians who periodically lose their protection from attack seems both logical and consistent with the practice of states engaged in non-international armed conflicts. This conclusion is reflected in a recently proposed manual of LOAC rules applicable to armed conflict between states and internal dissident forces authored by three of the most highly respected *jus belli* scholars in the international community.[39] In their Manual for Non–International Armed Conflict, Yoram Dinstein, Michael Schmitt, and Charles Garaway define non-state forces as "fighters", and indicate that use of force is authorized against "members of armed forces and dissident armed forces or other organized armed groups, or taking active (direct) part in hostilities."[40] The Manual then asserts that "[A]ttacks must be directed only against fighters or military objectives."[41] The Manual continues with an excellent analysis of both customary and conventional international law and concludes that the targeting principles—including distinction and proportionality—apply to regulate both international and non-international armed conflict.

Other emerging approaches to this non-state actor targeting dilemma appear to reinforce this approach of recognizing the existence of enemy forces in the context of non-international armed conflicts. These include the concept of Likely and Identifiable Threat currently being used in Afghanistan by Coalition forces for identifying individuals subject to "status" based targeting;[42] and

---

38. *See* Annual Meeting of the American Society of International Law Washington, DC, March 25, 2010, Harold Hongju Koh, *available at* http://www.state.gov/s/l/releases/remarks/139119.htm.; *see also* Military Commissions Act, 10 U.S.C. sec. 948a(1)(i) and (ii) (defining unlawful enemy combatant).

39. International Institute of Humanitarian Law, The Manual on the Law of Non–International Armed Conflict, Sanremo, March 2006 (hereinafter NIAC Manual).

40. *Id.* at ¶ 1.1.2.a.

41. *Id.* at ¶ 2.1.1.

42. INT'L & OPERATIONAL LAW DEP'T, THE JUDGE ADVOCATE GENERAL'S SCHOOL, U.S. ARMY, OPERATIONAL LAW HANDBOOK 86 (MAJ John Rawcliffe, ed., 2007) ("b. Declared Hostile Force. Any civilian, paramilitary or military force or terrorist that has been declared hostile by appropriate U.S. authority. Once a force is declared to be "hostile," U.S. units may engage it without observing a hostile act or demonstration of hostile intent; i.e., the basis for engagement shifts from

the concept of the "revolving door" of direct participation in hostilities recently endorsed by the Israeli High Court of Justice in the Targeted Killing decision (discussed in greater detail below).[43] Even the ICRC's Interpretive Guidance on the Notion of Direct Participation in Hostilities recognizes a new concept titled "Continuing Combat Function."[44] As the Guidance notes, even in the context of international armed conflicts, once civilians engage in a pattern of continuing combat function, they in effect become subject to status based targeting by virtue of that behavior.[45]

All of these approaches share a common element: they establish criteria whereby association with a hostile belligerent force justifies designating an individual as a lawful military objective *irrespective* of the individual's conduct at the time of targeting. They also, however, reveal the difficulty of defining lawful objects of attack based on status when fighting an opponent that does not fall within an accepted international legal definition of combatant. Thus, even assuming that a category of combatant can exist in what might be called a "traditional" non-international armed conflict (between government and internal dissident forces), extending the definition of armed conflict to military action against transnational terrorist organizations resulted in a further complication: unlike internal armed conflicts, organization is not a requirement for such conflicts. Indeed, the transnational armed conflict proposition is based in large part on the assumption that transnational non-state entities will often defy any notion of traditional military "organization." As a result, determining what members of such organizations are the lawful objects of attack based on an armed conflict theory is and remains especially challenging.

Applying LOAC targeting principles to justify status based targeting of terrorist operatives in the context of transnational armed conflict is therefore only the first step in the regulatory process. The much more difficult question is determining who falls into the category of enemy belligerent, and who is simply a civilian associated with those forces. If military operations against transnational terrorist entities are conceived purely as a form of extraterritorial law enforcement, the answer to this question would arguably be dictated by a human rights law, permitting the use of deadly

---

conduct to status."); CENTER FOR LAW AND MILITARY OPERATIONS, THE JUDGE ADVOCATE GENERAL'S LEGAL CENTER & SCHOOL, U.S. ARMY, LEGAL LESSONS LEARNED FROM AFGHANISTAN AND IRAQ VOLUME I MAJOR COMBAT OPERATIONS (11 SEPTEMBER 2001–1 MAY 2003) 312 (1 Aug. 2004) (sample ROE card for Operation Iraqi Freedom); Geoffrey S. Corn & Eric T. Jensen, *Transnational Armed Conflict: A "Principled" Approach to the Regulation of*

Counter–Terror Combat Operations, 42 ISRAEL L. REV. 45 (2009).

43. *See* Public Committee *supra* note 33, at para. 40.

44. *See* INTERPRETIVE GUIDANCE ON THE NOTION OF DIRECT PARTICIPATION IN HOSTILITIES, *supra* note 29.

45. *Id.*

force only in self-defense when no lesser means of subduing the opponent is feasible. This is not, however, how targeting against transnational terrorists has been treated by the United States. Indeed, the characterization of this struggle as a Global War on Terror was clearly intended to reject the strict limitations of law enforcement use of force that had dominated the U.S. response to terrorism prior to September 11th. Instead, because as a practical matter the use of status based targeting against terrorist enemies indicates an implicit invocation of the LOAC principle of military objective, the employment of armed force in response to the threat of transnational terrorism generally defies a law enforcement characterization. Accordingly, it would be fundamentally inconsistent with the implicit invocation of the targeting authority of the LOAC to limit the lawful objects of attack to only those individuals posing a direct and imminent threat or those causing actual harm[46].

Unfortunately, determining status is far more difficult for terrorist operatives than it is for uniformed enemy forces of an opposing state. This does not, however, require abandoning status based targeting altogether. Instead, a more tailored criterion for status must be developed and implemented. Because of the lack of an objective uniform criterion, this will almost invariably focus on the conduct of individual actors to justify the conclusion of group affiliation and belligerent function. This does not, however, transform the targeting decision making process from a status based to a conduct based equation. In the former context, conduct becomes the intelligence criteria for determining status, which then brings into force military objective based targeting authority. In the latter context, targeting is justified solely on the manifestation of hostile conduct. While both equations rely on conduct to trigger targeting authority, the significant distinction between the two is that when conduct produces a determination of status, the scope of the targeting authority is consistent with the principle of military objective and the LOAC writ large, and not constrained to a law enforcement type authority.[47]

The United States practice of conducting missile strikes against suspected al Qaeda operatives illustrates this critical distinction.

46. See Geoffrey Corn & Eric Jensen, *Untying the Gordian Knott: A Proposal for Determining Applicability of the Laws of War to the War on Terror*, 81 Temp. L. Rev. 787 (2008) ("a nation's adoption of status-based rules of engagement for its military in a particular military operation should constitute the trigger requiring that nation and its military to apply the laws of war to that operation . . . because status-based ROE require no justification for the use of force beyond threat recognition and identification, they indicate that the state views the nature of the military mission as sufficient to trigger the targeting authority of the laws of war.").

47. See generally Geoffrey S. Corn & Eric T. Jensen, *Transnational Armed Conflict: A "Principled" Approach to the Regulation of Counter–Terror Combat Operations*, 42 Israel L. Rev. 45 (2009).

These strikes are ostensibly conducted against individuals positively identified as members of the belligerent forces of a transnational terrorist group engaged in hostilities against the United States. Individuals targeted for attack do not wear distinctive uniforms or even bear arms openly. Instead, they seek to exploit the general immunity from attack extended to the civilian population by cloaking themselves as civilians. As a result, identifying individuals subject for attack focuses on a much more complex intelligence assessment, almost certainly involving analysis of the conduct of a particular individual. Where is he located? What times of day or night is he moving from location to location? Who else is he associating with? Who is he communicating with? All of these questions, and almost certainly others, contribute to the conclusion that the individual falls within the status of enemy combatant. Once that conclusion is reached, it triggers a use of force based not in response to a particular threatening action (although striking a target while engaged in such conduct would certainly confirm the status), but instead on the status itself. Thus, the individual may be attacked at any time, irrespective of the conduct engaged in at the time of the attack.[48]

There are additional complications associated with treating terrorist operatives as lawful objects of attack. These include the geographic scope of targeting authority, the method by which such an operative may surrender, and application of the proportionality principle to such attacks. Of all of these, the geographic scope question appears to be the most complex. Once an individual is identified as a member of a terrorist belligerent group, is there any geographic limitation on where he may be lawfully targeted? This question was highlighted by Justice Kennedy when during the oral argument in the case of *Rumsfeld v. Padilla*[49] addressing the authority of the government to detain Jose Padilla based on a determination that he was an unlawful enemy combatant.[50] Justice Kennedy asked the Acting Solicitor General a simple question: could Padilla have been shot on sight at Chicago O'Hare airport as he exited the plane? The government response was at best evasive, emphasizing that the ability to arrest him negated the relevance of the question. But Justice Kennedy had not asked *would* he be shot; he asked *could* he be shot? In so doing, Justice Kennedy exposed an apparent anomaly: if Padilla could be detained by virtue of his status as an enemy belligerent, why couldn't he be shot on sight?

This exchange exposed a potentially troubling consequence of treating terrorist operatives as enemy belligerents or combatants for purposes of targeting: if that status is legally legitimate, there is

48. *Id.*
49. 542 U.S. 426 (2004).
50. Rumsfeld v. Padilla, 542 U.S. 426 (2004).

no rational reason why the targeting authority it triggers should be confined to only certain geographic areas. The U.S. practice of targeting terrorist operatives in countries like Pakistan, Somalia, and Yemen certainly indicates a rejection of limiting such authority to the confines of a conventional battle space such as Iraq or Afghanistan. However, there is no publically available evidence that the U.S. has not exercised this authority within the confines of the United States. To date, all that can be deciphered from this record is that while the United States has been judicious in its invocation of this targeting authority beyond the boundaries of the ongoing armed conflict in Afghanistan and the associated tribal areas of Pakistan, it retains the prerogative to invoke this authority when and where it chooses to do so.[51]

The other two questions related to targeting terrorist operatives pursuant to the principle of military objective—how such operatives surrender and application of the principle of proportionality in relation to such attacks—are equally complex. This complexity is in large measure the result of the fact that positive law simply does not address these questions specifically (because the LOAC does not address the status or obligations of transnational non-state actors). However, applying existing legal principles by analogy provides some guidance on resolving these issues. Surrender by a terrorist operative should require an affirmative act that eliminates the relationship between the operative and the terrorist organization. Surrender is the historically accepted method by which enemy belligerents demonstrate this severance and thereby eliminate the presumption of hostility that renders them lawful objects of attack while they remain subject to the authority of the enemy command structure. Accordingly, once an individual is determined to be a belligerent member of an enemy terrorist organization, the burden is on the individual to demonstrate to opposing forces that he is no longer an operative of the terrorist group. Traditional surrender—laying down arms and submitting to the authority of enemy forces—would certainly satisfy this requirement. Other methods, such as accepting offers of amnesty offered by enemy forces or state authority, would arguably also effectively remove the individual from the status of lawful military objective. Ultimately, however, because the LOAC places the burden of manifesting a break from the authority of the enemy force on the individual member of the group, classic surrender is the ideal means to achieve this effect.

Application of the proportionality rule is also a critical aspect of targeting terrorist belligerent forces. This rule has also been char-

---

51. *See generally* Geoffrey S. Corn & Eric T. Jensen, *Transnational Armed Conflict: A "Principled" Approach to the* *Regulation of Counter–Terror Combat Operations,* 42 ISRAEL L. REV. 45 (2009).

acterized by the International Court of Justice as a cardinal principle of the LOAC and like the rule of military objective is applicable
in all armed conflicts.[52] Indeed, the principle of proportionality
operates as a critical complement to the principle of military
objective by ensuring that the collateral or incidental effects of an
otherwise lawful attack are not so excessive as to negate the
legitimacy of the attack.[53]

Proportionality in the armed conflict context also exposes another crucial difference between LOAC based targeting and law
enforcement based use of force. In the law enforcement context, the
principle of proportionality operates to protect the object of state
violence by allowing only that amount of force necessary to subdue
a hostile actor. Thus, when a police officer employs force against a
civilian, the officer is prohibited from using deadly force if less than
lethal force would suffice to reduce the threat. Immediate resort to
deadly force is therefore justified only when less than lethal force
would be ineffective to respond to the threat. In contrast, the LOAC
principle of proportionality is not intended and does not protect the
lawful object of state violence—the enemy combatant. Once that
status is determined, use of deadly force as a measure of first resort
is lawful precisely because the individual qualifies as a lawful
military objective. While use of less than lethal force may be
directed as a matter of command discretion (for example if a
military commander wanted to capture an enemy operative instead
of kill him in order to exploit potential information through interrogation), it is not mandated by the principle of proportionality.[54]
Instead, in the armed conflict context, this principle operates to
protect the anticipated but unavoidable collateral and incidental
innocent civilian victims of an otherwise lawful attack. Accordingly,
the principle prohibits launching an otherwise lawful attack (an
attack on a lawful military objective) when the commander antici-
pates that the collateral damage or incidental injury to civilians or
civilian property will be excessive in relation to the concrete and
direct military advantage anticipated by the attack.[55]

52. Advisory Opinion, *Legality of
the Threat or Use of Nuclear Weapons*,
ICJ, 8 July 1996; *see also* ROGERS, *supra*
note 13 at 3 ("The great principles of
customary law, from which all else
stems, are those of military necessity,
humanity, distinction and proportionality.").

53. Although this "proportionality"
test is used in Protocol I to define the
meaning of an indiscriminate attack, *see*
Protocol I, *supra* note 1, at Art. 51(5)(b);
and as a component of the Article 57
precautions in the attack obligations, *see*
id. at Art. 57(2)(a) and (b), it is a

"stand-alone" provision in Field Manual
27–10, which, in paragraph 41, indicates
that "... loss of life and damage to
property incidental to attacks must not
be excessive in relation to the concrete
and direct military advantage to be
gained." FM 27–10, *supra* note 17, at 5.

54. *See generally* Geoffrey S. Corn,
*Mixing Apples and Hand Grenades: The
Logical Limit of Applying Human
Rights Norms to Armed Conflict*, J.
INT'L. HUMANITARIAN LEGAL STUD. (forth-
coming).

55. *See generally* Matthew Lippman, *Conundrums of Armed Conflict:*

Because terrorist operatives routinely exploit the presence of civilians in an effort to shield themselves from attack, application of this principle is a major aspect of terrorist targeting operations. It requires attacking commanders to assess the risk that innocent civilians will be the incidental victims of an attack, and forego an otherwise lawful attack if that risk is considered excessive.[56] There is, however, no universal formula for assessing how much collateral damage is excessive. Instead, a wide range of factors play into the case-by-case application of this principle. These include not merely a numerical comparison of number of enemy casualties versus number of anticipated civilian casualties. Instead, factors such as the value of the enemy objective (the more important the enemy combatant, the higher the value), the likelihood of other opportunities to attack the enemy, the type of civilians anticipated to be injured (for example, children compared to non-combatant members of the enemy group), and the probability of successful attack all play into the analysis. This also drives consideration of alternative methods (tactics) and means (weapons) to achieve the same effect, such as delaying attack until it is less likely civilians will be present (night versus day) or using a weapon with a reduced risk of causing collateral consequences.

Ultimately, compliance with the proportionality principle is contingent on good faith judgments of attacking commanders. In fact, the complexity of complying with this principle in the context of counter-insurgency operations is a major factor in the imposition of policy based constraints on the use of combat power, such as command imposed restrictions on the use of indirect fire support (weapons that do not have line of sight with the intended target when fired, such as artillery) in civilian populated areas. It must, however, be emphasized that the imposition of such constraints in the form of command directives (normally rules of engagement) do not necessarily reflect the inherent illegality of causing civilian casualties in the effort to destroy military objectives. Instead, they reflect additional layers of operational restraint imposed on U.S. forces for a variety of political, strategic, and policy reasons.

D. RECENT SIGNIFICANT DEVELOPMENTS IN THE LAW OF TARGETING

Two recent developments have significantly influenced the contemporary discourse on targeting terrorist operatives: the Israeli High Court's "Targeted Killing" decision,[57] and the Interpretive

Criminal Defenses to Violations of the Humanitarian Law of War, 15 DICK. J. INT'L L. 1, 63 (1996).

56. *See* API, *supra* note 1, at art. 51(5)(b).

57. Public Committee *supra* note 33.

Guidance on the Meaning of Direct Participation in Hostilities,[58] a report published by the International Committee of the Red Cross after a series of discussions on this subject by high level experts. Both of these sources reflect the attempt to grapple with the complex question of what conduct justifies targeting a presumptive civilian during the course of armed conflict.

The Israeli High Court took on this issue in response to a challenge to the legality of what many characterized as targeted killings by the Israeli Defense Forces.[59] The Court was required to assess the legality of IDF missions, usually conducted by air assets employing precision guided munitions, directed against members of Hamas in the West Bank and Gaza.[60] These missions were, according to the IDF, justified by the determination that the targets were members of the military wing of Hamas, and therefore lawful objects of attack pursuant to the rule of military objective.[61] Opponents to the IDF practice of targeting such individuals with lethal forces as a measure of first resort challenged the legality of the practice on a number of grounds. First, they challenged the assertion that Israel was even engaged in an armed conflict with Hamas, asserting that instead the incapacitation of Hamas operatives was an act of law enforcement.[62] Second, they challenged the assertion that members of Hamas could be properly classified as lawful objects of attack in any situation other than when they were actually engaged in hostilities against the IDF.[63] Because these individuals did not belong to a regular armed force, the opponents asserted they were civilians, and therefore could only be made the object of attack while taking a direct part in hostilities.[64] Finally, the opponents challenged the legality of attacking such individuals even when they were directly participating in hostilities, arguing that the collateral damage and incidental injury to civilians resulting from such attacks ran afoul of the rule of proportionality.[65]

The High Court addressed each of these issues. First, it concluded that the situation between Israel and Hamas amounted to an armed conflict, thereby rejecting the assertion that Israel was limited to law enforcement authority to respond to the threat posed by Hamas.[66] However, the Court also concluded that the armed conflict was international in character (thereby bringing into force the full corpus of the LOAC in accordance with common article 2 of the Geneva Conventions).[67] Although Hamas was not a state party

58. IG *supra* note 32.

59. Public Committee *supra* note 33 at para. 2.

60. *Id.*

61. *Id.* at para. 23.

62. *Id.* at para. 4.

63. *Id.*

64. *Id.* at paras. 5, 6.

65. *Id.* at para. 8.

66. Public Committee, *supra* note 33, at para. 16.

67. *Id.* at para. 18.

to the Conventions, and therefore was not a participant in an inter-
state armed conflict, the fact that the hostilities were ongoing in
areas subject to Israeli belligerent occupation led the Court to
conclude the conflict fell within the scope of common article 2.[68]
The impact of this aspect of the decision is arguably limited to the
situation in Israel. The Court did not reach the international armed
conflict conclusion because it considered Hamas to be some kind of
quasi state. Instead, it was the unique occupation relationship
between the IDF and Hamas that led to this outcome. Accordingly,
it would be unjustified to rely on this aspect of the decision to
support an assertion that armed conflict with non-state terrorist
groups should be characterized as international in character.

A far more significant aspect of the decision was the Court's
analysis of the legality of targeting terrorist operatives in the
context of an armed conflict. Resolving this issue required the
Court to analyze the status of Hamas operatives in the context of
an international armed conflict. In a marked divergence from the
U.S. view that such operatives are properly characterized as unprivileged belligerents, the Court rejected the existence of such a
category of combatants.[69] Instead, the Court concluded that during
international armed conflicts, there are only two categories of
individuals for purposes of target legality analysis: combatants and
civilians.[70] Combatants, according to the Court, include members of
the regular armed forces and militia and volunteer corps personnel
associated with the armed forces, or what might be best understood
as "lawful" combatants (individuals qualified for status as prisoners of war pursuant to the Geneva Convention Relative to the
Treatment of Prisoners of War).[71] All other individuals are civilians.[72] Because there were no regular armed forces belonging to
Hamas, this led the Court to conclude that all Hamas operatives
must be considered civilians for purposes of targeting analysis.[73]

The Court then addressed when targeting a civilian during
international armed conflict would be legal.[74] The Court analyzed
the law on direct participation in hostilities, which led to two
conclusions. First, the Court reiterated the rule codified in Article
51 (3) of Additional Protocol I to conclude that although civilians
are presumptively protected from being made the deliberate object
of attack, that protection (or presumption) is rebutted when and for
such time as they take a direct part in hostilities.[75] Although Israel
is not a party to this treaty, the Court concluded that this direct

68. *Id.* at para. 20.

69. *Id.* at para. 28.

70. *Id.* at paras. 24–26.

71. Public Committee, *supra* note
33 at paras. 24, 25.

72. *Id.* at para. 26.

73. *Id.*

74. *Id.* at para. 29.

75. *Id.* at para. 30.

participation rule had ripened to a rule of customary international law.[76] Second, the Court took on the far more difficult question of what constitutes taking a direct part in hostilities,[77] a question that had been the subject of debate for years, but had never been addressed in the context of an actual judicial decision.

The Court rejected the narrow interpretation of direct participation in hostilities advanced by opponents to the IDF practice.[78] They argued that civilian protection is lost only when the civilian engaged in conduct that will cause immediate harm to the military, for example firing a weapon or detonating an explosive.[79] According to the Court, this interpretation was too narrow to address the reality of terrorist operations, and would essentially render immune from attack terrorist operatives essential to the execution of hostile operations, such as the individual who assembles the explosive or orders the execution of an attack.[80] Accordingly, the Court adopted a broader definition of direct participation in hostilities, including within that definition conduct that is essential for the planning and execution of hostile activities.[81]

The Court then turned to the "for such time" component of the Article 51 standard for assessing when an individual who takes a direct part in hostilities is subject to attack.[82] In an equally significant aspect of the opinion, the Court rejected the interpretation of this qualifier that civilians who directly participate in hostilities are subject to attack only while they are actually doing so.[83] According to the Court, applying this interpretation to all such civilians effectively sanctions a "revolving door" approach, allowing the civilian to routinely participate in hostilities but then claim the benefit of civilian protection as soon as that participation is terminated.[84] While the Court acknowledged that this narrow interpretation might be appropriately applied to a civilian whose participation in hostilities is a one-time occurrence, it is inappropriate for a civilian who is routinely participating in hostilities.[85] For that latter civilian, a broader definition of "for such time" is justified and necessary.[86] Accordingly, the Court concluded that civilians who routinely participate in belligerent activities on behalf of Hamas—for example, members of the military wing of Hamas—are lawfully subject to attack even while they are not actually engaged in such participation.[87] For the Court, such periods of inactivity are nothing

76. *Id.*

77. *Id.* at paras. 34–37.

78. *Id.*

79. *Id.*

80. *Id.*

81. *Id.*

82. Public Committee, *supra* note 33, at paras. 38–40.

83. *Id.* at para. 39.

84. *Id.* at para. 40.

85. *Id.*

86. *Id.*

87. *Id.*

more than brief respites in an otherwise ongoing participation in hostilities.[88]

Finally, the Court turned to the issue of proportionality.[89] Responding to the petitioner's argument that targeted killings would inevitably run afoul of the proportionality constraints of both the LOAC and international human rights law, the Court first made clear that it was the LOAC principle of proportionality that controlled resolution of this issue—a conclusion based on the determination that Israel and Hamas were engaged in an armed conflict.[90] According to the Court, the applicable proportionality principle establishes that:

> [an] attack upon innocent civilians is not permitted if the collateral damage caused to them is not proportionate to the military advantage (in protecting combatants and civilians). In other words, attack is proportionate if the benefit stemming from the attainment of the proper military objective is proportionate to the damage caused to innocent civilians harmed by it.[91]

The Court then emphasized that when reviewing a targeted killing mission, "[t]he question is whether the decision of the military commander falls within the zone of reasonable activity on the part of the military commander. If the answer is yes, the Court will not exchange the military commander's security discretion with the security discretion of the Court."[92] The Court further stated, "[t]he decision of the question whether the benefit stemming from the preventative strike is proportionate to the collateral damage caused to innocent civilians harmed by it is a legal question, the expertise about which is in the hands of the judicial branch."[93]

The Court then took an odd turn. After concluding that the LOAC principle of proportionality controlled resolution of the issue, the Court seemed to invoke a human rights based interpretation of that principle.[94] According to the Court, attacks against a civilian taking a direct part in hostilities are prohibited when the collateral damage and incidental injury to innocent bystanders is anticipated to be excessive. This reflects an application of the LOAC principle of proportionality, which provides protection for the innocent civilian, not the object of attack.[95] However, the Court then ruled that principle of proportionality also protects the object of attack, allowing resort to deadly force against the civilian directly participating

---

88. Id.

89. Public Committee, *supra* note 33, at paras. 45, 46.

90. Id. at para. 45.

91. Public Committee, *supra* note 33, para. 45.

92. Id. at para. 57.

93. Id. at para. 58.

94. Id.

95. Id.

in hostilities only when the armed forces determine that capturing that individual is not a viable course of action.[96] Because the LOAC proportionality principle in no way protects the lawful object of attack, this aspect of the decision is somewhat perplexing. However, it may be explained by the unique occupation relationship between the two parties to the conflict, a relationship that implicitly implicates law enforcement type authorities and constraints. Or perhaps the Court was tempering the effect of its broad interpretation of direct participation in hostilities, attempting to ensure that individuals not actually causing immediate harm to the IDF be subdued by less than lethal means when feasible. Ultimately, that aspect of the opinion, like the international armed conflict aspect, is arguably limited to the unique situation in the West Bank and Gaza.

The Israeli Supreme Court ultimately declined petitioners' request to strike down the Government's policy of target killings.[97] The decision itself reflects points of both consensus and divergence with the contemporary U.S. interpretation of targeting authority and terrorist operatives. First, as noted above, the conclusion that the conflict between Hamas and Israel is international in character is inconsistent with the conclusion by the U.S. that its conflict with al Qaeda is non-international. However, the fact that both the U.S. and Israel have formally determined their respective struggles against terrorism are armed conflicts is significant. Second, the conclusion that there are only two categories of individuals for purposes of targeting analysis—lawful combatants and civilians—is in stark opposition to the LOAC interpretation relied on by the U.S. to target terrorist operatives. U.S. practice reflects the view that there is indeed a category of unprivileged belligerent, and that the legal authority to attack such individuals is no different from the authority to attack lawful combatants. As a result, the U.S. does not analyze whether such individuals are subject to attack as a result of their direct participation in hostilities. Instead, it is their status as members of the enemy belligerent group that renders them lawful objects of attack. Third, there is no indication that the U.S. imposes a legally based 'capture instead of kill' qualification on targeting authority related to such enemy belligerent personnel. While the traditional LOAC proportionality analysis is certainly applicable to both U.S. and IDF forces (protecting innocent civilians from excessive collateral damage or incidental injury), for the U.S. status as an enemy belligerent triggers the use of deadly force as a measure of first resort.

The ICRC's Interpretive Guidance on the Notion of Direct Participation in Hostilities Under International Humanitarian

---

96. *Id.*   **97.** Public Committee, *supra* note 33, at para. 60.

Law[98] (IG) has also made a significant impact on the contemporary terrorist targeting discourse. That IG, completed after a series of meetings involving some of the most respected LOAC experts in the world, attempts to provide guidance on how to interpret the authority to target civilians directly participating in hostilities. It must be noted, however, that many of the participants in that process— including highly respected U.S. and U.K. LOAC experts-expressed opposition to certain aspects of the finally published IG. Furthermore, the IG itself emphasizes that it does not reflect a consensus view on all the issues it addresses.

Nonetheless, the IG includes several particularly significant LOAC interpretations. Perhaps the most significant for purposes of treating counter-terror operations as an armed conflict is the explicit recognition that non-state groups can be properly considered and treated as a "party" to a non-international armed conflict.[99] As the IG notes, the legal characterization of such groups has been a longstanding issue of uncertainty.[100] Because there is no positive provision for the status of such groups in a LOAC treaty, many experts have asserted that members of non-state belligerent groups must always be treated as civilians and therefore targeted only pursuant to the rule of direct participation in hostilities.[101] The ICRC IG categorically rejects this proposition, noting that a refusal to acknowledge the existence of non-state belligerent parties in such armed conflicts would fundamentally distort the functioning of the LOAC. According to the IG:

> While it is generally recognized that members of State armed forces in non-international armed conflict do not qualify as civilians, treaty law, State practice, and international jurisprudence have not unequivocally settled whether the same applies to members of organized armed groups (i.e. the armed forces of non-State parties to an armed conflict). Because organized armed groups generally cannot qualify as regular armed forces under national law, it might be tempting to conclude that membership in such groups is simply a continuous form of civilian direct participation in hostilities. Accordingly, members of organized armed groups would be regarded as civilians who, owing to their continuous direct participation in hostilities, lose protection against direct attack for the entire duration of their membership. However, this approach would seriously

---

98. Nils Melzer, Legal Adviser, International Committee of the Red Cross, Interpretive Guidance on the Notion of Direct Participation in Hostilities Under Int'l Humanitarian Law (May 2009), *available at* http://www.icrc.org/Web/

Eng/siteeng0.nsf/htmlall/p0990/$File/ICRC_002_0990.pdf

99. *Id.* at 16.

100. *Id.*

101. *Id.* at 17.

undermine the conceptual integrity of the categories of persons underlying the principle of distinction, most notably because it would create parties to non-international armed conflicts whose entire armed forces remain part of the civilian population. As the wording and logic of Article 3 GC I–IV and Additional Protocol II (AP II) reveals, civilians, armed forces, and organized armed groups of the parties to the conflict are mutually exclusive categories also in non-international armed conflict.[102]

Although the IG does not go as far as to acknowledge that transnational groups such as terrorist groups could fall into this category, the express recognition that belligerent forces of a non-state actor *are not* civilians for purpose of targeting analysis is consistent with the interpretation of the law that underlies the U.S. military response to terrorism. It also suggests that the "two category" approach adopted by the Israeli High Court is indeed properly limited to the context of international armed conflicts; in the context of non-international armed conflicts, this excerpt from the IG effectively endorses the concept of the unprivileged belligerent.

The IG tracks much more closely with the Israeli High Court opinion in almost all other respects. First, like that opinion, the IG concludes that in the context of an international armed conflict, there are only two categories of individuals for purposes of targeting: lawful combatants and civilians.[103] When connected with the extract above, this leads to the following equation: in all armed conflicts, there are combatants (members of armed belligerent groups of each party to the conflict) who are lawful objects of attack by virtue of their status, and civilians (all other individuals) protected from direct attack so long as they refrain from directly participating in hostilities, in which case their conduct establishes the legal basis for being made the object of attack. As a result, the IG implicitly rejects the concept of an unprivileged belligerent in the context of an international armed conflict—the characterization used by the United States *vis a vis* Taliban personnel during the armed conflict with Afghanistan.

The heart of the IG, however, addresses those activities that qualify as direct participation in hostilities resulting in a loss of protection from attack. Like the Israeli High Court opinion, the IG rejects a narrow interpretation of this term that limits direct participation to actions that will cause immediate harm to an armed force.[104] The IG begins by articulating a three part test for determining what constitutes direct participation:

102. *Id.* at 27.   **104.** *Id.* at 46.
103. IG *supra* note 32 at 24.

Acts amounting to direct participation in hostilities must meet three cumulative requirements: (1) a threshold regarding the harm likely to result from the act, (2) a relationship of direct causation between the act and the expected harm, and (3) a belligerent nexus between the act and the hostilities conducted between the parties to an armed conflict.[105]

The key to this three prong test is the focus on causation with a nexus to an armed conflict. First, the IG emphasizes that the harm element need not require death or destruction, but is satisfied by any degradation to the military capacity or capability of an opponent.[106] Second, there must be a direct causal link between the civilian and the requisite harm, although the IG concedes that the link need not be immediate to the harm:

> In the present context, direct causation should be understood as meaning that the harm in question must be brought about in one causal step. Therefore, individual conduct that merely builds up or maintains the capacity of a party to harm its adversary, or which otherwise only indirectly causes harm, is excluded from the concept of direct participation in hostilities.[107]
>
> . . .
>
> The required standard of direct causation of harm must take into account the collective nature and complexity of contemporary military operations. For example, attacks carried out by unmanned aerial vehicles may simultaneously involve a number of persons, such as computer specialists operating the vehicle through remote control, individuals illuminating the target, aircraft crews collecting data, specialists controlling the firing of missiles, radio operators transmitting orders, and an overall commander. While all of these persons are integral to that operation and directly participate in hostilities, only few of them carry out activities that, in isolation, could be said to directly cause the required threshold of harm. The standard of direct causation must therefore be interpreted to include conduct that causes harm only in conjunction with other acts. More precisely, where a specific act does not on its own directly cause the required threshold of harm, the requirement of direct causation would still be fulfilled where the act constitutes an integral part of a concrete and coordinated tactical operation that directly causes such harm. Examples of such acts would include, *inter alia*, the

---

105. *Id.*
106. *Id.* at 47.

107. *Id.* at 53.

identification and marking of targets, the analysis and
transmission of tactical intelligence to attacking forces,
and the instruction and assistance given to troops for the
execution of a specific military operation.[108]

This "collective" causation test is in many ways similar to the
"routine participation" test adopted by the Israeli High Court. The
IG therefore endorses a definition of direct participation that is
more expansive than a very narrow "immediate harm" test in
order to account for the nature of contemporary military operations.

Perhaps the most significant aspect of the Interpretive Guidance is treatment of the "revolving door" problem, the same
problem addressed by the Israeli High Court opinion.[109] Like the
Israeli High Court, the ICRC acknowledged that a definition of "for
such time" that limits the loss of civilian protection to periods of
actual belligerent conduct would incentivize such conduct by cloaking the civilian with protection from attack whenever she completed a mission and returned to non-belligerent activity.[110] The Guidance also emphasizes that the narrow "for such time" definition
was never intended to apply to a civilian who routinely participates
in belligerent conduct, but instead does so only sporadically.[111]
Accordingly, the Guidance articulates what it characterizes as the
Continuous Combat Function test: when a civilian continuously
performs belligerent acts, the accordant loss of protection from
attack applies for so long as the civilian remains a member of the
organized group conducting such activity.[112] According to the Guidance:

the restriction of loss of protection to the duration of
specific hostile acts was designed to respond to spontaneous, sporadic or unorganized hostile acts by civilians and
cannot be applied to organized armed groups. It would
provide members of such groups with a significant operational advantage over members of State armed forces, who
can be attacked on a continuous basis. This imbalance
would encourage organized armed groups to operate as
farmers by day and fighters by night . . .

Instead, where individuals go beyond spontaneous, sporadic, or unorganized direct participation in hostilities and
become members of an organized armed group belonging
to a party to the conflict, IHL deprives them of protection
against direct attack for as long as they remain members
of that group. In other words, the "revolving door" of

protection starts to operate based on membership. As stated earlier, membership in an organized armed group begins in the moment when a civilian starts *de facto* to assume a continuous combat function for the group, and lasts until he or she ceases to assume such function.[113]

This recognition that routine—or "continuous"—participation in belligerent conduct results in an ongoing loss of protection from attack is significant. Although the ICRC does not recognize that such conduct in the context of an international armed conflict results in such civilians becoming unprivileged belligerents, it does recognize that this continuous combat function provides a legal basis for these civilians to be targeted even when they are not performing a belligerent function. In essence, the ICRC continuous combat function concept is analogous to the approach followed by the Israeli High Court which treated periods of non-belligerent activity as brief pauses in an otherwise ongoing direct participation in hostilities. It must also be noted, however, that like the Israeli High Court, the Guidance then indicates that the law prohibits resort to deadly force against such civilians if it is feasible to subdue them with a less harmful level of force (capture instead of kill).[114]

While the ICRC Guidance is an important step forward in dealing with the reality of civilians who routinely engage in belligerent activities during armed conflict, it is by no means a blanket endorsement of the U.S. approach to targeting terrorists. First, the Guidance requires a nexus between the civilian activity and an ongoing armed conflict. As a result, it is unlikely the ICRC would concede that the direct participation test is even applicable to terrorists operatives located outside the geographic proximity of Afghanistan or Iraq. In contrast, the U.S. does not appear to self-impose any geographic nexus requirement to its targeting operations. Second, even the expanded concept of direct participation does not include conduct that has been relied on by the U.S. as a basis to designated individuals as unprivileged belligerents. More specifically, the ICRC Guidance explicitly rejects material support activities—to include providing financial resources or recruitment and training—as examples of direct participation. This is precisely the type of conduct that has been relied on by the United States to designate terrorist operatives as unprivileged belligerents.

In spite of these differences, the fact that a consensus is developing that a continuous combat function and conduct that does not produce immediate harm may qualify as direct participation in hostilities is significant. Perhaps even more significant is the explicit effort to address the "revolving door" problem in order

---

113. *Id.* at 71–72.   114. IG, *supra* note 32, at 78.

to bring the LOAC in line with the realities of asymmetric warfare and deprive individuals who routinely engage in belligerent conduct from an unjustified windfall of protection from attack.

E. HOW MUCH PROOF IS ENOUGH?

One final wrinkle to the terrorist targeting dilemma is determining when the proof is sufficient to justify a use of deadly force as a measure of first resort. This is particularly problematic in the context of drone attacks outside an area of active combat operations. Neither the ICRC Guidance nor the Israeli High Court opinion addressed the quantum of proof required to justify an attack on a civilian who directly participates in hostilities. However, at least one scholar has suggested that when such attacks are directed against suspected terrorist operatives outside of an area of active combat operations, proof beyond a reasonable doubt should be the required standard.[115]

This quantum of proof component to a lawful targeting decision has been generally overlooked in the law. The LOAC requires commanders to make reasonable judgments in relation to target selection and engagement, but it does not define how much proof renders a judgment reasonable. Jurisprudence from the International Criminal Tribunal for the Former Yugoslavia indicates that a reckless judgment is unreasonable, but again fails to indicate how much proof renders a judgment reasonable. The proposal for a proof beyond a reasonable doubt requirement for drone attacks of suspected terrorist operatives is most likely responsive to the widespread discomfort with subjecting individuals beyond an area of active combat operations to LOAC based targeting. While many experts reject the reliance on LOAC targeting law in such situations, the United States has and will most likely continue to treat certain terrorist operatives as lawful military objectives, even when they are attenuated from a more traditional battle-space. At this point, it is unclear whether this proof beyond a reasonable doubt standard has been adopted by the U.S., or for that matter, what standard of proof applies to target decision-making related to terrorist operatives.

---

115. *See* Scott Shane, *U.S. Approval of Killing of Cleric Causes Unease*, NEW YORK TIMES, (May 13, 2010), *available at* http://www.nytimes.com/2010/05/14/world/14awlaki.html (Another former C.I.A. lawyer, John Radsan, said prior judicial review of additions to the target list might be unconstitutional. "That sort of review goes to the core of presidential power," he said. But Mr. Radsan, who teaches at the William Mitchell College of Law in St. Paul, said every drone strike should be subject to rigorous internal checks to be "sure beyond a reasonable doubt" that the target is an enemy combatant.)

F.　CONTINUING INVOCATION OF THE LOAC PRINCIPLE OF MILITARY OBJECTIVE TO ATTACK TERRORIST OPERATIVES

When President Obama took office, he confronted the difficult and controversial question of whether to continue to embrace his predecessor's characterization of the struggle against transnational terrorism as an armed conflict and if so, how that continued characterization would be ultimately translated into operational measures. Though he has made no affirmative statement endorsing the Bush administration's policies with respect to preemptive self-defense, he has continued to utilize an armed conflict paradigm to justify self-help measures against terrorists. Illustrative of this approach are the continuing drone attacks against al Qaeda targets in Pakistan and Afghanistan. Although the question of international legality of such attacks is predominantly one related to the *jus ad bellum*, because it involves the application of combat power it also obviously implicates *jus in bello* considerations. Perhaps more importantly, it is a manifestation of President Obama's conception of the nature of the struggle against transnational terrorism as an armed conflict, and therefore has a direct impact on the resolution of many other issues related to the *jus in bello*. As President Bush's time in office was coming to an end, he transitioned to a policy of not requesting the permission of Pakistan before launching drone attacks against al Qaeda targets within Pakistan.[116] There is no indication that President Obama has changed this procedure. Further, during 2008, President Bush authorized 36 drone attacks. From the time President Obama took office in January until mid-September, he had already surpassed that number, authorizing 39 attacks.[117]

Certainly drone attacks are merely one indication of the extent to which President Obama will follow in the footsteps of his predecessor, but it clearly indicates that at least to some extent, President Obama has embraced the prior administration's self-defense theory. The use of self-help measures in prosecuting the fight against transnational terrorists will evidently continue. Targeting terrorist operatives pursuant to authority derived from the LOAC remains a complicated and controversial proposition. However, the continuing U.S. practice of invoking this authority, coupled with the ongoing efforts of LOAC experts, the ICRC, and other countries to develop a coherent legal framework to address the authority to target the members of groups such as al Qaeda,

116.　Greg Miller, *U.S. strikes stagger al Qaeda; Predator attacks in Pakistan have taken a toll, officials say*, L.A. TIMES, Mar. 22, 2009, at A1, *available in* LEXIS Nexis Library, CURNWS File.

117.　Karen DeYoung & Walter Pincus, *Success Against al-Qaeda Cited: Infiltration of Network Is a Factor as Administration Debates Afghanistan Policy*, WASH. POST, Sep. 30, 2009, *available in* LEXIS Nexis Library, CURNWS File, (where the authors state "a total of 39 such attacks have been launched between January and mid-September, according to news reports, compared with 36 under the Bush administration in 2008.)"

Hezbollah, and other transnational belligerent organizations indicate the significance of this issue. Perhaps more importantly, it indicates that there is no clear answer to the dilemma of defining the scope of use of force authority in response to the threat to such individuals.[118]

In the context of military operations to destroy, disable, or disrupt transnational terrorist organizations, whatever standard is devised for designating opposition groups subject to targeting must be consistent with the underlying purposes of the LOAC. Any state invoking the authority of the principle of military necessity and engaging in attacks based on the rule of military objective in order to attack a non-state enemy, must ensure that the complementary targeting principles of proportionality and minimization of civilian risk are also applied. Once a military commander is authorized to engage an opponent with combat power based solely on a determination of the status of that opponent (irrespective of the status determination criteria), that commander must understand his obligation to comply with the principles of the LOAC that operate to limit the suffering resulting from the application of that combat power. Such a balanced application of authority and humanity is central to the principle of military necessity from which targeting authority is derived.

---

118. *But see* Ronald Reagan, *The U.S. Decision Not to Ratify Protocol I to the Geneva Conventions on the Protec-* *tion, of War Victims: Letter of Transmital* 81 A.J.I.L. 910, 911 (Oct., 1987).

Chapter 4

DETENTION OF TERRORIST OPERATIVES*

A. DETENTION OF COMBATANTS AND THE GLOBAL WAR ON TERROR

On November 13, 2001, President Bush issued Military Order #1 titled "Detention, Treatment and Trial of Certain Non–Citizens in the War Against Terrorism." In that Order, the President determined that:

> International terrorists, including members of al Qaida, have carried out attacks on United States diplomatic and military personnel and facilities abroad and on citizens and property within the United States on a scale that has created a state of armed conflict that requires the use of the United States Armed Forces.[1]

With this determination, the President indicated that the United States would invoke the authorities derived from the law of armed conflict (LOAC)—the law establishing rights and obligations in the context of an armed conflict—to respond to the threat of international terrorism. Consistent with that invocation, the order established authority for the preventive military detention of individuals determined by the President to be members of al Qaida, other individuals associated with past or future terrorist activities directed against U.S. interests, or individuals who harbored these terrorists.[2]

Preventive detention of enemy belligerents is considered by the United States to be a fundamental incident of armed conflict authorized by customary international law.[3] Although preventive detention has been determined lawful in limited circumstances in

---

* With contributions from Colonel James A. Schoettler, U.S. Army.

1. Military Order of November 13, 2001—Detention, Treatment and Trial of Certain Non–Citizens in the War Against Terrorism, 66 Fed. Reg. 57,833 (2001).

2. *Id.*, sec. 2. While detention is authorized under the Military Order, few detainees were actually designated as subject to the Military Order for purpose of detention. Cong. Research Serv., Enemy Combatant Detainees: Habeas Corpus Challenges in Federal Courts Detentions (Order Code No. RL33180) at 9 n. 59 (last updated Jan. 29, 2009) *available at* http://www.fas.org/sgp/crs/natsec/RL 33180.pdf (last visited Mar. 9, 2009). Rather such detention generally occurs under the authority granted in the AUMF, which courts have interpreted to include the right to detain.

3. *See, e.g.,* Gherebi v. Obama, 609 F. Supp. 2d 43, 62 (D.D.C. 2009).

95

the non-conflict context, as a general proposition deprivation of liberty outside the armed conflict context is permitted only in relation to criminal process.[4] In the armed conflict context, preventive detention is an action justified by the principle of military necessity, a customary international law norm that permits belligerents to take all measures not otherwise prohibited by international law necessary to bring about the prompt submission of an opponent.[5]

It is axiomatic that preventing captured enemy belligerents from returning to hostilities is necessary to defeat the enemy.[6] Nonetheless, there is contemporary debate related to whether the authority for preventive detention is the same in both international and non-international armed conflicts. While several treaties, including most importantly, the Geneva Convention Relative to the Treatment of Prisoners of War (GPW)[7], which regulates the treatment of certain categories of combatants and civilians acting on behalf of enemy States in an international armed conflict, are clearly premised upon an international consensus that States have the legal authority to detain such individuals, few LOAC treaties address the treatment of enemy combatants in the context of non-international armed conflicts and none discuss the authority to detain. This has led some experts and even states to conclude that preventive detention, although an action justified by military necessity, is permitted in the context of non-international armed conflicts only when authorized by positive municipal law.[8] According to this interpretation of international law, absent statutory or other domestic legal authority, a State's preventive detention of non-State combatants in the context of a non-international armed conflict is inherently arbitrary unless pursued under the rules and procedures applicable to the detention of criminals.[9]

This is not the position of the United States. Instead, it is the U.S. position that the customary norm of military necessity provides the legal authority to detain enemy belligerents in any armed conflict, even absent a treaty or statute expressly authorizing preventive detention. As will be explained below, this interpretation of customary international law as a source of preventive detention

---

4. *See United States v. Salerno*, 481 U.S. 739 (1987) (holding that preventive detention does not violate the Fifth Amendment Due Process Clause nor the Eighth Amendment Excessive Fines Clause).

5. *See Id.*

6. *See, e.g.,* al-Marri v. Pucciarelli, 534 F.3d 213, 379 (4th Cir. S.C. 2008).

7. Geneva Convention Relative to the Treatment of Prisoners of War, Aug.

12, 1949, 6 U.S.T. 3316, 75 U.N.T.S. 135.

8. *See* Hamlily v. Obama, 616 F. Supp. 2d 63, 71 (D.D.C. 2009).

9. *See generally* Robert Chesney & Jack Goldsmith, *Terrorism and the Convergence of Criminal and Military Detention Models*, 60 STAN. L. REV. 1079, 1084 (2008).

authority is based on a seminal World War II era Supreme Court interpretation of the LOAC—the principal authority relied on by the Court when it endorsed the President's invocation of preventive detention authority in Military Order #1.

1. THE U.S. LEGAL FOUNDATION FOR PREVENTIVE DETENTION OF ENEMY BELLIGERENTS

In 1942, the Supreme Court decided the case of *Ex parte Quirin.*[10] *Quirin* involved the trial by secret military commission of nine German saboteurs arrested by the FBI after landing on Long Island and Florida, and dispersing to cities in the United States. The defendants had been selected by the German intelligence service because their proficiency in English and U.S. dialects resulting from having lived in the United States. They were all members of the German armed forces, and each had been trained to conduct sabotage missions in the United States. After coming ashore from a German U–Boat, they immediately discarded their uniforms and proceeded to various locations in the United States ostensibly to conduct their sabotage missions.[11]

Whether a result of their lack of zeal to perform their missions, a deliberate desire to be exposed, their amateurish conduct, or the fact that one of the saboteurs exposed the plot, all of the saboteurs were soon arrested by the FBI.[12] Although the Department of Justice began the process to bring them to trial in federal court, President Roosevelt chose instead to order their transfer for trial as war criminals by the U.S. armed forces.[13] A secret military commission was convened by order of the President, and the saboteurs were all brought before the commission on allegations of violations of the laws and customs of war, including espionage and operating as unlawful belligerents.[14]

The military lawyers detailed to represent the German defendants challenged the legality of trial by military commission through a writ of habeas corpus to the Supreme Court.[15] In a *per curium* opinion, the Court denied the writ and held that the military commission had lawful jurisdiction to try the saboteurs.[16] According to the Court, because the defendant's were enemy belligerents, they were subject to the laws and customs of war.[17] More importantly, the state of war between the United States and Germany permitted the government to invoke the law of war as a

10. 317 U.S. 1 (1942).

11. *See Id.* at 21.

12. *See Id.*

13. *See Id.* at 22–23.

14. *See Id.*

15. *See Id* at 20.

16. *Id.* at 24.

17. *Id.* at 37.

source of authority for the capture, detention, and trial of the defendants.[18]

Although the *Quirin* decision focused primarily on the legality of trial by military commission, it also addressed the authority for preventive detention. According to the opinion:

> By universal agreement and practice the law of war draws a distinction between the armed forces and the peaceful populations of belligerent nations and also between those who are lawful and unlawful combatants. Lawful combatants are subject to capture and detention as prisoners of war by opposing military forces. Unlawful combatants are likewise subject to capture and detention, but in addition they are subject to trial and punishment by military tribunals for acts which render their belligerency unlawful.[19]

This extract indicates that the Supreme Court did not consider it necessary that there be any positive law authorizing preventive detention of captured enemy belligerents. Instead, the Court relied on the customary law of war as the legal basis for such detention. Perhaps even more important for the events that transpired after September 11, 2001, the Court clearly considered this authority applicable to captured enemy belligerents irrespective of whether they qualified as 'lawful' combatants (captured enemy belligerent personnel qualified for status as prisoners of war pursuant to the Geneva Convention Relative to the Treatment of Prisoners of War).[20] This decision would provide the essential legal foundation for the Supreme Court's next foray into the preventive detention issue nearly sixty years later. This time, however, the nature of the conflict would be much different from the declared war between the United States and Germany in which *Quirin* and his comrades had been captured.

Almost as soon as the United States initiated military action against Taliban and al Qaida forces in Afghanistan following the terror attacks of September 11th, the U.S. military began detaining individuals they captured, or who were handed over to them by Afghan Northern Alliance allies. Pursuant to the President's "Military Order No. 1," many of these detainees were transferred to the newly established Military Detention Facility at Guantanamo Bay Naval Base in Cuba. Military Order No. 1 included a directive to establish this facility for the detention of "unlawful alien enemy combatants."[21] Accordingly, U.S. nationals were excluded from the

18. *See Id.* at 31.
19. *Id.*
20. *See infra* pp. 7–8.

21. Military Order of November 13, 2001—Detention, Treatment and Trial of Certain Non–Citizens in the War

category of captured personnel subject to detention at Guantanamo. The United States soon learned that one of the detainees that had been transferred from Afghanistan to Guantanamo, Yaser Esam Hamdi, was born in the United States and was therefore a U.S. citizen. This did not, however, result in his release or transfer to civilian custody for purposes of trial by federal court. Instead, his preventive detention continued, but only after he was immediately transferred to a military confinement facility in the United States.

Although Hamdi was held incommunicado, his father successfully petitioned the courts by writ of habeas corpus filed as a "next friend" on behalf of his son. The challenge to the legality of his son's detention culminated with the Supreme Court decision of *Hamdi v. Rumsfeld*.[22] This was the first post-September 11th case decided by the Supreme Court that directly addressed the legality of preventive detention in the context of the U.S.-proclaimed global war on terror.

Invoking *Quirin,* the Supreme Court endorsed Hamdi's continued preventive detention as an enemy belligerent.[23] Although the Court also held that Hamdi was entitled to more meaningful procedural protections than had been afforded by the Executive Branch, it rejected the assertion that Hamdi's detention was unlawful because he had not been captured in the context of a declared war against a state enemy. Instead, the Court concluded that because Hamdi had been captured in the context of an armed conflict conducted by the President with the statutory support of Congress (the 2001 Authorization for the Use of Military Force against those responsible for the terror attacks of September 11, 2001 or "AUMF"), and had been engaged in hostilities against U.S. and Coalition forces, Hamdi was legally indistinguishable from the defendants in *Quirin*. According to the Court:

> In light of these principles, it is of no moment that the AUMF does not use specific language of detention. Because detention to prevent a combatant's return to the battlefield is a fundamental incident of waging war, in permitting the use of "necessary and appropriate force," Congress has clearly and unmistakably authorized detention in the narrow circumstances considered here.[24]

Earlier in the opinion, the Court emphasized that the "principles" it referenced in the extract quoted above were the principles derived from the law of war permitting the preventive detention of

Against Terrorism, 66 Fed. Reg. 57,833 Sec. 3(a) (2001).
22.   542 U.S. 507 (2004).

23.   See *Hamdi*, 542 U.S. at 519.

24.   *Id*. at 519.

captured enemy personnel.[25] These principles, according to the Court, were implicitly invoked by Congress when it authorized the President to use all "necessary and appropriate" force against "nations, organizations, or persons associated with the September 11th terrorist attacks."[26] In short, Congress had authorized the President to invoke the same principle of military necessity that had been central to the *Quirin* Court's endorsement of preventive detention of the German saboteurs in 1942.

The *Hamdi* opinion laid a legal foundation that continues to be built upon today. By extending the *Quirin* holding to the armed conflict against individuals, organizations, and nations associated with the terrorist attacks of September 11th, the Court endorsed the invocation of the armed conflict legal framework to the struggle against transnational terrorism. However, by condemning the summary process relied upon by the Executive Branch to determine that Hamdi fell into the category of detainable enemy belligerents, the Court also set in motion a procedural revision process that continues to this day.[27] Thus, the preventive detention of terrorists pursuant to the law of armed conflict involves two distinct legal questions. First, from a substantive perspective, who falls within the scope of this preventive detention authority? Second, to what process are individuals alleged to fall within that scope entitled?

a.   The Substantive Component

As significant as *Hamdi*'s extension of the *Quirin* precedent was to the war on terror, the Court did not define with anything close to precision who fell within the scope of this preventive detention authority.[28] Instead, the Court addressed only what it characterized as the narrow question of whether a U.S. citizen falling into an accepted core definition of enemy combatant could be preventively detained:

> The threshold question before us is whether the Executive has the authority to detain citizens who qualify as "enemy combatants." There is some debate as to the proper scope of this term, and the Government has never provided any court with the full criteria that it uses in classifying individuals as such. It has made clear, however, that, for purposes of this case, the "enemy combatant" that it is seeking to detain is an individual who, it alleges, was "part of or supporting forces hostile

25. *Id.*
26. *See Id.* at 518.
27. *See, e.g.*, Benjamin Wittes, Robert M. Chesney, and Rabea Benhalim, *The Emerging Law of Detention: The Guantánamo Habeas Cases as Lawmaking*, Brookings, January 22, 2010, at 74.

28. *Id.* at 552 (Souter, J. concurring).

to the United States or coalition partners" in Afghanistan and who "engaged in an armed conflict against the United States" there. We therefore answer only the narrow question before us: whether the detention of citizens falling within that definition is authorized.[29]

Concluding Hamdi's detention did not violate substantive due process was accordingly based on the underlying conclusion that the U.S. government had the legal authority to preventively detain an enemy combatant in an armed conflict, even if, as in the case of Hamdi, the combatant was a U.S. citizen.[30] (This conclusion perforce means that such authority exists with respect to alien enemy combatants, given that aliens enjoy no more constitution protections than U.S. citizens). This conclusion is based on an axiom of the law of armed conflict: the authority of States to kill enemy combatants implies the authority of States to detain enemy combatants to prevent their return to hostilities. This axiom is central to the holding in *Hamdi*:

> We conclude that detention of individuals falling into the limited category we are considering, for the duration of the particular conflict in which they were captured, is so fundamental and accepted an incident to war as to be an exercise of the "necessary and appropriate force" Congress has authorized the President to use.[31]

While the *Hamdi* opinion therefore explicitly validated the legality of preventive detention of enemy combatants, it did not provide a comprehensive definition of the term "enemy combatant," which is laced with ambiguity in the context of counter-terror operations. Instead, the Court expressly left the definitional process to the lower courts, noting, "[t]he legal category of enemy combatant has not been elaborated upon in great detail. The permissible bounds of the category will be defined by the lower courts as subsequent cases are presented to them."[32]

The *Hamdi* Court clearly expected that in the process of considering habeas corpus petitions from Guantanamo detainees, the lower courts would define which terrorist operatives properly fell within the scope of the United States' preventive detention authority under LOAC. However, Congress quickly responded to *Hamdi* and the Supreme Court's decision in *Rasul v. Bush* that the federal habeas statute, 18 U.S.C. 2241, applied to detainees in Guantanamo, by restricting the access of Guantanamo detainees to

---

29. *Id.* at 516.

30. *See Id.* at 532–33.

31. *Id.* at 518.

32. *Id.* at 522 n.1.

habeas corpus review.[33] These restrictions were set forth in the Detainee Treatment Act (DTA)[34], which *inter alia* amended the habeas statute to effectively reverse the decision in *Rasul* and instead provide for an alternative form of review by the D.C. Circuit Court of Appeals. Then, in response to the Supreme Court's determination in its 2006 *Hamdan v. Rumsfeld*[35] decision, which permitted statutory habeas challenges to go forward even if pending at the time Congress passed the DTA, Congress enacted the Military Commission Act (MCA) of 2006[36], which, *inter alia*, amended the statute so that it was clear that the restrictions imposed on statutory habeas access by the DTA applied both prospectively and retrospectively.

The foregoing series of judicial decisions and countermanding statutory amendments set the stage for the Supreme Court's decision in *Boumediene v. Bush.*[37] *Boumediene* involved the questions of 1) whether non-resident aliens detained outside the territory of the United States at the Guantanamo detention facility were entitled to the constitutional privilege of habeas corpus; and, 2) if so, whether the DTA as amended by the MCA provided an adequate substitute for that privilege.[38] Writing for a five justice majority, Justice Kennedy held that the unique situation of these detainees—i.e., detained by the federal government, in an area outside the territorial sovereignty of the United States but subject to the exclusive control of the United States[39], with no viable alternative access to challenge the legality of their detention; facing a genuine prospect of generational deprivation of liberty, and far removed from the battlefield point of capture[40]—justified the conclusion that they were entitled to judicial review of their habeas petitions under the constitution.[41] Furthermore, the Court concluded that the review in the U.S. Court of Appeal for the District of Columbia, authorized by the DTA and MCA were an inadequate substitute for review of the petition by a court, as required by the U.S. Constitution.[42]

As a result of this decision, the process anticipated by Justice O'Connor in her *Hamdi* opinion, by which lower courts would add the proverbial "flesh to the bones" of the term "enemy combatant" finally began in earnest. Following the *Boumediene* decision, the

---

33. 542 U.S. 466 (2004).

34. Pub. L. No. 109–148, Title X; Pub. L. No. 109–163, Title XIV.

35. 548 U.S. 557 (2006).

36. Military Commissions Act of 2006, Pub. L. No. 109–366, § 3, 120 Stat. 2600 (2006).

37. 553 U.S. 723 (2008).

38. *See Id.* at 731.

39. *See Id.* at 768.

40. *See, e.g., Id.* at 797 ("Some of these petitioners have been in custody for six years with no definitive judicial determination as to the legality of their detention. Their access to the writ is a necessity to determine the lawfulness of their status, even if, in the end, they do not obtain the relief they seek.").

41. *See Id.* at 770.

42. *See Id.*

federal courts in the District of Columbia Circuit have entertained numerous habeas corpus challenges filed by Guantanamo detainees challenging the legality of their continued detention. Many of these challenges have required the courts to engage in the process of determining, first, how to define "enemy combatant" and second, which petitioners have been properly designated by the government as enemy combatants subject to lawful preventive detention.

The contours of the definition that is gradually emerging from this litigation process are sketchy at best. As a result, it is useful to conceptualize the LOAC preventive detention authority for terrorist operatives through the following analytical model. First, as the courts have recognized, the AUMF is the basis for the authority to preventively detain in the present conflict, the courts have focused their analysis on defining the groups that are the target of the AUMF, i.e., the Taliban, al Qaeda, and associated forces.[43] Second, in order to apply the AUMF authority, the courts have adopted a working definition of an "unlawful enemy belligerent" (the term adopted by President Obama as a substitute for the original "unlawful enemy combatant" used by President Bush), as more fully discussed below. Third, in applying the authority and definition in individual cases, the reviewing courts have sought to determine (i) whether the government, by a preponderance of the evidence, has alleged conduct by the detainee that is sufficient to bring the detainee within the definition of "unlawful enemy belligerent" and (ii) whether the government has provided sufficient evidence to support its allegations.[44] An affirmative finding with respect to (i) and (ii) results in the denial of habeas relief and continued preventive detention, at least until the Executive chooses to release the detainee through the Administrative Review Board process, which will be discussed in more detail below. A negative finding on either (i) or (ii) results in granting habeas relief and an order to release of the detainee (which does not result in actual release until the U.S. government has identified a nation willing to take the detainee.) This case-by-case approach to each detainee who wishes to challenge his detention is the focus of a process of complicated and time consuming habeas litigation before the U.S. District Court for the District of Columbia.

Developing a workable definition of "unlawful enemy belligerent" involves a complex synthesis of existing LOAC principles related to preventive detention of enemy belligerents and the

43. *See* Hamlily v. Obama, 616 F. Supp. 2d 63, 69–70 (D.D.C. 2009).

44. *See* Benjamin Wittes, Robert M. Chesney, and Rabea Benhalim, *The Emerging Law of Detention: The Guantánamo Habeas Cases as Lawmaking,* Brookings, January 22, 2010, at 13 (citing In re Guantanamo Bay Detainee Litig., 2008 WL 4858241, CMO § II.A (D.D.C. Nov. 6, 2008) ("The government bears the burden of proving by a preponderance of the evidence that the petitioner's detention is lawful.")).

realities of counter-terror operations. It is impossible to ignore the reality that the U.S. government has struggled in the face of the lack of clear LOAC authorities applicable to combating transnational terrorism, and the operational challenges of conducting effective counter-terrorism operations and has had difficulty developing a logical and clearly legitimate approach to preventive detention of transnational terrorists. As a result, the courts have been called upon to intervene to clarify the law, and are now decisively engaged in rendering decisions that eventually will provide clearer guidance on the scope of the authority of the U.S. government to detain terrorists.

i. The Traditional Legal Foundation for Detention of Enemy Belligerents

During periods of armed conflict, the authority to detain captured enemy belligerents is provided by the laws and customs of war, which today typically are called the LOAC.[45] The purpose of such detention is to prevent the belligerent from returning to hostilities against the detaining power; it is in no way punitive,[46] although a detainee, who does not belong to a State and otherwise does not meet the requirements of the GPW, also may be prosecuted by a State for the detainee's participation in hostilities against the State. The authority to detain is derived first and foremost from the determination that the captive is in fact an enemy belligerent, and not from the qualification of the captive as a "prisoner of war" under the GPW. While all prisoners of war are subject to preventive detention because they fall into the category of enemy belligerent, not all enemy belligerents meet the qualification for the special treatment afforded to prisoners of war under GPW. Thus, the determination by a capturing power that an individual is *not* qualified as a prisoner of war does not *ipso facto* result in a lack of authority to preventively detain.

The part of the laws and customs of war that provides the authority to preventively detain enemy belligerents includes both customary and conventional international law. Treaties that have addressed the treatment of enemy belligerents as "prisoners of war" are based on the premise that States have the right, in the exercise of military necessity, to preventively detain enemy belligerents belonging to an enemy State.[47] These treaties include the first multi-lateral convention addressing the qualification and status of

45. *See Id.*

46. In re Territo, 156 F.2d 142, 145 (9th Cir.1946) ("The object of capture is to prevent the captured individual from serving the enemy. He is disarmed and from then on must be removed as completely as practicable from the front, treated humanely, and in time, exchanged, repatriated or otherwise released.") (citations omitted).

47. *See Ex parte Quirin*, 317 U.S. 1, 29–30 (1942).

combatants, the 1907 successor of which remains in force to this day.[48] The treatment of enemy belligerents who qualify as prisoners of war in an international armed conflict was advanced substantially with the adoption in 1929 of a treaty dedicated to the treatment of prisoners of war, which was subsequently revised in the 1949 GPW, and further supplemented by certain provisions of The 1977 Protocol Additional to the Geneva Conventions of 12 August 1949 relating to the Protection of Victims of International Armed Conflicts (hereinafter Additional Protocol I or API).[49] Once qualified as a prisoner of war, captured enemy belligerents benefit from an extensive regulatory regime intended to protect their interests, prevent arbitrary treatment by the detaining power, and provide mechanisms for redress of perceived violation of treaty rights.

Each of these treaties focused almost exclusively, however, on providing an extensive regime of protections for enemy belligerents who meet treaty definitions of prisoners of war; no treaty purports to establish rules for all enemy belligerents. In addition, these treaties deal exclusively with captives in the context of international (or inter-State) armed conflicts, and do not address preventive detention in the context of non-international armed conflicts (with the exception of one clause in GPW that prescribes humane treatment for all those not actively participating in hostilities in a non-international conflict). Even in the context of an international armed conflict, not all enemy belligerents necessarily qualify for prisoner of war status. Instead, they must satisfy certain requirements, which include carrying arms openly; wearing a fixed distinctive symbol recognizable at a distance; operating under responsible command; and complying with the laws and customs of war.[50]

Article 44 of Additional Protocol I diluted the requirements by extending the protections afforded to prisoners of war, to enemy belligerents who only meet the requirement of carrying arms openly and complying with the laws and customs of war.[51] This provision effectively degraded the requirement that the enemy distinguish itself from the civilian population. For that reason, the United States rejected Article 44 and chose not to accede to API in large measure based on its objection to its dilution of the requirements

48. Regulations Respecting the Laws and Customs of War on Land, annexed to Convention Respecting the Laws and Customs of War on Land, Oct. 18, 1907, 36 Stat. 2277, 1 Bevans 631.

49. Geneva Convention Relative to the Treatment of Prisoners of War, art. 3, Aug. 12, 1949, 6 U.S.T. 3316, 75 U.N.T.S. 135 *entered into force* Oct. 21, 1950; *see also* Protocol (I) Additional to the Geneva Conventions of 12 August 1949, and Relating to the Protection of Victims of International Armed Conflicts, June 8, 1977, 1125 U.N.T.S. 3 *entered into force* Dec. 7, 1978.

50. Geneva Convention Relative to the Treatment of Prisoners of War, art. 4, Aug. 12, 1949, 6 U.S.T. 3316, 75 U.N.T.S. 135. *Entered into force* Oct. 21, 1950.

51. *Id.*

for prisoner of war treatment. As a result, although as a matter of policy the United States might afford GPW protection to a wider range of individuals, it is the United States' position, GPW only applies as a matter of law to enemy belligerents captured by the United States who satisfy a two part qualification equation. First, they must have been captured in an international armed conflict against the United States or States allied with the United States in such a conflict (the right type of conflict component);[52] second, they must satisfy the traditional four requirements listed above (the right type of person component).[53]

Because of this two-part POW qualification equation, POW status has been virtually irrelevant in relation to the detention of individuals captured by the United States in the struggle against transnational terrorism. The issue of whether these individuals qualified for such status was addressed by the U.S. government almost immediately following the initiation of preventive detention for these captives. In his February 7, 2002 Memorandum on the Humane Treatment of Taliban and al Qaeda Detainees, President Bush formalized findings he had made, after extensive debate within the Administration, that resulted in the inapplicability of POW status to the individuals the United States had begun capturing when it commenced military operations in Afghanistan in 2001. According to the President's memorandum, individuals associated with al Qaeda were conclusively excluded from POW status because they had engaged in a non-international armed conflict—an armed conflict that simply could not trigger the provisions of the POW Convention.[54] As for captured members of the Taliban, although President Bush grudgingly conceded that these individuals had in fact been captured in the context of an international armed conflict, he determined on behalf of the United States that because the Taliban forces failed to comply with the individual qualification requirements of the GPW (for example, the failure to distinguish themselves from civilians), all captured Taliban fighters were conclusively excluded from the status of prisoner of war under the GPW.[55]

These findings by President Bush sparked widespread criticism by legal experts, nongovernment organizations, and even some U.S. allies, including because he had conclusively determined the status of all fighters without engaging in any sort of individualized review of the facts surrounding the capture and conduct of each fighter. Nonetheless, the exclusion of individuals captured in the context of

52. *Id.* at art. 4.

53. *Id.*

54. White House Memorandum, "Humane Treatment of al Qaeda and Taliban Detainees" (February 7, 2002),

available at http://www.pegc.us/archive/White_House/bush_memo_20020207_ed.pdf. (last visited on Aug. 11, 2010).

55. *Id.* at 2(d).

the war on terror from the protections of the GPW has become a fundamental component of the legal foundation for the preventive detention regime adopted by the United States that continues in force to this day. To date, none of the individuals detained by the United States has successfully claimed entitlement to POW status. Thus, as a practical matter, the law related to the status and treatment of prisoners of war is essentially irrelevant for purposes of understanding the authority and obligations applicable to terrorist detained by the United States as unlawful enemy belligerents.

The inapplicability of the GPW and other treaties related to prisoners of war also had the effect of depriving the United States of a conventional source of authority to support the preventive detention of captured terrorists. It was this fact that necessitated the government's reliance on a claim of authority to detain under the more general "laws and customs of war" (i.e., customary law) as its source of authority to justify preventive detention. As noted above, the Supreme Court ultimately accepted this invocation in *Hamdi v. Rumsfeld,* holding that the preventive detention of enemy belligerents in the context of armed conflict is a necessary incident of war.[56]

Subjecting individuals captured during the struggle against terrorism to preventive detention based on the "laws and customs of war" has severely tested the efficacy of this law. As noted above, the United States continues to treat terrorist captives as subject, by virtue of their designation as enemy belligerents, to preventive detention for the duration of the conflict in the same manner as any other enemy soldier would be detained. But this invocation has produced an array of controversy and uncertainty. Among the many complicated and controversial issues that it triggered include: Is the United States even engaged in an armed conflict against terrorism? If so, how will the United States ever know when the conflict has terminated (a question so amorphous that Justice Kennedy concluded preventive detention in the context of this armed conflict may very well be "generational")?[57] What is the definition of unlawful enemy belligerent? If someone is preventively detained, what rights, if any, is that person entitled to? Finally, are terrorist detainees entitled to judicial review of the Executive's determination that they fall into a detainable category?

ii. Extending the Traditional Legal Basis to Terrorist Detainees

The *Hamdi* Court's holding that detention of enemy belligerents was a necessary incident of war provided an important founda-

---

56. *See* Hamdi v. Rumsfeld, 542 U.S. 507, 521 (2004).

57. *See* Boumediene v. Bush, 553 U.S. 723, 786 (2008).

tion for subjecting terrorists to preventive detention, but did not define who qualified as an enemy belligerent. Hamdi, having been captured on the field of battle after engaging U.S. and Coalition forces in combat, fell into the core of any definition that could be adopted. The United States, however, would extend the detention authority endorsed in *Hamdi* well beyond that core.

President Bush defined the category of individuals subject to wartime detention in his Military Order #1 directing the detention of captured terrorists at Guantanamo. That Order included the following definition of individuals subject to preventive detention:

(a) The term "individual subject to this order" shall mean any individual who is not a United States citizen with respect to whom I determine from time to time in writing that:

(1) there is reason to believe that such individual, at the relevant times;

(i) is or was a member of the organization known as al Qaida;

(ii) has engaged in, aided or abetted, or conspired to commit, acts of international terrorism, or acts in preparation therefore, that have caused, threaten to cause, or have as their aim to cause, injury to or adverse effects on the United States, its citizens, national security, foreign policy, or economy; or

(iii) has knowingly harbored one or more individuals described in subparagraphs (i) or (ii) of subsection 2(a)(1) of this order; and

(2) it is in the interest of the United States that such individual be subject to this order.[58]

This definition was clearly broader than the category of enemy belligerent analyzed by the *Hamdi* Court. Nonetheless, it provided the initial scope of detention authorization relied on by the United States. Of particular significance is that it included within its scope not only actual terrorist operatives captured during the planning, preparation, or execution of hostilities, but also individuals who

---

58. Military Order of November 13, 2001—Detention, Treatment and Trial of Certain Non–Citizens in the War Against Terrorism, 66 Fed. Reg. 57, 833 (2001). While detention is authorized under the Military Order, few detainees were actually designated as subject to the Military Order for purpose of detention; JENNIFER K. ELSEA & MICHAEL JOHN GARCIA, ENEMY COMBATANT DETAINEES: HA- BEAS CORPUS CHALLENGES IN FEDERAL COURTS DETENTIONS, CONG. RES. SERV. (Order Code No. RL33180) at 9 n. 59 (last updated Jan. 29, 2009) *available at* http://www.fas.org/sgp/crs/natsec/RL 33180.pdf (last visited Mar. 9, 2009). Rather, such detention generally occurs under the authority granted in the AUMF, which courts have interpreted to include the right to detain.

provide assistance to such operatives. Additionally, a determination of membership in al Qaida—however that determination would be made—would itself be sufficient to trigger preventive detention authority.

Although President Bush attempted to prohibit judicial review of the legality of the preventive detention regime he established in Military Order #1, it soon became clear that the federal courts were unwilling to acquiesce to his effort. In *Rasul v. Bush*,[59] the Supreme Court rejected the President's attempt to shield the Guantanamo detention operations from judicial scrutiny by interpreting the federal habeas corpus statute to run to the Guantanamo Naval Base. However, on the same day, the Court in *Hamdi* indicated that judicial review of detentions might not be necessary should the executive provide the type of minimal procedural protections the Court indicated were required for U.S. citizen detainees.[60] In response to the suggestion, the Department of Defense implemented a new procedure for assessing the belligerent status of individuals transported to Guantánamo.[61]

The process implemented by the Department of Defense involved two review tribunals for all individuals initially designated by the executive branch as subject to the president's detention order. The first tribunal was designated as a Combatant Status Review Tribunal (CSRT). This CSRT would make the initial determination of whether an individual transported to Guantánamo should continue to be detained preventively as the result of being an unlawful enemy combatant (the predecessor term to the currently used unprivileged enemy belligerent). The procedures adopted for the CSRT were based loosely on the procedures provided for in Army Regulation (AR) 190–8, which itself provided the procedures for conducting a review hearing required by the POW Convention when the POW status of a detainee is uncertain, but included procedural protections that were not set out in AR 190–8. In the context of POW determinations, these tribunals are known as article 5 tribunals (referring to the article of the GPW that calls for a tribunal to determine status in questionable cases). However, because President Bush had already determined that the individuals subjected to detention at Guantánamo could not qualify as POWs, a different characterization was adopted for the CSRT. Instead, of determining whether they were entitled to POW treatment, a CSRT would determine whether detainees were unlawful

59.   542 U.S. 466 (2004).

60.   *See Hamdi*, 542 U.S. at 533–34.

61.   *See* JENNIFER K. ELSEA, TREATMENT OF "BATTLEFIELD DETAINEES" IN THE WAR ON TERRORISM, CONG. RES. SERV., (Order Code No. RL31367) (last updated Jan. 23, 2007) *available at* http://www.fas.org/sgp/crs/terror/RL31367.pdf (last visited Aug. 11, 2010).

enemy combatants.[62] If an individual was designated as an unlawful enemy combatant, detention would be authorized indefinitely subject to an annual review to determine if detention remain justified. This annual review would be conducted by a second tribunal, which had been established prior to (and possibly in anticipation of) the *Rasul* and *Hamdi* decisions, known as the Administrative Review Board (ARB).[63]

The CSRTs would obviously need a standard to apply to determine who would remain in preventive detention and who had been improperly detained and transported to Guantánamo. The order issued by the Secretary of Defense directing the Secretary of the Navy (presumably because the Navy operates Guantanamo) to establish the CSRT included the following definition:

> a. *Enemy Combatant.* For purposes of this Order, the term "enemy combatant" shall mean an individual who was part of or supporting Taliban or al Qaeda forces, or associated forces that are engaged in hostilities against the United States or its coalition partners. This includes any person who has committed a belligerent act or has directly supported hostilities in aid of enemy armed forces. Each detainee subject to this Order has been determined to be an enemy combatant through multiple levels of review by officers of the Department of Defense.[64]

This definition did seem to establish the requirement for a more direct link between the detainee and the conduct of combat operations. However, by also including within the definition of detainable captive individuals who provided support to al Qaeda or the Taliban, the definition ultimately resulted in no significant difference between the controlling standard to be applied by the CSRTs and the President's initial definition.

Another definition that emerged in response to the initial detainee decisions by the Supreme Court was included in the MCA 2006.[65] This law was passed by Congress in response to the Supreme Court's decision in Hamdan striking down the military

---

62. *See* JENNIFER K. ELSEA & MICHAEL JOHN GARCIA, ENEMY COMBATANT DETAINEES: HABEAS CORPUS CHALLENGES IN FEDERAL COURTS DETENTIONS, CONG. RES. SERV., (Order Code No. RL33180) at 7 (last updated Jan. 29, 2009) *available at* http://www.fas.org/sgp/crs/natsec/RL33180.pdf (last visited Aug. 11, 2010).

63. *See Id.* n.130 and accompanying text.

64. Department of Defense Memorandum, "Order Establishing Combatant Status Review Tribunal" (July 7, 2004) *available at* http://www.defense.gov/news/Jul2004/d20040707review.pdf (last visited on Aug. 11, 2010).

65. *Supra* at note 36.

commission ordered established by President Bush in the same Military Order that directed the establishment of the detention facility at Guantanamo. Congress passed this law to both cure the procedural defects that had doomed that original military commission in Hamdan, and to ensure that unlawful enemy combatants detained at Guantánamo would in fact be subject to trial by military commission. Accordingly, it was necessary for Congress to provide its own definition of who fell into the category of unlawful enemy combatant subject to commission jurisdiction—a definition that by implication also covers the authority to preventively detain individuals because of their status as unlawful enemy combatants. Congress defined unlawful enemy combatant in 10 U.S.C. § 948a as:

> (i) a person who has engaged in hostilities or who has purposefully and materially supported hostilities against the United States or its co-belligerents who is not a lawful enemy combatant (including a person who is part of the Taliban, al Qaeda, or associated forces); or

> (ii) a person who, before, on, or after the date of the enactment of the Military Commissions Act of 2006, has been determined to be an unlawful enemy combatant by a Combatant Status Review Tribunal or another competent tribunal established under the authority of the President or the Secretary of Defense.[66]

What is most significant about both the definition adopted by the Department of Defense for purposes of the CSRTs, and the definition enacted by Congress in MCA 2006 for purposes of defining who would be subject to trial by military commission, is that each indicates that persons who materially support a terrorist group need not actually commit belligerent acts in order to be treated as enemy combatants.

This broad definition would remain the basis for U.S. detentions for as long as the detention process remained outside judicial scrutiny. Accordingly, the United States could, and often did, subject captured aliens believed to be part of or to have provided support to al Qaeda to detention without charge or trial.[67] The CSRTs did provide a limited check on this process, but only in relation to the weight of the evidence supporting the characteriza-

---

66. 10 U.S.C. § 948a (2006) (as enacted by Military Commissions Act of 2006, Pub. L. No. 109–366, § 3, 120 Stat. 2600 (2006)). To be subject to trial by military commission, a person meeting the definition of unlawful enemy combatant also must be an alien (i.e., not a U.S. citizen.) *Id.*

67. *See, e.g.,* Scott Shane and Adam Liptak, *Detainee Bill Shifts Power to President,* N.Y. Times, Sept. 30, 2006, at A1.

tion and not in relation to the definition that justified detention. Nor did a limited judicial review of CSRT decisions subsequently authorized in the Detainee Treatment Act provide detainees with a viable opportunity to challenge the scope of the enemy combatant definition; it merely authorized judicial review of whether the CSRT had followed its own established procedures.[68]

In June 2008, the efforts of the President and Congress to limit habeas review of preventive detention of Guantanamo detainees was nullified by the Supreme Court's decision of *Boumediene v. Bush*.[69] In a 5–4 decision, the Court held that (i) the detainees enjoyed a constitutional privilege to petition the federal courts for habeas corpus; (ii) the review procedures in the CSRTs and the Detainee Treatment Act were an insufficient substitute for this privilege; and (iii) the detainees could challenge their continued detention as a violation of both substantive and procedural due process.[70] This decision cleared the way for detainees to challenge not only the process they had been afforded to authorize their preventive detention, but perhaps more importantly the scope of the definition of enemy belligerent itself—the definition pursuant to which they were detained. The response by both the Executive Branch and the courts that began to decide these challenges is ongoing at the time of this writing, although the trend seems to be towards strengthening the link between the LOAC principle of military necessity and the definition that justifies preventive detention.

iii.   Attempting to Restore the Link Between the LOAC and Preventive Detention

Following the *Boumediene* decision, Guantanamo detainees initiated or revised judicial challenges to the legality of their continued detention. The primary challenge, *In re Guantanamo Detainees*[71], was a consolidation of challenges by a number of detainees. The Bush administration responded by asserting that determinations that individuals were members of al Qaeda or the Taliban at the time of their capture, or that they had materially supported those entities, justified continued detention. After President Obama took office, the Court requested the government to indicate whether it would modify its position on the legality of the detentions.

---

68. *See* JENNIFER K. ELSEA, TREATMENT OF "BATTLEFIELD DETAINEES" IN THE WAR ON TERRORISM, CONG. RES. SERV., 53–55, (Order Code No. RL31367) (last updated Jan. 23, 2007) *available at* http://www.fas.org/sgp/crs/terror/RL31367.pdf (last visited Aug. 11, 2010).

69. 553 U.S. 723 (2008).

70. *See Id.* at 786.

71. 355 F.Supp.2d 443 (D.D.C. 2005).

In response, the Department of Justice filed a memorandum offering the first significant indicator on how it would address the preventive detention issue President Obama inherited from the Bush administration.[72] In the memorandum, the government proposed the following "definitional framework" for its authority to detain persons held at Guantanamo Bay:

> The President has the authority to detain persons that the President determines planned, authorized, committed, or aided the terrorist attacks that occurred on September 11, 2001, and persons who harbored those responsible for those attacks. The President also has the authority to detain persons who were part of, or substantially supported, Taliban or al-Qaida forces or associated forces that are engaged in hostilities against the United States or its coalition partners, including any person who has committed a belligerent act, or has directly supported hostilities, in aid of such enemy armed forces.[73]

Although the continued assertion of preventive detention authority undoubtedly disappointed supporters of candidate Obama who had hoped he would abandon this policy, the new administration's position exposed two significant adjustments from that of the Bush administration. First is the express concession that the President's authority to continue to preventively detain the Petitioners is derived from the Authorization to Use Military Force (AUMF) enacted by Congress in response to the attacks on September 11, 2001.[74] This joint resolution authorized the use of "all necessary and appropriate force against those nations, organizations, or persons ... [the President] determines planned, authorized, committed, or aided the terrorist attacks that occurred on September 11, 2001, or harbored such organizations or persons, in order to prevent any future acts of international terrorism against the United States by such nations, organizations or persons."[75] This was the same authority relied on by the Supreme Court in *Hamdi,* and like that decision, the memorandum asserted that the all necessary and appropriate force language implicitly invokes the laws and customs of war, specifically the authority to detain enemy belligerents as an exercise of military necessity. Second, the memorandum abandoned the term "material support" and substituted the term "substantial

---

72. Respondent's Memorandum Regarding the Government's Detention Authority Relative to Detainees Held at Guantanamo Bay, In re: Guantanamo Bay Detainee Litigation, Misc. No. 08–442 (TFH) (Mar. 13, 2009).

73. *Id.* at 2.

74. Authorization for Use of Military Force, S.J. Res. 23, 107th Congress, 1st Sess. Pub. L. No. 107–40, 115 Stat. 224 (2001) [hereinafter AUMF].

75. *Id.* § 2(a).

support." This seems to indicate the Obama administration is moving towards a more restrictive scope of detention authority, requiring a more direct link between the authority to detain and the LOAC principle of military necessity. This conclusion is bolstered by the fact that the memorandum indicates that determining whether an individual was "part of" such a force depended on a "formal or functional analysis" of the individual's role in the groups subjected to the AUMF. To guide this analysis, the AUMF provides, "given the nature of the irregular forces, and the practice of their participants or members to try to conceal their affiliations, judgments about the detainability of a particular individual will necessarily turn on the totality of the circumstances."[76]

2. THE PROCEDURAL COMPONENT[77]

Related to the scope of a State's preventive detention authority in an armed conflict, is the question of what procedures apply to the process of determining whether particular individuals fall within the scope of that authority. If the question were whether these individuals qualify for treatment as prisoners of war under the GPW, the determination would be relatively uncomplicated. Moreover, a finding that an individual falls within the categories covered by the GPW is not punitive, as that treaty establishes a comprehensive regime of treatment and procedural protections for POWs. Effectively, those who are determined to be POWs are amply protected under international law, including being shielded from prosecution for their belligerent activities (unless those activities were war crimes) and, at the conclusion of hostilities, having the right to be repatriated to the State to which they belong.

President Bush's 2002 decision that al Qaeda, Taliban and other terrorist detainees do not qualify for POW status necessarily also excludes them from GPW protection framework, including the right to particularized determination of their status in appropriate cases under Article 5, GPW. Indeed, this was likely one of the primary reasons for interpreting the LOAC to support such exclusion. While this interpretation is arguably justified based on the failure of terrorists to satisfy the two prong POW qualification equation, it did create substantial uncertainty as to the required procedural framework to lawfully detain these unprivileged belligerents. While many experts asserted that exclusion from the GPW required detainees to be treated as civilians protected by the Geneva Convention Relative to the Protection of Civilian Persons in Time of War—an assertion based on an interpretation of the

76. *Id.* at 7.
77. This section is reproduced, with light edits, from James A. Schoettler, Jr., *Detention of Combatants and the* *Global War on Terror, in* THE WAR ON TERROR AND THE LAW OF WAR: A MILITARY PERSPECTIVE, 103–23 (Geoffrey S. Corn, ed., Oxford Univ. Press, 2009).

Conventions whereby all detainees must fall within the protections of either the GPW or the GCC[78]—this assertion is by no means supported by the language of the GCC (for reasons beyond the scope of this chapter), and in any case, has not been embraced by the U.S. government. Instead, by classifying terrorist detainees as unprivileged enemy belligerents, the United States effectively placed them in a category of belligerent detainees falling outside the scope of either GPW or GCC.

The initial U.S. approach to procedural aspects of detention was minimalist: the President, acting as Commander-in-Chief, possessed plenary authority to determine which captives were subject to preventive detention as enemy combatants. Accordingly, this determination was not subject to any type of external review, as emphasized by Military Order #1. Further pursuant to AR 190–8 and lower level guidance from U.S. military commanders, many detainees at Guantanamo had been subject to multiple reviews at various levels of the detention process before they arrived at Guantanamo; however many detention determinations were summary decisions made by military officials based almost exclusively on interrogation reports.

The combined effect of the Supreme Court's contemporaneous 2004 decisions in *Rasul v. Bush*[79] and *Hamdi v. Rumsfeld*[80] led to a modification of this process. *Rasul* opened the door to judicial review for detainees at Guantanamo; *Hamdi* called into question the sufficiency of the process being used by the Executive to classify detainees. Although *Hamdi* dealt with the process due for a U.S. citizen, in seeking to fashion procedures for non-citizen Guantanamo detainees that the U.S. government thought would meet judicial challenge allowed by the *Rasul* decision, the U.S. government believed that it would be sufficient to implement a process that met the guidance provided by the *Hamdi* decision for U.S. citizen detainees. This did not require a procedure identical to the procedure afforded in habeas proceedings in U.S. courts: Most notably, Justice O'Connor noted that the minimum due process in the context of detaining Hamdi included giving the detainee "some opportunity to present and rebut facts."[81]

According to the *Hamdi* decision, a status determination—which as a result of the *Rasul* decision had been made available to all Guantanamo detainees—could not be made "as a matter of law,

78. *See* LTC Paul Kantwill & Maj. Sean Watts, *Hostile Protected Persons or "Extra–Conventional Persons:" How Unlawful Combatants in the War on Terrorism Posed Extraordinary Challenges for Military Attorneys and Commanders*, 28 FORDHAM INT'L L.J. 681 (2005).

79. 542 U.S. 466 (2004).

80. 542 U.S. 507 (2004).

81. Hamdi v. Rumsfeld, 542 U.S. 507, 526 (2004).

without further hearing or factfinding necessary,"[82] It also could not be made under a highly deferential "some evidence" standard, which effectively would amount to relying exclusively on the government's evidence, a conclusion that effectively rejected the President's assertion of plenary and exclusive authority to determine who could be detained.[83] Although Justice O'Connor rejected the lower court conclusion that the process due should mirror that of a criminal trial,[84] minimally acceptable process must afford the detainee "notice of the factual basis for his classification" and "a fair opportunity to rebut the factual assertions before a neutral decision-maker."[85] In addition, "enemy combatant proceedings could be tailored to alleviate their uncommon potential to burden the Executive at time of ongoing military conflict."[86] Thus, "hearsay may need to be accepted as the most reliable evidence", and a rebuttable presumption in favor of government evidence might be provided.[87]

Because *Rasul* had opened the habeas door for detainees, *Hamdi's* articulation of minimally acceptable process for detention determinations, albeit in relation to U.S. citizens, seemed to indicate a broader application of that process to all detainees. It was also clear, however, that the *Hamdi* Court was cognizant of what it considered legitimate concerns of the Executive that judicial review of detention decisions might interfere with the ability to efficiently prosecute the armed conflict against terrorism. Accordingly, the Court not only rejected the criminal process model for detention determinations, but also qualified the holding in two other significant respects. First, Justice O'Connor emphasized that the procedural protections did not apply to "initial captures" on the battlefield, but rather only when a decision is being made to continue the detainee's captivity.[88] Second, and perhaps more importantly, Justice O'Conner suggested that Executive implementation of more robust internal detention classification procedures—procedures that she noted were ironically already provided for in Army Regulation 190–8—might negate the necessity of judicial review:

> There remains the possibility that the standards we have articulated could be met by an appropriately authorized and properly constituted military tribunal. Indeed, it is notable that military regulations already provide for such process in related instances, dictating that tribunals be made avail-

82. *Id.* at 526.

83. *Id.* at 527.

84. *Id.* at 528.

85. *Id.* at 533. Justice O'Connor characterized these as "core elements" of the petitioner's rights. *Id.*

86. *Id.*

87. *Id.* at 534; *See also* James A. Schoettler, Jr., *Detention of Combatants and the Global War on Terror*, in THE WAR ON TERROR AND THE LAW OF WAR: A MILITARY PERSPECTIVE, 103–23 (Geoffrey S. Corn, ed., Oxford Univ. Press, 2009).

88. *Id.* at 534.

able to determine the status of enemy detainees who assert prisoner-of-war status under the Geneva Convention. See Enemy Prisoners of War, Retained Personnel, Civilian Internees and Other Detainees, Army Regulation 190—8, § 1—6 (1997). In the absence of such process, however, a court that receives a petition for a writ of habeas corpus from an alleged enemy combatant must itself ensure that the minimum requirements of due process are achieved.[89]

Thus, while *Hamdi* did not expressly require the adoption of more robust procedures for detention determinations at Guantanamo, it did seem to suggest that by so doing the Executive might avoid judicial review for all detainees.

As noted earlier in this Chapter, the Bush Administration quickly responded by implementing a two-prong detention review process it considered consistent with Justice O'Connor's suggestion. The first level of review is the CSRT process to determine "whether the detainee is properly detained as an enemy combatant,"[90] employing a definition of "enemy combatant" similar to the definition adopted by Justice O'Connor in *Hamdi*.[91] The CSRT is modeled after the tribunal under AR 190–8, with "three neutral commissioned officers" to hear the evidence and a recorder ("preferably a judge advocate", as stipulated under AR 190–8) to handle administrative tasks.[92]

There are significant differences, however. First, the detainee is entitled to advance notice of the "unclassified factual basis" for his designation as an enemy combatant.[93] Second, in addition to the recorder, one of the CSRT members is a judge advocate (i.e., military lawyer).[94] Third, the detainee is entitled to be represented by a non-lawyer military officer acting as "personal representative".[95] The personal representative has the right to review any "reasonably available" evidence and can share any unclassified evidence with the detainee.[96] Fourth,

---

89. *Id.* at 538.

90. 2004 CSRT Order, *supra* note 64, para. (g)(12). The order makes clear that "[e]ach detainee subject to this Order has been determined to be an enemy combatant through multiple levels of review by officers of the Department of Defense." *Id.* para. a.

91. *Hamdi*, 542 U.S. at 516 ("[The Government] has made clear, however, that, for purposes of this case, the 'enemy combatant' that it is seeking to detain is an individual who, it alleges, was 'part of or supporting forces hostile to the United States or coalition partners' in Afghanistan and who 'engaged in an armed conflict against the United States' there.").

92. 2004 CSRT Order, *supra* note 64, para. e.

93. *Id.* para. g(1).

94. *Id.* para. e.

95. *Id.* para. c.

96. *Id.* para. c.

the Convening Authority is not a commander, but rather an appointee of the Secretary of the Navy.[97] Fifth, hearsay evidence is permitted "taking into account the reliability of such evidence in the circumstances." [98]Finally, there is a "rebuttable presumption" in favor of the government's evidence.[99]

An Administrative Review Board (ARB) procedure, which, as noted earlier this Chapter had been established prior to the *Rasul* decision, will "assess annually the need to continue to detain each enemy combatant during the course of the current and ongoing hostilities."[100] Like the CSRT, the ARB consists of three officers; but, unlike the CSRT, there is no requirement for a lawyer to be a member,[101] although a lawyer advises the ARB. Like the CSRT, the detainee may be given the assistance of a non-lawyer military officer, as well as a summary of the evidence. The detainee is permitted to present to the ARB information about "why he is no longer a threat to the United States and its allies in the ongoing armed conflict against al Qaida and its affiliates and supporters, why it is otherwise appropriate that he be released, or any other relevant information." The ARB makes its recommendation on retention to a designated civilian official or "DCO", who is "a presidentially-appointed Senate-confirmed civilian in the Department of Defense whom the Secretary of Defense has designated to operate and oversee the administrative review process." The ARB is available for all detainees except those pending charges before military commissions and those already pending transfer/release.[102]

Taken together, the process provided by the CSRT and the ARB seemed to meet if not exceed the standard articulated by Justice O'Connor as sufficient to satisfy the minimal process due to classify an individual as an unlawful enemy combatant. The CSRT itself includes procedures that are more extensive than not only those required by AR 190–8, but even what is contemplated by the

---

97. *Id.* para. f.

98. *Id.* para. g(9).

99. *Id.* para. g(12); *See also* James A. Schoettler, Jr., *Detention of Combatants and the Global War on Terror*, in THE WAR ON TERROR AND THE LAW OF WAR: A MILITARY PERSPECTIVE, 103–23 (Geoffrey S. Corn, ed., Oxford Univ. Press, 2009).

100. Dep'y Sec'y Defense, Order, Subject: Administrative Review Procedures for Enemy Combatants in the Control of the Department of Defense at Guantanamo Bay Naval Base, Cuba, para. 1 (May 11, 2004) *available at* http://www.defenselink.mil/news/May

2004/d20040518gtmoreview.pdf (last visited on March 9, 2009). The ARB procedures were already under development in early 2004 and in fact were adopted and put in place before either *Hamdi* or *Rasul* were handed down.

101. *Id.* para. 2.B.ii. At least one member must be an officer "experienced in the field of intelligence." *Id.*

102. Both the CSRT and ARB procedures were revised and updated in 2006. In addition, a procedure for reviewing new evidence about a detainee's enemy combatant status was adopted in 2007.

GPW for resolving uncertainty as to whether an individual is or is not a POW. The ARB was an additional level of procedural review not even contemplated by the Army Regulation or the GPW.[103]

Congress also acted to express its position on the adequacy of the CSRT/ARB process that had been created by the Administration. In response to the Supreme Court's interpretation of the federal habeas statute in *Rasul*, Congress passed the Detainee Treatment Act of 2005. Section 1005 of the DTA amended the habeas corpus statute to preclude courts from taking jurisdiction of petitions from detainees, or regarding detention, at Guantanamo. Instead, the D.C. Circuit Court of Appeals was rested with the authority to review CSRT decisions to determine:

i.   whether the status determination of the Combatant Status Review Tribunal with regard to such alien was consistent with the standards and procedures specified by the Secretary of Defense for Combatant Status Review Tribunals (including the requirement that the conclusion of the Tribunal be supported by a preponderance of the evidence and allowing a rebuttable presumption in favor of the Government's evidence); and

ii. to the extent the Constitution and laws of the United States are applicable, whether the use of such standards and procedures to make the determination is consistent with the Constitution and laws of the United States.[104]

The DTA was therefore intended to not only overrule the interpretation of the federal habeas statute adopted by the Supreme Court in the *Rasul* opinion, but also to indicate that the process provided to detainees by the CSRT is sufficient to satisfy any U.S. government obligation owed to them under U.S. law. *Hamdan v. Rumsfeld*[105] necessitated further amendment to the habeas statute after the Supreme Court ruled that the DTA amendment had not been intended to apply retroactively to habeas petitions that had been pending at the time the DTA was enacted. Responding to this interpretation of the statute, Congress once again amended the habeas statute when it passed MCA 2006. While MCA 2006 was focused primarily on providing a solid legal foundation for the military commissions that had been struck down by the Supreme Court in the *Hamdan* decision, it also included an

103. James A. Schoettler, Jr., *Detention of Combatants and the Global War on Terror*, in THE WAR ON TERROR AND THE LAW OF WAR: A MILITARY PERSPECTIVE, 103–23 (Geoffrey S. Corn, ed., Oxford Univ. Press, 2009).

104. Detainee Treatment Act, Pub. L. No. 109–148, § 1005(e)(2)(C), 119 Stat. 2680, 2742 (2005) (codified at 28 U.S.C.A. § 2241(e) (2005)). The DTA was amended by the MCA, *supra* note 36, § 8.

105. 548 U.S. 557 (2006).

amendment to the federal habeas statute which clearly indicated that the statute did not apply to Guantánamo detainees under any circumstances.[106] This provision of MCA 2006 applied not only to challenges to CSRT determinations regarding detainees at Guantanamo, but also to any enemy combatant determination made worldwide regarding persons in the custody of the United States.[107]

Although both the Administration and Congress clearly considered the CSRT process to satisfy procedural obligations related to the designation of an individual as a detainable enemy combatant, detainees did not share that opinion. In the view of the lawyers representing them and outside observers, the CSRT process was insufficient to protect the detainees from the risk of arbitrary and indefinite detention. Criticism of the CSRT process was both substantive and procedural. From a substantive perspective, the process itself was alleged to be insufficient to offset the risk of arbitrary detention resulting from a definition of unlawful enemy combatant that was far more expansive than the definition endorsed by the Supreme Court in the *Hamdi* decision. Procedurally, there were several aspects of the CSRT process that were considered to be inconsistent with the process outlined in *Hamdi*. First, the tribunals consisted of military officers selected to review the case by the Defense Department, which was the same organization that had decided to detain them in the first place. Second, while the Court had held that Hamdi unquestionably had a right to the assistance of counsel, none was provided in the CSRT process. Third, the procedures included presumptions in favor of the government that might be difficult to overcome, including because certain evidence could be withheld from the detainee on the grounds that it was not "reasonably available."[108] Finally, there was no explicit right to appeal the substance of the status determination to a court.

106. MCA, *supra* note 36, § 7, *codified at* 28 U.S.C. § 2241(e). The MCA also barred courts from considering "any other action against the United States or its agents relating to any aspect of the detention, transfer, treatment, trial, or conditions of confinement of an alien who is or was detained by the United States and has been determined by the United States to have been properly detained as an enemy combatant or is awaiting such determination." Although the Court in *Boumediene*, discussed *infra* notes 114–117 and accompanying text, invalidated, as an unconstitutional suspension of the writ of habeas corpus, the bar on habeas petitions to challenge the legality of detention at Guantanamo, lower courts have held that this did not affect the validity of the separate MCA provision barring other actions to challenge the conditions of detention; Khadr v. Bush, 587 F. Supp. 2d 225 (D.D.C. 2008).

107. James A. Schoettler, Jr., *Detention of Combatants and the Global War on Terror*, in THE WAR ON TERROR AND THE LAW OF WAR: A MILITARY PERSPECTIVE, 103–23 (Geoffrey S. Corn, ed., Oxford Univ. Press, 2009).

108. Some of these issues were addressed in a series of decisions by the Court of Appeals for the D.C. Circuit, which held that the D.C. Circuit in reviewing a CSRT's enemy combatant determination (under a limited right granted in the DTA, to appeal CSRT determinations to the D.C. Circuit) was entitled to all the information reason-

This combination of denial of statutory habeas access and continuing assertions of arbitrary deprivation of liberty would ultimately result in the Supreme Court's decision in *Boumediene v. Bush.*[109] This decision addressed the very narrow question of whether the detainees at Guantánamo were entitled to challenge their detention pursuant to the constitutional right of habeas corpus, and if so, whether the provisions of the DTA and MCA 2006 amounted to an unconstitutional suspension of that right.[110] The Supreme Court ruled in favor of the Guantánamo detainees on both of these questions. The Court concluded that because Guantánamo was outside the *de jure* territory of the United States, formal sovereignty should not dictate the reach of habeas corpus. Instead, what is required is,[111] a case by case determination involving the examination of "at least" three factors: "(1) the detainees' citizenship and status and the adequacy of the process through which that status was determined; (2) the nature of the sites where apprehension and then detention took place; and (3) the practical obstacles inherent in resolving the prisoner's entitlement to the writ."[112] Weighing

ably available to the Recorder in making his or her determination of the evidence to present to the CSRT. In support of a decision to deny rehearing en bank, Chief Justice Ginsburg noted various limitations of the CSRT:

> Unlike the final decision rendered in a criminal or an agency proceeding, which is the product of an open and adversarial process before an independent decisionmaker, a CSRT's status determination is the product of a necessarily closed and accusatorial process in which the detainee seeking review will have had little or no access to the evidence the Recorder presented to the Tribunal, little ability to gather his own evidence, no right to confront the witnesses against him, and no lawyer to help him prepare his case, and in which the decisionmaker is employed and chosen by the detainee's accuser.

Bismullah v. Gates, 514 F.3d 1291, 1296 (opinion of Chief Judge Ginsburg, joined

by three other judges, concurring in the denial of rehearing en banc).

109. 553 U.S. 723, 128 S.Ct. 2229, 2274 (2008).

110. *See* Boumediene, 128 S. Ct. at 2262. Article I, section 9, clause 2 of the Constitution provides: "The privilege of the Writ of Habeas Corpus shall not be suspended, unless when in Cases of Rebellion or Invasion the public Safety may require it."

111. In *Rasul*, 542 U.S. at 504, the Court similarly found the fact that Guantanamo was not sovereign U.S. territory did not preclude detainees from seeking a writ of habeas corpus under the habeas statute to challenge their detention in Guantanamo but Congress amended the habeas statute to specifically eliminate the detainee's ability to pursue a writ of habeas under the statute.

112. Boumediene, 128 S. Ct. at 2259. The Court based its ruling in part on *Eisentrager v. Johnson*, 339 U.S. 763 (1950), a post-World War II decision in which the Court held that German prisoners of war tried by the U.S. military commission in China and imprisoned in occupied Germany did not have a right to pursue a writ of habeas corpus to challenge their detention. Previously, however, *Eisentrager* had been cited for the proposition that aliens tried and imprisoned outside the territorial limits of

these factors in the case before it, the Court found that the constitutional right to the writ of habeas corpus extended to aliens held as enemy combatants at Guantanamo.[113]

The Court then rejected the government's argument that the CSRT process or the right to appeal the CSRT's findings to the D.C. Circuit provided an adequate substitute for habeas proceedings in a Federal court. The Court recognized that a CSRT provided "some process", but the CSRT did not provide for "a rigorous adversarial process", including a right to counsel, did not grant access to all evidence relied upon to detain him or her, and provided for liberal use of hearsay evidence (which meant that the "opportunity to question witnesses is likely to be more theoretical than real.")[114] The opportunity to appeal CSRT decisions to the D.C. Circuit also was not a sufficient substitute for habeas, because of the limited scope of the D.C. Circuit's review, the fact that it did not expressly have the authority to order the release of a detainee in the event detention was found to be unauthorized, and the lack of an opportunity for the detainee to present evidence discovered after the CSRT proceedings were complete.[115]

Ultimately, once the Court concluded that individuals detained as enemy combatants at Guantanamo were constitutionally entitled to challenge their detention through the writ of habeas corpus, the significant disparity between the CSRT process and standard habeas procedure was bound to lead to the conclusion that the detainees' constitutional rights had been improperly deprived. This once again cleared the way for judicial review of detention, although arguably limited to individuals at Guantanamo. The Court emphasized this limited scope of the Great Writ when it noted that "[o]ur holding . . . should not be read to imply that a habeas court should intervene the moment an enemy combatant steps in a territory where the writ runs." It also did not reject the CSRT process, holding instead that "[t]he Executive is entitled to a reasonable period of time to determine the detainee's status before a court entertains that detainees habeas corpus petition."[116] It also noted that "accommodations" could be made to reduce the burdens of habeas proceedings and to protect sources and methods of intelligence gathering.

These qualifiers in no way distract from the unavoidable conclusion that the Supreme Court had chosen to inject the judicial branch into a realm of decision-making historically immune from judicial oversight. One factor that ostensibly contributed to this

United States could not seek the writ, which was the formalistic approach rejected by the Court in *Boumediene*.

113. *See Id.* at 765, 771.

114. *Boumediene*, 553 U.S. at 764, 783–788.

115. *Id.* at 786–793.

116. *Id.* at 795.

outcome was the obvious discomfort felt by the Court with the application of wartime preventive detention authority in the context of a conflict that had no foreseeable end date. In this unique context, traditional doctrines of judicial restraint based on separation of powers principles were outweighed by the requirement for a judicial determination of the legality of continuing deprivations of liberty, which the *Boumediene* Court characterized as potentially "generational" in duration.[117] The Court noted that, while short conflicts in the past had made it possible to leave the "outer boundaries" of Executive wartime detention powers undefined, the "[C]ourt might not have this luxury" in the context of a conflict of indefinite duration. Therefore, it invited the Administration and Congress to "engage in a genuine debate about how best to preserve constitutional values while protecting the Nation from terrorism." [118]

However, the Court also limited its holding to the narrow question of access to habeas review, and left to the lower courts the responsibility to resolve the questions of substantive detention authority and requisite procedures, including (as noted above) the definition of the unlawful enemy combatant that would be subject to detention. In so doing, the Supreme Court opened a new chapter in the evolution of the law of terrorist detentions, a chapter that continues to be written today.

a. Post Boumediene Developments

The government's record in defending continued detentions based on this revised definition of detainability has to date been mixed.[119] "[B]ecause the Supreme Court acknowledged but did not clarify the uncertain "permissible bounds" of the Government's detention authority . . . the state of the law regarding the scope of the President's authority to detain petitioners remains unsettled."[120] Some D.C. Circuit courts' interpretation of the scope of detention permissible by the AUMF has been decidedly broader than others, with the focal point of their discussions turning on the "substantial support" term within the new Administration's definition. In *Gherebi v. Obama*,[121] the Court agreed with the government that "substantial support" for an enemy organization did provide a grounds for preventive detention under the AUMF, *so long as* the standard was applied only to members of the enemy's armed

117. *See* Boumediene v. Bush, 553 U.S. 723 (2008).

118. *Id.*

119. *See* Benjamin Wittes, Robert M. Chesney, and Rabea Benhalim, *The Emerging Law of Detention: The Guantánamo Habeas Cases as Lawmaking*, Brookings, January 22, 2010, at 14.

120. Al Odah v. United States, 648 F. Supp. 2d 1, 6 (D.D.C. 2009) (citing Hamdi v. Rumsfeld, 542 U.S. 507, 552 (2004)).

121. 609 F. Supp. 2d 43 (D.D.C. 2009).

forces.[122] The Court noted that, while it was impossible to precisely define the term, the standard itself was not "entirely nebulous."[123] The determination of who qualifies as a member of an enemy organization's "armed forces," the Court said, is governed by Article 4 of the Third Geneva Convention and Article 43 of Additional Protocol I, and requires that the force itself be organized and structured into a hierarchy.[124] Even though most terrorist organizations do not wear uniforms or "issue membership cards," each organization engaged in combat bears some sort of command structure, and the detainee must have a tie within that structure.[125] Under *Gherebi*, those "supporters" of enemy forces who have some sort of ' "structured' role in the 'hierarchy' of [that] enemy force" fall lawfully under the President's detention authority granted by the AUMF.[126] Additionally, "mere sympathy for or association with an enemy organization does not render an individual a member of that enemy organization's armed forces."[127]

Following the "substantial support" standard established by *Gherebi*, the Court in *Al–Adahi v. Obama*,[128] concluded that a captured Yemenite who, *inter alia*, was recruited by, received training from, bunked in the guesthouses of, and traveled under the orders of al-Qaida and Taliban leadership, was under the "command structure" of those enemy organizations and thus, was lawfully detained by the authority given the President under the AUMF.[129]

Other rulings of the D.C. Circuit have rejected the "substantial support" standard adopted by *Gherebi* in favor of a narrower interpretation of the President's detention authority under the AUMF. These courts have held that the Executive has authority, under the AUMF and laws of war, to detain persons who were *part of* the AUMF targeted organizations, but lacks authority to detain non-members who provide "support" to those organizations. In *Hamlily v. Obama*,[130] the Court rejected *Gherebi*'s substantial support standard as a valid independent basis for detention, holding instead that "[d]etention based on substantial or direct support of the Taliban, al Qaeda or associated forces, without more, is simply not warranted by domestic law or the law of war."[131] The court held that the government has the authority to detain members of "associated forces" as long as those forces would be considered co-belligerents [those who violate the law of neutrality] under the law

---

122. *See Id.* at 70 (emphasis added).

     123. *Id.* at 69.

     124. *Id.* at 68.

     125. *Id.*

     126. *Id.* at 70.

     127. *Id.*

128. 692 F. Supp. 2d 85 (D.D.C. 2010).

     129. *Id.* at 102.

130. 616 F. Supp. 2d 63 (D.D.C. 2009).

     131. *Id.* at 69.

of war.[132] The court found that attempting to detain those who had a peripheral connection to the enemy organizations (i.e. financial supporters) was an importation of domestic criminal law, and while the Court did not reject its policy rationale or foreclose the potential for later litigation of the issue, currently allowing such detention of supporters is "simply beyond what the law of war will support."[133]

The key inquiry then, is not necessarily whether one self-identifies as a member of the organization (although this could be relevant in some cases), but whether the individual functions or participates within or under the command structure of the organization—i.e., whether he receives and executes orders or directions.[134] Thus, as *Gherebi* observed, this could include an individual "tasked with housing, feeding, or transporting al-Qaeda fighters . . . but an al-Qaeda doctor or cleric, or the father of an al-Qaeda fighter who shelters his son out of familial loyalty, [is likely not detainable] assuming such individuals had no independent role in al-Qaeda's chain of command."[135]

Under this "command structure" analysis, this sect of the D.C. Circuit has been willing to recognize detentions authorized under the AUMF in circumstances where the detainee has trained with the enemy forces, traveled to the regions it frequents, taken up shelter in its camps, received its arms, met with its leaders, and traveled with its trainees.[136] Even where the detainee has not formally joined with the enemy force, yet participated in its hostile action, the Court has been willing to find his detention lawful under the AUMF.[137]

One post-*Boumediene* decision sparked particular controversy and raised concerns that the D.C. Circuit may have resurrected the expansive theory of preventive detention exemplified by the original Bush administration policies. In *Al–Bihani v. Obama,* the Petitioner challenged the legality of his detention by asserting, *inter alia,* that as a cook for a volunteer group associated with the Taliban he did not qualify as an enemy combatant[138], and that even if he had

132. *Id.* at 73.

133. *Id.* at 76.

134. *Id.* at 75 (citing *Gherebi v. Obama*, 609 F. Supp. 2d 43, 69 (D.D.C. 2009); Curtis A. Bradley & Jack L. Goldsmith, *Congressional Authorization and the War on Terrorism*, 118 Harv. L. Rev. 2047, 2109 (2005)).

135. *Id.* (citing *Gherebi*, 609 F. Supp. 2d at 69). Notably, this "command structure analysis" does not encompass those who unwittingly participate in hostilities on the side of al-Qaida

or its associated forces. Some element of knowledge is required. *Id.*

136. *See e.g.*, Al-Odah v. Obama, 648 F. Supp. 2d 1 (D.D.C. 2009).

137. *See* Awad v. Obama, 646 F. Supp. 2d 20, 23 (D.D.C. 2009) (*habeas* denied and detention held lawful where detainee had traveled to Afghanistan in 2001 to join the fight against U.S. forces and later barricaded himself in a hospital with al-Qaida fighters).

138. *See* Al-Bihani v. Obama, 590 F.3d 866, 871 (D.C. Cir. 2010).

been an enemy combatant at the time of his capture in 2001, he was captured in the context of the international armed conflict between the United States and the Taliban regime of Afghanistan, which was now over.[139] Because, al Bihani argued, the conflict with Afghanistan terminated at the time the Taliban regime was replaced by the Karzai regime, his detention was no longer justified by the laws and customs of war.[140] More specifically, al Bihani asserted that pursuant to a customary principle of LOAC that prisoners are repatriated upon termination of hostilities, he was entitled to release.[141] In addition, he asserted that pursuant to the LOAC (*i.e.*, Article 5 of GPW), he was entitled to a hearing to determine whether he was qualified as a POW and to be presumed to be a POW until such hearing found otherwise.[142]

The District Court rejected Al Bihani's request for habeas relief, concluding that his role in the volunteer group indicated he was a person who supported the Taliban and was therefore subject to the detention authority of the AUMF as interpreted by the Supreme Court's *Hamdi* decision.[143] Al Bihani appealed to the D.C. Circuit Court of Appeals. That court affirmed the District Court's decision. Like the lower court, the D.C. Circuit concluded that Al Bihani's LOAC-based arguments lacked merit.[144] However, the opinion also addressed the role of the customary laws of war in relation to the authority of the government to detain individuals like Al Bihani pursuant to the AUMF.[145] The D.C. Circuit acknowledged that, pursuant to *Hamdi*, the AUMF authorized detention as part of the "necessary and appropriate force" that the AUMF directed the President to use against al Qaeda terrorist and other groups.[146] However, the Court concluded that the LOAC "as a whole" had not been implemented into U.S. law and were not a source of authority for U.S. courts.[147] The D.C. Circuit saw no indication that the LOAC was an "extra-textual" limit on the President's power under the AUMF.[148] Indeed, the Court added that the LOAC was too "contestable and fluid" in its application to actual events in order to be relevant.[149] Therefore, the D.C. Circuit concluded that detainees like Al Bihani could not invoke the LOAC as a basis for challenging an exercise of detention authority. According to the opinion:

> Before considering these arguments in detail, we note that
> all of them rely heavily on the premise that the war powers

---

139. *See Id.*

140. *See Id.* at 874.

141. *See Id.* at 871, 875.

142. *See Id.* at 875.

143. *See* Al–Bihani v. Obama, 594 F. Supp 2d 35, 40 (D.D.C. 2009).

144. *See* Al–Bihani v. Obama, 590 F.3d 866, 875 (D.C. Cir. 2010).

145. *See, e.g., Id.* at 883.

146. *See Id.* at 871–72.

147. *Id.*

148. *Id.*

149. *Id.*

granted by the AUMF and other statutes are limited by the international laws of war. This premise is mistaken. . . . Therefore, while the international laws of war are helpful to courts when identifying the general set of war powers to which the AUMF speaks, *see Hamdi*, 542 U.S. at 520, their lack of controlling legal force and firm definition render their use both inapposite and inadvisable when courts seek to determine the limits of the President's war powers. Therefore, putting aside that we find Al–Bihani's reading of international law to be unpersuasive, we have no occasion here to quibble over the intricate application of vague treaty provisions and amorphous customary principles. The sources we look to for resolution of Al–Bihani's case are the sources courts always look to: the text of relevant statutes and controlling domestic case law. Under those sources, Al–Bihani is lawfully detained. . . .[150]

The D.C. Circuit provided only questionable authority for this interpretation of the role of the customary laws of war in relation to government authority; an interpretation that seems to be clearly at odds with how that law has historically been viewed by the United States. The Court also seemed to rely selectively on the *Hamdi* precedent, notably omitting the portion of that opinion that emphasized:

> Hamdi contends that the AUMF does not author-
> ize indefinite or perpetual detention. Certainly, we
> agree that indefinite detention for the purpose of
> interrogation is not authorized. Further, we un-
> derstand Congress' grant of authority for the use
> of "necessary and appropriate force" to include
> the authority to detain for the duration of the
> relevant conflict, and our understanding is based
> on longstanding law-of-war principles.[151]

How this portion of the *Hamdi* decision justifies the conclusion that the customary law of war is irrelevant for determining the rights of detainees is perplexing. It seems far more likely that the Supreme Court understood that the customary law of war serves not only as a source of authority but also as a source of constraint on the government's detention power. In fact, even the Department of Justice seems to disagree with D.C. Circuit's interpretation, noting in a subsequent filing that while it supports the ultimate conclusion of al Bihani's detainability, it did not agree with the conclusion that the customary law of war is relevant only for the

150. *Id*. at 885.   **151.** Hamdi v. Rumsfeld, 542 U.S. 507, 521 (2004).

purpose of defining government authority.[152] This was emphasized in the Government's response to al Bihani's petition for *en banc* rehearing, which indicated that:

> Petitioner cites the panel majority's statement that the "premise that the war powers granted by the [... (AUMF)] and other statutes are limited by the international laws of war * * * is mistaken." The Government agrees that this broad statement does not properly reflect the state of the law. The Government interprets the detention authority permitted under the AUMF, as informed by the laws of war. That interpretation is consistent with the Supreme Court's decision in *Hamdi v. Rumsfeld*, and with longstanding Supreme Court precedent that statutes should be construed as consistent with applicable international law.[153]

Al Bihani requested *en banc* review, a request that the D.C. Circuit rejected.[154] The decision rejecting the request included seven concurring opinions, and emphatically endorsed the original panel's rejection of customary international law as a source of constraint on the government's execution of war powers. Indeed, not only did Judge Brown in his lead opinion emphasize this lack of relevance of the customary international laws of war, he went even further by noting the potential logic of Congress authorizing measures inconsistent with that law in response to the unusual nature of the terrorist belligerent threat:

> There is no indication that the AUMF placed any international legal limits on the President's discretion to prosecute the war and, in light of the challenge our nation faced after September 11, 2001, that makes eminent sense. Confronted with a shadowy, non-traditional foe that succeeded in bringing a war to our doorstep by asymmetric means, it was (and still is) unclear how international law applies in all respects to this new context. The prospect is very real that some tradeoffs traditionally struck by the laws of war no longer make sense. That Congress wished the President to retain the discretion to recalibrate the military's strategy and tactics in light of circumstances not contemplated by our international obligations is therefore sensible, and reflects the traditional sovereign prerogative to violate international law or terminate international agreements.[155]

---

152. Al–Bihani v. Obama, Case No. 09–5051 (May 13, 2010), Government Response to Petition for Rehearing and Rehearing *en banc*.

153. *Id.*

154. Al–Bihani v. Obama, Case No. 1:05–cv–01312 (August 31, 2010), On Petition for Rehearing En Banc.

155. *Id.* at 13 (Brown, J., concurring).

In his concurring opinion, Judge Kavanaugh provided the rationale for the conclusion that courts cannot consider customary international law as a source of authority to constrain the President's war powers. While acknowledging that precedents from early in the nation's history did support such a role for customary international law, he concluded that the Supreme Court's seminal *Erie* decision rejecting the notion of federal common law nullified any future relevance of customary international law:

> *First*, international-law norms are not domestic U.S. law in the absence of action by the political branches to codify those norms. Congress and the President can and often do incorporate international-law principles into domestic U.S. law by way of a statute (or executive regulations issued pursuant to statutory authority) or a self-executing treaty. When that happens, the relevant international-law principles become part of the domestic U.S. law that federal courts must enforce, assuming there is a cognizable cause of action and the prerequisites for federal jurisdiction are satisfied. But in light of the Supreme Court's 1938 decision in *Erie Railroad Co. v. Tompkins*, 304 U.S. 64 (1938), which established that there is no federal general common law, international-law norms are not enforceable in federal courts unless the political branches have incorporated the norms into domestic U.S. law. None of the international-law norms cited by Al–Bihani has been so incorporated into domestic U.S. law.[156]

Judge Kavanaugh then concluded that nothing in the AUMF indicated Congress intended to incorporate customary international law norms into the grant of authority to the President to wage war against al Qaeda. Accordingly, the meaning of the AUMF's grant of authority for the President to use "necessary and appropriate" force is not be limited by the laws of war. Nor, according to Judge Kavanaugh, do the Geneva Conventions impose any limitations on the President (at least judicially enforceable limitations), because these four treaties are non-self executing.[157] Finally, in a footnote Judge Kavanaugh concludes that even if international law in the form of a non-self executing treaty or customary norms were judicially enforceable in theory, relief for Al Bihani would still be foreclosed because Congress' definition of detainability trumped those sources of law:

> Even if international law were a judicially enforceable constraint on the President's authority under the AUMF and even if international law prohibited detention of mere

156. *Id.* at 2 (Kavanaugh, J., concurring).

157. *Id.*

supporters of al Qaeda, Al–Bihani's argument that al Qaeda supporters cannot be detained would be unavailing. An enemy belligerent may be detained for the duration of these hostilities. *See Hamdi*, 542 U.S. at 518 (plurality opinion of O'Connor, J.) (interpreting scope of AUMF's detention authority). And in the Military Commissions Act of 2006 and the Military Commissions Act of 2009, Congress provided that the category of enemy belligerents includes those who "purposefully and materially supported hostilities against the United States or its coalition partners." A statute may of course override pre-existing statutes, including any statutes that incorporate international law. Therefore, as the panel opinion explained, the Military Commissions Act definitively establishes that those who purposefully and materially support al Qaeda may be detained for the duration of the hostilities, regardless of what international law might otherwise say about detention of such supporters.[158]

Unless the Supreme Court chooses to review the Al Bihani decision, this rejection of customary international law as a controlling source of authority for defining the scope of legitimate detentions will control all subsequent habeas challenges in the D.C. Circuit. Furthermore, the MCA must now be treated as providing the controlling definition of enemy belligerent subject to Hamdi's preventive detention authority. The fact that providing material support to al Qaeda may not in fact justify the conclusion that the detainee is an enemy belligerent within the broader meaning of the customary international law of war will simply be irrelevant to the courts reviewing habeas petitions.

It is difficult to understate the long-term significance of this decision if it remains in effect. Essentially, the government is now free from any constraints derived from the laws and customs of war, and need only convince reviewing courts that a petitioning detainee falls under the broad category of enemy combatant derived from an amalgamation of the AUMF and the various versions of the MCA. On the other hand, the decision suggests any attempt by the present Administration or a future Administration to exercise authority in connection with an armed conflict solely on the basis of the LOAC, without clear statutory authority that in some manner incorporated the provision or principles of the LOAC relevant to that exercise of presidential authority, could be overturned by the courts.

Regardless of the D.C. Circuit's holding, the Administration has not expressly abandoned its position that designating individu-

---

158. *Id.* at 28, n. 7 (internal citations omitted).

als who are part of, associated with, or supporting terrorist organizations as unprivileged enemy belligerents pursuant to the AUMF triggers the customary LOAC authority to preventively detain, and the *Hamdi* court's LOAC-based interpretation of the AUMF would appear to support that position.

This analysis of the post-*Boumediene* case law clearly illustrates the D.C. Circuit has left some key questions unresolved with regard to the rights of detainees challenging their detentions.[159] Can an individual be preventively detained for offering material support to a terrorist organization? Does the phrase "once al Qaeda, always al Qaeda" apply, or can a detainee denounce is affiliation to the group. If so, who has the burden of proving the detainees relationship to the group? Does the evidence offered by the government get the presumption of accuracy? How is the court to deal with hearsay or statements made by the detainee or fellow detainees that are alleged to be the product of torture or abuse?[160]

One factor that complicates judicial treatment of these questions is that to date Congress has failed to provide an express statutory definition of unprivileged belligerent subject to preventive detention. While both the Detainee Treatment Act and the Military Commission Act implicitly endorse detention of terrorist belligerents, neither statute was enacted to provide an express definition. While providing a statutory definition of who could lawfully be detained as an enemy belligerent would not guarantee that the government would prevail in subsequent legal challenges by detainees,[161] it would substantially bolster the government's assertion of legal justification.[162]

Congress has finally initiated the process of enacting such legislation. On August 4, 2010, Senator Graham introduced to the Senate the Terrorist Detention Review Reform Act[163] "to provide

159. Benjamin Wittes, Robert M. Chesney, and Rabea Benhalim, *The Emerging Law of Detention: The Guantánamo Habeas Cases as Lawmaking*, Brookings, January 22, 2010, at 2.

160. *Id.*

161. *In* United States v. Comstock, 130 S.Ct. 1949 (2010), the Supreme Court held that the necessary and proper clause of Article I vests Congress with broad power to authorize preventive detention. That case addressed the constitutionality of a statute authorizing preventive detention for mentally ill sex offenders who completed their punitive incarceration but were considered a threat to the community. The Court emphasized that as custodians of these inmates, the federal government not only

had "sound reasons" to provide for their continued detention to protect society, but perhaps even a duty to do so. This consideration seems particularly relevant to the current effort by Senator Graham to provide a statutory definition of unprivileged belligerents subject to preventive detention. Although the prior criminal conviction of these detainees distinguishes them from unprivileged belligerents, the case should bolster any future assertion of congressional power to authorize preventive detention of captured terrorist operatives.

162. *See* Youngstown Sheet & Tube Co. v. Sawyer, 343 U.S. 579, 634 (1952) (Jackson, J., concurring).

163. Terrorist Detention Review Reform Act, S. 3707, 111th Cong. (2010).

for habeas corpus review for certain enemy belligerents engaged in hostilities against the United States, and for other purposes."[164] This bill mandates that all applications for a writ of habeas corpus be consolidated for uniform treatment of common questions of law and fact, including procedural questions.[165] It puts the burden of proof on the government to show that the individual is a "covered individual"[166] but provides the government with the rebuttable presumption that the evidence it relies on is authentic.[167]

Perhaps most significantly, the bill defines an 'unprivileged enemy belligerent' as an individual who has engaged in hostilities, has purposefully and materially supported hostilities or who has operated on behalf of the Taliban, al Qaeda or associated forces.[168] If the government shows that the individual "knowingly obtained military-style training from the Taliban, al Qaeda, or associated forces," there is a rebuttable presumption that the individual is an unprivileged enemy belligerent.[169] This presumption can only be rebutted through clear and convincing evidence that the individual withdrew from the organization prior to capture.[170] With regard to statements made by the detainee, the bill provides they maybe entered into evidence *only* if "the statement was made incident to lawful conduct during military operations . . . and the interest of justice would be best served by admission of the statement into evidence or the statement was voluntarily given."[171] No statement obtained by torture (as defined by the Detainee Treatment Act of 2005[172]) is admissible in a habeas proceeding.[173]

Should this bill be enacted into law, it would not only streamline future habeas litigation, but would virtually disable the ability of detainees to successfully challenge the definition of unprivileged belligerent. In response to such challenges, the government would be armed with the almost insurmountable argument that litigants are detained pursuant to a definition of enemy belligerent and invocation of the nation's war powers reflecting the cooperative efforts of the two political branches of the government. Even if a reviewing court were to conclude the definition conflicted with a prior ratified treaty (which is extremely unlikely), the latter in time statute would be accorded precedence.[174] Like Boumediene, detainees could prevail in such challenges only be successfully convincing

---

164. *Id.*

165. *Id.* at § 2256(c)(3).

166. *Id.* at § 2256(a)(3).

167. *Id.* at § 2256(e)(1)(E).

168. *Id.* at § 2265(a)(6)(A–C).

169. *Id.* at § 2256(e)(1)(E)(i).

170. *Id.* at § 2256(e)(1)(E)(ii)(I).

171. *Id.* at § 2256(e)(4)(B)(i–ii) (emphasis added).

172. 42 U.S.C. § 2000dd.

173. Terrorist Detention Review Reform Act, S. 3707, 111th Cong. § 2256(e)(4)(A) (2010).

174. *See* Restatement (Third) Foreign Relations Law of The United States (1987) § 115.

a court that the statutory definition conflicts with a provision of the Constitution. Unlike Boumediene, the likelihood of prevailing on such an argument seems virtually non-existent.

i.   The Obama Administration: Holding the Line on Judicial Review

Challenges to the scope of preventive detention authority began prior to President Obama taking office. These challenges were the consequence of the Supreme Court's decision in *Boumediene* granting constitutional habeas corpus access to Guantanamo detainees.[175] Unsurprisingly, advocates for detainees in other locations sought to leverage the *Boumediene* decision on behalf of their own clients.

One of these challenges emerged from the long-term detention of individuals at the Bagram Air Force Base in Afghanistan. The U.S. military had maintained a detention facility at that location for as long as it has had the facility at Guantanamo. While the majority of detainees at Bagram were Afghan nationals, the population had always included a number of non-Afghans who had been captured by U.S. or Coalition forces during operations in that country, as well as individuals captured outside of Afghanistan and brought to Bagram for detention (presumably to avoid the legal issues associated with detention at Guantanamo). The case of *Fadi Al–Maqaleh v. Gates*[176] involved many of those non-Afghan detainees who had been captured in various locations and subsequently transferred to Afghanistan for detention.[177]

This challenge once again presented the Obama Administration with the opportunity to draw a clear distinction between detained battlefield enemy belligerents and individuals apprehended outside the zone of combat operations, an opportunity it declined. Instead, the government filings opposed extending *habeas* access to these detainees, arguing that unlike their counterparts in Guantanamo, detainees located in an actual theater of operations such as Afghan-

---

175. Boumediene v. Bush, 553 U.S. 723 (2008).

176. 604 F. Supp. 2d 205 (D.D.C. 2009).

177. *Id*. ("Petitioners, four detainees who were foreign nationals captured outside Afghanistan and held at the Bagram, Afghanistan, Internment Facility for six years, filed habeas corpus petitions, invoking the Suspension Clause, U.S. Const. art. I, § 9, cl. 2, to argue that § 7(a) of the Military Commissions Act of 2006, 28 U.S.C.S. § 2241(e)(1), was unconstitutional as applied. Respondent government officials filed motions to dismiss. Statutory jurisdiction was lacking, but 28 U.S.C.S. § 2241(e) was unconstitutional as to the three non-Afghan detainees. Those three could invoke the Suspension Clause and seek habeas relief. Accordingly, the motions to dismiss were denied as to those three detainees. The court deferred ruling on whether to dismiss the Afghan detainee's petition."). The D.C. Circuit ultimately reversed, holding that, under the Court's factor-based test in *Boumediene*, the district court's jurisdiction was lacking, and the habeas petitions should have been dismissed. *Al–Maqaleh v. Gates*, 605 F.3d 84, 99 (D.C. Cir. 2010).

istan should not be granted this privilege.[178] The District Court rejected this contention and ruled in favor of the detainee litigants, concluding that, 1) because the detainees, by nature of their status, were "not much different" than the Guantanamo detainees of *Boumediene;* and 2) were detained in an area under a very high "objective degree of control" by the United States, they (like their Guantanamo counterparts) lacked any other meaningful method to challenge the legality of their detention and were thus entitled to *habeas* review.[179]

In response, the Obama Administration appealed the District Court's decision. On May 21, 2010, in *Al–Maqaleh v. Gates*[180], the D.C. Circuit reversed the District Court decision and held that detainees held at Bagram Air Force Base in Afghanistan—even those who were captured outside of Afghanistan and transported to Bagram for detention—cannot bring *habeas corpus* challenges in U.S. courts. The Court relied on a number of factors articulated in the *Boumediene* decision to conclude that extending habeas corpus to detainees in Bagram—even those who had been rendered from outside of Afghanistan—was unjustified. While the location of detention in the area of active combat operations weighed in favor of the denying extension of the writ, that factor was ultimately not decisive. Instead, the court focused on the practical obstacles to extending the writ to Bagram, obstacles that it concluded were more significant than those related to extending the writ to Guantanamo. Because Bagram was in a theater of war, the court concluded that it fell more closely to the *Eisentrager* precedent than *Boumediene*.[181]

Ultimately, the combined effect of the facility being in an active theater of combat operations and not within the *de facto* or *de jure* jurisdiction of the United States resulted in the court distinguishing the situation from that of detentions in Guantanamo. Although the government prevailed in holding the line on habeas access, it also seems cognizant of the need to improve the procedural framework for detentions in Afghanistan. Perhaps in an effort to improve its appellate record prior to the D.C. Circuit decision, President Obama directed implementation of enhanced detainee review procedures in Afghanistan. These procedures effectively extend the CSRT process from Guantanamo to Bagram.[182]

178. Respondents' Motion to Dismiss Petition for Writ of Habeas Corpus and Complaint for Declaratory and Injunctive Relief, Bakri v. Bush, No. 08–1307 (D.D.C. Sept. 15, 2008).

179. *Al–Maqaleh*, 604 F. Supp. 2d at 220–21, 223.

180. 605 F.3d 84 (D.C. Cir. 2010).

181. *Id.*

182. Posting of Reagan Kuhn to Human Rights First Blog, Protecting the Rights of Afghans http://www.humanrightsfirst.org/blog/hrfblog/labels/Afghanistan.html (Dec. 1, 2009, 14:12 EST).

While critics continue to assert that this additional process is still insufficient to protect the fundamental rights of detainees against prolonged arbitrary detention, they also acknowledge this process represents a marked improvement from the pre-Obama detention regime in Afghanistan, which lacked any opportunity for meaningful review. Pursuant to President Obama's directive there is now an ongoing process to revise, enhance, and formalize detention procedures.[183] What effect, if any, this will have on the ultimate resolution of the Bagram habeas corpus cases is yet to be seen, although it seems that it will be difficult for the reviewing courts to ignore the President's efforts to enhance the process available to detainees without resort to judicial review.

An important sub-text of this narrative is the apparent continuing assertion that the U.S. authority to detain captured personnel in Afghanistan is in no way contingent on Afghan law. This reflects the fact that the United States has never conceded that its military operations in Afghanistan are being conducted exclusively in support of the Afghan government's non-international armed conflict against Taliban dissident forces. Detention operations have been ongoing in Afghanistan since the United States first put "boots on the ground." At no time did the United States consider detentions contingent on either a grant of Afghan legal authority or even Security Council authorization. Instead, like their Guantanamo counterparts, detainees were held pursuant to an implicit invocation of the principle of military necessity derived from the U.S. armed conflict with both the Taliban and al Qaeda.

The fall of the Taliban and the assumption of authority by the Karzai government led many experts to assert that the original armed conflict between the United States and Afghanistan terminated along with the authority to detain derived from that armed conflict.[184] The continued detentions by the United States indicate a different interpretation of authority. Furthermore, the resistance by the Obama Administration to extend habeas corpus review to detainees at Bagram demonstrates that there is no significant modification to the U.S. view that the ongoing armed conflict with the Taliban and al Qaeda provides sufficient authority to preventively detain captured personnel. Although many Coalition partners

183. Exec. Order No. 13,492 74 Fed. Reg. 13,492 (Jan. 27, 2009).

184. Human Rights First, *Fixing Bagram: Strengthening Detention Reforms to Align with U.S. Strategic Priorities*, 4 (Nov. 2009) *available at* http://www.humanrightsfirst.info/pdf/Fixing–Bagram–110409.pdf; David D. Coron & Jenny S. Martinez, *Availability of U.S. Courts to Review Decision to Hold U.S. Citizens as Enemy Combatants—Executive Power in War on Terror*, 98 A.J.I.L. 782, 787 (2004) ("any authority for detention provided by the Third Geneva Convention may possibly have ceased when the U.S.-friendly government of Hamid Karzai took control of Afghanistan, arguably ending the international armed conflict there.").

consider the armed conflict in Afghanistan to be a non-international conflict between Afghanistan and its Taliban opponents, in which
the United States is engaged at the invitation of the Afghan
government, and accordingly consider the authority to detain individuals contingent on Afghan law,[185] U.S. practice suggests a rejection of this legal theory. There is no indication President Obama
will alter this position.

b.   Treatment of War on Terror Detainees

Detention in the context of an armed conflict automatically
implicates detainee treatment issues. Like virtually all other aspects of preventive detention in the U.S. "war on terror", President
Bush's February 2002 decision that neither Al Qaeda nor the
Taliban qualify for POW status created uncertainty as to the source
of legal obligation related to the treatment of unprivileged enemy
belligerents. Unlike POWs, these detainees (or perhaps more appropriately those advocating on their behalf) could not invoke a well-
established treaty regime that detailed both substantive and procedural treatment standards. Instead, as the war on terror detentions
began, it became clear that the detainees found themselves in a
twilight zone of regulation that effectively left them at the mercy of
the policy determinations of the United States.

This reality became a matter of public knowledge when in 2004
the White House released President Bush's February 7, 2002 memorandum. In the memorandum, the President noted:

> I accept the legal conclusion of the Department of
> Justice and determine that none of the provisions
> of Geneva apply to our conflict with al Qaeda in
> Afghanistan or elsewhere throughout the world
> because, among other reasons, al Qaeda is not a
> High Contracting Party to Geneva.[186]

This determination obviously excluded al Qaeda detainees from the
protections of the GPW, a treaty intended to apply only to certain
categories of individuals fighting on behalf of a state. However,
accepting the conclusion that "none of the provisions of Geneva
apply to our conflict with al Qaeda" had a more expansive meaning:
it also excluded these detainees from the protections of common
article 3 to the four Geneva Conventions of 1949.[187] This provision

185. *See US must reform Afghani-stan detention policy as new facility opens,* AMNESTY INTERNATIONAL, Nov. 16, 2009, *available at* http://www.amnesty.org/en/news-and-updates/us-must-reform-afghanistan-detention-policy-new-facility-opens–20091116 (last visited Feb. 11, 2010).

186. White House Memorandum, "Humane Treatment of al Qaeda and Taliban Detainees" (Feb. 7, 2002), *available at* http://www.pegc.us/archive/White_House/bush_memo_20020207_ed.pdf (last visited on Aug. 11, 2010).

187. *Geneva Convention Relative to the Protection of Civilian Persons in Time of War,* art. 3, 75 U.N.T.S. 287,

is the only treaty provision to which the United States is a party that is specifically applicable to prisoners (and others not actively participating in hostilities) in a non-international armed conflict.

The Geneva Conventions form the treaty foundation for the protection of victims of war. They consist of four treaties, each focused on the protection of a specific category of war victims. The first treaty is the Convention for the Amelioration of the Wounded and Sick in the Field (GWS)[188]; the second treaty is the Convention for the Shipwrecked and Wounded at Sea (GWSS)[189]; the third treaty is the Convention Relative to the Treatment of Prisoners of War (GPW)[190]; the fourth treaty is the Convention Relative to the Treatment of Civilians in Time of War (GCC).[191] Each of these Conventions consists of numerous articles providing comprehensive regulation related to the protection of each of these categories of war victims. However, these Conventions also share a common limitation: they were developed primarily for the regulation of international (inter-state) armed conflicts. Accordingly, while some of the Conventions' provisions have evolved into norms of customary international law applicable to any armed conflict (international or non-international), with the exception of one article that is

August 12, 1949, provides in pertinent part:

> In the case of armed conflict not of an international character occurring in the territory of one of the High Contracting Parties, each Party to the conflict shall be bound to apply, as a minimum, the following provisions: (1) Persons taking no active part in the hostilities, including members of armed forces who have laid down their arms and those placed 'hors de combat' by sickness, wounds, detention, or any other cause, shall in all circumstances be treated humanely, without any adverse distinction founded on race, colour, religion or faith, sex, birth or wealth, or any other similar criteria. . . .

188. International Committee of the Red Cross (ICRC), *Geneva Conven-* *tion for the Amelioration of the Condition of the Wounded and Sick in Armed Forces in the Field (First Geneva Convention)*, 12 August 1949, 75 UNTS 31, *available at* http://www.unhcr.org/ref world/docid/3ae6b3694.html (last visited August 11, 2010).

189. International Committee of the Red Cross (ICRC), *Geneva Convention for the Amelioration of the Condition of Wounded, Sick and Shipwrecked Members of Armed Forces at Sea (Second Geneva Convention)*, 12 August 1949, 75 U.N.T.S. 85, *available at* http:// www.unhcr.org/refworld/docid/3ae6b 37927.html (last visited Aug. 11, 2010).

190. International Committee of the Red Cross (ICRC), *Geneva Convention Relative to the Treatment of Prisoners of War (Third Geneva Convention)*, 12 August 1949, 75 UNTS 135, *available at* http://www.unhcr.org/refworld/docid/3 ae6b36c8.html (last visited Aug. 11, 2010).

191. International Committee of the Red Cross (ICRC), *Geneva Convention Relative to the Protection of Civilian Persons in Time of War (Fourth Geneva Convention)*, 12 August 1949, 75 UNTS 287, *available at* http://www.unhcr.org/ refworld/docid/3ae6b36d2.html (last visited Aug. 11, 2010).

common to each of these Conventions[192], they are simply not applicable to non-international armed conflicts.

This focus on international armed conflict is explained by the reality of the context in which these treaties were developed. Recovering from the horrors of World War II, the primary focus of the delegates assembled by the International Committee of the Red Cross in 1947 to revise the Conventions was to prevent recurrence of many of the horrors associated with that war. By 1947, however, there was also a growing recognition that the suffering associated with armed conflict was not restricted to international wars. In fact, the inter-war experiences in Spain, China, and Russia provided compelling evidence that brutality and suffering could be just as extensive in the context of civil war as it was in the context of inter-state war.

Responding to the reality that warfare inflicts suffering irrespective of its international or non-international character, the ICRC proposed a simple solution: require compliance with all the Conventions in any type of armed conflict. This proposal never gained momentum, primarily because states that would bind themselves to the Conventions were unwilling to limit their sovereign prerogative to deal with internal dissident forces with such an extensive regime of regulation. Instead, the delegates agreed to include within each Convention a 'common article'—an article identical in each treaty—to address humanitarian concerns related to non-international armed conflicts. Thus, common article 3 emerged as sole article of the Conventions applicable to non-international armed conflicts.

Common article 3, which applies to "conflicts not of an international character", mandates the humane treatment of any individual who is not taking an active part in hostilities, or who has been rendered *hors de combat* (out of combat) by reason of wounds, capture, or illness. A non-exhaustive list of specific prohibition then follows, including *inter alia* the prohibition of murder; torture; cruel, inhuman, or degrading treatment; and "the passing of sentences and the carrying out of executions without previous judgment pronounced by a regularly constituted court, affording all the judicial guarantees which are recognized as indispensable by civilized peoples."[193] The ICRC commentaries to the Conventions—an authoritative source of interpretation—emphasize that the obligations imposed by common article 3 are minimalist and essentially

192. Geneva Convention Relative to the Treatment of Prisoners of War, art. 3, Aug. 12, 1949, 6 U.S.T. 3316, 75 U.N.T.S. 135. *Entered into force* Oct. 21, 1950.

193. *Id.*

redundant with the most basic human rights obligations applicable to states even in times of peace.[194]

Over time, many believed that common article 3 evolved into a customary international law standard of baseline treatment obligations during any armed conflict. This was emphasized by the International Court of Justice in *Nicaragua v. United States* when it characterized common article 3 as the "minimum yardstick" for regulating the treatment of individuals not or no longer actively participating in hostilities.[195] Common article 3 also became the centerpiece of U.S. military practice related to the treatment of civilians and detainees in all military operations, even those operations that did not rise to the level of armed conflicts (such as Haiti, Bosnia, and Kosovo). U.S. military lawyers were taught that compliance with the principles reflected in common article 3 was a non-negotiable aspect of all U.S. military operations.

President Bush's February 2002 memorandum was based upon the Department of Justice Office of Legal Counsel's analysis that the GPW, including common article 3, did not apply to the armed conflict with al Qaeda. That analysis concluded that common article 3 did not apply to the armed conflict with al Qaeda because the intent of the State parties who adopted the article was that it should apply exclusively to internal armed conflicts. Because the armed conflict with al Qaeda was 'international' in scope—i.e., not confined to the territory of the United States—and because al Qaeda was not a State party to the GPW, it fell outside the scope of application of the common article. However, although international in scope, because the armed conflict was not inter-state, it also fell outside the scope of common article 2 (the article of the Conventions that dictates application of all the remaining articles of the Conventions to inter-state, or 'international' armed conflicts). As for the conflict with the Taliban, the GPW also did not apply because, although the international conflict with the Taliban was with another State, the Taliban themselves did not qualify for treatment under GPW because they did not fit with any of the categories of combatants covered by the GPW.[196] Thus, the United

194. *See* General Commentary, *The Discussions at the Diplomatic Conference of 1949.* "[Common Article 3] ensures the application of the rules of humanity which are recognized as essential by civilized nations and provides a legal basis for interventions by the International Committee of the Red Cross or any other impartial humanitarian organization...." *available at* http://www.icrc.org/ihl.nsf/COM/375–590006?OpenDocument (last visited on August 10, 2010).

195. Case Concerning Military and Paramilitary Activities in and Against Nicaragua, (Nicaragua v. United States of America), 1986 I.C.J. 14, at par. 218.

196. The applicability of the GCC to the Taliban was not expressly addressed in the Office of Legal Counsel's analysis, but it is likely that the analysis would have concluded that the GCC by its terms does not apply to enemy combatants outside the territory of the capturing State or occupied territory.

States was engaged in an armed conflict that fell outside the scope of the key treaty dealing with captive enemy combatants, leaving al Qaeda and Taliban detainees in a legal twilight zone covered only by a policy mandate that they be treated humanely:

> As a matter of policy, the United States Armed Forces shall continue to treat detainees humanely and, to the extent appropriate and consistent with military necessity, in a manner consistent with the principles of Geneva.[197]

This interpretation was not without basis. As noted above, common article 3 had been developed primarily in response to the atrocities associated with civil wars, and the ICRC Commentary discussion on application of this treaty provision focused on the line between internal criminal disturbances and internal armed conflicts. Accordingly, prior to September 11th, the LOAC was generally understood as applying to only two situations: international armed conflict (in accordance with common article 2) or internal armed conflicts (in accordance with common article 3). This international/internal application interpretation was bolstered by the jurisprudence of the International Criminal Tribunal for the Former Yugoslavia. In its seminal decision in *Prosecutor v. Tadic*[198], the tribunal articulated a test for application of common article 3 that focused exclusively on internal armed conflicts.

However, there was also some evidence that the principle of humane treatment reflected in common article 3 was more broadly applicable. For several decades, as noted above, the armed forces of the United States had applied the principle of humane treatment to all military operations as a matter of Department of Defense policy. Ultimately, the intersection of the 'internal' interpretation of the concept of non-international armed conflict with the decision to designate the struggle against transnational terrorism as an international armed conflict exposed a lacunae in LOAC regulation that was identified and in view of many exploited by the legal interpretations endorsed by President Bush.

The consequence of the Bush Administration's interpretation of the inapplicability of common article 3 to the armed conflict with al Qaeda became increasingly apparent in the months following September 11th. Under the Bush Administration's interpretation, because the "war on terror" armed conflict was not the right type of conflict to trigger even the most basic LOAC humanitarian

197. White House Memorandum, "Humane Treatment of al Qaeda and Taliban Detainees" (Feb. 7, 2002), *available at* http://www.pegc.us/archive/White_House/bush_memo_20020207_ed.pdf. (last visited on Aug. 11, 2010).

198. Case No. IT–94–1–I, Decision on the Deference Motion for Interlocutory Appeal on Jurisdiction, ¶ 70 (Oct. 2, 1995).

protections, the United States was free to adopt treatment standards consistent with the LOAC but considered justified by President Bush' concept of military necessity. Furthermore, because these individuals were considered wartime detainees, the United States concluded they fell outside the scope of fundamental human rights protections. This was the result of two aspects of the U.S. interpretation of human rights obligations. First, human rights treaties are generally considered by the United States not to apply extraterritorially (but instead to apply only as a limitation on U.S. government action within U.S. territory). Second, the United States traditionally treats the LOAC as a *lex specialis* that fully occupies the field of conflict regulation, effectively excluding application of human rights norms during armed conflict.[199]

This combination of interpreting the LOAC as the exclusive source of international regulation of the treatment of al Qaeda and Taliban detainees while rejecting the application of human rights treaties to the detainees produced a genuine legal black hole: As belligerent operatives of a transnational non-State enemy, detainees were excluded from the protections of the full GPW and even the minimum humanitarian protections of common article 3. But because they had been captured in the context of an armed conflict and were detained outside the territory of the United States, they were also excluded from the protections afforded by human rights treaties. In short, they were protected only as a matter of policy, and as the President noted in his February 7, 2002 memorandum, that protection was subject to the dictates of military necessity. This ultimately led to development of an interrogation policy authorizing techniques inconsistent with humane treatment mandate of common article 3. Although the government never conceded the approved interrogation techniques were in fact inconsistent with that mandate, it was clear that the scope of authorized interrogation measures exceeded the type of interrogation techniques authorized by service regulations and manuals for use against prisoners of war.[200]

Concern over the inapplicability of any humanitarian protections for al Qaeda and Taliban detainees led ultimately in 2005 to legislation intended to provide such protection. Proposed somewhat ironically by Sen. John McCain, one of the staunchest supporters of

---

199. *See* United States Army, Judge Advocate General's Operational Law Handbook, 2007, at Ch. 3; *see also* Geoffrey S. Corn, *Mixing Apples and Hand Grenades: The Logical Limit of Applying Human Rights Norms to Armed Conflict,* (forthcoming in the Journal of International Humanitarian Legal Studies), *available at:* http://papers.ssrn.com/sol3/papers.cfm?abstract_id=1511954.

200. *See generally* Dick Jackson, *Interrogation and Treatment of Detainees in the Global War on Terror, in* THE WAR ON TERROR AND THE LAW OF WAR: A MILITARY PERSPECTIVE, (Geoffrey S. Corn ed., 2009).

the war on terror, but who had also been subject to torture while held as a POW during the Vietnam War, the DTA, also known as the McCain amendment, directed that no person held in the custody of the United States would be subject to cruel inhumane or degrading treatment. According to section 1003 of the amendment:

> (a) No individual in the custody or under the physical control of the United States Government, regardless of nationality or physical location, shall be subject to cruel, inhuman, or degrading treatment or punishment.[201]

Unlike common article 3, however, the DTA also included a statutory definition of cruel, inhumane, or degrading treatment. According to the same section of the act:

> (d) In this section, the term 'cruel, inhuman, or degrading treatment or punishment' means the cruel, unusual, and inhumane treatment or punishment prohibited by the Fifth, Eighth, and Fourteenth Amendments to the Constitution of the United States, as defined in the United States Reservations, Declarations and Understandings to the United Nations Convention Against Torture and Other Forms of Cruel, Inhuman or Degrading Treatment or Punishment done at New York, December 10, 1984.[202]

This definition was a source of substantial criticism, because in the view of many it endorsed the use of harsh interrogation techniques that had been approved pursuant to the original legal interpretations adopted by President Bush in his February 7, 2002 memorandum.[203] However, a different section of the act provided what was in operational terms a far more significant link to pre-existing authority. Section 1002 prohibited the use of any interrogation technique for individuals held in the custody or under the effective control of the Department of Defense or in a Department of Defense facility that was not authorized by the Army Regulation on interrogation of prisoners of war and other detainees.[204] In so doing, the DTA placed significant limitations on the scope of discretion available to the President and the Department of Defense in adopting aggressive interrogation techniques. This is because the interrogation techniques approved in the Army Regulation had all been based on the assumption that they must comply not only with common article 3, but with even more protective requirements of the GPW. This reliance on the GPW as the point of

201. 42 USCS § 2000dd (2005).

202. *Id.*

203. *See supra* note 186 and accompanying text.

204. 109 P.L. 148, 1002 (2005).

reference for authorized interrogation techniques effectively restored the shield of humane treatment to all detainees in Department of Defense custody, regardless of the nature of the conflict in which they were captured.

President Bush opposed this legislative effort to restrict his discretion, and asserted that selecting interrogation techniques (and interpreting the scope of the Geneva conventions) fell squarely within his vested authority as Commander-in-Chief of the Armed Forces and Chief Executive of the nation. Ultimately however, the President agreed to sign the DTA into law, and it was included as an amendment to the Defense appropriations act of 2005. However, President Bush also attached a signing statement which asserted his continued authority to authorize interrogation techniques inconsistent with the statute in those situations in which he determined the statute impermissibly intruded upon his exclusive vested authority as Commander-in-Chief:

> The executive branch shall construe Title X in Division A of the Act, relating to detainees, in a manner consistent with the constitutional authority of the President to supervise the unitary executive branch and as Commander in Chief and consistent with the constitutional limitations on the judicial power, which will assist in achieving the shared objective of the Congress and the President, evidenced in Title X, of protecting the American people from further terrorist attacks.[205]

This was an obvious effort to preserve freedom of action vis-à-vis the selection of interrogation techniques for captured al Qaeda operatives. However, his effort to preserve flexibility took an even more serious blow when the Supreme Court issued its decision in *Hamdan*. Hamdan's challenge to the legality of the military commission was based primarily on an assertion that the procedures established for that tribunal violated the humane treatment obligation of common article 3. Accordingly, in order to resolve his challenge, it was necessary that the Court confront the Administration's position that common article 3 did not apply to the conflict with al Qaeda, which was the foundation for the flexibility in detainee treatment policies that the Bush Administration was seeking to preserve.

Hamdan had raised the same challenge to the Administration's position in the lower courts, arguing that because he had been

205. President's Statement on Signing H.R. 2863, the "Department of Defense, Emergency Supplemental Appropriations to Address Hurricanes in the Gulf of Mexico, and Pandemic Influenza Act, 2006," 41 Weekly Comp. Pres. Doc. 52, 1918 (Dec. 30, 2005) *available at* http://georgewbush-whitehouse.archives.gov/news/releases/2005/12/print/20051230–8.html.

captured in the context of a non-international armed conflict, he was entitled as a matter of treaty obligation to the protections established in common article 3. The majority of DC Circuit reject-ed this argument and instead concluded—like the Bush administra-tion—that common article 3 was inapplicable to the armed conflict with al Qaeda because that armed conflict transcended national boundaries of the United States.[206] In so doing, the lower court set the stage for what would become perhaps the most profound judicial intervention into the conduct of the armed conflict with al Qaeda since the "war on terror" began.

Writing for a majority of five justices, Justice Stevens rejected the interpretation of common article 3 first adopted by the Bush administration in February of 2002 and subsequently endorsed by the DC Circuit. Justice Stevens relied on the plain text of common article 3—that it applies to armed conflicts "not of an international character"—to conclude that contrary to these prior interpreta-tions, the article is applicable to any armed conflict that did not fall within common article 2's international armed conflict definition. According to Justice Stevens, the use of the term "non-internation-al" within common article 3 indicated that it was intended to apply in "contradistinction" to common article 2.[207] The consequence of this interpretation of common article 3 was that arguably no armed conflict fell outside the regulatory provisions of the Geneva Conven-tions: armed conflicts between States would continue to be regulat-ed by Geneva Conventions in full (which provides more extensive protections than common article 3), while all other armed conflicts, including conflicts between states and non-state groups, or even conflicts between two non-state groups, would fall within the scope of common article 3. Accordingly, no individual detained in the context of an armed conflict could ever fall outside the minimum humanitarian protection afforded by common article 3.

Immediately following this opinion, Undersecretary for Defense Gordon England issued a memorandum to all elements of the Department of Defense, confirming that all existing DOD orders, policies, orders and doctrine comply with common article 3, other than the commission procedures that the *Hamdan* court found to violate common article 3, and directing that all DOD personnel adhere to the humane treatment standards of common article 3.[208] The memorandum directed that the leadership of all DOD elements ensure that all DOD personnel adhere to the standards of common

206. Hamdan v. Rumsfeld, 415 F.3d 33, 41 (D.C. Cir. 2005).

207. Hamdan v. Rumsfeld, 548 U.S. 557, 630 (2006).

208. Department of Defense Memo-randum, "Application of Common Arti-cle 3 of the Geneva Conventions to the Treatment of Detainees in the Depart-ment of Defense" (July 7, 2006) *avail-able at* http://www.defense.gov/pubs/pdfs /DepSecDef%20memo%20on%20common

article 3 and directed them to promptly review "all relevant directives, regulations, policies, practices and procedures under your purview to ensure that they comply with the standards of Common Article 3."[209] In so doing, the memorandum ensured that common article 3's humane treatment mandate thereafter would apply vis-à-vis all detainees within the custody of the Department of Defense.

Of course, the precise meaning of humane treatment remained somewhat uncertain. As a result, the definition contained in the DTA and the limitations on authorized interrogation techniques it imposed remained quite significant in implementation of this new mandate. However, one thing was clear: Not only was torture prohibited (a point that had never been disputed by the Administration), but anything that arguably came close to qualifying as cruel treatment would not be a permissible interrogation or treatment technique from that point forward, as such conduct is clearly inconsistent with the obligations established by both the DTA and the now clearly applicable mandate of common article 3.

For detainees in the custody of the Department of Defense, the combination of the DTA and the Supreme Court's interpretation of common article 3 in the *Hamdan* opinion would seem to effectively provide a shield against officially sanctioned cruel, inhumane, or degrading treatment. However, MCA 2006 added another level of uncertainty to treatment standards when Congress used that statute to amend the War Crimes Act[210], a federal criminal statute penalizing the commission of certain war crimes when committed by or against a U.S. national. According to that amendment, only what Congress defined as "grave breach" of common article 3 provides a basis for criminal sanction pursuant to the War Crimes Act. The amendment then defined "cruel, inhumane, or degrading treatment" for purposes of establishing a criminal violation of common article 3 as follows:

> The act of a person who commits, or conspires or attempts to commit, an act intended to inflict severe or serious physical or mental pain or suffering (other than pain or suffering incidental to lawful sanctions), including serious physical abuse, upon another within his custody or control.[211]

However, the amendment later provides that "[t]he definitions in this subsection are intended only to define the grave breaches of common Article 3 and not the full scope of United States obligations under that Article."[212] This meant that, while the United

%20article%203.pdf (last visited Aug. 11, 2010).

209. *Id.*

210. 18 U.S.C. § 2441.

211. *Id.* at (d)(1)(b).

212. *Id.* at (d)(5).

States might have broader obligations as a nation pursuant to common article 3, an individual would only be subject to punishment under the War Crimes Act for a violation of common article 3 if it was proven that he or she violated the more specific standards of that Act.

How this amendment impacts the treatment standard for detainees is somewhat confusing. The amendment establishes two distinct definitions of cruel, inhumane, and degrading treatment for purposes of compliance with common article 3. The first definition provides the standard for conduct that violates the WCA, and is quite restrictive. Only 'grave breaches'—or what might be better understood as severe violations of common article 3—provide a basis for prosecution as a federal offense. The second definition is a broader one that imposes a standard of humane treatment under common article 3 which, if violated might be considered a breach of U.S. obligations as a State, but not provide a basis for criminal sanction in federal court of those who committed the violation of common article 3.

When coupled with another provision of the MCA 2006's amendment to the War Crimes Act, which applied this dual definition of common article 3 retroactively, it is difficult to avoid the conclusion that Congress was attempting to shield government officials from criminal sanction for authorizing interrogation techniques that may have violated common article 3. In essence, Congress appeared to have decided that while many of the techniques used prior to the *Hamdan* decision may have in fact violated common article 3, prosecution for violation of the War Crimes Act would not be justified unless the interrogation techniques were 'grave' violations according to the more limited definition provided by the amendment. However, by emphasizing that common article 3's prohibition against cruel, inhumane, and degrading treatment was broader for non-criminal regulatory purposes than what was included in the War Crimes Act, Congress seemed to be emphasizing that the United States, as a government, was not abandoning the broader standards imposed by common article 3 on all State parties to the Geneva Conventions.

Ultimately, this schizophrenia regarding the controlling definition of cruel, inhumane, and degrading treatment rendered the original link between acceptable treatment standards and the U.S. Army field manual on interrogation contained in the DTA the most important source of detainee protection. Because Congress had mandated compliance with the field manual, which was drafted to be consistent with common article 3, detainees were effectively protected from interrogation techniques inconsistent with common article 3, and if the techniques adopted met a certain higher threshold, those involved could be punished under the War Crimes

Act (or, for that matter, under the Uniform Code of Military Justice, which provides criminal sanction for any member of the armed forces participates in maltreatment of detainees.) Ultimately, the combined effect of all these sources, and in particular the *Hamdan* Court's rejection of the legal black hole that the Bush Administration's legal analysis had created for al Qaeda and Taliban detainees, protected all unprivileged enemy belligerents from any type of abusive interrogation treatment going forward.

One area of uncertainty persisted as the result of the fact that not all al Qaeda detainees were in the custody of the Department of Defense. Instead some of the most senior members of al Qaeda were in the custody of what is euphemistically referred to within the U.S. government as "Other Government Agencies", or "OGA's"—the standard euphemism for the Central Intelligence Agency ("CIA").[213] The treatment standards related to these detainees became the next focal point for critics of harsh interrogation techniques and/or torture.

President Bush asserted that detainees in the custody of the CIA could, if determined necessary, be subjected to interrogation techniques not authorized by the Army field manual for interrogation and that were therefore inconsistent with the DTA.[214] This led Congress to propose an amendment to the DTA that would extend its application to any individual detained by the United States in the custody of an agency of the United States or contractor working on behalf of the United States. In response, President Bush indicated that he would veto any such legislation based on his conclusion that it would impermissibly intrude upon his inherent executive authority.

The potential dispute between Congress and President Bush on the applicability of the DTA and common article 3 to detainees in the custody of OGA's never reached a loggerhead. President Bush left office prior to being confronted with legislation imposing the humane treatment obligation on these detainees. In addition, in an effort to moot the issue, President Bush directed that the high-value al Qaeda detainees in the custody of the CIA be transferred to the custody of the Department of Defense at Guantánamo Bay.[215] As a result, the question of permissible CIA interrogation techniques became more theoretical than actual, as these detainees fell

213. Evan Thomas, *The Debate Over Torture*, http://www.newsweek.com/2005/11/20/the-debate-over-torture.html.

214. *See* Arsalan M. Suleman, *Recent Developments: Detainee Treatment Act of 2005*, 19 HARV. HUM. RTS. J. 260 (Spring 2006) ("[I]f the Administration wants to use harsher interrogation methods on a detainee, it simply has to transfer that detainee to a non-[Department of Defense] facility and into the custody or control of another department, such as the CIA").

215. Remarks on War on Terror, 42 Weekly Comp. Pres. Doc. 36, 1573 (Sep. 6, 2006).

under the authority of the DTA and Undersecretary England's memorandum once they were transferred to DOD custody.

Even this theoretical expanded scope of CIA interrogation authority was eliminated when President Obama took office in January of 2010. One of the new President's first actions terminated all debate on the permissibility of cruel or other harsh interrogation techniques *vis a vis* al Qaeda detainees. To this end, shortly after inauguration, he issued an Executive Order banning the torture of any individual in U.S. custody or control (irrespective of what government agency is in control of the detainee), and included water-boarding within the definition of torture.[216] This was undoubtedly an important step in restoring the United States to its historic role as a proponent of fundamental protections for all individuals adversely impacted by armed conflict or any other type of military operation. What it undoubtedly means is that the traditional policy followed by the United States for years prior to the initiation of the global war on terror—that any person detained by the United States would be protected by the minimum humanitarian protections reflected in common article 3 of the four Geneva Conventions—is once again the controlling standard for the treatment of detainees, including those responsible for the most heinous acts of terrorism in the history of our nation.

It is important to note, however, that the application to all detainees of at least the common article 3 humane treatment mandate in no way deprives the United States of its right or ability to interrogate detainees in order to obtain valuable information. Indeed, the Army manual on interrogation incorporated by reference into the DTA was developed specifically to facilitate the exploitation of captured and detained enemy personnel consistent with the obligations of the Geneva Conventions. Accordingly, U.S. intelligence operatives can, and will continue to, exploit these sources of potentially critical intelligence information. All that these developments mean is that in so doing, these United States operatives may not transgress minimal humanitarian treatment standards established to protect all victims of war, and determined by the Supreme Court to be applicable to any armed conflict.

B. CONCLUSION

The capture and detention of enemy belligerents in time of war has always been fundamental to military and national success in such struggles. However, the bulk of treaty provisions related to preventive detention of enemy belligerents applies to combatants belonging to a State and captured in the context of an international armed conflict. In contrast, there is virtually no express treaty provisions providing for analogous preventive detention of enemy

---

216. Exec. Order No. 13,491, 74 Fed. Reg. 13,491 (Jan. 27, 2009).

belligerents who are not within the scope of the GPW and other LOAC treaties dealing with POWs, because they were captured in the context of a non-international armed conflict, or even if captured in an international armed conflict, because they failed to meet the individual qualification requirements for protection under the GPW (see discussion above).

In the weeks and months following the initiation of the 'global war on terror', U.S. policy makers were confronted with the legal uncertainty resulting from the lack of treaty provisions applicable to detainees captured in a conflict with transnational terrorists. The solution was to invoke the customary LOAC principle of military necessity as a legal basis to detain these captured terrorists. Because of the lack of treaty law, determining who is an enemy combatant, what process they are due in relation to that determination, and the conditions of their detention and treatment is in many ways analogous to painting on a blank canvas.

The portrait that initially emerged from the Bush Administration's attempt to fill out the canvas reflected an attempt to exercise almost plenary executive power. President Bush asserted this plenary authority in his February 2002 memorandum when he determined, who should be detained without the benefit of a tribunal. The President, or other Administration leaders, also unilaterally determined, where the detainees should be detained, what process they were due (or not due), and how they were to be treated while in detention. In essence, the Bush administration had invoked the authority of the LOAC to justify preventive detention, but disavowed any constraints under the LOAC on the exercise of that authority. Thus, while President Bush directed that detainees be treated humanely, consistent with GPW, this humane treatment was subject to the dictates of military necessity.

The Bush Administration's initial portrait, however, was incomplete. Contrary to Bush's view that the President was the only "artist" entitled to contribute to the portrait, Congress and the Supreme Court added their contributions. This ultimately led to a substantial alteration of the Bush Administration's interpretation of its authority to detain and the obligations it owed to detainees in terms of their treatment. In the view of many, the revised interpretation was far more balanced. Access to judicial review, in particular, added a new artist to the process—the D.C. Circuit—whose holdings have actually not given the LOAC a significant role in the regulation of preventive detention. Nevertheless, a number of appeals are still pending and the portrait remains a work in progress.

Certain aspects of the legal picture are now clear. First, all three branches of the U.S. government endorse treating the struggle against transnational terrorism as an armed conflict. As such, the struggle should trigger the rights and obligations of the LOAC. Second, captured enemy belligerents are subject to preventive detention as a necessary incident of war, even if they do not qualify as prisoners of war entitled to protection under the GPW. Third, the preventive detention authority of the customary LOAC was implicitly invoked on behalf of the nation when Congress enacted the 2001 Authorization for the Use of Military Force, an authority that remains in effect to this day. Fourth, determining whether an individual detained at Guantanamo has been properly designated as an enemy belligerent subject to preventive detention requires both meaningful Executive branch review and judicial scrutiny of the decision to detain. Finally, detainees are entitled as a matter of law to be treated humanely pursuant to, at a minimum, common article 3 of the Geneva Conventions, and as a result only interrogation techniques that comply with that article (i.e., those authorized by the U.S. Army field manual on interrogation) may be employed to exploit these detainees.

The preventive detention of terrorist operatives has been and remains perhaps the most controversial aspect of treating the struggle against transnational terrorism as an armed conflict. Since his election, President Obama has made it clear that the United States will not abandon reliance on preventive detention as a basis to incapacitate terrorist operatives. This has undoubtedly disappointed many. However, the evolution of this detention process now reflects a far more balanced application of legal authority and obligation than was first invoked by President Bush, and in that regard has restored a substantial degree of legitimacy to the process.

It is clear that the United States will not abandon the use of preventive detention to protect the nation against the threat of transnational terrorism any time soon. How courts, and perhaps Congress, will build upon the legal foundation established over the past nine years will undoubtedly impact the balance of government and individual interests implicated by this practice. How it might impact the broader law of armed conflict is much more difficult to predict. While it is true that U.S. practice stressed certain core aspects of this law (most notably the principle of humane treatment), the evolution of that practice has in fact confirmed perhaps the most important norm of that law: the exercise of wartime power must always be complimented with respect for wartime constraint.

Chapter 5
TRIAL BY MILITARY TRIBUNAL*

A. INTRODUCTION

The terms 'war crime'[1] and 'terrorism'[2] share common connections: they both refer to the unjustified infliction of suffering, they both connote the victimization of the innocent, and they both trigger criminal sanction. But these two terms also differ in certain legally substantial ways. The most significant difference is the nature of the legal proscription—the source of law that operates to condemn the conduct alleged as criminal. War crimes are quintessential international law violations—crimes that are defined by international humanitarian law and subject to criminal sanction either through international tribunals or domestic tribunals applying the substance of international law. Terrorism, in contrast, although ostensibly universally condemned, is primarily the subject of domestic criminal proscription adjudicated in domestic criminal courts applying domestic criminal law.

Prior to September 11th, 2001 these differences had virtually no practical significance: war crimes and terrorism were prosecuted as distinct classes of crime. However, when President Bush issued his now infamous Military Order Number 1[3] directing the Secretary of Defense to establish a military commission to try certain individuals captured in the context of the newly proclaimed war on terror, the significance of these differences assumed profound proportions.

A military commission is a military criminal court historically created out of a necessity to fill a jurisdictional gap or to provide battlefield commanders a forum to hold captured enemy personnel accountable for pre-capture violations of the laws and customs of war. In *Hamdan v. Rumsfeld,*[4] the Supreme Court, citing William Winthrop's seminal treaties of American military law[5] noted that,

---

* This chapter is based (with substantial revisions) on Geoffrey S. Corn and Rick Talbot Jensen, war crimes, In the War on Terror & The Law of War: A Military Perspective (Oxford Univ. Press (2009).

1. *See, e.g.* Convention Relative to the Treatment of Prisoners of War, art. 130 (addressing prosecution obligations for certain war crimes), opened for signature Aug. 12, 1949, 6 U.S.T. 3316, 75 U.N.T.S. 135, reprinted in ADAM ROBERTS & RICHARD GUELFF, DOCUMENTS ON THE LAWS OF WAR (3d. ed. Oxford 2000).

2. *See, e.g.* 18 U.S.C. § 2339B (defining the federal offense of Providing Material Support to Terrorism).

3. Military Order, November 13, 2001, Detention, Treatment, and Trial of Certain non-Citizens in the War Against Terrorism, Sec. 1(a), 66 Fed. Reg. 57833 (Nov. 16, 2001).

4. Hamdan v. Rumsfeld, 548 U.S. 557 (2006).

5. W. WINTHROP, MILITARY LAW AND PRECEDENTS 831 (rev. 2d ed. 1920).

The military commission, a tribunal neither mentioned in the Constitution nor created by statute, was born of military necessity. Though foreshadowed in some respects by earlier tribunals like the Board of General Officers that General Washington convened to try British Major John André for spying during the Revolutionary War, the commission "as such" was inaugurated in 1847. As commander of occupied Mexican territory, and having available to him no other tribunal, General Winfield Scott that year ordered the establishment of both " '*military commissions*' " to try ordinary crimes committed in the occupied territory and a "*council of war*" to try offenses against the law of war.

When the exigencies of war next gave rise to a need for use of military commissions, during the Civil War, the dual system favored by General Scott was not adopted. Instead, a single tribunal often took jurisdiction over ordinary crimes, war crimes, and breaches of military orders alike . . . [E]ach aspect of that seemingly broad jurisdiction was in fact supported by a separate military exigency. Generally, though, the need for military commissions during this period—as during the Mexican War—was driven largely by the then very limited jurisdiction of courts-martial: "The *occasion* for the military commission arises principally from the fact that the jurisdiction of the court-martial proper, in our law, is restricted by statute almost exclusively to members of the military force and to certain specific offences defined in a written code."[6]

This led the Court to conclude that military commissions serve three distinct functions. First, it has been as a substitute for normal civilian criminal courts during martial law when those courts are not functioning (although as the Court noted, this use has never been without controversy). Second, it has been used to adjudicate allegations of criminal misconduct by the population of enemy territory under the control of a U.S. military commander during periods of belligerent occupation. Third, it has been used as a forum to adjudicate allegations of violations of the laws of war (today the law of armed conflict, or LOAC) by members of the U.S. military and captured enemy belligerents, what the Supreme Court characterized as a "law-of-war military commission."[7] Because the function of the law-of-war military commission function is to adjudicate allegations of battlefield misconduct, it's jurisdiction has historically been extremely narrow.[8]

6. *Hamdan*, 548 U.S. at 590.
7. *Hamdan*, 548 U.S. at 595.
8. *Hamdan*, 548 U.S. at 596.

Military commissions had essentially become dormant in U.S. military legal practice upon the completion of the post World War II war crimes trials. Although some experts argued for the continuing viability of this tribunal,[9] because both General Courts–Martial (GCM) and federal courts were available forums for the prosecution of war crimes, others doubted the continuing relevance of the military commission as a law of war tribunal.[10] However, once the United States chose to invoke its war powers in response to the terror attacks of September 11th, the proverbial door was opened for the President to resurrect this prosecutorial forum. In November of 2001 President Bush did so, issuing Military Order Number 1,[11] which first asserted that the United States was engaged in an armed conflict against al Qaeda and associated terrorist personnel, and then directed the Secretary of Defense to create a military commission to try captured terrorist operatives for violations of the laws of war.[12]

The military commission created by the Department of Defense pursuant to this order essentially resurrected the trial process last used in the aftermath of World War II. This process was substantially less defendant favorable than the process provided to U.S. service-members tried by courts-martial (a process that had undergone substantial improvement in the sixty years following World War II), and was also perceived as inconsistent with minimal fair trial requirements of both domestic and international law.[13] These perceived procedural defects would prove highly controversial, draw fire from numerous legal experts,[14] and ultimately lead to judicial invalidation of the President's commission.[15]

Equally controversial was the assertion of war crimes jurisdiction to try terrorist operatives. The mere designation of the struggle against armed conflict was and remains highly charged. However, as would be revealed by the *Hamdan* decision, once Congress enacted the Authorization for the Use of Military Force against al Qaeda, this issue was effectively settled for the United States. However, what was far less certain was the subject-matter jurisdic-

9. Michael A. Newton, Continuum Crimes: Military Jurisdiction over Foreign Nationals Who Commit International Crimes, 153 MIL. L. REV. 1, 13 (1996).

10. Jan E. Aldykiewicz & Geoffrey S. Corn, *Authority to Court Martial Non–U.S. Military Personnel for Serious Violations of International Humanitarian Law Committed during Internal Armed Conflicts*, 167 MIL. L. REV. 74, 145–148 (2001).

11. Military Order, November 13, 2001, Detention, Treatment, and Trial of Certain non-Citizens in the War Against Terrorism, Sec. 1(a), 66 Fed. Reg. 57833 (Nov. 16, 2001).

12. *Id.*

13. Neal K. Katyal & Laurence H. Tribe, *Waging War, Deciding Guilt: Trying the Military Tribunals*, 111 YALE L.J. 1259 (2002).

14. Geoffrey S. Corn, *Taking the Bitter with the Sweet: A Law of War Based Analysis of the Military Commission*, 35 STETSON L.REV. 811 (2006).

15. Hamdan v. Rumsfeld, 548 U.S. 557 (2006).

tion triggered by this conflict. First, did the armed conflict begin on September 11th? Or did it pre-date that infamous day? Because the existence of armed conflict would be identified by the *Hamdan* majority as a jurisdictional predicate to trial by military commission sitting as a law of war court, this would become a critical question. Second, what offenses qualify as violations of the law of war? This was a second jurisdictional predicate identified by *Hamdan,* an issue that continues to create substantial uncertainty.

Salim Hamdan, Osama Bin Laden's driver, challenged the legality of his trial by the military commission created pursuant to Military Order Number 1.[16] Procedural and jurisdictional defects led the Supreme Court to invalidate that commission. However, the decision also sowed the seeds for the current battles over commission prosecutions when it essentially invited Congress to provide a statutory authorization for trial by military commission ("The charge's shortcomings are not merely formal, but are indicative of a broader inability on the Executive's part here to satisfy the most basic precondition—*at least in the absence of specific congressional authorization*—for establishment of military commissions: military necessity."[17]). Congress responded to *Hamdan* by enacting the Military Commission Act of 2006.[18] As will be explained below, this Act cured most of the procedural and evidentiary defects of the original commission. However, by enumerating offenses subject to trial by military commission, the Act also exacerbated concerns over subject-matter jurisdiction legitimacy, and added a new level of complexity to that debate: what limits, if any, exist on congressional authority to establish the subject-matter jurisdiction of a military commission?[19]

The most recent chapter in the military commission story began following the election of President Barak Obama. Contrary to expectations, President Obama chose not to abandon the military commission option for the trial of terrorist operatives. Instead, as will be explained below, he focused his efforts on enhancing the procedural and evidentiary standards for the commission. However, neither the revised Military Commission Act (MCA)[20] he proposed and signed into law, nor his administration's decisions on who and what to charge for trial by military commission, have alleviated the fundamental jurisdictional uncertainty of these trials.

16. Hamdan v. Rumsfeld, 548 U.S. 557 (2006).

17. *Hamdan*, 548 U.S. at 598.

18. Military Commissions Act of 2006, Pub. L. 109–366, 120 Stat. 2600, codified at 10 U.S.C. ch. 47, amended by Pub. L. 111–87, H.R. 2647–385 (2009).

19. GEOFFREY S. CORN & ERIC TALBOT JENSEN, WAR CRIMES, IN THE WAR ON TERROR & THE LAW OF WAR: A MILITARY PERSPECTIVE 103–23 (Geoffrey S. Corn ed., Oxford Univ. Press, 2009).

20. Military Commissions Act of 2006, Pub. L. 109–366, 120 Stat. 2600, codified at 10 U.S.C. ch. 47, amended by Pub. L. 111–87, H.R. 2647–385 (2009).

B. MILITARY COURTS AND MILITARY COMMISSIONS

Military courts have always been recognized as legitimate forums to adjudicate allegations of criminal misconduct by members of the U.S. armed forces.[21] Allegations of LOAC violations by captured enemy forces have also fallen under the jurisdiction of U.S. military courts.[22] The most commonly used type of U.S. military court is the court-martial, a tribunal established pursuant to the Uniform Code of Military Justice[23] (a statute enacted by Congress pursuant to its enumerated power to "make rules for the land and naval forces."[24]). Article 18 of the UCMJ (and its predecessor the Articles of War[25]) vests General Courts–Martial with jurisdiction to try "any person who, by the law of war, is subject to trial by military tribunal."[26] In 1942 the Supreme Court addressed the jurisdiction of U.S. military courts to try captured enemy belligerents during times of war. In *Ex parte Quirin*, the Court relied on the Articles of War predecessor to Article 18 of the UCMJ to conclude Congress had vested U.S. military courts with authority to try enemy belligerents for violations of the laws of war.[27] However, the Quirin defendants were not facing trial by General Court–Martial, but instead by a secret military commission established pursuant to the order of President Roosevelt. In support of the holding that jurisdiction over the defendants could also be exercised by the military commission, the Court relied on another provision of the Articles of War, Article 15.[28] An identical version of Article 15 is now codified as Article 21 of the UCMJ, which is identical to the Article considered by the Court in 1942 and provides:

> The provisions of this chapter conferring jurisdiction upon courts-martial do not deprive military commissions, provost courts, or other military tribunals of concurrent

21. Military Commissions Act of 2006, Pub. L. 109–366, 120 Stat. 2600, codified at 10 U.S.C. ch. 47, amended by Pub. L. 111–87, H.R. 2647–385 (2009).

22. *See* Jan E. Aldykiewicz & Geoffrey S. Corn, *Authority to Court Martial Non–U.S. Military Personnel for Serious Violations of International Humanitarian Law Committed during Internal Armed Conflicts*, 167 MIL. L. REV. 74, 145–148 (2001); Michael A. Newton, *Continuum Crimes: Military Jurisdiction over Foreign Nationals Who Commit International Crimes*, 153 MIL. L. REV. 1 (1996).

23. Uniform Code of Military Justice, 64 Stat. 109, 10 U.S.C. ch. 47 [hereinafter UCMJ].

24. U.S. CONST. art. I § 8, cl. 14.

25. MILITARY LAWS OF THE UNITED STATES 702, (3d ed. 1898). 1920 Articles of War, Bul. No. 25, W.D., 1920 (June 4, 1920).

26. 10 U.S.C. § 818.

27. Ex parte Quirin, 317 U.S. 1 (1942).

28. *See Hamdan v. Rumsfeld*, 548 U.S. 557, 593, at n.22 ("Article 15 was first adopted as part of the Articles of War in 1916. See Act of Aug. 29, 1916, ch. 418, § 3, Art. 15, 39 Stat. 652. When the Articles of War were codified and re-enacted as the UCMJ in 1950, Congress determined to retain Article 15 because it had been "construed by the Supreme Court (Ex Parte Quirin, 317 U.S. 1 (1942))." S. Rep. No. 486, 81st Cong., 1st Sess., 13 (1949).").

jurisdiction with respect to offenders or offenses that by statute or by the law of war may be tried by military commission, provost court, or other military tribunals.[29]

The *Quirin* Court held that this provision provided statutory authority for the use of military commissions to try enemy belligerents for alleged war crimes.[30] This interpretation of the effect of Article 21 has always been questionable, and many experts believe that it merely recognized that the common law of war authorizes the President to convene military commissions when necessary.[31] Justice Stevens called the *Quirin* interpretation of this provision of the military code into question when he highlighted the uncertain effect of Article 21 in *Hamdan v. Rumsfeld*. Responding to the President's assertion that his vested authority as Commander in Chief provided authority to convene military commissions, Justice Stevens noted:

> We have no occasion to revisit *Quirin*'s controversial characterization of Article of War 15 as congressional authorization for military commissions. Contrary to the Government's assertion, however, even *Quirin did not view the authorization as a sweeping mandate for the President to "invoke military commissions when he deems them necessary." Rather, the Quirin Court recognized that Congress had simply preserved what power, under the Constitution and the common law of war, the President had had before 1916 to convene military commissions—with the express condition that the President and those under his command comply with the law of war.*[32]

Whether then Article 15 and today Article 21 of the UCMJ authorizes the President to convene military commissions to try enemy belligerents, or whether it merely acknowledges his authority to do so pursuant to the common law of war, one conclusion is clear: through both the Articles of War and the UCMJ, Congress has recognized the legitimate authority of U.S. military tribunals to exercise jurisdiction over enemy belligerents for pre-captured LOAC violations.

Sixty four years after the Court endorsed military commission over war crimes, the Court again confronted this issue. In *Hamdan v. Rumsfeld*,[33] the Supreme Court again relied on the U.S. military

---

29. 10 U.S.C. § 821.

30. *Quirin*, 317 U.S. at 27.

31. *See* Jan E. Aldykiewicz & Geoffrey S. Corn, *Authority to Court Martial Non–U.S. Military Personnel for Serious Violations of International Humanitarian Law Committed during Internal Armed Conflicts*, 167 MIL. L. REV. 74,

145–148 (2001); Michael A. Newton, *Continuum Crimes: Military Jurisdiction over Foreign Nationals Who Commit International Crimes*, 153 MIL. L. REV. 1 (1996).

32. *Hamdan*, 548 U.S. at 592.

33. Hamdan v. Rumsfeld, 548 U.S. 557 (2006).

code to conclude Congress endorsed the trial of captured enemy belligerents by military commission. The Court avoided the question of whether congressional authorization for the use of military commissions was necessary, an issue raised when the President asserted inherent authority to convene such tribunals in times of armed conflict to try captured enemy belligerents as an exercise of command authority.[34] Instead, the Court concluded that by invoking the war powers of the nation with enactment of the Authorization for the Use of Military Force[35] against al Qaeda, Congress had "activated the President's war powers, and that those powers include the authority to convene military commissions in appropriate circumstances . . . "[36] This led the Court to focus on the legal predicates for a legitimate invocation of military commission jurisdiction.

Justice Stevens began his analysis of this issue by noting that "The common law governing military commissions may be gleaned from past practice and what sparse legal precedent exists."[37] Based primarily on this historical practice, the Court concluded that:

> Commissions historically have been used in three situations. First, they have substituted for civilian courts at times and in places where martial law has been declared. Their use in these circumstances has raised constitutional questions. Second, commissions have been established to try civilians "as part of a temporary military government over occupied enemy territory or territory regained from an enemy where civilian government cannot and does not function." Illustrative of this second kind of commission is the one that was established, with jurisdiction to apply the German Criminal Code, in occupied Germany following the end of World War II.

> The third type of commission, convened as an "incident to the conduct of war" when there is a need "to seize and subject to disciplinary measures those enemies who in their attempt to thwart or impede our military effort have violated the law of war," has been described as "utterly different" from the other two.[38]

Having identified these three distinct uses of military commission, the Court next concluded that the commission subject matter jurisdiction depends on the purpose for which it is being used. As a

---

34. *See generally* Curtis Bradley & Jack Goldsmith, *Congressional Authorization and the War on Terrorism*, 118 HARV. L. REV. 2047 (2005).

35. Authorization for the Use of Military Force, Pub. L. 107–40, 115 Stat. 224 (2001).

36. *Hamdan*, 548 U.S. at 593.

37. *Id.*

38. *Hamdan*, 548 U.S. at 595.

martial law court, jurisdiction ostensibly includes offenses established by the military commander asserting martial rule. As an occupation court, jurisdiction extends to all offenses incorporated from local law and promulgated by the occupation commander pursuant to the Geneva Convention for the Protection of Civilians. As Hamdan did not implicate either of these uses, the Court provided little additional insight into the limits on jurisdiction in these contexts.

Instead, the Court focused on the third type of military commission, what it called a "law-of-war military commission".[39] According to the Court, this

> [t]hird type of commission, convened as an "incident to the conduct of war" when there is a need "to seize and subject to disciplinary measures those enemies who in their attempt to thwart or impede our military effort have violated the law of war," has been described as "utterly different" from the other two. Not only is its jurisdiction limited to offenses cognizable during time of war, *but its role is primarily a factfinding one—to determine, typically on the battlefield itself, whether the defendant has violated the law of war.*[40]

As will be explained in greater detail below, this conclusion that the type of military commission convened by President Bush could exercise only limited subject-matter jurisdiction set the conditions for a plurality of the Court to conclude conspiracy fell outside that jurisdiction.[41]

Both *Quirin* and *Hamdan* considered the legality of the law of war type military commission and the scope of permissible jurisdiction when used to adjudicate allegations of war crimes. In neither case had the commission been convened pursuant to express statutory authority. As a result, the alleged offenses in both cases were, according to each opinion, derived from the common law of war. According to Justice Stevens,

> As we explained in *Quirin*, that [the absence of a statutory definition of the alleged war crime] is not necessarily fatal to the Government's claim of authority to try the alleged offense by military commission; Congress, through Article 21 of the UCMJ, has "incorporated by reference" the common law of war, which may render triable by military commission certain offenses not defined by statute.[42]

---

39. *Hamdan*, 548 U.S. at 597.

40. *Id.*

41. *Id.* at 611–12.

42. *Hamdan*, 548 U.S. at 601.

However, Justice Stevens then concluded that a charge based on this common law must be subjected to significant scrutiny, implying that a statutory enumeration of offenses falling within the jurisdiction of a military commission should receive greater judicial deference.

> When, however, neither the elements of the offense nor the range of permissible punishments is defined by statute or treaty, the precedent must be plain and unambiguous. To demand any less would be to risk concentrating in military hands a degree of adjudicative and punitive power in excess of that contemplated either by statute or by the Constitution.[43]

Prior to 2006, Congress had never provided express statutory authority to convene military commissions as law of war courts (or for any purpose), nor had it enumerated offenses subject to the jurisdiction of a military commission convened for the trial of captured enemy belligerents. Both *Quirin* and *Hamdan* suggested Congress possessed the authority to do so through an exercise of its vested power to "define and punish . . . Offences against the Law of Nations"[44] Congress did not respond to that suggestion after the *Quirin* decision, most likely because the Court upheld the exercise of commission jurisdiction. However, in response to the Court's decision in *Hamdan* striking down the military commission created by order of President Bush, Congress did respond, enacting the MCA, which it amended in 2009.[45] This statute authorized trial of certain terrorist operatives by military commission, established procedural and evidentiary rules for these trials, and expressly enumerated offenses subject to military commission jurisdiction. As will be explained below, the MCA did not eliminate uncertainty related to the subject-matter jurisdiction of the military commission. Instead, it shifted the focus to the question of whether Congress can include within that jurisdiction offenses that are not well accepted violations of the law of war. This issue has become a major source of contention in the current military commission litigation.[46]

---

43. *Id.*

44. U.S. Const. art. I, § 8, cl. 10.

45. Military Commissions Act of 2006, Pub. L. 109–366, 120 Stat. 2600, codified at 10 U.S.C ch. 47, amended by Pub. L. 111–87, H.R. 2647–385 (2009).

46. *See, e.g.,* United States v. al Bahlul, Brief on Behalf of Appellee, CMCR Case No. 09–001 (Oct. 21, 2009); United States v. Hamdan, Brief on Behalf of Appellee, CMCR Case No. 09–0002 (Dec. 4, 2009) p. 6–7 (citing Winthrop, supra, at 5); United States v. Sal-

im Ahmed Hamdan, CMCR Case No. 09–002, *available at* http://www.defense. gov/news/CMCRHamdan.html; United States v. Omar Ahmed Khadr, *available at* http://www.defense.gov/news/ commissionsKhadr.html; United States v. Mohammed Jawad, CMCR Case No. 08–004, *available at*: http://www.defense. gov/news/CMCRJAWAD1.html; United States v. al Bahlul, CMCR Case No. 09–00, *available at* http://www.defense.gov/ news/CMCRHAMZA.html; *see also* Geoffrey S. Corn and Eric Talbot Jensen,

Procedurally, military commissions have varied throughout history. Congress, however, has generally linked the process for trial by military commission with the process established for trial by court-martial. This was an apparent effort to ensure that the process afforded to captured enemy belligerents is fundamentally fair. Article 36 of the UCMJ:

> [p]laces two restrictions on the President's power to promulgate rules of procedure for courts-martial and military commissions alike. First, no procedural rule he adopts may be "contrary to or inconsistent with" the UCMJ—however practical it may seem. Second, the rules adopted must be "uniform insofar as practicable." That is, the rules applied to military commissions must be the same as those applied to courts-martial unless such uniformity proves impracticable.[47]

This "mirror image" method of ensuring fair process for captured enemy belligerents subject to trial by military commission for alleged war crimes is consistent with the method used in the Geneva Convention Relative to the Treatment of Prisoners of War.[48] Article 102 of this treaty provides:

> A prisoner of war can be validly sentenced only if the sentence has been pronounced by the same courts according to the same procedure as in the case of members of the armed forces of the Detaining Power . . .[49]

Although individuals within the jurisdiction of both the military commission convened by order of President Bush and pursuant to the MCA did not qualify for POW status, the analogy between these two provisions is significant. While Article 36 does provide more flexibility than the GPW (through its impracticability qualifier), it does not permit the President to adopt procedures fundamentally less favorable for trial of enemy belligerents than those provided to U.S. service-members by tried by courts-martial. This limitation that would prove central to the Supreme Court's ruling in *Hamdan* that the President's military commission failed to satisfy minimum procedural standards required not only by the law of war, but also by the UCMJ.[50]

War Crimes, in THE WAR ON TERROR AND THE LAW OF WAR: A MILITARY PERSPECTIVE (Geoffrey S. Corn, ed., Oxford Univ. Press, 2009).

47. *Hamdan*, 548 U.S. at 620 (citing 10 U.S.C. § 836).

48. Convention Relative to the Treatment of Prisoners of War, art. 3 opened for signature Aug. 12, 1949, 6 U.S.T. 3316, 75 U.N.T.S. 135, reprinted in ADAM ROBERTS & RICHARD GUELFF, DOCUMENTS ON THE LAWS OF WAR (3d. ed. Oxford 2000).

49. *Id.* at art. 102.

50. 10 U.S.C. § 836.

The Congress clearly heeded the requirement of Article 36 when it enacted the MCA of 2006, and amended that statute in 2009. The MCA provides extensive procedural and evidentiary rules for trial by military commission, substantially enhancing the procedural framework for commission proceedings. It also reflects an effort by Congress to bring military commission process in line with courts-martial process wherever feasible.[51] The MCA, and its impact on commission proceedings will be discussed in greater detail below. However, more generally the current commission is an adversarial tribunal with a jury composed of military officers presided over by a qualified military judge.[52] Defendants (designated as the "accused" by the MCA) benefit from a presumption of innocence, requiring the prosecution to prove all defined elements beyond a reasonable doubt.[53] Defendants have a right to detailed military defense counsel appointed by the government, confrontation and compulsory process, and a privilege against self-incrimination (although not as extensive as provided for in the UCMJ).[54] In a major improvement from the original military commission, the MCA created a military appellate court, and granted defendants an appeal of right. This court is also empowered to act on extraordinary writs.[55] The MCA provides for discretionary appeal to the Court of Appeals for the District of Colombia and subsequently to the Supreme Court of the United States.[56]

As noted above, the subject matter jurisdiction of a military commission convened as a law of war court over captured enemy belligerents is concurrent with that of General Courts–Martial. Because the process for trial by courts-martial is both well established and highly respected as an example of legitimate military justice, that forum was considered by many as preferable to trial before a newly created military tribunal.[57] This led many to question why the government chose the military commission option. There is unequivocal answer to this question. When first used by the United States, military commissions were relied on to try

---

51. *See* JENNIFER K. ELSEA, CONG. RESEARCH SERV., RL33688, THE MILITARY COMMISSIONS ACT OF 2006: ANALYSIS OF PROCEDURAL RULES AND COMPARISON WITH PREVIOUS DOD RULES AND THE UNIFORM CODE OF MILITARY JUSTICE (2007).

52. Military Commissions Act of 2006, Pub. L. 109–366, 120 Stat. 2600, codified at 10 U.S.C. ch. 47, amended by Pub. L. 111–87, H.R. 2647–385 (2009) at §§ 948j(b), 948(m) [hereinafter MCA].

53. *Id.* at § 949l(c)1.

54. *Id.* at §§ 948k(3), 948r.

55. *Id.* at § 7.

56. *Id.* at § 950c.

57. *See* JENNIFER ELSEA, CONG. RESEARCH SERV., RL 31191, TERRORISM AND THE LAW OF WAR: TRYING TERRORISTS AS WAR CRIMINALS BEFORE MILITARY COMMISSIONS (2001); *see also* Neal K. Katyal & Laurence H. Tribe, *Waging War, Deciding Guilt: Trying the Military Tribunals*, 111 YALE L.J. 1259 (2002); Jan E. Aldykiewicz & Geoffrey S. Corn, *Authority to Court Martial Non–U.S. Military Personnel for Serious Violations of International Humanitarian Law Committed during Internal Armed Conflicts*, 167 MIL. L. REV. 74 (2001).

captured enemy personnel because courts-martial jurisdiction was limited to U.S. service-members.[58] Although Congress expanded court-martial jurisdiction to include captured enemy belligerents who committed violations of the laws and customs of war prior to World War II, the practice of trying enemy belligerents by military commission continued during and after that conflict.[59]

One possible explanation of why President Bush chose to convene the military commission in lieu of using the established process of the General Court–Martial is that he wanted to deprive terrorist defendants of the substantial procedural and evidentiary protections applicable to courts-marital. These protections include access to judicial review, a right expressly prohibited by the military order President Bush used to direct the creation of the commission. This explanation is certainly compelling, but arguably incomplete. Some credit must be afforded to the President's asserted motivation, which was that the process for trial of war crimes must be tailored to the unique challenges of such cases. When Congress enacted the MCA, it rejected the Bush administration effort to resurrect a military commission process substantially less defendant protective than the court-martial. However, the MCA also reflects a congressional judgment that trial by court-martial, although possible, is not the appropriate method to deal with allegations of war crimes by captured terrorists detained as enemy belligerents. Perhaps an even more significant indication that the decision by President Bush was at least partially justified is the fact that his successor, President Obama, chose not to abandon the military commission prosecutorial option. As will be explained below, this decision by the political branches of the government to move continue to prosecute terrorist operatives by military commission has resulted in continuing questions as to the legitimacy of both the substantive and procedural aspects of the process established by the MCA.

C. MILITARY COMMISSIONS AND THE WAR ON TERROR

Perhaps the most unanticipated consequence of characterizing the struggle against transnational terrorism as an armed conflict was the subsequent invocation of military jurisdiction to criminally sanction terrorist operatives. Before President Bush issued his Military Order Number 1[60] directing the Secretary of Defense to

58. *See* W. Winthrop, Military Law and Precedents 832 (rev. 2d ed. 1920); *see also* Michael O. Lacey, *Military Commissions: A Historical Survey*, 2002 Army Law. 41 (Mar. 2002); John Bickers, Military *Commissions are Constitutionally Sound: A Response to Professors*

Katyal and Tribe, 34 Tex. Tech. L. Rev. 899 (2002–2003).

59. Michael O. Lacey, *Military Commissions: A Historical Survey*, 2002 Army Law. 41(Mar. 2002).

60. Military Order, November 13, 2001, Detention, Treatment, and Trial

detain unlawful alien enemy combatants and to try by military commission those determined to have violated the laws of war, civilian criminal process had been the exclusive method used by the United States to prosecute alleged terrorists. In fact, the United States had not used a military commission to try captured enemy personnel since the end of World War II, and even the use during that war generated legal controversy.[61] The decision to convene military commissions demonstrated unequivocally that President Bush viewed struggle against terrorism no longer as merely crime, but an armed conflict triggering LOAC rights and obligations.[62] Accordingly, terrorist operatives determined to have acted as enemy belligerents would be tried for violations of the LOAC no differently than captured enemy belligerents had been tried in conflicts past: by military commission. This newly embraced characterization of terrorism and terrorist operatives was highly controversial, and in the view of many legal experts utterly invalid. Thus, the November 13, 2001 Bush military order to resurrect this forum for the trial of captured personnel not only took many by surprise, it also initiated a wave of legal uncertainty that continues to this day.[63]

The legal basis to subject alleged terrorists to the jurisdiction of a military commission was uncertain at best. A tribunal of extremely limited jurisdiction, military commissions had normally been used as law of war courts in close proximity (geographically and temporally) to the field of battle to adjudicate allegations that a defendant who participated in armed conflict violated applicable LOAC rules or norms (what the Supreme Court characterized in *Quirin* as the "common law of war"[64]). The fact that terrorist are

of Certain non-Citizens in the War Against Terrorism, Sec. 1(a), 66 Fed. Reg. 57833 (Nov. 16, 2001).

61. See Jennifer Elsea, Cong. Research Serv., RL 31191, Terrorism and the Law of War: Trying Terrorists as War Criminals before Military Commissions (2001); see also Michael O. Lacey, *Military Commissions: A Historical Survey*, 2002 Army Law. 41, (Mar. 2002); John Bickers, *Military Commissions are Constitutionally Sound: A Response to Professors Katyal and Tribe*, 34 Tex. Tech. L. Rev. 899 (2002–2003); Geoffrey S. Corn, *Taking the Bitter with the Sweet: A Law of War Based Analysis of the Military Commission*, 35 Stetson L. Rev. 811 (2006).

62. Jennifer Elsea, Cong. Research Serv., RL 31191, Terrorism and the Law of War: Trying Terrorists as War Criminals before Military Commissions (2001).

63. See generally Amicus Brief before the Supreme Court in the Hamdan case by Professors Fletcher and Cassese; United States v. Hamdan, Amicus Curiae Brief of Professors Geoffrey Corn and Victor M. Hansen in Support of Appellant, CMCR Case No. 09–002 (Dec. 4, 2009); United States v. Hamdan, Brief of Amici Curiae, Prof. Dr. Terry Gill and Dr. Gentian Zyberi, CMCR Case No. 09–002 (Dec. 4, 2009); United States v. Hamdan, Brief of Constitutional Law Scholars as Amici Curiae in Support of the Petitioner, CMCR Case No. 09–002; Center for Constitutional Rights, Military Commissions Act of 2006: A Summary of the Law (July 23, 2006); Neal K. Katyal & Laurence H. Tribe, *Waging War, Deciding Guilt: Trying the Military Tribunals*, 111 Yale L.J. 1259 (2002); David Glazier, *Playing by the Rules: Combating Al Qaeda Within the Law of War*, 51 Wm. & Mary L. Rev. 957 (2009).

64. *Quirin*, 317 U.S. at 34.

not members of armed forces qualified for status as lawful combatants pursuant to the LOAC, coupled with the fact that they operate in a manner considered by many experts as not triggering the LOAC,[65] produced complex issues?[66] Could the conduct of terrorists violate the laws and customs of war? Could terrorism itself be characterized as a war crime? When do acts of terrorism fall within the legitimate jurisdiction of a 'law of war court'? If terrorists were to be tried by such courts, would these courts be legally obligated to comply with the fundamental trial rights guaranteed by the law of armed conflict?[67] Would defendants have a right to judicial review? What happens to defendant's acquitted by a military commission? Each of these issues has and continues to generate almost more questions than answers.

The debate related to these issues unfolded in the months and years following issuance of Military Order 1.[68] Legal challenge to the commissions, coupled with congressional intervention in defining offenses and process for trial by military commission produced a substantial evolution of military commission process. Substantively, however, the legal determination that provided the foundation for President Bush's initial order to try terrorist by military commission—that acts of transnational terrorism are legitimately designated as war crimes subject to the jurisdiction of military commissions even when civilian criminal courts provide a viable prosecutorial alternative—remains as controversial today as it did when President Bush issued Military Order Number 1.

Perhaps more importantly, the designation of the struggle against terrorism as an armed conflict continues to provide the legal foundation for the continued use of military commissions to try captured terrorist operatives. Neither the enactment of the MCA nor the assumption of responsibility by President Obama substantially altered this theory of military commission jurisdiction. Indeed, in many ways the actions by Congress and President Obama have affirmed the decision by President Bush to order the use of military commission for such trials. Accordingly, captured al Qaeda operatives have and will continue to be subjected to trial by military commission for not only violations of accepted LOAC proscriptions, but also for terrorism type offenses designated by the

---

65. *See* International Law Association, Use of Force Committee, Final Report on the Meaning of Armed Conflict in International Law, 25–28 (2010), *available at* http://www.ila-hq.org/en/committees/index.cfm/cid/1022.

66. Spencer J. Crona & Neil A. Richardson, *Justice for War Criminal of Invisible Armies: A New Legal and Military Approach to Terrorism,* 21 OKLA. CITY U.L. REV. 349 (1996).

67. Hereinafter LOAC.

68. Military Order, November 13, 2001, Detention, Treatment, and Trial of Certain non-Citizens in the War Against Terrorism, Sec. 1(a), 66 Fed. Reg. 57833 (Nov. 16, 2001).

MCA as either war crimes, or "other offenses subject to trial by military commission."[69]

Controversy surrounding the trial of alleged terrorists by military commission does not, however, indicate that such tribunals are inherently invalid. In fact, there is nothing fundamentally irrational about the use of military courts to try war crimes. War crimes themselves are derived from a history of trying captured enemy belligerents by military tribunals vested with jurisdiction to sit in judgment of violations of the laws and customs of war.[70] As the United States Supreme Court noted in *Ex parte Quirin,* one of its rare opinions addressing the legality of military commissions: "by universal agreement . . . Unlawful combatants are likewise subject to capture and detention, but in addition they are subject to trial and punishment by military tribunals for acts which render their belligerency unlawful."[71]

Although a technically viable forum for trial of enemy belligerents for their pre-capture LOAC violations, following World War II military commissions receded into proverbial hibernation. This dormancy, coupled with the ascendance of *ad hoc* international civilian war crimes tribunals in the decade preceding the terror attacks of September 11th, led to an assumption that use of military tribunals, and in particular a military commission to try captured enemy personnel by military tribunal in future conflicts was highly unlikely. Even the small circle of experts analyzing military jurisdiction for war crimes considered such use almost purely theoretical.[72] When President Bush chose to resurrect this tribunal the controversy he generated was not based on the conclu-

69. *See* Military Commissions Act of 2006, Pub. L. 109–366, 120 Stat. 2600, codified at 10 U.S.C. ch. 47, amended by Pub. L. 111–87, H.R. 2647–385 (2009); *see also* United States v. Salim Ahmed Hamdan, CMCR Case No. 09–002, *available at* http://www.defense.gov/news/CMCRHamdan.html; United States v. Omar Ahmed Khadr, *available at* http://www.defense.gov/news/commissionsKhadr.html; United States v. Mohammed Jawad, CMCR Case No. 08–004, *available at* http://www.defense.gov/news/CMCRJAWAD1.html; United States v. al Bahlul, CMCR Case No. 09–00, *available at* http://www.defense.gov/news/CMCRHAMZA.html.

70. *See* Jennifer Elsea, Cong. Research Serv., RL 31191, Terrorism and the Law of War: Trying Terrorists as War Criminals before Military Commissions (2001); *see also* Michael O. Lacey, *Military Commissions: A Historical Survey,* 2002 Army Law. 41 (Mar. 2002); John Bickers, Military *Commissions are Constitutionally Sound: A Response to Professors Katyal and Tribe,* 34 Tex. Tech. L. Rev. 899 (2002–2003); Geoffrey S. Corn, *Taking the Bitter with the Sweet: A Law of War Based Analysis of the Military Commission,* 35 Stetson L. Rev. 811 (2006).

71. Ex parte Quirin, 317 U.S. 1 (1942).

72. *See, e.g.,* Jan E. Aldykiewicz & Geoffrey S. Corn, *Authority to Court Martial Non–U.S. Military Personnel for Serious Violations of International Humanitarian Law Committed during Internal Armed Conflicts,* 167 Mil. L. Rev. 74, 145–148 (2001); Michael A. Newton, *Continuum Crimes: Military Jurisdiction over Foreign Nationals Who Commit International Crimes,* 153 Mil. L. Rev. 1 (1996).

sion military commissions are inherently invalid. Instead, the controversy resulted from the perceived jurisdictional and procedural defects produced by the uncertain fit between terrorism and war crimes and the resurrection of a trial process based on standards of military justice that had been eclipsed in the six decades since the last use of the commission.

Substantively, the characterization of transnational terrorism as an armed conflict with the accordant assertion of war crimes jurisdiction over the conduct of terrorist operatives was a novel extension of traditionally accepted definitions of war crimes.[73] Procedurally, the resurrection of a trial framework last utilized in World War II turned back the clock of fundamental fairness and was considered by most observers as a denied of procedural protections inconsistent with due process, the UCMJ, and the LOAC itself.[74]

The debate over procedural obligations related to the use of military tribunals to try terrorism offenses has been in large measure resolved by a combination of the Supreme Court decision in *Hamdan v. Rumsfeld*[75] and subsequent enactment of the MCA of 2006 as amended by the MCA of 2009.[76] Substantive clarity, however, remains elusive. Although the MCA enumerates offenses subject to military commission jurisdiction, internal statutory contradictions coupled with the continuing judicial challenge to the scope of jurisdiction established by Congress cast doubt on the ultimate resolution of this debate. This jurisdictional uncertainty is ultimately produced by the invocation of the historically valid exercise of law of war jurisdiction to address the conduct of terrorist operatives. What offenses fall within the lawful jurisdiction of such courts, and what limits if any apply to Congress' authority to vest a

73. *See* JENNIFER ELSEA, CONG. RESEARCH SERV., RL 31191, TERRORISM AND THE LAW OF WAR: TRYING TERRORISTS AS WAR CRIMINALS BEFORE MILITARY COMMISSIONS (2001); *see also* Michael O. Lacey, *Military Commissions: A Historical Survey*, 2002 ARMY LAW. 41, (Mar. 2002); John Bickers, Military *Commissions are Constitutionally Sound: A Response to Professors Katyal and Tribe*, 34 Tex. TECH. L. REV. 899 (2002–2003); Geoffrey S. Corn, *Taking the Bitter with the Sweet: A Law of War Based Analysis of the Military Commission,* 35 STETSON L. REV. 811 (2006).

74. *See, e.g.,* JORDAN PAUST & M.C. BASSIOUNI ET. AL, HUMAN RIGHTS MODULE: CRIMES AGAINST HUMANITY, GENOCIDE, OTHER CRIMES AGAINST HUMAN RIGHTS, AND WAR CRIMES (2001); Gabor Rona, *When is a war not a war?—The proper role of the*

law of armed conflict in the "global war on terror", "International Action to Prevent and Combat Terrorism"—Workshop on the Protection of Human Rights While Countering Terrorism, Copenhagen, 15–16 March 2004—Presentation given by Gabor Rona, Legal Adviser-*available at the ICRC's Legal Division, at* http://www.icrc.org/Web/Eng/siteeng0.nsf/iwpList575/3C2914F52152E565C12 56E60005C84C0 (last accessed 10 August, 2010); Mary Ellen O'Connell, *When is War Not a War? The Myth of the Global War on Terror*, 12 ILSA J. OF INT'L & COMP. L. 2 (2005).

75. Hamdan v. Rumsfeld, 548 U.S. 557 (2006).

76. Military Commissions, 10 U.S.C. §§ 948a–950w (2006).

military commission with subject-matter jurisdiction, has become the primary focus of legal challenges to the commissions.[77]

D. PROCEDURAL ASPECTS OF TRIAL OF TERRORISTS BY MILITARY COURTS

The procedural framework for trial by military commission was the primary focus of criticism and challenge to the commission created pursuant to Military Order Number 1. The process established by the Department of Defense to implement Military Order 1[78] resulted in condemnation from numerous military, criminal, and international law experts, and would ultimately lead to the demise of the commission in *Hamdan v. Rumsfeld*.[79] However, almost all of these defects have been cured. This was the result of the combined effect of judicial challenge, the determination by the Supreme Court that these tribunals must comply with the fair trial guarantees of Common Article 3, and the decision by Congress to provide a statutory framework for trial by military commission adopting procedural and evidentiary standards generally analogous to those used during trial by courts-martial.[80]

When President Bush first ordered the use of military commissions, he included within his Order certain procedural requirements for these trials. Although defendants would benefit from a presumption of innocence and a proof beyond a reasonable doubt standard, the overall process outlined by the President's order was far short of the standards established by Congress for trial of U.S. military personnel by courts-martial. This divergence was exacerbated by the implementing directives and instructions promulgated by the Department of Defense. As a result, it became clear that the government had resurrected the process used for trial by military commission last used in the aftermath of World War II.[81]

Perhaps the resurrection of this decades old process was somewhat explained by the fact that this was the first time since World War II that a military commission was convened. What was inexpli-

---

77. *See* United States v. Hamdan, CMCR Case No. 09–002, *available at* http://www.defense.gov/news/CMCR Hamdan.html; United States v. Khadr, *available at* http://www.defense.gov/news/commissionsKhadr.html; United States v. Jawad, CMCR Case No. 08–004, *available at* http://www.defense.gov/news/CMCRJAWAD1.html; United States v. al Bahlul, CMCR Case No. 09–00, *available at* http://www.defense.gov/news/CMCRHAMZA.html.

78. *See* Military Commissions Order No. 1 (MCO No. 1), March 21, 2002; nine Military Commission Instructions (MCI), April 30, 2003; MCO No. 3, February 5, 2004; and MCI 10, March 24, 2006.

79. Hamdan v. Rumsfeld, 548 U.S. 557 (2006).

80. *See* Jennifer K. Elsea, Cong. Research Serv., RL33688, The Military Commissions Act of 2006: Analysis of Procedural Rules and Comparison with Previous DOD Rules and the Uniform Code of Military Justice (2007).

81. *See* Geoffrey S. Corn, *Taking the Bitter with the Sweet: A Law of War Based Analysis of the Military Commission,* 35 Stetson L. Rev. 811 (2006).

cable, however, was how this resurrection effectively disregarded the significant developments in U.S. military justice law over six decades since 1945. During this time period, both the UCMJ and the LOAC evolved to provide certain guideposts for the use of military tribunals to prosecute captured enemy belligerents.

At the international level, the humane treatment mandate of Common Article 3 to the four Geneva Conventions—the treaty provision adopted to address the treatment of captured personnel in non-international armed conflicts—included within its mandate the requirement that any sentence imposed on such a captive be issued "by a regularly constituted court, affording all the judicial guarantees which are recognized as indispensable by civilized peoples."[82] Domestically, Congress had not only significantly improved the process for trial by courts-martial (the primary objective of enacting the UCMJ),[83] but as noted previously had also included in UCMJ a requirement that military commissions generally follow the same procedures applicable to trial by courts-martial.[84] Finally, international human rights law has evolved to prohibit states from using any criminal tribunal that fails to offer fundamental procedural guarantees to criminal defendants (although the U.S. has always asserted that humanitarian law, and not human rights law, is the exclusive source of regulation during periods of armed conflict).[85]

This disparity between the process established for the original military commissions and contemporary international and domestic legal obligations related to trial of captured enemy belligerents provided the impetus for the Supreme Court's decision in *Hamdan v. Rumsfeld*.[86] This case arose out of Hamdan's assertion, *inter alia,* that the rule that permitted his exclusion from his trial for reasons of security violated both Common Article 3 and Article 36 of the UCMJ.[87] The government responded that Hamdan could not claim the protections of Common Article 3 because common article 3 did not apply to the armed conflict with al Qaeda, and that the President was not bound by Article 36 of the UCMJ because

---

82. Convention for the Amelioration of the Condition of the Wounded and Sick in Armed forces in the Field, art. 3 opened for signature Aug. 12, 1949, 6 U.S.T. 3114, 75 U.N.T.S. 31; Convention of the Amelioration of the Condition of the Wounded, Sick, and Shipwrecked Members of Armed Forces at Sea, art 3 opened for signature Aug. 12, 1949, 6 U.S.T. 3217, 75 U.N.T.S. 85; Convention Relative to the Treatment of Prisoners of War, art. 3 opened for signature Aug. 12, 1949, 6 U.S.T. 3316, 75 U.N.T.S. 135; Convention relative to the Protection of Civilian Persons in Time of War, art. 3 opened for signature August 12, 1949, 6 U.S.T. 3516, 75 U.N.T.S. 287, reprinted in ADAM ROBERTS & RICHARD GUELFF, DOCUMENTS ON THE LAWS OF WAR (3d ed. Oxford 2000).

83. *See generally* LAWRENCE J. MORRIS, MILITARY JUSTICE: A GUIDE TO THE ISSUES, 1–14 (Santa Barbara, CA 2010).

84. 10 U.S.C. § 836.

85. Hamdan v. Rumsfeld, 548 U.S. 557, 620 n.48 (2006).

86. *See* Hamdan v. Rumsfeld, 548 U.S. 557 (2006).

87. *Id.* at 567.

Hamdan was not a prisoner of war.[88] The Supreme Court rejected both of these arguments.[89]

First, the Court held that Common Article 3 applied in "contradistinction" from Common Article 2 and therefore applied to any armed conflict that was not international in the meaning of common article 2, namely inter-state.[90] Second, it rejected the suggestion that the President was not bound by the UCMJ, but instead concluded that Congress, pursuant to its vested authority to make rules for the land and naval forces,[91] had placed limits on the discretion of the President to make rules of procedure for military commissions. Because the government had cited no compelling justification to deviate from procedures established for trial by courts-martial, and because the Court determined that these procedures provided a logical example of a "regularly constituted tribunal" within the meaning of Common Article 3, the Court concluded the process established by the President and the Department of Defense violated both domestic and international law.[92]

In response to the holding, the government terminated all proceedings initiated pursuant to the President's Military Order. Although the Bush Administration sought to resurrect the commission by asking Congress to provide a statutory endorsement to the Military Order, Congress chose instead to enact a comprehensive statutory authorization for trial by military commission; including substantial improvements in the process for such trials: Military Commissions Act of 2006 (MCA).[93]

In choosing to enact military commission procedures analogous to those applicable in courts-martial, Congress must have cognizant the alternate option of resurrecting the Bush military commission risk invalidation. Even had Congress provided statutory authorization for the original commission, thereby opting out of the requirements of Article 36, the process would not have complied with the humane treatment obligation the *Hamdan* Court held applied to the armed conflict with al Qaeda. Nor was Common Article 3 the only source of international humanitarian law relevant to the question of adequate process. Both Additional Protocol I[94] and Additional Protocol II,[95] treaties developed to supplement the Gene-

---

88. *Id.* at 621.

89. *See Id.* at 621–25.

90. *Id.* at 630–31.

91. U.S. Const. art. I, § 8, cl. 14.

92. *Hamdan*, 548 U.S. at 729.

93. MCA at § 3, 10 U.S.C. § 948b(a) (2006).

94. Protocol Additional to the Geneva Conventions of 12 August 1949, and Relating to the Protection of Victims of International Armed Conflict, art. 75, June 8, 1977, 1125 U.N.T.S. 3.

95. Protocol Additional to the Geneva Conventions of 12 August 1949, and Relating to the Protection of Victims of Non–International Armed Conflict, art. 4, June 8, 1977, 1125 U.N.T.S. 609.

va Conventions, include articles that add meaning to the common article 3 fair trial requirement. According to Article 75:

> No sentence may be passed and no penalty may be executed on a person found guilty of a penal offence related to the armed conflict except pursuant to a conviction pronounced by an impartial and regularly constituted court respecting the generally recognized principles of regular judicial procedure . . .[96]

Although the United States is not a party to either of these treaties, a plurality of the *Hamdan* Court nonetheless considered Article 75 a relevant source to assist in defining the meaning of common article 2. As Justice Stevens noted:

> Inextricably intertwined with the question of regular constitution is the evaluation of the procedures governing the tribunal and whether they afford 'all the judicial guarantees which are recognized as indispensable by civilized peoples." Like the phrase "regularly constituted court," this phrase is not defined in the text of the Geneva Conventions. But it must be understood to incorporate at least the barest of those trial protections that have been recognized by customary international law. Many of these are described in Article 75 of Protocol I to the Geneva Conventions of 1949, adopted in 1977. Although the United States declined to ratify Protocol I, its objections were not to Article 75 thereof. Indeed, it appears that the Government "regards the provisions of Article 75 as an articulation of safeguards to which all persons in the hands of an enemy are entitled."[97]

Additional Protocol II includes an analogous provision, expressly applicable to armed conflicts not of an international character (traditionally interpreted by the United States to apply to any armed conflict subject to the regulation of common article 3[98]). According to Article 6, "[N]o sentence shall be passed and no penalty shall be executed on a person found guilty of an offence except pursuant to a conviction pronounced by a court offering the essential guarantees of independence and impartiality."[99]

---

96. Protocol Additional to the Geneva Conventions of 12 August 1949, and Relating to the Protection of Victims of International Armed Conflict, art. 75, June 8, 1977, 1125 U.N.T.S. 3.

97. *Hamdan*, 548 U.S. at 633.

98. *See* Geoffrey S. Corn, *Hamdan, Fundamental Fairness, and the Signifi-* *cance of Additional Protocol II*, THE ARMY LAWYER (Aug. 2006).

99. Protocol Additional to the Geneva Conventions of 12 August 1949, and Relating to the Protection of Victims of Non–International Armed Conflict, art. 4, June 8, 1977, 1125 U.N.T.S. 609.

The *Hamdan* majority clearly considered Article 75 relevant to its assessment of whether the procedures established for trial by military commission complied with the LOAC. The Court held that the military commissions as then constituted "dispense[d] with the principles, articulated in Article 75 and indisputably part of the customary international law, that an accused must, absent disruptive conduct or consent, be present for his trial and must be privy to the evidence against him."[100] The Court was also very concerned about the wholesale disregard for evidentiary protections in the military commissions order. These three failings of the military commissions were sufficient to render them inconsistent with international obligations. The remedy suggested by the decision was to comply with the requirement of Article 36 of the UCMJ: develop procedures analogous to those established for courts-martial. According to the opinion, "[A]t a minimum, a military commission can be "regularly constituted" by the standards of our military justice system only if some practical need explains deviations from court-martial practice."[101] Where following such standards was impracticable, evidence to support that assertion would need to be presented.[102]

Congress heeded the Court's holding when it enacted the MCA. The procedures enacted by the Act were intended to not only resurrect the commissions, but to ensure future trials would be conducted consistent with the requirements of domestic and international law. The MCA indicates that "[T]he procedures for military commissions set forth in this Chapter are based upon the procedures for trial by general courts-martial under Chapter 47 of this title (Uniform Code of Military Justice)."[103] The Act further asserts "[A] military commission established under this chapter is a regularly constituted court affording all the necessary 'judicial guarantees which are recognized as indispensable by civilized peoples' for purposes of common Article 3 of the Geneva Conventions."[104] While this assertion is not necessarily accepted by all critics, particularly by those facing trial by military commissions, it does indicate that the United States now accepts the Common Article 3 as the applicable standard for procedural fairness in for trial by military commission.

The MCA also responded to the three specific objections implicated in *Hamdan*, though again with varying credibility in the view of academics and practitioners. In response to the requirement that the accused be present at trial, section 949d(b) of the MCA provides

100. *See* Hamdan v. Rumsfeld, 548 U.S. 557, 634 (2006).

101. *See* Hamdan v. Rumsfeld, 548 U.S. 557, 632–33 (2006).

102. *See* Hamdan v. Rumsfeld, 548 U.S. 557, 622–24 (2006).

103. MCA 120 Stat. at § 948b(c).

104. MCA 120 Stat. at § 948b(f).

that "[E]xcept as provided in subsections (c) and (e), all proceedings of a military commission under this chapter, including any consultation of the members with the military judge or counsel shall—(A) be in the presence of the accused, defense counsel, and trial counsel, and (B) be made part of the record."[105] Subsection (c) exempts the deliberations on guilt or innocence by the members of the commission (the jury), and subsection (e) allows the judge to "exclude the accused from any portion of a proceeding upon a determination that, after being warned by the military judge, the accused persists in conduct that justifies exclusion from the courtroom—(1) to ensure the physical safety of individuals; or (2) to prevent disruption of the proceedings by the accused."[106]

An accused's access to evidence was also a defect noted by the Supreme Court. The MCA attempts to strike a balance between the protection of national security information and an accused's ability to prepare a defense. Section 949(f) of the 2006 Act contains the provisions on protection of classified information and allows the government to protect the disclosure of "sources, methods, or activities by which the United States acquired the evidence if the military judge finds that (i) the sources, methods, or activities by which the United States acquired the evidence are classified, and (ii) the evidence is reliable."[107] The judge may require the trial counsel to produce an unclassified summary if practicable. As noted below, this section was amended in 2009 to provide even more protection for an accused.

Congress also addressed the difficult issue of statements obtained by torture or coercion, attempting to strike a balance between fairness and the ability to introduce reliable evidence against an accused. The 2006 Act prohibited the introduction of any evidence obtained by torture, but permitted the use of statements obtained by coercion short of torture if made prior to December 30, 2005 (the date the Detainee Treatment Act[108] came into force). However, such statements would be admitted only if the military judge finds that "(1) the totality of the circumstances renders the statement reliable and possessing sufficient probative value; and (2) the interests of justice would best be served by admission of the statement into evidence."[109] For evidence obtained by coercion after that date, a third element was also required—"the interrogation methods used to obtain the statement do not amount to cruel, inhuman, or degrading treatment prohibited by section 1003 of the

---

105. MCA 120 Stat. at § 949d(b).

106. MCA 120 Stat. at § 949d(e).

107. MCA 120 Stat. at § 949d(f)(2)(B).

108. Detainee Treatment Act of 2005, Pub. L. No. 109–148, § 1005(e), 119 Stat. 2680 [hereinafter DTA].

109. MCA 120 Stat. at § 948r(c).

Detainee Treatment Act of 2005."[110] The admissibility of statements obtained by coercion was later prohibited absolutely by the 2009 amendment to the Act.

As will be discussed in greater detail below, as a result of the combined effect of the 2006 and 2009 versions of the MCA, procedures for trial by military commission are now widely considered consistent with all domestic and international legal obligations.[111] This has not, however, eliminated controversy related to the legality of these trials. Instead, it merely shifted the focus of critique to questions related to the jurisdiction for trial by military commission established by Congress.

E. THE LAW OF ARMED CONFLICT, SUBJECT MATTER–JURISDICTION, AND MILITARY TRIBUNALS

The LOAC is and has always been inherently responsive to changing realities of warfare. In a very real sense, rules developed for the regulation of armed hostilities are never truly validated or discredited until they are tested in the "battle laboratory."[112] As a result, some of the most significant developments in the law have occurred in the aftermath of wars. Most experts—indeed many laymen—could identify the post World War II war crimes trials as marking one of these landmark developments: that individuals, and not only the states they serve, bear responsibility for violations of international humanitarian law.[113]

It was not, however, until the end of the Cold War that the concept of individual criminal responsibility for violations of LOAC norms applicable in the context of non-international armed conflicts became a significant component of international legal regulation. In response to the brutal internal conflict in the former Yugoslav republics of Bosnia–Herzegovina and Croatia, the United Nations established the first *ad hoc* international war crimes tribunal since the end of World War II.[114] Like its post-World War II predecessors the International Criminal Tribunal for the Former Yugoslavia (ICTY) was established to impose individual criminal responsibility on participants in those armed conflicts for commis-

110. MCA 120 Stat. at § 948r(d).

111. *See* JENNIFER K. ELSEA, CONG. RESEARCH SERV., THE MILITARY COMMISSIONS ACT OF 2006: ANALYSIS OF PROCEDURAL RULES AND COMPARISON WITH PREVIOUS DOD RULES AND THE UNIFORM CODE OF MILITARY JUSTICE 12 (Sept. 27, 2007).

112. *See generally* LESLIE C. GREEN, THE CONTEMPORARY LAW OF ARMED CONFLICT 59–61 (2d ed. 2000); *see also* INT'L & OPERATIONAL LAW DEP'T, THE JUDGE ADVO-

CATE GEN.'S SCH., LAW OF WAR WORKSHOP DESKBOOK (Bill J. Brian et al. eds., 2004).

113. GARY D. SOLIS, THE LAW OF ARMED CONFLICT: INTERNATIONAL HUMANITARIAN LAW IN WAR (Cambridge Univ. Press 2010).

114. S.C. Res. 827, U.N. Doc. S/RES/827 (May 25, 1993), *available at* http://www.icty.org/x/file/Legal% 20Library/Statute/statute_827_1993_en.pdf.

sion of, *inter alia*, serious LOAC violations.[115] The ICTY would rule that its jurisdiction was not limited to offenses committed in the context of an inter-state armed conflict. Instead, for the first time in history, the concept of individual criminal responsibility for violating the law of armed conflict was extended to the realm of intra-state, or non-international armed conflicts.[116]

In light of the brutality historically associated with non-international armed conflicts, and in particular civil wars, this extension seemed pragmatic and justified. Nonetheless, it represented a landmark development in both the LOAC and the concept of individual criminal responsibility. Added to this extension of jurisdiction was an expanded scope of norms applicable to these armed conflicts. In its first opinion, the ICTY concluded that many rules developed to regulate the conduct of hostilities during international armed conflicts had "migrated" into the realm of non-international armed conflicts.[117] This established both the foundation for enhanced accountability for individuals participating in these type conflicts, and expansion of the LOAC regulation of non-international armed conflicts generally.[118]

The jurisprudence of the ICTY and its sister tribunal the International Criminal Tribunal for Rwanda unleashed a new wave of LOAC development. This development addressed the reality that the regulation of hostilities and the protection of war victims must be driven by the existence of armed conflict, irrespective of its characterization as internal or international.[119] In fact, in the years following the ICTY's first decision of *Prosecutor v. Tadic*,[120] a remarkable shift in the law occurred. Prior to that decision, the law of non-international armed conflict was understood as a minor offshoot of the law of international armed conflict, focused almost exclusively on the most fundamental protections of individuals not participating in hostilities.[121] Today, the understanding is inversed:

---

115. S.C. Res. 827, ¶ 2, U.N. Doc. S/RES/827 (May 25, 1993).

116. Updated Statute of the International Criminal Tribunal for The Former Yugoslavia art. 5, Sept. 29, 2008, *available at* http://www.icty.org/x/file/Legal%20Library/Statute/statute_sept 08_Den.pdf.

117. *See* Prosecutor v. Tadic, Case No. IT–94–1–AR72, Appeal on Jurisdiction (Oct. 2, 1995), at para. 70, *reprinted in* 35 I.L.M. 32 (1996).

118. GARY D. SOLIS, THE LAW OF ARMED CONFLICT: INTERNATIONAL HUMANITARIAN LAW IN WAR (Cambridge Univ. Press 2010); *see* also Geoffrey S. Corn, Taking the Bitter with the Sweet: A Law of War Based Analysis of the Military

Commission, 35 STETSON L. REV. 811 (2006).

119. *See generally* S.C. Res. 955, U.N. Doc. S/RES/955 (Nov. 8, 1994), *available at* http://69.94.11.53/ENGLISH/Resolutions/955e.htm.

120. Prosecutor v. Tadic, Case No. IT–94–1, Appeals Chamber Judgment, (July 15, 1999).

121. *See* Commentary: I Geneva Convention for the Amelioration of the Condition of the Wounded and Sick in Armed Forces in the Field 19–23 (Jean S. Pictet ed., 1960). A similar Commentary was published for each of the four Geneva Conventions. Because Articles 2 and 3 are identical—or common—to

the fundamental norms applicable to both types of armed conflict have become in large measure synonymous, and it is the disparities between LOAC norms applicable to these two types of armed conflicts that are increasingly minor.[122]

The operative word is norms, for the applicability of treaty rules established to regulate international armed conflicts-including all but one article in each of the Geneva Conventions[123]—cannot simply be extended to the realm of non-international armed conflict by fiat. But because so many of these rules and those of other LOAC treaty provisions reflect underlying customary LOAC norms, the difference between operational standards applicable to all armed conflicts has become virtually transparent.[124] More simply, armed conflict triggers battlefield regulation, and when states or non-state groups use the tools of war, they must follow the rules of war.

These developments of the law also planted the seed for the next step forward in realm of individual criminal responsibility: extending this liability to transnational terrorist operatives. When in response to the terrorist attacks of September 11th 2001 President Bush determined that the United States was engaged in an armed conflict, the prior extension of international criminal responsibility to non-international armed conflict provided the foundation for a new approach to prosecuting terrorists. President Bush explicitly signaled this intersection of war crimes jurisdiction and a revised assessment of the nature of the struggle against transnational terrorism when he issued Military Order Number 1 directing the Secretary of Defense to create a military commission for the trial of terrorist operatives as war criminals. In that order, the President determined it was necessary:

---

each Convention, however, the Commentary for these articles is also identical in each of the four Commentaries.

122. *See* MICHAEL N. SCHMITT, CHARLES H.B. GARRAWAY & YORAM DINSTEIN, THE MANUAL ON THE LAW OF NON-INTERNATIONAL ARMED CONFLICT WITH COMMENTARY (San Remo–International Institute of Humanitarian Law 2006); *see also Geoffrey S. Corn & Eric T. Jensen, Transnational Armed Conflict: A 'Principled' Approach to the Regulation of Counter–Terror Combat Operations,* (Israel Law Review, forthcoming), *available at* http://papers.ssrn.com/sol3/papers.cfm?abstract_id=1256380; *see also* GARY D. SOLIS, THE LAW OF ARMED CONFLICT: INTERNATIONAL HUMANITARIAN LAW IN WAR (Cambridge Univ. Press 2010)

123. For example, of the 143 articles in the Prisoner of War Convention, only one (common article 3) applies to non-international armed conflicts.

124. The most significant exception to this trend is qualification for status as a prisoner of war and the accordant combatant immunity derived from that status. This status is and will almost certainly continue to be restricted to belligerents involved in international armed conflicts. *See* Major Geoffrey S. Corn & Major Michael L. Smidt, *"To Be Or Not To Be, That Is The Question",* *Contemporary Military Operations and the Status of Captured Personnel,* 1999 ARMY LAWYER 1 (1999).

for individuals subject to this order pursuant to section 2 hereof to be detained, and, when tried, to be tried for violations of the laws of war and other applicable laws by military tribunals.[125]

An analogous invocation of LOAC based liability provided the jurisdictional foundation for the MCA of 2006, which provides:

PURPOSE.—This chapter establishes procedures governing the use of military commissions to try alien unprivileged enemy belligerents for violations of the law of war and other offenses triable by military commission.[126]

This assertion of war crimes jurisdiction has already been the basis for several trials and convictions of *al Qaeda* operatives.[127]

The scope of criminal prohibition derived from the law of non-international armed conflict is not, however, unlimited. Historically, military commissions were used to try violations of the laws and customs of war. Accordingly, even assuming *arguendo* that an armed conflict exists between the United States and al Qaeda it must, by virtue of the fact that al Qaeda is not a state, be a non-international armed conflict. As a result, only offenses derived from LOAC norms applicable to this type of armed conflict should legitimately be subject to trial by military commission. However, the subject-matter jurisdiction of both the original military commission established by President Bush, and the subsequent military commission established by the MCA, challenged this premise through an expansive definition of offenses subject to trial by the commissions.

The limited nature of military tribunal jurisdiction over captured enemy belligerents is central to the UCMJ's provision for the use of such tribunals.[128] While the Code vests General Courts–Martial with jurisdiction to try captured enemy belligerents for pre-capture misconduct, it explicitly limits that jurisdiction to violations of the laws and customs of war.[129] Furthermore, as noted by the *Hamdan* majority, Article 21 of the Code includes an analogous limitation on the exercise of concurrent jurisdiction of military commissions to try captured enemy belligerents ("there is nothing in the text or legislative history of the AUMF even hinting that

125. Military Order, November 13, 2001, Detention, Treatment, and Trial of Certain non-Citizens in the War Against Terrorism, Sec. 1(a), 66 Fed. Reg. 57833 (Nov. 16, 2001).

126. 10 U.S.C. § 948b.

127. 10 U.S.C. §§ 948a–950w; *see generally* U.S. v. Mohammed, U.S. v. Binalshibh, U.S. v. Ali, U.S. v. al Hawsawi, U.S. v. Hicks, *available at* http://www.defenselink.mil/news/commissions.html.

128. UCMJ 10 U.S.C. §§ 801–950 (2000).

129. *Id.* at § 818.

Congress intended to expand or alter the authorization set forth in Article 21 of the UCMJ."[130]).

The authority to convene military tribunals for the trial and punishment of alleged war crimes committed by *any* person is consistent with the historic function of these tribunals As the U.S. Supreme Court recognized in *Hamdan*, this history provides a sufficient foundation for the use of military courts to try war crimes. The Court also emphasize, however, the jurisdiction of such tribunals is therefore limited to acts or omissions that violate the laws of war, a conclusion that was equally central in *Ex parte Quirin*.[131] As the Court noted in that opinion:

> We have no occasion now to define with meticulous care the ultimate boundaries of the jurisdiction of military tribunals to try persons according to the law of war ... *We hold only that those particular acts constitute an offense against the law of war which the Constitution authorizes to be tried by military commission.*[132]

Not even *Hamdan's* plurality seriously questioned this basic jurisdictional premise of an armed conflict between the United States and al Qaeda, at least beginning on September 11, 2001.[133] Indeed, by focusing on the nature of the allegation of conspiracy and the procedural defects of the commission, *Hamdan v. Rumsfeld* was, if anything, an implicit endorsement of the treatment of the struggle as an armed conflict subject to the LOAC.[134] Accordingly, assuming terrorist operatives are in fact engaged in a non-international armed conflict, complying with this limitation required alleging offenses derived from the LOAC applicable to such conflicts. This provides a limited, although increasingly expanding body of treaty rules and norms for which war crimes liability may be imposed. The most obvious source of liability would be violations of the principle of humanity as reflected in Common Article 3.[135]

130. *Hamdan*, 548 U.S. at 593.

131. Ex parte Quirin, 317 U.S. 1 (1942).

132. *Id.* at 45–46 (emphasis added).

133. *See Hamdan*, 548 U.S. 557.

134. *Id.* There may be rational explanations for why the Court seemed to avoid any meaningful critique of the jurisdictional foundation of trial of *al Qaeda* terrorists as war criminals—first among these the apparent concession of jurisdiction by Hamdan's lawyers. In its opinion, the Court noted that "[Petitioner] concedes that a court-martial constituted in accordance with the Uniform Code of Military Justice (UCMJ) ... would have authority to try him." Because such court-martial jurisdiction could be based only on applicability of the law of war to Hamdan, this one sentence reveals that the jurisdictional predicated for trying Hamdan as a war criminal was never challenged by his lawyers.

135. *See* Geneva Convention for the Amelioration of the Condition of the Wounded and Sick in Armed Forces in the Field, August 12, 1949, art. 3, T.I.A.S. 3362 [hereinafter GWS], *reprinted in* Department of the Army Pamphlet 27–1, TREATIES GOVERNING LAND WARFARE, (December 1956); Geneva Convention for the Amelioration of the Condition of Wounded, Sick, and Shipwrecked Members at Sea, August 12,

Common Article 3's humane treatment mandate represents a "compulsory minimum"[136] standard of conduct for any and all participants in any armed conflict—not necessarily as a matter of treaty obligation,[137] but as a customary principle of international law. This conclusion is only reinforced by the fact that humane treatment represents the very purpose of the Geneva Conventions.[138] It prohibits any act of inhumanity directed against individuals not actively participating in hostilities, and is considered a universal obligation for participants in armed conflict. In the context of any armed conflict, common article 3 therefore provides a basis for imposing criminal responsibility in response to almost all conduct that would fall under the pragmatic definition of terrorism when such acts of terror are presumptively directed against noncombatants.

Offenses based on violations of common article 3 could therefore include the taking of the airline passengers as hostages; the targeting of structures filled with civilians, or, in the language of the law, the targeting of "persons taking no active part in hostilities"; the terrorizing of the civilian population; and the killing of the thousands of innocent civilians on September 11th. If the attacks of September 11th occurred in the context on a non-

1949, art. 3, T.I.A.S. 3363 [hereinafter GWS Sea], *reprinted in* Department of the Army Pamphlet 27–1, TREATIES GOVERNING LAND WARFARE, (December 1956); Geneva Convention Relative to the Treatment of Prisoners of War, August 12, 1949, art. 3, T.I.A.S. 3364 [hereinafter GPW], *reprinted in* Department of the Army Pamphlet 27–1, TREATIES GOVERNING LAND WARFARE, (December 1956); Geneva Convention Relative to the Treatment of Civilian Persons in Time of War, August 12, 1949, art. 3, T.I.A.S. 3365 [hereinafter GC], *reprinted in* Department of the Army Pamphlet 27–1, TREATIES GOVERNING LAND WARFARE, (December 1956).

136. Prosecutor v. Tadic, Case No. IT–94–1–AR72, Appeal on Jurisdiction, ¶ 94 (Oct. 2, 1995), *reprinted in* 35 I.L.M. 32, 62 (1996) at 37.

137. It is certainly plausible to assert the applicability of Common Article 3, and not merely the principles reflected therein, to any armed conflict not of an international character, even if not occurring in the territory of a High Contracting Party. *See* Derek Jinks, *September 11 and the Laws of War*, 28 YALE J. INT'L L. 1 (2003) (citing Harold Hongju Koh, *The Spirit of the Laws*, 43 HARV. INT'L L. J. 23, 26 (2002)).

In this regard, it is also worth noting that the subject of the binding nature of Common Article 3 has been a significant issue for the ICRC. In fact, in the September–October, 1978 edition of the *International Review of the Red Cross*, the International Committee for the Red Cross along with the League of Red Cross Societies published the *Fundamental Rules of Humanitarian Law Applicable In Armed Conflicts*, 206 INTERNATIONAL REVIEW OF THE RED CROSS 246 (September–October 1978), *reprinted in* Adam Roberts and Richard Guelff, DOCUMENTS ON THE LAWS OF WAR, 469–470 (1989). The International Committee for the Red Cross and the League of Red Cross Societies, while emphasizing the informal nature of the rules, noted the rules "express in useful condensed form some of the most fundamental principles of international humanitarian law governing armed conflicts." The rules are based on the four Geneva Conventions of 1949, the two Protocols Additional to the Geneva Conventions of 1977, the Hague Regulations, and customary international law.

138. Common Article 3, *supra* note 135.

international armed conflict, the LOAC proscribed any act that deliberately targeted civilians or civilian property. Accordingly, those who planned, encouraged, and supported them, violated this minimum LOAC standard of wartime conduct.[139]

Other LOAC norms considered fundamental or foundational have, in the language of the ICTY, "migrated" from the realm of international to non-international armed conflicts.[140] These norms extend beyond the humane treatment obligation to regulate methods and means of warfare. Prohibitions against deliberate targeting of civilians or civilian property, launching attacks expected to produce excessive incidental injury to civilians, use of indiscriminate weapons, and use of weapons calculated to cause unnecessary suffering would all fall into this category.[141] In addition, LOAC

---

139. It is the opinion of these authors that the offense of "unlawful belligerency" would be both much more difficult to sustain, and unnecessary to charge due to the clear applicability of Common Article 3 as a basis for criminal prosecution. The essence of a charge of "unlawful belligerency" is that individuals engaged in armed conflict without satisfying the international law standard for identifying themselves as members of a combatant force. In support of this offense, there has been much said and much written about the "four criteria" from the Geneva Prisoner of War Convention's Article 4 that must be satisfied by conflict participants. However, the criteria relied upon to assert that members of Al Quida and the Taliban engaged in unlawful belligerency—that they failed to carry arms openly, wear fixed insignia recognizable from a distance, operate under effective command, and comply with the law of war—are requirements that apply, by the terms of the Convention, only to conflicts of an international (state versus state) character, and not to internal armed conflicts.

This is illustrated by the fact that these criteria are used to determine when a member of a insurgent or militia group becomes entitled to status as an enemy prisoner of war. However, by the terms of both treaty and customary international law, warriors who engage in non-international armed conflicts are not now, nor have they ever been, legally entitled to prisoner of war status (and the accompanying combatant immunity) upon capture, regardless of their uniform or conduct. It is a simple fact of international law that such warriors receive no immunity for their warlike acts,

and therefore are fully susceptible to prosecution for violation of domestic law based on the actions they engaged in while involved in conflict. Based on this, it is difficult to understand how engaging in warlike activities while in civilian clothes during a non-international armed conflict amounts to an offense under international law. There simply is no requirement to be in uniform because there is no benefit of combatant immunity for wearing a uniform.

It seems that the true objection to the conduct of al Qaeda and their Taliban sponsors was not so much who they were, but what they did. Their attacks on non-combatants were certainly unlawful. While they may have therefore been "unlawful belligerents" in the pragmatic sense of the term, they were not in the legal sense of the term. Instead, their crimes were violations of Common Article 3, and it is this provision of the law of war which should form the basis for any subsequent prosecution.

140. Statute of the International Tribunal for the former Yugoslavia, adopted by S.C. Res. 827, U.N. SCOR, 48th Sess., 3217th mtg., U.N. Doc. S/RES/827 (1993); see also Geoffrey S. Corn & Eric Talbot Jensen, *Transnational Armed Conflict: A 'Principled' Approach to the Regulation of Counter–Terror Combat Operations*, 42 ISRAEL L. REV. 45 (2009).

141. *See generally* Geoffrey S. Corn & Eric Talbot Jensen, *Transnational Armed Conflict: A 'Principled' Approach to the Regulation of Counter–Terror Combat Operations*, 42 ISRAEL L. REV. 45

prohibitions against perfidy and treachery, such as feigning surrender or misuse of a protected emblem, are also applicable to non-international armed conflicts.[142] Accordingly, violation of these norms in the context of non-international armed conflict provides an equally legitimate basis for war crimes accountability of transnational terrorist operatives.

All of these offenses are reflected in the punitive articles of the MCA.[143] Although the assertion that the struggle against terrorism triggers the law of non-international armed conflict remains highly controversial, and therefore even these offenses are considered invalid by many experts, they are at least based on accepted norms of international law. What is far more contentious is the inclusion by Congress in the punitive articles offenses that lack a connection to accepted principles of international law. Whether Congress may properly vest the military commission with jurisdiction over such offenses is a far more complicated issue, and one that is the focal point of current litigation.

At the most basic level, a war crime is a violation of the laws and customs of war subjecting the violator to individual criminal responsibility. Some experts assert that any violation of the law of war amounts to a war crime,[144] an assertion that finds support in the U.S. Army Field Manual 27–10, the Law of Land Warfare.[145] This assertion is overbroad,[146] and contradicted by both provisions of the Geneva Conventions establishing obligations for the suppression of certain treaty breaches, and on the exclusion of certain minor violations of the law of war from the definition of war crimes enacted by Congress in amendments to the War Crimes Act.[147] Prior to November of 2002, however, there was virtually no debate that the jurisdiction of a military commission over the pre-capture conduct of enemy personnel was limited to violations of the laws and customs of war, a conclusion emphasized by the Supreme Court in *Hamdan* when Justice Stevens noted that the function of a

(2009); *see also* MICHAEL N. SCHMITT, CHARLES H.B. GARRAWAY & YORAM DINSTEIN, THE MANUAL ON THE LAW OF NON-INTERNATIONAL ARMED CONFLICT WITH COMMENTARY (San Remo–International Institute of Humanitarian Law 2006).

142. *See generally* Geoffrey S. Corn & Eric Talbot Jensen, *Transnational Armed Conflict: A 'Principled' Approach to the Regulation of Counter–Terror Combat Operations,* 42 ISRAEL L. REV. 45 (2009); *see also* MICHAEL N. SCHMITT, CHARLES H.B. GARRAWAY & YORAM DINSTEIN, THE MANUAL ON THE LAW OF NON-INTERNATIONAL ARMED CONFLICT WITH COMMENTARY (San Remo–International Institute of Humanitarian Law 2006).

143. MCA 120 Stat. at § 948q.

144. JORDAN PAUST & M.C. BASSIOUNI ET. AL, HUMAN RIGHTS MODULE: CRIMES AGAINST HUMANITY, GENOCIDE, OTHER CRIMES AGAINST HUMAN RIGHTS, AND WAR CRIMES (2001).

145. U.S. Dept. of Army, Field Manual 27–10, The Law of Land Warfare, para. 499 (July 1956).

146. Gary D. Solis, The Law of Armed Conflict: International Humanitarian Law in War (Cambridge Univ. Press 2010).

147. *See* MCA 120 Stat. at § 6(b)(1).

military commission was limited to determining "whether the defendant has violated the law of war."[148]:

This jurisdictional limitation seems logical. Trial of captured enemy personnel by the detaining power's own military tribunals for pre-capture misconduct is based on two assumptions. First, the pre-capture misconduct was subject to the proscriptions of international law—or more precisely the LOAC. Second, the use of a military tribunal is logically related to the necessity of holding enemy belligerents accountable for their pre-capture violation of the rules that regulate the conduct of hostilities. Historic use of military tribunals by U.S. military commanders to prosecute captured enemy belligerents—dating as far back as the American Revolution and continuing through World War II—confirms the significance of these two assumptions.[149]

As Justice Steven's noted in *Hamdan,* military commissions have also been used in other situations: to try civilians during periods of belligerent occupation and as courts of last resort during periods of domestic martial law.[150] Use in these situations did not require a link between the laws and customs of war and legitimate subject-matter jurisdiction. Instead, subject-matter jurisdiction extended to the prohibitions established by the occupation or martial law commander.

When, however, a military commission is used as what the Supreme Court characterized in *Hamdan* as a law of war court, establishing that the alleged offense is derived from the law of war has always been regarded as an essential jurisdictional predicate for the legitimate use of such tribunals. According to a plurality of the Justices in *Hamdan,* in order to satisfy this predicate, the allegation must rest on a two prong foundation: first, that the LOAC applied at the time of the alleged misconduct; second, that the defendant's acts or omissions violated an established and internationally accepted LOAC proscription established.[151]

In *Hamdan v. Rumsfeld,* the Supreme Court held that the military commission established pursuant to Military Order Number 1 violated the law upon which the commission is based: the common law of war. A majority of Justices held that the trial process created by the Department of Defense pursuant to the Order[152] violated not only Article 36 if the UCMJ, but also common

148. *Hamdan,* 548 U.S. at 596.

149. *See* Michael O. Lacey, *Military Commissions: A Historical Survey,* 2002 ARMY LAW. 41, 47 (Mar. 2002); *see also* JENNIFER ELSEA, CONG. RESEARCH SERV., RL 31191, TERRORISM AND THE LAW OF WAR: TRYING TERRORISTS AS WAR CRIMINALS BEFORE MILITARY COMMISSIONS (2001).

150. *Hamdan,* 548 U.S. at 597.

151. *Hamdan,* 548 U.S. at 598–604.

152. The Department of Defense promulgated several orders and instructions setting out the applicable law and procedures for trial by military commission, including Military Commissions Order No. 1 (MCO No. 1), March 21,

article 3's requirement that when trying individuals captured in the context of non-international armed conflicts, "judgement [is] pronounced by a regularly constituted court, affording all the judicial guarantees which are recognized as indispensable by civilized peoples."[153]

Only a plurality of the Court addressed the legitimacy of the subject-matter jurisdiction established by the Department of Defense, specifically whether conspiracy to violate the law of war qualified as an offense within the jurisdiction of a military commission. Justice Stevens began this portion of the opinion by emphasizing those two critical predicates for establishing valid commission jurisdiction: that the alleged misconduct had to occur within the context of an armed conflict (not in a time period prior to the initiation of armed conflict); and that when used as a law of war court, offenses be based on established violations of the law of war. According to the plurality, the government failed to carry the burden to prove either of these predicates. First, it failed to establish the existence of an armed conflict between the United States and al Qaeda dating as far back as 1998 (the date the alleged conspiracy began). Second, it failed to convince the plurality that conspiracy to violate the laws of war qualified as a well accepted violation of the laws and customs of war.

Justice Kennedy broke from the majority for this aspect of the decision.[154] As a result, the proper scope of military commission subject matter jurisdiction remains uncertain. In addition, Justice Stevens included in the plurality opinion a qualifier of potentially profound significance: the lack of express statutory authorization for the commission. According to the opinion,

> The charge's shortcomings are not merely formal, but are indicative of a broader inability on the Executive's part here to satisfy the most basic precondition—*at least in the absence of specific congressional authorization*—for establishment of military commissions: military necessity.[155]

Whether this qualification means that statutory authorization eliminates the need for a link to the LOAC, or that such authorization justifies the use of military commissions to try war crimes far removed in time and distance from the field of battle is unclear. Because the Court placed such emphasis on the limited nature of

2002; nine Military Commission Instructions (MCI), April 30, 2003; MCO No. 3, February 5, 2004; and MCI 10, March 24, 2006.

153. Convention Relative to the Treatment of Prisoners of War, art. 3 opened for signature Aug. 12, 1949, 6 U.S.T. 3316, 75 U.N.T.S. 135, reprinted in ADAM ROBERTS & RICHARD GUELFF, DOCUMENTS ON THE LAWS OF WAR (3d. ed. Oxford 2000).

154. *Hamdan*, 548 U.S. at 655 (Kennedy, J., concurring).

155. *Id.* at 612 (plurality opinion) (emphasis added).

military jurisdiction throughout the opinion, it seems unlikely that the plurality was endorsing an expansion of subject-matter jurisdiction beyond well accepted war crimes. Nonetheless, even if these Justices consider the violation of an established LOAC rule a jurisdictional requirement even when offenses are enumerated by statute, there was not sufficient consensus on this point to garner a majority vote.

Although lacking the votes necessary to be part of the holding, the plurality's emphasis on the limited jurisdiction of a military commission appears to have influenced the congressional response to the decision. Almost immediately following *Hamdan*, Congress resurrected the military commission by enacting the MCA of 2006. However, Congress rejected the President's request to simply provide a statutory endorsement of his Military Order Number 1, and instead used the MCA to cure many of the procedural flaws of Bush's military commission. Subject matter jurisdiction was also a major component of the Act, and in an apparent effort to ensure that future offenses would be endorsed by the judiciary, Congress provided that:

> This chapter establishes procedures governing the use of military commissions to try alien unlawful enemy combatants engaged in hostilities against the United States for violations of the law of war *and other offenses* triable by military commission.[156]

In a separate provision of the Act, Congress emphasized that the offenses enumerated in the punitive articles of the statute were not new and had always been subject to trial by military commission. This reveals a potential internal inconsistency. First, Congress establishes jurisdiction for offenses that are *not* violations of the law of war. In fact, the punitive articles of the MCA include many offenses that have never been alleged as war crimes in any other context and are not included among the war crimes enumerated as part of the Rome Statute for the International Criminal Court.[157] These offenses include, among others, hijacking, material support to terrorism, perjury, and obstruction of justice.[158] However, the Act then declares that all of the offenses enumerated are offenses traditionally subject to trial by military commission, implying that it merely codified existing war crimes.[159] As will be explained below, this latter provision has led the government to proffer a unique definition of the law of war in support of a number of offenses

---

156. 10 U.S.C. § 948b(a) (2006) (emphasis added).

157. Rome Statute of the International Criminal Court, July 17, 1998, 2187 U.N.T.S. 3.

158. MCA at § 950v.

159. 10 U.S.C. § 950p.

arguably not recognized by the broader international community as war crimes.[160]

The MCA has certainly added important clarity to the government's position on the jurisdictional foundation for the use of military commissions. First, it indicates congressional support for treating the struggle against al Qaeda as an armed conflict by invoking the laws and customs of war as a source of criminal proscription applicable to captured al Qaeda operatives. Second, it reflect the express determination by Congress that many of the offenses defined by the statute qualify as violations of the law of war in the context of the armed conflict with al Qaeda.

However, not only did inclusion "other offenses triable by military commission" in the MCA create legal uncertainty for the ongoing commission trials. Other provisions of the Act also exacerbate the concerns that the MCA reflects an overbroad assertion of military jurisdiction. Most significantly, the Act fails to define when the armed conflict with al Qaeda began, a determination that according to the *Hamdan* plurality operates as a critical demarcation point for the initiation of military commission jurisdiction. Instead, the Act imposes responsibility for making this determination on the finder of fact by including "in the context of an armed conflict" within the material elements of each offense. Because the *Hamdan* plurality treated this fact as a jurisdictional requirement, it seems odd that the Act defines this as a factual element instead of a question of law.

Had Congress limited the subject-matter jurisdiction of the military commission to violations of Common Article 3 and those fundamental LOAC norms considered applicable to non-international armed conflicts, much of the contemporary criticisms to commission prosecutions might have been averted. What seems almost certain is that objections to jurisdiction would have been focused almost exclusively on the legitimacy of characterizing the struggle against terrorism as an armed conflict. Because this question was arguably resolved in favor of the government by *Hamdan*, it would have been virtually impossible for defendants to effectively challenge the jurisdiction of the commission.

However, this was not the case. Instead, expanding the range of offenses available to military prosecutors beyond this limited source of international proscription exacerbated the criticism of the commission's jurisdiction. The questionable nature of this expan-

---

160. *See* United States v. Ali Hamza Ahmed Suliman, United States Court of Military Commission Review, CMCR Case No. 09–001 (Brief on behalf of Respondent), (21 October 2009) (in which the government argues *inter alia* that Congress is authorized to adopt a broader definition of war crimes than that of the international community and that such definition is entitled to substantial judicial deference).

sion is exemplified by two offenses that have been central to military commission prosecutions: murder in violation of the laws of war and material support to terrorism.[161]

F. STRETCHING THE LIMITS OF SUBSTANTIVE LEGITIMACY[162]

1. MURDER IN VIOLATION OF THE LAW OF WAR

Few would doubt that murder in violation of the law of war should be subject to criminal sanction, nor that such an offense falls within the jurisdiction of a military commission convened as a law of war court. The law of war certainly does not sanction all killings, but instead only those justified by the necessity of war. As a result, it is an axiom of the LOAC that deliberate killings not justified by the necessities of war fall outside the scope of immunity afforded to lawful combatants. Accordingly, the perpetrator of such killings should (or perhaps must) be subject to criminal sanction for violation of the law that proscribes such killings.

However, when Congress enacted the MCA and included the offense of Murder in Violation of the Law of War in the punitive articles, it resulted in a somewhat misleading effect. The title of the offense suggests that the LOAC provides the source of criminal proscription for the offense. While it is axiomatic that all killings unjustified by the necessities of war are unlawful, and equally axiomatic that non-state belligerents are not entitled to claim the benefit of lawful combatant immunity[163] (thereby subjecting them to criminal sanction for their violent acts even when committed pursuant to a claim of military necessity), the fact that a killing is a violation of law does not *ipso facto* render it a violation of *international* law. However, this is precisely the theory of criminal liability invoked by this provision of the Act.

The current offense of Murder in Violation of the Law of War is the successor to an offense established by Department of Defense Instruction for the original military commission: Murder by an Unprivileged Belligerent.[164] The thread that connects these offenses is the asserted legal theory of international criminality: any killing by a belligerent who does not qualify for the legal privilege of participating in hostilities (a privilege reserved for state actors) is

161. *See generally* 10 U.S.C. § 950v(15), (25) (2006).

162. For an excellent analysis of the legitimate scope of military commission jurisdiction (with a particular emphasis on the history of exercising such jurisdiction), *see generally* David W. Glazier, *Still a Bad Idea: Military Commissions Under the Obama Administration*, (forthcoming), *available at:* http://papers.ssrn.com/sol3/papers.cfm?abstract_id=1658590

163. United States v. Lindh, 210 F. Supp. 2d 780 (E.D. Va. 2002).

164. U.S. Dep't of Defense, Military Commission Instruction No. 2 § 6(B)(3) (April 30, 2003), *available at* http://www.defenselink.mil/news/May2003/d20030430milcominstno2.pdf.

ipso facto a violation of the LOAC, *per se* unlawful, and therefore murder subject to trial by military commission. This theory is reflected in the following explanation for this offense contained in the Manual for Military Commissions, the regulation that implements the MCA: "A 'violation of the law of war,' may be established by proof of the status of the accused as an unlawful combatant ..."[165] It is also reflected in this excerpt from the Manual:

> It is generally accepted international practice that unlawful enemy combatants may be prosecuted for offenses associated with armed conflicts, such as murder; such unlawful enemy combatants do not enjoy combatant immunity because they have failed to meet the requirements of lawful combatancy under the law of war.[166]

The focal point for debate over whether this theory is in fact "generally" accepted, or is a distortion of the LOAC, is the case of *United States v. Omar Ahmed Khadr*.[167] Khadr is charged with a violation of Section 948t(15) of the MCA, which defines this offense as follows:

> MURDER IN VIOLATION OF THE LAW OF WAR.—Any person subject to this chapter who intentionally kills one or more persons, including privileged belligerents, in violation of the law of war shall be punished by death or such other punishment as a military commission under this chapter may direct.[168]

The allegations stem from a firefight in Afghanistan. Khadr, at that time 14 years old, participated in defending an alleged al Qaeda safe house under attack by U.S. military forces. During the engagement, it is alleged that Khadr threw a hand grenade that killed one of the assaulting U.S. soldiers. Nothing in the allegation indicates Khadr engaged in any treachery or perfidy; in effect, Khadr is charged with the war crime of murder for killing an attacking opponent during a 'fair fight'.

Khadr contests the assertion that his conduct violated the law of war. Contrary to the comment extracted above, he asserts that there is no "general acceptance" for such an offense in the context of non-international armed conflict. While he concedes that participating in hostilities without the privilege afforded to lawful combatants results in liability for violations of domestic law (the law of the state where the act occurred or the law of the state of the victim

165. U.S. Dep't of Defense, The Manual for Military Commissions § 6(a)(16)(c) (Jan. 18, 2007), *available at* http://www.defenselink.mil/pubs/pdfs/The%20Manual%20for%20Military%20Commissions.pdf.

166. *Id.* at § 6(a)(13)(d).

167. United States v. Khadr, *available at* http://www.defense.gov/news/commissionsKhadr.html.

168. 10 U.S.C. § 948t(15).

through some long arm statute), he argues that the mere act of fighting without privilege is not a violation of international law.

This theory of international criminal liability is dubious. Even if participation in hostilities without privilege is a violation of *international* law in the context of international armed conflict (a theory that is derived from the U.S. Supreme Court's *Quirin*[169] decision, which upheld the trial of German saboteurs for the war crime of "unlawful belligerency" during the Second World War), it has never been extended to the context of non-international armed conflict.[170] Even in the context of international armed conflict this offense has never been widely or "generally" endorsed.[171]

Khadr (and other defendant's facing similar allegations) has challenged the government to identify contemporary precedent for extending the theory to non-international armed conflict, a challenge that the government has been unable to answer. Instead, the government has responded with two arguments. First, that any defense challenge was foreclosed once Congress codified the offense in the MCA. According to the government, Congress' authority to define and punish offenses in violation of the law of nations justifies substantial deference to the decision to characterize this conduct as a violation of the law of war, which is based not on the define and punish clause but on the aggregate war powers vested in the political branches of the government:

> In its Response to the Government's Supplemental Brief, the Defense argues that Congress' authority to confer subject matter jurisdiction on military commissions is strictly limited to offenses against the Law of Nations. The Defense reaches this conclusion because it mistakenly locates the source of Congress' power to authorize military commissions in the Define and Punish clause of the U.S. Constitution. U.S. Const. Art. I, § 8, cl.10. In fact, the constitutional authority for the use of military commissions derives from the War Powers of the political branches. Of course, when Congress deals with conduct that violates the Law of Nations, it is *additionally* exercising its power to define and punish under Article 1, Section 8,

---

169. Ex parte Quirin, 317 U.S. 1 (1942).

170. There has never been an indictment alleging the act of participation in hostilities by a non-state actor as a war crime brought before either the International Criminal Tribunal for the Former Yugoslavia nor the International Criminal Tribunal for Rwanda. *See* The ICTY, "Cases", *available at* http://www.

icty.org/action/cases/4; The ICTR, "Cases", *available at* http://liveunictr. altmansolutions.com/Cases/tabid/204/Default.aspx.

171. There is no such offense included within the enumerated war crimes or the International Criminal Court. *See* Rome Statute of the International Criminal Court, July 17, 1998, 2187 U.N.T.S. 3.

clause 10; the foundational constitutional authority for military commissions, however, remains the War Powers.[172]

Second, the government argues that this offense is merely a contemporary analogue to the offense of operating as a "marauder" during the Civil War, and offense routinely subject to military commission jurisdiction. Accordingly, the meaning of the term "in violation of the law of war" must not be restricted to the internationally accepted definition of war crimes, but instead on the unique U.S. common law of war, which includes these precedents:

> In its *Ex Parte Quirin* decision, the Supreme Court did *not* hold that *only* violations of the Law of Nations may be tried before military commissions. Rather, the Court observed that "[f]rom the very beginning of its history, this Court has recognized and applied the law of war as *including* that part of the law of nations which prescribes, for the conduct of war, the status, rights and duties of enemy nations as well as of enemy individuals." *Ex Parte Quirin*, 317 U.S. at 27. (emphasis added). The Court's use of "including" indicates that the part of the Law of Nations prescribing rules for the conduct of war is only a part of the larger category of the "law of war" cognizable by U.S. military commissions.[173]

This latter argument appears to ignore two important considerations. First, the plurality opinion in *Hamdan* emphasized the jurisdictional requirement that the government establish an offense brought before a military commission is an *internationally* recognized violation of the law of war.[174] Second, the prosecution of marauders by military commission during the Civil War may have implicated other sources of commission jurisdiction, such as martial law or the law of belligerent occupation. How the courts will respond to these arguments is unknown, although it does appear that the government has effectively acknowledged that their theory of criminal liability is not firmly rooted in international law.

This theory of criminality is also problematic for another reason. Extending international criminal responsibility to the realm of non-international armed conflicts based on operating as an unprivileged belligerent produces an anomaly: in the context of an international armed conflict, the offense provides an international sanction (criminal responsibility) for failing to comply with the requirements for gaining the benefit of international law: POW

---

172. *See* United States v. Khadr, P009, Reply to Defense Response to Government's Supplemental Brief in support of the Government's Motion for Findings Instructions on Charges I, II, and III, (2 August, 2010) (internal citations omitted) (copy on file with author).

173. *Id.*

174. *Hamdan*, 548 U.S. at 695.

status and its accordant combatant immunity. However, because non-state belligerents can never qualify for lawful belligerent status,[175] it imposes *international* legal sanction without a complimentary *international* legal reward. As a result, this theory of criminal liability mixes the benefits of status with the consequence of participation in non-international armed conflict, thereby distorting the impact of failing to qualify for combatant immunity. Non-state belligerents cannot qualify for this immunity, a privilege reserved for state armed forces engaged in international armed conflicts. But this does not result in the conclusion that acting as a belligerent without qualification for combatant immunity is *ipso facto* a war crime. Instead, this simply permits the assertion of domestic criminal jurisdiction to the acts and omissions of the belligerent. In short, the lack of qualification deprives the belligerent of combatant immunity, subjecting him to the criminal jurisdiction of the state in which his conduct occurs, which for a warrior could include murder, assault, arson, kidnapping, etc.

However, in order to qualify as a war crime, the acts of a non-state belligerent must violate not only applicable domestic law (such as prohibitions against murder, assault, arson, kidnapping, mayhem, etc.), but also *international* law, or more specifically the LOAC. Because mere participation in a non-international armed conflict by a non-state actor has never been considered a LOAC violation, imposing international criminal liability for such participation seems invalid. Instead, international criminal liability exists only when those acts or omissions violate norms of conduct applicable to non-international armed conflicts.

2. MATERIAL SUPPORT TO TERRORISM

Perhaps even more controversial is the offense of providing Material Support to Terrorism.[176] The Act defines this offense as follow:

> Any person subject to this chapter who provides material support or resources, knowing or intending that they are to be used in preparation for, or in carrying out, an act of terrorism (as set forth in paragraph (24) of this section), or who intentionally provides material support or resources to an international terrorist organization engaged in hostilities against the United States, knowing that such organization has engaged or engages in terrorism (as so set

---

175. *See* Department of Justice, Office of Legal Counsel, Memorandum for the Office of the President, "Status Of Taliban Forces Under Article 4 Of The Third Geneva Convention Of 1949," (Feb. 7, 2002), *available at* http://www.usdoj.gov/olc/2002/pub-artc4potus determination.pdf; *see also* INTERNATIONAL AND OPERATIONAL LAW DEP'T, THE JUDGE ADVOCATE GENERAL'S LEGAL CTR. & SCH., LAW OF WAR DESKBOOK 120 (2010) *available at* http://www.loc.gov/rr/frd/Military_Law/pdf/LOW–Deskbook.pdf.

176. 10 U.S.C. § 948t(25).

forth), shall be punished as a military commission under this chapter may direct.[177]

This offense has been a prime weapon in the arsenal of military commission prosecutors. It is also the subject of several appeals currently pending before the Court of Appeals for the Military Commissions (the military appellate court established by the MCA). In each of the three cases involving convictions for this offense, *U.S. v. Jawad*,[178] *U.S. v. Bahlul*,[179] and U.S. v. Hamdan,[180] appellants are challenging the validity of vesting a military commission with jurisdiction over this crime. Even if the government prevails at this initial appellate level, it is unlikely the question will be definitively resolved. Instead, the appellants will almost certainly pursue discretionary appeal and perhaps also collateral attack.

The primary argument presented by appellants is that this offense is neither a violation of the law of war nor an offense traditionally tried by military commission, and therefore Congress exceeded its authority when it included the offense in the MCA. Counsel for Hamdan was able to cite both the Congressional Research Service and the General Counsel to the Department of Defense. According to the Congressional Research Service, "defining as a war crime the 'material support for terrorism' does not appear to be supported by historical precedent."[181] This conclusion was even endorsed by counsel to the Secretary of Defense: "the President has made clear that military commissions are for law of war offenses. We believe it would be best for material support to be removed from the list of offenses triable by military commissions . . ."[182]

In response, the government response is similar to its defense of the crime of murder in violation of the law of war. The first line of defense is that the definition of offenses subject to military commission jurisdiction is entrusted by the Constitution to the two political branches. According to one appellate pleading, "the treatment of captured enemy combatants during war is a matter committed to the political branches under their enumerated wars

177. *Id.*

178. United States v. Jawad, CMCR Case No. 08–004, *available at* http://www.defense.gov/news/CMCRJAWAD1.html

179. United States v. al Bahlul, CMCR Case No. 09–001, *available at* http://www.defense.gov/news/CMCRHAMZA.html

180. United States v. Hamdan, CMCR Case No. 09–002, *available at* http://www.defense.gov/news/CMCRHamdan.html

181. *See* JENNIFER K. ELSEA, CONG. RESEARCH SERV., THE MILITARY COMMISSIONS ACT OF 2006: ANALYSIS OF PROCEDURAL RULES AND COMPARISON WITH PREVIOUS DOD RULES AND THE UNIFORM CODE OF MILITARY JUSTICE 12 (Sept. 27, 2007).

182. Prepared Statement of Jeh C. Johnson, General Counsel, Department of Defense, before the Senate Armed Services Committee, July 7, 2009.

powers.''[183] The government relies on William Winthrop's seminal treaties on U.S. military law to bolster this position, in which Winthrop noted that "[t]he [military] commission is simply an instrumentality for the more efficient execution of the war powers vested in Congress and the power vested in the President as commander-in-chief in war.''[184]

This is a curious theory considering *Hamdan* represents a very different Supreme Court perspective. Of course, unlike that case, the offenses being defended by the government were not defined exclusively by the President, but reflect the collective judgment of the two political branches. Whether this will be decisive is yet to be determined. However, the government theory is certainly in a stronger posture as the result of the MCA than at the time of the *Hamdan* decision.

The government argues that material support to terrorism is, like murder in violation of the law of war, merely a contemporary analogue to an offense historically subject to military commission jurisdiction. In *United States v. Bahlul*, the government argued that:

> Just as terrorism is a well-established war crime, so too is providing material support therefor. Long before Appellant began supporting al Qaeda, providing material support for terrorism violated both U.S. and international law. The law of war has long prohibited the provision of material support to groups of unlawful combatants. Since at least the Civil War, the United States has considered it a war crime to materially support groups of unlawful combatants by providing them one's personal services. So, in 1865, the Attorney General opined that "to unite with banditti, jayhawkers, guerillas, or any other unauthorized marauders is a high offence against the laws of war; **the offence is complete when the band is** organized or **joined**." Likewise, numerous people were tried by military commission for joining or being a guerilla.

> During the Civil War, "numerous rebels ... furnish[ed] the enemy with arms, provisions, clothing, horses and means of transportation; [such] insurgents [we]re banding together in several of the interior counties for the purpose of assisting the enemy to rob, to maraud and to lay waste to the country. All such persons are by the laws of war in every civilized country liable to capital punish-

---

183. United States v. al Bahlul, Brief on Behalf of Appellee, CMCR Case No. 09–001 (Oct. 21, 2009) 17.

184. United States v. Hamdan, Brief on Behalf of Appellee, CMCR Case

No. 09–002 (Dec. 4, 2009) p. 6–7 (citing Winthrop, supra, at note 831).

ment." Likewise, in describing violations of the "laws and usages of war cognizable by military tribunals," Colonel Winthrop includes:

> running a blockade, unauthorized contracting, trading or dealing with enemies, furnishing them with money, arms, provision, medicines, etc., conveying to or from them dispatches, letters or other communications, . . . aiding the enemy by harboring his spies, emissaries, etc. . . . acting as a guide to his troops . . . secretly recruiting for his army, negotiating and circulating his currency or securities . . . publications or declarations calculated to excite opposition to the federal government or sympathy with the enemy . . .

Although the words "material support for terrorism" were not used, it has historically violated the law of war to provide oneself, or any other material support, to an outlaw organization, such as al Qaeda, whose principal purpose is the "killing [and] disabling . . . of peaceable citizens or soldiers." Thus, providing material support for terrorism is, and was prior to the enactment of the MCA, a violation of the law of war. The MCA's codification of that prohibition does not violate the prohibition against ex post facto laws.[185]

It will be interesting to see how appellate courts respond to these precedents. While Winthrop is unquestionably a persuasive source of authority, conditions related to the Civil War call into question the relevance of the cited examples. It is not even clear whether the Civil War should be considered analogous to international or non-international armed conflict (at the time of the war, the Confederacy was recognized as a belligerent by other states, suggesting the precedents are primarily relevant to international armed conflicts). Furthermore, those commission prosecutions may have reflected an amalgamation of law of war and martial law jurisdiction. It is however clear that in contrary to the suggestion by the DOD General Counsel, the government is not abandoning this offense.

G. THE MOST ELUSIVE ISSUE: THE SOURCE AND LIMITS OF CONGRESSIONAL AUTHORITY TO DEFINE AND PUNISH

By vesting the military commission with authority to try "other offenses triable by military commission", Congress sowed the seeds for the inevitable challenge to its authority to authorize

---

185. United States v. Ali Hamza Ahmad Suliman al Bahlul, CMCR Case   No. 09–00, (Brief on behalf of Appellee) (21 October 2009).

criminal prosecutions by an Article I military court for offenses not tethered to the law of war. In *Hamdan,* the Court indicated by implication that the define and punish clause of Article I vests Congress with the authority to enumerate offenses subject to trial by military commission,

> [h]ere is no suggestion that Congress has, *in exercise of its constitutional authority to "define and punish ... Offences against the Law of Nations,"* U. S. Const., Art. I, § 8, cl. 10, positively identified "conspiracy" as a war crime. As we explained in *Quirin,* that is not necessarily fatal to the Government's claim of authority to try the alleged offense by military commission; Congress, through Article 21 of the UCMJ, has "incorporated by reference" the common law of war, which may render triable by military commission certain offenses not defined by statute.[186]

Contrasting Article 21's incorporation by reference of the common law of war with an exercise of the define and punish power seems to indicate that when enumerating offenses subject to trial by military commission, Congress is limited to codifying international law violations.[187] This theory has been proffered by defendants and appellants to support the argument that Congress exceeded its authority by vesting the military commission with jurisdiction over terrorism offenses, as there is no accepted international legal definition of terrorism. For example, in the appellate brief filed on behalf of Salim Hamdan challenging the military commission jurisdiction over the offense of material support to terrorism, appellant argued that

> [I]t is important to recognize that the military commissions authorized by the MCA are Article I courts established pursuant to Congress's power to "punish ... Offenses against the Law of Nations." That limited grant of authority and jurisdiction must be enforced. To go beyond that—for example, to confer jurisdiction on the military commission to try the purely *domestic* offense of Material Support to Terrorism set forth in Title 18 of the U.s. Code—would offend Article III of the Constitution, which confers the judicial power of the United States on Article II

186. *Hamdan,* 548 U.S. at 601 (emphasis added).

187. *See* Beth Stephens, *Federalism and Foreign Affairs: Congress's Power to "Define and Punish ... Offenses Against the Law of Nations,"* 42 Wm. & Mary L. Rev. 447, 474 (2000) ("Congress [has] the power to punish only actual violations of the law of nations, not to create new offenses."); *see also* Stephen I. Vladeck, *The Laws of War as a Constitutional Limit on Military Commission Jurisdiction,* 4 J. Nat'l Sec. L. & Pol'y (forthcoming 2010).

courts with structural guarantees of independence that are not present in the commission.

. . .

While military trials are permissible under certain Article I provisions—for example the Offenses Clause and the power to "make Rules for the Government and Regulation of the land and naval forces"—the Supreme Court has always "been alert to ensure that Congress does not exceed the constitutional bounds and bring within the jurisdiction of military courts matters beyond that jurisdiction, and properly within the realm of judicial power.[188]

Thus, the issue as framed by Hamdan (and other defendants) is whether Congress may vest an Article I military criminal court with jurisdiction over non-military domestic offenses.

The government response asserts first that these offenses are in fact violations of the law of war, second that Congress's judgment on whether these offenses violate the law of war is entitled to substantial deference, and third, that the MCA is an exercise not merely of the define and punish clause, but instead of the aggregate war powers vested by the Constitution in the government.

How this issue is ultimately resolved holds perhaps the greatest potential to impact the future of military jurisdiction. A determination that the offenses enumerated by the MCA in fact codify violations of the law of war will undoubtedly be criticized as invalid. However, such an outcome will at least theoretically preserve the link between military commission jurisdiction and armed conflict. If, however, these offenses are validated as an exercise of congressional authority to invoke the jurisdiction of the military commission for offenses not considered violations of international law, it adds an entirely new category to commission jurisdiction. In effect, such an outcome will endorse the use of the military commission as an Article I 'national security court.'

These ongoing challenges indicate that the treatment of terrorism as a war crime, or in the alternative, subjecting terrorism offenses to the jurisdiction of a military commission not as war crimes but as "other offenses" triable by military commission, is no less controversial today than it was on the day President Bush issued Military Order Number 1. Nor is there any indication that President Obama intends to significantly modify this theory of military jurisdiction. This conclusion is bolstered by the fact that his administration sought no significant jurisdictional amendments

188. United States v. Salim Ahmed Hamdan, CMCR Case No. 09–002, (Brief on behalf of Appellant).

to the MCA of 2006 when it proposed and then signed into law the MCA of 2009. Ultimately, the trial of al Qaeda operatives by military commission with the accordant appellate process will influence the resolution of the most important jurisdiction question related to the military commissions: if the military component of the struggle against transnational terrorism is an armed conflict, what war crimes liability is derived from this armed conflict?

H. PRESIDENT OBAMA AND THE MILITARY COMMISSION ACT OF 2009[189]

Only two defendants were tried by the military commission established by the MCA during the Bush administration.[190] However, President Bush's commitment to the military commission option never wavered. In contrast, while campaigning for President, Barack Obama frequently criticized the use of military commissions to try captured terrorists. He called the military commission system an "enormous failure" and vowed to "reject the Military Commissions Act."[191] On August 7, 2008, he stated "I have faith in America's courts. I have faith in our JAGs. As president, I'll close Guantanamo, reject the Military Commissions Act, adhere to the Geneva Conventions. Our Constitution and our Uniform Code of Military Justice provide a framework for dealing with the terrorists."[192]

As President, Barack Obama adopted a very different approach to the military commission trial option. Despite his campaign criticisms, on May 15, 2009 he announced that he would not terminate these trials, but would instead propose amendments to the MCA in order to improve the rights of defendants and the legitimacy of the commission process.[193] Unsurprisingly, this disappointed many of his campaign supporters and triggered significant criticisms.[194]

189. This section is based on Geoffrey S. Corn & Eric Talbot Jensen, *The Obama Administration's First Year and IHL: A Pragmatist Reclaims the High Ground,* Yearbook of International Humanitarian Law (forthcoming), *available at* http://papers.ssrn.com/sol3/papers.cfm?abstract_id=1596962.

190. John P. McLoughlin et al., *Security Detention in Practice: Security Detention, Terrorism and the Prevention Imperative,* 40 Case W. Res. J. Int'l L. 463, 505 n.19 (2009) ("The only military commissions completed as of November 2008 were the guilty plea of the Australian David Hicks and the conviction of Salim Hamdan (a.k.a. 'bin Laden's driver') for providing material support.").

191. Peter Baker & David M. Herszenhorn, *Obama Planning to Re-* tain Military Tribunal System for Detainees, N.Y. Times, May 15, 2009, at A.18 ("Mr. Obama called the military commission system put in place by Mr. Bush 'an enormous failure' and vowed to 'reject the Military Commissions Act.' ").

192. Michael D. Shear and Peter Finn, *Obama to Revamp Military Tribunals,* Wash. Post, May 16, 2009, *available in* LEXIS Nexis Library, CURNWS File.

193. Michael D. Shear and Peter Finn, *Obama to Revamp Military Tribunals,* Wash. Post, May 16, 2009, *available in* LEXIS Nexis Library, CURNWS File.

194. *Obama Breaks Major Campaign Promise as Military Commissions*

Responding to the President's proposal, Congress enacted the Military Commissions Act of 2009 (MCA 2009).[195] While the new Act substantially improved procedural and evidentiary aspects of the military commissions, it also triggered criticism from both proponents and opponents of the military commission. Proponents condemned the 2009 MCA for providing excessive legal protections to terrorists; opponents condemned the decision to continue use of the military commission. Nonetheless, the newly enacted version of the MCA included significant changes from the 2006 predecessor.

According to the new Act, individuals subject to trial by military commission will no longer be designated as unlawful enemy combatants. Instead, the term unprivileged enemy belligerent is used.[196] This may seem merely semantic, but it does eliminate an inference of guilt in the characterization of the status itself. Furthermore, the commission itself must determine whether a detainee falls within this status and is therefore subject to trial by military commission, and cannot rely on a determination made by a different tribunal such as the prior Combat Status Review Tribunals.[197] The limitation on the ability to invoke the Geneva Conventions to claim a remedy is carried over from the 2006 Act. However, the prohibition now extends only to private rights of action rather than the previous more general prohibition of invocation as a source of any rights.[198] While defendants before the Commission have always been provided a detailed military defense counsel, the new Act provides enhanced assistance of counsel rights. The Act provides for an enhanced opportunity for an accused to select both military and civilian defense counsel,[199] and the defendant is granted a right to the assistance of a "learned" defense counsel in capital cases.[200]

Evidentiary issues were also addressed in the new Act. Eliminating one of the few remaining sources of criticism in the 2006 MCA, the new Act extends the exclusionary rule for statements obtained by torture to any statement obtained by torture or cruel, inhuman, or degrading treatment,[201] and establishes voluntariness as the standard of admissibility of statements generally.[202]

Hearsay evidence is also limited to certain exceptions, and the prosecution bears the burden to establish reliability as a predicate

Resume, Says Amnesty International, PR NEWSWIRE, May 15, 2009, *available in* LEXIS Nexis Library, CURNWS File.

195. Military Commissions Act of 2009, U.S. Code 10 (2009) [hereinafter MCA 2009].

196. MCA 2009 at § 948a(7)(B).

197. *Id.* § 948c.

198. *Id.* § 948b(e).

199. *Id.* § 949c.

200. *Id.* § 949a(b)(2)(C)(ii).

201. *Id.* § 948r(a).

202. *Id.* § 948r(d).

to admissibility.[203] Compulsory process and discovery rights are also enhanced. The opportunity to obtain witnesses is improved,[204] and the Act imposes increased responsibility on the prosecution to disclose exculpatory evidence,[205] including evidence that might impeach government witnesses[206] and evidence that might be presented as mitigation at sentencing.[207]

Like the rule applicable to courts-martial, there is now an explicit prohibition against unlawful influence on members of the military commissions and the Court of Military Commission Review (CMCR).[208] The Act also includes revised classified information rules that are generally analogous to the Classified Information Procedures Act[209] provisions used in Article III courts, including the established jurisprudence.[210] The CMCR is authorized to review both facts and law,[211] and the United States Court of Appeals for the DC Circuit will have its traditional scope of review as opposed to its prior, more limited scope.[212]

This latest version of the MCA more closely aligns military commission process with courts-martial process. In this sense, it is one more step towards satisfying *Hamdan's* implied mandate, at least procedurally. The process is not, however, identical to courts-marital process. Nor has the revised Act addressed substantive jurisdiction concerns. It is therefore not surprising that critics continue to assert both that the military commissions remain procedurally defective and fail to sufficiently provide for a fundamentally fair trial. The degree of improvement from the original military commission established by President Bush, coupled with the *Hamdan* decision's degree of division among the Justices, it is highly unlikely that procedural attacks against the commission will prevail in the future. However, criticisms and challenges to the jurisdiction of the commission remain as viable under the new Act as they did before it was enacted.[213, 214] Other issues of concern include the fact that the law allows for the prosecution of child-

---

203. *Id.* § 949a(b)(3)(D).

204. *Id.* § 949j(a).

205. *Id.* § 949j(b)(1).

206. *Id.* § 949j(b)(2).

207. *Id.* § 949j(b)(3).

208. *Id.* § 949b.

209. Classified Information Procedures Act, Pub. L. No. 96–456, 94 Stat. 2025 (1980).

210. MCA 2009, at § 949p.

211. *Id.* at § 950f(d).

212. *Id.* at § 950g.

213. Deborah Pearlstein, *Revised— Military Commissions, Round 3*, BALKANIZATION, Oct. 23, 2009, *available in* LEX-

IS Nexis Library, CURNWS File; *US: Revised Military Commissions Remain Substandard; Legislation Lacks Reforms Obama Had Sought*, STATE NEWS SERVICE, Oct. 28, 2009 *available in* LEXIS Nexis Library, CURNWS File. Attorney Gen. of the U.S. Attorney General Announces Forum Decision for Guantanamo Detainees, Nov. 13, 2009, (transcript available at http://www.justice.gov/ag/speeches/2009/ag-speech–091113.html).

214. Steve Vladick, *MCA 2009: (Accidentally) Opening the Collateral Review Floodgates*, PRAWFSBLAWG, Oct. 23, 2009 *available in* LEXIS Nexis Library, CURNWS File.

soldiers (such as Omar Khadr who was captured while 15 years old),[215] allows for the use of confessions that are not considered voluntary pursuant to the U.S. Constitution,[216] fails to provide for any type of pre-trial hearing or grand jury,[217] and fails to include a sunset provision.

Shortly after signing the 2009 Act into law, the Obama Administration signaled a potentially significant policy shift concerning the long-term prosecutorial strategy for certain Guantanamo detainees. On November 13, Attorney General Holder announced that the alleged planners of the September 11, 2001 attacks would be tried in the federal district court in the Southern District of New York, in New York City.[218] This decision triggered intense controversy, and has yet to be implemented, with an increasingly apparent possibility it will be reversed. It did, however, highlight a possible narrowing of the military commission prosecutorial option.

The cases proposed for transfer from the commission to federal court all involve acts of terror that inflicted harm on U.S. territory, not in Afghanistan or Iraq or some other "extension" of those battlefields. During the prior administration, President Bush went to great lengths to emphasize the "global" nature of the battlefield. He christened the conflict the "Global War on Terror" and drew no distinctions between those captured in Afghanistan and other places around the world.[219] By prosecuting the planners of the 9/11 attack in the federal courts for crimes committed on U.S. territory,

215. William Fisher, *Rights—US: "New" Military Courts Still Lack Basic Safeguards*, INTERPRESS SERVICE, Nov. 19, 2009 *available in* LEXIS Nexis Library, CURNWS File; Peter Finn, *Former boy soldier, youngest Guantanamo detainee, heads toward military tribunal*, WASH. POST, Feb. 10, 2010, *available at* http://www.washingtonpost.com/wp-dyn/content/article/2010/02/09/AR2010020904020.html?wpisrc=nl_headline; *See also* Prosecutor v. Dyilo, ICC–01/04–01/06 (trial commenced Jan. 26, 2009) (trying Dyilo for using child-soldiers under the age of 15 in the Patriotic Forces for the Liberation of Congo and making them fight in conflicts both of international and non-international character as prohibited by articles 8(2)(b)(xxvi) and 8(2)(e)(vii), respectively, of the Rome Statute).

216. *Congressional Conferees Approve Changes to Guantanamo Detainee Policay and Military Commissions*, TARGETED NEWS SERVICE, Oct. 7, 2009 *available in* LEXIS Nexis Library, CURNWS File.

217. William Fisher, *Rights—US: Obama's Terrorism Courts Still "Fatally Flawed"*, INTERPRESS SERVICE, Nov. 9, 2009 *available in* LEXIS Nexis Library, CURNWS File.

218. Eric H. Holder, Jr., Attorney Gen. of the U.S. Attorney General Announces Forum Decision for Guantanamo Detainees, Nov. 13, 2009, (transcript available at http://www.justice.gov/ag/speeches/2009/ag-speech–091113.html). Though this decision was subsequently put in doubt. (*See* Michael Barbaro & Al Baker, *Bloomberg Balks at 9/11 Trial, Dealing Blow to White House*, N.Y. TIMES, Jan. 27, 2010, *available at* http://www.nytimes.com/2010/01/28/nyregion/28bloomberg.html?adxnnl=1&adxnnlx=1265924510–+fDlGSvxYpmPz2efhsSnPQ), there has been no decision by the Obama administration that signals a change from the issues as discussed in the text.

219. David E. Sanger, *Bush Orders Heavy Bombers Near Afghans; Demands Bin Laden Now, Not Negotiations*, N.Y. TIMES, Sep. 20, 2001, at 1, *available in* LEXIS Nexis Library, CURNWS File.

it appears that President Obama is distinguishing between them and others detainees whose acts of violence occurred outside the United States and/or against U.S. military interests. Attorney General Holder stated that he based the forum decisions on a protocol between the Department of Defense and Department of Justice,[220] but the provisions of that protocol have not been made public. This decision may indicate an emerging prosecutorial distinction between these two categories of terrorist violence. At a minimum, it seemed to be motivated by President Obama's efforts to adopt a more restrictive conception of the scope of the conflict with terrorism.

The decision also indicates President Obama has adopted another important aspect of his predecessor's view of the nature of the struggle against terrorism. Like President Bush, President Obama has chosen to assert that the armed conflict against terrorism pre-dates the terror attacks of September 11th. As the *Hamdan* decision held, establishing that conduct alleged as a war crime occurred in the time of armed conflict is a jurisdictional predicate for trial by military commission, a predicate that a plurality of the Justices concluded the government failed to satisfy when it charged offenses as far back as 1998.[221] Nonetheless, neither President Bush (by resurrecting those charges against Hamdan in his subsequent trial pursuant to the MCA of 2006[222]) nor President Obama have abandoned this temporal interpretation of the armed conflict with al Qaeda. A charging decision announced by Attorney General Holder on the same day as he announced the transfer of the high value detainee cases to federal court clearly signaled this interpretation. Abd al-Rahim al-Nashiri, an al Qaeda detainee suspected of complicity in the bombing of the USS Cole will be tried by military commission.[223] Thus, while President Obama seems to be struggling to establish some rational limits on his use of the military commission as a forum to try terrorist operatives, he has in no way abandoned the jurisdictional theories for such trials that proved so controversial for his predecessor.

I. CONCLUSION

Trials by military commissions date back to the inception of our nation, and have been explicitly endorsed as a valid exercise of

---

220. Holder, Jr., *supra* note 218; *Proposals on Reform to the Military Commissions System: Hearing before the House Committee on the Judiciary Subcommittee on the Constitution, Civil Rights and Civil Liberties,* (July 30, 2009) (testimony of Jeh Charles Johnson, Gen. Counsel, Dep't of Def.), *available at* http://judiciary.house.gov/hearings/pdf/Johnson090730.pdf.

221. *Hamdan,* 548 U.S. at 569–571.

222. *See United States Department of Defense, Military Commissions, United States v. Hamdan (Charge Sheet), available at:* http://www.defense.gov/news/Jul2004/d20040714hcc.pdf. http://www.defense.gov/news/commissions Hamdan.html.

223. Holder, Jr., *supra* note 218.

government power by the Supreme Court. However, use of a military commission has also always been viewed as an extremely limited authority. As Justice Stevens noted in his opinion for the *Hamdan* majority, only three situations have justified this use of this tribunal: belligerent occupation, martial law, and the trial of captured enemy belligerents for violations of the laws of war committed in the context of armed conflict. Only these situations of necessity justify rebutting the powerful presumption that federal civilian process will be used to try allegations of criminal misconduct.

The designation of the struggle against terrorism as an armed conflict by the United States following the terror attacks of September 11th opened the door for this use of this unique criminal tribunal. Acting pursuant to his inherent constitutional authority, President Bush ordered the creation of a military commission to try captured terrorist operative for violations of the law of war. This decision produced a virtual avalanche of legal uncertainty and a barrage of criticism that continues to this day. Ultimately, the decision by the Bush administration to resurrect a commission process last used in the aftermath of World War II and to charge offenses lacking an adequate foundation in contemporary international law resulted in the *Hamdan* decision invalidating the commissions.[224] However, that decision sowed the seeds for another chapter in the military commission debate by essentially inviting Congress to cure the defects of the military commission created by the President.

Congress responded to the Court by enacting the Military Commission Act of 2006.[225] For the first time in the nation's history, a military commission was established by statute. The MCA effectively addressed many of the procedural defects that plagued the original commission. It also included an enumeration of offenses available for trial before the newly created commission. It did not however terminate the legal and policy debates surrounding the validity of the commission process, nor legal challenges to the commission. Instead, it focused these challenges on the validity of *personam* and subject-matter jurisdiction established by the Act, challenges that continue to this day. Accordingly, the conditions are again set for the courts to decide who may be tried by military commission, what they may be tried for, and when their acts fall within that jurisdiction.

President Obama did not, as had been expected by many, abandon this prosecutorial option. Choosing instead to move for-

---

224. *See, e.g.,* Hamdan v. Rumsfeld, 548 U.S. 557 (2006).

225. Military Commissions Act of 2006, Pub. L. 109–366, 120 Stat. 2600 (2006).

ward with the commission process, he proposed additional procedural and evidentiary improvements, enacted by Congress in the
Military Commission Act of 2009.[226] However, this revised Act did
nothing to assuage the concerns over the nature of jurisdiction
vested in the military commissions, and the battles over this issue
rage as intensely today as they did in 2002. How these issues are
resolved will inevitably impact the future use of this unique criminal tribunal, and perhaps the development of international law
more broadly. It is clear, however, that there is no foreseeable end
in sight for trial terrorist operatives by military commission.

226. Military Commissions Act of
2009, 10 U.S.C. ch. 47A (2009).

Part II
THE LAW ENFORCEMENT
RESPONSE

Chapter 6

GATHERING COUNTER–TERRORISM INTELLIGENCE INFORMATION

A. FOREIGN INTELLIGENCE SURVEILLANCE ACT, 50 U.S.C. §§ 1801 *ET SEQ.*

1. STATUTORY FRAMEWORK

a. General Overview

The Foreign Intelligence Surveillance Act (FISA), 50 U.S.C. §§ 1801 *et seq.*, enacted in 1978, provides a statutory framework for the use of electronic surveillance to gather foreign intelligence information.[1] Following the terrorist attacks of September 11, 2001, FISA, as amended, has become a prominent tool used by the Government to collect foreign intelligence information to prevent terrorist attacks and conduct international terrorism investigations. As originally enacted, FISA governed the collection of foreign intelligence information through the use of electronic surveillance of "foreign powers" and "agents of foreign powers" as those terms were defined under the Act.[2] Subsequent legislation expanded FISA to address gathering foreign intelligence information through the use of physical searches,[3] pen registers and trap and trace devices,[4] and access to certain business records and other "tangible things."[5]

1. Foreign Intelligence Surveillance Act of 1978, P.L. 95–511, 92 Stat. 1783 (October 25, 1978), 50 U.S.C. §§ 1801 *et seq.*

2. As enacted in 1978, FISA defined the term "foreign power" to include "a group engaged in international terrorism or activities in preparation therefor." 50 U.S.C. § 1801(a)(4). The term "agent of a foreign power" was defined to include a member of such a group and any person who "knowingly engages in sabotage or international terrorism, or activities that are in preparation therefor, on behalf of a foreign power." *Id.* at § 1801(b)(2)(C).

3. *See* Intelligence Authorization Act for Fiscal Year 1995, Pub. L. No. 103–359, § 807, 108 Stat. 3423, 3443 (1994) (codified as amended 50 U.S.C. 1822–6 (2008)).

4. *See* Intelligence Authorization Act for Fiscal Year 1999, Pub. L. No.

105–272, § 601, 112 Stat. 2396, 2405 (codified as amended at 50 U.S.C. §§ 1841–46 (2008)). Pen registers capture the numbers dialed on a targeted phone line; trap and trace devices identify the originating number of a call on a targeted telephone line. *See* 18 U.S.C. § 3127(3)–(4) (2008).

5. *See e.g.*, Intelligence Authorization Act for Fiscal Year 1999, § 602, 112 Stat. at 2410 (codified at 50 U.S.C. §§ 1861–62) (authorizing orders to compel production of certain business records); *see also* Uniting and Strengthening America by Providing Appropriate Tools Required to Intercept and Obstruct Terrorist (USA PATRIOT) Act of 2001, P.L. 107–56, § 215, 115 Stat. at 2410 (codified at 50 U.S.C. §§ 1861–62) (2008) (deleting former §§ 1861–3 and adding new §§ 1861–62 authorizing orders to compel production of "any tangible things").

FISA was a response by Congress to three related concerns: "(1) the judicial confusion over the existence, nature and scope of a foreign intelligence exception to the Fourth Amendment's warrant requirement that arose in the wake of the Supreme Court's 1972 decision in *United States v. United States District Court*, 407 U.S. 297 (1972); (2) the Congressional concern over perceived Executive Branch abuses of such an exception;[6] and (3) the felt need to provide the Executive Branch with an appropriate means to investigate and counter foreign intelligence threats."[7] Congress sought to accommodate these concerns by establishing detailed procedures the Executive Branch must follow to obtain court orders allowing it to collect foreign intelligence information "without violating the rights of citizens of the United States."[8]

Three terms are critical to understanding FISA's scope and application: "foreign intelligence information," "foreign power," and "agent of a foreign power." The term "foreign intelligence information" is defined to cover two broad categories of information. Section 1801(e)(1) includes "counterintelligence" or "protective" foreign intelligence information.[9] Such information relates to the ability of the United States to protect against "(A) actual or potential attack or other grave hostile acts of a foreign power or an agent of a foreign power; (B) sabotage, international terrorism, or the international proliferation of weapons of mass destruction by a foreign power or an agent of a foreign power; or (C) clandestine intelligence activities by an intelligence service or network of a foreign power or by an agent of a foreign power."[10] The term "foreign intelligence information" also includes "positive" or "affirmative" foreign intelligence information.[11] Section 1801(e)(2) includes information with respect to a "foreign power or foreign territory" that relates to "the national defense or the security of the United States" or "the conduct of the foreign affairs of the United States."[12]

---

6. FISA was enacted in response to the revelations of the Committee to Study Government Operations with Respect to Intelligence Activities (known as the "Church Committee") regarding past abuses of electronic surveillance for national security purposes.

7. United States v. Rosen, 447 F.Supp.2d 538, 542–3 (E.D. Va. 2006) (internal citations omitted). *See also* William C. Banks and M.E. Bowman, *Executive Authority for National Security Surveillance,* 50 AM. U. L. REV. 1, 75–6 (2000) (describing the reasons motivating FISA).

8. United States v. Hammoud, 381 F.3d 316, 332 (4th Cir. 2004) (en banc), *vacated on other grounds,* 543 U.S. 1097, *reinstated in pertinent part,* 405 F.3d 1034 (2005).

9. Patricia L. Bellia, *The "Lone Wolf" Amendment and the Future of Foreign Intelligence Surveillance Law,* 50 VILL. L. REV. 425, 438 (2005) (discussing FISA's statutory structure) [hereinafter *The "Lone Wolf" Amendment*].

10. 50 U.S.C. § 1801(e)(1)(A)–(C).

11. *The "Lone Wolf" Amendment, supra* note 9, at 438.

12. 50 U.S.C. § 1801(e)(2)(A)–(B).

The term "foreign power" includes traditional state or state-related entities, such as a foreign government, a faction of a foreign nation, or an entity that is acknowledged by a foreign government to be directed or controlled by such foreign government.[13] The definition of "foreign power" also includes non-state entities, such as groups engaged in international terrorism or international proliferation of weapons or mass destruction.[14] "International terrorism" means activities that "involve violent acts or acts dangerous to human life that are a violation of the criminal laws of the United States," that appear intended to intimidate or coerce a civilian population or a government, or affect the conduct of a government by assassination or kidnaping, and occur totally outside the United States or transcend national boundaries.[15]

The definition of "agent of a foreign power" differs depending on whether the FISA target is a "United States person."[16] If the target is someone other than a U.S. person, "agent of a foreign power" means a person who (A) acts as an officer, employee, or member of a foreign power; (B) acts for or on behalf of a foreign power engaged in clandestine activities in the United States; (C) engages in international terrorism or related activities; (D) engages in the international proliferation of weapons of mass destruction or related activities; or (E) engages in the international proliferation of weapons of mass destruction or related activities on behalf of a foreign power.[17] There is no requirement of a connection to a foreign power, if the target engages in international terrorism or international proliferation of weapons of mass destruction.[18] At the same time, the term "agent of a foreign power" covers *any* person, including a U.S. person, who (A) knowingly engages in clandestine intelligence gathering activities on behalf of a foreign power, "which activities involve . . . a violation of the criminal statutes of the United States"; (B) pursuant to the direction of an intelligence service or network or a foreign power, knowingly engages in any other clandestine intelligence activities on behalf of a foreign power, "which activities involve or are about to involve a violation of

13. *Id.* at § 1801(a)(1)–(3). *See also The "Lone Wolf" Amendment, supra* note 9, at 439.

14. 50 U.S.C. §§ 1801(a)(4), (7). The term "foreign power" also means "a foreign-based political organization, not substantially composed of United States persons" or "an entity that is directed and controlled by a foreign government." *Id.* at §§ 1801(a)(5), (6).

15. *Id.* at §§ 1801(c), 1821(1).

16. For FISA purposes, "United States person" means "a citizen of the United States, an alien lawfully admitted for permanent residence, an unin-

corporated association a substantial number of members of which are citizens of the United States or aliens lawfully admitted for permanent residence, or a corporation which is incorporated in the United States, but does not include a corporation of association which is a foreign power, as defined in subsection (a)(1), (2), or (3) of this section." *Id.* at § 1801(i) (internal citations omitted).

17. 50 U.S.C. at §§ 1801(b)(1)(A)–(E).

18. *See* §§ 1801(b)(1)(C), (D).

the criminal statutes of the United States"; (C) knowingly engages in sabotage or international terrorism or related activities on behalf of a foreign power; (D) knowingly enters the United States under a false or fraudulent identity or, while in the United States, knowingly assumes a false or fraudulent identity, on behalf of a foreign power; or (E) aids or abets any person or conspires with any person to engage in prohibited activities enumerated under the statute.[19] In each case, the FISA target must act for or on behalf of a foreign power.

b. Application for Court Orders, 50 U.S.C. § 1804

An application for an order approving electronic surveillance of a foreign power or an agent of a foreign power must be made by a federal officer "in writing upon oath or affirmation" to a judge of the Foreign Intelligence Security Court (FISC).[20] The FISC consists of eleven district court judges selected by the Chief Justice of the United States Supreme Court from at least seven judicial circuits.[21] At least three of the FISC's judges must reside within twenty miles of Washington, D.C.[22] These eleven judges have jurisdiction over applications for orders approving electronic surveillance,[23] physical searches,[24] pen registers or trap and trace devices,[25] or orders for production of documents or tangible things.[26] In the event that a FISA application is denied by a judge of the FISC, the Government may seek review of such denial before the Foreign Intelligence Surveillance Court of Review (FISCR), comprised of three judges designated by the Chief Justice.[27] The FISCR judges may be designated from the U.S. district courts or U.S. courts of appeal.[28] The judges of the FISC and FISCR serve for seven-year terms and may not be redesignated.[29]

Each application must include the identify of the federal officer making the application[30] and the identity, if known, or a description of the target of the electronic surveillance.[31] Such application shall also include a statement of facts relied upon by the applicant to justify his belief that the target of the electronic surveillance is a foreign power or an agent of a foreign power, and his belief that each of the facilities at which the electronic surveillance is directed is being used, or about to be used, by a foreign power or agent of a

19. *Id.* at §§ 1801(b)(2)(A)–(E).

20. 50 U.S.C. § 1804(a).

21. *Id.* at § 1803(a)(1). As enacted in 1978, the FISC was made up of seven judges. Section 208 of P.L. 107–56 increased the number of judges to eleven.

22. 50 U.S.C. § 1803(a)(1).

23. *Id.* at § 1802(b).

24. *Id.* at § 1822(c).

25. *Id.* at § 1842(b) and (d).

26. *Id.* at § 1861(b) and (c).

27. *Id.* at § 1803(b).

28. *Id.*

29. *Id.* at § 1803(d).

30. 50 U.S.C. § 1804(a)(1).

31. *Id.* at § 1804(a)(2).

foreign power.[32] Additionally, each application must contain a statement of proposed "minimization procedures":[33] and a description of the nature of the information sought and the type of communications or activities to be subjected to surveillance.[34] The "minimization procedures" are specific procedures adopted by the Attorney General that are reasonably designed to minimize the acquisition and retention, and prohibit the dissemination, of nonpublic information which is not foreign intelligence information.[35]

An application for electronic surveillance must also contain a "certification" by a designated executive branch official, such as the Director of the Federal Bureau of Investigation, that the information sought is foreign intelligence information;[36] that a "significant purpose" of the surveillance is to obtain foreign intelligence information;[37] and that such information cannot "reasonably be obtained by normal investigative techniques."[38] The USA PATRIOT Act amended the national security certification required for electronic surveillance and physical searches. Rather than requiring that a national security official certify that "the purpose" of the FISA surveillance was to gather foreign intelligence information, the amended statute requires certification that a "significant purpose" of the surveillance or search is to obtain foreign intelligence information.[39] Thus, if gathering foreign intelligence information is a "significant purpose," another purpose such as criminal prosecution could be primary.[40]

The certification also must designate the "type of foreign intelligence information being sought,"[41] and include a statement that describes the basis for the certification that the information sought is the type of foreign intelligence information designated, and that such information could not reasonably be obtained by normal investigative techniques.[42] Further, each application must contain a statement of the means by which the surveillance will be effected,[43] a statement of the period of time for which the electronic

32. *Id.* at § 1804(3)(A)–(B).

33. *Id.* at § 1804(4).

34. *Id.* at § 1804(5).

35. *Id.* at § 1801(h)(1). *See also* In re Sealed Case, 310 F.3d 717, 731 (Foreign Int.Surv.Ct.Rev. 2002) (minimization procedures are "designed to protect, as far as reasonable, against the acquisition, retention, and dissemination of nonpublic information which is not foreign intelligence information").

36. 50 U.S.C. § 1804(6)(A).

37. *Id.* at § 1804(6)(B).

38. *Id.* at § 1804(6)(C).

39. USA PATRIOT Act § 218, 115 Stat. at 291 (codified at 50 U.S.C. §§ 1804(a)(6)(B), 1823(a)(6)(B) (2008)).

40. *See* In re Sealed Case, 310 F.3d 717, 734 (Foreign Int.Surv.Ct.Rev. 2002). The FISCR found that the term "significant" "imposed a requirement that the government have a measurable foreign intelligence purpose, other than just criminal prosecution of even foreign intelligence crimes...." *Id.* at 735.

41. 50 U.S.C. § 1804(6)(D).

42. *Id.* at § 1804(6)(E)(i)–(ii).

43. *Id.* at § 1804(7).

surveillance is required,[44] and whether any previous applications have been made to any judge involving any of the persons, facilities, or places specified in the application and the action taken on each previous application.[45] Finally, such an application must be approved by the Attorney General (or Acting Attorney General), the Deputy Attorney General, or upon the designation of the Attorney General, the Assistant Attorney General for National Security.[46]

c. Issuance of Order, 50 U.S.C. § 1805

After review of the application, a judge of the FISC must enter an *ex parte* order granting the Government's application for electronic surveillance of a foreign power or agent of a foreign power provided the judge makes specific findings. The judge must find that on the basis of the facts submitted by the applicant there is probable cause to believe that (1) the target of the electronic surveillance is a foreign power or an agent of a foreign power, and (2) each of the facilities or places at which the electronic surveillance is directed is being used, or is about to be used, by a foreign power or an agent of a foreign power.[47] In determining whether probable cause exists, a judge may consider past activities of the target, as well as facts and circumstances related to current or future activities of the surveillance target.[48] An order approving electronic surveillance must describe the target, the nature and location of each of the facilities or places at which the electronic surveillance will be directed, the information sought, the means of acquiring such information, and set forth the period of time during which the electronic surveillance is approved.[49] For both electronic surveillance and physical searches, an order may be granted for a period of ninety days, though extensions may be granted if the Government submits another application to the FISC.[50] However, if the target is a foreign power as defined in sections 1801(a)(1), (2), or (3) (foreign government, faction of a foreign nation, or entity that is acknowledged by a foreign government to be directed and controlled by a foreign government) the order may extend for up to

44. *Id.* at § 1804(9).

45. *Id.* at § 1804(8).

46. *Id.* at § 1801(g).

47. *Id.* at § 1805(a)(2)(A)–(B). In addition to these probable cause findings, the FISC judge must also find that: (1) the President has authorized the Attorney General to approve applications for electronic surveillance for foreign intelligence information; (2) that the application has been made by a Federal officers and approved by the Attorney General; (3) that the proposed minimization procedures meet the respective definitions of minimization procedures

for electronic surveillance; and (4) that the application contains all the statements and certifications required by 50 U.S.C. § 1804 for electronic surveillance and, if the target is a United States person, the certifications are not clearly erroneous on the basis of the statement made under section 1804(6)(E). *See United States v. Rosen,* 447 F.Supp.2d 538, 544 n.6 (E.D. Va. 2006) (citing 50 U.S.C. § 1805(a)).

48. 50 U.S.C. §§ 1805(b).

49. *Id.* at § 1805(c)(1)(A)–(E).

50. *Id.* at §§ 1805(d)(1), (2), 1824(d)(1), (2).

one year.[51] If the target is an agent of a foreign power who is not a U.S. person as defined in section 1801(b)(1), the order may be approved for a period not to exceed 120 days.[52] An order authorizing installation of a pen register or trap and trace device may not exceed 90 days.[53] If the target is not a U.S. person, an order may be for a period to exceed one year.[54]

The requirements for an order authorizing a physical search for foreign intelligence information are included in 50 U.S.C. § 1823, and strongly parallel those procedures applicable to electronic surveillance under 50 U.S.C. § 1804(a)(1)–(9).[55] However, to obtain a court order to install a pen register or trap and trace device, as well as to obtain business records, the USA PATRIOT Act eliminated the requirement that the foreign intelligence information be connected to a foreign power or agent of a foreign power. Each type of order may now be granted upon a showing that information is relevant to an authorized investigation to obtain foreign intelligence information not concerning a U.S. person, or to protect against international terrorism or clandestine activities.[56]

Finally, FISA provides criminal sanctions for intentionally engaging in electronic surveillance or conducting a physical search under color of law not authorized by FISA, or disclosing information obtained under color of law by electronic surveillance or physical search, knowing or having reason to know that such information was not authorized by statute.[57] FISA also authorizes civil liability, where an aggrieved person has been subjected to electronic surveillance or whose property has been subjected to a physical search, or where information was gathered by such means concerning an aggrieved person and disclosed in violation of FISA.[58]

d. Roving Wiretaps

Section 206 of the USA PATRIOT Act amended FISA to permit "roving" wiretaps, which target persons rather than places.[59] Prior to the enactment of § 206, a FISA court order authorizing electronic surveillance had to identify the location or facility subject to

51. Id.
52. Id.
53. Id. at § 1842(e)(1). An extension may be granted for a period not to exceed 90 days. Id.
54. Id. at § 1842(e)(2). Such an order may be extended for a period not to exceed one year. Id.
55. See id. at § 1823.
56. See USA PATRIOT Act § 214(a)(2), 115 Stat. at 286 (codified at 50 U.S.C. §§ 1842(c)(2), 1861(b)(2) (2008)).
57. See 50 U.S.C. §§ 1809, 1827. Such violation is punishable by imprisonment of not more than five years or a maximum fine of $10,000, or both.
58. Id. at §§ 1819, 1828. A person who commits such violation may be ordered to pay actual damages, punitive damages and reasonable attorney's feed and court costs.
59. See USA PATRIOT Act of 2001, P.L. 107–56, § 206 (2001) (codified at 50 U.S.C. § 1805(c)(2)(B) (2008)).

surveillance.[60] Also, only identifiable third parties could be directed by the government to furnish the information, facilities, or technical assistance necessary to accomplish the electronic surveillance.[61] In cases where the location or facility was unknown, the identity of the persons needed to assist the Government for electronic surveillance could not be specified in the order.[62] Therefore, the inability to identify the persons that could be directed to assist the Government effectively limited the reach of electronic surveillance to "known and identifiable locations."[63] Section 206 of the USA PATRIOT Act amended section 1805(c)(2)(B) to authorize FISA orders to direct "other persons" to assist with electronic surveillance if "the Court finds, based on the specific facts provided in the application, that the actions of the target of the application may have the effect of thwarting the identification of a specified person."[64] Further, in a technical amendment that followed, the requirement that the order specify the location of the facilities or places at which the electronic surveillance will be directed was also changed, so that this requirement only applies if such facilities or places are known.[65] These amendments permit FISA orders to direct unspecified individuals ("other persons") to assist the Government in performing electronic surveillance of places and locations that are unknown at the time the order is issued.[66]

Congress provided the following explanation for these changes:

> The multipoint wiretap amendment to FISA in the USA PATRIOT Act (section 206) allows the FISA court to issue generic orders of assistance to any communications provider. This change permits the Government to implement new surveillance immediately if the FISA target changes providers in an effort to thwart surveillance. The amendment was directed

---

60. *See* 50 U.S.C. § 1805(c)(1)(B) (2001) (requiring FISA warrants to identity the "nature and location of each of the facilities or places at which electronic surveillance will be directed").

61. *See id.* at § 1805(c)(2) (2001). Section 1805(c)(2) then provided:

... that, upon the request of the applicant, a specified communication or other common carrier, landlord, custodian, or other *specified person* furnish the applicant forthwith all information, facilities, or technical assistance necessary to accomplish the electronic surveillance in such a manner as will protect its secrecy and produce a minimum of interference with the services that such carrier, landlord, custodian, or other person is providing that target of electronic surveillance.

Id. (emphasis added).

62. *See* Anna C. Henning & Edward C. Liu, Cong. Research Serv., R40138, Amendments to the Foreign Intelligence Surveillance Act (FISA) Set to Expire February 28, 2010, at 7 (2010) (discussing the "roving" wiretap amendment to FISA) [hereinafter Amendments to the Foreign Intelligence Surveillance Act].

63. *Id.*

64. 50 U.S.C. § 1805(c)(2)(B) (2008).

65. P.L. 107–108, § 314(a)(2)(A) (codified at 50 U.S.C. § 1805(c)(1)(B)). *See also* Amendments to the Foreign Intelligence Surveillance Act, *supra* note 57, at 7.

66. *See* 50 U.S.C. §§ 1805(c)(1)(B), 1805(c)(2)(B).

at persons who, for example, attempt to defeat surveillance by changing wireless telephone providers or using pay phones.

Currently, FISA requires the court to "specify" the "nature and location of each of the facilities or places at which the electronic surveillance will be directed." 50 U.S.C. § 1805(c)(1)(B). Obviously, in certain situations under current law, such a specification is limited. For example, a wireless phone has no fixed location and electronic mail may be accessed from any number of locations.

To avoid ambiguity and clarify Congress' intent, the conferees agreed to a provision which adds the phrase, "if known," to the end of 50 U.S.C. § 1805(c)(1)(B). The "if known" language, which follows the model of 50 U.S.C. § 1805(c)(1)(A), is designed to avoid any uncertainty about the kind of specification required in a multipoint wiretap case, where the facility to be monitored is typically not known in advance.[67]

The USA PATRIOT Improvement and Reauthorization Act of 2005 amended section 1805(c) to require that the FISC be notified within 10 days after "surveillance begins to be directed at any new facility or place."[68] In addition, the Government is required to notify the FISC of (A) the nature and location of each new facility or place at which the electronic surveillance is directed, (B) the facts and circumstances relied upon to justify the new surveillance, (C) a statement of any proposed minimization procedures—i.e., rules to limit the Government's acquisition and dissemination of information involving U.S. citizens—that differ from those contained in the original application or order, and (D) the total number of locations and facilities subject to electronic surveillance under the present order.[69]

Critics of FISA roving wiretaps may argue that orders authorizing such surveillance do not comport with the requirement contained in the Fourth Amendment that warrants shall "particularly describe[e] the place to be searched."[70] However, similar roving wiretaps have been permitted under Title III of the Omnibus Crime Control and Safe Streets Act. In *United States v. Petti,* the Ninth Circuit rejected a legal challenge to a roving wiretap under Title III

---

67. Conference Report on H.R. 2338, Intelligence Authorization Act for Fiscal Year 2002 (which became P.L. 107–108), H.Rept. 107–328, at 24.

68. P.L. 109–177, § 108(b)(4) (codified at 50 U.S.C. § 1805(c)(3) (2008)). Upon a finding of good cause, notice to the FISC may be delayed up to 60 days. 50 U.S.C. § 1805(c)(3).

69. 50 U.S.C. § 1805(c)(3)(A)–(D). Section 206 of the USA PATRIOT Act was originally scheduled to sunset on December, 31, 2005, and extended to February 28, 2010. P.L. 108–177, § 103; P.L. 111–118, § 1004. However, the sunset date has been extended to February 28, 2011. P.L. 109–177, § 103.

70. U.S. Const. amend. IV.

on the grounds that such wiretaps do not satisfy the Fourth
Amendment particularity requirement.[71] The court noted that

> the test for determining the sufficiency of the warrant descrip-
> tion is whether the place to be searched is described with
> sufficient particularity to enable the executing officer to locate
> and identify the premises with reasonable effort, and whether
> there is any reasonable probability that another premise might
> be mistakenly searched.[72]

Applying this test, the Ninth Circuit upheld the constitutionality of roving wiretaps under Title III.[73] The court reasoned that
targets of roving wiretaps had to the identified, satisfying the
particularity requirement of the Fourth Amendment.[74] Further, the
court found that the use of roving wiretaps was limited under Title
III and only permitted where the target's actions indicated an
intent to thwart electronic surveillance.[75]

e. Access to Business Records or Other "Tangible Things," 50 U.S.C. §§ 1861–2

Section 215 of the USA PATRIOT Act broadened the scope of
records that may be sought under FISA, and lowered the standard
for a court order compelling their production.[76] In 1998, Congress
amended FISA to authorize the production of documents not available through National Security Letters (NSLs).[77] Four categories of
documents were accessible, records from common carriers, public
accommodation facilities, storage facilities, and vehicle rental businesses.[78] The FISC would issue an order if the application contained
"specific and articulable facts giving reason to believe that the
person to whom the records pertain is a foreign power or an agent
of a foreign power."[79] Section 215 expanded the scope of records
subject to compulsory production under FISA, authorizing the
production of "any tangible things" for an investigation to obtain
foreign intelligence information not concerning U.S. persons or to
protect against international terrorism or clandestine intelligence
activities.[80]

---

71. United States v. Petti, 973 F.2d
1441 (9th Cir. 1992). *See also* AMEND-
MENTS TO THE FOREIGN INTELLIGENCE SUR-
VEILLANCE ACT, *supra* note 54, at 9 (discussing *United States v. Petti*).

72. *United States v. Petti*, 973 F.2d
at 1444 (internal quotations omitted).

73. *Id.* at 1445.

74. *Id. See also* United States v.
Bianco, 998 F.2d 1112, 1124 (2d Cir.
1993) (upholding the constitutionality of
roving wiretaps under Title III).

75. *United States v. Petti*, 973 F.2d
at 1445.

76. USA PATRIOT Act of 2001,
P.L. 107-56 (2001), § 215 (codified at 50
U.S.C. §§ 1861(a)(2) (2008)).

77. P.L. 105–272, § 602, 112 Stat.
2411–12 (1998).

78. 50 U.S.C. § 1862(a) (2001).

79. *Id.* at § 1862(b)(2)(B) (2001).

80. *Id.* at § 1861(a)(1) (2008).

The expanded scope of documents subject to FISA was strongly criticized by members of the library community who feared that such access would have a chilling effect on the exercise of First Amendment rights and violate areas protected by the Fourth Amendment.[81] In response to these concerns, a "library-specific amendment" to section 215 was enacted by the USA PATRIOT Improvement and Reauthorization Act of 2005.[82] Pursuant to this amendment, if the application for a FISA order requires the production of "library circulation records, library patron lists, book sales records, book customer lists, firearm sales records, tax return records, educational records, or medical records containing information that would identify a person," it must be approved by one of three high-ranking national security officials, the Director of the FBI, the Deputy Director of the FBI, or the Executive Assistant Director for National Security.[83] Further, this approval authority cannot be delegated to some lower-level government official.[84]

Section 215 of the PATRIOT Act also lowered the standard for an order compelling the production of documents. Prior to the enactment of section 215, the Government had to have "specific and articulable facts giving reason to believe that the person to whom the records pertain is a foreign power or agent of a foreign power."[85] Section 215 eliminated the requirement that the requested documents be connected to a foreign power or agent of a foreign power. Under section 215, the applicant only need "specify that the records concerned are sought for a [foreign intelligence, international terrorism, or espionage investigation.]"[86]

In 2005, the FISA procedures for obtaining business records were amended. The standard was modified to require "a statement of facts showing that there are reasonable grounds to believe that the tangible things sought are *relevant* to a [foreign intelligence, international terrorism, or espionage investigation.]"[87] Under this standard, such records are presumptively relevant if they pertain to

(i) a foreign power or agent of a foreign power;

(ii) the activities of a suspected agent of a foreign power who is the subject of such authorized investigation; or

81. *See* AMENDMENTS TO THE FOREIGN INTELLIGENCE SURVEILLANCE ACT, *supra* note 54, at 10. *See also* Ulrika Ekman Ault, *The FBI's Library Awareness Program: Is Big Brother Reading Over Your Shoulder?*, 65 N.Y.U. L.Rev. 1532 (1990).

82. USA PATRIOT Improvement and Reauthorization Act of 2005, P.L. 109–177, § 106(b).

83. 50 U.S.C. § 1861(a)(3) (2008).

84. *Id.*

85. *Id.* at § 1862(b)(2)(B) (2001).

86. P.L. 107–56, § 215.

87. USA PATRIOT Act Improvement and Reauthorization Act of 2005, P.L. 109–177, § 106(b) (codified at 50 U.S.C. § 1861(b)(2)(A) (2008)) (emphasis added).

(iii) an individual in contact with, or known to, a suspected agent of a foreign power who is the subject of such authorized investigation.[88]

Orders issued pursuant to section 215 are accompanied by a nondisclosure order prohibiting the recipients from disclosing that the FBI has sought or obtained tangible things pursuant to a FISA order.[89] However, the recipient may discuss the FISA order with persons to whom disclosure is necessary to comply with such order, with an attorney to obtain legal advice or assistance with respect to the order, and other persons as permitted by the FBI.[90]

The USA PATRIOT Improvement and Reauthorization Act of 2005 provides a recipient of a production order under 50 U.S.C. § 1861 a process for judicial review of the legality of such order and related nondisclosure order.[91] A person receiving a production order may challenge the legality of that order by filing a petition with the pool of the FISC established by 50 U.S.C. § 1803(e)(1).[92] Once a petition for review is submitted, a FISC judge must determine whether the petition is frivolous within 72 hours.[93] If the petition is frivolous, the order must be affirmed.[94] The order may be modified or set aside only if the judge finds that such order does not meet the requirements of FISA or is otherwise unlawful.[95] Either party may appeal the decision of the FISC to the FISCR and the Supreme Court.[96]

The recipient of a FISA order for production of documents may also challenge the nondisclosure order.[97] However, he must wait at least one year after issuance of that order to file a petition to modify or set aside the nondisclosure order.[98] A petition to set aside the nondisclosure order may be granted if the judge finds that there is no reason to believe that disclosure may endanger the national security of the United States, interfere with a criminal, counterterrorism, or counterintelligence investigation, interfere with diplomatic relations, or endanger the life or physical safety of any person.[99]

A petition to set aside a nondisclosure order may be denied if the Attorney General, Deputy Attorney General, an Assistant Attorney General, or the Director of the FBI certifies that disclosure may endanger the national security of the United States or inter-

88. 50 U.S.C. § 1861(b)(2)(A)(i)–(iii) (2008). The sunset date has been extended for section 215 to February 28, 2011. P.L. 111–141.

89. *Id.* at § 1861(d)(1).

90. *Id.* § 1861(d)(1)(A)–(C).

91. *Id.* at § 1861(f)(2)(A)(i).

92. *Id.*

93. *Id.* at § 1861(f)(2)(A)(ii).

94. *Id.*

95. *Id.* at § 1861(f)(2)(B).

96. *Id.* at § 1861(f)(3).

97. *Id.* at § 1861(f)(2)(A)(i).

98. *Id.*

99. *Id.* at § 1861(f)(2)(C)(i).

fere with diplomatic relations.[100] Absent a finding that certification
was made in bad faith, such certification is to be treated as
conclusive by the FISC.[101] Finally, if a petition to modify or set aside
a nondisclosure is denied, the recipient may not file another such
petition for one year.[102]

f. "Lone Wolf" Terrorists

In 2004, Congress amended FISA to expand the government's
authority to conduct electronic surveillance and physical searches of
suspected international terrorists.[103] Commonly referred to as the
"lone wolf" amendment, section 6001(a) of the Intelligence Reform
and Terrorism Prevention Act (IRTPA) broadened the definition of
an "agent of a foreign power" to include any non-U.S. person who
"engages in international terrorism or activities in preparation
therefor."[104] The "lone wolf" provision was prompted by an investigation of Zacarias Moussaoui, one of the individuals believed to be
responsible for the 9/11 terrorist attacks.[105] FBI agents suspected
that Moussaoui had planned a terrorist attack involving the pilot-
ing of commercial airliners, and detained him on an immigration
violation.[106] The FBI agents then sought a FISA court order to
examine the contents of Moussaoui's laptop computer and other
possessions.[107] However, the agency concluded that it lacked sufficient information to prove that Moussaoui was an agent of a foreign
power as then required by FISA.[108]

Prior to the "lone wolf" amendment, FISA authorized the
FISC to approve applications for physical searches only if probable
cause existed to believe that the premises to be searched were
owned or controlled by a foreign power or its agent.[109] The defini-

100. *Id.* at § 1861(f)(2)(C)(ii).

101. *Id.* However, in Doe v. Mukasey, 549 F.3d 861, 882 (2d Cir. 2008),
the Second Circuit considered a similar
provision involving judicial review of national security letters, holding that there
is no meaningful judicial review "of the
decision of the Executive Branch to prohibit speech if the position of the Executive Branch that speech would be harmful is 'conclusive' on the reviewing
court, absent only a demonstration of
bad faith." *Id.*

102. 50 U.S.C. § 1861(f)(2)(C)(iii).

103. Intelligence Reform and Terrorism Prevention Act of 2004, P.L. No.
108–458, § 6001, 118 Stat. 3638, 3742
(2004).

104. *See* IRTPA, § 6001(a), 118
Stat. at 3742 (codified at 50 U.S.C.
§ 1801(b)(1)(C)).

105. *See* AMENDMENTS TO THE FOREIGN
INTELLIGENCE SURVEILLANCE ACT, *supra* at
note 59, at 5 (discussing the connection
between the Moussaoui investigation
and the "lone wolf" provision); "LONE
WOLF" AMENDMENT, *supra* note 9, at 3
(discussing the historical context of the
"lone wolf" provision).

106. *See* NATIONAL COMMISSION ON
TERRORIST ATTACKS UPON THE UNITED
STATES, THE 9/11 COMMISSION REPORT, at
273–74 (W.W. Norton & Company 2004),
available at http://www.9–11commission.
gov/report/911Report.pdf   [hereinafter
"9/11 REPORT"].

107. *Id.*

108. *Id.* at 274.

109. 50 U.S.C. § 1821(4) (2001).

tion of "foreign power" included "groups engaged in international terrorism or activities in preparation therefor."[110] Further, individuals involved in acts of international terrorism for or on behalf of such groups were considered "agents of a foreign power."[111] Because the FBI was unable to establish probable cause to believe that Moussaoui was acting for or on behalf of a terrorist group, it was not able to obtain a FISA order to search his belongings.[112]

Following these revelations, Congress enacted section 6001 of the IRTPA, which provides that persons, other than U.S. citizens or permanent residents of the U.S., who are engaged in international terrorism are considered to be "agents of a foreign power."[113] The "lone wolf" provision eliminates any need to provide an evidentiary connection between the target of a FISA application and a foreign government or terrorist organization.[114] The proponents of the provision contend that "the increased self-organization among terror networks has made proving connections to identifiable groups more difficult. Thus, a 'lone wolf' provision is necessary to combat terrorists who use a modern organizational structure or who are self-radicalized."[115] Further, it should be emphasized that the expanded definition of an "agent of a foreign power" does not extend to U.S. persons.[116] Therefore, a FISA warrant could not be obtained to conduct surveillance of a U.S. citizen under the "lone wolf" provision.

g. Electronic Surveillance Without a Court Order

Electronic surveillance under FISA generally requires a court order, unless the surveillance fits within one of three statutory exceptions. The first exception involves electronic surveillance of certain foreign powers without a court order upon Attorney General certification that specific criteria have been met. Under 50 U.S.C. § 1802, the President, through the Attorney General, may authorize electronic surveillance to acquire foreign intelligence information for up to one year without a court order if two criteria are satisfied. First, the Attorney General must certify in writing under oath that:

> (A) the electronic surveillance is solely directed at—
>
> > (i) the acquisition of the contents of communications transmitted by means of communication used exclusively

---

110. *Id.* at § 1801(a)(4) (2001).

111. *Id.* at § 1801(b)(2)(C) (2001).

112. *See* 9/11 COMMISSION REPORT, *supra* note 103, at 274.

113. P.L. 108–458, § 6001(a) (codified at 50 U.S.C. § 1801(b)(1)(C) (2008)).

114. *Id.* The sunset date for § 6001 has been extended to February 28, 2011. P.L. 111–118, § 1004.

115. AMENDMENTS TO THE FOREIGN INTELLIGENCE SURVEILLANCE ACT, *supra* note 59, at 7.

116. 50 U.S.C. § 1801(b)(1)(C).

between or among foreign powers as defined in [50 U.S.C. § 1801(a)(1), (2), or (3)]; or

(ii) the acquisition of technical intelligence, other than the spoken communications of individuals, from property or premises under the open and exclusive control of a foreign power, as defined in [50 U.S.C. § 1801(a)(1), (2), or (3)];

(B) there is not substantial likelihood that the surveillance will acquire the contents of any communication to which a United States person is a party; and

(C) the proposed minimization procedures with respect to such surveillance meet the definition of minimization procedures under [50 U.S.C. § 1801(h)].[117]

Second, the Attorney General must report—

such minimization procedures and any changes thereto to the House Permanent Select Committee on Intelligence and the Senate Select Committee on Intelligence at least thirty days prior to their effective date, unless the Attorney General determines immediate action is required and notifies the committees immediately of such minimization and the reason for their becoming effective immediately.[118]

Under section 1802, electronic surveillance authorized without a court order may be directed against only three categories of "foreign powers." Those categories include "(1) a foreign government or any component thereof, whether or not recognized by the United States; (2) a faction of a foreign nation or nations, not substantially composed of United States persons; or (3) any entity that is openly acknowledged by a foreign government or governments to be directed or controlled by such foreign government or governments."[119] Further, such electronic surveillance must be conducted in accordance with the Attorney General's certification and the minimization procedures adopted by him.[120] Finally, a copy of the certification must be transmitted under seal by the Attorney General to the FISC.[121]

The second exception to the FISC order requirement is authorized in emergency situations. Section 1805(e)(1) provides that notwithstanding any other provisions of FISA, if the Attorney General "reasonably determines that an emergency situation exists with respect to the employment of electronic surveillance to obtain foreign intelligence information before an order authorizing such surveillance can with due diligence be obtained," he may authorize

117. 50 U.S.C. § 1802(a)(1)(A)–(C).
118. Id. at § 1802(a)(1)(C).
119. Id. at §§ 1801(a)(1), (2), (3).
120. Id. at § 1802(a)(2).
121. Id. at § 1802(a)(3).

electronic surveillance if specified steps are taken.[122] First, the Attorney General must reasonably determine that the factual basis for issuing an order to approve such electronic surveillance exists.[123] Second, at the time of the Attorney General's emergency authorization, he or his designee must inform a FISC judge that the decision to employ emergency electronic surveillance has been made.[124] Next, the Attorney General must ensure that the minimization procedures required for a judicial order are followed.[125] Finally, an application for a court order must be made as soon as practicable, but not more than 72 hours after the Attorney General authorizes such surveillance.[126] In the absence of a judicial order approving the electronic surveillance, the surveillance must terminate when the information sought is obtained, when the application for the order is denied, or after the expiration of seven days from the time of the Attorney General's authorization, whichever is earliest.[127]

The third and final statutory exception to the FISA warrant requirement is set forth in 50 U.S.C. § 1811. Section 1811 provides that the President, through the Attorney General, may authorize involves electronic surveillance without a court order to acquire foreign intelligence information for up to15 days following a congressional declaration of war.[128]

h. Targeting Non–U.S. Persons Outside the United States

The FISA Amendments Act of 2008 ("FAA"), 50 U.S.C. § 1881a, amended FISA by creating a new framework for certain federal officials to seek approval from the FISC to authorize surveillance targeting non-U.S. persons located outside the United States to acquire foreign intelligence information.[129] Under the FAA, "[n]otwithstanding any other provision of law, upon the issuance of an order in accordance with [50 U.S.C. § 1881a(i)(3)] or a determination under [50 U.S.C. § 1881a(c)(2)], the Attorney

122. *Id.* at § 1805(e)(1). The Attorney General may also authorize an emergency FISA search pursuant to the requirements set forth in 50 U.S.C. § 1824(e)(1). *See* United States v. Gowadia, 2009 WL 1649709 (D. Hawaii) (upholding FISA emergency search).

123. 50 U.S.C. § 1805(e)(1)(B).

124. *Id.* at § 1805(e)(1)(C).

125. *Id.* at § 1805(e)(2).

126. *Id.* at § 1805(e)(1)(D).

127. *Id.* at § 1805(e)(3).

128. *Id.* at § 1811.

129. P.L. 95–511, Title VII, § 702, as added P.L. 110–261, Title I, § 101(a)(2), July 10, 2008, 122 Stat. 2438. The FAA also added 50 U.S.C. § 1881b approving the targeting of a U.S. person reasonably believed to be located outside the United State to acquire foreign intelligence information, if the acquisition constitutes electronic surveillance, stored electronic communications, or stored electronic data, and such acquisition is conducted within the United States. *See* 50 U.S.C. §§ 1881b. Further, the FAA added section 1881c, authorizing the targeting of a U.S. person, where there is probable cause to believe that the person is reasonably believed to be located outside the United States, and such person is a foreign power, an agent of a foreign power, or an officer or employee of a foreign power. *Id.* at 1881c.

General and the Director of National Intelligence may authorize jointly, for a period of up to 1 year from the effective date of the authorization, the targeting of persons reasonably believed to be located outside the United States to acquire foreign intelligence information."[130]

i. The Application Process

In order to authorize electronic surveillance outside the United States under the FAA, the Attorney General and the Director of National Intelligence must apply for and obtain an order authorizing such surveillance from the FISC.[131] Unlike section 1804, which only requires approval by the Attorney General, an application for a FISA surveillance order under section 1881a requires the joint approval of the Attorney General and Director of National Intelligence.[132] Under section 1881a, the application consists of providing a written certification and supporting affidavit, under oath and under seal to the FISC.[133] The certification must attest, among other things, that there are procedures in place that have been approved or have been submitted for approval by the FISC that are reasonably designed to ensure that the acquisition of foreign intelligence information is limited to targeting persons reasonably believed to be located outside of the United States, and prevent the intentional acquisition of any communications as to which the sender and intended recipients are known to be located in the United States.[134] The certification must also attest that the Government has targeting and minimization procedures in place that have been approved, have been submitted for approval, or will be submitted with the certification for approval by the FISC.[135] Further, such procedures and guidelines must be consistent with the requirements of the Fourth Amendment.[136] "Targeting procedures" are procedures reasonably designed to ensure that the requested surveillance is limited to targeting persons reasonably believed to be located outside the United States and to prevent the intentional acquisition of communications known to be domestic communications at the time of the surveillance.[137] "Minimization procedures" under the FAA must meet the minimization procedures for purposes of electronic surveillance set forth under section 1801(h) or

---

130. 50 U.S.C. § 1881a(a).
131. *Id.* at §§ 1881a(a), (i)(3).
132. *Id.* at § 1804(a).
133. *Id.* at § 1881a(g)(1)(A).
134. *Id.* at § 1881a(g)(2)(A)(i).
135. *Id.* at § 1881a(g)(2)(A)(ii).
136. *Id.* at § 1881a(g)(2)(A)(iv). The explicit requirement that electronic surveillance be conducted in a manner consistent with the Fourth Amendment is new and not included in the FISA procedures governing the collection of foreign intelligence information domestically.

137. 50 U.S.C. §§ 1881a(d)(1), (g)(2)(A)(i)(I)–(II).

1821(4) of FISA.[138] The certification must also attest that a "significant purpose" of the requested surveillance is to obtain foreign intelligence information;[139] that the surveillance involves obtaining such information from or with the assistance of an electronic communications service provider;[140] and that the surveillance complies with certain limitations set forth in § 1881a(b).[141]

The statute imposes certain limitations or restrictions on the requested surveillance. Pursuant to section 1881a(b), the surveillance may not intentionally target: (1) any person known at the time of the surveillance to be located in the United States; (2) any person reasonably believed to be located outside of the United States if the purpose of such surveillance is to target a particular, known person reasonably believed to be in the United States; or (3) any U.S. person reasonably believed to be located outside the United States.[142] Moreover, the limitations imposed by section 1881a(b) prohibit the intentional acquisition of communications known at the time of the surveillance to be domestic communications.[143] Further, section 1881a(b) provides that the requested surveillance must be conducted in a manner consistent with the Fourth Amendment.[144] The certification must be supported by the affidavit of any appropriate official in the area of national security who is appointed by the President, by and with the advice and consent of the Senate, or who is the head of an element of the intelligence community,[145] and include an effective date for the authorization that is at least 30 days after the submission of the certification to the FISC, or, if the acquisition has begun or the effective date is less that 30 days after the submission of the certification to the FISC, the date the acquisition began or the effective date of the acquisition.[146]

Finally, in applying for an order from the FISC under the FAA, the certification is not required to identify the specific facilities, places, premises, or property at which the surveillance will be directed or conducted.[147] The Government is also not required to identify the targets of the requested surveillance or establish probable cause to believe that the targets of the surveillance are foreign powers or agents of a foreign power.[148] This represents a major departure from section 1805, which requires the FISC to find on the basis of the facts submitted by the applicant that there is probable cause to believe that (1) the target of the electronic

138. *Id.* at § 1881a(e).
139. *Id.* at § 1881a(g)(2)(A)(v).
140. *Id.* at § 1881a(g)(2)(A)(vi).
141. *Id.* at § 1881a(g)(2)(A)(vii).
142. *Id.* at §§ 1881a(b)(1)–(3).
143. *Id.* at § 1881b(1)(4).
144. *Id.* at § 1881a(b)(5).
145. *Id.* at § 1881a(g)(2)(C).
146. *Id.* at § 1881a(g)(2)(D).
147. *Id.* at § 1881a(g)(4).
148. *See* Amnesty Intern. USA v. McConnell, 646 F. Supp.2d 633, 641 (S.D.N.Y. 2009).

surveillance is a foreign power or an agent of a foreign power and (2) each of the facilities or places at which the electronic surveillance is directed is being used, or is about to be used, by a foreign power or an agent of a foreign power.[149]

ii. Issuance of an Order

The FISC has jurisdiction to review a certification for electronic surveillance under the FAA, including the targeting and minimization procedures adopted by the Attorney General and the Director of National Intelligence.[150] If the FISC finds that the certification and the targeting and minimization procedures are in compliance with the statute and the Fourth Amendment, the court must enter an order granting the Government approval to authorize the requested surveillance.[151] However, the FISC must complete its review and issue an order not later than 30 days after the date on which such certification and the targeting and minimization procedures are submitted for approval.[152]

2. LEGAL CHALLENGES TO FISA

a. Standing

In order to reach the merits of a legal challenge to a FISA surveillance order, the court must first determine whether the plaintiffs have standing to bring such cause of action. "Standing is an aspect of justiciability."[153] The court must initially determine whether the plaintiff has standing to invoke the jurisdiction of the federal courts to decide the merits of the underlying dispute.[154] Article III of the Constitution limits the jurisdiction of federal courts to "Cases" and "Controversies."[155] To establish standing, a plaintiff must establish that "(1) [he] has suffered an actual or imminent injury in fact, that is concrete and particularized, and not conjectural or hypothetical; (2) there is a causal connection between the injury and the defendant's actions; and (3) it is likely that a favorable decision in the case will address the injury."[156] Because the judicial power of federal courts "exists only to redress or otherwise protect against injury to the complaining party," a federal court's jurisdiction "can be invoked only when the plaintiff . . . has suffered 'some threatened or actual injury resulting from the

---

149. 50 U.S.C. § 1805(a)(2)(A)–(B).

150. *Id.* at § 1881a(i)(1)(A).

151. *Id.* at § 1881a(i)(3)(A).

152. *Id.* at § 1881a(i)(1)(B).

153. ACLU v. NSA, 493 F.3d 644, 652 (6th Cir. 2007). *See also* Warth v. Seldin, 422 U.S. 490, 498 (1975); Daimler Chrysler Corp. v. Cuno, 547 U.S. 332 (2006); Amnesty Intern. USA v. McCon-

nell, 646 F. Supp.2d 633, 643 (S.D.N.Y. 2009) (internal citations omitted).

154. *See ACLU v. NSA,* 493 F.3d at 652; *Amnesty Intern. USA v. McConnell,* 646 F. Supp.2d at 643.

155. Lujan v. Defenders of Wildlife, 504 U.S. 555, 559 (1992).

156. *Id.* at 560–61. *See also* Steel Co. v. Citizens for a Better Env't, 523 U.S. 83, 102–03 (1998).

putatively illegal action. . . .' "[157] Further, the party invoking the jurisdiction of the court bears the burden of establishing standing.[158] Finally, the plaintiff must generally assert his own rights, and cannot establish standing on the basis of the legal rights or interests of third parties.[159]

Plaintiffs attempting to challenge the constitutionality of FISA surveillance orders have struggled to establish standing to litigate such actions. In *ACLU v. NSA*, the plaintiffs claimed that the Terrorist Surveillance Program ("TSP") conducted by the National Security Agency ("NSA") violated their First Amendment and Fourth Amendment rights.[160] The TSP involved the warrantless interception of telephone and email communications where one party to the communication was located outside the United States and the NSA had "a reasonable basis to conclude that one party to the communication is a member of al Qaeda, affiliated with al Qaeda, or a member of an organization affiliated with al Qaeda, or working in support of al Qaeda."[161] The plaintiffs included journalists, academics, and lawyers who regularly communicated with individuals located overseas, whom they believed the NSA suspected of being affiliated with al Qaeda and therefore likely to be monitored under the TSP.[162] Plaintiffs claimed that overseas clients, witnesses, and other sources were unwilling to communicate by telephone or email, due to their fear that the NSA will intercept the communications.[163] However, the plaintiffs did not assert that any of their own communications had ever been intercepted.[164] Instead, they alleged only a belief that their communications were being intercepted, based on their own assessment of their overseas contacts as people who are likely to fall within the TSP.[165]

Plaintiffs alleged that the NSA had, by conducting warrantless surveillance, violated their First Amendment free speech and freedom of association rights.[166] Plaintiffs claimed that the TSP had a chilling effect on telephone and email communications with overseas clients, witnesses and other associates, which constituted protected speech under the First Amendment.[167] The Sixth Circuit held that plaintiffs lacked standing to pursue their First Amendment claim.[168] More specifically, the court concluded that the plaintiffs failed to show that they suffered some actual or threatened injury

157. *Warth*, 422 U.S. at 499 (quoting Linda R.S. v. Richard D., 410 U.S. 614, 617 (1973)). *See also Steel Co.*, 523 U.S. at 103.

158. *See Lujan v. Defenders of Wildlife*, 504 U.S. at 561.

159. *Warth*, 422 U.S. at 499.

160. ACLU v. NSA, 493 F.3d 644 (6th Cir. 2007).

161. *Id.* at 648–9.

162. *Id.*

163. *Id.* at 665.

164. *Id.* at 673.

165. *Id.*

166. ACLU v. NSA, 493 F.3d 644, 659 (6th Cir. 2007).

167. *Id.* at 660.

168. *Id.* at 673.

as a result of the Government's conduct. In reaching its conclusion, the court relied on the Supreme Court's ruling in *Laird v. Tatum*.[169] In *Laird*, the Supreme Court considered a First Amendment challenge to an Army surveillance program that entailed "the collection of information about public activities that were thought to have at least some potential for civil disorder," and the dissemination and storage of such information within the Army.[170] Plaintiffs argued that they had standing to challenge the program because it chilled the exercise of their First Amendment rights.[171] The Supreme Court rejected the argument, reasoning that plaintiffs had failed to connect the existence of surveillance program to their own speech. The Supreme Court framed the issue as "whether the jurisdiction of a federal court may be invoked by a complainant who alleges that the exercise of his First Amendment rights is being chilled by the mere existence, without more, of a governmental investigative and data-gathering activity."[172] While plaintiffs may have suffered a "subjective chill," the Court stated, they did not allege a sufficiently concrete, actual and imminent injury to demonstrate standing.[173] The Court held that "[a]llegations of a subjective 'chill' are not an adequate substitute for a claim of specific present objective harm or a threat of specific future harm[.]"[174] Finally, the Supreme Court distinguished its prior cases finding standing, explaining that "in each of these cases, the challenged exercise of governmental power was regulatory, proscriptive, or compulsory in nature, and the complainant was either presently or proscriptively subject to the regulations, proscriptions, or compulsions that he was challenging."[175]

Applying the reasoning in *Laird*, the Sixth Circuit posited that to allege a sufficient injury under the First Amendment, a plaintiff must establish that he is "regulated, constrained, or compelled directly by the government's actions, instead of by his ... subjective chill."[176] The court found that plaintiffs' alleged injury was based on two purely subjective and speculative fears: "(1) that the NSA will actually intercept the plaintiffs' particular communications, and (2) that armed with the fruit of those interceptions, the NSA will take action detrimental to the contacts."[177] Ultimately, the court could find no basis to distinguish *Laird* from the First Amendment claims raised by the plaintiffs. The court held:

169. Laird v. Tatum, 408 U.S. 1 (1972).

170. *Id*. at 9.

171. *Id*.

172. *Id*. at 15.

173. *Id*.

174. *Id*. at 13–4 & n. 7.

175. Laird v. Tatum, 408 U.S. 1, 11 (1972).

176. *ACLU v. NSA*, 493 F.3d at 661.

177. *Id*. at 662.

The plaintiffs' first alleged injury, arising from a personal subjective chill, is no more concrete, actual, or imminent than the injury alleged in *Laird*. The injury in *Laird* was insufficient to establish standing for a First Amendment cause of action; the plaintiffs' first injury is less than or, at best, equal to that in *Laird*; and [therefore] ... likewise insufficient to establish standing.[178]

The court in *ACLU v. NSA* also rejected plaintiffs' second alleged injury; the unwillingness of their overseas clients, witnesses and other associates to communicate by telephone or email, due to their "fear" that the NSA will intercept the communications. The court held that plaintiffs failed to satisfy either of two criteria required to prove standing—causation or redressability.[179] Plaintiffs claimed that the "putatively illegal action" involved the NSA's interception of overseas communications without FSIA warrants, and the "threatened or actual injury" included the added cost of in-person communications with their overseas contacts and the diminished performance resulting from the inability to communicate.[180] According to plaintiffs, the absence of a FISA warrant has chilled the plaintiffs and their overseas contacts from communicating by telephone or email.[181] The court was skeptical of plaintiffs' claim, stating that "it is not clear whether the chill can fairly be traced to the absence of a warrant, or if the chill would still exist without regard to the presence of absence of a warrant."[182] Moreover, the court noted "the plaintiffs have not proffered any types or topics of communication, from which they are currently refraining, but about which—upon the imposition of FISA limitations and protections—they would thereafter 'freely engage in conversations and correspond[ence] via email.' "[183] Thus, the court held that "the plaintiffs had not shown a sufficient causal connection between the complained-of conduct (i.e., the absence of a warrant or FISA protection) and the alleged harm (i.e., the inability to communicate)."[184]

The court also held that the plaintiffs had failed to satisfy the redressability element for proving standing. The court stated that

---

178. *Id.* at 665. *See also* United Presbyterian Church in the United States of America v. Reagan, 738 F.2d 1375 (D.C. Cir. 1984) (rejecting standing based on fear of surveillance); Amnesty Intern. USA v. McConnell, 646 F. Supp.2d 633, 647 (S.D.N.Y. 2009) ("[Plaintiffs] have failed to allege a concrete harm 'apart from' the chilling effect on their international communications, and the chilling effect is their subjective fear of being surveilled which is insufficient in the absence of evidence that they are subject to surveillance under the statute.").

179. *Id.* at 670–1.

180. *Id.* at 667.

181. *Id.* at 667–8.

182. ACLU v. NSA, 493 F.3d 644, 668 (6th Cir. 2007).

183. *Id.* at 669 (internal citations omitted).

184. *Id.* at 670.

"redressability rests on the premise that the NSA's compliance with FISA's warrant requirement will entice the plaintiffs and their contacts to 'freely engage in conversations and correspond vial email without concern.' "[185] The court concluded that even with the imposition of a warrant requirement, the plaintiffs' fear will not be abated.[186] The "remedy" would therefore not address the injuries alleged.[187] Thus, the court held that plaintiffs lack standing to pursue their First Amendment claim because their alleged injury is not redressable by the remedy they seek.[188]

Finally, the court rejected plaintiffs' Fourth Amendment claim for lack of standing. The court stated that "it would be unprecedented for this court to find standing for plaintiffs to litigate a Fourth Amendment cause of action without any evidence that the plaintiffs themselves have been subjected to an illegal search or seizure."[189] Further, the concurring opinion rejected plaintiffs' standing argument relying on *United Presbyterian Church*.[190] In *United Presbyterian Church*, the D.C. Circuit denied standing to plaintiffs seeking to challenge the constitutionality of Executive Order 1233, which created a framework within which intelligence agencies could apply to the Attorney General for approval to collect, retain of disseminate certain kinds of intelligence information.[191] The plaintiffs were political and religious organizations that claimed that they were likely to be subject to surveillance under the Executive Order.[192] The D.C. Circuit rejected plaintiffs' attempt to rely upon the "threat" of surveillance for standing to challenge the Executive Order, explaining that "[t]he problem with [the plaintiffs'] attempt to rely upon this sort of harm to establish standing . . . is that they have not adequately averred that any specific action is threatened or even contemplated against them."[193] The D.C. Circuit stated that "[t]o give these plaintiffs standing on the basis of threatened injury would be to acknowledge, for example, that all churches would have standing to challenge a statute which provides that search warrants may be sought for church property if there is a reasonable belief that felons have taken refuge there. This is not the law."[194]

In *ACLU v. NSA*, the concurring opinion distinguished cases involving "[a] genuine threat of enforcement of a policy against a plaintiff who is demonstrably subject to that policy," which supports standing, from cases "in which a plaintiff cannot establish

---

185. *Id.* at 671.

186. *Id.*

187. *Id.*

188. ACLU v. NSA, 493 F.3d 644, 673 (6th Cir. 2007).

189. *Id.* at 673–74.

190. *Id.* at 690–91.

191. United Presbyterian Church in the United States of America v. Reagan, 738 F.2d 1375 (D.C. Cir. 1984).

192. *Id.* at 1380.

193. *Id.*

194. *Id.*

that he is subject to the policy but merely fears that he is subject to the policy that may be enforced, which cannot support standing."[195] The plaintiffs in the *NSA* case, like the plaintiffs in *United Presbyterian Church,* failed to show that they are subject to the surveillance policy they seek to challenge.[196] In the absence of such a showing, the Sixth Circuit held that the plaintiffs' fear that they will suffer harm is insufficient to support standing.[197]

b. Fourth Amendment

FISA warrants have been challenged as a violation of the Fourth Amendment. Several arguments have been raised in support of these claims. Petitioners maintain that FISA procedures (1) lack a particularity requirement, (2) lack reasonable durational limits, and (3) fail to provide adequate notice. However, every court that has considered the issue except for one has rejected such claims, finding that FISA does not violate the Fourth Amendment.[198]

The Fourth Amendment protects the right "to be secure . . . against unreasonable searches and seizures."[199] Whether warrantless electronic surveillance conducted for the purpose of gathering foreign intelligence information violates the Fourth Amendment has never been squarely addressed by the United States Supreme Court. In *Olmstead v. United States,* decided in 1928, the Supreme Court held that a wiretap installed without trespassing onto private property did not violate the Fourth Amendment.[200] According to the *Olmstead* Court, the constitutionality of electronic surveillance turned on whether placement of the electronic surveillance device involved trespassory conduct.[201] Approximately forty years later the

---

195. ACLU v. NSA, 493 F.3d 644, 689 n.2 (6th Cir. 2007) (Gibbons, J., concurring).

196. *Id.* at 691 (Gibbons, J., concurring).

197. *Id.* at 674. *See also* Amnesty Intern. USA v. McConnell, 646 F. Supp.2d 633, 652 (S.D.N.Y. 2009) ("The plaintiffs in this case have failed to show that they are subject to the statute other than by speculation and conjecture, which is insufficient for standing.").

198. *See, e.g.,* In re Directives Pursuant to Sec. 105B, 551 F.3d 1004 (Foreign Int.Surv.Ct. Rev. 2008); United States v. Wen, 477 F.3d 896, 898 (7th Cir. 2007); United States v. Damrah, 412 F.3d 618, 625 (6th Cir. 2005); In re Sealed Case, 310 F.3d 717, 742–46 (Foreign Int.Surv.Ct. Rev. 2002); United States v. Pelton, 835 F.2d 1067, 1075

(4th Cir. 1987); United States v. Cavanaugh, 807 F.2d 787, 790–91 (9th Cir. 1987); United States v. Duggan, 743 F.2d 59 (2d Cir. 1984); United States v. Abu–Jihaad, 531 F. Supp.2d 299, 309 (D. Conn. 2008); United States v. Mubayyid, 521 F. Supp.2d 125, 140–1 (D. Mass. 2007); United States v. Holy Land Found. for Relief & Dev., 2007 WL 2011319, at *5–6 (N.D. Tex. (2007); United States v. Sattar, 2003 WL 22137012, at *3–5 (S.D.N.Y. 2003); American Civil Liberties Union v. United States Dep't of Justice, 265 F. Supp.2d 20, 32 & n.12 (D.D.C. 2003). *But see* Mayfield v. United States, 504 F. Supp.2d 1023, 1036–43 (D. Or. 2007).

199. U.S. CONST. amend. IV.

200. Olmstead v. United States, 277 U.S. 438 (1928).

201. *Id.*

Supreme Court overturned its previous holding in *Olmstead*. In *Katz v. United States,* the Court abandoned the trespass approach, ruling that "the Government's activities in electronically listening to and recording petitioner's words violated the privacy upon which he justifiably relied while using a telephone booth and thus constituted a 'search and seizure' within the meaning of the Fourth Amendment."[202] The Court reasoned that the fact that the electronic device employed to record the conversation did not penetrate the wall of the phone booth was constitutionally irrelevant.[203] The Court declared: "[O]nce it is recognized that the Fourth Amendment protects people—and not simply 'areas'—against unreasonable searches and seizures, it becomes clear that the reach of that Amendment cannot turn upon the presence or absence of a physical intrusion into any given enclosure."[204]

The Supreme Court in *Katz*, however, did not extend its holding to national security cases.[205] In a footnote, the Court stated that "[w]hether safeguards other than prior authorization by a magistrate would satisfy the Fourth Amendment in a situation involving the national security is a question not presented by this case."[206] In fact, the Justices were strongly divided on whether the Fourth Amendment warrant clause applies to the seizure of foreign intelligence information. Justice White argued that "[w]e should not require the warrant procedure and the magistrate's judgment if the President of the United States or his chief legal officer, the Attorney General, has considered the requirements of national security and authorized electronic surveillance as reasonable."[207] Justice Douglas, joined by Justice Brennan, disagreed, claiming that Justice White sought to grant "a wholly unwarranted green light for the Executive Branch to resort to electronic eavesdropping without a warrant in cases which the Executive Branch itself labels 'national security' matters."[208]

In *United States v. United States District Court*, commonly known as the *Keith* case (the name of the district court judge against whom the Government sought a writ of mandamus), the Supreme Court addressed the constitutionality of the use of war-

---

202. Katz v. United States, 389 U.S. 347, 353 (1967).

203. *Id.*

204. *Id.* The test that has evolved from *Katz* has become known as the "reasonable expectation of privacy" test, which has two requirements: "first that a person [has] exhibited an actual (subjective) expectation of privacy and, second that the expectation [is] one that society is prepared to recognize as 'reasonable.'" *Id.* at 361 (Harlan, J., concurring). This formulation has been

adopted in subsequent cases. *See, e.g.,* Smith v. Maryland, 442 U.S. 735, 740 (1979).

205. *Katz*, 389 U.S. at 358 n.23.

206. *Id.*

207. *Id.* at 364 (White, J., concurring). *See also The "Lone Wolf" Amendment, supra* note 9, at 432–33 (discussing *Katz* and its application to FISA).

208. *Id.* at 359 (Douglas, J., concurring).

rantless electronic surveillance against a purely domestic target.[209] Justice Powell, writing for the *Keith* Court, framed the matter before the Court as follows:

> The issue before us is an important one for the people of our country and their Government. It involves the delicate question of the President's power, acting through the Attorney General, to authorize electronic surveillance in internal security matters without prior judicial approval. Successive Presidents for more than one-quarter of a century have authorized such surveillance in varying degrees, without guidance from Congress or a definitive decision of this Court. This case brings the issue here for the first time. Its resolution is a matter of national concern, requiring sensitivity both to the Government's right to protect itself from unlawful subversion and attack and to the citizen's right to be secure in his privacy against unreasonable Government intrusion.[210]

Ultimately, the Court held that, in the case of intelligence gathering involving purely domestic surveillance, prior judicial approval was required to satisfy the Fourth Amendment.[211] However, the Court emphasized that its holding was limited to cases involving only the domestic aspects of national security.[212] The Court declared: "We have not addressed, and express no opinion as to, the issues which may be involved with respect to activities of foreign powers or their agents."[213]

While the Supreme Court has not decided the matter, the FISCR has directly addressed the issue, rejecting claims that FISA violates the Fourth Amendment. In *In re Sealed Case*, the FISCR held that electronic surveillance authorized by FISA satisfies the Fourth Amendment's reasonableness requirement.[214] The FISCR began its analysis by comparing the requirements for obtaining a surveillance order under FISA and Title III, which allows a court to issue an *ex parte* order for electronic surveillance for domestic law enforcement purposes.[215] The court noted that the Fourth Amendment's Warrant Clause has been interpreted to require three elements: (1) prior judicial review by a neutral and disinterested magistrate; (2) probable cause to believe that the evidence sought will aid in apprehension and prosecution for a particular offense; and (3) that the warrant particularly describe the "things to be seized" and the place to be searched.[216] Addressing the first ele-

---

209. United States v. United States District Court, 407 U.S. 297 (1972).

210. *Id.* at 299.

211. *Id.* at 321.

212. *Id.*

213. *Id.* at 321–2.

214. In re Sealed Case, 310 F.3d 717, 746 (Foreign Int.Surv.Ct.Rev. 2002).

215. *Id.* at 737–38.

216. *Id.* at 738 (quoting Dalia v. United States, 441 U.S. 238, 255 (1979)).

ment, the FISCR held that both FISA and Title III require prior judicial review of an application for an order authorizing electronic surveillance.[217] Further, there is no dispute, the court stated, that a FISA judge satisfies the Fourth Amendment's requirement of a "neutral and detached magistrate."[218]

Other courts have embraced this view, finding that the FISA court provides "neutral and responsible oversight of the government's activities in intelligence surveillance."[219] In *United States v. Mubayyid*, the court reasoned:

> Although judicial review of FISA applications is certainly more circumscribed than that of search warrant applications generally, it is far from a meaningless rubber-stamp. The requisite certifications must be made by high-ranking executive branch officers, providing an important check against reckless and arbitrary actions by law enforcement officers, particularly those in the field. . . . [A] judicial officer plainly has the ability to deny a request intended solely for domestic law enforcement purposes, or where the foreign intelligence purpose is not signifcant. Furthermore, the statute provides the judicial officer the opportunity to require additional information.[220]

Thus, because FISA interposes a neutral and detached judicial officer between the Government and the target of the surveillance, the courts have consistently held that FISA satisfies the requirement of review by a neutral and disinterested magistrate.[221]

Turning to the probable cause requirement, the FISCR in *In re Sealed Case* noted that FISA and Title III differ to some extent in their probable cause showings.[222] Title III allows a court to enter an *ex parte* order if it finds "there is probable cause for belief that an individual is committing, has committed, or is about to commit" a specified predicate crime.[223] FISA requires a showing of probable cause that the target is a foreign power or agent of a foreign power

---

217. *In re Sealed Case,* 310 F.3d at 738 (citing 50 U.S.C. §§ 1805, 2518).

218. *In re Sealed Case*, 310 F.3d at 738 (citations omitted).

219. United States v. Cavanagh, 807 F.2d 787, 790 (9th Cir. 1987).

220. United States v. Mubayyid, 521 F. Supp.2d 125, 136 (D. Mass. 2007).

221. *See* United States v. Spanjol, 720 F.Supp. 55, 58 (E.D. Pa. 1989) ("FISA's procedure for obtaining judicial authorization of the Government's electronic surveillance for foreign intelligence purposes interposes a neutral and detached judicial officer between the Government and the target of the surveillance. As such, it satisfies the war-

rant requirement of the Fourth Amendment."); United States v. Megahey, 553 F.Supp. 1180, 1190 (E.D.N.Y. 1982) ("[T]he FISA warrant is a warrant within the meaning of the Fourth Amendment, since it provides for the interposition of independent judicial magistrates between the executive and the subject of the surveillance which the warrant requirement was designed to assure."), *aff'd sub nom.* United States v. Duggan, 743 F.2d 59 (2d Cir. 1984).

222. In re Sealed Case, 310 F.3d 717, 738 (Foreign Int.Surv.Ct.Rev. 2002).

223. *Id.* (quoting 18 U.S.C. § 2518(3)(a)).

and that each of the facilities or places at which electronic surveillance is directed is being used by a foreign power or agent of a foreign power.[224] However, the court found that the differences were not constitutionally significant. While the two probable cause standards differ, the differences appear reasonably adapted to the particular challenges of foreign intelligence gathering.[225] The court stated that FISA is sufficiently limited and applies only "to certain carefully delineated, and particularly serious foreign threats to national security."[226] Thus, the court concluded that FISA does not violate the Fourth Amendment's probable cause requirement.[227]

Addressing the particularity requirement of the Warrant Clause, the FISCR noted that while Title III requires probable cause to believe that particular communications concerning the specified crime will be obtained through electronic surveillance, FISA requires an official to delineate the type of foreign information being sought, and to certify that such information is foreign intelligence information.[228] Further, to ensure that only relevant information is sought, FISA requires that the certification must be made by a national security officer and approved by the Attorney General or Deputy Attorney General.[229] FISA also requires probable cause to believe that each of the facilities or places at which the surveillance is directed is being used by a foreign power or agent.[230] When compared to the Title III warrant requirements, the court concluded that "FISA requires less of a nexus between the facility and the pertinent communications than Title III, but more of a nexus between the target and the pertinent communications."[231] Accordingly, the FISCR held that FISA's particularity requirements, while different from those of Title III, satisfy the Fourth Amendment.[232]

The FISCR considered other elements of Title III that some circuits have determined to be constitutionally significant: necessi-

224. *Id.* (citing 50 U.S.C. § 1805(a)(3)).

225. *In re Sealed Case*, 310 F.3d at 738.

226. *Id.* at 739.

227. *Id.* at 738–39. *See also* United States v. Pelton, 835 F.2d 1067, 1075 (4th Cir. 1987) (holding FISA "compatible with the Fourth Amendment," despite allowing surveillance on "less than traditional probable standard," because "FISA's numerous safeguards provide sufficient protection for the rights guaranteed by the Fourth Amendment"); *Duggan*, 743 F.2d at 74 (FISA does not violate the probable cause requirement of the Fourth Amendment); *United States v. Mubayyid*, 521 F. Supp.2d at 137 (same). *But see Mayfield*, 504 F. Supp.2d at 1038–39 (holding that FISA violates the probable cause requirement of the Fourth Amendment).

228. In re Sealed Case, 310 F.3d 717, 739 (Foreign Int.Surv.Ct.Rev. 2002).

229. *Id.*

230. *Id.* at 740.

231. *Id.*

232. *Id. See also Cavanagh*, 807 F.2d at 791 ("We reject appellant's suggestion that FISA violates the Fourth Amendment's particularity requirement. . . ."); *Mubayyid*, 521 F. Supp.2d at 138 (FISA satisfies the particularity requirement of the Fourth Amendment).

ty, duration of surveillance and minimization.[233] The court concluded that both Title III and FISA have a "necessity" provision, which requires the court to find that the information sought is not available through normal investigative procedures.[234] The statutes also have durational provisions; Title III orders may last for 30 days, while FISA orders may last for up to 90 days for U.S. persons.[235] However, the court stated that the longer period for FISA orders is justified based on the nature of national security surveillance, which is "often long range and involves the interrelation of various sources and types of information."[236] The court also noted that FISA requires minimization procedures governing the acquisition, retention, and dissemination of non-public information.[237] Further, the court posited that the reasonableness of minimization procedures depends on the facts and circumstances of each case.[238]

Finally, the FISCR focused on the differences between FISA and Title III concerning notice.[239] Title III requires notice to the target once the surveillance order expires.[240] FISA does not require notice to a person whose communications were intercepted unless the government "intends to enter into evidence or otherwise use or disclose" such communications in a criminal trial or other enumerated proceeding against the target.[241] However, the court stated that FISA's notice requirements are not unreasonable, given the balance of competing interests.[242] Congress concluded, the court stated, that nondisclosure was justified to preserve secrecy for sensitive counterintelligence sources and methods.[243] Thus, the FISCR held that FISA's notice provisions are reasonable and do not violate the Fourth Amendment.[244] Ultimately, the court concluded that "the procedures and government showings under FISA, if they do not meet the minimum Fourth Amendment warrant standards, certainly come close."[245] Balancing the competing interests of protecting an individual's privacy interests against the nation's need to obtain foreign intelligence information, the court held that FISA's surveil-

233. *In re Sealed Case*, 310 F.3d at 740.

234. *Id.* (citing 18 U.S.C. § 2518(3)(c); 50 U.S.C. §§ 1804(a)(7)(E)(ii), 1805(a)(5)).

235. *Id.* (citing 18 U.S.C. § 2518(5), 50 U.S.C. § 1805(e)(1)).

236. *Id.* (quoting *Keith*, 407 U.S. at 332).

237. *Id.*

238. *Id.*

239. *Id.*

240. *Id.* at 741.

241. *Id.* (citing 50 U.S.C. § 1806(c)).

242. *Id.*

243. *Id.*

244. *Id.* at 741–42. *See also Mubayyid*, 521 F. Supp.2d at 139 (FISA's notice provisions do not violate the Fourth Amendment).

245. *In re Sealed Case*, 310 F.3d at 746.

lance provisions satisfy the Fourth Amendment's reasonableness requirement.[246]

The FISCR also maintained that FISA surveillance orders could be upheld under the "special needs" exception to the warrant requirement.[247] The Supreme Court has approved warrantless searches that are designed to serve the government's "special needs, beyond the normal need for law enforcement."[248] FISA surveillance warrants are for the purpose of gathering foreign intelligence information and protecting national security, the court noted; these interests are beyond the ordinary needs of law enforcement.[249]

In *In re Directives Pursuant to Sec. 105B*, a communications service provider challenged directives issued by the Government pursuant to the Protect America Act (PAA), commanding petitioner to assist in warrantless surveillance of certain customers reasonably believed to be located outside the United States.[250] The FISCR upheld the warrantless surveillance authorized under FISA, rejecting petitioner's Fourth Amendment challenge on two grounds.[251] First, the FISCR found that a FISA surveillance order falls within the "special needs" exception to the Fourth Amendment's Warrant Clause.[252] Second, the court held that in light of the governmental interest at stake and the procedural protections provided in the statute, surveillance under FISA satisfies the Fourth Amendment's reasonableness requirement.[253] To fall within the "special needs" exception to the warrant requirement, the Government must prove that (1) the purpose behind the search and seizure is beyond the normal needs for law enforcement and (2) insisting upon a warrant would materially interfere with the accomplishment of that pur-

---

246. *Id.*

247. *Id.* at 745–6.

248. *Id.* at 745 (quoting Vernonia School Dist. 47J v. Acton, 515 U.S. 646, 653 (1995) (quoting Griffin v. Wisconsin, 483 U.S. 868, 873 (1987)).

249. *In re Sealed Case*, 310 F.3d at 746.

250. In re Directives Pursuant to Sec. 105B, 551 F.3d 1004 (Foreign Int. Surv.Ct.Rev. 2008). The PAA provisions sunset on February 16, 2008, and were repealed on July 10, 2008. However, provisions authorizing surveillance targeting non-U.S. persons located outside of the United States to acquire foreign intelligence information were enacted as part of the FISA Amendments Act (FAA) of 2008 (codified at 50 U.S.C.

§ 1881a). However, section 1881a requires that an application for electronic surveillance conducted abroad be submitted to the FISC for approval. *See* 50 U.S.C. § 1881a(i)(1).

251. The FISCR held that petitioner had standing to mount a challenge to the legality of the FISA directives based on the Fourth Amendment rights of third-party customers. *Id.* at 1008. The court reasoned that petitioner "faces an injury in the nature of the burden that it must shoulder to facilitate the government's surveillances of its customers; that injury is obviously and indisputably caused by the government through the directives; and this court is capable of redressing the injury." *Id.*

252. *Id.* at 1012.

253. *Id.* at 1016.

pose.[254] Applying the two-part test, the FISCR concluded that the central purpose of the FISA surveillance order was to collect foreign intelligence information.[255] The court stated: "There is no indication that the collections of information are primarily related to ordinary criminal-law enforcement purposes."[256] Thus, the purpose of the Government's actions was beyond routine law enforcement, satisfying the first prong of the two-prong test.[257] Next, the court posited that there was a high degree of probability that requiring a warrant would hinder the government's ability to gather time-sensitive information, undermining vital national security interests.[258] Compliance with the warrant requirement would frustrate the government's efforts to collect foreign intelligence information in a timely manner, potentially jeopardizing national security.[259] For these reasons, the FISCR held that the "foreign intelligence exception to the Fourth Amendment's warrant requirement exists when surveillance is conducted to obtain foreign intelligence for national security purposes and is directed against foreign powers or agents of foreign powers reasonably believed to be located outside the United States."[260]

The FISCR also held that the warrantless surveillance of persons believed to be located abroad constitutes a reasonable exercise of government power under the Fourth Amendment. The FISCR stated that to determine the reasonableness of the government's actions, the court must consider the totality of the circumstances.[261] Further, the totality of the circumstances model requires the court to balance the competing interests at stake.[262] In balancing the competing interests involving the privacy rights of the targeted persons and governmental interests of national security, the FISCR stated that national security is an interest of the "highest order or magnitude."[263] The court emphasized the procedural protections spelled out in the PAA and those mandated under

254. *Id.* at 1010. *See also* Vernonia Sch. Dist. 47J v. Acton, 515 U.S. 646, 653 (1995) (holding that drug testing of high school athletes and explaining that the exception to the warrant requirement applies "when special needs, beyond the normal need for law enforcement, make the warrant and probable-cause requirement[s] impracticable") (quoting Griffin v. Wisconsin, 483 U.S. 868, 873 (1987)); Skinner v. Railway Labor Execs. Ass'n, 489 U.S. 602, 620 (1989) (upholding regulations instituting drug and alcohol testing of railroad workers based on safety considerations, not law enforcement concerns); *cf.* Terry v. Ohio, 392 U.S. 1, 23–4 (1968) (upholding stop and patdown for weapons to protect safety of officers without a warrant).

255. *In re Directives Pursuant to Sec. 105B*, 551 F.3d at 1011.

256. *Id.*

257. *Id.*

258. *Id.*

259. *Id.*

260. *Id.* at 1012.

261. *Id. See also* Samson v. California, 547 U.S. 843, 848 (2006); Tennessee v. Garner, 471 U.S. 1, 8–9 (1985).

262. *In re Directives Pursuant to Sec. 105B*, 551 F.3d at 1012.

263. *Id.*

the certifications and directives.[264] Those safeguards, the court stated, comprise at least five components: "targeting procedures, minimization procedures, a procedure to ensure that a significant purpose is to obtain foreign intelligence information, procedures incorporated through Executive Order 12333, § 2.5, and procedures outlined in an affidavit supporting the certifications."[265] The FISCR found that collectively these procedures require a showing of particularity, a meaningful probable cause determination, a showing of necessity, and a reasonable duration time limit not to exceed 90 days.[266] Thus, the court stated that "[b]alancing these findings against the vital nature of the government's national security interest and the manner of the intrusion, we hold that the surveillances at issue satisfy the Fourth Amendment's reasonableness requirement."[267]

c.   Suppression of FISA Evidence in Criminal Prosecutions

FISA explicitly authorizes the use of evidence obtained or derived from electronic surveillance, physical searches, pen registers or trap and trace devices in a criminal prosecution, so long as the use comports with FISA procedures.[268] FISA evidence can be used in a criminal proceedings before federal, state and local courts only with the advance authorization of the Attorney General.[269] Evidentiary use of FISA evidence is permitted in criminal proceedings, provided that proper notice is given to the court and each "aggrieved person" against whom the information is to be used.[270] Upon receiving such notice, an aggrieved person may seek to suppress use of any FISA-derived evidence on the grounds that the evidence was unlawfully acquired, or the electronic surveillance, physical search, pen register or trap and trace device was not conducted in conformity with an order of authorization or approval.[271] Pursuant to 50 U.S.C. §§ 1806(f), 1825(g) and 1845(f), the

---

264. *Id.* at 1013.

265. *Id.*

266. *Id.* at 1016.

267. *Id.*

268. *See* 50 U.S.C. §§ 1806(b) (electronic surveillance), 1825(c) (physical search), and 1845(b) (pen register and trap and trace device).

269. *Id.* at §§ 1806(c), 1825(d), 1845(c).

270. *Id.* FISA defines "aggrieved person" to mean "a person who is the target of an electronic surveillance or any other person whose communications or activities were subject to electronic surveillance." 50 U.S.C. § 1801(k). With respect to physical searches, "aggrieved person" means a "person whose premis-

es, property, information, or material is the target of physical search or any other person whose premises, property, information, or material was subject to physical search." *Id.* at 1821(2). Finally, for use of evidence derived from a pen register or trap and trace device, "aggrieved person" means any person— "(A) whose telephone line was subject to the installation or use of a pen register or trap and trace device, or (B) whose communication instrument or device was subject to the use of a pen register or trap and trace device." *Id.* at § 1841(3)(A)–(B).

271. *See* United States v. Abu–Jihaad, 531 F. Supp.2d 299, 303–04 (D. Conn. 2008); United States v. Rosen, 447 F. Supp.2d 538, 545 (E.D. Va. 2006)

defendant may move to compel disclosure of FISA materials, including FISA applications, affidavits, court orders, and extensions, as well as any other documents related to the FISA surveillance and search.[272] Access to such materials is necessary in order for the defendant to file a factually specific motion to suppress and protect his rights to due process and effective assistance of counsel.[273]

If an aggrieved person moves to suppress or obtain FISA evidence, the Attorney General may oppose such a request for disclosure by filing an affidavit stating that the disclosure "would harm the national security of the United States."[274] Upon filing such an affidavit, the district court must review the FISA warrant application and related materials *in camera* and *ex parte* to determine whether the surveillance was "lawfully authorized and conducted."[275] After an *in camera* review, the court has the discretion to disclose portions of the documents, under appropriate protective procedures, "only where such disclosure is necessary to make an accurate determination of the legality of the surveillance [or physical search or use of the pen register or trap and trace device]."[276] According to the D.C. Circuit in *Belfield*, disclosure should occur—

> only where the court's initial review of the application, order, and fruits of the surveillance indicates that the question of legality may be complicated by factors such as "indications of possible misrepresentations of fact, vague identification of the persons to be surveilled, or surveillance records which include a significant amount of nonforeign intelligence information, calling into question compliance and minimization standards contained in the order.[277]

In fact, no court has found it necessary to disclose FISA materials in order to make a determination of the lawfulness of FSIA surveillance or searches.[278] Courts uniformly hold that FISA's

(citing 50 U.S.C. §§ 1806(e) and 1825(f)). Section 1845(e) authorizes an aggrieved person to file a motion to suppress evidence derived from the use of a pen register or trap and trace device. 50 U.S.C. § 1845(e).

272. 50 U.S.C. §§ 1806(f), 1825(g), 1845(f).

273. *See* United States v. Mubayyid, 521 F. Supp.2d 125, 129–30 (D. Mass. 2007).

274. 50 U.S.C. §§ 1806(f), 1825(g), 1845(f).

275. *Id.*

276. *Id. See also* United States v. Damrah, 412 F.3d 618, 624 (6th Cir. 2005); United States v. Duggan, 743

F.2d 59, 78 (2d Cir. 1984); United States v. Islamic Am. Relief Agency, 2009 WL 5169536, at *3 (W.D. Mo. 2009); *United States v. Abu–Jihaad,* 531 F. Supp.2d at 310; *United States v. Mubayyid,* 521 F. Supp.2d at 130.

277. United States v. Belfield, 692 F.2d 141, 147 (D.C. Cir. 1982) (quoting S. Intelligence Rep. At 64). *See also United States v. Islamic Am. Relief Agency,* 2009 WL 5169536, at 3–4; United States v. Rosen, 447 F. Supp.2d 538, 546 (E.D. Va. 2006).

278. *See, e.g.,* United States v. Squillacote, 221 F.3d 542, 553–54 (4th Cir. 2000); United States v. Islamic American Relief Agency, 2009 WL 5169536 at *4 (W. D. Mo.); United

in camera review procedures do not deprive a defendant of due process.[279] While defendants are significantly disadvantaged by not being able to review the materials needed to effectively challenge a FISA warrant, the courts contend that in devising the procedures that govern court review of FISA materials, Congress made a reasonable effort to balance the competing interests in privacy and national security. As the D.C. Circuit observed in *Belfield*:

> We appreciate the difficulties of appellants' counsel in this case. They must argue that the determination of legality is so complex that an adversary hearing with full access to relevant materials is necessary. But without access to the relevant materials their claim of complexity can be given no concreteness. . . .
>
> Congress was also aware of these difficulties. But it chose to resolve them through means other than mandatory disclosure. . . . [I]t cannot be said that this exclusion [of defendants from the process] rises to the level of a constitutional violation.[280]

Ex parte and *in camera* inspections also have been upheld against a constitutional challenge alleging a violation of the Sixth Amendment right of confrontation.[281]

If the district court finds that the surveillance or search was not lawfully authorized or conducted, it must suppress the FISA evidence and any evidence derived therefrom.[282] The district court's review of FISA materials is *de novo*.[283] Thus, no deference is accorded to the FISC's probable cause determination, but there is a presumption of validity accorded to certifications contained in the

States v. Warsame, 547 F. Supp.2d 982, 987 (D. Minn. 2008) ("No United States District Court or Court of Appeals has ever determined that disclosure to the defense of such materials was necessary to determine the lawfulness of surveillance or searches under FISA."); *United States v. Rosen*, 447 F. Supp.2d at 546 (listing cases).

279. *See* United States v. Damrah, 412 F.3d 618, 624–25 (6th Cir. 2005); United States v. Ott, 827 F.2d 473, 476 (9th Cir. 1987); United States v. Badia, 827 F.2d 1458, 1464 (11th Cir. 1987); United States v. Duggan, 743 F.2d 59, 78 (2d Cir. 1984); *United States v. Abu–Jihaad*, 531 F. Supp.2d at 310; *United States v. Mubayyid*, 521 F. Supp.2d at 131.

280. United States v. Belfield, 692 F.2d 141, 148 (D.C. Cir. 1982). *See also United States v. Abu–Jihaad*, 531 F.

Supp.2d at 310; *United States v. Mubayyid*, 521 F. Supp.2d at 131.

281. *See* United States v. Isa, 923 F.2d 1300, 1307 (8th Cir. 1991) (Sixth Amendment right of confrontation not violated by FISA's *in camera* review procedures); *United States v. Belfield*, 692 F.2d at 148.

282. 50 U.S.C. § 1806(g), 1825(h), 1845(g).

283. *See* United States v. Hammoud, 381 F.3d 316, 332 (4th Cir. 2004) (conducting *de novo* review of FISA materials), *vacated on other grounds,* 543 U.S. 1097 (2005); United States v. Squillacote, 221 F.3d 542, 554 (4th Cir. 2000); United States v. Gowadia, 2009 WL 1649709, *4 (D. Hawaii); *United States v. Islamic Am. Relief Agency*, 2009 WL 5169536, at *4; *United States v. Rosen*, 447 F. Supp.2d at 545.

application.[284] Further, when reviewing the denial of a motion to suppress, the court of appeals reviews a district court's findings of fact for clear error and its conclusions of law *de novo*.[285] Defendants' attack on the lawfulness of the FISA surveillance generally focuses on two issues: (1) whether the FISC had probable cause to believe that the targets of the surveillance were "agents of a foreign power," as required by FISA, and (2) whether there was proper compliance with the minimization procedures subsequent to the surveillance.[286] "The showing of probable cause necessary to justify a FISA surveillance or search is not necessarily analogous to the probable cause standard applicable in the general criminal context."[287] In a criminal case, the judge makes a determination, based on the totality of circumstances, of whether there is a fair probability that evidence of a crime will found at the place to be searched.[288] However, a FISC judge must determine whether there is probable cause to believe that "the target of the electronic surveillance is a foreign power or an agent of a foreign power" and that "each of the facilities or places at which the electronic surveillance is directed is being used, or is about to be used, by a foreign power or agent of a foreign power."[289] In making a probable cause determination, the FISC judge may not consider a U.S. person an agent of a foreign power "solely upon the basis of activities protected by the First Amendment."[290] The legislative history, as well as the statute's plain language, clearly establish that First Amendment activities cannot form the sole basis for concluding that a U.S. person is an agent of a foreign power.[291] However, "the probable cause determi-

284. *United States v. Islamic Am. Relief Agency*, 2009 WL 5169536, at *4. *See also Hammoud*, 381 F.3d at 332 (citing *Squillacote*, 221 F.3d at 554); *United States v. Rosen*, 447 F. Supp.2d at 545.

285. *See* United States v. Damrah, 412 F.3d 618, 624 (6th Cir. 2005); United States v. Foster, 376 F.3d 577, 583 (6th Cir. 2004).

286. *See United States v. Islamic Am. Relief Agency*, 2009 WL 5169536, at *4; *United States v. Rosen*, 447 F. Supp.2d at 547.

287. *United States v. Islamic Am. Relief Agency*, 2009 WL 5169536, at *5 (internal citations omitted).

288. *See* Illinois v. Gates, 462 U.S. 213, 238 (1983).

289. 50 U.S.C. § 1804(a)(3). *See United States v. Hammoud*, 381 F.3d at 332 (upholding probable cause finding that Hammoud was an agent of Hizballah).

290. 50 U.S.C. § 1805(a)(2)(A).

291. *United States v. Rosen*, 447 F. Supp.2d at 548. The legislative history illustrates this point:

The Bill is not intended to authorize electronic surveillance when a United States person's activities, even though secret and conducted for a foreign power, consist entirely of lawful acts such as lobbying or the use of confidential contacts to influence public officials, directly or indirectly, through the dissemination of information. Individuals exercising their right to lobby public officials or to engage in political dissent from official policy may well be in contact with representatives of foreign governments and groups when the issues concern foreign affairs or international economic matters.

They must continue to be free to communicate about such issues and to obtain information or exchange views

nation may rely in part on activities protected by the First Amendment, provided the determination also relies on activities not protected by the First Amendment."[292] Finally, in making a probable cause determination, a FISA judge may "consider past activities of the target, as well as facts and circumstances relating to current or future activities of the target."[293]

In support of a motion to suppress FISA evidence, defendants often argue that the Government failed to follow the applicable minimization procedures.[294] The minimization procedures are "designed to protect, as far as reasonable, against the acquisition, retention, and dissemination of nonpublic information which is not foreign intelligence information."[295] Thus, for example—

> [M]inimization at the acquisition stage is designed to insure that the communications of non-target U.S. persons who happen to be using a FISA target's telephone, or who happen to converse with the target about non-foreign intelligence information, are not improperly disseminated. Similarly, minimization at the retention stage is intended to ensure that "information acquired, which is not necessary for obtaining, producing, or disseminating foreign intelligence information, be destroyed where feasible. Finally, the dissemination of foreign intelligence information, "needed for an approved purpose . . . should be restricted to those officials with a need for such information.[296]

However, it is not fatal that the Government may have recorded and stored an overbroad selection of electronic communications, so long as the Government acted in good faith to minimize the acquisition and retention of irrelevant information.[297] In *Mubayyid*, the court stated:

with representatives of foreign governments or with foreign groups, free from any fear that such contact might be the basis of probable cause to believe they are acting at the direction of a foreign power thus triggering the government's power to conduct electronic surveillance.
S. Rep. No. 95–701, at 29 (1978), 1978 U.S.C.C.A.N. 3873, 3990–91.

292. *United States v. Rosen,* 447 F. Supp.2d at 548 (finding ample probable cause to believe that targets were agents of a foreign power apart from their First Amendment lobbying activities).

293. 50 U.S.C. § 1805(b).

294. *See, e.g., United States v. Islamic Am. Relief Agency,* 2009 WL 5169536, at *5; *United States v. Rosen,* 447 F. Supp.2d at 550. The minimiza-

tion procedures for electronic surveillance are found at 50 U.S.C. § 1801(h). Section 1821(4) governs minimization procedures for physical searches.

295. In re Sealed Case, 310 F.3d 717, 731 (Foreign Int.Surv.Ct.Rev. 2002). *See also United States v. Rosen,* 447 F. Supp.2d at 550 ("Congress intended these minimization procedures to act as a safeguard for U.S. persons at the acquisition, retention and dissemination phases of electronic surveillance and searches.").

296. *Rosen,* 447 F. Supp.2d at 551 (internal citations omitted).

297. *See* United States v. Hammoud, 381 F.3d 316, 334 (4th Cir. 2004) (en banc); *United States v. Mubayyid,* 521 F. Supp.2d at 134–35.

[I]n construing [existing electronic surveillance law] "it is . . . obvious that no electronic surveillance can be so conducted that innocent conversations can be totally eliminated.". . . . Absent a charge that the minimization procedures have been disregarded completely, the test of compliance is "whether a good faith effort to minimize was attempted."[298]

The courts have also denied a motion to suppress on the grounds that the Government violated minimization procedures by retaining FISA evidence for long periods of time. In *Mubayyid,* the court observed that

> in intelligence as in law enforcement, leads must be followed. Especially in counterintelligence cases where often trained professional foreign intelligence personnel are involved, a lead which initially ends in a "dry hole" can hardly be considered a dead issue, although it may be temporarily shelved to divert limited resources to other leads. Therefore . . . a significant degree of latitude [must] be given in counterintelligence and counterterrorism cases with respect to the retention of information and the dissemination of information between and among counterintelligence components of the Government.[299]

The court held that the Government's retention of electronic intercepts for more than ten years prior to the indictment did not violate FISA minimization procedures.[300]

B. NATIONAL SECURITY LETTERS

1. LEGISLATIVE HISTORY

Five statutory provisions require businesses to produce specified records to federal officials (principally the Federal Bureau of Investigation (FBI)) in national security investigations.[301] These requests for documents, which are comparable to administrative subpoenas, are known as "National Security Letters" (NSLs).[302] NSLs seek certain business records in national security investigations from electronic communication service providers (ECSPs),[303]

---

298. *United States v. Mubayyid,* 521 F. Supp.2d at 135 (quoting United States v. Armocida, 515 F.2d 29, 44 (3d Cir. 1975)) (internal citations omitted).

299. *Mubayyid,* 521 F. Supp.2d at 134 (quoting H.R. Rep. No. 95–1283, pt. I, at 59 (1978)).

300. *Mubayyid,* 521 F. Supp.2d at 134.

301. The five statutory provisions include: section 114(a)(5) of the Right to Financial Privacy Act (12 U.S.C. § 3414(a)(5)); sections 626 and 627 of the Fair Credit Reporting Act (15 U.S.C. §§ 1681u, 1681v); section 2709 of title

18 of the United States Code; and section 802 of the National Security Act (50 U.S.C. § 436).

302. *See* CHARLES DOYLE, CONG. RESEARCH SERV., RL33320, NATIONAL SECURITY LETTERS IN FOREIGN INTELLIGENCE INVESTIGATIONS: LEGAL BACKGROUND AND RECENT AMENDMENTS, CRS REPORT FOR CONGRESS 1 (2009) [hereinafter NATIONAL SECURITY LETTERS IN FOREIGN INTELLIGENCE INVESTIGATIONS].

303. ECSPs include telephone companies and Internet service providers. *See* Doe v. Mukasey, 549 F.3d 861, 864 (2d Cir. 2008).

financial institutions and credit agencies.[304] Like orders issued
pursuant to FISA, NSLs are justified by national security concerns.
However, NSLs differ from FISA orders in several important respects. First, FISA orders must be obtained from the FISC.[305] NSLs
are issued by federal government agencies responsible for foreign
intelligence investigations and do not require a court order.[306]
Second, FISA court orders provide access to any documents, records
and tangible things relevant to national security.[307] The scope of
documents and information which may be obtained pursuant to a
NSL is more limited. As mentioned, NSLs are authorized by five
federal statutes, each of which is limited to a narrow category of
documents.[308] Finally, as a practical matter, NLS are issued much
more frequently than FISA orders. In 2006, for example, less than
50 FISA orders were issued, while the FBI issued more than 50,000
NSLs.[309]

The first NSL statute was enacted by Congress in 1986 as an
amendment to the Right to Financial Privacy Act, authorizing the
FBI to access financial institution records in foreign intelligence
cases.[310] Next, in the Electronic Communications Privacy Act, Congress gave the FBI comparable access to telephone company and
other communications service provider customer information.[311]

304. *Id. See also* NATIONAL SECURITY LETTERS IN FOREIGN INTELLIGENCE INVESTIGATIONS, *supra* note 304, at 1.

305. ANNA C. HENNING & EDWARD C. LIU, CONG. RESEARCH SERV., R40138, AMENDMENTS TO THE FOREIGN INTELLIGENCE SURVEILLANCE ACT (FISA) SET TO EXPIRE FEBRUARY 28, 2011, at 4 (2010) [hereinafter AMENDMENTS TO THE FOREIGN INTELLIGENCE SURVEILLANCE ACT].

306. *Id.*

307. *Id.*

308. *Id.* at 4 n. 29.

309. *Id.* at 4.

310. P.L. 99–569, § 404, 100 Stat. 3197 (1986), 12 U.S.C. § 3414(a)(5)(A) (1988 ed.). Section 12 U.S.C. § 3414(a)(5)(A) provides:

Financial institutions, and officers, employees, and agents thereof, shall comply with a request for a customer's or entity's financial records made pursuant to this subsection by the Federal Bureau of Investigation when the Director of the Federal Bureau of Investigation (or the Director's designee in a position not lower than Deputy Assistant Director at Bureau headquarters or a Special Agent in Charge in a Bureau field office designated by

the Directory) certifies in writing to the financial institution that such records are sought for foreign counter intelligence purposes to protect against international terrorism or clandestine intelligence activities....

12 U.S.C. § 3414(a)(5)(A).

311. 18 U.S.C. § 2709 (1988 ed.). Subsections 2709(a)–(b) provides:

(a) Duty to provide. A wire or electronic communication service provider shall comply with a request for subscriber information and toll billing records information, or electronic communication transactional records in its custody or possession made by the Director of the Federal Bureau of Investigation under subsection (b) of this section.

(b) Required Certification. The Director of the Federal Bureau of Investigation, or his designee in a position not lower than Deputy Assistant Director at Bureau headquarters or a Special Agent in Charge in a Bureau file office designated by the Director, may—

(1) request the name, address, length of service, and local and long distance toll billing records of a person or enti-

"Together the two NSL provisions afforded the FBI access to communications and financial business records under limited circumstances—customer and customer transaction information held by telephone carriers and banks pertaining to a foreign power or its agents relevant to a foreign counter-intelligence investigation."[312]

In the mid–1990s, Congress enacted two other NSL provisions. The National Security Act, 50 U.S.C. § 436, permits NSL use to access financial institution records and credit reports, as well as travel records of federal employees suspected of leaking classified information.[313] Passed in the wake of the Ames espionage case, use of NSLs under the Act are limited to investigations involving the disclosure of classified information.[314] The Federal Credit Reporting Act, 15 U.S.C. § 1681u(a), grants the FBI access to credit agency records.[315] More specifically, a consumer reporting agency is required to furnish to the FBI the names and addresses of all

ty if the Director (or his designee) certifies in writing to the wire or electronic communication service provider to which the request is made that the name, address, length of service, and toll billing records sought are relevant to an authorized investigation to protect against international terrorism or clandestine intelligence activities, provided that such an investigation of a United States person is not conducted solely on the basis of activities protected by the first amendment to the Constitution of the United States; and

(2) request the name, address, and length of service or a person or entity if the Director (or his designee) certifies in writing to the wire or electronic communication service provider to which the request is made that the information sought is relevant to an authorized investigation to protect against international terrorism or clandestine intelligence activities, provided that such an investigation of a United States person is not conducted solely upon the basis of activities protected by the first amendment of the Constitution of the United States.

18 U.S.C. § 2709(a)–(b).

312. NATIONAL SECURITY LETTERS IN FOREIGN INTELLIGENCE INVESTIGATIONS, *supra* note 302 at 2–3 (citing 18 U.S.C. § 2709 (1988 ed.); 12 U.S.C. § 3414(a)(5)(A) (1988 ed.)).

313. 50 U.S.C. § 436 (1994 ed.).

314. *Id.* Section 436 provides that NSL requests may be made for certain

records pertaining to a person who is or was a federal employee where "there are reasonable grounds to believe, based on credible information, that the person is, or may be, disclosing classified information in an unauthorized manner to a foreign power or agent of a foreign power." *Id.*

315. 15 U.S.C. § 1681u. Section 1681u states in relevant part:

[A] consumer reporting agency shall furnish to the Federal Bureau of Investigation the names and addresses of all financial institutions (as that term is defined in section 3401 of Title 21) at which a consumer maintains or has maintained an account, to the extent that information is in the files of the agency, when presented with a written request for that information, signed by the Director of the Federal Bureau of Investigation, or the Director's designee in a position not lower than Deputy Assistant Director at Bureau headquarters or a Special Agent in Charge of a Bureau field office designated by the Director, which certifies compliance with this section. The Director or the Director's designee may make such a certification only if the Director or the Director's designee has determined in writing, that such information is sought for the conduct of an authorized investigation to protect against international terrorism or clandestine intelligence activities. . . .

15 U.S.C. § 1681u.

financial institutions at which a consumer maintains or has maintained an account, to the extent that information is in the files of the credit agency.[316] The FBI requested access to credit agency records to enable it to make more effective use of its authority to access financial records:

> FBI's right of access under the Right of Financial Privacy Act cannot be effectively used, however, until the FBI discovers which financial institutions are being utilized by the subject of a counterintelligence investigation. Consumer reports maintained by credit bureaus are a ready source of such information, but, although such report[s] are readily available to the private sector, they are not available to FBI counterintelligence investigators. . . .[317]

Both the National Security Act and Fair Credit Reporting Act NSL sections contain dissemination restrictions,[318] and safe harbor (immunity) provisions.[319]

The USA PATRIOT Act amended three of the four NSL provisions and added a fifth. In the three NLS statutes available exclusively to the FBI—the Electronic Communications Privacy Act (18 U.S.C. § 2709), the Right to Financial Privacy Act (12 U.S.C. § 3414(a)(5)), and the Fair Credit Reporting Act (15 U.S.C. § 1681u)—section 505 of the PATRIOT Act:

- expanded FBI issuing authority beyond FBI headquarter officials to include the heads of the FBI field offices (i.e., Special Agents in Charge (SAC));

- eliminated the requirement that the record information sought pertain to a foreign power or the agent of a foreign power;

- required instead that the NSL request be relevant to an investigation to protect against international terrorism or foreign spying;

- added the caveat that no such investigation of an American can be predicated exclusively on First Amendment protected activities.[320]

The PATRIOT Act amendments enhanced the use of NSLs in two important ways. First, NSL authority could be employed more quickly because prior approval from FBI headquarters was no

---

316. *Id.*

317. H.R. 104–427, at 36 (1996). *See also* National Security Letters in Foreign Intelligence Investigations, *supra* note 302, at 3.

318. 50 U.S.C. § 436(e); 15 U.S.C. § 1681u(f).

319. 50 U.S.C. § 436(c); 15 U.S.C. § 1681u(k).

320. National Security Letters in Foreign Intelligence Investigations, *supra* note 302, at 4 (citing P.L. 107–56, § 505, 115 Stat. 365–66 (2001)).

longer required. A written request for documents could now be issued by a Special Agent in Charge of a Bureau field office.[321] Second, NSLs could be used more widely because the requirement that the information sought pertain to a foreign power or agent of a foreign power was eliminated.[322] The amendments authorized the issuance for NSLs of documents relevant to an investigation to protect against international terrorism or foreign spying.

Section 358(g) of the USA PATRIOT Act, codified at 15 U.S.C. § 1681v, amended the Fair Credit Reporting Act by adding a fifth NSL section.[323] The amendment expanded the use of NSLs beyond the FBI to any governmental agency authorized to conduct an investigation or analysis related to international terrorism. Section 358(g) provides:

> Notwithstanding section 1681b of this title or any other provision of this subchapter, a consumer reporting agency shall furnish a consumer report of a consumer and all other information in a consumer's file to a government agency authorized to conduct investigations of, or intelligence or counterintelligence activities or analysis related to, international terrorism when presented with a written certification by such governmental agency that such information is necessary for the agency's conduct or such investigation, activity or analysis.[324]

In 2004, Congress amended the Right of Financial Privacy Act by expanding the definition of "financial institution" to include not only banks and credit unions but also car dealers, jewelers, real estate agents, and brokers or dealers in securities or commodities, among others.[325] Thus, NSL authority was extended to these non-traditional financial institutions under the Act.[326]

In 2006, Congress created a judicial enforcement mechanism and judicial review procedure for NSL recipients to challenge the requests and nondisclosure requirements.[327] Further, the amendments established specific penalties for failure to comply with an NSL request or observe the nondisclosure requirements,[328] made it clear that the nondisclosure requirements did not preclude the recipient from consulting an attorney,[329] and provided a process for

---

321. See 12 U.S.C. § 3414(a)(5)(A); 15 U.S.C. § 1681u; 18 U.S.C. § 2709(b). See also NATIONAL SECURITY LETTERS IN FOREIGN INTELLIGENCE INVESTIGATIONS, supra note 302, at 4.

322. Id.

323. P.L. 107–56, § 358(g), 115 Stat. 327 (2001).

324. 15 U.S.C. § 1681v(a).

325. P.L. 108–177, § 374, 117 Stat. 2628 (2004), 12 U.S.C. § 3414(d). Sec-

tion 3414(d) adopted the definition of "financial institution" set forth in 31 U.S.C. § 5312(a)(2).

326. Id.

327. 18 U.S.C. § 3511.

328. 18 U.S.C. §§ 3511(c), 1510(e).

329. 12 U.S.C. § 3414(a)(3)(A); 15 U.S.C. § 1681v(c)(1), 1681u(d)(1); 18 U.S.C. § 2709(c)(1); 50 U.S.C. § 436(b)(1).

a recipient to petition the court for an order modifying or setting aside a nondisclosure requirement.[330] Finally, the 2006 amendments expanded congressional oversight and required an Inspector General's audit of the use of NSL authority.[331]

2. STATUTORY FRAMEWORK

While the five NSL statutes share a number common attributes, they differ with respect to the nature of the businesses to whom they may be addressed. For example, under the Electronic Communication Privacy Act, NSLs are addressed to electronic communication service providers (ECSPs), which are typically telephone companies or Internet service providers.[332] NSLs issued under the Right to Financial Privacy Act are directed at financial institutions, which include banks and credit unions as well as nontraditional financial institutions such as car dealers, real estate agencies, securities brokers and dealers, and other enumerated entities that are likely to engage in large currency transactions.[333] Recipients of Fair Credit Reporting Act NSLs are addressed to consumer credit reporting agencies.[334] Finally, recipients of NSLs authorized under the National Security Act may include financial institutions or consumer credit reporting agencies as well commercial entities with information concerning a federal employee's travel.[335]

Under each of the five NSL provisions, government agents are required to provide a certification for issuance of an NSL. If NSLs are requested under the Electronic Communications Privacy Act, the Right to Financial Privacy Act, or the Fair Credit Reporting Act, issuance requires the certification of either the Director of the FBI, a senior FBI official (no lower than the Deputy Assistant Director), or the Special Agent in Charge of an FBI field office.[336] Certification authority is much broader under the other two statutes. Under the National Security Act, each NSL request must be accompanied by a written certification signed by "the department or agency head or deputy department or agency head concerned, or by a senior official designated ... by the department or agency head concerned (whose rank shall be no lower than Assistant Secretary or Assistant Director)" of an agency whose employee is under investigation for disclosure of classified information.[337] A designated supervisory official of an agency authorized to conduct

330. 18 U.S.C. § 3511(b).
331. P.L. 109–177, §§ 118–19.
332. See 18 U.S.C. § 2709.
333. See 12 U.S.C. § 3414(a), (d).
334. See 15 U.S.C. §§ 1681u(a), 1681v(a).
335. See 50 U.S.C. § 436(a).
336. See 18 U.S.C. § 2709(b), U.S.C. 3414(a)(5)(A); 15 U.S.C. 12 § 1681u(b).
337. See 50 U.S.C. § 436(a)(3).

an international terrorism investigation may certify a NSL request under the more recent section of the Fair Credit Reporting Act.[338]

The purpose of each NSL is to acquire information related to national security concerns. The certification must provide that the information sought is for such limited purpose. For example, under the Electronic Communications Privacy Act, 18 U.S.C. § 2709(b), the designated senior FBI official must certify that "[the information] sought [is] relevant to an authorized investigation to protect against international terrorism or clandestine intelligence activities. . . ."[339] The certifications required under the Fair Credit Reporting Act, 15 U.S.C. § 1681u, and the Right of Financial Privacy Act, 21 U.S. 3414(a)(5)(A), are quite similar.[340] The newer provision of the Fair Credit Reporting Act, 15 U.S.C. § 1681u(a), provides that "such information is sought for the conduct of an authorized investigation to protect against international terrorism or clandestined intelligence activities. . . ."[341] The information must be sought "to conduct investigations of, or intelligence or counterintelligence activities or analysis related to, international terrorism. . . ."[342] Finally, the National Security Act requires a certification that the information is sought to conduct "any authorized law enforcement investigation, counterintelligence inquiry, or security determination. . . . ."[343]

Each of the five NSL statutes contains a nondisclosure or confidentiality requirement. The recipient of a NSL may not disclose to any person that the requesting agency has sought or obtained access to certain information or records if the agency certifies that disclosure may jeopardize national security, interfere with a criminal, counterterrorism, or counterintelligence investigation, interfere with diplomatic relations, or endanger the life or physical safety of any person.[344] However, the recipient may disclose the NSL to those persons necessary to comply with the request and to an attorney for legal advice and assistance with respect to the request.[345] Further, any recipient disclosing to those persons is required to inform them of the nondisclosure requirement.[346] Per-

---

338. *See* 15 U.S.C. § 1681v(b).

339. 18 U.S.C. § 2709(b).

340. 15 U.S.C. § 1681u ("information is sought for the conduct of an authorized investigation to protect against international terrorism or clandestine intelligence activities"); 12 U.S.C. § 3414(a)(5)(A) ("records are sought for foreign counter intelligence purposes to protect against international terrorism or clandestine intelligence activities").

341. *See* 15 U.S.C. § 1681u(a).

342. *See* 15 U.S.C. § 1681v(a). *See also* NATIONAL SECURITY LETTERS IN FOREIGN INTELLIGENCE INVESTIGATIONS, *supra* note 302, at 8.

343. 50 U.S.C. § 436(a)(1).

344. *See* 12 U.S.C. § 3414(a)(5)(D)(i); 15 U.S.C. §§ 1681u(d), 1681v(c)(1); 18 U.S.C. § 2709(c); 50 U.S.C. § 436(b)(1).

345. *Id.*

346. *See* 12 U.S.C. § 3414(a)(5)(D)(iii); 15 U.S.C. §§ 1681u(d)(3),

sons receiving disclosure are subject to the same prohibitions on disclosure.[347] A breach of the confidentiality requirement committed knowingly and with an intent to obstruct justice is punishable by imprisonment of not more than five years, a fine of not more than $250,000 (not more than $500,000 for an organization), or both.[348]

If filed within one year of the request for records, a recipient may petition the court for an order to modify or set aside such a nondisclosure requirement.[349] To grant such a petition, the court must find "there is no reason to believe that disclosure may endanger the national security of the United States, interfere with a criminal, counterterrorism, or counterintelligence investigation, interfere with diplomatic relations, or endanger the life or physical safety of any person."[350] However, if, at the time of the petition, the government agency certifies that disclosure may endanger national security or interfere with diplomatic relations, the court is required to treat such certification as conclusive unless the court finds that the certification was made in bad faith.[351] The bad faith requirement sets an extremely high bar for the recipient to prevail in a petition challenging NSL nondisclosure requirements.[352]

A recipient of a NSL may also seek judicial review of the underlying request. A court may modify or set aside the NSL request if compliance would be unreasonable, oppressive, or otherwise unlawful.[353] At the same time, the government may invoke the court's authority to enforce a NSL against a noncompliant recipient and failure to comply is punishable as contempt of court.[354]

Dissemination of information acquired in response to NSLs is restricted by four of the five NSL statutes. Guidelines approved by the Attorney General govern the sharing of information acquired under the Right to Financial Privacy and the Electronic Communications Privacy Act NSL provisions.[355] Under the Fair Credit Re-

1681v(c)(3); 18 U.S.C. § 2709(c)(3); 50 U.S.C. § 436(b)(3).

347. *Id.*

348. 18 U.S.C. §§ 1510(e), 3571, 3559.

349. 18 U.S.C. § 3511(b)(2).

350. *Id.*

351. *Id.*

352. *See* Doe v. Mukasey, 549 F.3d 861, 882 (2d Cir. 2008) (finding there is no meaningful judicial review "of the decision of the Executive Branch to prohibit speech if the position of the Executive Branch that speech would be harmful is 'conclusive' on the reviewing

court, absent only a demonstration of bad faith").

353. 18 U.S.C. § 3511(a).

354. *Id.* at § 3511(c).

355. *See* 12 U.S.C. § 3414(a)(5)(B) ("The Federal Bureau of Investigation may disseminate information obtained pursuant to this paragraph only as provided in guidelines approved by the Attorney General for foreign intelligence collection and foreign counterintelligence investigations conducted by the Federal Bureau of Investigation, and, with respect to dissemination to an agency of the United States, only if such information is clearly relevant to the authorized responsibilities of such agency."); *see also* 18 U.S.C. § 2709(d).

porting Act sections, the FBI may disseminate information to other Federal agencies as may be necessary to conduct a foreign counter-intelligence investigation or to military authorities in order to conduct a joint foreign counterintelligence investigation of a member of the Armed Forces.[356] The National Security Act limits the dissemination of NSL information outside the requesting agency:—"(1) to the agency employing the employee who is the subject of the records or information; (2) to the Department of Justice for law enforcement or counterintelligence purposes; or (3) with respect to dissemination to an agency of the United States, if such information is clearly relevant to the authorized responsibilities of such agency."[357] The Fair Credit Reporting Act, 15 U.S.C. § 1681v, has no explicit provision restricting dissemination.[358] Finally three of the NSL statutes offer immunity from civil liability,[359] and two statutes offer fees to deter the costs of compliance.[360]

3. LEGAL CHALLENGES

In *Doe v. Mukasey*, an Internet service provider brought an action raising First Amendment challenges to the constitutionality of statutes governing the issuance and review of NSLs.[361] The FBI delivered a NSL directing the plaintiffs, an Internet service provider, "to provide the [FBI] the names, addresses, lengths of service and electronic communication transactional records, to include [other information] (not to include message content and/or subject fields) for [a specific] email address."[362] The written request certified that the information sought was relevant to an international terrorism investigation or clandestine intelligence activities.[363] The request for documents was authorized by 18 U.S.C. § 2709, which imposes a duty on ECSPs to comply with requests from the FBI for specified information about a subscriber.[364] Further, the NSL advised the recipient that the law "prohibit[ed] any officer, employee or agent" of the company from "disclosing to any person that the FBI has sought or obtained access to information or records" pursuant to the NSL provisions.[365] At the time, section 2709(c) imposed a blanket nondisclosure requirement prohibiting an ECSP

---

356. 15 U.S.C. § 1681u(f).

357. 50 U.S.C. § 436(e)(1)–(3).

358. 15 U.S.C. § 1681v.

359. 15 U.S.C. §§ 1681u(k), 1681v(e); 50 U.S.C. § 436(c)(2).

360. 15 U.S.C. § 1681u(e), 50 U.S.C. § 436(d).

361. Doe v. Mukasey, 549 F.3d 861 (2d Cir. 2008). *See also* Doe v. Gonzales, 386 F.Supp.2d 66, 73–75, 82 (D. Conn. 2005) (finding that section 2709(c) was unconstitutional under the First Amend-

ment because it imposed an unjustified prior restraint and content-based restriction on speech).

362. *Id.* at 865.

363. *Id.*

364. 18 U.S.C. § 2709(a). However, the statute does not require disclosure of the content of electronic communications. *Id.*

365. *Mukasey*, 549 F.3d at 865.

from disclosing receipt of an NSL.[366]

While the case was pending, Congress enacted the USA PATRI-OT Improvement and Reauthorization Act of 2005, which amended the nondisclosure provision to require nondisclosure only upon certification by a senior FBI official that "otherwise there may result a danger to the national security of the United States, interference with a criminal, counterterrorism, or counterintelligence investigation, interference with diplomatic relations, or danger to the life or physical safety of any person."[367] The Reauthorization Act also added provisions for judicial review, permitting a recipient of an NSL to petition the district court for an order modifying or setting aside the NSL and the nondisclosure requirement.[368] Pursuant to 18 U.S.C. § 3511(a), the district court may modify or set aside a NSL if "compliance would be unreasonable, oppressive, or otherwise unlawful."[369] Further, under subsection 3511(b)(2) the nondisclosure requirement may be modified or set aside if the district court "finds that there is no reason to believe that disclosure may endanger that national security of the United States" or cause other enumerated harms set forth in the statute.[370] Finally, the subsection provides that if the Attorney General or other senior agency official certifies at the time of the petition that disclosure may endanger national security or interfere with diplomatic relations, such certification shall be treated as "conclusive" unless the court finds that the certification was made in "bad faith."[371]

On appeal, plaintiffs raised two principal issues. First, plaintiffs maintained that the nondisclosure requirement of section 2709(c) is a content-based prior restraint on the freedom of speech.[372] In their view, section 2709(c) prohibits disclosure of the fact and details of the issuance of an NSL, and is a prior restraint because it is imposed before an NLS recipient has an opportunity to

---

366. *Id.* at 865–66. Subsection (c), in 2004, provided:

> (c) Prohibition of certain disclosure. No wire or electronic communication service provider, or officer, employee, or agent thereof, shall disclose to any person that the Federal Bureau of Investigation has sought or obtained access to information or records under this section.

18 U.S.C. § 2709(c) (2000).

367. USA PATRIOT Improvement and Reauthorization Act of 2005, § 115, Pub.L. No. 109–177, 120 Stat. 192, 211–14 (March 9, 2006), *amended by* USA Patriot Act Additional Reauthorizing Amendments Act of 2006, § 4(b), Pub.L. No. 109–178, 120 Stat. 278, 280 (March 9, 2006), codified at 18 U.S.C. § 2709(c) (West Supp. 2008). There is an exception to the nondisclosure prohibition for persons to whom disclosure is necessary to comply with the NSL or an attorney for the purpose of seeking legal advice and assistance with respect to the request. See 18 U.S.C. § 2709(c)(1).

368. 18 U.S.C. § 3511(a), (b)(1).

369. *Id.* at § 3511(a).

370. *Id.* at § 3511(b)(2).

371. *Id.*

372. Doe v. Mukasey, 549 F.3d 861, 873 (2d Cir. 2008).

speak.[373] Second, the plaintiffs challenged section 3511(b) on the grounds that "(1) the judicial review provisions do not require the Government to initiate judicial review and to sustain a burden of proof and (2) certification of certain risks by senior governmental officials is entitled to a conclusive presumption (absent bad faith)."[374] Plaintiffs alleged that section 3511(b) violates First Amendment procedural standards.[375]

The Second Circuit panel posited that a content-based restriction is subject to review under the strict scrutiny standard, requiring a demonstration that the restriction is "narrowly tailored to promote a compelling Government interest."[376] Further, where expression is subject to a prior restraint, the First Amendment requires procedural protections to guard against censorship.[377] The court noted that the Supreme Court in *Freedman v. Maryland* identified three procedural requirements: "(1) any restraint imposed prior to judicial review must be limited to 'a specified brief period'; (2) any further restraint prior to final judicial determination must be limited to 'the shortest fixed period compatible with sound judicial resolution'; and (3) the burden of going to the court to suppress speech and the burden of proof in court must be placed on the government."[378]

While the Second Circuit panel could not agree on whether section 2709(c) constituted a prior restraint subject to strict scrutiny analysis or should be judged under a less demanding standard, the lack of consensus proved of little consequence because the Government conceded that the strict scrutiny standard is the applicable standard, and the court agreed that the result would be the same under the factor common to both standards—whether the nondisclosure requirement is as "narrowly tailored" as possible to protect national security.[379] Under strict scrutiny review, the Government must demonstrate that the nondisclosure requirement is "narrowly tailored to promote a compelling Government interest," and that there is no "less restrictive alternatives [that] would be at least as effective in achieving the legitimate purpose that the statute was enacted to serve."[380] Since no governmental interest is more compelling than U.S. national security, the Second Circuit posited that the principal strict scrutiny issue turns on whether the

373. *Id.*

374. *Id.*

375. *Id.* at 873–74.

376. *Id.* at 871 (quoting United States v. Playboy Entertainment Group, Inc., 529 U.S. 803, 813 (2000)).

377. *Id.*

378. *Id.* at 871 (quoting Freedman v. Maryland, 380 U.S. 51, 58–59 (1965)).

379. Doe v. Mukasey, 549 F.3d 861, 878 (2d Cir. 2008). *See also* NATIONAL SECURITY LETTERS IN FOREIGN INTELLIGENCE INVESTIGATIONS, *supra* note 302, at 16–17.

380. *Mukasey*, 549 F.3d at 878 (internal quotations and citations omitted).

narrow tailoring requirement is met.[381] The court held that in the absence of Government-initiated judicial review, subsection 3511(b) is not narrowly tailored to conform to First Amendment procedural standards.[382] To withstand a First Amendment challenge, the Second Circuit posited that subsection 3511(b) must be interpreted to place the burden on the Government "to show a 'good' reason to believe that disclosure may result in an enumerated harm, i.e., a harm related to 'an authorized investigation to protect against international terrorism or clandestine intelligence activities,' and to place on a district court an obligation to make the 'may result' finding only after consideration, albeit deferential, of the Government's explanation concerning the risk of an enumerated harm."[383]

Further, the Second Circuit deemed inconsistent with either the strict scrutiny or a less demanding standard of review the provision of subsections 3511(b)(2) and (b)(3) specifying that a certification by senior governmental officials that disclosure may "endanger the national security of the United States or interfere with diplomatic relations ... shall be treated as conclusive unless the court finds that the certification was made in bad faith."[384] The court posited:

> There is not meaningful judicial review of the decision of the Executive Branch to prohibit speech if the position of the Executive Branch that speech would be harmful is "conclusive" on a reviewing court, absent only a demonstration of bad faith. To accept deference to that extraordinary degree would be to reduce strict scrutiny to no scrutiny, save only in the rarest of situations where bad faith could be shown. Under either traditional strict scrutiny or a less exacting application of that standard, some demonstration from the Executive Branch of the need for secrecy is required in order to conform the nondisclosure requirement to First Amendment standards.[385]

While judicial review may occur *ex parte* and *in camera*, the court stated that such review may not be bound by the executive's "conclusive" certification of harm clause set forth in section 3511(b).[386]

Finally, while the Second Circuit acknowledged that it lacked the authority to "interpret" or "revise" the NSL statutes to create the constitutionally required obligation of the Government to initiate judicial review, the court suggested that the Government could

---

381. *Id.*
382. *Id.* at 881.
383. *Id.*
384. *Id.* at 882 (quoting 18 U.S.C. § 3511(b)(2)).

385. *Id.* at 882.
386. *Id.*

assume such an obligation.[387] In an effort to salvage the NSL secrecy provisions, the court proposed the following procedures for judicial review:

> The Government could inform each NSL recipient that it should give the Government prompt notice, perhaps within ten days, in the event that the recipient wishes to contest the nondisclosure requirement. Upon receipt of such notice, the Government could be accorded a limited time, perhaps 30 days to initiate a judicial review proceeding to maintain the nondisclosure requirement, and the proceeding would have to be concluded within a prescribed time, perhaps 60 days.[388]

The court added:

> If the Government uses the suggested reciprocal notice procedure as a means of initiating judicial review, there appears to be no impediment to the Government's including notice of a recipient's opportunity to contest the nondisclosure requirement in an NSL. If such notice is given, time limits on the nondisclosure requirement pending judicial review, as reflected in *Freedman*, would have to be applied to make the review procedure constitutional. We would deem it to be within our judicial authority to conform subsection 2709(c) to First Amendment requirements, by limiting the duration of the nondisclosure requirement ... to the 10–day period in which the NSL recipient decides whether to contest the nondisclosure requirement, the 30–day period in which the Government considers whether to seek judicial review, and a further period of 60 days in which a court must adjudicate the merits, unless special circumstances warrant additional time. If the NSL recipient declines timely to precipitate Government-initiated judicial review, the nondisclosure requirement would continue, subject to the recipient's existing opportunities for annual challenges to the nondisclosure requirement provided by subsection 3511(b). If such an annual challenge is made, the standards and burden of proof that we have specified for an initial challenge would apply, although the Government would not be obliged to initiate judicial review.[389]

Ultimately, the Second Circuit struck down the conclusive presumption clause of subsections 3511(b)(2) and (b)(3), and invalidated subsection 2709(c) and the remainder of subsection 3511(b) only to the extent that they fail to provide for Government-initiated judicial review.[390] The court concluded that the Government could respond to this partial invalidation ruling by using the suggested

---

387. *Id*. at 883.
388. *Id*. at 879.
389. *Id*. at 883–84 (internal citations omitted).

390. *Id*. at 884.

reciprocal notice procedures. If these procedures were followed, the court held that subsections 2709(c) and 3511(b) would survive First Amendment challenge.[391]

4. CONCLUSION

Acts of terrorism directed at the United States at home and abroad constitute a preeminent national security threat. To counter these attacks, the Government has employed existing criminal investigation techniques while developing a new legal framework to adapt to the evolving threats of global terrorism. The Foreign Intelligence Surveillance Act (FISA) and National Security Letters (NSLs) have proven to be invaluable investigative tools enabling the Government to discover and prevent terrorist plots before they mature. FISA allows the Government to gather counterterrorism intelligence information through the use of electronic surveillance, physical searches, pen registers, trap and trace devices, as well as access business records and other tangible things. At the same time, FISA imposes important procedural safeguards to protect against abuse by law enforcement, including minimization procedures and a requirement that a significant purpose of the FISA order is to obtain foreign intelligence information. Further, FISA interposes a neutral and detached judicial officer between the Government and the target of the surveillance, providing an important check against reckless and arbitrary actions by law enforcement. Among other things, the FISA judge must find probable cause that the target is a foreign power or agent of a foreign power and that each of the facilities or places at which electronic surveillance is directed is being used by a foreign power or agent. However, while the courts have found these checks and balances sufficient to protect privacy interests, individuals challenging FISA orders face virtually insurmountable legal hurdles to compel disclosure of FISA materials to support a motion to suppress evidence or challenge a nondisclosure order. As the courts have repeatedly emphasized, there is no interest more compelling than national security.[392] As a result, under FISA, concerns for national security often take precedence over individual civil liberties.

NSLs have also become a critical investigative tool in combating terrorism. The ability to access business records from electronic communication service providers, financial institutions and credit agencies is extremely important in national security investigations. Moreover, the advantage of being able to access such records without a court order has resulted in NSLs being issued more

391. *Id.*

392. *See* In re Directives Pursuant to Sec.105B, 551 F.3d 1004, 1012 (Foreign Int.Surv.Ct.Rev. 2008) (national security is an interest of the "highest order of magnitude"); In re Sealed Case, 310 F.3d 717, 746 (Foreign Int. Surv.Ct.Rev. 2002).

frequently than FISA orders. However, recipients of NSLs have been successful in challenging NSL nondisclosure orders on First Amendment grounds. The Second Circuit has held that the NSL statute is not narrowly tailored to conform to First Amendment procedural standards.[393] Furthermore, review of an NSL nondisclosure order may not be bound by the executive's "conclusive" certification regarding the potential of harm to national security posed by disclosure, the court ruled.[394] According to the Second Circuit, in order to conform to constitutional standards, NSL statutes must be interpreted to require the Government to provide notice to each NSL recipient of its statutory right to contest the nondisclosure requirement.[395]

In short, there is a constant tension between protecting national security and individual liberties. While FISA orders and NSLs are critical to gathering counterterrorism intelligence information and preventing terrorist attacks, the courts must remain vigilant to protect against violating the constitutional rights of U.S. citizens in the name of national security. However, achieving the proper balance between these competing interests remains an elusive goal.

393. *See* Doe v. Mukasey, 549 F.3d 861 (2d Cir. 2008).

394. *Id.* at 882.

395. *Id.* at 879, 883–84.

Chapter 7

PROSECUTING TERRORIST SPONSORS AND FACILITATORS

A. MATERIAL SUPPORT STATUTES, 18 U.S.C. §§ 2339A AND 2339B[1]

Congress has enacted significant legislation aimed at combating international terrorism.[2] The principal federal criminal provisions used to prosecute international terrorists are the "material support" statutes, 18 U.S.C. §§ 2339A and 2339B.[3] The material support statutes are preventive measures, which "criminalize not terrorist attacks themselves, but aid that makes the attacks more likely to occur."[4] Sections 2339A and 2339B enable federal prosecutors to punish those individuals who provide "material support or resources," including money, weapons, expertise in constructing explosive devices, and other assistance to terrorists and designated foreign terrorist organizations (FTOs).[5] Congress recognized that "[c]utting off 'material support or resources' from terrorist organizations deprives them of the means with which to carry out acts of terrorism and potentially leads to their demise."[6]

1. STATUTORY FRAMEWORK

Section 2339A was enacted in 1994 as part of the Violent Crime Control and Law Enforcement Act.[7] The statute makes it a

1. The discussion of the material support statutes is taken in part from Jimmy Gurulé, UNFUNDING TERROR: THE LEGAL RESPONSE TO THE FINANCING OF GLOBAL TERRORISM, at ch. 10, (Edward Elgar 2008) hereinafter [UNFUNDING TERROR]

2. *See, e.g.,* 18 U.S.C. § 2332a (use of weapons of mass destruction); 18 U.S.C. § 2332b (acts of terrorism transcending national boundaries); 18 U.S.C. § 2332f (anti-terrorist bombing statute); 18 U.S.C. § 2339 (harboring or concealing terrorists); 18 U.S.C. § 2339C (anti-terrorist financing statute); and 18 U.S.C. § 2339D (receiving military-type training from a foreign terrorist organization).

3. 18 U.S.C. § 2339A (West 2008); 18 U.S.C. § 2339B (2000 & Supp. IV 2004).

4. Holder v. Humanitarian Law Project, 130 S.Ct. 2705, 2728 (2010).

5. 18 U.S.C. § 2339A (West 2008) and 18 U.S.C. § 2339B (2000 & Supp. IV 2004). The term "material support or resources" is a term of art and bans various types of assistance and support to terrorists and terrorist groups. *See* discussion *infra,* note 20.

6. Humanitarian Law Project v. Mukasey, 552 F.3d 916, 931 (9th Cir. 2009), *overturned on other grounds,* Holder v. Humanitarian Law Project, 130 S.Ct. 2705, 2728 (2010).

7. Violent Crime Control and Law Enforcement Act of 1994, Pub. L. No. 103–322, § 12005(a), 108 Stat. 1796, 2022–3 (1994) (codified at 18 U.S.C. § 2339A).

crime to provide "material support or resources" "knowing or intending" that they be used to prepare for or carry out one of the statute's enumerated predicate offenses.[8] For example, section 2339A prohibits the provision of financial assistance "knowing or intending" that the funds be used in preparation for, or in carrying out, a plot to kill or injure persons or damage property outside the United States, in violation of 18 U.S.C. § 956.[9] To convict under section 2339A, the Government must prove four elements: "(1) the defendant knowingly (2) provided "material support or resources," (3) knowing or intending that the provision of 'material support or resources' be used in preparation for, or in carrying out (4) one or more of the violent crimes specified in the statute."[10]

In 1996, Congress added section 2339B as part of the Antiterrorism and Effective Death Penalty Act.[11] Section 2339B makes it unlawful to "provide[ ] material support or resources to a foreign terrorist organization, or attempt[ ] or conspire[ ] to do so...."[12] The statute prohibits the provision of material support or resources to foreign organizations designated by the Secretary of State for engaging in terrorist activities.[13] Section 2339B is aimed at depriving terrorist groups of funding and other resources.[14] The prohibition is based on a finding by Congress that terrorist organizations "are so tainted by their criminal conduct that any contribution to such an organization facilitates that conduct."[15]

In *Humanitarian Law Project v. Gonzales*, the court examined the legislative history of section 2339B, commenting:

> Congress enacted § 2339B in order to close a loophole left by § 2339A. Congress, concerned that terrorist organizations

---

8. 18 U.S.C. § 2339A. Section 2339A punishes—

Whoever provides material support or resources or conceals or disguises the nature, location, source, or ownership of material support or resources, knowing or intending that they are to be used in preparation for, or in carrying out, a violation of section 32, 37, 81, 175, 229, 351, 831, 842(m) or (n), 844(f) or (i), 930(c), 956, 1091, 1114, 1116, 1203, 1361, 1362, 1363, 1366, 1751, 1992, 2155, 2156, 2280, 2281 2332, 2332a, 2332b, 2332f, 2340A, or 2442 of this title, section 236 of the Atomic Energy Act of 1954, (42 U.S.C. 2284), section 46502 or 60123(b) of title 49, or any offense listed in section 2332b(g)(5)(B) (except for section 2339A and 2339b) or in preparation for, or in carrying out, the concealment of an escape from the commission of any such violation, or attempts

or conspires to do such an act, shall be fined under this title, imprisoned not more that 15 years, or both, and, if the death of any person results, shall be imprisoned for any term of years or for life.

9. *See* United States v. Chandia, 514 F.3d 365, 373 (4th Cir. 2008).

10. Unfunding Terror, supra note 1, at 279.

11. Antiterrorism and Effective Death Penalty Act, Pub. L. No. 104–132, § 303, 110 Stat. 1214, 1250.

12. 18 U.S.C. § 2339B(a)(1).

13. *Id.*

14. Unfunding Terror, *supra* note 1, at 279.

15. AEDPA, *supra* note 11, note following 18 U.S.C. § 2339B (Findings and Purpose).

would raise funds "under the cloak of a humanitarian or charitable exercise," sought to pass legislation that would "severely restrict the ability of terrorist organizations to raise much needed funds for their terrorist acts within the United States" [citations omitted]. As § 2339A was limited to donors intending to further the commission of specific federal offenses, Congress passed § 2339B to encompass donors who acted without the intent to further federal crimes.[16]

To sustain a conviction under section 2339B, the Government must prove that the defendant acted with knowledge that the foreign group has been designated an FTO,[17] or has engaged in or engages in acts of terrorism.[18] "Unlike section 2339A, section 2339B does not require for conviction proof that the defendant has provided support or resources with the knowledge or intent that such resources be used to commit specific violent crimes."[19] According to one commentator:

> To prove a violation of section 2339B, the defendant must have knowledge that the organization is a designated [FTO] or engages or has engaged in acts of terrorism. The Government is not required to prove that the defendant intended to further the illegal aims of the FTO by the provision of material support or resources. Under § 2339B, the donor is criminally liable even if he intended to fund the *humanitarian* activities of the organization, if he had knowledge that the group had been designated an FTO or engaged or engages in terrorist activities.[20]

For purposes of both sections 2339A and 2339B, "material support or resources" is defined to include:

---

16. Humanitarian Law Project v. Gonzales, 380 F. Supp.2d 1134, 1146 (C.D. Cal. 2005). The court further observed:

> [T]he AEDPA sought to prevent the United States from becoming a base for terrorist fundraising. Congress recognized that terrorist groups are often structured to include political or humanitarian components in addition to terrorist components. Such an organizational structure allows terrorist groups to raise funds under the guise of political or humanitarian causes. Those funds can then be diverted to terrorist activities.

Id. at 1137.

17. *Id.* 8 U.S.C. § 1189 authorizes the Secretary of State to designate an entity as an FTO. *See* discussion *infra* at notes 21–2, and accompanying text.

18. 18 U.S.C. § 2339B (2000 & Supp. IV 2004).

19. United States v. Stewart, 590 F.3d 93, 116 (2d Cir. 2009). See also Holder v. Humanitarian Law Project, 130 S.Ct. 2705, 2717 (2010).

20. UNFUNDING TERROR, *supra* note 1, at 281 (Edward Elgar 2008) (citations omitted) (emphasis in original). However, section 2339B does not render section 2339A obsolete. "[A] prosecutor may file charges under § 2339A rather than § 2339B if the material-support type activity was not undertaken on behalf of a particular designated FTO or where the provision of material support benefitted a terrorist group that has not been designated an FTO." *Id.*

any property, tangible or intangible, or service, including currency or monetary instruments or financial securities, financial services, lodging, training, expert advice or assistance, safehouses, false documentation or identification, communications equipment, facilities, weapons, lethal substances, explosives, personnel (1 or more individuals who may be or include oneself), and transportation, except medicine or religious materials.[21]

Upon conviction, both sections 2339A and 2339B impose a fine or a term of imprisonment of not more than 15 years, or both, and, if the death of any person results, incarceration for any term of years or for life.[22] In addition, assets involved in violations of §§ 2339A and 2339B are subject to civil forfeiture under 18 U.S.C. § 981[23]

Finally, multiple punishment for violations of sections 2339A and 2339B arising from a single course of conduct does not violate the Double Jeopardy Clause.[24] Historically, the Double Jeopardy Clause has been interpreted to protect against three distinct abuses: "(1) a second prosecution for the same offense after acquittal; (2) a second prosecution for the same offense after conviction; and (3) multiple punishment for the same offense."[25] The protection against multiple punishment prohibits the Government from "punishing twice, or attempting a second time to punish criminally for the same offense."[26]

It is well settled that "[w]hen a single course of conduct violates multiple statutes, multiple punishments may be imposed without violating the Double Jeopardy Clause, if that is what Congress intended."[27] Further, if the statutory elements "do not

21. 18 U.S.C. § 2339A(b)(1) (2000); *see also id.* § 2339B(g)(4) (2000) ("[T]he term 'material support or resources' has the same meaning given that term in section 2339A. . . .").

22. 18 U.S.C. §§ 2339A, 2339B. Section 2339B provides:

Whoever knowingly provides material support or resources to a foreign terrorist organization, or attempts or conspires to do so, shall be fined under this title or imprisoned not more then 15 years, or both, and, if the death of any person results, shall be imprisoned for any term of years or for life. . . .

23. 18 U.S.C. § 981 (West, 2008).

24. The Double Jeopardy Clause of the Fifth Amendment provides: "[N]or shall any person be subject for the same

offense to be twice put in jeopardy of life or limb." U.S. CONST. amend. V.

25. JIMMY GURULÉ, SANDRA GUERRA THOMPSON & MICHAEL O'HEAR, THE LAW OF ASSET FORFEITURE 338 (LexisNexis, 2d ed. 2004) (citing North Carolina v. Pearce, 395 U.S. 711, 717 (1969)); United States v. Dixon, 509 U.S. 688, 696 (1993).

26. Witte v. United States, 515 U.S. 389, 115 S.Ct. 2199, 2204 (1995) (quoting Helvering v. Mitchell, 303 U.S. 391, 399 (1938)).

27. United States v. Chandia, 514 F.3d 365, 372 (4th Cir. 2008) (rejecting defendant's argument that conviction on three counts of providing material support to terrorists and terrorist organizations in violation of 18 U.S.C. §§ 2339A, 2339B violated the Double Jeopardy Clause) (citing Albernaz v. United States, 450 U.S. 333, 344 (1981)).

overlap, then multiple punishments are presumed to be authorized absent a showing of contrary intent."[28] The elements of sections 2339A and 2339B do not overlap.[29] Section 2339B requires proof that the defendant (1) knowingly provided material support (2) to an organization designated as a foreign terrorist organization (3) with knowledge of the organization's status as an FTO, or knowing that it engages in terrorism.[30] By contrast, section 2339A requires proof that the defendant provided material support or resources, "knowing or intending that they were to be used in preparation for, or in carrying out, a violation of" statutorily enumerated violent crimes.[31] Because each statute requires proof of an element that the other does not, there is a presumption that Congress authorized multiple punishments.[32] Absent a showing of clear congressional intent to overcome the presumption, imposing multiple punishment for violations of sections 2339A and 2339B does not violate the Double Jeopardy Clause.[33]

2. FTO DESIGNATION PROCESS

The authority to designate an entity a "foreign terrorist organization" resides with the Secretary of State.[34] Under 8 U.S.C. § 1189, the Secretary of State, in consultation with the Secretary of Treasury and the Attorney General, may designate a foreign organization upon finding that "(1) the organization is a foreign organization, (2) the organization engages in terrorist activity or retains the capability and intent to engage in terrorist activity, and (3) the terrorist activity threatens national security or the security of United States nationals."[35] In making an FTO determination, the Secretary of State compiles an "administrative record" and makes "findings" based on this record.[36] The FTO designation may be based on "classified information" which is unavailable for review by the designated party.[37] Further, the Secretary is not required to notify an organization prior to designation as an FTO.[38] Seven days

28. *Chandia*, 514 F.3d at 372 (citations omitted). *See also* Blockburger v. United States, 284 U.S. 299, 304 (1932).

29. *Chandia,* 514 F.3d at 372.

30. 18 U.S.C. § 2339B.

31. *Id.* at § 2339A.

32. *Chandia*, 514 F.3d at 372.

33. *Id.*

34. 8 U.S.C. § 1189(a)(1), (d)(4). The Secretary of State has designated 45 groups as FTOs. *See* Foreign Terrorist Organizations, Office of the Coordinator for Counterterrorism, U.S. Dep't of State (Jan. 19, 2010), *available at* http://www.state.gov/s/ct/rls/other/des/123085.htm (last visited July 6, 2010).

35. *Id.* at § 1189(a)(1)(A)–(C). " '[N]ational security' means the national defense, foreign relations, or economic interests of the United States." *Id.* at § 1189(d)(2).

36. 8 U.S.C. § 1189(a)(3)(A).

37. *Id.* at § 1189(a)(3)(B). *See also* People's Mojahedin Org. of Iran v. Department of State, 327 F.3d 1238, 1240–41 (D.C. Cir. 2003) (*"PMOI"*); National Council of Resistance of Iran v. Department of State, 251 F.3d 192, 209 (D.C. Cir. 2001).

38. The absence of pre-designation notice has been challenged in the courts. In National Council of Resistance of Iran v. Department of State, 251 F.3d

before designating an organization as an FTO, the Secretary must submit to key Congressional leaders and committee members a "classified communication" detailing the Secretary's findings.[39] The designation is then published in the Federal Register.[40]

An FTO seeking to challenge its designation can only seek judicial review of the designation in the D.C. Circuit and must do so no later than 30 days after the Secretary of State publishes the designation in the Federal Register.[41] The D.C. Circuit has exclusive jurisdiction to review FTO designations.[42] The appellate court may review only the first two prongs of the three-prong standard for FTO designation. The court may review the Secretary's findings that the entity is a "foreign" organization and that it engages in "terrorist activity."[43] However, whether the organization "threatens the security of United States nationals or the national security of the United States" is a nonjusticiable question.[44] Further, the D.C. Circuit's review is limited to the administrative record and any classified information submitted to the court by the Government *ex parte* and *in camera*.[45] The D.C. Circuit will set aside an FTO designation only if it finds it to be "(1) arbitrary, capricious, an abuse of discretion, or otherwise not in accordance with the law; (2) contrary to constitutional right, power, privilege, or immunity; (3) in excess of statutory jurisdiction, authority, or limitation, or short of statutory right; (4) lacking substantial support in the administrative record taken as a whole or in classified information submitted to the court; or (5) not in accord with the procedures required by law."[46] Finally, pursuant to section 1189(a)(8), "a defendant in a criminal action . . . shall not be permitted to raise any question concerning the validity of the issuance of such designation as a

192, 209 (D.C. Cir. 2001) ("*NCRI*"), the D.C. Circuit ruled that due process requires that the Secretary afford entities under consideration notice that the designation is impending. *Id.* at 208. However, notice may be delayed until after designation where pre-designation notice would jeopardize national security or foreign policy. *Id. See* discussion of *NCRI infra*, at note 213, and accompanying text.

39. 8 U.S.C. § 1189(a)(2)(A)(i).

40. *Id.* at § 1189(a)(2)(A)(ii). An FTO designation may be revoked in three ways: "(1) Congress blocks or revokes a designation, 8 U.S.C. § 1189(a)(5); (2) the Secretary revokes the designation based on a finding that changed circumstances or national security warrants such a revocation, 8 U.S.C. § 1189(a)(6)(A); or (3) the D.C. Circuit sets aside the designation under 8

U.S.C. § 1189(c)(3)." United States v. Taleb–Jedi, 566 F. Supp.2d 157, 163 (E.D.N.Y. 2008).

41. 8 U.S.C. § 1189(c)(1).

42. *Id.*

43. *See* People's Mojahedin Org. of Iran v. Department of State, 327 F.3d 1238, 1240–1 (D.C. Cir. 2003).

44. *Id.* ("Such questions concerning the foreign policy decisions of the Executive Branch present political judgments, decisions of a kind for which the Judiciary has neither aptitude, facilities nor responsibilities and have long been held to belong in the domain of political power not subject to judicial intrusion or inquiry.").

45. 8 U.S.C. § 1189(c)(2).

46. United States v. Taleb–Jedi, 566 F. Supp.2d 157, 163 (E.D.N.Y. 2008) (citing 8 U.S.C. § 1189(c) (3)(A)–(E)).

defense or an objection at any trial or hearing."[47] Consequently, in a criminal prosecution for violating section 2339B, the defendant is prohibited from collaterally attacking the validity of the FTO designation.[48]

The consequences of being designated an FTO are severe. Financial institutions are required to freeze the assets of an FTO located in the United States,[49] and representatives and members of the FTO are prohibited from entering the United States.[50] Finally, section 2339B imposes severe criminal sanctions upon whoever knowingly provides "material support or resources" to an FTO.[51]

3. EXTRATERRITORIAL JURISDICTION

Section 2339B, but not section 2339A, has extraterritorial application. Pursuant to section 2339B(d)(2), federal courts may properly exercise jurisdiction for violations of section 2339B(a)(1) that occurred outside of the United States.[52] A penal statute may be applied extraterritorially if (1) Congress intended the statute to apply to acts committed outside of the United States, and (2) the extraterritorial application of the statute would not violate international law.[53] Congress is empowered to attach extraterritorial effect to a statute so long as the statute does not violate the Due Process Clause of the Fifth Amendment.[54] To withstand a due process challenge, "there must be a sufficient nexus between the defendant and the United States."[55] In the case of section 2339B, Congress's intent to apply the statute extraterritorially is clear from language of the statute. Section 2339B(d)(2) expressly provides: "There is extraterritorial Federal jurisdiction over an offense under this

47. 8 U.S.C. § 1189(a)(8).

48. *See, e.g.,* United States v. Hammoud, 381 F.3d 316, 331 (4th Cir. 2004) (*en banc*) ("Congress has provided that the *fact* of an organization's designation as an FTO is an element of § 2339B, but the *validity* of the designation is not.") (emphasis in original), *vacated on other grounds*, 543 U.S. 1097 (2005), *reinstated in relevant part*, 405 F.3d 1034 (4th Cir. 2005); United States v. Afshari, 426 F.3d 1150, 1159 (9th Cir. 2005) ("[T]he element of the crime that the prosecutor must prove in a § 2339B case is the predicate fact that a particular organization was designated at the time the material support was given, not whether the government made a correct designation."); *United States v. Taleb–Jedi*, 566 F. Supp.2d at 170–71 ("Congress delegated the authority to make such distinctions to the Secretary of State and specifically took this policymaking 'out of the hands of United States Attorneys

and juries.' ") (*quoting Afshari*, 426 F.3d at 1155).

49. 18 U.S.C. § 2339B(a)(2).

50. 8 U.S.C. § 1189(a)(3)(B)(i).

51. 18 U.S.C. § 2339B(a)(1) (2000).

52. *See* 18 U.S.C. § 2339B(d)(2).

53. Jimmy Gurulé, Complex Criminal Litigation: Prosecuting Drug Enterprises and Organized Crime 444 (LEXIS, 2d ed. 2000) [hereinafter "Complex Criminal Litigation"]. *See also* Restatement (Third) of Foreign Relations Law §§ 401–2.

54. *See* United States v. Vasquez–Velasco, 15 F.3d 833, 839 (9th Cir. 1994); United States v. Larsen, 952 F.2d 1099, 1100 (9th Cir. 1991).

55. United States v. Caicedo, 47 F.3d 370, 371 (9th Cir. 1995) (quoting United States v. Davis, 905 F.2d 245, 248–49 (9th Cir. 1990), *cert. denied*, 498 U.S. 1047 (1991)).

section."[56] Further, courts have interpreted the "sufficient nexus" requirement rather liberally; they have found that the nexus requirement was satisfied in cases where the evidence indicated that the defendant intended to smuggle drugs into the United States.[57] If the intent to smuggle drugs into the U.S. constitutes a "sufficient nexus," the nexus requirement would clearly be met where the provision of material support or resources occurred outside of the United States, but the foreign terrorist organization intended to engage in terrorist acts killing innocent civilians within the country.

The law of nations permits the exercise of jurisdiction under five principles: territorial, national, protective, universal, and passive personality.[58] The "territorial" principle involves conduct which takes place within the territorial limits of a nation or occurred outside of the territory but was intended to have detrimental effects within the country.[59] When criminal acts are committed within the territory of the state asserting jurisdiction, the "subjective" form of the territorial principle is implicated.[60] The "objective" theory of the territorial principle applies where acts committed outside of the asserting state's territory were intended to have detrimental effects within its borders.[61] In *Strassheim v. Daily*, Justice Holmes stated: "Acts done outside a jurisdiction, but intended to produce and producing effects within it, justify a State in punishing the cause of the harm as if he had been present at the effect, if the State should succeed in getting him within its power."[62] However, the Government need not prove that the acts committed outside its territory actually had detrimental or harmful effects within its borders. A mere showing of intent to produce detrimental effects within the United States may support extrater-

---

56. *Id.* at § 2339B(d)(2).

57. *See* United States v. Khan, 35 F.3d 426, 429–30 (9th Cir. 1994) ("To meet this requirement, the government must show that the plan for shipping drugs was likely to have effects in the United States."); United States v. Aikins, 946 F.2d 608, 613 (9th Cir. 1990) ("A sufficient nexus exists where the ship with drugs is bound ultimately for the United States."); United States v. Gonzalez, 810 F.2d 1538, 1542 (11th Cir. 1987) (sufficient nexus requires "that the [ships] intended destination was the United States or that the crew members' purpose was to send [the drugs] into this country").

58. COMPLEX CRIMINAL LITIGATION, *supra* note 23, at 453.

59. RESTATEMENT (THIRD) OF FOREIGN RELATIONS LAW, § 401(1)(a), (1)(b).

60. *Id.* at § 402(1)(a) ("[A] state has jurisdiction to prescribe law with respect to conduct, that, wholly or in substantial part, takes place within its territory.").

61. *See* United States v. Vasquez–Velasco, 15 F.3d 833, 841 (9th Cir. 1994) ("Our circuit has repeatedly approved extraterritorial application of statutes that prohibit the importation and distribution of controlled substances in the United States because these activities implicate national security interests and create a detrimental effect in the United States.").

62. Strassheim v. Daily, 221 U.S. 280, 285 (1911).

ritorial jurisdiction. According to the RESTATEMENT (THIRD) OF FOR-
EIGN RELATIONS LAW:

> [A] state may recognize jurisdiction based on effects in the
> state, where the effect or intended effect is substantial and the
> exercise is reasonable under § 403. Cases involving intended
> but unrealized effects are rare, but international law does not
> preclude jurisdiction in such instances, subject to the principle
> of reasonableness. When the intent to commit the proscribed
> act is clear and demonstrated by some activity, and the effect
> to be produced by the activity, is substantial and foreseeable,
> the fact that a plan or conspiracy was thwarted does not
> deprive the target state of jurisdiction to make its law applica-
> ble.[63]

Under the territorial principle, the exercise of extraterritorial
jurisdiction would be proper where the defendant provided material
support to an FTO outside of the United States, knowing that the
terrorist group intended to engage in terrorist attacks against
civilians within the United States.

The "nationality" principle authorizes extraterritorial jurisdiction for offenses committed by nationals of the asserting country.[64]
Nationality-based jurisdiction is based on the proposition that "nationals of a state remain under its sovereignty and owe their
allegiance to it, even though traveling or residing outside its territory."[65] In *Skiriotes v. Florida,* the Supreme Court posited: "The
United States is not debarred by any rule of international law from
governing the conduct of its own citizens upon the high seas or
even in foreign countries when the rights of other nations or their
nationals are not infringed."[66] Thus, a state has jurisdiction to
prescribe penal laws punishing the conduct of a national of the
state wherever the conduct occurs.[67] Further, the nationality principle has been extended to include jurisdiction based on "domicile or
residence."[68]

Under the "protective" principle, extraterritorial jurisdiction is
based on whether "the national interest or national security is
threatened or injured by the conduct in question."[69] The protective

---

63. RESTATEMENT (THIRD) OF FOREIGN RELATIONS LAW § 402 cmt. d.

64. RESTATEMENT (THIRD) OF FOREIGN RELATIONS LAW § 402(2), cmt. (e) and Re-porter's Note 1.

65. CHRISTOPHER L. BLAKESLEY, TER-RORISM, DRUGS, INTERNATIONAL LAW, AND THE PROTECTION OF HUMAN LIBERTY 125 (1992).

66. Skiriotes v. Florida 313 U.S. 69, 73 (1941).

67. *See* RESTATEMENT (SECOND) OF FOREIGN RELATIONS LAW § 30 (1965) ("A State has jurisdiction to prescribe a rule of law . . . attaching legal consequences to conduct of a national of the state wherever the conduct occurs. . . .").

68. *See* RESTATEMENT (THIRD) OF FOR-EIGN RELATIONS LAW §§ 411, 484.

69. United States v. Felix–Gutier-rez, 940 F.2d 1200, 1204 (9th Cir. 1991), *cert. denied,* 508 U.S. 906 (1993). *See*

principle has been applied to support extraterritorial jurisdiction over violent crimes committed against a U.S. Congressman and federal law enforcement officers perpetrated abroad, and other offenses that threaten the integrity of governmental functions, such as espionage, counterfeiting, and falsification of official documents.[70]

The "universal" principle recognizes jurisdiction over crimes so heinous and universally condemned by all nations that "any state if it captures the offender may prosecute and punish that person on behalf of the world community regardless of the nationality of the offender or victim or where the crime was committed."[71] The RESTATEMENT (THIRD) OF FOREIGN RELATIONS LAW recognizes the universal principle. Section 404 provides:

> A state may exercise jurisdiction to define and punish certain offenses recognized by the community of nations as of universal concern, such as piracy, slave trade, attacks on or hijacking of aircraft, genocide, war crimes, and perhaps terrorism, even where none of the bases of jurisdiction indicated in § 402 is present.[72]

Finally, the passive personality principle authorizes a state to assert jurisdiction over the offenses committed against their citizens abroad. Jurisdiction is based on the nationality of the victim. In *United States v. Yunis*, the D.C. Circuit stated. "Under the passive personality principle, a state may punish non-nationals for crimes committed against its nationals outside of its territory, at least where the state has a particularly strong interest in the crime."[73] The passive personality principle is the most controversial of the five sources of jurisdiction. The RESTATEMENT (SECOND) OF FOREIGN RELATIONS LAW rejects a state exercising extraterritorial jurisdiction based on the nationality of the victim alone.[74] However, the passive personality principle has received greater acceptance when applied to acts of terrorism.[75]

also RESTATEMENT (THIRD) OF FOREIGN RELATIONS LAW at § 402(3)m cmt., (f).

70. *See, e.g.,* United States v. Layton, 855 F.2d 1388, 1393 (9th Cir. 1988) (extraterritorial jurisdiction upheld under the protective principle for the murder of a U.S. Congressman); *United States v. Felix–Gutierrez*, 940 F.2d at 1206 (court had extraterritorial jurisdiction under the protective principle for the murder of a DEA agent in Mexico). *See also* RESTATEMENT (THIRD) OF FOREIGN RELATIONS LAW § 402(3) cmt., (f).

71. United States v. Yunis, 681 F.Supp. 896, 900 (D.D.C. 1988). *See also* RESTATEMENT (THIRD) OF FOREIGN RELATIONS LAW, at § 404.

72. RESTATEMENT (THIRD) OF FOREIGN RELATIONS LAW § 404. *See also* United States v. Yunis, 924 F.2d 1086, 1091 (D.C. Cir. 1991) (holding that the universal principle supports asserting extraterritorial jurisdiction for hostage taking and aircraft piracy).

73. *United States v. Yunis*, 924 F.2d 1086 at 1091.

74. *See* RESTATEMENT (SECOND) OF FOREIGN RELATIONS LAW § 30(2) (1965).

75. *See* RESTATEMENT (THIRD) OF FOREIGN RELATIONS LAW § 402, cmt. (g) ("The principle has not been generally accepted for ordinary torts or crimes, but it is increasingly accepted as applied to ter-

Section 2339B(d) authorizes jurisdiction based on the subjective theory of the territorial principle; there is jurisdiction over a violation of section 2339B if "the offense occurs in whole or in part within the United States."[76] However, the statute does not explicitly authorize jurisdiction under the objective theory form of the territorial principle.

Further, the statute confers jurisdiction based on the nationality principle. Pursuant to section 2339B(d)(1)(A), a court may exercise jurisdiction if an offender is a national of the United States, regardless of where the offense takes place.[77] The exercise of jurisdiction is also authorized based on the defendant's domicile, implicating the nationality principle. Under the statute, there is jurisdiction over an offense if the defendant is an alien lawfully admitted for permanent residence in the United States or a stateless person whose habitual residence is in the United States.[78]

Extraterritorial jurisdiction is also permitted based on the universal principle. Under section 2339B(d)(1)(C), there is jurisdiction over an offense if "an offender is brought into or found in the United States, even if the conduct required for the offense occurs outside the United States."[79] In such a case, extraterritorial jurisdiction attaches regardless of the location of the offense (territorial principle), the nationality of the offender (nationality principle) or victim (passive personality principle), and regardless of whether the offense threatens the national security or governmental functions of the United States (protective principle). Jurisdiction based solely on the offender's presence in the United States, supports the view that the provision of material support or resources to an FTO is a universal crime.

Finally, there is jurisdiction over an offense committed under section 2339B if an offender aids and abets or conspires with any person over whom jurisdiction exists under section 2339B(d).[80] In other words, if extraterritorial jurisdiction is authorized under the statute for the actual perpetrator of the offense, jurisdiction extends with equal force to his aiders and abettors and co-conspirators.[81] The statute does not implicate either the protective or passive personality principles.

rorist and other organized attacks on a state's nationals by reason of their nationality, or to assassination of a state's nationals by reason of their nationality, or to assassination of a state's diplomatic representatives or other officials.").

76. 18 U.S.C. § 2339B(d). The statute also authorizes jurisdiction if the offense occurs in or affects interstate or foreign commerce. *See* 18 U.S.C. § 2339B(d)(1)(E).

77. *Id.* at § 2339B(d)(1)(A).

78. *Id.* at § 2339B(d)(1)(A)–(B).

79. *Id.* at § 2339B(d)(1)(C). *See* United States v. Yunis, 924 F.2d 1086, 1092 (D.C. Cir. 1991) (upholding the exercise of extraterritorial jurisdiction where hijacking of aircraft was committed outside the United States and defendant was "present in" the territory).

80. *Id.* at § 2339B(d)(1)(F).

81. *Id.*

4. LEGAL CHALLENGES

a. *First Amendment*

i. *Freedom of Association*

In the Intelligence Reform and Terrorism Prevention Act of 2004 (IRTPA), Congress amended section 2339B to clarify the mental state necessary to sustain a violation of the statute, requiring knowledge of the foreign group's designation as an FTO or the group's commission of terrorist acts.[82] Despite the amendment imposed by the IRTPA, defendants have challenged the constitutionality of the material support statute. Defendants argue that section 2339B violates the First Amendment right of freedom of association because, in the absence of a specific intent element, the statute imposes guilt by association.[83] It is well settled that the First Amendment "restricts the ability of the state to impose liability on an individual solely because of his association with another."[84] Defendants contend that section 2339B impermissibly criminalizes mere membership in, or association with, a terrorist organization.[85]

In *Holder v. Humanitarian Law Project*, the United States Supreme Court rejected plaintiffs' First Amendment freedom of association claims.[86] In that case, two U.S. citizens and six domestic organizations challenged the constitutionality of the material support statute, 18 U.S.C. § 2339B.[87] Plaintiffs claimed that they wished to provide support for the humanitarian and political activities of the Partiya Karkeran Kurdistan (PKK) and the Liberation Tigers of Tamil Eelam (LTTE), organizations which had been designated as "foreign terrorist organizations" by the Secretary of State.[88] However, plaintiffs maintained that they could not do so for fear of prosecution under section 2339B.[89] They argued that the material-support statute should be interpreted, when applied to speech, to require proof that a defendant intended to further a foreign terrorist organization's illegal activities.[90] The Supreme Court disagreed, holding that under section 2339B, proof of plaintiffs' knowledge that the organizations were designated as FTOs was sufficient.[91]

82. Intelligence Reform and Terrorist Prevention Act of 2004 (IRTPA), § 6603, 118 Stat. 3762–4.

83. *See, e.g.*, Holder v. Humanitarian Law Project, 130 S.Ct. 2705 (2010); *United States v. Warsame*, 537 F. Supp.2d at 1013.

84. NAACP v. Claiborne Hardware Co., 458 U.S. 886, 918–9 (1982).

85. *See United States v. Warsame*, 537 F. Supp.2d at 1013.

86. Holder v. Humanitarian Law Project, 130 S.Ct. 2705 (2010).

87. *Id.*

88. *Id.* at 2712.

89. *Id.* at 2714.

90. *Id.* at 2717.

91. *Id.* at 2717.

The Supreme Court advanced three arguments in support of its holding. First, the Court maintained that plaintiff's interpretation of section 2339B was inconsistent with the text of the statute. The Court noted that section 2339B prohibits "knowingly" providing material support.[92] The statute then specifically describes the type of knowledge that is required: "To violate this paragraph, a person must have knowledge that the organization is a designated terrorist organization . . ., that the organization has engaged or engages in terrorism . . ."[93] The Court concluded: "Congress plainly spoke to the necessary mental state for a violation of § 2339B, and it chose knowledge about the organization's connection to terrorism, not specific intent to further the organization's terrorist activities."[94]

Second, the Supreme Court posited that plaintiffs' interpretation was untenable in light of sections 2339A(a) and 2339C(a)(1), both of which refer to specific intent to further terrorist activity. The Court observed that section 2339A(a) establishes criminal liability for one who "provides material support or resources . . . knowing or intending that they are to be used in preparation for, or in carrying out, a violation of" one of the listed statutes proscribing violent terrorist acts.[95] Further, section 2339C(a)(1) provides criminal penalties for one who "unlawfully and willfully provides or collects funds with the intention that such funds be used, or with the knowledge that such funds are to be used, in full or in part, in order to carry out" other criminal acts.[96] The Court stated: "Congress enacted § 2339A in 1994 and § 2339C in 2002. Yet Congress did not import the intent language of those provisions into § 2339B, either when it enacted § 2339B in 1996, or when it clarified § 2339B's knowledge requirement in 2004."[97] Because Congress clearly knows how to include a specific intent requirement when it so desires, as evidenced by sections 2339A and 2339C, the Court concluded that Congress deliberately excluded such an intent from section 2339B.[98]

Finally, the Supreme Court distinguished *Scales v. United States*, the case on which plaintiffs most heavily relied.[99] *Scales*

92. Holder v. Humanitarian Law Project, 130 S.Ct. 2705, 2717 (2010).

93. *Id.* at 2717 (quoting 18 U.S.C. § 2339B).

94. *Id.* at 2717.

95. *Id.* at 2717 (quoting 18 U.S.C. § 2339A(a)).

96. *Id.* at 2718 (quoting 18 U.S.C. § 2339C(a)(1)).

97. *Id.*

98. *Id.* at 2718. *See also* United States v. Warsame, 537 F. Supp.2d 1005, 1013 (D. Minn. 2008) ("Congress's inclusion of an explicit *mens rea* requirement in § 2339A strongly suggests that it chose not in include a specific intent requirement in § 2339B."); United States v. Taleb–Jedi, 566 F. Supp.2d 157, 174 (E.D.N.Y. 2008) ("Congress is capable of and knows how to include a specific intent requirement when it so desires, and courts should not infer a different intent than what Congress specifically provides for in a statute.").

99. *See* Scales v. United States, 366 U.S. 978 (1961).

involved a constitutional challenge to the Smith Act, which prohibited membership in the Communist Party, a group advocating the violent overthrow of the Government.[100] Defendant maintained that the Smith Act unconstitutionally imputed guilt based on associational membership alone.[101] In *Scales*, the Supreme Court held that a person could not be convicted under the Smith Act absent knowledge of the group's illegal advocacy *and* a specific intent to further the organization's unlawful goals.[102] The Court in *Holder* distinguished *Scales* noting that section 2339B does not criminalize mere membership in a designated foreign terrorist organization, but prohibits the *conduct* of providing material support or resources to such a group.[103] As such, the statute is qualitatively different from laws that punish a defendant solely because of his membership in a group or association with others.[104] The Court limited the specific intent requirement in *Scales* to statutes that criminalize mere membership in a group that advocates criminal activity.[105] Since section 2339B does not punish mere membership in an FTO, the statute does not require proof of specific intent to further the groups' terrorist activities.[106] According to the Court, "[n]othing about *Scales* suggests the need for a specific intent requirement in such a case [as *Holder*]."[107]

Plaintiffs made a related claim arguing that the material support statute violates their First Amendment freedom of association by criminalizing the mere fact of their associating with the PKK and LTTE, which the Court easily dismissed.[108] The Court held that the statute does not prohibit being a member of an FTO or vigorously promoting or supporting the political goals of such groups.[109] What section 2339B prohibits is the affirmative act of providing material support to designated terrorist groups.[110] Thus, the cases cited by plaintiffs, which imposed criminal penalties on

100. *Id.* at 226, n. 18.

101. *Id.* at 229.

102. *Id.* at 220–2.

103. Holder v. Humanitarian Law Project, 130 S.Ct. 2705, 2718 (2010). *See also* United States v. Chandia, 514 F.3d 365, 371 (4th Cir. 2008); *Hammoud*, 381 F.3d at 329 (the material support statute "does not prohibit mere association; it prohibits the conduct of providing material support to a designated FTO"); People's Mojahedin Org. of Iran v. Department of State, 327 F.3d 1238, 1244 (D.C. Cir. 2003); United States v. Taleb–Jedi, 566 F. Supp.2d 157, 175 (E.D.N.Y. 2008) ("The Court concurs with each of the Courts of Appeals that has considered this issue and similarly finds that the statute does not punish individuals for advocating or sympathizing with the goals of organizations like the PMOI."); *United States v. Warsame*, 537 F. Supp.2d at 1015 ("Section 2339B does not criminalize expression or association.").

104. Holder v. Humanitarian Law Project, 130 S.Ct. 2705, 2718 (2010).

105. *Id.*

106. *Id.*

107. *Id.*

108. *Id.* at 2730–31.

109. *Id.*

110. Holder v. Humanitarian Law Project, 130 S.Ct. 2705 (2010). *See supra* note 64 for list of cases.

simple association or assembly, were inapposite.[111] The Court also held that plaintiffs' right of freedom of association is not violated because the material support statute prevents them from providing support to designated FTOs, but not to other groups. The Court stated that "Congress is not required to ban material support to every group or none at all."[112]

ii.　Freedom of Speech

In *Holder v. Humanitarian Law Project*, the Supreme Court also considered whether the material support statute, as applied to plaintiffs, violates the freedom of speech guaranteed by the First Amendment.[113] The Court began its analysis by discussing what kind of speech is prohibited under the statute. The Court posited that section 2339B does not prohibit independent advocacy or expression of any kind. The Court stated that plaintiffs "may speak and write freely about the PKK and LTTE, the government of Turkey and Sri Lanka, human rights, and international law. They may advocate before the United Nations."[114] Further, the Court noted that section 2339B does not prevent plaintiffs from becoming members of the PKK and LTTE.[115] Rather, according to the Court, the statute is carefully drawn to cover only a narrow category of speech "to, under the direction of, or in coordination with foreign groups that the speaker knows to be terrorist organizations."[116] At the same time, the Court rejected the Government's view that the material support statute only covers noncommunicative conduct. Instead, the Court found that section 2339B regulates speech on the basis of its content.[117] The Court reasoned that if plaintiffs' speech to the PKK and LTTE imparts a "specific skill" or communicates advice derived from "specialized knowledge," such as training on the use of international law or on petitioning the United Nations for relief, it would be barred under the statute.[118] Because the material support statute regulates "content-based" speech, the Court rejected the standard of review articulated in *United States v. O'Brien*,[119] which applies when a facially neutral statute restricts

111.　*Id.*

112.　*Id.*

113.　*Id.* at 2722–30.

114.　*Id.* at 2722.

115.　*Id.*

116.　*Id.*

117.　Holder v. Humanitarian Law Project, 130 S.Ct. 2705, 2722 (2010).

118.　*Id.*

119.　United States v. O'Brien, 391 U.S. 367 (1968). If a statute is directed not at speech but rather at conduct, thus invoking the intermediate scrutiny standard, the statute is valid—

if it is within the constitutional power of the Government; if it furthers an important or substantial governmental interest; if the governmental interest is unrelated to the suppression of free expression; and if the incidental restriction on alleged First Amendment freedoms is no greater than is essential to the furtherance of that interest.

Id. at 377.

some expressive conduct.[120] The Court explained: "The law here may be described as directed at conduct, . . . but as applied to plaintiffs the conduct triggering coverage under the statute consists of communicating a message."[121] Thus, the Court held that a more demanding, strict scrutiny standard of review must be applied, requiring the Government to demonstrate a compelling governmental interest.[122]

The Court found that "combating terrorism was an urgent objective of the highest order."[123] However, plaintiffs maintained that the objective of combating terrorism does not justify prohibiting their speech because their support would advance only the legitimate activities of the PKK and LTTE.[124] The Court disagreed, stating that when Congress enacted section 2339B, it made specific findings that "any" contribution to a foreign terrorist organization facilitates their unlawful activities. Specifically, Congress determined that "foreign organizations that engage in terrorist activity are so tainted by their criminal conduct that *any contribution to such an organization* facilitates that conduct."[125] Further, Congress's findings were embraced by the Executive Branch in a State Department affidavit, stating that "it is highly likely that any material support to these terrorist organizations will ultimately inure to the benefit of their criminal, terrorist functions—regardless of whether such support was ostensibly intended to support non-violent, non-terrorist activities."[126] The Court found these views persuasive, positing that material support, even for humanitarian purposes, "frees up other resources within the organization that may be put to violent ends. It also importantly helps lend legitimacy to foreign terrorist groups—legitimacy that makes it easier for those groups to persist, to recruit members, and to raise funds—all of which facilitate terrorist attacks."[127] Further, "money is fungible," the Court stated, and "money a terrorist group such as the PKK obtains using the techniques plaintiffs propose to teach could be redirected to funding the group's violent activities."[128] Ultimately, the Court concluded that Congress's and the Executive's assessment of the threat posed by providing any form of material support to a terrorist group was reasonably supported by the evidence and should be entitled to deference.[129] The Court stated:

120. *Holder*, at 2723.

121. *Id*. at 2724.

122. *Id*.

123. *Id*.

124. Holder v. Humanitarian Law Project, 130 S.Ct. 2705, 2725 (2010).

125. *Id*. at (quoting AEDPA § 301(a)(7)) (emphasis added).

126. *Id*. at 2727 (quoting State Department affidavit).

127. *Holder*, at 2725.

128. *Id*. at 2729.

129. *Id*. at 2727.

At bottom, plaintiffs simply disagree with the considered judgment of Congress and the Executive that providing material support to a designated foreign terrorist organization—even seemingly benign support—bolsters the terrorist activities of that organization. That judgment, however, is entitled to significant weight, and we have persuasive evidence before us to sustain it.[130]

The Supreme Court held that, in prohibiting the particular forms of support that plaintiffs intended to provide to the PKK and LTTE, section 2339B does not violate the freedom of speech.[131]

iii. Overbreadth

Some defendants argue that section 2339B violates the First Amendment because it is unconstitutionally overbroad, indiscriminately criminalizing both protected speech and unprotected conduct.[132] A statute is overbroad if it "punishes a substantial amount of protected free speech, judged in relation to the statute's plainly legitimate sweep."[133] The Supreme Court has "insisted that a law's application to protected speech be 'substantial,' not only in an absolute sense, but also relative to the scope of the law's plainly legitimate application, before applying the strong medicine of overbreadth invalidation."[134] Because the overbreadth doctrine allows for facial invalidation, an overbreadth challenge will rarely succeed against a statute that does not specifically regulate speech.[135] The courts have consistently rejected defendants' overbreadth challenge to section 2339B, holding that the statute does not punish a substantial amount of free speech in relation to its plainly legitimate sweep. For example, in *United States v. Hammoud*, the Fourth Circuit denied an overbreadth challenge to section 2339B despite the fact that it prohibits some plainly legitimate activity, teaching members of an FTO how to apply for grants to finance

130. *Id.* at 2728.

131. *Id.* at 2730.

132. *See, e.g.,* United States v. Hammoud, 381 F.3d 316, 330 (4th Cir. 2004) (*en banc*), *vacated on other grounds*, 543 U.S. 1097 (2005), *reinstated in relevant part*, 405 F.3d 1034 (4th Cir. 2005). United States v. Warsame, 537 F. Supp.2d 1005, 1017 (D. Minn. 2008); United States v. Awan, 459 F. Supp.2d 167, 180–81 (E.D.N.Y. 2006); United States v. Assi, 414 F. Supp.2d 707, 716 (E.D. Mich. 2006); Humanitarian Law Project v. Gonzales, 380 F. Supp.2d 1134, 1153 (C.D. Cal. 2005); United States v. Sattar, 314 F. Supp.2d 279, 305 (S.D.N.Y. 2004).

133. Virginia v. Hicks, 539 U.S. 113, 118–9 (2003). *See also* United States v. Amawi, 545 F. Supp.2d 681, 683 (N.D. Ohio 2008) ("To be invalid for overbreadth, the statute's reach into the zone of protected speech must be real and substantial 'judged in relation to [its] legitimate sweep.' ") (citations omitted).

134. *Virginia v. Hicks*, 539 U.S. at 119–20 (internal quotation marks and citations omitted).

135. *Id.* at 124; United States v. Afshari, 412 F.3d 1071, 1079 (9th Cir. 2005) (noting that section 2339B regulates non-expressive financial contributions and therefore is subject to less exacting scrutiny).

their humanitarian activities.[136] In *United States v. Assi*, the court held that the material support statute advances the legitimate governmental aim of depriving terrorists of the weapons, explosive and other means of carrying out their deadly mission.[137] Because there is no constitutionally protected right to provide material support or resources to terrorists or FTOs, the section 2339B does not infringe on constitutionally protected conduct.[138]

b. Fifth Amendment

i. Vagueness

The material support statute has been challenged on the grounds that it is unconstitutionally vague in violation of the Fifth Amendment Due Process Clause. "[T]he void-for vagueness doctrine requires that a penal statute define the criminal offense with sufficient definiteness that ordinary people can understand what conduct is prohibited and in a manner that does not encourage arbitrary and discriminatory enforcement."[139] The doctrine serves two purposes. First, it ensures fair notice by requiring that a statute "give the person of ordinary intelligence a reasonable opportunity to know what is prohibited, so he may act accordingly."[140] Second, the doctrine aims to provide standards for law enforcement to discourage "arbitrary and discriminatory enforcement."[141] A party may challenge a statute on unconstitutional vagueness grounds by arguing either that the statute is vague as applied to the relevant conduct at issue, or that the statute is

---

136. *United States v. Hammoud*, 381 F.3d at 330. *See also* Humanitarian Law Project v. Mukasey, 509 F.3d 1122, 1136–37 (9th Cir. 2007) (terms "training," "personnel," "expert advice or assistance" and "service" as used in section 2339B not overbroad), *overturned on other grounds*, Holder v. Humanitarian Law Project, 130 S.Ct. 2705 (2010); *United States v. Amawi*, 545 F. Supp.2d at 683 (defendant's "speculation about some unspecified circumstance in which § 2339A could infringe lawful expression is not a basis for finding the section impermissibly overbroad"); *United States v. Awan*, 459 F. Supp.2d at 180 (defendants "failed to describe any situation in which even an insubstantial amount of speech may be restrained because of § 2339A(a)'').

137. *United States v. Assi*, 414 F. Supp.2d at 717; *see also United States v. Sattar*, 314 F. Supp.2d at 305 (section 2339A is a legitimate exercise of Con-

gress' power to enact criminal laws that reflect "legitimate state interests in maintaining comprehensive controls over harmful, constitutionally unprotected conduct"); *United States v. Awan*, 459 F. Supp.2d at 180 (citing *Sattar* with approval).

138. *See United States v. Assi*, 414 F. Supp.2d at 717.

139. Kolender v. Lawson, 461 U.S. 352, 357 (1983). *See also* United States v. Williams, 553 U.S. 285, 304 (2008) ("A conviction fails to comport with due process if the statute under which it is obtained fails to provide a person of ordinary intelligence fair notice of what is prohibited, or is so standardless that it authorizes or encourages seriously discriminatory enforcement.").

140. Columbia Natural Res., Inc. v. Tatum, 58 F.3d 1101, 1104–5 (6th Cir. 1995).

141. *Id.*

facially vague.[142] In an as-applied vagueness challenge, where a party has notice of the criminality of his own conduct from the challenged statute, he may not attack it on grounds that "the language would not give similar fair warning with respect to other conduct which might be within its broad and literal ambit. One to whose conduct a statute clearly applies may not successfully challenge it for vagueness."[143] In a facial vagueness case, a court may strike down a statute only if it is "impermissibly vague in all of its applications."[144] However, laws that implicate constitutional rights are subject to a more stringent facial vagueness test.[145] In the First Amendment context, for example, courts may strike down a statute as facially vague if the law reaches a substantial amount of protected conduct, even if the law is not vague in all its applications.[146]

The due process vagueness claims relating to the material support statute have principally focused on the following terms: "service," "training," "expert advice or assistance," and "personnel." In the IRTPA, Congress added the term "service" to the definition of "material support or resources",[147] and defined "training" to mean "instruction or teaching designed to impart a specific skill, as opposed to general knowledge."[148] The IRTPA also defined "expert advice or assistance" to mean "advice or assistance derived from scientific, technical or other specialized knowledge."[149] In addition, the IRTPA changed "personnel" in section 2339A to "personnel (1 or more individuals who may be or include oneself.)"[150] This amendment was intended to clarify that a person can provide himself as personnel.[151] Finally, the IRTPA added a definition of "personnel" to section 2339B:

> No person may be prosecuted under [§ 2339B] in connection with the term "personnel" unless that person has knowingly provided, attempted to provide, or conspired to provide a foreign terrorist organization with 1 or more individuals (who may be or include himself) to work under that terrorist organization's direction or control or to organize, manage, supervise, or otherwise direct the operation of that organization. Individuals who act entirely independently of the foreign terrorist

---

142. *See* Parker v. Levy, 417 U.S. 733, 756 (1974) (discussing an as-applied vagueness challenge); Village of Hoffman Estates v. Flipside, 455 U.S. 489, 494–95 (1982) (discussing claims of facial vagueness).

143. *Parker v. Levy*, 417 U.S. at 756.

144. *Village of Hoffman Estates v. Flipside*, 455 U.S. at 494–5.

145. *Id.* at 499.

146. *Id.*; *Parker v. Levy*, 417 U.S. at 760.

147. 18 U.S.C. § 2339A(b)(1).

148. *Id.* at § 2339A(b)(2).

149. *Id.* at § 2339A(b)(3).

150. IRTPA, § 6603(b), 118 Stat. at 3762 (codified at 18 U.S.C. § 2339A(b)(1)).

151. United States v. Abu–Jihad, 600 F. Supp.2d 362, 397 (D. Conn. 2009).

organization to advance its goals or objectives shall not be considered to be working under the foreign terrorist organization's direction and control.[152]

However, unlike the other IRTPA amendments to the definition of "material support or resources," this detailed definition of "personnel" was added to section 2339B, but not to section 2339A.[153]

In *Holder v. Humanitarian Law Project*, the Supreme Court granted *certiorari* to decide whether the material support statute, as applied to plaintiffs, was impermissibly vague under the Fifth Amendment Due Process Clause.[154] Plaintiffs' vagueness claims focused on the terms "training," "expert advice or assistance," "personnel," and "service."[155] Plaintiffs wanted to train members of the PKK, a designated FTO, on the use of humanitarian and international law to peacefully resolve disputes, and teach PKK members how to petition international bodies such as the United Nations for relief.[156] However, they argued that the application of the statutory terms to their proposed conduct was unclear.[157] Because the plaintiffs did not argue that the material-support statute grants too much enforcement discretion to the Government, the Supreme Court only addressed whether the statute "provide[s] a person of ordinary intelligence fair notice of what is prohibited."[158]

According to the Court, most of the activities in which plaintiffs sought to engage readily fall within the scope of the terms "training" and "expert advice or assistance."[159] The Court found that those terms were not unconstitutionally vague as applied to plaintiffs' proposed conduct, stating:

> A person of ordinary intelligence would understand that instruction on resolving disputes through international law falls within the statute's definition of "training" because it imparts a "specific skill," not "general knowledge." Plaintiffs' activities also fall comfortably within the scope of "expert advice or assistance": A reasonable person would recognize that teaching the PKK how to petition for humanitarian relief before the

---

152. IRTPA, § 6603(f), 118 Stat. at 3763 (codified at 18 U.S.C. § 2339B(h)).

153. At least one court has held that the definition of "personnel" is limited to prosecutions under section 2339B, and does not apply to section 2339A. *See United States v. Abu–Jihad*, 600 F. Supp.2d at 397 ("'[T]he fact that Congress chose not to apply the more detailed definition to § 2339A causes the Court to believe that the definition Congress provided for § 2339B should not apply to § 2339A.'").

154. Holder v. Humanitarian Law Project, 130 S.Ct. 2705 (2010).

155. *Id.* at 2720.

156. *Holder*, at 2720.

157. *Id.* at 2718–19.

158. *Id.* at 2719 (quoting *United States v. Williams*, 553 U.S. at 304).

159. Holder v. Humanitarian Law Project, 130 S.Ct. 2705, 2720 (2010).

United Nations involves advice derived from ... "specialized knowledge."[160]

Plaintiffs also maintained that they wanted to engage in "political advocacy" on behalf of Kurds living in Turkey and Tamils living in Sri Lanka.[161] Addressing the term "personnel," the Court noted that Congress limited the definition in the IRPTA.[162] Providing material support that constitutes "personnel" is defined as knowingly providing a person "to work under that terrorist organization's direction or control or to organize, manage, supervise, or otherwise direct the operation of that organization."[163] Further, the statute explicitly provides that "personnel" does not cover independent advocacy.[164] Section 2339B(h) expressly provides: "Individuals who act entirely independently of the foreign terrorist organization to advance its goals or objectives shall not be considered to be working under the foreign terrorist organization's direction and control."[165] The Court found that plaintiffs' proposed "political advocacy" on behalf of the Kurds and Tamils is not barred under the statutes for two reasons. First, the plaintiffs would not be working under the FTOs' direction and control.[166] Second, the statute does not punish independent advocacy.[167] Thus, the Court held that "personnel" is not unconstitutionally vague as applied to plaintiffs' proposed conduct.[168]

The Court held that the meaning of the term "service" is also sufficiently clear. The Court stated that "service" refers to concerted activity, not independent advocacy.[169] Thus, any independent advocacy by plaintiffs is not prohibited by section 2339B.[170] On the other hand, "a person of ordinary intelligence would understand the term 'service' to cover advocacy performed in coordination with, or at the direction of, a foreign terrorist organization."[171] Such conduct is clearly punishable under the statute. Finally, regarding how much direction and coordination is necessary for an activity to constitute a "service," the Court concluded that adjudication of those issues must await a concrete fact situation.[172]

Unconstitutional vagueness challenges to the term "personnel" have been dismissed in other cases. In *United States v. Warsame*, the district court held that the term "personnel" is not vague as applied to defendant's alleged participation in an al Qaeda training

160. *Id.* (internal citations omitted).

161. *Id.* at 2721.

162. *Id.*

163. *Id.* (quoting 18 U.S.C. § 2339B(h)).

164. *Holder*, at 2721.

165. 18 U.S.C. § 2339B(h).

166. *Holder*, at 2721.

167. *Id.*

168. Holder v. Humanitarian Law Project, 130 S.Ct. 2705, 2721-22 (2010).

169. *Id.* at 2721.

170. *Id.*

171. *Id.*

172. *Id.* at 2721–22.

camp.[173] Participation in a terrorist training camp is unambiguously encompassed within the plain meaning of "personnel."[174] In *United States v. Lindh*, the district court rejected a vague challenge to "personnel" where defendant allegedly fought in combat on behalf of the Taliban.[175] The court concluded that:

> providing "personnel" to HUM [Humanitarian Law Project] or al Qaeda necessarily means that the persons provided to the foreign terrorist organization work under the direction and control of that organization. One who is merely present with other members of the organization, but is not under the organization's direction and control, is not part of the organization's "personnel." . . . Simply put, the term "personnel" does not extend to independent actors. Rather, it describes employees or employee-like operatives who serve the designated group and work at its command or . . . who provide themselves to serve the organization.[176]

Although *Lindh* was decided before the IRTPA of 2004 added the more detailed definition of "personnel" to section 2339B, the district court's interpretation of "personnel" is entirely consistent with the statutory definition. Section 2339B(h) requires the person "to work under that terrorist organization's direction or control or to organize, manage, supervise, or otherwise direct the operation of that organization," and does not apply to "[i]ndividuals who act entirely independently of the foreign terrorist organization to advance its goals and objectives."[177] The *Lindh* court also interpreted the term "personnel" to require the defendant to work under the "direction and control" of the FTO, and excludes from coverage "independent actors."[178]

In *United States v. Shah*, the court upheld the application of the term "personnel" to a doctor alleged to have provided medical support to members of al Qaeda.[179] In *Shah*, the court noted that section 2339B exempts from criminal prosecution the provision of "medicine" to a designated FTO.[180] However, the court concluded that Congress intended the term "medicine" to be limited to the

---

173. United States v. Warsame, 537 F. Supp.2d 1005, 1018 (D. Minn. 2008). *See also* United States v. Goba, 220 F. Supp.2d 182, 194 (W.D.N.Y. 2002) (rejecting vagueness challenge to "personnel," where defendants allegedly attended terrorist training camps in Afghanistan).

174. *Warsame*, 537 F. Supp.2d at 1018.

175. United States v. Lindh, 212 F. Supp.2d 541, 574 (E.D. Va. 2002).

176. *Id.* at 572.

177. 18 U.S.C. § 2339B(h). *But see* United States v. Sattar, 314 F. Supp.2d 279 (S.D.N.Y. 2004) (finding a lawyer guilty of providing "personnel" who had acted in concert with others to make a coconspirator available, despite the fact that she was not acting as an employee or quasi-employee of the FTO).

178. *Lindh*, 212 F. Supp.2d at 572.

179. United States v. Shah, 474 F. Supp.2d 492, 497–98 (S.D.N.Y. 2007).

180. *Id.* at 495. *See also* 18 U.S.C. § 2339A(b)(1).

medicine itself.[181] The court held that the provision of English language lessons to nurses at al Qaeda clinics does not fall within the "medicine" exception.[182]

However, providing prohibited classified information to a terrorist organization does not constitute the provision of personnel. In *United States v. Abu–Jihaad*, a U.S. Navy Signalman aboard a naval destroyer disclosed classified information to Azzam Publications, an organization that exhorted its readers to assist in violent jihad.[183] The district court rejected the Government's theory that by providing classified information to Azzam, "Mr. Abu–Jihaad provided personnel—that is, Abu–Jihaad himself—to Azzam, knowing that he or his assistance would be used to prepare for, or carry out, the killing of U.S. nationals," in violation of section 2339A.[184] The court stated:

> [M]erely providing an organization with a resource, even a prohibited resource, is not necessarily the same thing as providing personnel to prepare for or carry out the prohibited purposes of the statute through some form of coordinated or joint action. For if that were the case, then much of the definition of "material support or resources" would be entirely redundant; providing weapons, explosives, or anything else on the list would also automatically constitute the provision of personnel as well.[185]

The courts have also consistently rejected claims that section 2339B's prohibition on "training" is unconstitutionally vague as applied. In *Warsame*, the prosecution maintained that defendant provided "training" to al Qaeda by teaching English at an al Qaeda clinic in Kandahar, Afghanistan, in part, to assist nurses in reading English-language medicine labels.[186] In support of the conclusion that "training" is not unconstitutionally vague as applied to this conduct, the court posited that "[t]he alleged English-language training in this case has direct application to an FTO's terrorist activities, as it would likely speed the healing and eventual return of terrorist militants to Al Qaeda training camps."[187] Further, the court emphasized that because the conduct was closely tied to terrorist activity, the defendant would likely understand his conduct to be criminalized as "training" under section 2339B.[188] How-

181. *Shah*, 474 F. Supp.2d at 495 (quoting H.R. Rep. 104–518, at 114 (1996), U.S. Code Cong. & Admin. News 1996, pp. 944, 947).

182. *Shah*, 474 F. Supp.2d at 497.

183. United States v. Abu–Jihaad, 600 F. Supp.2d 362, 401 (D. Conn. 2009).

184. *Id.*

185. *Id.*

186. *United States v. Warsame*, 537 F. Supp.2d at 1018–9.

187. *Id.* at 1019.

188. *Id.* However, the court stated that allegations that the defendant taught English at an al Qaeda clinic, without evidence tying that conduct to terrorist activity, would not survive a vagueness challenge. *Id.* The court posit-

ever, while evidence that the training was closely tied to terrorist activity is highly relevant on the issue of notice, even training unrelated to such activities could survive a vagueness challenge.[189]

Finally, the courts have consistently held that "[t]here is nothing at all vague about the term 'currency.' "[190] In *United States v. Hammoud*, the Fourth Circuit (*en banc*) upheld defendant's conviction for violating section 2339B for making a monetary donation to Hizballah, a designated FTO, rejecting defendant's vagueness challenge.[191]

ii. Due Process and Scienter

Defendants have challenged the constitutionality of section 2339B, arguing that it violates the Fifth Amendment Due Process Clause by imposing criminal liability in the absence of personal guilt.[192] According to *Scales v. United States*, a statute violates due process if it "impermissibly imputes guilt to an individual merely on the basis of his associations and sympathies, rather than because of some concrete, personal involvement in criminal conduct."[193] The Supreme Court has found that:

> In our jurisprudence guilt is personal, and when the imposition of punishment on a status or on conduct can only be justified by reference to the relationship of that status or conduct to other concededly criminal activity . . ., that relationship must be sufficiently substantial to satisfy the concept of personal guilt to withstand attack under the Due Process Clause of the Fifth Amendment.[194]

Ultimately, the Supreme Court required proof of a heightened *mens rea* because without it, the Act in question would have been interpreted as criminalizing membership in a group advocating the

ed: "For example, an individual who teaches English so that patients in the clinic can teach the Koran in the English language is unlikely to understand that conduct to be prohibited as 'training,' since such activity has no direct connection with underlying military or terrorist activities." *Id.* at 1020.

189. *See* Holder v. Humanitarian Law Project, 130 S.Ct. 2705, 2720–22 (2010) (rejecting plaintiffs' vagueness argument involving proposed humanitarian activities on behalf of FTOs).

190. *United States v. Hammoud*, 381 F.3d at 330–1.

191. *Id. See also United States v. Warsame*, 537 F. Supp.2d at 1017 (finding that the material support statute

clearly applies to defendant's repayment of a loan to an al Qaeda member).

192. This argument is closely connected to the previous discussion on the First Amendment freedom of association discussed *supra* at notes 35–58 and accompanying text. However, the Fifth Amendment argument is concerned with the issue that criminal sanctions not be "imposed on persons who are related by status or conduct to a proscribed organization," while the First Amendment prohibits punishment by reason of membership or association alone. Humanitarian Law Project v. United States Dept. of Justice, 352 F.3d 382, 394–5 (9th Cir. 2003).

193. Scales v. United States, 367 U.S. 203, 220 (1961).

194. *Id.* at 224–5.

overthrow of the government by force and violence.[195] However, that is not the case here. "Section 2339B does not criminalize mere membership or association with a designated FTO."[196] Rather, the statute prohibits the conduct of providing material support or resources to these organizations.[197] This provision of support amounts to what *Scales* referred to as "concrete, personal involvement in criminal conduct," and not merely membership or association alone.[198] Thus, the reasons for a heightened *scienter* requirement in *Scales* do not apply to section 2339B.

Several reasons have been advanced by the courts for rejecting the argument that section 2339B imposes criminal liability in the absence of personal guilt and thereby violates due process under the Fifth Amendment. First, the statute prohibits "knowingly" providing material support or resources.[199] Although the statutory language of section 2339A includes a specific intent requirement to further illegal activities, the language of section 2339B lacks any such requirement. Second, when Congress enacted the IRTPA it had the opportunity to incorporate into section 2339B a specific intent requirement, but chose instead to "clarify that the only *mens rea* required under § 2339B is that a donor know that the recipient is a foreign terrorist organization."[200] In *Holder v. Humanitarian Law Project*, the Supreme Court stated: "Congress plainly spoke to the necessary mental state for a violation of § 2339B, and it chose knowledge about the organization's connection to terrorism, not specific intent to further the organization's terrorist activities."[201] Third, the legislative history indicates that Congress enacted section 2339B to close a loophole left by section 2339A. Congress was concerned that FTOs would raise funds "under the cloak of a humanitarian or charitable exercise"[202] and made a legislative finding that "foreign organizations that engage in terrorist activity are so tainted by their criminal conduct that any contribution to such an organization facilitates that conduct," regardless of the donor's intent.[203] Finally, "although section 2339B does not require a heightened *scienter*, it does provide for some showing of *scienter* that is sufficient to meet the due process standard of personal

195. *Id.* at 226 n.18, 228.

196. United States v. Taleb–Jedi, 566 F. Supp.2d 157 (E.D.N.Y. 2008). *See also supra* note 64 for list of cases.

197. 18 U.S.C. § 2339B.

198. Scales v. United States, 367 U.S. 203, 220 (1961).

199. 18 U.S.C. § 2339B.

200. Humanitarian Law Project v. Gonzales, 380 F. Supp.2d 1134, 1146 (C.D. Cal. 2005). *See also United States v. Taleb–Jedi*, 566 F. Supp.2d at 179

("[T]he 2004 IRTPA amendment dispenses with any argument that Congress accidentally omitted a specific intent requirement."); United States v. Assi, 414 F. Supp.2d 707, 723 (E.D. Mich. 2006) (advancing the same argument).

201. *See* Holder v. Humanitarian Law Project, 130 S.Ct. 2705, 2717 (2010).

202. H.R. Rep. 104–383, at 43 (1995).

203. AEDPA, *supra* note 9, at § 301(a)(7), 110 Stat. 1214, 1247.

guilt."[204] To convict under the statute, the Government must prove that the donor provided material support to an FTO, knowing either that the organization was designated as an FTO, or that it engaged in or engages in terrorist activity.[205] Thus, a defendant must make a knowledgeable choice to violate the law, establishing personal guilt.[206]

Only one district court that has addressed the issue has concluded that section 2339B's knowledge *scienter* requirement is insufficient. In *United States v. Al–Arian*, the district court held that section 2339B raised constitutional concerns that could only be avoided by construing the statute to require that the defendant "knew (had specific intent) that the support would further the illegal activities of an FTO."[207] However, several other courts have rejected this view.[208]

c.   *Challenging the FTO Designation*

i.   *Notice and a Hearing*

Defendants contend that the FTO designation procedure under 8 U.S.C. § 1189(a) violates due process because it does not provide an organization with meaningful notice or judicial review of its designation. As a general proposition, foreign entities receive constitutional protections only when "they come with the territory of the United States and [have] developed substantial connections with this country."[209] Thus, the threshold question is whether a foreign entity has a presence in the United States and has sufficient connections with the United States.[210] In *People's Mojahedin Organization v. Dept. of State ("PMOI")*, the D.C. Circuit upheld the FTO designation because it was a "foreign entity without property or presence in this country" and thus "ha[d] no constitutional

---

204. *United States v. Taleb*, 566 F. Supp.2d at 179. *See also United States v. Warsame*, 537 F. Supp.2d at 1021 ("[T]he Court finds that assigning criminal liability to a donor who knows the recipient is a terrorist organization, or that it engages in terrorism, satisfies minimal requirements of due process.").

205. 18 U.S.C. § 2339B(a)(1).

206. *See United States v. Taleb*, 566 F. Supp.2d at 179; *Assi*, 414 F. Supp.2d at 723–4; United States v. Paracha, 2006 WL 12768, at *29 (S.D.N.Y. 2006) ("The statutory definition of 'material support or resources' limits what constitutes assistance sufficiently blameworthy to attach criminal liability.").

207. United States v. Al–Arian, 308 F. Supp.2d 1322, 1307–8, *reconsidera-*

tion denied, 329 F. Supp. 2d 1294 (M.D. Fla. 2004).

208. *See United States v. Taleb–Jedi*, 566 F. Supp.2d at 179; *Warsame*, 537 F. Supp.2d at 1021–22; *United States v. Paracha*, 2006 WL 12768, at *25; *Assi*, 414 F. Supp.2d at 723–4; United States v. Marzook, 383 F. Supp.2d 1056, 1070 (N.D. Ill. 2005).

209. United States v. Verdugo–Urquidez, 494 U.S. 259, 271 (1990).

210. *Id. See also* 32 County Sovereignty Comm. v. Department of State, 292 F.3d 797, 799 (D.C. Cir. 2002) (holding that "[a] foreign entity without property or presence in this country has no constitutional rights, under the due process clause or otherwise").

rights under the due process clause."[211] However, in *National Council of Resistance of Iran v. Department of State* (*"NCRI"*), since the NCRI had a presence in the United States, the D.C. Circuit held that due process requires that the Secretary of State "afford to the entities under consideration notice that the designation is pending" and "the opportunity to be heard at a meaningful time and in a meaningful manner."[212] The notice to the prospective FTO need not disclose classified information to be presented *in camera* and *ex parte* to the court under the statute.[213] Further, post-designation notice may comport with due process. The D.C. Circuit stated that "[u]pon an adequate showing to the court, the Secretary may provide this notice *after* the designation where earlier notification would impinge upon the security and other foreign policy goals of the United States."[214] Finally, compliance with the hearing requirement does not mandate a hearing closely approximating a trial. Instead, the Secretary must "afford entities considered for imminent designation the opportunity to present, at least in written form, such evidence to rebut the administrative record or otherwise negate the proposition that they are foreign terrorist organizations."[215]

ii. Collateral Attack of the FTO Designation

Under 8 U.S.C. § 1189(a)(8), a defendant in a criminal action under section 2339B is precluded from raising any question regarding the validity of an organization's designation as an FTO during the criminal proceedings.[216] Defendants argue that the FTO designation procedure unconstitutionally deprives them of a right to a jury determination of guilt on each element of the charged offense. The Fifth and Sixth Amendments require that criminal convictions be based upon "a jury determination that the defendant is guilty of every element of the crime with which he is charged, beyond a reasonable doubt."[217] Defendants' constitutional challenge has been

211. People's Mojahedin Organization v. Department of State, 182 F.3d 17, 22 (D.C. Cir. 1999).

212. National Council of Resistance of Iran v. Department of State, 251 F.3d 192, 200, 209 (D.C. Cir. 2001) (*"NCRI"*). The court set a low bar for determining whether the two designated organizations had developed substantial connections with the United States. The court found that the designated organizations had "an overt presence within the National Press Building in Washington, D.C. . . . and . . . claim[ed] an interest in a small bank account," which satisfied the "substantial connection" test. *Id.* at 201. *But see 32 County Sovereignty*

Comm, 292 F.3d at 799 (evidence that some of the organization's members rented post office boxes and utilized a bank account to transmit funds to the organization, but did not possess any controlling interest in property located in the U.S., did not establish sufficient connections with the U.S. to trigger due process protection).

213. *NCRI*, at 208.

214. *Id.* (emphasis added).

215. *Id.* at 209.

216. 8 U.S.C. § 1189(a)(8).

217. United States v. Gaudin, 515 U.S. 506, 510 (1995).

rejected by the courts on two grounds. First, the courts hold that defendants lack standing to challenge the FTO designation procedure on behalf of a third party not before the court.[218] Under the doctrine of prudential standing, a plaintiff must assert his own legal rights and cannot rest his claim on the legal rights of others.[219] Thus, for example, a defendant lacks standing to challenge the validity of an FTO designation on behalf of al Qaeda, the Taliban, or some other designated FTO.[220]

Second, the courts unequivocally hold that the relevant element of section 2339B is the *fact* of an organization's designation as an FTO, not the *validity* of the designation. In *United States v. Afshari*, the Ninth Circuit held that "the element of the crime that the prosecutor must prove in a § 2339B case is the predicate fact that a particular organization was designated at the time the material support was given, not whether the government made a correct designation."[221] The Ninth Circuit reasoned:

> The defendants are right that § 1189(a)(8) prevents them from contending, in defense of the charges against them under 18 U.S.C. § 2339B, that the designated terrorist organization is not really terrorist at all. No doubt Congress was well aware that some might claim that "one man's terrorist is another man's freedom fighter." Congress clearly chose to delegate policymaking authority to the President and Department of State with respect to designation of terrorist organizations, and to keep such policymaking authority out of the hands of United States Attorneys and juries. Under § 2339B, if defendants provide material support for an organization that has been designated under § 1189, they commit the crime, and it does not matter whether the designation is correct or not.[222]

Because the validity of an FTO designation is not an element of the offense, defendant's inability to challenge the validity under section 1189(a)(8) does not deprive him of his constitutional rights.[223]

218. *See* United States v. Warsame, 537 F. Supp.2d 1005, 1022 (D. Minn. 2008).

219. *See* Valley Forge Christian Coll. v. Americans United, 454 U.S. 464, 474–5 (1982); *Warsame*, 537 F. Supp.2d at 1022.

220. *See Warsame*, 537 F. Supp.2d at 1022.

221. United States v. Afshari, 426 F.3d 1150, 1159 (9th Cir. 2005).

222. *Id.* at 1155–6.

223. *See* United States v. Hammoud, 381 F.3d 316, 331 (4th Cir. 2004) (finding that "Congress has provided that the *fact* of an organization's designation as an FTO is an element of § 2339B, but the *validity* of the designation is not") (emphasis in original); United States v. Chandia, 514 F.3d 365, 371 (4th Cir. 2008) (citing *Hammoud* with approval); United States v. Afshari, 412 F.3d 1071, 1076 (9th Cir. 2005); *Warsame*, 537 F. Supp.2d at 1021.

B. COUNTER–TERRORIST FINANCING STATUTE, 18 U.S.C. § 2339C

1. STATUTORY OVERVIEW

In 2002, Congress passed the terrorist financing statute, 18 U.S.C. § 2339C.[224] The statute was intended to implement the International Convention for the Suppression of the Financing of Terrorism,[225] which requires State signatories to enact domestic legislation to punish the provision or collection of funds with the intent or knowledge that they be used to carry out terrorist acts.[226] Section 2339C makes it a crime to "unlawfully and willfully" "provide or collect" funds with the intention or knowledge that they are to be used to carry out acts which constitute an offense within the scope of nine counterterrorism treaties enumerated in the statute, or any other act intended to cause death or serious bodily injury to a civilian, when the purpose of such act is "to intimidate a population, or to compel a government or an international organization to do or to abstain from doing any act."[227] Criminal liability extends not only to the actual perpetrators, but also to persons who attempt or conspire to commit an offense under the statute.[228] Further, the terrorist financing statute does not require that the funds be traced to a particular terrorist attack. The statute expressly provides that "[f]or an act to constitute an offense . . . it shall *not* be necessary that the funds were used to carry out a predicate act."[229]

Section 2339C punishes the act of providing or collecting funds for terrorist purposes.[230] The statute defines "provide" to include "giving, donating, and transmitting," and "collect" to include both "raising and receiving."[231] Thus, the statute punishes not only donors, but fundraisers and persons who solicit donations, as well as persons who receive and transmit the terrorist-related funds, such as bank employees. In *Linde v. Arab Bank*, the court upheld the application of section 2339C against bank officials allegedly transmitting funds to Hamas.[232] The court held that "the banking

---

224. 18 U.S.C. § 2339C (West 2008).

225. International Convention for the Suppression of the Financing of Terrorism, Dec. 9, 1999, T.I.A.S. No. 13075, 2178 U.N.T.S. 229. On June 26, 2002, the United States Senate ratified the treaty. There are 173 signatories to the treaty.

226. *See* Pub. L. 107–197, Title II, § 203, June 25, 2002, 116 Stat. 727. *See also* H.R. Rep. No. 107–307, at 6–7 (2001), 147 Cong. Rec. E2397 (daily ed. Dec. 19, 2001).

227. 18 U.S.C. § 2339C (West 2008).

228. *Id.* at § 2339C(a)(2).

229. *Id.* at § 2339C(a)(3) (emphasis added).

230. The term "funds" is broadly construed to mean "assets of every kind, whether tangible or intangible, movable or immovable, . . . and legal documents or instruments . . . evidencing title to, or interest in, such assets, including coin, currency, bank credits, travelers checks, bank checks, money orders, shares, securities, bonds, drafts, and letters of credit."

231. *Id.* at § 2339C(e)(4), (5).

232. Linde v. Arab Bank, 384 F. Supp.2d 571, 588 (E.D.N.Y. 2005). It should be noted that *Arab Bank* involved a civil cause of action under the

activities of receiving deposits and transmitting funds between accounts" where "the accounts (and funds) belong to groups engaged in terrorist activity" or are "charity fronts that operate as agents of [terrorist organizations]" serve as a basis for liability under section 2339C.[233]

Section 2339C is limited to providing or collecting funds for certain predicate acts, including offenses within the scope of nine counter-terrorism treaties. For purposes of section 2339C, the term "treaty" refers to the following international conventions ratified by the United States:

(A) Convention for the Suppression of Unlawful Seizure of Aircraft, done at The Hague on December 16, 1970;

(B) the Convention for the Suppression of Unlawful Acts against the Safety of Civil Aviation, done at Montreal on September 23, 1971;

(C) the Convention on the Prevention and Punishment of Crimes against Internationally Protected Persons, including Diplomatic Agents, adopted by the General Assembly of the United Nations on December 14, 1973;

(D) the International Convention against the Taking of Hostages, adopted by the General Assembly of the United Nations on December 17, 1979;

(E) the Convention on the Physical Protection of Nuclear Material, adopted at Vienna on March 3, 1980;

(F) the Protocol for the Suppression of Unlawful Acts of Violence at Airports Serving International Civil Aviation, supplementary to the Convention for the Suppression of Unlawful Acts against the Safety of Civil Aviation, done at Montreal on February 24, 1988;

(G) the Convention for the Suppression of Unlawful Acts against the Safety of Maritime Navigation, done at Rome on March 10, 1988;

(H) the Protocol for the Suppression of Unlawful Acts against the Safety of Fixed Platforms located on the Continental Shelf, done at Rome on March 10, 1988; or

(I) the International Convention for the Suppression of Terrorist Bombings, adopted by the General Assembly of the United Nations on December 15, 1997.[234]

Thus, a person is criminally liable under section 2339C if he provides or collects funds with the intent or knowledge that the

Anti–Terrorism Act, 18 U.S.C. § 2332.   **234.**   18 U.S.C. § 2339C(e)(7).
Id.

    233.   *Linde,* 384 F. Supp.2d at 588.

funds are to be used to commit an offense under any of these counterterrorism treaties.

Section 2339C requires proof of a more heightened *scienter* than section 2339B. To sustain a conviction under the terrorist financing statute, the Government must prove that the defendant acted "with the intention that such funds be used, or with the knowledge that such funds are to be used . . . in order to carry out" a statutorily enumerated predicate offense.[235] However, it is not necessary to prove that the defendant had the specific intent to commit specific acts of terrorism.[236] It is enough to convict if the defendant provided funds with the intention that they be used to fund terrorist activities that constitute a predicate offense under the statute. Further, section 2339C "only require[s] knowledge *or* intent that the resources given to terrorists are to be used in the commission of terrorist acts."[237] The defendant is criminally liable if he either acted with the specific intent to carry out acts of terrorism *or* had knowledge that the funds would be used for such purposes.[238] By contrast, section 2339B requires proof that the defendant provided material support or resources with knowledge that the organization is a designated FTO or engages in terrorist activity.[239] Under section 2339B, the Government is not required to prove that the defendant acted with the specific intent or knowledge that the material support be used to carry out terrorist acts.[240] The only *mens rea* requirement is knowledge that the recipient is connected to terrorism.[241] Finally, a conviction under section 2339C carries a severe penalty. The statute provides that whoever violates section 2339C shall be fined or imprisoned for not more than 20 years, or both.[242]

2. EXTRATERRITORIAL JURISDICTION

Section 2339C authorizes jurisdiction for offenses committed outside of the United States.[243] The statute confers extraterritorial jurisdiction under the nationality principle, which provides that a State may prescribe laws regulating the conduct of its nationals wherever the conduct occurs.[244] The nationality principle has been expanded to permit jurisdiction based on "domicile or residence,"

---

235. *Id.* at § 2339C(a)(1).

236. *Linde,* 384 F. Supp.2d at 586 ("None of these provisions [sections 2339A–C] . . . requires specific intent to commit specific acts of terrorism.").

237. *Id.* at 586 n. 9 (emphasis added). *But see* Boim v. Quranic Literacy Inst. & Holy Land Found. for Relief & Dev., 291 F.3d 1000, 1023–4 (7th Cir. 2002) (requiring proof of specific intent to sustain a violation of section 2339C).

238. *Linde,* 384 F. Supp.2d at 586 n. 9.

239. 18 U.S.C. § 2339B(a)(1).

240. *Id.*

241. *Id.*

242. *Id.* at § 2339C(d)(1).

243. *Id.* at § 2339C(b)(2).

244. *See* Skiriotes v. Florida, 313 U.S. 69, 73 (1941).

rather than exclusively on the perpetrator's nationality.[245] Consistent with this broader application of the nationality principle, section 2339C confers extraterritorial jurisdiction where the offense was committed abroad by a U.S. national or the offender's habitual residence is in the United States.[246] The statute also authorizes extraterritorial jurisdiction based on the universal principle. Section 2339C(b)(2)(B) confers jurisdiction regardless of where the offense took place if the perpetrator was found in the United States.[247] The exercise of jurisdiction based solely on the perpetrator's presence within the United States supports the view that terrorist financing is a universal crime.[248]

Section 2339C confers extraterritorial jurisdiction based on the objective theory of the territorial principle. Under the statute, extraterritorial jurisdiction may be exercised where the offense takes place outside of the United States, but was directed toward or resulted in the carrying out of a predicate offense against "any person or property within the United States," "any national of the United States or the property of such national," or "any property of any legal entity organized under the laws of the United States."[249] In such scenarios, while the offense took place outside the United States, it was intended to have or had detrimental effects within the territory, implicating the objective theory. The terrorist financing statute also implicates the subjective theory of territorial jurisdiction. Extraterritorial jurisdiction exists where the unlawful acts occur within the territorial confines of a State, including a State's embassies and consulates, or on vessels or aircraft subject to its "flag" jurisdiction.[250] Under the statute, jurisdiction extends to offenses committed abroad and directed toward carrying out a terrorist offense against a U.S. embassy or other U.S. diplomatic or consular premises, or offenses committed on board a vessel flying the flag of the U.S., or an aircraft registered under the laws of the U.S.[251]

245. *See* RESTATEMENT (THIRD) OF FOREIGN RELATIONS LAW §§ 411, 484, cited in cmt. e.

246. 18 U.S.C. § 2339C(b)(2)(A).

247. *Id.* at § 2339C(b)(2)(B).

248. As previously noted, 173 states are signatories to the International Convention for the Suppression of the Financing of Terrorism, which condemns the provision or collection of funds with the intention or knowledge that such funds be used to carry out terrorist activities, *supra* note 224. The international condemnation of terrorist financing by 173 states makes a compelling case for the view that terrorist financing is a universal crime for which universal jurisdiction is permitted. *See also* RESTATEMENT (THIRD) OF FOREIGN RELATIONS LAW § 404 (states may exercise jurisdiction under the universal principle to punish acts of terrorism).

249. *Id.* at § 2339C(b)(2)(C)(ii)–(iv).

250. JORDAN J. PAUST, M. CHERIF BASSIOUNI, ET AL., INTERNATIONAL CRIMINAL LAW, CASES AND MATERIALS 178–79 (Carolina Academic Press, 3d ed. 2007).

251. *Id.* at § 2339C(b)(2)(C)(i). Extraterritorial jurisdiction is also authorized for offenses committed on board an aircraft which is operated by the U.S. *Id.* at § 2339C(b)(4).

The statute also authorizes jurisdiction based on the nationality of the victim, implicating the passive personality principle. Under section 2339C(b)(2)(C)(iii), jurisdiction exists if the terrorist financing offense takes place outside the United States and resulted in the carrying out of a predicate offense against a U.S. national.[252] In such a case, the court would have jurisdiction even though the terrorist financing offense and the predicate offense that was directed against a U.S. national took place outside the United States.[253]

Finally, section 2339C authorizes the exercise of jurisdiction based on the protective principle. Under the protective principle, "jurisdiction is asserted over foreigners for an act committed outside the United States that may impinge on the territorial integrity, security or political independence of the United States."[254] Section 2339C(b)(2)(5) confers jurisdiction if the offense takes place outside the United States and "the offense was directed toward or resulted in the carrying out of a predicate act committed in an attempt to compel the United States to do or abstain from doing any act."[255] Arguably, for example, financing acts of terrorism committed for the purpose of compelling the United States to withdraw its military forces from Iraq and Afghanistan would have a potentially adverse effect upon the foreign policy and national security of the United States.[256] Thus, exercising extraterritorial jurisdiction would be justified under section 2339C(b)(2)(5).

Despite section 2339C's extraterritorial reach, the statute seldom has been used to prosecute terrorist financing cases.[257] Section 2339C's *scienter* requirement that the defendant provided or collected funds with the intention or knowledge that the funds be used to carry out terrorist acts likely has caused prosecutors to favor filing terrorist financing cases under 18 U.S.C. § 2339B. Section 2339B prohibits the provision of material support or resources to an FTO, which includes money and financial services.[258] However, section 2339B only requires knowledge that the recipient of the material support or resources was an FTO or engaged in terrorist

---

252. 18 U.S.C. § 2339C(b)(2)(C)(iii).

253. *Id.*

254. United States v. Vasquez–Velasco, 15 F.3d 833, 840 (9th Cir. 1994). *See also* United States v. Felix–Gutierrez, 940 F.2d 1200, 1204 (9th Cir. 1991), *cert. denied*, 508 U.S. 906 (1993);United States v. Benitez, 741 F.2d 1312, 1316 (11th Cir. 1984), *cert. denied*, 471 U.S. 1137 (1985); United States v. Pizzarusso, 388 F.2d 8, 10 (2d Cir. 1968), *cert. denied*, 392 U.S. 936 (1968).

255. 18 U.S.C. § 2339C(b)(5).

256. *United States v. Benitez*, 741 F.2d at 1316.

257. *See* Nina J. Crimm, *High Alert: The Government's War on the Financing of Terrorism and Its Implications for Donors, Domestic Charitable Organizations, and Global Philanthropy*, 45 Wm. & Mary L. Rev. 1341, 1422 (2004) ("To date, no indictments have been brought under 18 U.S.C. § 2339C against either individuals or organizations.").

258. 18 U.S.C. § 2339B.

activities.[259] The statute does not require proof that the defendant acted with the intention or knowledge that the material support or resources would be used to commit terrorist acts.[260] Further, if the Government proceeds under section 2339C(a)(1)(B), contending that the funds were intended to be used to commit an act intended to cause death or serious bodily injury, not covered by one of the counterterrorism treaties enumerated in section 2339C, the prosecution must prove that the violent act was committed with the purpose "to intimidate a population, or to compel a government or an international organization to do or to abstain from doing any act."[261] This theory of prosecution impose an additional *mens rea* requirement on the Government—that the defendant acted with a specific purpose to compel a population, or to compel a government or international organization to do or abstain from doing any act. The imposition of these additional *mens rea* requirements impose a substantial obstacle to prosecutions under section 2339C.

3. CONCEALMENT

Section 2339C(c) makes it a separate offense to "knowingly conceal or disguise the nature, location, source, ownership, or control of any material support or resources, or any funds or proceeds of such funds," if such acts were done knowing or intending that the funds, material support or resources, were provided in violation of either 18 U.S.C. §§ 2339B or 2339C.[262] Further, the statute confers extraterritorial jurisdiction for offenses committed by U.S. nationals outside of the U.S.[263] A violation of section 2339C(c) is punishable by a fine, imprisonment of not more than 10 years, or both.[264] However, there are no reported district court or court of appeals decisions discussing section 2339C(c), suggesting that the concealment provision is not widely used by federal prosecutors to combat international terrorism.

4. CONCLUSION

The material support statutes, 18 U.S.C. §§ 2339A and 2339B, are an extremely effective tool for prosecutors to combat international terrorism. The ability to punish individuals who provide material support or resources to terrorists is critical to depriving them of the means with which to carry out deadly terrorist attacks. Section 2339B's extraterritorial jurisdiction provision is particularly important to that effort because it allows the United States to hold

---

259. *Id.*

260. *Id.*

261. *Id.* at § 2339C(a)(1)(B).

262. 18 U.S.C. § 2339C(c)(2)(A)–(B).

263. *Id.* at § 2339C(a)(1)(B). The statute also extends jurisdiction to crim-

inal offenses committed outside of the U.S. by "a legal entity organized under the laws of the United States (including any of its States, districts, commonwealths, territories, or possessions)." *Id.*

264. *Id.* at § 2339C(d)(2).

individuals and entities accountable for providing material support to terrorist groups wherever those acts of assistance occur.[265] For example, raising money for designated foreign terrorist groups that occurs wholly outside of the United States is punishable under section 2339B. Further, while the material support statutes have been the subject of extensive litigation, including First Amendment freedom of speech and freedom of association, as well as Fifth Amendment vagueness challenges, many of those legal issues were resolved by the Supreme Court in *Holder v. Humanitarian Law Project*.[266] The resolution of those legal issues in favor of the Government will make it easier for federal prosecutors to obtain criminal convictions under the material support statutes in the future. In short, the Supreme Court's decision in *Holder* ensures that prosecutions under the material support statutes will remain the centerpiece of the federal law enforcement response to international terrorism. At the same time, the terrorist financing statute, 18 U.S.C. § 2339C, has been a relatively ineffective and under-utilized criminal statute. Congress should consider amending the statute to remove the specific purpose requirement contained in subsection 2339C(a)(1)(B).[267]

265. *Id.* at § 2339B(d).

266. Holder v. Humanitarian Law Project, 130 S.Ct. 2705 (2010).

267. 18 U.S.C. § 2339C(a)(1)(B).

Part III
ECONOMIC SANCTIONS

Chapter 8
DOMESTIC ECONOMIC SANCTIONS

A central component of the U.S. government's counterterrorism strategy is to deprive terrorists and terrorist organizations such as al Qaeda and the Taliban of funding. Money is critical to financing terrorist operations (operational costs) as well as sustaining the organizational infrastructure of terrorist groups (organizational costs).[1] Terrorists cannot pursue sophisticated operations like the 9/11 terror attacks without adequate funding. The 9/11 attacks are estimated to have cost as much as $500,000 to stage.[2] Further, terrorists "need money to finance their organizational activities, including paying operatives, recruiting and training new members, bribing government officials, forging ties with other [terrorist groups], paying travel and communications expenses, and acquiring military weapons, explosives and radiological materials to construct a nuclear device or 'dirty bomb'."[3] Simply stated, "terrorists need money to terrorize."[4]

Starving terrorists and terrorist organizations of funding is critical to preventing terrorist attacks. However, going after the money is important for other reasons as well. Investigating terrorist financial networks may "expose terrorist financing 'money trails' that may generate leads to previously unknown terrorist cells and financiers."[5] Blocking the assets of front companies, shutting down corrupt charities and arresting terrorist financiers

---

1. JIMMY GURULÉ, UNFUNDING TERROR: THE LEGAL RESPONSE TO THE FINANCING OF GLOBAL TERRORISM 21 (Edward Elgar Publ. 2008) [hereinafter UNFUNDING TERROR] (discussing the domestic economic sanctions regime to deprive terrorists of funding).

2. *See* NATIONAL COMMISSION ON TERRORIST ATTACKS, THE 9/11 COMMISSION REPORT: FINAL REPORT OF THE NATIONAL COMMISSION ON TERRORIST ATTACKS UPON THE UNITED STATES 169 (W.W. Norton & Company 2004) (going after terrorist finances "has decreased the amount of money available to al Qaeda and has increased the costs and difficulty in raising and moving that money"), *available at* http://www.9-11commission.gov/

report/911Report.pdf [hereinafter THE 9/11 COMMISSION REPORT].

3. UNFUNDING TERROR, *supra* note 1, at 21.

4. *Id.* at 40. *See also* Financial Action Task Force, Terrorist Financing (Feb. 28, 2008), *available at* http://www.fatf-gafi.org/dataoecd/28/43/40285899.pdf.

5. U.S. Dep't of Treasury, National Money Laundering Strategy 7 (2003), *available at* http://www.treasury.gov/offices/enforcement/publications/ml2003.pdf. *See also* THE 9/11 COMMISSION REPORT, *supra* note 2, at 382 ("The government has recognized that information about terrorist money helps us to understand their networks, search them out, and disrupt their operations.").

may deter terrorist sympathizers from providing financial assistance to terrorist organizations.[6] Further, disrupting the channels of funding may force terrorists to use more risky and less efficient and reliable means to move money globally to finance terrorist activities.[7] In short, "depriving [terrorists] of funding is just as important as targeting the operational cells themselves."[8]

Since the September 11, 2001 terrorist attacks, the U.S. Treasury Department has blocked the assets of over 500 individuals and entities determined to be acting for or on behalf of, sponsoring, providing support or services to, or otherwise associated with suspected terrorists or terrorist organizations.[9] The legal authority to block terrorist assets derives from the International Emergency Economic Powers Act (IEEPA) and the Presidential Executive Order 13224.[10] Publicly designating individuals and organizations for asset freeze "notifies the U.S. public and the world that these parties are either actively engaged in or supporting terrorism or that they are being used by terrorists and their organizations."[11] Public designation also exposes and isolates these parties and denies them access to the U.S. financial system.[12] Further, blocking actions have several important legal consequences. First, all property and interests in property of designated parties that are in the United States or that come within the United States, or within the possession of control of U.S. persons, are blocked.[13] Second, any transaction or dealing by any U.S. persons in blocked property is prohibited.[14] More specifically, U.S. persons are prohibited from "making or receiving . . . any contribution of funds, goods, or services to or for the benefit" of persons determined to be subject

6. *See* UNFUNDING TERROR, *supra* note 1 at 22.

7. *Id. See also* THE 9/11 COMMISSION REPORT, *supra* note 2, at 382.

8. UNFUNDING TERROR, *supra* note 1, at 22.

9. *See* Office of Foreign Assets Control list of specially designated global terrorists (SDGTs), *available at* http:// www.treas.gov/offices/enforcement/ofac/ programs/terror/terror.pdf (last visited May 30, 2010). *See also Terrorist Assets Report, Eighteenth Annual Report to Congress on Assets in the United States of Terrorist Countries and International Terrorism Program Designees 4,* Office of Foreign Assets Control, U.S. Dep't of Treasury (2009) (as of December 31, 2009, a total of 539 individuals and entities have been identified or designated as "Specially Designated Global Terrorists" or "SDGTs" and their assets have been blocked or frozen) [hereinafter *Terrorist Assets Report*].

10. *See* International Emergency Economic Powers Act, 50 U.S.C. §§ 1701–7. *See also* Blocking Property and Prohibiting Transactions with Persons Who Commit, Threaten to Commit, or Support Terrorism, Exec. Order No. 13,244, 66 Fed.Reg. 49,079 (Sept. 23, 2001), 31 C.F.R. 786–90 (2001), reprinted as amended in 50 U.S.C. § 1701 note (Supp. IV 2004), as amended by Exec. Orders No. 13,268, 67 Fed.Reg. 44–751 (July 2, 2002) and No. 13,372, 70 Fed. Reg. 8499 (Feb. 16, 2005). [hereinafter E.O. 13224].

11. TERRORIST ASSETS REPORT, *supra* note 9.

12. *Id.*

13. *See* E.O. 13224, § 1, *supra* note 10.

14. *Id.* § 2(a).

to asset freeze under Executive Order 13224.[15] Third, any transaction by any U.S. person that evades or avoids, or has the purpose of evading or avoiding any of the prohibitions of the Executive Order is prohibited.[16] Finally, severe civil and criminal penalties may be assessed for violations of any license, order, or regulation issued pursuant to the Executive Order. A civil penalty not to exceed $50,000 per violation may be imposed for a violation of E.O. 13224.[17] Whoever willfully violates any license, order or regulation issued under the Order shall be fined not more than $50,000 and imprisoned for not more than 20 years, or both.[18]

The blocking actions have been highly controversial and the subject of extensive legal challenges. Persons subject to asset freeze maintain that blocking orders violate the right of freedom of association and free exercise of religion under the First Amendment.[19] One group argues that blocking assets "substantially burdens" religious freedom because donations are intended to fulfill the religious obligation of their members to engage in charitable giving and blocking those funds interferes with that religious expression.[20] Critics also maintain that such blocking orders constitute an unreasonable seizure for purposes of the Fourth Amendment.[21] They argue that blocking orders require a judicial warrant based on probable cause.[22] Also, blocking orders have been criticized for failing to provide adequate notice and a hearing to the property owner prior to his assets being blocked, in violation of the Due Process Clause.[23] Finally, plaintiffs assert that the authority to block assets based on an entity's support of and association with groups that have never engaged in terrorism is unconstitutionally overbroad and vague.[24]

15. *Id. See also* Humanitarian Law Project v. United States Treasury Dept., 578 F.3d 1133, 1140 (9th Cir. 2009); KindHearts v. Geithner, 647 F. Supp.2d 857, 866 (N.D. Ohio 2009) (E.O. 13224 "prohibits all transactions with designated entities, including making or receiving any contribution of funds, goods or services to or for the benefit of those persons.").

16. *See* E.O. 13224, *supra* note 10, at ¶ 2(b).

17. *See* 31 C.F.R. § 594.701(a)(1) (2007).

18. *Id.* § 594.701(a)(2).

19. *See* Islamic American Relief Agency v. Gonzales, 477 F.3d 728, 736 (D.C. Cir. 2007) (rejecting plaintiff's claims that government blocking actions violated organization's First Amendment right to freedom of association);

Holy Land Found. for Relief & Dev. v. Ashcroft, 333 F.3d 156, 166 (D.C. Cir. 2003) ("[T]here is no First Amendment right nor any other constitutional right to support terrorists [with funding].").

20. *See Gonzales*, 477 F.3d at 737.

21. *See* KindHearts v. Geithner, 647 F. Supp.2d 857, 872 (N.D. Ohio 2009) (blocking action violated plaintiff's Fourth Amendment rights by failing to obtain a warrant based on probable cause); *but see* Al Haramain Islamic v. United States Dept. of Treasury, 2009 WL 3756363, *14–15 (D. Or.) (blocking action was a seizure but reasonable under the Fourth Amendment because it was supported by the special needs of the government).

22. *See KindHearts v. Geithner*, 647 F. Supp.2d at 884.

23. *Id.* at 906–8.

The legal authority to block terrorist assets and the legal challenges to such blocking actions will be discussed in Chapter 8.

A. INTERNATIONAL EMERGENCY ECONOMIC POWERS ACT

The IEEPA was enacted in 1977 to amend the Trading with the Enemy Act (TWEA).[25] In 1917, Congress enacted TWEA authorizing the President to control financial transactions of foreign persons and entities and impose other economic sanctions regardless of the state of foreign affairs (peace or war time).[26] Specifically, the TWEA granted the President authority to "investigate, regulate, ... prevent or prohibit ... transactions" in times of war or national emergency.[27] Its purpose is to deprive the enemy of economic benefits by restricting their ability to trade in the United States.[28] In 1977, Congress enacted the IEEPA to delineate the Executive Branch's exercise of emergency economic powers in response to wartime and peacetime crises. "The IEEPA limited the TWEA's application to periods of declared wars and to certain existing TWEA programs, while the IEEPA was applicable during other times of declared national emergencies."[29]

IEEPA authorizes the President to declare a national emergency "to deal with any unusual and extraordinary threat, which has its source in whole or in substantial part outside the United States, to the national security, foreign policy, or economy of the United States."[30] When such a national emergency is declared, the Presi-

---

24. *See* Global Relief Found., Inc. v. O'Neill, 207 F. Supp.2d 779, 806 (N.D. Ill. 2002), *aff'd* 315 F.3d 748 (7th Cir. 2002) (E.O. 13224 is not overbroad under the First Amendment because it neither "directly regulates speech or expression" and does not grant discretion to "determine whether particular items of expression may be prohibited on the basis of their content"); *Al Haramain Islamic v. U.S. Dept. of Treasury*, 585 F. Supp.2d at 1269–70 (rejecting plaintiff's overbreadth argument and finding that the term "services" is not impermissibly vague, but holding that the term "material support" is unconstitutionally vague); see also Humanitarian Law Project v. United States Treasury Dept., 578 F.3d 1133 (9th Cir. 2009) (ban on providing services to designated terrorist organizations was not unconstitutionally vague); Kind-hearts v. Geithner, 647 F. Supp.2d 857, 895 (N.D. Ohio 2009) ("The term 'service' in E.O. 13224 is not unconstitutionally vague.").

25. *See* Trading with the Enemy Act of 1917, ch. 106, 40 Stat. 411 (codified as amended at 50 U.S.C. §§ 1–44 (2007)).

26. *Id.*

27. *Id.*

28. *See KindHearts v. Geithner*, 647 F. Supp.2d at 875.

29. Islamic Am. Relief Agency v. Unidentified FBI Agents, 394 F. Supp.2d 34, 41 (D.D.C. 2005); *see also* Regan v. Wald, 468 U.S. 222, 227–8 (1984).

30. 50 U.S.C. § 1701(a). IEEPA authorizes the President to impose trade embargoes against foreign countries with which the United States has engaged in hostilities. *See id.* § 1707(a). In response to the seizure of the American embassy in Tehran in 1979, President Carter issued a series of Executive Orders authorizing the Office of Foreign Assets Control, a federal agency located within the U.S. Department of the Trea-

dent may block the transfer of any property in which "any foreign country or a national thereof has any interest . . ."[31] and may prohibit "transfers of credit or payments between, by, through, or to any banking institution . . . involv[ing] any interest of any foreign country or a national thereof."[32] Simply stated, "once the President has declared a national emergency, the IEEPA authorizes the blocking of property to protect against that threat."[33]

The IEEPA authorizes the President to block the transfer of any property in which a foreign national has "any interest."[34] The term "interest" means "an interest of any nature whatsoever, direct or indirect."[35] Further, the terms "property" and "property interest" have been defined to include currency, negotiable instruments, "evidence of title," and "contracts of any nature whatsoever, and any other property, real, personal, or mixed, tangible or intangible, or interest or interests therein, present, future or contingent."[36] The courts have broadly construed the phrase "any interest" as used in the IEEPA.[37] The statute does not require that a foreign national have a legally enforceable interest in targeted assets.[38] "A beneficial interest in the entity's assets may suffice."[39] Further, "any interest" covers domestic corporations where foreign nationals occupy key executive positions or were members of the entity's board of directors.[40] According to *Kindhearts v. Geithner*, "[t]his satisfies the requirement . . . that a foreign national have an

---

sury, to promulgate regulations blocking transactions with Iran. *See* Dames & Moore v. Regan, 453 U.S. 654, 662–63 (1981).

31. 50 U.S.C. § 1702(a)(1)(B). Pursuant to § 1702(a)(1)(B), the President may:

[I]nvestigate, block during the pendency of an investigation, regulate, direct and compel, nullify, void, prevent or prohibit, any acquisition, holding, withholding, use, transfer, withdrawal, transportation, importation or exportation of, or dealing in, or exercising any right, power, or privilege with respect to, or transactions involving, any property in which any foreign country or a national thereof has any interest by any person, or with respect to any property, subject to the jurisdiction of the United States. . . .

50 U.S. § 1702(a)(1)(B).

32. *Id.* § 1702(a)(1)(A)(ii).

33. Islamic American Relief Agency v. Gonzales, 477 F.3d 728, 735 (D.C. Cir. 2007).

34. *See* 50 U.S.C. § 1702(a)(1)(B); Holy Land Found. for Relief & Dev. v.

Ashcroft, 219 F.Supp.2d 57, 67 (D.D.C. 2002).

35. 31 C.F.R. § 535.312.

36. *Id.* at § 535.311.

37. *See e.g.,* Regan v. Wald, 468 U.S. 222, 225–26, 233–4 (1984) (the phrase "any interest" must be broadly construed); KindHearts v. Geithner, 647 F. Supp.2d 857, 887 (N.D. Ohio 2009).

38. *See* Global Relief Found. v. O'Neill, 315 F.3d 748, 753 (7th Cir. 2002); *KindHearts*, 647 F. Supp.2d at 887.

39. *KindHearts*, 647 F. Supp.2d at 887 (citing *Global Relief Found.*, 315 F.3d at 753).

40. *See Global Relief Found.*, 315 F.3d at 752–3 (two of the board members were foreign nationals); *KindHearts*, 647 F. Supp.2d at 887 (the President of KindHearts was a foreign national); Al Haramain Islamic v. United States Dept. of Treasury, 585 F. Supp.2d 1233, 1261 (D. Or. 2008) (foreign nationals served as the President and the Treasurer).

interest in the organization" for purposes of freezing the entity's assets pending investigation.[41]

While IEEPA authorizes the imposition of economic sanctions against any foreign country or a national thereof, the statute "does not require that the foreign nation be sanctioned prior to blocking the assets of a foreign national,"[42] or that the foreign person or entity itself poses an "unusual or extraordinary threat" to national security.[43] The courts have consistently rejected the argument that the IEEPA requires that blocked individuals have a nexus with a sanctioned nation to be blocked.[44] Thus, the IEEPA permits sanctions against a national of a foreign country the United States has never, or does not currently have, sanctioned.[45]

In any judicial review of a determination made under the IEEPA, the government may submit to the court *ex parte* and *in camera* any classified information on which it relied.[46] Further, when the President exercises his authority, he must immediately provide a report to Congress identifying the reasons for his emergency declaration, including why the circumstances "constitute an unusual and extraordinary threat[.]"[47]

IEEPA recognizes a humanitarian exception. The authority granted to the President does not extend to regulating or prohibiting donations of food, clothing and medicine intended to be used to relieve human suffering, unless the President determines that such donations would "seriously impair his ability to deal with any national emergency."[48] Finally, § 1704 provides that "[t]he President may issue such regulations, including regulations prescribing definitions, as may be necessary for the exercise of the authorities granted . . . ."[49]

Under § 1705(a) it is "unlawful for a person to violate, attempt to violate, conspire to violate, or cause a violation of any license, order, regulation or prohibition" issued under the IEEPA.[50] The Act provides for a civil penalty of not more than $250,000 or twice the amount of the culpable transaction.[51] A willful violation of IEEPA is a criminal offense. A person who "willfully" violates, attempts, conspires to commit, or aids and abets a violation of any

---

41. *Kind-hearts*, 647 F. Supp.2d at 887.

42. Al Haramain Islamic v. U.S. Dept. of Treasury, 585 F. Supp.2d at 1260.

43. *See Islamic American Relief Agency v. Gonzales,* 477 F.3d at 735 (D.C. Cir. 2007).

44. *See Al Haramain Islamic v. U.S. Dept. of Treasury,* 585 F. Supp.2d at 1260; KindHearts v. Geithner, 647 F. Supp. 2d 857, 886 (N.D. Ohio 2009).

45. *Id.* American citizenship does not immunize a party from blocking. *See* Global Relief Found. v. O'Neill, 315 F.3d 748, 753 (7th Cir. 2002).

46. 50 U.S.C. § 1702(c).

47. Id. § 1703.

48. *Id.* § 1702(b)(2).

49. *Id.* at § 1704.

50. *Id.* § 1705(a).

51. *Id.* § 1705(b).

license, order, regulation, or prohibition issued under IEEPA can be subject to a fine of not more than $1,000,000 or imprisonment for not more than 20 years, or both.[52] In order to sustain a conviction for a willful violation, the government has to prove beyond a reasonable doubt that the defendant acted with knowledge "that his conduct was unlawful," but need not prove that the defendant was aware of a specific statutory or regulatory duty.[53] However, no mens rea is required for IEEPA's civil provisions.[54]

B. EXECUTIVE ORDER 13224

1. INTRODUCTION

On September 23, 2001, President George W. Bush declared a national emergency, pursuant to IEEPA, and signed Executive Order 13224.[55] The Executive Order was issued in response to the "grave acts of terrorism and threats of terrorism committed by foreign terrorists, including the terrorist attacks in New York, Pennsylvania, and the Pentagon committed on September 11, 2001 . . . and the continuing and immediate threat of further attacks on . . . the United States."[56] By this executive order, the President authorized the Secretary of the Treasury to block the property of twenty-seven individuals and groups identified in an annex to Executive Order 13224.[57] The list included "core members of al Qaeda, affiliated terrorist groups, Islamic charities suspected of funding al Qaeda, and other businesses believed to be a front for al Qaeda."[58] The executive order was later amended to include the Taliban and its leader, Mohammed Mullah Omar.[59] Any person or group whose property is blocked pursuant to Executive Order

---

52. *Id.* § 1705(c).

53. United States v. Mousavi, 604 F.3d 1084, 1093–94 (9th Cir.). *See also* Humanitarian Law Project v. United States Treasury Dept., 578 F.3d 1133 (9th Cir. 2009) ("'[IEEPA's] criminal provisions raise no constitutional concerns as they include willfulness, or knowledge of unlawfulness, as an element.'").

54. *See* Humanitarian Law Project v. United States Treasury Dept., 578 F.3d 1133, 1138 (9th Cir. 2009).

55. E.O. 13224, *supra* note 2. *See also* Proclamation No. 7463, 66 Fed.Reg. 48199 (Sept. 14, 2001) (declaring national emergency).

56. E.O. 13224, *supra* note 10.

57. *Id.* at § 1(a).

58. JIMMY GURULÉ, UNFUNDING TERROR: THE LEGAL RESPONSE TO THE FINANCING OF GLOBAL TERRORISM 195 (Edward Elgar Publ. 2008). Pursuant to IEEPA's requirement that he provide a report to Congress, on September 24, 2001, President Bush declared in a Message to Congress:

> I have identified in an Annex to this order eleven terrorist organizations, twelve individual terrorist leaders, three charitable or humanitarian organizations that operate as a front for terrorist financing and support. I have determined that each of these organizations and individuals have committed, supported, or threatened acts of terrorism that imperil the security of the United States.

President Declares National Emergency, Sept. 24, 2001, *available at* http://www.whitehouse.gov/news/releases/2001/09/20010924.html.

59. *See* Exec. Order No. 13268, 67 Fed.Reg. 44751 (July 2, 2002).

13224 is known as a "specially designated global terrorist" or SDGT.[60]

In the executive order, the President also delegated authority to the Secretary of the Treasury to designate other foreign groups or individuals as SDGTs that are determined:

(a) to be owned or controlled by, or act for or on behalf of those persons listed in the Annex to the Order or persons determined to be subject to the Order;[61]

(b) to assist in, sponsor, or provide financial, material, or technological support for, or financial or other services to or in support of, acts of terrorism or individuals or entities designated under the Order;[62] or

(c) to be otherwise associated with designated individuals or entities under the Order.[63]

In *Humanitarian Law Project v. U.S. Dept. of Treasury*, the court held that the "otherwise associated" criterion was unconstitutionally vague.[64] In response, the Treasury Department issued a regulation that defined the provision to mean: "(a) To own or control; or (b) To attempt, or conspire with one or more persons, to act for or on behalf of, or to provide financial, material, or technological support, or financial or other services to."[65] The court reconsidered its ruling and changed it after the Treasury regulation cured the defects.[66]

Executive Order 13224 also authorizes blocking all property and interests in property of foreign persons determined by the Secretary of State, in consultation with the Secretary of Treasury and the Attorney General, "to have committed or to pose a significant risk of committing, acts of terrorism that threaten the security of U.S. nationals or the national security, foreign policy, or economy of the United States."[67] Thus, the Secretary of State as well as the Treasury Secretary may initiate designations and asset freeze

---

60. 31 C.F.R. § 594.310 (SDGT is defined to mean "any foreign person or persons listed in the Annex or designated pursuant to Executive Order 13224 of September 23, 2001.")

61. *Id.* at § 1(c), *supra* note 10.

62. *Id.* at § d(i). The Treasury regulations do not define the term "services," but they do contain a non-exhaustive list of examples: "legal, accounting, financial, brokering, freight forwarding, transportation, public relations, or other services." 31 C.F.R. § 594.406.

63. *Id.* at § d(ii). *See also* U.S. Dep't of State, Fact Sheet: Executive Order 13224 (Dec. 20, 2002), *available at* http://www.state.gov/s/ct/rls/fs/2002/161 81.htm.

64. Humanitarian Law Project v. United States Dept. of Treasury, 463 F. Supp.2d 1049, 1070–1 (C.D. Cal. 2006).

65. 31 C.F.R. § 594.316.

66. *See* Humanitarian Law Project v. United States Dep't of Treasury, 484 F. Supp.2d 1099, 1104–07 (C.D. Cal. 2007).

67. E.O. 13224, § 1(b), *supra* note 10.

under the executive order.[68] Further, while Executive Order 13224 was certainly directed at members of al Qaeda, it is much broader in coverage, authorizing blocking all property and interests in property, of all persons who pose a threat of future terrorist attacks and threaten the national security, foreign policy, and economy of the United States.[69]

2. DESIGNATION PROCESS

The Department of the Treasury's Office of Foreign Assets Control (OFAC) is the lead agency responsible for implementing economic sanctions targeting international terrorists and terrorist organizations and their supporters.[70] In coordination with other federal agencies such as the Departments of State, Justice, and Homeland Security, OFAC identifies persons and groups for designation and asset freeze.[71] However, blocking terrorist-related assets is an administrative, rather than a criminal action. Designation does not require that the party be criminally prosecuted and convicted, or even charged with committing acts of terrorism. Because designations and blocking orders are administrative in nature, the Government is not required to satisfy the criminal standard of proof beyond a reasonable doubt. Instead, a lower standard of proof is applied. An individual may be designated and his assets frozen if there is "reason to believe" that he may have engaged in activities that violate E.O. 13224.[72] Further, a decision to designate a party as an SDGT may be based on classified information, including foreign governments' intelligence reports.[73] In any judicial review of a determination made under E.O. 13224,

---

68. The list of individuals and entities designated under Executive Order 13224 has grown from the original 27 names to 539 designations. For a comprehensive list of individuals and entities designated as SDGTs on the Office of Foreign Assets Control website, see U.S. Dep't of Treasury Office of Foreign Assets Control, Terrorism: What You Need to Know About U.S. Sanctions (updated May 30, 2010), *available at* http://www.treas.gov/offices/enforcement/ofac/programs/terror/terror.pdf.

69. E.O. 13224, *supra* note 10.

70. *See* TERRORIST ASSETS REPORT, *supra* note 38, at 1.

71. *Id.*

72. *See* Al Haramain Islamic Found. v. United States Department of Treasury, 2009 WL 3756363, *14 (D. Or.) ("Such a standard is appropriate in cases of this kind, especially since '[t]he standard of probable cause is particularly related to criminal investigations, not

routine, non-criminal procedures.' ") (internal citations omitted); Al Haramain Islamic v. United States Dept. of Treasury, 585 F. Supp.2d 1233, 1253 (D. Or. 2008) ("Contrary to AHIF–Oregon's contention, the government need not show AHIF–Oregon intended to support terrorism, merely that OFAC held a reasonable belief that AHIF–Oregon is a component of a larger organization that funds terrorism."); Holy Land Found. for Relief and Dev. v. Ashcroft, 333 F.3d 156, 161–62 (D.C. Cir. 2003). *But see* KindHearts v. Geithner, 647 F. Supp.2d 857, 893 (N.D. Ohio 2009) ("OFAC may only block pending investigation on a showing of *probable cause* that the target entity has violated prohibitions of the IEEPA and E.O. 13224....") (emphasis added).

73. *See* Holy Land Found. for Relief & Dev. v. Ashcroft, 219 F. Supp.2d 57, 71 (D.D.C. 2002) (it was reasonable for OFAC to rely on Israeli intelligence reports in deciding to designate HLF).

such classified information may be "submitted to the reviewing court *ex parte* and *in camera*."[74]

Once a designation is made under E.O. 13224, OFAC provides notice of blocking actions through press releases, by updating its website, and by publishing a notice in the Federal Register.[75] The individual or entity is also added to OFAC's list of SDGTs. Once the designation is made public, holders of blocked property are required to take appropriate steps to freeze the property, including placing blocked funds into an interest-bearing account in accordance with OFAC regulations.[76] Further, when opening a new account, financial institutions are required to consult the Treasury Department list of SDGTs to determine whether a person seeking to open an account appears on the list.[77] If so, the bank should refuse to open an account for such person. In short, U.S. persons are forbidden from doing any business with the SDGTs, essentially isolating them from the U.S. financial system.[78]

3. BLOCKING PENDING INVESTIGATION

Section 7 of E.O. 13224 authorizes the Secretary of the Treasury to take such actions, including the promulgation of rules and regulations, and to employ all powers granted to the President by the IEEPA and the United Nations Participation Act (UNPA) in order to carry out the purposes of the Order.[79] In October 2001, the Patriot Act amended IEEPA by authorizing the blocking of proper-

---

74. 50 U.S.C. § 1702(c).

75. *See* Al Haramain Islamic Foundation v. United States Dep't of Treasury, 2009 WL 3756363, *13 (D. Or.); Al–Aqeel v. Paulson, 568 F. Supp.2d 64, 71 (D.D.C. 2008) (OFAC posted press release announcing designation on the Treasury Department website, which provided adequate notice of plaintiff's designation).

76. *See* 31 C.F.R. § 594.203(b)(1)(i) (2007). Financial institutions have a legal duty and obligation to prevent money laundering and terrorist financing, which includes not engaging in transactions with suspected terrorists or terrorist organizations. *See* 31 U.S.C. §§ 5318(h), (*l*)(2)(C).

77. *See* 31 U.S.C. § 5318(*l*)(2)(C), which provides that when opening an account financial institutions shall comply with Treasury Department regulations and procedures for "consulting lists of known or suspected terrorists or terrorist organizations provided to the financial institution by any government agency to determine whether a person

seeking to open an account appears on any such list."

78. *See* E.O. 13224, § 2(a), *supra* note 9.

79. *Id.* at § 7. The UNPA authorizes the President to implement U.N. Security Council measures by prohibiting economic relations between any foreign country or any national thereof and any persons subject to U.S. jurisdiction. See 22 U.S.C. § 287c. The statute provides:

[W]henever the United States is called upon by the [United Nations] Security Council to apply measures which said Council has decided ... the President may, ... under such orders, rules, and regulations as may be prescribed by him, ... prohibit, in whole or in part, economic relations ... between any foreign country or any national thereof or any person therein and the United States or any person subject to the jurisdiction thereof, or involving any property subject to the jurisdiction of the United States.

22 U.S.C. § 287c(a).

ty and the interests in property of persons or entities "during the pendency of an investigation."[80] While E.O. 13224 does not specifically mention any power to block pending investigation, the catch-all provision of § 7 delegates the President's authority under IEEPA to block pending an investigation to the Treasury Department.[81] Thus, the amendment permits the Treasury Secretary to freeze an organization's assets indefinitely without designating the organization as an SDGT.[82] In order to issue a blocking order, "[t]he Treasury only needs to assert that it is investigating whether the entity should be designated."[83]

4. PETITION FOR ADMINISTRATIVE RECONSIDERATION

OFAC has promulgated regulations that permit a person to seek "administrative reconsideration" of a designation.[84] Review of a designation may be sought on multiple grounds. First, a person may seek removal of a blocking order based on an insufficient basis for the designation.[85] Under 31 C.F.R. § 501.807(a), the blocked person is permitted to "submit arguments or evidence that the person believes establishes an insufficient basis exists for the designation."[86] Second, a blocked person may seek to have his designation rescinded claiming that the circumstances resulting in the designation no longer apply.[87] "In determining whether to remove the petitioner's name from the OFAC list based on these latter grounds, the critical consideration is whether the person has made a demonstrable break with the designated entity. For example, if a person was designated an SDGT because he served on the board of directors of an Islamic charity suspected of raising money for a terrorist organization, the designee might file a petition for administrative reconsideration or delisting, claiming that he lacked knowledge that charitable donations were being used to finance terrorist activities and, upon learning of such activity, he severed all ties with the corrupt charity."[88] Almost all removals have involved cases where the petitioner claimed that he was no longer engaged in the activity that initially supported his designation.[89]

---

80. Uniting and Strengthening America by Providing Appropriate Tools Required to Intercept and Obstruct Terrorism Act of 2001, Pub. L. No. 107–56, 115 Stat. 272 (codified at 50 U.S.C. § 1702(a)(1)(B)).

81. *See* KindHearts v. Geithner, 647 F. Supp.2d 857, 891 (N.D. Ohio 2009).

82. *Id.* at 866.

83. *Id.*

84. Pursuant to 31 C.F.R. § 501.807, a "person may seek administrative reconsideration of his, her or its

designation . . . and thus seek to have the designation rescinded."

85. *Id.* at § 501.807(a).

86. *Id.*

87. *Id.*

88. *See* UNFUNDING TERROR, *supra* note 1, at 201.

89. OFAC removed two Somali Swedes from its list of designated entities after they severed all ties with a foreign money remitter suspected of financing al Qaeda. *See* JOHH ROTH, ET AL., NATIONAL COMMISSION ON TERRORIST AT-

After receiving a petition for reconsideration, OFAC may request additional information from the petitioner and conduct an internal investigation to establish or refute petitioner's claim. An exchange of correspondence, additional fact-finding, and various meetings with the petitioner may occur before OFAC decides whether to grant or deny the petition for removal. Moreover, a designated party is entitled to request a hearing.[90] Finally, after conducting its review, OFAC is required to submit a written determination of its decision to the designated party.[91]

Finally, Executive Order 13224 allows a party to challenge a blocking order based on mistaken identity.[92] In such a case, the petitioner must submit a written request to OFAC to release the blocked funds. A petition for release of funds should include:

(1) the name of the financial institution in which the funds are blocked;

(2) the amount blocked;

(3) the date of the blocking;

(4) the identity of the original remitter of the funds and any intermediary financial institutions;

(5) the intended beneficiary of the blocked transfer;

(6) a description of the underlying transaction including copies of related documents (e.g., invoices, bills of lading, promissory notes, etc.);

(7) the nature of the applicant's interest in the funds; and

(8) a statement of the reasons why the applicant believes the funds were blocked due to mistaken identity.[93]

Ultimately, the Director of OFAC decides whether to release the funds.[94]

5. LICENSING

Not all transactions with an SDGT are prohibited. Pursuant to regulations issued by OFAC, a designated party may seek a license to engage in any transaction involving a blocked property.[95] These regulations authorize OFAC to issue both "general" and "specific" licenses permitting certain types of transactions otherwise prohibited under Executive Order 13224.[96] The purpose of issuing a license

TACKS UPON THE UNITED STATES, MONOGRAPH ON TERRORIST FINANCING: STAFF REPORT TO THE COMMISSION 86 (Washington, D.C.: Gov't Printing Office 2004), *available at* http://www.govinfo.library.unt.edu/911/staff_statements911_TerrFin_Monograph.pdf.

90. 31 C.F.R. § 501.807(c) (2007).

91. *Id.* at § 501.807(d).

92. *See* 31 C.F.R. § 501.806.

93. *Id.* at § 501.806(d) (2007).

94. *Id.* at § 501.806(f).

95. *See* 31 C.F.R. § 501.801.

96. *Id.* at § 501.801(a), (b) (2007).

is to ameliorate the harsh effects of OFAC blocking actions. While granting a license is discretionary with OFAC, such decisions cannot be "arbitrary or capricious."[97]

OFAC has issued several general licenses authorizing transactions in which HAMAS has an interest. In October 2001, HAMAS was designated an SDGT.[98] After parliamentary elections in the West Bank and Gaza, HAMAS members formed the majority party within the Palestinian Legislative Council. As a result of these elections, OFAC determined that HAMAS has a property interest in the transactions of the Palestinian Authority. Accordingly, pursuant to E.O. 13224, U.S. persons are prohibited from engaging in any transactions with the Palestinian Authority, including the provision of humanitarian aid. To minimize the unintended consequences of the executive order, OFAC issued seven general licenses authorizing U.S. persons to engage in certain transactions with the Palestinian Authority.[99] One of those general licenses authorized in-kind donations of medicine, medical services and medical devices to the Palestinian Authority Ministry of Health.[100] OFAC has also issued general licenses for the provision of legal services,[101] non-scheduled emergency medical services,[102] transactions related to telecommunications,[103] and transactions incident to the receipt or

97. KindHearts v. Geithner, 647 F. Supp.2d 857, 916–7 (N.D. Ohio 2009).

98. *See* OFAC, U.S. Dep't of Treasury, SDGT designations, *available at* http://www.treasury.gov/offices/enforcement/ofac/actions/2001.shtml.

99. The discussion of general licenses issued by OFAC regarding transactions with the Palestinian Authority is taken in part from Unfunding Terror, supra note 1, at 199–200. OFAC has issued the following seven general licenses dealing with the Palestinian Authority:

(1) General License 1—official activities of certain international organizations. 31 C.F.R. § 594.510 (2007).

(2) General License 2—authorizing U.S. persons to engage in transactions with the Palestinian Authority that are "ordinarily incident to their travel to and from, employment, residence or personal maintenance within, the jurisdiction of the Palestinian Authority." *Id.* at § 594.511.

(3) General License 3—authorizing U.S. persons to pay taxes and fees to, and purchase or receive permits or public utility services from, the Palestinian Authority. *Id.* at § 594.412.

(4) General License 4—authorizing U.S. persons to engage in transactions with certain Palestinian government agencies. *Id.* at § 594.513.

(5) General License 5—authorizing transactions and activities necessary to conclude ongoing contracts or programs with the Palestinian Authority. *Id.* at § 594.514.

(6) General License 6—authorizing U.S. persons to "provide in-kind donations of medicine, medical devices, and medical services to the Palestinian Authority." Id. at § 594.515.

(7) General License 7—broad authorization for U.S. persons to engage in all transactions otherwise prohibited by the terrorism sanctions programs with the Palestinian Authority. *See* Office of Foreign Assets Control, U.S. Dep't of Treasury, General License No. 7, *available at* http://www.treas.gov/offices/enforcement/ofac/programs/terror.shtml.

100. *See* 31 C.F.R. § 594.515 (2007).

101. *Id.* at § 594.506.

102. *Id.* at § 594.507.

103. *Id.* at § 594.508.

transmission of mail between U.S. person and persons whose property or interests in property are blocked.[104] OFAC has also issued a general license with respect to Sudan, a designated state sponsor of terrorism.[105]

OFAC regulations also permit a designated party to seek a "specific license" to engage in a particular transaction involving blocked property.[106] In *Global Relief Foundation, Inc. v. O'Neill*, OFAC exercised its discretion quite liberally, granting a U.S.-based Islamic charity licenses to pay legal fees, establish a legal defense fund, pay employees' salaries, payroll taxes, health insurance, rent, utilities, and other recurring expenses.[107] At the same time, the denial of a license is not final. A party may refile an application with OFAC at a later date.

6. LEGAL CHALLENGES

a. Administrative Procedure Act

A person designated by OFAC as a SDGT bears a heavy burden to overturn the designation on the grounds of insufficient evidence. Under the Administrative Procedure (APA), the court may overturn an agency action only if the action was "arbitrary, capricious, an abuse of discretion, or otherwise not in accordance with law."[108] In determining whether an agency action is arbitrary and capricious, courts will "consider whether the decision was based on the relevant factors and whether there has been a clear error of judgment."[109] Review under this standard is highly deferential, and the court may not substitute its judgment for OFAC's, but require it to "examine the relevant data and articulate a satisfactory explanation for its action including a rational connection between the facts found and the choice made."[110] The court must review the administrative record assembled by the agency to determine wheth-

---

104. *Id.* at § 594.509.

105. The Sudan general license authorizes the exportation of agricultural commodities, medicine and medical devices to specified areas of Sudan, *available at* http://www.ustreas.gov/offices/enforcement/ofac/actions/2008.shtml. *See also* 31 C.F.R. § 538.

106. 31 C.F.R § 501.801(b).

107. *See* Global Relief Found., Inc. v. O'Neill, 207 F. Supp.2d 779, 786, 788, 805 (N.D. Ill. 2002). *See also* KindHearts v. Geithner, 647 F. Supp.2d 857, 916 (N.D. Ohio 2009) (upholding policy on granting licenses for attorney fees, but finding that application of that policy against KindHearts was arbitrary and capricious).

108. 5 U.S.C. § 706(2)(A); *see also* Marsh v. Oregon Natural Resources Council, 490 U.S. 360, 377 (1989). See also Unfunding Terror, supra note 1, at 201–02 (discussing legal challenges to OFAC designations under the APA).

109. *Marsh,* 490 U.S. at 378.

110. Islamic American Relief Agency v. Gonzales, 477 F.3d 728, 732 (D.C. Cir. 2007) (quoting Motor Vehicle Mfrs. Ass'n of the U.S., Inc. v. State Farm Mut. Auto. Ins. Co., 463 U.S. 29, 43 (1983)); *see also* Oregon Natural Resources Council v. Lowe, 109 F.3d 521, 526 (9th Cir. 1997); O'Keeffe's, Inc. v. United States Consumer Product Safety Comm., 92 F.3d 940, 942 (9th Cir. 1996).

er the agency's decision was supported by a rational basis.[111] Further, "in an area at the intersection of national security, foreign affairs, and administrative law," judicial review of an agency decision is extremely deferential.[112]

The courts have consistently upheld OFAC's SDGT designations. In *Holy Land Found. for Relief & Dev. v. Ashcroft,* the D.C. Circuit Court of Appeals affirmed the district court's ruling that OFAC's designation of the Holy Land Foundation for Relief and Development (HLF) was supported by substantial evidence and was not arbitrary and capricious.[113] The Treasury Department maintained that HLF was the principal fundraiser in the United States, for Hamas.[114] Further, prior to the action taken against HLF, the Treasury Department had designated Hamas as an SDGT.[115] The district court found that the administrative record contained evidence that

> (1) HLF has had financial connections to Hamas since its creation in 1989; (2) HLF leaders have been actively involved in various meetings with Hamas leaders; (30 HLF funds Hamas-controlled charitable organizations; (4) HLF provides financial support to the orphans and families of Hamas martyrs and prisoners; (5) HLF's Jerusalem office acted on behalf of Hamas; and (6) FBI informants reliably reported that HLF funds Hamas.[116]

The D.C. Circuit affirmed, holding that the "Treasury's decision to designate HLF as an SDGT was based on ample evidence in a massive administrative record."[117]

In *Islamic American Agency v. Gonzales,* the Islamic American Relief Agency (IARA–USA) challenged the district court's decision upholding the blocking of its assets.[118] The Treasury Department

111. *See* Camp v. Pitts, 411 U.S. 138, 142 (1973); Holy Land Found. for Relief & Dev. v. Ashcroft, 333 F.3d 156, 162 (D.C. Cir. 2003).

112. Islamic American Relief Agency v. Gonzales, 477 F.3d 728, 734 (D.C. Cir. 2007); *see also* Holy Land Found. for Relief & Dev. v. Ashcroft, 333 F.3d 156 (D.C.Cir. 2003) (reviewing an SDGT designation "involv[es] sensitive issues of national security and foreign policy"); Humanitarian Law Project v. Reno, 205 F.3d 1130, 1137 (9th Cir. 2000) (where a "regulation involves the conduct of foreign affairs, we owe the executive branch even more latitude than in the domestic context" and a high degree of judicial deference to the decision to designate an entity as an FTO "is a necessary concomitant of the foreign affairs

power"); Al Haramain Islamic v. United States Dept. of Treasury, 585 F. Supp.2d 1233, 1249 (D. Or. 2008) (in the area of foreign policy deference due to the government agency is "at its zenith").

113. Holy Land Found. for Relief & Dev. v. Ashcroft, 333 F.3d 156 (D.C. Cir. 2003).

114. *See* Holy Land Found. for Relief & Dev. v. Ashcroft, 219 F. Supp.2d 57, 64 n. 2 (D.D.C. 2002).

115. *Id.*

116. *Id.* at 69.

117. *Holy Land Found. for Relief & Dev. v. Ashcroft,* 333 F.3d at 162.

118. Islamic American Relief Agency v. Gonzales, 477 F.3d 728 (D.C. Cir. 2007).

concluded that the IARA–USA was a branch office of IARA.[119] In 2004, OFAC designated IARA as a SDGT on the grounds that it "provides financial support or other services to persons who commit, threaten to commit or support terrorism," in violation of E.O. 13224.[120] The D.C. Circuit upheld the designation, rejecting IARA–USA's theory that blocking its assets based on the designation of IARA was proper only if IARA "dominates and controls" IARA–USA.[121] The court posited that the " 'dominates and controls' " test is appropriate for reviewing the existence of a principal-agent relationship because, where there is sufficient evidence to find an agency relationship, substantial evidence of the principal's unlawful activity is sufficient to justify the designation or blocking of the agent."[122] However, OFAC's theory was that IARA–USA and IARA comprised a single global organization.[123] Therefore, the court reasoned that "if the record contains substantial evidence that IARA–USA is a branch of IARA, then it was proper for OFAC to subject IARA–USA to the blocking as a result of IARA's designation"[124] Ultimately, the court found substantial evidence from several different sources, and covering an extended period of time, supporting OFAC's conclusion that IARA–USA is part of IARA.[125] Accordingly, OFAC's decision to designate IARA–USA was not arbitrary and capricious.[126]

b. First Amendment Claims

The federal courts have consistently rejected plaintiffs' claims that OFAC designations and blocking orders violate their First Amendment rights to freedom of association and speech.[127] In *Holy Land Found. for Relief and Dev. v. Ashcroft*, plaintiff argued that the designation and blocking order were unconstitutional under *NAACP v. Claiborne Hardware Co.*, because the Government imposed guilt by association and because it failed to establish that HLF had a "specific intent" to further Hamas' illegal aims.[128] The court rejected these claims, stating that OFAC's action was not taken against HLF for "reason of association alone."[129] The court

119. *Id.* at 730.

120. *Id.* at 731.

121. *Id.* at 732.

122. *Id.* at 733.

123. Islamic American Relief Agency v. Gonzales, 477 F.3d 728 (D.C. Cir. 2007).

124. *Id.*

125. *Id.* at 734.

126. *Id.*

127. *See, e.g.,* FEC v. Colorado Republican Federal Campaign Committee, 533 U.S. 431, 440 (2001) (contributions of money fall within the First Amendment's protection of speech and political association); McConnell v. Federal Election Commission, 540 U.S. 93, 135 (2003); Nixon v. Shrink Missouri Gov't PAC, 528 U.S. 377 (2000); Buckley v. Valeo, 424 U.S. 1 (1976).

128. Holy Land Found. for Relief & Dev. v. Ashcroft, 219 F. Supp.2d 57, 80 (D.D.C. 2002), *aff'd* Holy Land Foundation v. Ashcroft, 333 F.3d 156 (D.C. Cir. 2003).

129. *Holy Land Found.*, 219 F. Supp.2d at 80.

reasoned that OFAC's designation and blocking order do not prohibit membership in Hamas or endorsement of its views, and therefore do implicate HLF's associational rights.[130] Instead, OFAC's actions prohibit HLF from providing financial support to Hamas, and the court stated that "there is no constitutional right to facilitate terrorism."[131] Thus, the Treasury agency's action did not violate the First Amendment right of association.

The court also held that the First Amendment does not require the Government to establish that HLF had a "specific intent" to further Hamas' unlawful activities.[132] The court distinguished *Clairborne Hardware*, where the Supreme Court imposed the specific intent requirement on Government restrictions that establish liability on the basis of association alone.[133] Because the Government had not imposed guilt by association, the court in *Holy Land Found. for Relief and Dev.*, held that the specific intent requirement was not applicable.[134] Moreover, the court reasoned that imposing a "specific intent" requirement on the Government's authority to issue blocking orders would substantially undermine the purpose of the economic sanctions program.[135] The court stated that "[r]egardless of HLF's intent, it cannot effectively control whether support given to Hamas is used to promote that organization's unlawful activities."[136]

Finally, the court rejected HLF's contention that the Government violated its First Amendment right to freedom of speech by prohibiting it from making any humanitarian donations by blocking its assets.[137] The court found that HLF's financial contributions to Hamas implicate both speech and nonspeech elements and therefore applied the intermediate scrutiny standard of review laid out in *United States v. O'Brien*.[138] In that case, the Supreme Court rejected a First Amendment challenge to a conviction under a statute prohibiting the destruction of draft cards, even though O'Brien had burned his draft card in protest against the draft.[139] Under the intermediate scrutiny standard, the government restriction is lawful if:

---

130. *Id.* at 81.

131. *Id.* (quoting Humanitarian Law Project v. Reno, 205 F.3d 1130, 1133 (9th Cir. 2000)). *See also* Islamic Relief Agency v. Gonzales, 477 F.3d 728, 735 (D.C.Cir. 2007) ("[T]here is no First Amendment right nor any other constitutional right to support terrorists"); Holy Land Foundation v. Ashcroft, 333 F.3d 156, 166 (D.C. Cir. 2003) (same).

132. *Holy Land Found.*, 219 F. Supp.2d at 81.

133. *Id.*

134. Holy Land Found. for Relief & Dev. v. Ashcroft, 219 F. Supp.2d 57, 81 (D.D.C. 2002).

135. *Id.*

136. *Id.*

137. *Id.*

138. *Holy Land Found.*, 219 F. Supp.2d at 81 (citing United States v. O'Brien, 391 U.S. 367 (1968)).

139. *O'Brien,* 391 U.S. at 370, 376, 382.

(1) it is within the constitutional power of the Government; (2) it furthers an important or substantial government interest; (3) the government interest is unrelated to the suppression of free speech; and (4) the incidental restriction on alleged First Amendment freedoms is no greater than is essential to the furtherance of that interest.[140]

Applying the test articulated in *O'Brien*, the district court held that the Government's action passes intermediate scrutiny.[141] First, the President was authorized to issue the E.O. pursuant to IEE-PA.[142] Moreover, the IEEPA and the E.O. both grant OFAC the authority to designate HLF and block its assets.[143] Second, the court found that OFAC's blocking orders promote an important and substantial government interest—"that of combating terrorism by undermining its financial base."[144] Third, the Government's interest in preventing terrorist attacks is unrelated to suppressing free expression, according to the court.[145] The court stated: "[T]he Government has merely restricted HLF's ability to provide financial support to Hamas. It has not restricted HLF's ability to express its viewpoints, even if these views include endorsement of Hamas."[146] Fourth and finally, the court held that the incidental restriction on speech is no greater than necessary to further the Government's interest.[147] The court posited: "Money is fungible, and the Government has no other, narrower, means of ensuring that even charitable contributions to a terrorist organization are actually used for legitimate purposes."[148] Accordingly, the court held that the Government's restriction was "narrowly enough tailored to only further its interest in stopping the flow of American dollars to Hamas."[149]

The D.C. Circuit Court of Appeals affirmed the district court's ruling, ruling that OFAC's designation and blocking order did not violate HLF's First Amendment right of freedom of association and

---

140. *Holy Land Found.*, 219 F. Supp.2d at 82 (citing *United States v. O'Brien*, 391 U.S. at 367–7). *See also* Texas v. Johnson, 491 U.S. 397, 403 (1989) ("If the [Government's] regulation is not related to expression, then the less stringent standard we announced in *United States v. O'Brien* for regulations of noncommunicative conduct controls. If it is, then we are outside of *O'Brien's* test, and we must [apply] a more demanding standard.").

141. *Holy Land Found.*, 219 F. Supp.2d at 82.

142. *Id.*

143. *Id.*

144. *Id.*

145. *Id.*

146. Holy Land Found. for Relief & Dev. v. Ashcroft, 219 F. Supp.2d 57, 82 (D.D.C. 2002).

147. *Id.*

148. *Id. See also* Humanitarian Law Project v. Reno, 205 F.3d 1130, 1136 (9th Cir. 2000) (finding that the restrictions imposed by the material support statute are no greater than necessary because money is fungible and even contributions earmarked for humanitarian purposes can be used by terrorists for criminal purposes).

149. *Holy Land Found.*, 219 F. Supp.2d at 82.

free speech.[150] In dismissing plaintiff's First Amendment claims, the court declared: "[T]here is no First Amendment right nor any other constitutional right to support terrorists."[151] Other courts that have decided the issue have reached the same result.[152]

c. Fourth Amendment Claims

The courts are divided on whether blocking assets constitutes an unreasonable seizure under the Fourth Amendment. More specifically, the courts that have considered the issue disagree on whether the freezing of assets is a "seizure" for purposes of the Fourth Amendment.[153] Further, those courts that hold that blocking constitutes a seizure, are split on whether such action is unreasonable absent a warrant.[154] The Fourth Amendment provides that the "right of the people to be secure in their persons, house, papers and effects, against unreasonable searches and seizures, shall not be violated . . . ."[155] In *Holy Land Foundation for Relief and Development v. Ashcroft*, the court held that blocking assets is not a seizure for Fourth Amendment purposes.[156] However, the court's analysis centered on whether a OFAC blocking constitutes a taking under the Takings Clause of the Fifth Amendment.[157] The court cited authority for the proposition that blocking within the context of IEEPA and TWEA do not constitute takings with the meaning of the Fifth Amendment Takings Clause.[158] For example, the court relied on *Tran Qui Than v. Regan*, which rejected a takings claim

150. Holy Land Foundation v. Ashcroft, 333 F.3d 156 (D.C. Cir. 2003).

151. *Id.* at 166.

152. *See e.g.,* Islamic American Relief Agency v. Gonzales, 477 F.3d 728, 735 (D.C. Cir. 2007) ("[W]here an organization is found to have supported terrorism, government actions to suspend that support are not unconstitutional."); Global Relief Found., Inc. v. O'Neill, 207 F. Supp.2d 779, 806 (N.D. Ill. 2002) (Holding that E.O. 13224 clearly meets the standard of review enunciated in United States v. O'Brien, 391 U.S. 367, 376–7 (1968) for determining whether regulations on protected speech violate the First Amendment); United States v. Al–Arian, 308 F. Supp.2d 1322, 1342 (M.D. Fla. 2004).

153. *See* Islamic Am. Relief Agency v. Unidentified FBI Agents, 394 F. Supp.2d 34, 47–48 (D.D.C. 2005) (freezing assets is not a seizure entitled to Fourth Amendment protection); Holy Land Found. for Relief & Dev. v. Ashcroft, 219 F. Supp.2d 57, 79 (D.D.C.

2002) (same). *But see* KindHearts v. Geithner, 647 F. Supp.2d 857, 872 (N.D. Ohio 2009) ("An OFAC block interferes with possessory rights, and is, in Fourth Amendment terms a seizure."); Al Haramain Islamic v. United States Dept. of Treasury, 585 F. Supp.2d 1233, 1263 (D. Or. 2008) (same).

154. *See KindHearts v. Geithner,* 647 F. Supp.2d at 884 (blocking actions do not fit with the special needs or exigent circumstances exceptions to the warrant requirement). *But see* Al Haramain Islamic Found. v. United States Dept. of Treasury, 2009 WL 3756363 (D. Or.) (OFAC's blocking action falls within the special needs exception to the probable cause and warrant requirement).

155. U.S. Const. amend. IV.

156. *See Holy Land Found. for Relief & Dev. v. Ashcroft,* 219 F. Supp.2d at 79.

157. *Id.*

158. *Id.*

because blocking under TWEA is not equivalent to vesting.[159] Likewise, the court relied on *IPT Co., Inc. v. Dep't of Treasury* rejecting a takings claim because IEEPA blocking is temporary.[160] Finally, *Islamic Am. Relief Agency v. Unidentified FBI Agents*, followed similar reasoning, holding that freezing of assets is not a seizure under the Fourth Amendment.[161]

In contrast to *Holy Land Found. for Relief and Dev.* and *Islamic Am. Relief Agency*, the district court in *Al Haramain Islamic v. U.S. Dept. of Treasury* held that OFAC asset-blocking is a seizure subject to Fourth Amendment analysis.[162] The district court stated that reliance on the Takings Clause was misplaced, because "[t]he Fourth Amendment imposes a lower threshold than does the Fifth Amendment."[163] The court applied the standard articulated in *Soldal v. Cook County*, where the Supreme Court stated that a seizure of property occurs when there is some "meaningful interference with an individual's possessory interests in that property."[164] Further, the district court opined that "[e]ven a temporary deprivation of property, as a blocking is, constitutes a meaningful interference with property and qualifies as a 'seizure' for purposes of the Fourth Amendment."[165]

The court observed that OFAC's blocking order against Al Haramain Islamic Foundation (AHIF–Oregon) prohibits "[a]ny and all transactions" including "the sale and conveyance of title or deed" unless specifically licensed by OFAC.[166] Further, the blocking notice to AHIF–Oregon provided that "any transfer, withdrawal, export, payment or other dealing in AHIF–Oregon's blocked assets was prohibited with OFAC's prior authorization."[167] Thus, the court held that the blocking order deprives AHIF–Oregon of the benefit of the property, which constitutes a "meaningful interference with a possessory interest."[168]

The courts that agree that asset-blocking is a seizure for purposes of the Fourth Amendment are divided on whether such action is unreasonable absent a warrant. In *Al Haramain Islamic*

159. *Id.* (quoting Tran Qui Than v. Regan, 658 F.2d 1296, 1301 (9th Cir. 1981).

160. *See* Holy Land Found. for Relief & Dev. v. Ashcroft, 219 F. Supp.2d at 79 (quoting IPT Co., Inc. v. Department of Treasury, 1994 WL 613371, at *5–6 (S.D.N.Y. Nov. 4, 1994).)

161. *Islamic Am. Relief Agency v. Unidentified FBI Agents*, 394 F. Supp.2d at 47–8.

162. *Al Haramain Islamic v. U.S. Dept. of Treasury*, 585 F. Supp.2d at 1262–3.

163. *Id.* at 1262.

164. *Id.* (quoting Soldal v. Cook County, 506 U.S. 56, 61 (1992)).

165. *Al Haramain Islamic*, 585 F. Supp.2d at 1263.

166. *Id.* at 1262.

167. *Id.* (internal citation omitted).

168. *Id.* at 1263. *See also* Kind-Hearts v. Geithner, 647 F. Supp.2d 857 (N.D. Ohio 2009) ("An OFAC block interferes with possessory rights, and is, in Fourth Amendment terms a seizure.").

Foundation v. U.S. Dept. of Treasury (*Al Haramain II*), the court held that OFAC blocking actions fall within the "special needs" exception to the Fourth Amendment requirement of probable cause and a warrant.[169] However, the court in *Kindhearts v. Geithner*, reached the opposite conclusion.[170] The special needs exception was first articulated in Justice Blackmun's concurring opinion in *New Jersey v. T.L.O.*[171] He stated:

> Only in those exceptional circumstances in which special needs, beyond the normal need for law enforcement, make the warrant and probable-cause requirement impracticable, is a court entitled to substitute its balancing of interests for that of the Framers.[172]

Three factors must be present for the special needs exception to apply. First, the primary purpose of the seizure must be beyond the need for law enforcement.[173] Second, a warrant and probable cause must be impracticable.[174] Third, there must be sufficient safeguards in place that act as a "constitutionally adequate substitute for a warrant".[175] When analyzing the government's action under the first factor, courts review whether the "purpose actually served . . . is ultimately indistinguishable from the general interest in crime control."[176] Courts consider the "programmatic purpose" and "distinguish[ ] general crime control programs and those that have another particular purpose, such as protection of citizens against special hazards or protection of our borders. . . . The nature of the 'emergency' . . . take the matter out of the realm of ordinary crime control."[177]

---

169. Al Haramain Islamic Foundation v. United States Dept. of Treasury, 2009 WL 3756363 (D. Or.) [hereinafter *Al Haramain II*].

170. *KindHearts v. Geithner*, 647 F. Supp.2d at 878–4 (blocking assets violated the Fourth Amendment because OFAC did not obtain prior judicial review, and neither the special needs nor exigency exception applied).

171. New Jersey v. T.L.O., 469 U.S. 325 (1985).

172. *Id.* at 351. The special needs exception has been applied in various non-criminal searches such as searches of prisoners, parolees, probationers, border searches, immigration stops and searches, airport security, and administrative searches. *See* 2 John Wesley Hall, Jr., *Search and Seizure* § 38.2 (3d Ed. 2000); *see also KindHearts v. Geithner*, 647 F. Supp.2d at 880–81 (special needs search includes administrative searches,

searches and seizures that occur at roadblock checkpoints and border crossings).

173. *See* Ferguson v. City of Charleston, 532 U.S. 67, 81–6 (2001); City of Indianapolis v. Edmond, 531 U.S. 32, 41–7 (2000); United States v. Heckenkamp, 482 F.3d 1142, 1147 (9th Cir. 2007).

174. *See* Griffin v. Wisconsin, 483 U.S. 868, 873 (1987); *T.L.O.*, 469 U.S. at 351 (Blackmun, J., concurring).

175. New York v. Burger, 482 U.S. 691, 703 (1987).

176. *Ferguson v. City of Charleston*, 532 U.S. at 81–2 (internal citation and quotations omitted).

177. In re Sealed Case, 310 F.3d 717, 745–46 (FISA Ct. Rev. 2002); *see also Heckenkamp*, 482 F.3d at 1147 (whether the search and seizure is "motivated by a need to collect evidence for law enforcement purposes or at the request of law enforcement agents"); *Ed-*

Addressing the first factor, *Al Haramain II* stated that the primary focus of the asset seizure scheme is not for criminal law enforcement purposes.[178] The court observed that "[t]he purpose of the asset seizure scheme is not to obtain information about whether the asset owner has committed an act of terrorism, but rather is to withhold assets to ensure future terrorist acts are not committed."[179] The court disagreed with the ruling in *KindHearts v. Geithner*.[180] In *Kindhearts*, the court considered the "method" and "modus operandi" of the asset seizure program, which it stated more closely resembles traditional law enforcement investigative activity than warrantless searches allowed under the special needs exception.[181] In *Al Haramain II*, the court argued that the focus of the inquiry should be on the programmatic purpose of the search, not the method by which the activity is carried out.[182] Since the purpose of the blocking action is preventive in nature, the court concluded that it serves a purpose beyond normal criminal law enforcement.[183]

As for the second factor, *Al Haramain II* agreed with the government's argument that obtaining a warrant would be impracticable.[184] The court stated that it would be difficult to meet the specificity requirements in an application for a warrant.[185] The court reasoned that OFAC has authority to seize a wide variety of property interests, "ranging from money to mortgages, options to insurance policies, merchandise to accounts payable, located both in the United States and elsewhere, the existence of which are not always known to the agency at the time of the blocking order."[186] As a result, the court stated that it would be difficult to apply for a warrant for every asset in each jurisdiction in which the asset might be located.[187] Further, such a requirement would interfere with OFAC's ability to act quickly to block assets that are often liquid and could be easily transferrable.[188] Next, the court engaged in a balancing test to determine the reasonableness of the search, weighing the intrusion on AHIF–Oregon's privacy interests against the government's interest in seizing the assets of organizations

mond, 531 U.S. at 41 (whether the "primary purpose [is] to detect evidence of ordinary criminal wrongdoing" or approved purposes such as "policing the border" or "ensuring roadway safety").

178. *Al Haramain II, supra* note 169, at *12.

179. *Id.*

180. *KindHearts v. Geithner*, 647 F. Supp.2d at 881.

181. *Id.*

182. *Al Haramain II, supra* note 169, at *12 n. 8.

183. *Id.* at 12.

184. *Id.* at *13. *But see KindHearts v. Geithner*, 647 F. Supp.2d at 881 (ruling that the government had failed to provide an explanation as to why the probable cause warrant requirements were impracticable to the case).

185. *Al Haramain II, supra* note 169, at *12.

186. *Id.* at *13.

187. *Id.*

188. *Id.*

with ties to international terrorist groups.[189] The court found that "the government's interest in stopping the financing of terrorism outweighs AHIF–Oregon's privacy interests."[190]

Finally, the court addressed the third factor, whether there are safeguards that act as "constitutionally adequate substitute[s] for a warrant."[191] The court observed that OFAC froze AHIF–Oregon's assets due to its "reason to believe" that AHIF "may be engaged in activities that violate" the IEEPA.[192] The court held that "because individualized suspicion is required before OFAC undertakes an asset seizure, no additional safeguards are necessary to act as a substitute for a warrant."[193] Thus, OFAC's seizure of AHIF–Oregon's assets was reasonable under the Fourth Amendment because it fell within the special needs exception to the probable cause and warrant requirements.[194]

In *KindHearts v. Geithner*, the court found that OFAC's asset-blocking violated the Fourth Amendment because OFAC failed to obtain a judicial warrant, and neither the special needs nor exigency exception applied.[195] In *KindHearts II*, the court held that the appropriate remedy for such violation was a post-hoc probable cause determination.[196] The court held that "this post-hoc probable cause determination, though not typical, provides a necessary check on otherwise unrestrained executive discretion."[197] However, because this is not a conventional criminal case, the court stated that the typical Fourth Amendment probable cause standard is inapplicable.[198] Thus, the government need not show probable cause to believe that the blocking or seizure of KindHearts' assets will disclose evidence of a crime.[199] Instead, the government must show that "at the time of the original seizure, it had probable cause-that is, a reasonable ground-to believe that KindHearts ... was subject to designation under E.O. 13224 § 1."[200]

189. *Id.*

190. *Id. But see* KindHearts for Charitable Humanitarian Development v. Geithner, 710 F.Supp.2d 637, 646 (N.D. Ohio 2010) ("Given the substantial intrusion on KindHearts' interest, the seizure here was not reasonable under the Fourth Amendment based on the totality of the circumstances.").

191. *Al Haramain II, supra* note 169, at *14 (internal citations omitted).

192. *Id.* at *14. *But see KindHearts v. Geithner,* 647 F. Supp.2d at 881 ("OFAC's blocking power entails no built-in limitations curtailing executive

discretion and putting individuals on notice that they are subject to blocking.").

193. *Al Haramain II, supra* note 169, at *14.

194. *Id.*

195. *KindHearts v. Geithner,* 647 F. Supp.2d at 878–84.

196. KindHearts v. Geithner, 710 F.Supp.2d 637, 648 24 (N.D. Ohio).

197. *Id.* at 652.

198. *Id.*

199. *Id.*

200. *Id.*

d. Fifth Amendment Violations

OFAC designations and blocking orders have been challenged on due process grounds. Plaintiffs have advanced multiple legal theories. First, plaintiffs maintain that OFAC actions fail to provide two fundamental requirements of due process: meaningful notice and an opportunity to be heard. Second, parties subject to blocking argue that the use of classified information violates due process. Third, plaintiffs claim that OFAC's authority under the IEEPA and E.O. 13224 is unconstitutionally vague. Finally, plaintiffs assert that OFAC blocking actions constitute an unconstitutional taking under the Takings Clause of the Fifth Amendment.

i. Meaningful Notice and a Hearing

The Due Process Clause of the Fifth Amendment guarantees that "[n]o person shall ... be deprived of life, liberty, or property, without due process of law."[201] The due process clause generally requires the government to afford notice and a meaningful opportunity to be heard before depriving a person of his property.[202] According to the Supreme Court: "Constitutionally sufficient notice must be reasonably calculated, under all the circumstances, to apprise interested parties of the pendency of the action and afford them an opportunity to present their objections."[203] However, the requirement of pre-seizure notice and a hearing is not absolute and an exception is recognized in "extraordinary" situations where some valid government interest justifies postponing notice and a hearing until after the event.[204] In *Calero–Toledo v. Pearson Yacht Leasing Co.*, the Supreme Court articulated a three-part test to justify delaying notice until after the seizure.[205] Postponement of notice and hearing does not deny due process when "(1) the deprivation was necessary to secure an important government interest; (2) there has been a special need for very prompt action; and (3) the party initiating the deprivation was a government official responsible for determining, under the standards of a nar-

201. U.S. Const. amend. V.

202. *See* United States v. James Daniel Good Real Property, 510 U.S. 43, 62 (1993); Mathews v. Eldridge, 424 U.S. 319, 333 (1976).

203. Mullane v. Central Hanover Bank & Trust Co., 339 U.S. 306, 314–5 (1950). See also KindHearts v. Geithner, 647 F. Supp.2d 857, 901 (N.D. Ohio 2009) ("The party must be able to know the conduct on which the government bases its action, so that it can explain the conduct or otherwise respond to the allegations.").

204. *See* James Daniel Good Real Property, 510 U.S. 43, 53 (1993); Calero–Toledo v. Pearson Yacht Leasing Co., 416 U.S. 663, 679–80 (1974); *see also* National Council of Resistance v. Department of State, 251 F.3d 192 (D.C. Cir. 2001) ("Upon an adequate showing to the court, the Secretary may provide this notice after the [FTO] designation where the earlier notification would impinge upon the security and other foreign policy goals of the United States.").

205. Calero–Toledo v. Pearson Yacht Leasing Co., 416 U.S. 663, 678 (1974).

rowly drawn statute, that it was necessary and justified in the particular instance."[206]

To date, no court has interpreted the Due Process Clause to require OFAC to provide notice *prior* to issuing a blocking order under the IEEPA and E.O. 13224.[207] In *Holy Land Found. for Relief & Dev. v. Ashcroft*, the district court held that OFAC's failure to provide plaintiff pre-designation notice did not violate due process.[208] Applying the *Calero–Toledo* three-part test, the court found that OFAC's designation and blocking order served an important government interest—"combating terrorism by cutting off its funding."[209] Further, prompt action by the government was necessary, the court stated, to prevent the Holy Land Foundation from transferring the assets subject to the blocking order.[210] The court declared: "Money is fungible, and any delay or pre-blocking notice would afford a designated entity the opportunity to transfer, spend, or conceal its assets, thereby making the IEEPA sanctions program virtually meaningless."[211] Third and finally, the court held that OFAC initiated the blocking action pursuant to IEEPA and E.O. 13224 that specifically authorize such action in limited circumstances.[212]

The Due Process Clause requires OFAC to provide meaningful notice *after* blocking assets. However, divergent views have emerged on whether OFAC's method of post-designation notice is constitutionally adequate and comports with procedural due process. In *Al–Aqeel v. Paulson*, the District Court for the District of Columbia rejected plaintiff's due process challenge.[213] In *Al–Aqeel*, the former chairman of Al–Haramain Islamic Foundation (AHF), an Islamic charity based in Saudi Arabia, brought action against the Secretary of the Treasury and other government officials, alleging that his designation as an SDGT by OFAC violated his due

---

206. *See* Holy Land Found. for Relief & Dev. v. Ashcroft, 219 F. Supp.2d 57, 76 (D.D.C. 2002) (citing *Calero–Toledo v. Pearson Yacht Leasing Co.*, 416 U.S. at 678).

207. It should be noted that E.O. 13224 expressly provides for designation and blocking of assets in the absence of prior notice and a hearing. The order provides:

[B]ecause of the ability to transfer funds or assets instantaneously, prior notice to such persons of measures to be taken pursuant to this order would render theses measures ineffectual.... [F]or these measures to be effective in addressing the national emergency declared in this order, there need be no prior notice of a listing or determination made pursuant to this order. E.O. 13224, at § 10.

208. Holy Land Found. for Relief & Dev. v. Ashcroft, 219 F. Supp.2d 57 (D.D.C. 2002).

209. *Id.* at 76.

210. *Id.* at 77.

211. *Id. See also* Global Relief Foundation, Inc. v. O'Neill, 207 F. Supp.2d 779, 804 (N.D. Ill. 2002) ("[p]re-deprivation notice would, in fact, be antithetical to the objectives of [the IEEPA] sanctions program[ ]").

212. *See Holy Land Found. for Relief & Dev. v. Ashcroft*, 219 F. Supp.2d at 77.

213. Al–Aqeel v. Paulson, 568 F. Supp.2d 64 (D.D.C. 2008).

process rights.[214] Plaintiff claimed that OFAC's method of notice—posting a press release on the Treasury Department website-was inadequate and did not provide him with an understanding of the allegations against him in order to prepare a defense.[215] The press release stated that a variety of sources and reports had identified Al–Aqeel as the Chairman, Director General and President of AHF, a designated SDGT.[216] Further, the press release stated that as AHF's founder and leader, Al–Aqeel was responsible for all of AHF's activities, including its support for terrorism.[217] Moreover, during settlement negotiations, OFAC provided Al–Aqeel with a copy of the unclassified and non-privileged portions of the administrative record developed by OFAC during the designation process.[218] The court held that OFAC's method of notice was constitutionally adequate to give him notice of the reasons for his designation.[219]

The court also found that the administrative reconsideration process provided Al–Aqeel a meaningful opportunity to be heard as required by due process.[220] The court observed that plaintiff was able to challenge his designation through OFAC's administrative reconsideration process.[221] Pursuant to 31 C.F.R. § 501.807, a "person may seek administrative reconsideration of his or her or its designation . . . and thus seek to have the designation rescinded."[222] Under the regulation, the plaintiff is permitted to "submit arguments or evidence that the [blocked] person believes establishes that insufficient basis exists for the designation."[223] Further, plaintiff was entitled to request a hearing, pursuant to 31 C.F.R. § 501.807(c), and to receive a written determination of his request for reconsideration, under 31 C.F.R. § 501.807(d).[224] However, the critical factor in the case, the court found, was that plaintiff did not avail himself of this process.[225]

In *Holy Land Foundation v. Ashcroft*, the D.C. Circuit affirmed the district court's ruling that the Treasury Department did not violate HLF's due process rights.[226] In that case, HLF was initially designated in 2001, which arguably violated HLF's due process

214. *Id.* at 68. At various times, OFAC had designated the national branches of AHF, including the Oregon branch located in the United States, as SDGTs. *Id.* at 67.

215. *Id.* at 67–8.

216. *Id.*

217. Al–Aqeel v. Paulson, 568 F. Supp.2d 64, 68 (D.D.C. 2008).

218. *Id.*

219. *Id.*

220. *Id. See also* Holy Land Found. for Relief & Dev. v. Ashcroft. 219 F.

Supp.2d 57, 66 (D.D.C. 2002) (post-designation notice and an opportunity to present evidence to OFAC satisfied due process).

221. *Al–Aqeel v. Paulson*, 568 F. Supp.2d at 71.

222. 31 C.F.R. § 501.807.

223. *Id.* at § 501.807(a).

224. *Id.*

225. *Id.*

226. Holy Land Foundation v. Ashcroft, 333 F.3d 156, 163–4 (D.C. Cir. 2003).

rights.[227] However, HLF was subsequently notified by Treasury that it was reopening the administrative record and considering whether to redesignate HLF as an SDGT on the basis of additional evidence linking HLF to Hamas, a designated foreign terrorist organization.[228] HLF was then given thirty-one days to respond to the new evidence and the redesignation.[229] The D.C. Circuit held that OFAC provided HLF with the requisite notice and opportunity for response necessary to satisfy due process requirements.[230] The court posited that the Due Process Clause does not require an agency to provide procedures which approximate a judicial trial.[231] Further, the blocked person does not have the right to confront and cross-examine witnesses.[232] Finally, the notice "need not disclose the classified information to be presented *in camera* and *ex parte* to the court."[233]

In *KindHearts v. Geithner*, the district court reached the opposite result, holding that OFAC's notice violated plaintiff's due process rights.[234] The court noted that to the extent that OFAC provided notice, it did so in a piecemeal, untimely manner.[235] According to the court, the initial blocking order pending investigation simply recited the criteria from E.O. 13224 and referenced the IEEPA.[236] The court found that OFAC did not disclose any of the unclassified administrative record or afford KindHearts access to any of the documents seized during a search of its premises.[237] More than a year later, OFAC notified KindHearts that it had completed its investigation and provisionally determined to designate it as a SDGT.[238] OFAC's notice of provisional designation included numerous unclassified, non-privileged exhibits, which constituted the administrative record on which OFAC based its provisional determination.[239] The disclosed documents included court opinions and indictments, articles on Hamas, various OFAC press releases, newspaper articles, KindHearts' Newsletters and its organizational chart.[240] However, OFAC failed to explain how those exhibits related to the charges against KindHearts.[241] Several months later, OFAC released redacted versions of internal reports on which it

227. *Id.* at 163.

228. *Id.* at 164.

229. *Id.*

230. *Id.*

231. *Id.*

232. Holy Land Found. v. Ashcroft, 333 F.3d 156, 164 (D.C. Cir. 2003).

233. *Id.*

234. KindHearts v. Geithner, 647 F. Supp.2d 857, 906 (N.D. Ohio 2009).

235. *Id.* at 901.

236. *Id.*

237. *Id.* at 902.

238. *Id.* at 865.

239. KindHearts v. Geithner, 647 F. Supp.2d 857, 902 (N.D. Ohio 2009).

240. *Id.* at 903.

241. *Id.* at 902. *See also* Al–Haramain Islamic v. United States Dept. of Treasury, 585 F. Supp.2d 1233, 1255–6 (D. Or. 2008) (holding that the government failed to provide constitutionally adequate notice when it provided documents supporting its designation and redesignation but failed to explain the significance of that evidence).

relied in reaching its provisional determination and declassified portions of the administrative record supporting its blocking action.[242] In reaching its conclusion that OFAC failed to provide meaningful notice, the court stated: "To comply with due process requirements, OFAC should, at the very least, have promptly given KindHearts the unclassified administrative record on which it relied in taking its blocking action."[243]

Finally, according to the court, OFAC should have provided its estimate of the approximate amounts of donations, or what portions of KindHearts' funds went to Hamas or individuals and entities related to Hamas, and which recipients of funds were fronts for Hamas.[244] Without such information, the court stated, OFAC's invitation to send a letter challenging the blocking action held out no hope that any such challenge would be successful.[245] No other court has interpreted the Due Process Clause so broadly.

In *KindHearts*, the district court also held that OFAC's procedures failed to provide a meaningful opportunity to be heard.[246] The court stated that "[p]romptness is an important aspect of the due process right to be heard."[247] While there is no bright-line gauge for determining whether the government has provided a hearing with sufficient promptness, courts are to examine several factors, including the "importance of the private interest and the harm to this interest occasioned by delay; the justification offered by the government for delay and its relation to the underlying governmental interest; and the likelihood that the interim decision may have been mistaken."[248] The court found that KindHearts had a substantial private interest-the loss of access to its assets.[249] Further, OFAC was primarily responsible for the delay KindHearts encountered in its efforts to be heard.[250] OFAC waited fifteen months after the blocking pending investigation to make a provisional determination and provide KindHearts access to an unclassified administrative record.[251] Finally, while the material provided to KindHearts may reasonably support OFAC's allegations, the court stated that does not justify the length of the government's delay in giving KindHearts an opportunity to be heard.[252] In sum, a party whose assets are blocked pending investigation is entitled to prompt notice of the reasons for the blocking action. More specifically, a fifteen month

242. *KindHearts v. Geithner*, 647 F. Supp.2d at 903.

243. *Id.* at 905.

244. *Id.* at 904.

245. *Id.* at 905.

246. *Id.* at 907–08.

247. KindHearts v. Geithner, 647 F. Supp.2d 857, 906 (N.D. Ohio 2009).

248. *Id.* at 907 (quoting Federal Deposit Ins. Corp. v. Mallen, 486 U.S. 230, 242 (1988)).

249. *KindHearts*, 647 F. Supp.2d at 907.

250. *Id.*

251. *Id.*

252. *Id.* at 908.

delay in notifying the plaintiff of the reasons for the asset freeze is not consistent with due process principles.

KindHearts raised one last due process issue, arguing that a hearing before the Director of OFAC constitutes a violation of its due process right to a neutral decision-maker.[253] However, the court rejected this claim, citing *Withrow v. Larkin*, where the Supreme Court held that members of administrative agencies typically receive the results of investigations and "approve the filing of charges or formal complaints instituting enforcement proceedings, and then ... participate in the ... hearings."[254] The Supreme Court held that such procedures do not violate the Due Process Clause.[255] Thus, a hearing before the Director of OFAC does not violate due process.[256]

ii. Disclosure of Classified Information

The IEEPA expressly authorizes *ex parte* and *in camera* review of classified information in "any judicial review of a determination made under this section [that] ... was based on classified information."[257] Plaintiffs have challenged OFAC designations and blocking orders maintaining that disclosure of classified information only to the court *ex parte* and *in camera* violates due process. However, the federal courts have been unreceptive to plaintiffs' arguments, rejecting their due process claims. In *Holy Land Foundation v. Ashcroft*, the D.C. Circuit held that denying HLF access to classified evidence did not violate due process.[258] According to the court, due process does not prevent OFAC from designating a party as a SDGT based on classified information disclosed only to the court *ex parte* and *in camera*.[259] In support of its decision, the D.C. Circuit relied on its earlier ruling in *People's Mojahedin Organization of Iran v. Dep't of State*, where the court rejected plaintiffs' claim that use of classified information in the designation of a foreign terrorist organization that had been disclosed only to the court offended due process.[260] The court justified withholding classified information from plaintiffs "emphasiz[ing] the primacy of the Executive in controlling and exercising responsibility over access to classified information," and the Executive's " 'compelling interest' in withholding national security information from unauthorized persons in

253. *Id.* at 908 n. 29.

254. *Id.* (citing Withrow v. Larkin, 421 U.S. 35, 56 (1975)).

255. *KindHearts*, 647 F. Supp.2d at 908 n. 29.

256. *Id.*

257. 50 U.S.C. § 170(c) (2000 & Supp. IV 2004). This discussion is taken in part from Unfunding Terror, supra note 1, at 205–06.

258. Holy Land Found. v. Ashcroft, 333 F.3d 156, 164 (D.C. Cir. 2003).

259. *Id.*

260. People's Mojahedin Organization of Iran v. Department of State, 327 F.3d 1238, 1242 (D.C. Cir. 2003).

the course of executive business.''[261] The HLF court found the reasoning in *People's Mojahedin Organization of Iran* equally applicable to a designation under E.O. 13224. The court opined:

> That the designation comes under an Executive Order issued under a different statutory scheme makes no difference. HLF's complaint, like that of the Designated Foreign Terrorist Organization in the earlier cases, that due process prevents its designation based upon classified information to which it has not had access is of no avail.[262]

Thus, OFAC designations may be supported by classified information not disclosed to the designated individual or entity.

In *Global Relief Found., Inc. v. O'Neill,* the court reached the same conclusion.[263] The district court applied a balancing test, balancing the nature of the government's interest against the plaintiff's interest in challenging an erroneous deprivation of property.[264] Deciding in favor the Government, the district court stated that "[a]lthough Global Relief does have a substantial interest in being able to study and respond to the evidence against it ... the defendants have demonstrated a compelling state interest in national security which outweighs Global Relief's interest in this case.''[265]

The Seventh Circuit affirmed the district court's ruling, noting that *ex parte* and *in camera* review of classified information is not unprecedented.[266] For example, *ex parte* review of information is common in criminal cases where the identity of an informant might otherwise be revealed.[267] Also, *ex parte* judicial review of classified information under the Foreign Intelligence Surveillance Act is constitutionally proper.[268] Further, the court reasoned that disclosure of classified information to alleged terrorist sympathizers would be contrary to public policy, possibly jeopardizing innocent lives. The court stated: "The Constitution would indeed be a

---

261. *Id.*

262. *Holy Land Foundation v. Ashcroft,* 333 F.3d at 164.

263. Global Relief Found., Inc. v. O'Neill, 315 F.3d 748, 754 (7th Cir. 2002). *See also* Al–Aqeel v. Paulson, 568 F. Supp.2d 64, 72–3 (D.D.C. 2008) (denying plaintiff's request for disclosure of classified portions of the administrative record to challenge OFAC's designation).

264. *Global Relief Found., Inc. v. O'Neill,* 315 F.3d at 754.

265. Global Relief Found., Inc. v. O'Neill, 207 F. Supp.2d 779, 808 (N.D. Ill. 2002). The district also rejected a

Sixth Amendment Confrontation Clause argument advance by plaintiff. The court held that the Confrontation Clause does not apply to IEEPA blocking actions. *Id.* at 807–8. The Sixth Amendment is not applicable because plaintiff was not charged in a criminal prosecution and facing criminal sanctions. *Id.*

266. *Global Relief Found., Inc. v. O'Neill,* 315 F.3d 748.

267. *See* Roviaro v. United States, 353 U.S. 53, 60–62 (1957).

268. *See* United States v. Ott, 827 F.2d 473, 476 (9th Cir. 1987); United States v. Belfield, 692 F.2d 141, 147 (D.C. Cir. 1982).

suicide pact if the only way to curtail enemies' access to assets were to reveal information that might cost lives."[269]

iii.   Unconstitutional Vagueness

Plaintiffs have challenged the ban imposed by E.O. 13324 on "services" claiming that the term is unconstitutionally vague.[270] Section 1(d)(i) of the E.O. permits the Secretary of the Treasury to designate individuals and entities who "provide . . . financial or other services to or in support of" acts of terrorism or to SDGTs.[271] Section 2(a) prohibits "any transaction or dealing by U.S. persons or within the United States in property or interests in property blocked" pursuant to E.O. 13224, "including but not limited to . . . services, to of for the benefit of" an SDGT.[272] While the Treasury regulations do not provide a concise definition of "services," they do contain a non-exhaustive list of examples of prohibited conduct: "legal, accounting, financial, brokering, freight forwarding, transportation, public relations, or other services."[273]

According to the Supreme Court, "[a] conviction fails to comport with due process if the statute under which it is obtained fails to provide a person of ordinary intelligence fair notice of what is prohibited, or is so standardless that it authorizes or encourages seriously discriminatory enforcement."[274] "But, 'perfect clarity and precise guidance have never been required even of regulations that restrict expressive activity.' "[275] Statutes that are insufficiently clear are void for three reasons: "(1) to avoid punishing people for behavior that they could not have known was illegal; (2) to avoid subjective enforcement of the laws based on 'arbitrary and discriminatory enforcement' by government officers; and (3) to avoid any chilling effect on the exercise of First Amendment freedoms."[276]

In *Humanitarian Law Project v. U.S. Treasury Dept.*, the Ninth Circuit held that the ban on "services" is not unconstitutionally vague.[277] Rejecting plaintiff's facial challenge, the court observed

269. *Global Relief Found., Inc.*, 315 F.3d at 754 (citations omitted).

270. *See* Humanitarian Law Project v. United States Treasury Dept., 578 F.3d 1133, 1147 (9th Cir. 2009) (the term "service" in E.O. 13224 is not unconstitutionally vague); *accord* Al Haramain v. United States Department of Treasury, 2009 WL 3756363 (D. Or.); KindHearts v. Geithner, 647 F. Supp.2d 857, 895 (N.D. Ohio 2009).

271. E.O. 13224, *supra* note 10, at § 1(d)(i).

272. *Id.* at § 2(a).

273. 31 C.F.R. § 594.406.

274. United States v. Williams, 553 U.S. 285, 304 (2008).

275. *Id.* at 304 (quoting Ward v. Rock Against Racism, 491 U.S. 781, 794 (1989)).

276. Grayned v. City of Rockford, 408 U.S. 104, 108 (1972).

277. Humanitarian Law Project v. United States Treasury Dept., 578 F.3d 1133, 1147 (9th Cir. 2009).

that the Treasury regulations clarify the term "services" by offering examples of what is contemplated.[278] The court commented:

> They make clear that legal and educational services are prohibited. They also indicate that one should not perform a useful professional or business task for a terrorist organization. For these reasons, even if the term "services" standing alone would be ambiguous, the examples alert a person of ordinary intelligence to the services that should not be provided to or for the benefit of SDGTs. In these circumstances, it is clear what the term "services" proscribes in the vast majority of intended applications.[279]

Further, the court could find no basis for supposing that the term "services" "could ensnare independent advocacy undertaken for the benefit of" terrorist organizations.[280] The court relied on the Treasury's assertion that the "designation criteria [under E.O. 13224] will be applied in a manner consistent with pertinent Federal law, including, where applicable the First Amendment to the United States Constitution."[281] The Ninth Circuit stated: "This reflects the Treasury Department's intent to interpret its own regulations, including the ban on 'services,' to exclude independent advocacy because independent advocacy is always protected under the First Amendment."[282] Finally, the court noted that the plaintiff could identify "no instance where any person engaged in independent advocacy has been subject to civil or criminal penalties under IEEPA for engaging in such conduct."[283] Thus, the court held that HLP's facial challenge fails.[284]

The Ninth Circuit also held that the ban on "services" is not unconstitutionally vague as-applied to HLP's proposed activities. The court posited that even if HLP's activities in which it intends

---

278. *Id.* at 1146. The parties disputed whether the First Amendment or non-First Amendment test for facial vagueness applies. The court stated: "When a statute 'clearly implicates free speech rights,' it will survive a facial challenge so long as 'it is clear what the statute proscribes 'in the vast majority of its intended applications.' " *Id.* (quoting California Teachers Ass'n v. State Bd. of Educ., 271 F.3d 1141, 1149, 1151 (9th Cir. 2001) (quoting Hill v. Colorado, 530 U.S. 703, 733 (2000)). Outside the First Amendment context, the court observed that a plaintiff alleging facial vagueness must show that "the enactment is impermissibly vague in all its applications." *Humanitarian Law Project v. U.S. Treasury Dept.*, 578 F.3d at 1147 (quoting Hotel & Motel Ass'n of Oakland v. City of Oakland, 344 F.3d

959, 972 (9th Cir. 2003) (quoting Village of Hoffman Estates v. Flipside, Hoffman Estates, Inc., 455 U.S. 489, 495 (1982)). Ultimately, the court found it unnecessary to resolve the dispute, finding that HLP could not succeed even under the more relaxed standard. *Humanitarian Law Project v. U.S. Treasury Dept.*, 578 F.3d at 1146.

279. *Humanitarian Law Project*, 578 F.3d at 1146–47.

280. *Id.* at 1147.

281. *Id.* (quoting 72 Fed.Reg. 4,206 (January 30, 2007)).

282. *Humanitarian Law Project*, 578 F.3d at 1147.

283. *Id.*

284. *Id.*

to engage for the benefit of SDGTs are not linked to the carrying out of terrorist activity, the proposed activities clearly constitute prohibited services.[285] The Supreme Court has stated that "[o]ne to whose conduct a statute clearly applies may not successfully challenge it for vagueness."[286] In other words, if the statute covers the plaintiff's conduct, a vagueness challenge may not be raised based on its application in some other context.[287]

The Ninth Circuit's decision is consistent with the ruling in *Holder v. Humanitarian Law Project*, where the Supreme Court held that the term "services," as used in the material support statute, is not unconstitutionally vague as applied.[288] The material support statute, 18 U.S.C. § 2339B, makes it a federal crime to "knowingly provide material support or resources to a foreign terrorist organization."[289] The term "material support or resources" is defined to include a ban on the provision of "services" to foreign organizations that engage in terrorist activity.[290] In rejecting HLP's vagueness challenge, the Supreme Court stated that the statute reaches only material support coordinated with or under the direction of a designated foreign terrorist group.[291] Independent advocacy is not covered.[292] Ultimately, the Court held that "a person of ordinary intelligence would understand the term 'service' to cover advocacy performed in coordination with, or at the direction of, a foreign terrorist organization."[293] Thus, the material support statute is not unconstitutionally vague.

E.O. 13224 also prohibits providing "material support" to terrorist acts and SDGTs.[294] However, the term is not defined in the E.O. or in the implementing regulations. In *Al Haramain Islamic v.*

---

285. *Id.* at 1148.

286. *Id.* (quoting Parker v. Levy, 417 U.S. 733, 756 (1974)).

287. *Humanitarian Law Project* v. *U.S. Treasury Dept.*, 578 F.3d at 1148. The court also rejected plaintiff's overbreadth argument. The court stated that the ban imposed by E.O. 13224 is not aimed at speech or conduct necessarily associated with speech, but at stopping aid to terrorists. *Id.* The prohibition of services to terrorist organizations is a legitimate government regulation of constitutionally unprotected conduct, the court concluded. *Id.* "That some particular instances of protected speech may fall within the Executive Order does not make those instances substantial compared to its legitimate scope." *Id.*

288. For a more detailed discussion *See* Holder v. Humanitarian Law Project, 130 S.Ct. 2705 (2010), supra Chapter 7.

289. 18 U.S.C. § 2339B(a)(1).

290. The term "material support or resources" means "any property, tangible or intangible, or service, including currency or monetary instruments or financial securities, financial services, lodging, training, expert advice or assistance, safehouses, false documentation or identification, communications equipment, facilities, weapons, lethal substances, explosives personnel (1 or more individuals who may be or include oneself), and transportation, except medicine or religious materials." 18 U.S.C. § 2339A(b)(1).

291. *Holder v. Humanitarian Law Project*, at 2726.

292. *Id.*

293. *Id.* at 2709–10.

294. E.O. 13224, *supra* note 10, at § 1(d)(i).

U.S. Dept. of Treasury, the district court held that "material support" is unconstitutionally vague both as applied and facially.[295] The Government argued that "material support" should be interpreted in the context of its larger clause, which is to "provide financial, material, or technological support for, or financial or other services. . . ."[296] According to the Government, "material support" means providing support in a way that is similar to providing financial or technological support or services.[297] The district court rejected the Government's argument. Further, the court was unwilling to use the definition of "material support" found in the material support statute, 18 U.S.C. § 2339A(b),[298] or the Immigration and Nationality Act, 8 U.S.C. § 1182(a)(3)(B)(iv)(VI).[299] The court held that the term "material support" is not "sufficiently clear so as not to cause persons 'of common intelligence . . . necessarily [to] guess at its meaning and [to] differ as to its applications'."[300] Accordingly, OFAC was prohibited from basing a designation and blocking order on a theory of "material support."

iv. *Fifth Amendment Taking's Clause*

Blocking orders issued under E.O. 13224 have been challenged as an uncompensated taking, in violation of the Takings Clause of the Fifth Amendment. The Fifth Amendment provides that no "private property [shall] be taken for public use, without just compensation."[301] The federal district courts have dismissed these challenges on two grounds. First, federal district courts lack subject matter jurisdiction over plaintiffs' Fifth Amendment takings claims.[302] The courts maintain that such cases must be brought before the Court of Federal Claims pursuant to the Tucker Act, 28 U.S.C. § 1491.[303] Second, the courts hold that blocking orders issued under E.O. 13224 are temporary deprivations that do not, as a matter of law, constitute takings within the meaning of the Fifth Amendment. Since blocking does not vest the blocked property in the Government, it does not constitute a constitutionally cognizable

---

295. Al Haramain Islamic v. United States Dept. of Treasury, 585 F. Supp.2d 1233, 1269 (D. Or. 2008).

296. *Id.* at 1268 (quoting E.O. 13224, § 1(d)(i)).

297. *Al Haramain Islamic*, 585 F. Supp.2d at 1268.

298. 18 U.S.C. § 2339A(b) (2006).

299. 8 U.S.C. § 1182(a)(3)(B)(iv)(VI).

300. *Al Haramain Islamic*, 585 F. Supp.2d at 1269 (internal citations omitted).

301. U.S. CONST. amend. V.

302. *See* Islamic Am. Relief Agency v. Unidentified FBI Agents., 394 F. Supp.2d 34, 51 (D.D.C. 2005); Holy Land Found. for Relief and Dev. v. Ashcroft, 219 F. Supp.2d 57, 77 (D.D.C. 2002).

303. *See e.g.,* 28 U.S.C. § 1491(a)(1) ("[t]he United States Court of Federal Claims shall have jurisdiction to render judgment upon any claims against the United States founded either upon the Constitution, or any Act of Congress or any regulation of an executive department . . ."); Dames & Moore v. Regan, 453 U.S. 654, 688–89 (1981) (the Court of Federal Claims is the proper forum for claims alleging an unconstitutional taking).

taking.[304] Courts have consistently rejected these claims in the IEEPA and TWEA context.[305]

In *Holy Land Found. for Relief and Dev. v. Ashcroft*, the district rejected plaintiff's claim that OFAC's blocking action violated the Takings Clause of the Fifth Amendment.[306] However, the court stated: "Plaintiff may . . . some day have a credible argument that the long-term blocking order has ripened into a vesting of property into the United States."[307] However, because HLF's assets had only been blocked for eight months, the court concluded that the current deprivation had not reached too far, so as to constitute a taking.[308] Unfortunately, the court offered no guidance regarding how much time is required for a blocking action to ripen into an unconstitutional taking.

e. Religious Freedom Restoration Act

Claims that OFAC designations and blocking orders substantially burden the exercise of religion in violation of the Religious Freedom Restoration Act (RFRA), 42 U.S.C. § 2000bb–1, have been rejected by the court.[309] The RFRA prohibits the Government from placing a "substantial burden" on the exercise of religion "even if the burden results from a rule of general applicability," unless the Government demonstrates a "compelling governmental interest," and used the "least restrictive means" of furthering that interest.[310] In passing the RFRA, Congress expressed its purpose "to restore the compelling interest test . . . and to guarantee it application in all cases where free exercise of religion is substantially burdened."[311]

In *Holy Land Foundation v. Ashcroft*, the D.C. Circuit held that OFAC's blocking action against HLF did not violate the RFRA.[312] The court found that OFAC's designation and blocking order imposed a burden on HLF's ability to raise funds to finance

304. *See Islamic Am. Relief Agency v. Unidentified FBA Agents*, 394 F. Supp.2d at 51; *Holy Land Found. for Relief and Dev. v. Ashcroft*, 219 F. Supp.2d at 78.

305. *See* Propper v. Clark, 337 U.S. 472 (1949) (blocking is not a taking because it is temporary in nature); Tran Qui Than v. Regan, 658 F.2d 1296, 1301 (9th Cir. 1981) (rejecting takings claims because blocking action under TWEA is not equivalent to vesting); *Islamic Am. Relief Agency v. Unidentified FBI Agents*, 394 F. Supp.2d at 51; *Holy Land Found. for Relief and Dev. v. Ashcroft*, 219 F. Supp.2d at 78; Global Relief

Found., Inc. v. O'Neill, 207 F. Supp.2d 779, 801–02 (N.D. Ill. 2002) (finding that IEEPA blocking actions are temporary).

306. *Holy Land Found. for Relief & Dev. v. Ashcroft*, 219 F. Supp.2d at 78.

307. *Id.*

308. *Id.*

309. *See* Holy Land Foundation v. Ashcroft, 333 F.3d 156, 166–67 (D.C. Cir. 2003).

310. 42 U.S.C. § 2000bb–1(a), (b).

311. *Holy Land Foundation v. Ashcroft*, 333 F.3d at 166–67.

312. *Id.* at 167.

Hamas, a designated foreign terrorist organization, not to practice its religion.[313] The court stated:

> No one on behalf of Holy Land Foundation has forwarded the proposition that the fomenting and spread of terrorism is mandated by the religion of Islam.... Acting against the funding of terrorism dos not violate the free exercise rights protected by RFRA and the First Amendment. There is no free exercise right to fund terrorists.[314]

Accordingly, the D.C. Circuit held that HLF's activities do not fall within the RFRA's protection and granted summary judgment for the Government.[315]

313. *Id.*

314. *Id.*

315. *Id.*

Chapter 9
INTERNATIONAL ECONOMIC SANCTIONS

A. INTERNATIONAL COUNTER– TERRORISM RESOLUTIONS

The U.N. Security Council and U.N. General Assembly have adopted several resolutions intended to prevent and suppress acts of terrorism. Shortly after the September 11, 2001 attacks on the World Trade Center and the Pentagon, the U.N. Security Council adopted Resolution 1368, condemning these terrorist acts in the strongest possible terms.[1] Resolution 1368 stressed that terrorism poses a serious threat to international peace and security and called on "all States to work together urgently to bring to justice the perpetrators, organizers, and sponsors of these terrorist attacks."[2] The Security Council's efforts to prevent terrorism and bring terrorists to justice, however, predates the 9/11 attacks. In October 1999, the Security Council adopted Resolution 1267, demanding that the Taliban "cease the provision of sanctuary and training for international terrorists and . . . take appropriate effective measures to ensure that the territory under its control is not used for terrorist installations and camps, or for the preparation or organization of terrorist acts . . . and cooperate with efforts to bring indicted terrorists to justice."[3] In the second paragraph of the resolution the Security Council demanded that the Taliban turn over Usama bin Laden to the appropriate authorities within a country where he will be arrested and prosecuted.[4] Resolution 1267 imposed various anti-terrorism measures on member states, including a travel ban prohibiting states from permitting any aircraft, owned or controlled by the Taliban, to take off or land in their

---

1. S.C. Res. 1368, U.N. Doc. S/RES/ 1368 (Sept. 12th, 2001). Resolution 1368 also suggests that the September 11, 2001 attacks constituted an "armed attack" under principles of international humanitarian law, implicating the inherent right of individual or collective self-defense. *Id.* On a parallel track, on the evening of September 11, 2001, the NATO Council invoked Article 5 of the North Atlantic Treaty, which states that "an armed attack against one or more of the Allies in Europe or North America shall be considered an attack against them all." NATO Press Release (2001) 124, Sept. 12, 2001. *See also An Attack on Us All: NATO's Response to Terrorism* (Oct. 10, 2001), *available at* http:// www.nato.int/cps/en/natolive/opinions.

2. S.C. Res. 1368, ¶ 3 (Sept. 12th, 2001).

3. S.C. Res. 1267, ¶ 1, U.N. Doc. S/RES/1267 (Oct. 15th, 1999).

4. *Id.* at ¶ 2.

territory.[5] Further, the resolution imposed a duty on states to freeze funds and other financial resources owned or controlled by the Taliban.[6]

In December 2000, the Security Council adopted Resolution 1333, demanding that the Taliban comply with Resolution 1267, and, in particular, that they cease providing sanctuary and training camps for international terrorists.[7] Resolution 1333 imposes a weapons ban on states, prohibiting them from supplying, selling and transferring weapons and ammunition, military vehicles and equipment to the Taliban.[8] The resolution also prohibits states from providing military training and technical advice to armed personnel under the control of the Taliban.[9] Further, Resolution 1333 strengthened the asset freeze measure by extending the economic sanctions beyond the members of the Taliban. Under Resolution 1333, states are required to freeze "without delay" the funds and other financial assets of Usama bin Laden, members of al Qaeda and their associates, and ensure that no funds or financial resources are made available to them or any entities owned or controlled by bin Laden, or individuals and entities associated with him, including the al Qaeda organization.[10] Since the 9/11 terrorist attacks, the Security Council has adopted more than a dozen counterterrorism resolutions intended to strengthen the measures imposed under Resolutions 1267 and 1333.[11]

The Security Council resolutions affirm the illegality of all forms of terrorism regardless of their motivation, whenever and by whomever committed. More specifically, Resolution 1526 (2004) reiterated the Council's "unequivocal condemnation of all forms of terrorism and terrorist acts."[12] Further, in Resolution 1566 (2004), the Security Council condemned attacks against civilians intended to intimidate a civilian population, irrespective of their motivation.[13] Resolution 1566 states, in pertinent part:

> [C]riminal acts, including against civilians, committed with the intent to cause death or serious bodily injury, or taking of hostages, with the purpose to provoke a state of terror in the general public or in a group of persons or particular persons, intimidate a population or compel a government or an interna-

5. *Id.* at ¶ 4(a).

6. *Id.* at ¶ 4(b). Resolution 1267 established a Committee of the Security Council consisting of all the members of the Council to oversee the implementation of the Taliban travel ban and asset freeze measures imposed by the resolution.

7. S.C. Res. 1333, U.N. Doc. S/RES/ 1333 (Dec. 19th, 2000).

8. *Id.* at ¶ 5(a).

9. *Id.* at ¶ 5(b).

10. *Id.* at ¶ 8(c).

11. *See infra* note 62, listing the post–9/11 Security Council anti-terrorism resolutions.

12. S.C. Res. 1526, U.N. Doc. S/RES/1526 (January 30th, 2004).

13. S.C. Res. 1566, U.N. Doc. S/RES/1566 (October 8th, 2004).

tional organization to do or to abstain from doing any act, which constitute offences within the scope of and as defined in the international conventions and protocols relating to terrorism, are under no circumstances justifiable by considerations of a political, philosophical, ideological, racial, ethnic, religious or other similar nature....[14]

More recently, in Resolution 1904 (2009), the Security Council reaffirmed that "terrorism in all its forms and manifestations constitutes one of the most serious threats to peace and security and that any acts of terrorism are criminal and unjustifiable regardless of their motivations, whenever and by whomever committed."[15] Thus, there is a strong international consensus that terrorism poses a serious threat to international peace and security and terrorist acts committed for whatever purpose, are condemned and should be punished.

The Security Council has also adopted resolutions intended to prevent nuclear proliferation. Since 2006, the U.N. Security Council has adopted three resolutions intended to stop Iran from acquiring nuclear weapons.[16] The international community fears that if allowed to develop such weapons, Iran would deploy them against Israel or share such weapons and technology with terrorists and terrorist organizations, such as Hizbollah and Hamas.[17] In Resolution 1696, the Security Council demanded that Iran suspend its nuclear enrichment-related and reprocessing activities and called on states to prevent the transfer of any items, materials, goods and technology that could contribute to such activities, including Iran's ballistic missile programs.[18] The last two resolutions imposed limited economic sanctions against Iran, including constraints on Iran's arms exports, restrictions on nuclear trade with Iran, and a ban on financial dealings with individuals and entities involved in Iran's nuclear weapons programs.[19] Resolution 1737 requires governments worldwide "to prevent the provision to Iran of any technical assistance or training, financial assistance, ... and the transfer of financial resources or services, related to the supply, sale, transfer, manufacture, or use of prohibited items, materials, equipment, goods and technology" associated with Iran's nuclear and missile

---

14. *Id.* at ¶ 3.

15. S.C.Res. 1904, U.N. Doc. S/RES/1904 (Dec. 19th 2009).

16. *See* S.C.Res. 1696, U.N. Doc. S/RES/1696 (July 31th, 2006); Sec. Res. 1737, U.N. Doc. S/RES/1737 (Dec. 27, 2006); Sec. Res. 1747, U.N. Doc. S/RES/1747 (Mar. 24th, 2007).

17. See Daniel Benjamin, Coordinator, Office of the Coordinator for Counterterrorism, *Confronting 21st Century*

Terrorism: Challenges for U.S. Policy (May 3rd, 2010), transcription available at http://www.state.gov/s/ct/rls/rm/2010/141443.htm.

18. S.C. Res. 1696, U.N. Doc. S/RES/1696 (July 31st, 2006).

19. *See* Philip H. Gordon, Iran Sanctions and Regional Security, Brookings Institution (Oct. 23rd, 2007), *available at* http://www.brookings.edu/testimony, 2007.

programs.[20] Finally, under Resolutions 1737 and 1747, States are required to freeze the assets of designated individuals and entities providing support for Iran's nuclear proliferation activities.[21]

The U.N. General Assembly has also condemned international terrorism and directed states to undertake various counterterrorism measures. In 2006, the General Assembly adopted Resolution 60/288, which reaffirmed that "acts, methods and practices of terrorism in all its forms and manifestations are activities aimed at the destruction of human rights, fundamental freedoms and democracy, threatening territorial integrity, security of States and destabilizing legitimately constituted Governments, and that the international community should take the necessary steps to enhance cooperation to prevent and combat terrorism."[22] The General Assembly resolution further directs states "to refrain from organizing, instigating, facilitating, participating in, financing, encouraging or tolerating terrorist activities and to take appropriate practical measures to ensure that ... territories are not used for terrorist installations or training camps, or for the preparation or organization of terrorist acts....".[23] Also, Resolution 60/288 calls on member states to become parties to all existing international conventions and protocols against terrorism, and to implement all General Assembly and Security Council resolutions on measures to eliminate international terrorism.[24] Several other anti-terrorism resolutions adopted by the U.N. General Assembly also strongly condemn acts of terrorism.[25]

While General Assembly Resolution 60/288 has no binding legal effect on member states, it reflects a general consensus of the international community that terrorist acts, particularly those involving the killing of innocent civilians, are unlawful regardless of

20. S.C. Res. 1737, ¶ 6, U.N. Doc. S/RES/1737 (Dec. 27th, 2006). *See also* Daniel Glaser, Deputy Assistant Secretary for Terrorist Financing and Financial Crimes, & Adam J. Szubin, Director of the Office of Foreign Assets Control, U.S. Dep't of Treasury, *Isolating Proliferators and Sponsors of Terrorism: The Use of Sanctions and the International Financial System to Change Regime Behavior*, Joint Testimony before the House Foreign Affairs Subcomm. on Terrorism, Nonproliferation, and Trade, and the Financial Services Subcomm. on Domestic and International Monetary Policy, Trade, and Technology, at 5 (Apr. 18, 2007).

21. *See* S.C. Res. 1737, U.N. Doc. S/RES/1737 (Dec. 27th, 2006), at 12; *see also* S.C. Res. 1747, art. 4, U.N. Doc. S/RES/1747 (Mar. 24th, 2007).

22. G.A. Res. 60/288, U.N. Doc. A/RES/60/288 (Sept. 20th, 2006), United Nations Global Counter–Terrorism Strategy.

23. *Id.* at Annex Plan of Action, ¶ II(1).

24. *Id.* at ¶¶ 1(b)–(c).

25. *See, e.g.*, Human Rights and Terrorism, U.N. G.A. Res. 59/195, ¶ 1 (20 December 2004); Protection of Human Rights and Fundamental Freedoms While Countering Terrorism, U.N. G.A. Res. 59/191, preamble (December 20th, 2004); Declaration on Measures to Eliminate International Terrorism, U.N. G.A. Res. 49/60, ¶ 1 (9 December, 1994); U.N. G.A. Res. 46/51, U.N. Doc. A/46/654 (December 9th, 1991).

their motivation. Further, in Resolution 60/288, states agree to cooperate fully in the fight against terrorism, deny terrorists a safe haven and bring terrorists and their sponsors to justice.[26] In short, Resolution 60/288 demonstrates a commitment by the international community to eradicate terrorism and cooperate in achieving that purpose.

Security Council resolutions, on the other hand, are binding on all member states. Under Article 24(1) of the U.N. Charter, the Security Council is delegated the primary responsibility for the maintenance of international peace and security.[27] When carrying out its duties under this responsibility, the Security Council acts on behalf of the members of the United Nations.[28] Once the Security Council determines the existence of any threat to the peace, it then must decide what measures to be taken in accordance with Article 41 (measures not involving the use of armed force) and Article 42 (measures involving the use of armed force) to maintain or restore international peace and security.[29]

Pursuant to Article 25 of the U.N. Charter, member states agree to "accept and carry out the decisions of the Security Council."[30] State compliance with Security Council resolutions is therefore obligatory, not discretionary under the U.N. Charter. Further, pursuant to Article 49, member states are required to cooperate and afford mutual assistance in implementing measures decided

---

26. *See* G.A. Res. 60/288, Annex Plan of Action, ¶ II(1)–(2).

27. U.N. Charter, art. 24(1) provides: "In order to ensure prompt and effective action by the United Nations, its Members confer on the Security Council primary responsibility for the maintenance of international peace and security, and agree that in carrying out its duties under this responsibility the Security Council acts on their behalf."

28. *Id.*

29. Article 39 provides: "The Security Council shall determine the existence of any threat to the peace, breach of the peace, or act of aggression and shall . . . decide what measures shall be taken . . . to maintain or restore international peace and security."

Article 41 provides:

The Security Council may decide what measures not involving the use of armed force are to be employed to give effect to its decisions, and it may call upon the Members of the United Nations to apply such measures. These may include complete or partial interruption of economic relations and of rail, sea, air, postal, telegraphic, radio, and other means of communication, and the severance of diplomatic relations.

Article 42 states:

Should the Security Council consider that measures provided for in Article 41 would be inadequate or have proved inadequate, it may take such action by air, sea, or land forces as may be necessary to maintain or restore international peace and security. Such action may include demonstrations, blockade, and other operations by air, sea, or land forces of Members of the United Nations.

30. U.N. Charter, art. 25. Further, article 48(2) provides that the decisions of the Security Council for the maintenance of international peace and security "shall be carried out by the Members of the United Nations directly and through their action in the appropriate international agencies of which they are members."

upon by the Security Council.[31] Moreover, Security Council resolutions have priority over and trump other international treaty obligations. Article 103 provides that "[i]n the event of a conflict between the obligations of the Members of the United Nations under the present Charter and their obligations under any other international agreement, their obligations under the present Charter shall prevail."[32] Finally, because U.N. Security Council resolutions concern commitments under the U.N. Charter, which is a multilateral treaty, they have the same force in international law as other treaty obligations.[33]

B. INTERNATIONAL COUNTER–TERRORISM TREATIES

The international community has adopted thirteen major multilateral treaties that specifically address the threat of international terrorism.[34] Those conventions prohibit the following: aircraft hijacking; aircraft sabotage; attacks against ships and fixed platforms in the ocean; attacks at airports; violence against officials and diplomats; hostage-taking; theft of nuclear material; use of unmarked plastic explosives; terrorist bombing; and the financing of terrorism.[35]

31. *See* U.N. Charter, art. 49.

32. U.N. Charter, art. 103.

33. The issue of the primacy of actions taken pursuant to U.N. Security Council resolutions was challenged by the European Court of Justice in Kadi and Al Barakaat International Foundation v. Council and Commission, C–402/05 P and C–415/05 P (Sept. 3, 2008). The *Kadi* case is discussed *infra* notes 144–186 and accompanying text.

34. International anti-terrorism treaties include: the Convention of Offenses and Certain Other Acts Committed on Board Aircraft, Sept. 14, 1963, 20 U.S.T. 2941, 704 U.N.T.S. 219; the Convention for the Suppression of Unlawful Seizure of Aircraft, Dec. 16, 1970, 22 U.S.T. 1643, 860 U.N.T.S. 105; the Convention for the Suppression of Unlawful Acts against the safety of civil aviation, Sept. 23, 1971, 24 U.S.T. 564, 974 U.N.T.S. 177; the Convention of the Prevention and Punishment of Crimes against Internationally Protected Persons, Including Diplomatic Agents, Dec. 14, 1973, 28 U.S.T. 1975, 1035 U.N.T.S. 167; the International Convention against the Taking of Hostages, Dec. 14, 1973, 28 U.S.T. 1975, 1035 U.N.T.S. 167; the Convention on the Physical Protection of Nuclear Material, Mar. 3, 1980, T.I.A.S. No. 11080, 1456 U.N.T.S. 101; the Protocol for the Suppression of Unlawful Acts of Violence at Airports Serving International Civil Aviation, Feb. 24, 1988, 1589 U.N.T.S. 474; the Convention for the Suppression of Unlawful Acts against the Safety of Maritime Navigation, Mar. 10, 1988, S. Treaty Doc. No. 101–1, 1678 U.N.T.S. 221; the protocol for the Suppression of Unlawful Acts against the Safety of Fixed Platforms located on the Continental Shelf, Mar. 10, 1988, S. Treaty Doc. No. 110–8, 1678 U.N.T.S. 304; Convention on the Making of Plastic Explosives for the Purpose of Detection, Mar. 1, 1991, S. Treaty Doc. No. 103–8, 2122 U.N.T.S. 359; International Convention for the Suppression of Terrorist Bombings, Dec. 15, 1997, S. Treaty Doc. No. 106–6, 2149 U.N.T.S. 256; International Convention for the Suppression of the Financing of Terrorism, Dec. 9, 1999, T.I.A.S. No. 13075, 2178 U.N.T.S. 229; International Convention for the Suppression of Acts of Nuclear Terrorism, Apr. 13, 2005, 44 I.L.M. 815.

35. *See* JORDAN PAUST, ET AL., INTERNATIONAL CRIMINAL LAW, CASES AND MATERIALS 845 (Carolina Academic Press, 3d ed. 2007).

The counterterrorism conventions seek to prevent and suppress proscribed acts of terrorism by establishing a framework for international cooperation among states. The basic components of the framework require states: (1) to establish as a criminal offense under its domestic law the offense proscribed by the international convention; (2) to make the offense punishable by appropriate penalties which take into account the grave nature of the offense; (3) to take necessary measures to establish its jurisdiction over the proscribed offense; (4) to ensure the presence for purposes of extradition or prosecution of any person who is alleged to have committed such offense and who may be present in its territory; (5) to submit the case without undue delay to its competent authorities for the purpose of prosecution, if it does not extradite an alleged offender present in its territory; (6) to treat the offense proscribed as an extraditable offense in any extradition treaty existing between any of the states parties; and (7) to afford one another the greatest measure of assistance in connection with investigations or criminal or extradition proceedings involving the covered offense, including assistance in obtaining evidence necessary for the proceedings.

This general framework is set forth in each of the counterterrorism conventions, including the International Convention for the Suppression of Terrorist Bombing ("Terrorist Bombing Convention").[36] In 1997, the United Nations General Assembly adopted the Terrorist Bombing Convention.[37] It has been ratified by over 120 countries, including the United States (June 26, 2002).[38] The United States has implemented the Terrorist Bombing Convention in the Terrorist Bombings Convention Implementation Act of 2002.[39] The Terrorist Bombing Convention specifically makes it an offense to bomb public places, a State or government facility, a public transportation system, or an infrastructure facility with the intent to cause death or serious bodily injury or with the intent to cause extensive destruction of such a place, where such destruction results in or is likely to result in major economic loss.[40] A person is

36. International Convention for the Suppression of Terrorist Bombings, G.A. Res. 52/164, U.N. Doc. A/RES/52/164 (Dec. 15th, 1997).

37. *Id.*

38. International Convention for the Suppression of Terrorist Bombings, Dec. 15, 1997, 2149 U.N.T.S. 256, S. Treaty Doc. No. 106–6 (1999).

39. *See* Terrorist Bombings Convention Implementation Act of 2002, Pub. L. No. 107–197, 116 Stat. 721 (2002), enacting 18 U.S.C. § 2339C(f) (making it a federal crime to engage in conduct prohibited by the Terrorist Bombing Convention).

40. Terrorist Bombing Convention, art. 2. Article 2 states in pertinent part:

1. Any person commits an offence within the meaning of this Convention if that person unlawfully and intentionally delivers, places, discharges or detonates an explosive or other lethal device in, into or against a place of public use, a State or government facility, a public transportation system or an infrastructure facility:

criminally liable if he attempts to commit such a crime or participates as an accomplice in such offense.[41] Further, any person who
organizes or directs others to commit such offense is criminally
liable,[42] as well as those persons who in any other way contribute to
the commission of a terrorist bombing by a group of persons acting
with a common purpose.[43] Further, the Terrorist Bombing Convention specifies that such acts are not justifiable by any political,
philosophical, ideological, racial, ethnic, religious, or other similar
considerations.[44]

The Terrorist Bombing Convention imposes various duties and
obligations on states parties to prevent and suppress terrorist
bombing attacks. Article 4 imposes a duty on each state party to
make terrorist bombing a criminal offense under its domestic law
and to make the offense punishable by penalties which take into
account the gravity of the offense.[45] Article 6 authorizes a state
party to exercise extraterritorial jurisdiction over terrorist bombing.[46] Article 6(a) provides that each state party *shall* take such
measures as may be necessary to establish its jurisdiction over the
offense when committed in the territory of that state (territorial
principle) or committed by a national of that state (nationality
principle).[47] Further, each state party *shall* take such measures as
may be necessary to establish its jurisdiction over the offense
"where the alleged offender is present in its territory and it does
not extradite that person to any of the States Parties which have
established jurisdiction" under the treaty (universal principle).[48]
However, a state party *may* establish its jurisdiction over the
offense when committed against a national of that state (passive
personality principle), or a State or government facility of that
State located abroad, including an embassy or other diplomatic or
consular premises of that State (protective principle).[49]

(a) With the intent to cause death or
serious bodily injury; or

(b) With the intent to cause extensive
destruction of such place, facility or
system, where such destruction results in or is likely to result in major
economic loss.

41. Article 2(2) extends criminal liability to persons who attempt to commit an offense set forth in Article 2(1).
Article 2(3)(a) punishes aiders and abettors of a terrorist bombing offense.

42. *Id.* at art. 2(3)(b).

43. *Id.* at art. 2(3)(c). Such contribution must be intentional and either
made with the aim of furthering the
general criminal activity or purpose of
the group or made with knowledge of
the intention of the group to commit the
offense. *Id.*

44. *Id.* at art. 5.

45. *Id.* at art. 4(a)–(b).

46. "The law of nations permits the
exercise of criminal jurisdiction by a nation under five general principles: territorial, national, protective, universality,
and passive personality." JIMMY GURULÉ,
COMPLEX CRIMINAL LITIGATION: PROSECUTING
DRUG ENTERPRISES AND ORGANIZED CRIME,
¶ 9–3 at 453 (Lexis Publ. 2d ed., 2000).

47. *See* Terrorist Bombing Convention, art. 6(1)(a), (c).

48. Art. 6(4).

49. *Id.* art. 6(2)(a)–(b).

A state party in whose territory the offender is present has a duty to arrest or take other appropriate measures to ensure that person's presence for the purpose of prosecution or extradition.[50] Further, Article 8 adopts the customary law principle *aut dedere aut judicare*. If a state party does not extradite the alleged offender, it must submit the case to its competent authorities for the purpose of prosecution.[51] The most important goal of the Terrorist Bombing Convention is to ensure prosecution of the accused. To this end, the convention states, quite strongly, the alternative obligation either to extradite or submit the accused for prosecution.[52] Article 9 makes terrorist bombing an extraditable offense in any existing extradition treaty between any of the state parties. Finally, Article 10 requires states parties to afford one another the "greatest measure of assistance" in connection with an investigation or criminal or extradition proceedings involving terrorist bombing.[53]

Two years after the Terrorist Bombing Convention was adopted by the U.N. General Assembly, the International Convention for the Suppression of the Financing of Terrorism ("Terrorist Financing Convention") was also adopted by the General Assembly.[54] It has been ratified by over 130 countries, including the United States (June 26, 2002).[55] The United States implemented the Terrorist Financing Convention via the Suppression of the Financing of Terrorism Convention Implementation Act of 2002.[56] The Convention makes it an offense to provide or collect funds to finance terrorist acts, including those proscribed in the Terrorist Bombing Convention.[57] The Terrorist Financing Convention imposes the same or similar duties on states parties as those set forth in the Terrorist Bombing Convention.[58]

50. *Id.* art. 7(2).

51. *Id.* art. 8(1).

52. John F. Murphy, *The Future of Multilateralism and Efforts to Combat International Terrorism*, 25 COLUM J. TRANS. L. 35,(1986).

53. *Id.* at art. 10(1).

54. International Convention for the Suppression of the Financing of Terrorism, G.A. Res. 54/109, U.N. Doc. A/RES/54/109 (Dec. 9th, 1999).

55. International Convention for the Suppression of the Financing of Terrorism, Dec. 9th 1999, T.I.A.S. No. 2178 U.N.T.S. 229.

56. *See* 18 U.S.C. § 2339C, discussed *supra* in Chapters 7, at 284–90.

57. Article 2 of the Terrorist Financing Convention states:

1. Any person commits an offence within the meaning of this Convention if that person by any means, directly or indirectly, unlawfully and wilfully, provides or collects funds with the intention that they should be used or in the knowledge that they are to be used, in full or in part, in order to carry out:

(a) An act which constitutes an offence within the scope of and as defined in [the Terrorist Bombing Convention]; or

(b) Any other act intended to cause death or serious bodily injury to a civilian, or to any other person not taking an active part in the hostilities in a situation of armed conflict, when the purpose of such act, by its nature or context, is to intimidate a population, or to compel a Government or an international organization to do or abstain from doing any act.

58. *See* art. 4 (requires states parties to establish terrorist financing as a

C. INTERNATIONAL ASSET FREEZE

The United Nations Security Council has played a central role in the global fight against terrorism. The centerpiece of that effort has been the development by an economic sanctions regime to deprive al Qaeda, the Taliban, and other terrorist organizations of funding and economic resources. An effective anti-terrorist financing regime is critical to successfully combating the threat of terrorism. Freezing terrorist-related assets:

(a) Deters non-designated parties who might otherwise be willing to finance terrorist activity.

(b) Exposes terrorist financing "money trails" that may generate leads to previously unknown terrorist cells and financiers.

(c) Encouraging designated persons to disassociate themselves from terrorist activity and renounce their affiliation with terrorist groups.

(d) Terminates terrorist cash flows by shutting down the pipelines used to move terrorist related funds or other assets.

(e) Forces terrorists to use more costly and higher risk means of financing their activities, which makes them more susceptible to detection and disruption.[59]

However, the economic sanctions regime developed by the Security Council has come under attack, particularly in Europe, for not providing adequate procedural protections for persons whose assets are subject to asset freeze. The apparent lack of due process in Security Council listing and delisting procedures has prompted numerous legal challenges.[60] These legal actions have undermined the effectiveness of the anti-terrorist financing regime. Unless a compromise can be reached to address the due process concerns,

criminal offense under its domestic laws and punish by appropriate penalties); art. 7 (take measures necessary to establish its jurisdiction over the offense); art. 9 (ensure alleged offender's presence for the purpose of prosecution or extradition); art. 10 (submit case to proper authorities for prosecution, if state does not extradite alleged offender); art. 11 (treat terrorist financing as an extraditable offense under existing extradition treaties); and art. 12 (requires state parties to afford one another the greatest measure of assistance in connection with a criminal investigation, or prosecution or extradition proceedings).

59. International Best Practices—Freezing of Terrorist Assets, ¶ 6 (June 23, 2009), *available at* http://www.fatf-gafi.org/dataoecd/30/43/34242709.pdf.

60. *See, e.g.,* Kadi and Al Barakaat Int'l Found. v. Council of the European Union and Commission of the European Comm'n, joined cases C–402/05 P and C–415/05 P (European Court of Justice, 3 September 2008); HM Treasury v. Mohammed Jabar Ahmed, [2010] UKSC 2; Abdelrazik v. Canada (Minister of Foreign Affairs, 2009 FC 580.

the U.N. economic sanctions program to deprive terrorists of funding may collapse.

The international economic sanctions program has its origins in three important Security Council resolutions: 1267, 1333, and 1373.[61] While the Security Council has adopted a number of related resolutions intended to strengthen Resolutions 1267, 1333, and 1373, these three resolutions constitute the cornerstone of the sanctions regime against the financing of terrorism.[62]

1.   U.N. SECURITY COUNCIL RESOLUTIONS 1267 (1999)

Following the terrorist attacks on the U.S. embassies in Nairobi, Kenya, and Dar es Salaam, Tanzania in 1998, the U.N. Security Council demanded that the Taliban, the *de facto* government in Afghanistan, surrender Usama bin Laden to appropriate authorities for prosecution in connection with the embassy bombings.[63] Further, the Security Council demanded that the Taliban close all

61. S.C. Res. 1267, U.N. Doc. S/RES/1276 (Oct. 15th, 1999), S.C. Res. 1333, U.N. Doc. S/RES/1333 (Dec. 19th, 2000), and S.C. Res. 1373, U.N. Doc. S/RES/1373 (Sept. 28th, 2001).

62. The Security Council resolutions adopted to strengthen and enhance the measures imposed under Resolutions 1267 and 1333 include: S.C. Res. 1390, U.N. Doc. S/RES/1390 (Jan. 28th, 2002) (expanding the financial embargo); S.C. Res. 1452, U.N. Doc. S/RES/1452 (Dec. 20th, 2002) (recognizing humanitarian exemptions to asset freeze); S.C. Res. 1455, U.N. Doc. S/RES/1455 (Aug. 15th, 2003) (requesting updated reports from States on implementation of measures imposed by Resolutions 1267 and 1333); S.C. Res. 1526 (Jan. 30th, 2004) (creating an Analytical Support and Sanctions Monitoring Team); S.C. Res. 1617, U.N. Doc. S/RES/1617 (July 29th, 2005) (providing a definition of "associated with" and requiring member states to provide a statement of the case when submitting names for the Consolidated List); S.C. Res. 1699, S/RES/1699 (Aug. 8th, 2006) (requests the Secretary General to take steps to increase cooperation between U.N. and Interpol); S.C. Res.1730, U.N. Doc. S/RES/1730 (Dec. 19th, 2006) (establishing "focal point" to handle delisting requests); S.C. Res. 1735, U.N. Doc. S/RES/1735 (Dec. 22nd, 2006) (providing for a "cover sheet" to be used when proposing names for listing, requiring notification of those listed, and establishing formal delisting criteria); S.C. Res. 1822, U.N. Doc. S/RES/1822 (Jun. 30th, 2008) (requires the posting on the 1267 Committee's website of narrative summaries explaining the bases for each designation and calls for a comprehensive review of all the names on the Consolidated List); and S.C. Res. 1904, U.N. Doc. S/RES/1904 (Dec. 17th, 2009) (creates an "Ombudsperson" to receive delisting requests from designated parties and to assist the 1267 Committee in considering these requests).

The Security Council Resolutions relevant to Resolution 1373 (Sept. 28th, 2001) include: S.C. Res. 1535, U.N. Doc. S/RES/1535 (Mar. 26th, 2004) (creating the Counter–Terrorism Committee Executive Directorate (CTED)); S.C. Res. 1566, U.N. Doc. S/RES/1566 (Oct. 8th, 2004) (creating a working group); S.C. Res. 1624, U.N. Doc. S/RES/1624 (Sept. 14th, 2005) (prohibiting the incitement to commit acts of terrorism); S.C. Res. 1631, U.N. Doc. S/RES/ 1631 (Oct. 7th, 2005) (encouraging enhanced cooperation between U.N. and regional and subregional organizations); S.C. Res. 1787, U.N. Doc. S/RES/1787 (Dec. 10th, 2007) (extending the mandate of the CTED); and S.C. Res. 1805, U.N. Doc. S/RES/ 1805 (Mar. 20th, 2008) (extending the CTED's mandate until Dec. 31, 2010).

63. *See* S.C. Res. 1214, ¶ 13, U.N. Doc. S/RES/1214 (Dec. 8th, 1998). The discussion of Resolution 1267 is taken in part from Jimmy Gurulé Unfunding Terror: The Legal Response to the Financing of Global Terrorism (Edward Elgar 2008) at 237–38 [herein after "Unfunding Terror"].

terrorist training camps and stop providing sanctuary for members of al Qaeda.[64] After the Taliban ignored all requests for cooperation, the Security Council unanimously adopted Resolution 1267, which imposed various obligations on member states, including a travel ban involving aircraft owned, leased or operated by or on behalf of the Taliban and a duty to freeze the funds and other financial resources owned or controlled by the Taliban.[65] Paragraph 4(b) required states to "[f]reeze funds and other financial resources, including funds derived or generated from property owned or controlled directly or indirectly by the Taliban, or by any undertaking owned or controlled by the Taliban, as designed by the Committee" established by Resolution 1267.[66]

Resolution 1267 created a committee, known as the Al–Qaida and Taliban Sanctions Committee ("Sanctions Committee"), consisting of all the members of the Security Council, to monitor action taken by member states to implement the measures imposed by the Security Council and to submit periodic reports to the Council on the impact of the measures imposed by the resolution.[67] Further, the Sanctions Committee was delegated the responsibility for designating individuals and entities for asset freeze under paragraph 4(b) of the Resolution.[68] Initially, the Committee's mandate was limited to the Taliban, but was extended to include Usama bin Laden, al Qaeda, and their associates by Resolutions 1333 and 1390.[69]

In 2004, to strengthen the mandate of the Sanctions Committee, the Security Council established an eight-person Analytical Support and Sanctions Monitoring Team ("Monitoring Team").[70] The Monitoring Team, which operates under the direction of the Sanctions Committee, was initially mandated to monitor and make recommendations on implementation of the measures imposed by Resolution 1267.[71] The group was further tasked with submitting independent reports to the Sanctions Committee on implementation by states of the measures imposed by Resolution 1267, including recommendations for improved implementation and possible new measures.[72]

64. *Id.*

65. *See* S.C. Res. 1267, ¶¶ 4(a), (b), U.N. Doc. S/RES/1267 (Oct. 15th, 1999).

66. *Id.* at ¶ 4(b).

67. *See* S.C. Res. 1267, ¶ 6. The Committee was initially known as the "1267 Committee." However, in September 2003, it was officially titled the "Al–Qaida and Taliban Sanctions Committee." *See* U.N. Doc. SC/7865 (Sept. 4, 2003). *See also* Al–Qaida and Taliban Sanctions Committee, *available at* http://

www.un.org/sc/committees/1267/index.shtml.

68. *See* S.C. Res. 1267, ¶ 6(e), U.N. Doc. S/RES/1267 (Oct.15th, 1999).

69. S.C. Res. 1333, U.N. Doc. S/RES/1333 (Dec.19th, 2000) and S.C. Res. 1390, U.N. Doc. S/RES/1390 (Jan. 28th, 2002).

70. *See* S.C. Res. 1526, ¶¶ 6–7., U.N. Doc. S/RES/1526 (Jan. 30th, 2004).

71. *Id.*

72. *Id.* at ¶ 8. To date, the Monitoring Team has submitted a total of ten

2. U.N. SECURITY COUNCIL RESOLUTION 1333 (2000)

On October 12, 2000, al Qaeda launched an attack against the USS Cole, docked in Aden, Yemen, killing 17 American sailors and wounding at least 40 others.[73] In response to the attack and other terrorist activities by al Qaeda, the Security Council adopted Resolution 1333.[74] Resolution 1333 extends beyond the Taliban, imposing sanctions on individuals and non-State entities, requiring states to "freeze without delay" the funds and other financial assets of Usama bin Laden and individuals and entities "associated with" him.[75] The purpose of the asset freeze provision is to deprive bin Laden and al Qaeda of funding by isolating them and their associates from the international financial community.[76]

The duty to freeze assets has since been expanded to require States to freeze the "economic resources" of Usama bin Laden, al Qaeda and the Taliban.[77] States are required to freeze non-monetary assets such as real estate, vehicles, aircraft, ships, equipment, precious stones, and other personal property owned or controlled by designated individuals and entities.[78] Further, Resolution 1333

reports to the Al–Qaida and Taliban Sanctions Committee. *See generally* TENTH REPORT OF THE ANALYTICAL SUPPORT AND SANCTIONS MONITORING TEAM, U.N. Doc. S/2009/502 (Oct. 2nd, 2009).

73. *See* THE NATIONAL COMMISSION ON TERRORIST ATTACKS, THE 9/11 COMMISSION REPORT: FINAL REPORT OF THE NATIONAL COMMISSION ON TERRORIST ATTACKS UPON THE UNITED STATES 190 (W.W. Norton & Company 2004), *available at* http://www.9–11commission,gov/report/911Report.pdf [hereinafter 911 COMMISSION REPORT].

74. *See* S.C. Res. 1333, U.N. Doc. S/RES/1333 (Dec. 19th, 2000). The discussion of Resolution 1333 is taken in part from Unfunding Terror, supra note 63, at 239.

75. Paragraph 8(c) of Security Council Resolution 1333 requires all States to take measures:

> To freeze without delay funds and other financial assets of Usama bin Laden and individuals and entities associated with him as designated by the Committee, including those in the Al–Qaida organization, and including funds derived or generated from property owned or controlled directly or indirectly by Usama bin Laden and

individuals and entities associated with him, and to ensure that neither they nor any other funds or financial resources are made available, by their nationals or by any persons within their territory, directly or indirectly for the benefit of Usama bin Laden, his associates or any entities owned or controlled, directly or indirectly, by Usama bin Laden or individuals and entities associated with him including the Al–Qaida organization and requests the Committee to maintain an updated list . . . of individuals and entities designated as being associated with Usama bin Laden, including those in the Al–Qaida organization.

76. Resolution 1333 also imposes a travel ban on any aircraft designated by the Al–Qaida and Taliban Sanctions Committee as being under Taliban control. *Id.* at ¶ 11. Resolution 1333 also prohibits providing weapons and military training, technical advice and assistance to the Taliban. *See id.* at ¶¶ 5(a)–(b).

77. *See* S.C. Res. 1617, ¶ 1, U.N. Doc. S/RES/1617 (July 29th, 2005).

78. *See* U.N. SECURITY COUNCIL, ANALYTICAL SUPPORT AND SANCTIONS MONITORING TEAM, SEVENTH REPORT OF THE SANCTIONS MONITORING TEAM, ¶¶ 82, 84, U.N. Doc.

broadened the scope of the duty to freeze terrorist assets and economic resources. Under the resolution, states are not only required to freeze the assets and financial resources of Usama bin Laden, members of al Qaeda and the Taliban, but individuals and entities "associated with" them.[79] Activities that indicate that an individual or group is "associated with" bin Laden, al Qaeda and the Taliban include:

(a) participating in the financing, planning, facilitating, preparing, or perpetrating of acts or activities by, in conjunction with, under the name of, on behalf of, or in support of;

(b) supplying, selling or transferring arms and related material to;

(c) recruiting for; or

(d) otherwise supporting acts or activities of;

al Qaeda, bin Laden, or the Taliban, or any cell, affiliate, or splinter group.[80]

Paragraph 8(c) of Resolution 1333 requires the Sanctions Committee established pursuant to Resolution 1267 "to [establish and] maintain an updated list, based on information provided by States and regional organizations, of the individuals and entities designated as being associated with Usama bin Laden, including those in the Al–Qaida organization."[81] Resolution 1333 encourages States to submit to the Sanctions Committee the names of individuals and entities associated with bin Laden and al Qaeda (including members of the Taliban) for designation and placement on a list, referred to as the "Consolidated List."[82] After inclusion on the List, states are required to "freeze without delay" the funds and other financial assets and economic resources of those individuals and entities.[83]

3.   U.N. SECURITY COUNCIL RESOLUTION 1373 (2001)

a.   Overview

In the aftermath of the 9/11 terrorist attacks, the U.N. Security Council unanimously adopted Resolution 1373, which imposes several important duties on member states to combat the threat of international terrorism.[84] Pursuant to Resolution 1373, States are

S/2007/677 (Nov. 29th, 2007), *available at* http://www.un.org/sc/committees/1267/monitoringteam.shtml [hereinafter SEVENTH REPORT OF THE SANCTIONS MONITORING TEAM].

79.   *See* S.C. Res. 1333, ¶ 8(c), U.N. Doc. S/RES/1333 (Dec. 19th, 2000).

80.   S.C. Res. 1617, ¶ 2. The definition of "associated with" was reaffirmed

by the Security Council in 2008. *See* S.C. Res. 1822, ¶ 2, U.N. Doc. S/RES/1822, (2008).

81.   *Id.* at ¶ 8(c).

82.   *Id.*

83.   *Id.*

84.   S.C. Res. 1373, U.N. Doc. S/RES/1373 (Sept. 28th, 2001). The dis-

required to prevent the movement of terrorists by effective border controls and controls on the issuance of travel documents (travel ban),[85] to prevent the supply of weapons to terrorists (arms embargo),[86] and to deny safe haven to those who plan, support or commit terrorist acts (safe haven ban).[87] Further, Resolution 1373 imposes various duties on states to prevent and suppress the financing of terrorism.[88] First, states are required to criminalize the wilful provision and collection of terrorist-related funds.[89] Second, states must ensure that any person who finances terrorist acts is criminally prosecuted.[90] Third, states must prohibit persons and entities from making financial assets, economic resources and financial services available to terrorists.[91] Finally, Resolution 1373 authorizes states to "freeze without delay funds and other financial assets or economic resources" of terrorists, terrorist organizations and their financial sponsors.[92]

Unlike Resolutions 1267 and 1333, Resolution 1373 is not limited to freezing the financial assets and economic resources of bin Laden, al Qaeda, the Taliban, and individuals and entities associated with them, but extends to other terrorists and terrorist organizations. For example, "Resolution 1373 authorizes States to freeze the assets of HAMAS, Hizballah, the Liberation Tigers of Tamil Elam (LTTE), the Revolutionary Armed Forces of Colombia (FARC), and other terrorist groups not controlled by al Qaeda, bin Laden, and the Taliban."[93] Resolution 1373 differs from Resolutions 1267 and 1333 in two other important respects. First, Resolution 1373 does not create a list of terrorist organizations, individuals and entities subject to asset freeze. While States are obliged to freeze the funds, financial assets and other economic resources of persons and entities involved in the commission of terrorist acts, Resolution 1373 does not require that their names be placed on a U.N. administered list.[94] The Consolidated List created by Resolution 1333, targeting bin Laden, al Qaeda, the Taliban, and individuals and entities associated with them, is the only U.N.-administered terrorist-financing list.[95] Second, the Counter–Terrorism Committee (CTC) created to oversee the implementation of measures imposed

cussion of Resolution 1373 is taken in part from Unfunding Terror, supra note 63, at 238–240.

85. *Id.* at ¶ 2(g).

86. *Id.* at ¶ 2(a).

87. *Id.* at ¶ 2(c). *See also* ALISTAIR MILLAR & ERIC ROSAND, ALLIED AGAINST TERRORISM 16 (Century Foundation Press 2006).

88. S.C. Res. 1373, ¶ 1(a) (Sept. 28th, 2001).

89. *Id.* at ¶ 1(b).

90. *Id.* at ¶ 2(e).

91. *Id.* at ¶ 1(d).

92. *Id.* at ¶ 1(c).

93. Unfunding Terror, supra note 63, at 239.

94. *Id. See also* S.C. Res. 1373, U.N. Doc. S/RES/1373 (Sept. 28th, 2001).

95. *See* UNFUNDING TERROR, at 239.

by Resolution 1373is not a sanctions body.[96] The CTC is not responsible for designating individuals and entities for asset freeze.

b. Designation Under Resolution 1373

Under Resolution 1373, a decision to freeze the assets of suspected terrorists takes place on two levels. First, a competent *national* authority decides whether certain assets should be frozen pursuant to paragraph 1(c) of the Resolution. Second, other States must then decide, in the exercise of their discretion, whether to impose an asset freeze on the party concerned. The CTC does not decide who should be designated for asset freeze. Because asset freeze is a preventive measure, rather than punishment for the commission of a crime, the criminal standard of proof beyond a reasonable doubt does not apply. To comply with Resolution 1373, assets should be frozen based on "reasonable grounds, or a reasonable basis, to suspect or believe that such funds or other assets could be used to finance terrorist activity."[97]

c. Designation Under Resolutions 1267 and 1333

Designation under Resolutions 1267 and 1333 involves a two-step process: "(1) Member States submit the names of persons and entities for inclusion on the Consolidated List to the Al–Qaida and Taliban Sanctions Committee, and (2) the Committee reviews the submissions and makes a final determination on whether to add the names to the List."[98] All names on the Consolidated List have been submitted to the Committee by member states for designation and asset freeze.[99] When proposing names for inclusion on the Consolidated List, states are required to use the Cover Sheet for Member State Submission to the Committee ("Cover Sheet"), attached to the Guidelines of the Committee for the Conduct of Its Work ("Committee Guidelines").[100] The Cover Sheet, which was created

---

96. S.C. Res. 1373, ¶ 6. The Security Council established the CTC to monitor implementation of the duties imposed on Member States by Resolution 1373. One of the CTC's most important functions is to help States get the technical assistance needed to implement the provisions of Resolution 1373. *See* UN-FUNDING TERROR, at 241.

97. Interpretive Note to FATF Special Recommendation III: Freezing and Confiscating Terrorist Assets, ¶ 2 [hereinafter INSR III].

98. UNFUNDING TERROR, at 243 (discussing the designation process). The Consolidated List of individuals and entities associated with al Qaeda and the Taliban has been characterized as the

"cornerstone" of the Al–Qaida and Taliban sanctions regime. *See* U.N. SECURITY COUNCIL, ANALYTICAL SUPPORT AND SANCTIONS MONITORING TEAM, TENTH REPORT OF THE SANCTIONS MONITORING TEAM, ¶ 10, U.N. Doc. S/2009/502 (Oct. 2nd, 2009) [hereinafter TENTH REPORT OF THE MONITORING TEAM].

99. *See* S.C. Res. 1735, ¶ 8, U.N. Doc. S/RES/1735 (Dec. 22nd, 2006) (directing the Committee to encourage States to submit names for inclusion on the Consolidated List).

100. Guidelines of the Committee for the conduct of its work (amended on Dec. 9, 2008), *available at* http://www.un.org/sc/committees/1267/pdf/1267_guidelines.pdf.

by Resolution 1735, is intended to simplify the designation process and enhance the quality of the identifier information submitted with state proposals for designation.[101] For individuals, states are required to include in their submissions: "family name/surname, given names, other relevant names, date of birth, place of birth, nationality/citizenship, gender, aliases, employment/occupation, residence, passport or travel document and national identification number, current and previous addresses, website addresses, and current location."[102] For entities, the following identifier information should be provided: "name, acronyms, address, headquarters, subsidiaries, affiliates, fronts, nature of business or activity, leadership, tax or other identification number and other names by which it is known or was formerly known" and website address.[103] If the identifier information is found to be insufficient, the Committee retains discretion to request additional information or refuse to approve the designation until additional identifier information is provided.

i.   Statement of the Case

The Committee Guidelines require states to provide a "statement of the case" with their submissions that establishes the justification for the designation and asset freeze. The "statement of the case" should provide as much information as possible for listing, including:

(1) specific findings demonstrating the association or activities alleged;

(2) the nature of the supporting evidence (e.g., intelligence, law enforcement, judicial, media, admission by subject, etc.);

(3) supporting evidence or documents that can be supplied . . . [and]

(4) the details of any connection with a currently listed individual or entity.[104]

States are also required to indicate to the Committee what portions of the statement of the case may be released to the public or other member states.[105]

101. S.C. Res.1735, ¶ 8, U.N. Doc. S/RES/1735 (Dec. 22nd, 2006). S.C. Res. 1735 was updated by S.C. Res. 1822, ¶ 14, U.N. Doc. S/RES/1822 (June 30th, 2008).

102. Al–Qaida and Taliban Sanctions Committee, Guidelines of the Committee for the Conduct of Its Work (adopted Nov. 7, 2002, as amended most recently on Feb. 12, 2007), ¶ 6(e), *available at* http://www.un.org/sc/committees/1267/pdf/1267_guidelines.pdf [hereinafter Guidelines of the Committee].

103. *Id.*

104. *Id.* at ¶ 6(d).

105. *See* S.C. Res. 1822, ¶ 12, S/RES/1822, (June 30th, 2008).

Asset freeze is a preventative measure intended to deprive terrorists of funding, rather than punish the owner for the commission of a crime.[106] Thus, the criminal standard of proof beyond a reasonable doubt does not apply. Instead, the standard for asset freeze is whether there are "reasonable grounds" or a "reasonable basis" to believe that the person or entity meets the criteria for designation under the relevant resolution.[107]

ii. Final Determination by the Committee

Once a state submits a name for designation and asset freeze, it is circulated to all fifteen members of the Al–Qaida and Taliban Sanctions Committee for their consideration. The members of the Committee have five working days to raise any objection.[108] If there is no objection, the designation is approved. The decision to designate an individual or entity is made by consensus of the Sanction Committee members.[109] All U.N. Member States are thereafter required to "freeze without delay" any assets or economic resources owned or controlled by the designated party.[110] States should notify appropriate authorities, government agencies, and financial institutions within their respective jurisdictions so that action can be taken to implement the freeze order "without delay," which ideally means within a few hours of a designation by the Al–Qaida and Taliban Sanctions Committee.[111] Obviously, any delay between the publication of the notice to freeze assets and implementation of that order affords the listed party an opportunity to conceal the funds and avoid the financial sanctions. Further, the

---

106. *See* Al–Qaida and Taliban Sanctions Committee, Fact Sheet on Listing, *available at* http://www.un.org/sc/committees/1267/fact_ sheet_ listing. shtml [hereinafter Fact Sheet on Listing]. *See also* FATF, The Interpretative Notes to the Special Recommendations on Terrorist Financing, Interpretive Note to Special Recommendation III: Freezing and Confiscating Terrorist Assets, ¶ 2 (Oct. 3, 2003), *available at* http://www.fatf-gafi.org/dataoecd/53/32/34262136.pdf. [hereinafter Interpretive Note to Special Recommendation III].

107. *See* Interpretive Note to Special Recommendation III, *supra* note 44, ¶¶ 2, 6; *see also* International Best Practices—Freezing of Terrorist Assets, ¶ 7(b) (June 23, 2009), *available at* http://www.fatf-gafi.org/dataoeced/30/43/34242709.pdf.

108. *See* Guidelines of the Committee, *supra* note 100, ¶ 4(b).

109. *Id.* at ¶ 4(a).

110. *See* Interpretive Note to Special Recommendation III, *supra* note at 44, ¶ 6, which provides:

> The term *freeze* means to prohibit the transfer, conversion, disposition or movement of funds or other assets on the basis of, and for the duration of the validity of, an action initiated by a competent authority or a court under a freezing mechanism. The frozen funds or other assets remain the property of the person(s)or entity(ies) that held an interest in the specialized funds or other assets at the time of the freezing and may continue to be administered by the financial institution or other arrangements designated by such person(s) or entity(ies) prior to the initiation of an action under a freezing mechanism. (emphasis added).

111. *See* Interpretive Note to Special Recommendation III, *supra* note 44, ¶ 47.

duty to freeze assets and refrain from engaging in financial transactions with designated parties is an ongoing obligation. Therefore, for example, when opening a new account, banks should check the name of the new customer against the names on the Consolidated List. As of May 11, 2010, there were 511 entries on the List:137 individuals associated with the Taliban, and 258 individuals and 103 entities associated with al Qaeda.[112] Finally, the Committee is required to periodically review all names on the Consolidated List in order to ensure that it is as updated and accurate as possible and to confirm that the listing remains appropriate.[113]

iii. Notice of Designation

After a name is added to the Consolidated List, the Committee is required to make accessible on its website a narrative summary of the reasons for listing the individual or entity.[114] However, the narrative summary does not provide information that the designating state regards as classified or privileged.[115] The purpose of the narrative summary is to notify the listed parties of the reasons for designation. Further, after publication, but within one week after a name is added to the Consolidated List, the Secretariat is required to notify the Permanent Mission of the country where the individual or entity is believed to be located, and the country of which the person is a national.[116] Such member states are thereafter required, in accordance with their domestic laws and practices, to notify in timely manner the listed individual or entity of the designation and include with this notification a copy of the portion of the statement of the case that may be released to the public, any reasons for listing available on the Committee's website, as well as a description of the effects of designation, the procedures for considering delisting requests, and provisions regarding available exemptions.[117]

iv. Delisting Process

Security Council Resolution 1735 establishes formal criteria for delisting. When determining whether to remove names from the Consolidated List, the Sanctions Committee may consider, among other things: "(i) whether the individual or entity was placed on

---

112. *See* TENTH REPORT OF THE SANCTIONS MONITORING TEAM, *supra* note 72, ¶ 11.

113. See S.C. Res. 1822, ¶ 25, U.N. Doc. S/RES/1822, (June 30th, 2008).

114. *Id.* at ¶ 13. Drafts of the narrative summaries are prepared by the Monitoring Team but must be approved by the designating State before submission to the Committee for publication. *See* U.N. Security Council, *Analytical Support and Sanctions Monitoring*

Team, Ninth Report of the Analytical Support and Sanctions Monitoring Team, ¶ 50, U.N. Doc. S/2009/245 (May 13, 2009) [hereinafter *Ninth Report of the Sanctions Monitoring Team].*

115. *See Ninth Report of the Sanctions Monitoring Team,* ¶ 51.

116. *See* S.C. Res. 1735, ¶ 10, S/RES/1735, (Dec. 22nd, 2006).

117. *See* S.C. Res. 1822, ¶ 17, U.N. Doc. S/RES/1822, (June 30th, 2008).

the Consolidated List due to a mistake of identity; or (ii) whether the individual or entity no longer meets the criteria set out in the relevant resolutions."[118] In deciding whether to grant a petition for delisting, the Committee members may consider whether the individual or entity has severed all association with al Qaeda, Usama bin Laden, the Taliban, and their supporters.[119] A petition for delisting must be submitted to the Office of the Ombudsperson.[120] The Ombudsperson serves as an intermediary between the designated party, the members of the Al–Qaida and Taliban Sanctions Committee, designating states, the state of residence and nationality or incorporation, relevant United Nations bodies, and any other states deemed relevant by the Ombudsperson.[121]

v. Information Gathering Period

The Ombudsperson forwards the delisting request to the Monitoring Team. Within two months, the Monitoring Team is required to provide the Ombudsperson, with the following:

(a) All information available to the Monitoring Team that is relevant to the delisting request, including court decisions and proceedings, news reports, and information that States or relevant international organizations have previously shared with the Committee or Monitoring Team.

(b) Fact-based assessments of the information provided by the petitioner that is relevant to the delisting request; and,

(c) Questions or requests for clarifications that the Monitoring Team would like asked of the petitioner regarding the delisting request.[122]

At the end of the two-month information gathering period, the Ombudsperson is required to submit a written report to the Committee on the progress to date.[123]

vi. Dialogue Period

Upon completion of the information gathering period, the Ombudsperson engages in a two-month period of engagement with the petitioner.[124] During this period of engagement, the Ombudsper-

118. S.C. Res. 1735, ¶ 14, U.N. Doc. S/RES/1735, (Dec. 22nd, 2006).

119. *Id.*

120. *See* S.C. Res. 1904, ¶ 20, U.N. Doc. S/RES/1904, Annex II, ¶ 1 (Dec. 17th, 2009). The Office of the Ombudsperson was created by Resolution 1904.

121. *Id.* at ¶ 2.

122. *Id.* at ¶ 3.

123. *Id.* at ¶ 4. The period for submitting the progress report to the Com-

mittee once for up to two months if the Ombudsperson determines that more time is needed for information gathering. *Id.*

124. *Id.* at ¶ 5. The two-month engagement period may also be once for up to two months based on an assessment by the Ombudsperson that more time is required for engagement and drafting the Comprehensive Report to the Committee. *Id.*

son may seek additional information from the petitioner that may assist or facilitate the Committee's consideration of the delisting request. Further, the Ombudsperson forwards to the petitioner any questions or information requests received from relevant states, the Committee and the Monitoring Team.[125] In turn, the Ombudsperson forwards replies from the petitioner back to the relevant states, the Committee and the Monitoring Team, and coordinates any further inquiries of, or responses to, the petitioner.[126] Upon the completion of the engagement period, the Ombudsperson is required to submit to the Sanctions Committee a Comprehensive Report that summarizes and specifies the sources of all information available to the Ombudsperson that is relevant to the delisting request.[127] The report also describes the Ombudsperson's activities with respect to the delisting requst, including dialogue with the petitioner, and based on an analysis of all relevant information available to the Ombudsperson, sets forth the principal arguments concerning the petition for delisting.[128]

vii.   Decision by the Sanctions Committee

After the Sanctions Committee has had thirty days to review the Comprehensive Report, the matter is placed on the Committee's agenda for consideration.[129] When the Committee considers the delisting request, the Ombudsperson, aided by the Monitoring Team, is required to present the Comprehensive Report in person and answer any questions by the Committee members regarding the request.[130] The Sanctions Committee is required to decide whether to grant the delisting request within two months. If the petition for delisting is granted, the Committee informs the Ombudsperson of its decision. The Ombudsman shall then inform the petitioner of this decision and remove the designation from the Consolidated List. If, on the other hand, the Sanctions Committee denies the delisting request, the Committee will convey its decision to the Ombudsperson, including "explanatory comments, any further relevant information about the Committee's decision, and an updated narrative summary of the reasons for the listing."[131] Finally, after the Committee has informed the Ombudsperson of its decision denying the delisting request, the Ombudsperson is required to send the petitioner, within fifteen days, a letter that:

(a) Communicates the Committee's decision for continued listing;

125. *Id.* at ¶ 6(a).
126. *Id.* at ¶¶ 6(b)–(c).
127. *Id.* at ¶ 7(a).
128. *Id.* at ¶¶ 7(b)–(c).
129. *Id.* at ¶ 8.
130. *Id.* at ¶ 9.
131. *Id.* at ¶ 12.

(b) Describes, to the extent possible and drawing upon the Ombudsperson's Comprehensive Report, the process and publicly releasable factual information gathered by the Ombudsperson; and,

(c) Forwards from the Committee all information about the decision provided to the Ombudsperson [by the Sanctions Committee for rejecting the delisting request].[132]

viii. Humanitarian Exception

Resolution 1452 recognizes a humanitarian exception to the freezing of assets necessary to cover basic living expenses such as food, housing, public utilities, medicines and medical treatment, and reasonable professional fees, including legal fees.[133] In *Ayadi v. Council of the European Union,* the Court of First Instance interpreted the humanitarian exception to prohibit asset freeze of "any kind of funds or economic resources ... for the carrying on of employed or self-employed professional activities and the funds received or receivable in connection with such activity."[134] More specifically, the Court found that granting the applicant a taxi-driver's license, permitting him to use his car for business purposes, and allowing him to keep the receipts produced by working as a taxi driver were properly exempted from asset freeze under the humanitarian exception.[135]

d. Legal Challenges to the U.N. Sanctions Regime

Despite improvements to the listing and delisting process, there are continuing concerns regarding the lack of procedural protections afforded designated parties.[136] In 2006, a comprehensive report on "Targeted Sanctions and Due Process" was published by Bardo Fassbender of Humboldt University, Berlin, Germany.[137] The

---

132. *Id.* at ¶¶ 13(a)–(c).

133. S.C. Res. 1452, *supra* note 2, ¶ 1(a). Resolution 1452 exempts funds, financial assets and economic resources needed to pay

basic expenses, including payments for foodstuffs, rent or mortgage, medicines and medical treatment, taxes, insurance premiums, and public utility charges, or exclusively for payment of reasonable professional fees and reimbursement of incurred expenses associated with the provision of legal services, or fees or service charges for routine holding or maintenance of frozen funds or other financial assets or economic resources.... *Id.*

134. Case T–253/02, Ayadi v. Council of the E.R., 2006 ECR II–2139, ¶ 130.

135. *Id.* at ¶ 131.

136. *See* Strengthening Targeted Sanctions Through Fair and Clear Procedures, Watson Institute Targeted Sanctions Project, 9–23 (Providence: Watson Institute for International Studies, Brown University, March 2006), *available at* http://www.watsoninstitute.org/pub/Strengthening_Targeted_Sanctions.pdf.

137. Bardo Fassbender, *Targeted Sanctions and Due Process: The responsibility of the UN Security Council to ensure that fair and clear procedures are made available to individuals and entities targeted with sanctions under Chapter VII of the UN Charter* (Study commissioned by the UN Office of Legal Affairs, Office of the Legal Counsel,

report was commissioned by the Office of Legal Counsel of the UN Office of Legal Affairs.[138] In the case of sanctions imposed on individuals and entities pursuant to Security Council resolutions, Fassbender maintains that international due process should include the following:

(a) the right of a person or entity against whom measures have been taken to be informed about those measures by the Council, as soon as this is possible without thwarting their purpose;

(b) the right of such a person or entity to be heard by the Council, or a subsidiary body, within a reasonable time;

(c) the right of such a person or entity of being advised and represented in his or her dealings with the Council;

(d) the right of such a person or entity to an effective remedy against an individual measure before an impartial institution of body previously established.[139]

According to Fassbender, the procedures adopted by the 1267 Sanctions Committee do not afford designated parties adequate due process. Fassbender states:

Individuals or entities are not granted a hearing by the Council or a committee. The de-listing procedures presently being in force place great emphasis on the States particularly involved ("the original designating government" which proposed the listing, and "the petitioned government" to which a petition for de-listing was submitted by an individual or entity) resolving the matter by negotiation. Whether the respective committee, or the Security Council itself, grants a de-listing request is entirely within the committee's or the Council's discretion; no legal rules exist that would oblige the committee or the Council to grant a request if specific conditions are met.[140]

The UN Special Rapporteur on the Promotion and Protection of Human Rights and Fundamental Freedoms While Countering Terrorism has also expressed serious concerns about the lack of due process protections. In August 2006, the Special Rapporteur submitted a report to the UN General Assembly criticizing the lack of effective judicial review of decisions to freeze terrorist-related assets.[141] More specifically, the Special Rapporteur complained that individuals and entities whose assets are frozen pursuant to Securi-

Humboldt University of Berlin, Germany (March 2006)), *available at* http://www.un.org/law/counsel/Fassbender_study.pdf. [hereinafter *Targeted Sanctions and Due Process*].

138. *Id.*

139. *Id.* at 8, 28.

140. *Id.* at 4.

141. *See* UN General Assembly, Report of the Special Rapporteur [Martin Scheinin] on the Promotion and Protection of Human Rights and Fundamental Freedoms while Countering Terrorism, A/61/267, New York, 16 August 2006, ¶ 40.

ty Council Resolutions 1267 and 1333 are not afforded a hearing before an independent and impartial tribunal to challenge the asset freeze order.[142] Other commentators have also expressed deep reservations regarding the absence of fundamental due process protections.[143]

i.   The Kadi Decision

In September 2008, the European Court of Justice (ECJ)—the highest court in the European Union (EU)—delivered a devastating blow to the United Nations sanctions program to deprive terrorists of funding and other financial resources. In *Kadi and Al Barakaat International Foundation v. Council of the European Union,* the ECJ ruled that the EU's application of UN economic sanctions against Yassin Kadi, a wealthy Saudi businessman, and Al Barakaat International Foundation, a money remitter based in Sweden, violated their basic rights, and held the action illegal under EU law.[144] Although the judgment applies only to these two parties, the ruling of the ECJ has far-reaching implications, not only of the EU but also the entire anti-terrorist financing sanctions regime. According to Richard Barrett, coordinator of the UN's Al–Qaida and Taliban Monitoring Team, without the support of the twenty-seven EU member states, the UN sanctions regime may collapse.[145]

In *Kadi and Al Barakaat International Foundation v. Council of the European Union,* the ECJ reversed a lower court ruling of the European Court of First Instance (CFI), which had rejected the legal challenges raised by Kadi and Al Barakaat.[146] The CFI upheld the EU procedures adopted to implement Resolutions 1267 and 1333, granting substantial deference to actions taken by the Security Council to freeze terrorist-related assets.[147] In the lower court's view, measures adopted by the Security Council acting under Chapter VII of the UN Charter are binding on Member States, including the EC. The ECJ reversed, annulling the EC regulations, holding that such measures violated fundamental rights protected by the

---

142. *Id.*

143. *See, e.g.,* Iain Cameron, The European Convention on Human Rights, Due Process and United Nations Security Council Counter–Terrorism Sanctions (report prepared by Professor Iain Cameron for the European Council on Human Rights, Council of Europe, 6 February 2006)).

144. *See* Joined Cases C–402/05 P and C–415/05 P, Kadi and Al Barakaat Int'l Found. v. Council of the European Union and Comm'n of the E.C. (E.C.J. Judgment), Sept. 3, 2008, *available at* http://curia.europa.eu/en/content/juris/

index.htm [hereinafter *Kadi and Al Barakaat (ECJ)*].

145. *See* RICHARD BARRETT, *Al–Qaeda and Taliban Sanctions Threatened,* The Washington Institute of Near East Policy (Oct. 6, 2008).

146. *Kadi and Al Barakaat (ECJ), supra* note 144.

147. *See* Case T–306/01, Yusuf and Al Barakaat Int'l Found. v. Council of the E.U, 2005 E.C.R. II–3533; and Case T–315/01, Kadi v. Council & Comm'n, 2005 E.C.R. II–3649 [hereinafter the *Kadi (CFI)*].

EC legal order.[148] The ECJ granted virtually no deference to decisions by the Security Council, holding that the implementing measures violated general principles of EC law, which rank at the top of the EC's normative hierarchy.[149] According to the ECJ, if measures adopted by the Security Council conflict with principles of EC law, the latter prevails.[150]

Kadi and Al Barakaat brought actions before the CFI seeking annulment of an EC regulation that automatically applied financial sanctions to any individual or entity placed on the UN Consolidated List.[151] The parties maintained that the regulations infringed on their fundamental rights, including the right of notice and a fair hearing.[152] The applicants further complained that the sanctions constituted an unjustified restriction on their right to property.[153] The CFI rejected all the pleas raised by Kadi and Al Barakaat and upheld the validity of the EC measures.[154] In so doing, the CFI ruled that in accordance with customary international law and Article 103 of the UN Charter, the obligations of member states under the Charter prevail over every other obligation of domestic or international treaty law, including those imposed under EC treaties.[155] This principle was characterized as the "rule of primacy," which the CFI stated extends to measures imposed by Security Council resolutions.[156] In support of its position, the CFI stressed that in accordance with Article 25 of the UN Charter, member states "agree to

---

148. *Kadi and Al Barakaat (ECJ),* at ¶¶ 348–49.

149. *Id.* at ¶ 282.

150. *Id.*

151. *See Kadi (CFI), supra* note 147. The CFI opinions in *Kadi* and *Al Barakaat* discuss many of the same issues and the legal analysis is essentially identical. I discuss here only the issues raised in the *Kadi* case, although it was subsequently joined with *Al Barakaat* on appeal to the ECJ.

Regulation (EC) No. 881/2002 orders EU member states to freeze the funds and other economic resources of persons and entities designated by the 1267 Sanctions Committee and listed in Annex I to that Regulation. *See* Council Regulation (EC) No. 881/2002, art. 2 (May 27, 2002). However, practice has varied with EU member states as to whether to implement their obligations under Security Council Resolutions 1267, 1333, and related resolutions by relying on Regulation 881 alone or by enacting domestic legislation which runs in parallel with the Regulation. *See* HM Treasury v. Ahmed, [2010] UKSC 2, ¶ 22.

152. *See* Case T–315/01, Kadi v. Council & Comm'n, 2005 E.C.R. II–3649 at ¶ 190.

153. *Id.* at ¶ 284.

154. *Id.* at ¶¶ 303, 321, 330, 346.

155. *Id.* at ¶¶ 231–33. Under Article 27 of the Vienna Convention on the Law of Treaties, "a party may not invoke the provisions of its internal law as justification for its failure to performs a treaty." *Id.* at ¶ 232. The rule of primacy is expressly set forth in Article 103 of the U.N. Charter, which provides:

> In the event of a conflict between the obligations of the Members of the United Nations under the present Charter and their obligations under any other international agreement, their obligations under the present Charter shall prevail.

The CFI posited that all treaties, regional, bilateral, and multilateral, are subject to the provisions of Article 103 of the U.N. Charter. *Id.* at ¶ 233.

156. *Kadi,* 2005 E.C.R. II–3649, at ¶¶ 232, 234.

accept and carry out the decisions of the Security Council."[157] The CFI further noted that pursuant to Article 307 of the EC Treaty, rights and obligations arising from international agreements previously entered into by member states of the EU are not affected by the provisions of the Treaty.[158] In other words, the EC Treaty does not trump or override the duties of member states imposed under previously entered into international agreements.[159]

The CFI stated that even though the EC itself is not directly bound by the UN Charter, it is *indirectly* bound by those obligations in the same way as its member states, by virtue of provisions of the EC Treaty.[160] The CFI reasoned that when member states entered into the Treaty establishing the European Economic Community, they were bound by their obligations under the UN Charter.[161] The duty to fulfill their obligations under the UN Charter is made clear by Article 224 of the EC Treaty. Article 224 provides:

> Member States shall consult with each other with a view to taking together the steps needed to prevent the functioning of the common market being affected by measures which a Member State may be called upon to take . . . in order to carry out obligations it has accepted for the purpose of maintaining peace and international security.[162]

The CFI stated that by conferring those powers on the Community, the EC member states demonstrated their willingness to be bound by the obligations entered into by them under the UN Charter.[163] Following this reasoning, the CFI concluded:

> first, that the Community may not infringe the obligations imposed on its Member States by the Charter of the United Nations or impede their performance and, second, that in the exercise of its powers it is bound, by the very Treaty by which it was established, to adopt all the measures necessary to enable its Member States to fulfill those obligations.[164]

Having established that the Community was required to give effect to the Security Council resolutions concerned, the CFI proceeded to define the scope of its review. Applicants argued that the

---

157. Art. 25, U.N. Charter.

158. *Kadi,* 2005 E.C.R. II–3649, at ¶ 235. Article 307 of the EC Treaty states:

> The rights and obligations arising from agreements concluded before 1 January 1958 or, for acceding States, before the date of their accession, between one or more Member States on the one hand, and one or more third countries on the other, shall not be affected by the provisions of this Treaty.

159. *Kadi,* 2005 E.C.R. II–3649, at ¶ 235.

160. *Id.* at ¶¶ 242–43.

161. *Id.* at ¶ 244.

162. Art. 224 of the EC Treaty.

163. *Kadi,* 2005 E.C.R. II–3649, at ¶ 250.

164. *Id.* at ¶ 254.

CFI should annul the contested regulation on the ground that the act infringes their fundamental rights.[165] The Council of the EU and Commission of the EC asked the CFI to decline all jurisdiction to undertake such review of the lawfulness of those resolutions.[166] In the alternative, they maintained that the CFI's review should be confined to ascertaining whether the rules and procedural requirements and jurisdiction imposed on the Community institutions were observed and whether the Community measures at issue were appropriate and proportionate in relation to the Security Council resolutions which they were designed to implement.[167] The CFI was reluctant to second guess the actions taken by the Security Council, acting through the Al–Qaida and Taliban Sanctions Committee, to freeze the assets of Kadi and Al Barakaat. The CFI noted that the resolutions at issue were adopted under Chapter VII of the UN Charter, which authorizes the Security Council *alone* to determine what constitutes a threat to international peace and security and the measures required to confront such a threat.[168] Moreover, the freeze orders were measures undertaken to implement those resolutions and binding on members of the United Nations, in accordance with Article 48 of the Charter.[169] The CFI held that the claim that it has jurisdiction to review indirectly the lawfulness of such a decision based on a violation of fundamental rights as recognized by the Community legal order, cannot be justified either on principles of international law or Community law.[170] Such jurisdiction would be incompatible with Articles 25, 48, and 103 of the U.N. Charter, as well as Article 27 of the Vienna Convention on the Law of Treaties.[171] The CFI held that "the resolutions of the Security Council at issue fall, in principle, outside the ambit of the Court's judicial review and that the Court has no authority to call in question, even indirectly, their lawfulness in the light of Community law."[172] However, the CFI did not completely defer to the authority of the

165. *Id.* at ¶ 267.

166. *Id.* at ¶ 268.

167. *Id.*

168. *Id.* at ¶ 270. Article 39 of the U.N. Charter provides:

> The Security Council shall determine the existence of any threat to the peace, breach of the peace, or act of aggression and shall make recommendations, or decide what measures shall be taken in accordance with Articles 41 and 42, to maintain of restore international peace and security.

169. *Kadi,* at ¶ 271. Article 48 provides:

1. The action required to carry out the decisions of the Security Council for the maintenance of international peace and security shall be taken by all the Members of the United Nations or by some of them, as the Security Council may determine.

2. Such decisions shall be carried out by the members of the United Nations directly and through their action in the appropriate international agencies of which they are members.

170. *Kadi,* at ¶ 272.

171. *Id.* at ¶ 273. The Court further opined that exercising such jurisdiction would be contrary to Articles 5, 19, and 297 of the EC Treatry. *Id.* at ¶ 274.

172. *Id.* at ¶ 276.

Security Council. The Court stated that it retained jurisdiction to review measures adopted by the Security Council to determine whether they violated peremptory norms of international law known as *jus cogens,* which are binding on all persons, and from which derogation is prohibited.[173] Such principles are further binding on the members of the United Nations and its bodies.[174]

With respect to the right of property, the CFI stated that only an arbitrary deprivation of that right may be regarded as contrary to *jus cogens.*[175] Ultimately, the Court found that Kadi had not been arbitrarily deprived of his right to property.[176] The CFI also rejected Kadi's claim of a breach of his right to be heard. The Court stated that the limitation of the applicant's right to access to a court is "justified both by the nature of the decisions that the Security Council is led to take under Chapter VII of the Charter of the United Nations and by the legitimate objective pursued."[177] Moreover, the question of whether an individual or entity poses a threat to international peace and security "entails a political assessment and value judgments which in principle fall within the exclusive competence of the authority to which the international community has entrusted primary responsibility for the maintenance of international peace and security."[178] In short, the CFI asserted that it would be impossible to conduct such a judicial hearing without trespassing on the Security Council's prerogatives under Chapter VII of the UN Charter in relation to determining whether the targeted individual or entity poses a threat to international peace and security.[179]

Kadi and Al Barakaat appealed the judgments of the CFI to the European Court of Justice.[180] The ECJ rejected the CFI's view that the contested regulation, since designed to give effect to a resolution adopted by the Security Council under Chapter VII of the U.N. Charter, could not be subject to judicial review, except with regard to its compatibility with the norms of *jus cogens.*[181] The ECJ stated:

> [T]he Community is based on the rule of law, inasmuch as neither its Member States nor its institutions can avoid review of the conformity of their acts with the basic constitutional charter, the EC Treaty, which established a complete system of

173. *Id.* at ¶ 277.
174. *Id.* at ¶ 280. *See also* Article 24(2) of the U.N. Charter, which provides that when discharging its duties for the maintenance of international peace and security, the Security Council must act "in accordance with the Purposes and Principles of the United Nations."
175. *Kadi,* at ¶ 293.

176. *Id.* at ¶ 294.
177. *Id.* at ¶ 344.
178. *Id.* at ¶ 339.
179. *Id.*
180. *Kadi and Al Barakaat (ECJ), supra* note 144.
181. *Id.* at ¶ 327.

legal remedies and procedures designed to enable the Court of Justice to review the legality of acts of the institutions.[182]

According to the ECJ, not only do EC courts have jurisdiction to review actions taken to implement measures by the Security Council, they are obliged to do so, in order to ensure that such actions conform with the EC Treaty. The review of any Community measure by the Court must be considered to be an expression of a constitutional guarantee stemming from the EC Treaty as "an autonomous legal system which is not to be prejudiced by an international agreement."[183] The ECJ declared that "the obligations imposed by an international agreement cannot have the effect of prejudicing the constitutional principles of the EC Treaty."[184] Thus, if the EC court finds that a contested regulation designed to give effect to a Security Council resolution offends the EC Treaty, such regulation must be annulled even if that results in noncompliance by EC Member States with measures adopted by the Security Council under Chapter VII of the U.N. Charter. While a judgment annulling a Council regulation intended to implement a Security Council resolution would not necessarily constitute a review of the lawfulness of such resolution, it would have the effect of blocking its implementation and thereby infringing on the rule of primacy. The ECJ also held that the inclusion of the appellants' names on the EU list of persons and entities whose funds are to be frozen violated the rights of defense, in particular the right to be heard and right to an effective judicial review.[185] Finally, the ECJ concluded that the freezing of funds belonging to Kadi and Al Barakaat constituted an unjustified restriction on the right to property.[186]

ii. Decisions Post–Kadi and Al Barakaat International Foundation

The ECJ is not alone in finding that the procedures for listing and delisting administered by the 1267 Sanctions Committee are incompatible with international due process principles. In *Abdelrazik v. The Minister of Foreign Affairs*, the Federal Court of Canada held that the procedures for imposing sanctions under Security Council Resolutions 1267 and 1333 violated the applicant's rights under the Canadian Charter of Rights and Freedoms.[187] Judge Zinn stated:

182. *Id.* at ¶ 281.
183. *Id.* at ¶ 316.
184. *Id.* at ¶ 285.
185. *Id.* at ¶ 348.
186. *Id.* at ¶ 370. *See also* Case T–318/01, Othman v. Council of the European Union (June 11, 2009) (following Kadi and Al Barakaat (ECJ), the Court of First Instance struck down an order freezing the assets of radical Muslim cleric Abu Qatada, also known as Omar Mohammed Othman, holding that his fundamental rights had been breached).

187. Abdelrazik v. Canada (Minister of Foreign Affairs), 2009 FC 580, [2010] 1 F.C.R. 267.

I add my name to those who view the 1267 Committee regime as a denial of basic legal remedies and as untenable under the principles of international human rights. There is nothing in the listing or delisting procedure that recognizes the principles of natural justice or that provides for basic procedural fairness.... It can hardly be said that the 1267 Committee process meets the requirements of independence and impartiality when ... the nation requesting the listing is one of the members of the body that decides whether to list or, equally as important, to de-list a person. The accuser is also the judge.[188]

In *Her Majesty's (HM) Treasury v. Ahmed*, the UK Supreme Court quashed two executive orders issued by HM Treasury to implement sanctions imposed under Security Council Resolutions 1267,1333 and successor resolutions.[189] The case concerns the legality of Terrorism (United Nations Measures) Order 2006 (TO) and Al–Qaida and Taliban (United Nations Measures) Order 2006 (AQO).[190] The TO and AQO were issued by HM Treasury pursuant to § 1 of the United Nations Act of 1946, which authorizes the making of such Orders in Council as are "necessary or expedient" to give effect to UN Security Council resolutions.[191] Section 1 of the 1946 Act enables Orders to be made by the executive without any Parliamentary scrutiny.[192] The Orders were made to give effect to the resolutions of the Security Council which were designed to suppress and prevent the financing of terrorism.[193] They provide for the freezing of the funds, economic resources and financial services available to persons and entities who have been designated.[194]

The Court found that the freezing measures under the TO and AQO imposed severe limitations on the ability of designated parties to deal with their property.[195] Further, designation under the relevant resolutions have an extremely grave effect upon their freedom of movement.[196] The Court held that the legislative history of the

---

188. *Id.* at ¶ 51.

189. HM Treasury v. Ahmed [2010] UKSC 2. In order to give effect to Security Council Resolutions 1267 and 1333 within the European Community, the Council adopted Regulation (EC) No 881/2002 ordering the freezing of the funds and other economic resources of the persons and entities whose names appear on a list annexed to the Regulation. Reports of the member states to the 1267 Committee indicate that eleven of the 27 EU member states appear to have relied on Regulation 881 alone to authorize freezing the assets of individuals and entities on the Consolidated List. However, the remaining sixteen members, including the United Kingdom have adopted their own domestic legislative measures which run parallel with the Regulation. *Id.* at ¶ 22.

190. *Id.* at ¶ 4.

191. *Id.* at ¶ 12.

192. *Id.* at ¶ 5.

193. HM Treasury v. Ahmed [2010] UKSC 2, at ¶¶ 25, 27.

194. The TO was issued to give effect to Resolutions 1373 (2001) and 1452 (2002). *Id.* at ¶ 25. The AQO was intended to implement sanctions imposed pursuant to Resolutions 1267 and 1333. *Id.* at ¶ 29.

195. *Id.* at ¶ 60.

196. *Id.*

United Nations Act of 1946 demonstrates that Parliament did not intend that the Act should be used to authorize such coercive measures that interfere fundamental rights.[197] Further, the Court held that the TO should be quashed as *ultra vires*.[198] The Court reasoned that the relevant Security Council resolutions did not address the standard of proof for imposing asset freezes. By introducing a test of "reasonable suspicion" to the TO, the Court ruled that the Treasury exceeded the power conferred by § 1 of the 1946 Act.[199]

The *Ahmed* Court also struck down the AQO, but for different reasons. The Court held that the AQO is *ultra vires* and unlawful by virtue of § 6(1) of the Human Rights Act of 1998 because it deprives designated parties an effective judicial remedy to challenge a listing by the 1267 Committee.[200] According to the Court, the listing system administered by the Sanctions Committee is incompatible with the fundamental right that there should be an opportunity for a review by an independent and impartial tribunal. The Court held "What [appellant] needs if he is to be afforded an effective remedy is a means of subjecting that listing to judicial review. This is something that, under the system that the 1267 Committee currently operates, is denied to him."[201] Ultimately, the Court ruled that the AQO is *ultra vires* because § 1 of the 1946 Act does not give authority for overriding such fundamental rights.[202]

e.   *U.N. Security Council Options*

The central criticism of the 1267 sanctions regime is that it deprives listed parties of an effective judicial remedy.[203] The critics maintain that individuals and entities whose names are placed on the Consolidated List should be afforded an opportunity to challenge the decision to have their assets frozen before an independent and impartial tribunal.[204] Further, the failure to provide to an effective legal remedy violates guarantees of fundamental human rights.[205] However, the defenders of the current system maintain

197. *Id.* at ¶¶ 16, 44.

198. *Id.* at ¶ 83.

199. *Ahmed,* at ¶¶ 58–61.

200. *Id.* at ¶ 81.

201. *Id.*

202. *Id.* at ¶ 76.

203. *See Targeted Sanction and Due Process, supra* note 137; *see also Kadi and Al Barakaat (EJC), supra* note 144.

204. *See e.g., HM Treasury v. Ahmed* [2010] UKSC 2, at ¶ 81; *Abdelra-zik v. Canada (Minister of Foreign Affairs,* 2009 FC 580 at ¶ 51 [2010].

205. *See* European Convention for the Protection of Human Rights and Fundamental Freedoms, art. 6 (guaranteeing the right to an effective judicial remedy). *See also* Universal Declaration of Human Rights, art. 8 ("Everyone has the right to an effective remedy by the competent national tribunals for acts violating the fundamental rights granted him by the constitution or by law."); International Covenant of Civil and Political Rights, art. 14 ("everyone shall be entitled to a fair and public hearing by a

that an independent judicial review would interfere with the Security Council's mandate under Chapter VII of the UN Charter.[206] Pursuant to Article 39, the Security Council "shall determine the existence of any threat to the peace, breach of the peace, or act of aggression, or decide what measures shall be taken . . . to maintain or restore international peace and security."[207] Under the UN Charter, member states have delegated the responsibility for maintaining international peace and security to the Security Council. For an independent body to overturn a decision of the Security Council undertaken pursuant to Chapter VII would interfere with the Council's mandate.[208] Another problem is how relevant national security information might be handled. Much of the information about terrorists and terrorist groups is obtained from intelligence agencies, and few jurisdictions around the world would permit such sensitive information to be disclosed to designated parties for fear that it would end up in the hands of terrorists.[209] According to the UN Sanctions Monitoring Team: "States will be reluctant to allow foreign nationals, however well qualified, access to their secret information, and they will be even more reluctant to allow them to examine the likely veracity of the sources."[210]

In response to the legal challenges to and criticisms of the designation process, the UN Security Council adopted Resolution 1904, creating an "Ombudsperson" to receive delisting requests and assist the Committee in considering such requests.[211] The Ombudsman is to deal with requests for delisting in accordance with specific procedures outlined in an annex to the resolution.[212] While these improvements are to be welcomed, any recommendations made by the Ombudsperson are not binding on the Sanctions Committee. Further, the designated party is still denied a formal hearing before the Sanctions Committee or independent body.[213] Thus, listed individuals and entities are still deprived of an oppor-

competent, independent and impartial tribunal established by law").

206. *See* Richard Barrett, *Al–Qaeda and Taliban Sanctions Threatened,* The Washington Institute of Near East Policy (Oct. 6, 2008); TENTH REPORT OF THE ANALYTICAL SUPPORT AND SANCTIONS MONITORING TEAM, S/2009/502, ¶ 45 (Oct. 2, 2009) (a review body outside of the Security Council could erode the authority of the Security Council).

207. UN Charter, art. 39.

208. *See* Richard Barrett, *Al–Qaeda and Taliban Sanctions Threatened,* The Washington Institute for Near East Policy (Oct. 6, 2008) ("it is impossible to imagine [the Security Council] permitting an independent body to overturn its

decisions"). Richard Barrett is the coordinator of the UN's Al–Qaida and Taliban Analytical Support and Sanctions Monitoring Team.

209. *Id.*

210. TENTH REPORT OF THE ANALYTICAL SUPPORT AND SANCTIONS MONITORING TEAM, S/2009/502, ¶ 45 (Oct. 2, 2009).

211. *See* S.C. Res. 1904, ¶ 20, U.N. Doc. S/RES/1904 (2009).

212. *Id.* at ¶ 21.

213. *See* TENTH REPORT OF THE ANALYTICAL SUPPORT AND SANCTIONS MONITORING TEAM, S/2009/502, ¶ 46 (Oct. 2, 2009) ("such a mechanism is unlikely to satisfy calls for effective and independent judicial review").

tunity to appear before an independent and impartial tribunal to challenge the designation and asset freeze orders.[214]

The legal controversy over the procedural protections afforded parties placed on the Consolidated List seriously threatens the future of the UN sanctions regime. Although the *Kadi* and *Al Barakaat* judgment applies to only those two parties, the ruling has far-reaching consequences. Unless the twenty-seven EU member states find a way to implement Security Council Resolutions 1267 and 1333 in a manner that satisfies the EU courts, the UN sanctions regime may collapse.[215] Further, *Kadi* and *Al Barakaat International Foundation* create an untenable situation for EU member states, requiring them to choose between implementing measures imposed by relevant Security Council resolutions or following the ECJ decision. The UN sanctions process has further been complicated by recent court decisions in *HM Treasury v. Ahmed* and *Abdelrazik v. Canada (Minister of Foreign Affairs).*[216] Following these court rulings, both the UK and Canada face serious legal hurdles to the implementation of UN anti-terrorist financing sanctions. Finally, leaving the matter unresolved will have deleterious effects. States will be reluctant to submit names for listing and freeze the assets of individuals and entities designated by the Sanctions Committee out of concern that such actions may be illegal or lead to legal challenges.[217] Ultimately, non-compliance by member states will lead to the demise of the UN sanctions regime to deprive terrorists of funding.

214. *See HM Treasury v. Ahmed* [2010] UKSC 2, at ¶ 78 (the creation of an Ombudsman to assist the 1267 Committee in handling delisting requests does not afford designated parties an effective judicial remedy). Several other options have been proposed for the creation of an effective legal review mechanism, such as an advisory panel of independent, impartial and judicial qualified persons to review delisting decisions. *See George A. Lopez, David Cortright, Alistair Millar, and Linda Gerber–Stellingwerf, Overdue Process: Protecting Human Rights while Sanctioning Alleged Terrorists,* A report to Cordaid from the Fourth Freedom Forum and Kroc Institute for International Peace Studies, University of Notre Dame (April 2009). The review panel members would be appointed by the Security Council upon

nomination by the Secretary–General and would render opinions on delisting requests. *Id.* However, it is highly unlikely that the Security Council would be willing to surrender its Chapter VII authority to or allow its decisions to be second-guessed by such a panel. *See* Richard Barrett, *Al–Qaida and Taliban Sanctions Threatened,* The Washington Institute for Near East Policy (Oct. 6, 2008).

215. *See Al–Qaida and Taliban Sanctions Threatened.*

216. *See* HM Treasury v. Ahmed [2010] UKSC 2; Abdelrazik v. Minister of Foreign Affairs, 2009 FC 580, 81 [2010].

217. *See Protecting Human Rights while Sanctioning Alleged Terrorists, supra* note 138, at 6.

Part IV
CIVIL CAUSES OF ACTION

Chapter 10

CIVIL LIABILITY—PRIVATE ACTIONS AGAINST TERRORISTS AND THEIR SPONSORS

Congress has enacted several statutes authorizing civil liability for personal injury or death caused by acts of international terrorism. The civil statutes include the Antiterrorism Act ("ATA"),[1] Alien Tort Claims Act ("ATCA"),[2] Torture Victim Protection Act ("TVPA"),[3] and the state-sponsored terrorism exception to the Foreign Sovereign Immunities Act ("FSIA").[4] Civil lawsuits filed under these statutes advance numerous important goals. First, the civil actions benefit the victims of terrorism by affording them the remedies of American tort law, including the recovery of damages, attorney's fees and court costs.[5] If terrorists or their financial sponsors have assets within the United States, victims of terrorism will have the power to seize them. Second, civil terrorism lawsuits suits can be effective in deterring and preventing acts of terrorism.[6] While the prospect of large civil monetary judgments may have

---

1. This discussion is taken in part from Jimmy Gurulé Unfunding Terror: The Legal Response to the Financing of Global Terrorism, 324-69 (Edward Elgar 2008), [hereinafter Unfunding Terror]. Sections 2331 and 2333 were initially enacted as the Antiterrorism Act of 1990, Pub. L. No. 101–519, § 132, 104 Stat. 2240, 2250 (1990). However, these sections were subsequently repealed and re-enacted as part of the Federal Courts Administration Act of 1992, Pub. L. No. 102–572, § 1003, 106 Stat. 4506 (1992).

2. 28 U.S.C. § 1350. The ATCA is also referred to as the Alien Tort Statute ("ATS").

3. Torture Victim Protection Act of 1991, Pub. L. No. 102–256, § 2(a)(1)–(2), 106 Stat. 73 (1992), codified in 28 U.S.C. § 1350 note § 2(a).

4. 28 U.S.C. § 1605A(a).

5. Boim v. Quranic Literacy Inst. & Holy Land Found. (*Boim I*), 291 F.3d 1000, 1010 (7th Cir. 2002). The judicial procedural history of the *Boim* case is set forth *infra*, note 49.

6. *See* 136 Cong. Rec. S4568–01, at S4593 (1990) (statement of Sen. Grassley) ("With the enactment of this legislation [the ATA], we set an example to the world of how the United States legal system deals with terrorists. If terrorists have assets within our jurisdictional reach, American citizens will have the power to seize them."); Antiterrorism Act of 1990: Hearing Before the Subcomm. on Courts and Administrative Practice of Comm. on the Judiciary, 101st Cong., 2d Sess. 79 (1990) [hereinafter *Senate Hearing*] (Statement of Joseph Morris) ("[A]nything that could be done to deter ... money laundering in the United States, the repose of assets in the United States ... would not only help benefit victims, but would also help deter terrorism."). *See also* Boim v. Holy Land Found. (*Boim III*), 549 F.3d 685, 691 (7th Cir. 2008) (*en banc*) ("'[civil] suits against financiers of terrorism can cut the terrorists lifeline'").

little or no deterrent value for the actual perpetrators of terrorist attacks, the same may not be true for individuals, organizations, and businesses engaged in secondary conduct, such as providing financial and logistical support or other resources to foreign terrorist organizations.[7] Such individuals and entities residing and conducting business in the United States are more likely to have assets and economic resources that could be attached pursuant to a civil judgment.[8] Attachment of those assets could make it extremely costly to provide material support and resources to terrorists and terrorist groups. Even the possibility of civil damages could act as a disincentive to supporting terrorism.[9] At a minimum, such civil actions " 'may deter terrorist groups from maintaining assets in the United States, from benefitting from investments in the U.S. and from soliciting funds within the U.S.' "[10]

Finally, money is the "lifeblood" of terrorists.[11] Terrorist organizations cannot successfully implement their deadly agenda without adequate financial resources.[12] Disrupting terrorist financial networks is essential to prevent terrorism. Cutting off the flow of money to terrorists can "disrupt their short-term operations and while undermining their long-term capabilities."[13] Civil lawsuits "serve an invaluable role in supplementing the traditional criminal law process and helping to facilitate government efforts to bankrupt foreign terrorist organizations."[14] Such actions empower pri-

---

7. *Boim III,* 549 F.3d at 690 ("Damages are a less effective remedy against terrorists and their organizations than against their financial angels.").

8. *See* Note, *The Antiterrorism Act of 1990: Bringing International Terrorists to Justice the American Way,* 15 SUFFOLK TRANSNAT'L L.J. 726, 743 (1992) [hereinafter *Bringing International Terrorists to Justice*] ("The organizations, businesses, and nations that support, train, and supply the terrorists and actually husband the financial assets are the entities which victims most often need to pursue.").

9. *See Senate Hearing, supra* note 6, at 79 (Statement of Joseph Morris) ("[A]nything that could be done to deter ... money laundering in the United States, the repose of assets in the United States, and so on, would not only help benefit victims, but would also help deter terrorism.").

10. *Boim I,* 291 F.3d at 1012 (quoting *Senate Hearing, supra* note 6, at 17) (Statement of Alex Kreczko, Deputy Legal Advisor, Dep't of State).

11. NATIONAL STRATEGY FOR COMBATING TERRORISM 17 (2003), *available at* http://www.cia.gov/news-information/cia-the-war-on-terrorism/counter_terrorism_strategy.pdf.

12. Unfunding Terror, supra note 1, at 21.

13. *Id.* at 21. *See also* NATIONAL COMMISSION ON TERRORIST ATTACKS, THE 9/11 COMMISSION REPORT: FINAL REPORT OF THE NATIONAL COMMISSION ON TERRORIST ATTACKS UPON THE UNITED STATES, 382 (W.W. Norton & Company 2004), *available at* http://www.9–11commission.gov/report/911Report.pdf [hereinafter THE 9/11 COMMISSION REPORT] ("The government has recognized that information about terrorist money helps us to understand their networks, search them out, and disrupt their operations.").

14. John D. Shipman, *Taking Terrorism to Court: A Legal Examination of the New Front in the War on Terrorism,* 86 N.C. L. REV. 526, 529 (2008). *See also* Halberstam v. Welch, 705 F.2d 472, 489 (D.C. Cir. 1983) (discussing the important role of civil suits in bankrupting terrorist organizations).

vate citizens to aid in combating terrorism.[15] As one commentator observed: "[T]he time has come for private citizens to enter the battle on civil grounds through lawsuits aimed at crippling terrorist organizations at their foundation."[16]

A. SUING NON–STATE SPONSORS OF TERRORISM

1. ANTITERRORISM ACT

a. Statutory Overview

The Antiterrorism Act affords civil remedies to United States nationals and their estates, survivors, and heirs for injuries suffered by reason of an act of "international terrorism."[17] The ATA permits "any national of the United States . . . [injured by reason of] an act of international terrorism . . . [to] sue . . . in any appropriate district court of the United States."[18] By enacting the ATA, Congress intended to deter and punish acts of international terrorism by "remov[ing] the jurisdictional hurdles . . . and . . . empower[ing] victims with all the weapons available in civil litigation."[19] The legislative history, in combination with the language of the statute, evidences an intent by Congress to codify general common law tort principles and to extend civil liability for acts of international terrorism to the full reaches of traditional tort law."[20] Under the statute, recovery of civil damages is authorized for injury to the person, property or business caused by a terrorist attack.[21] Further, liability is not limited to *physical* injuries. Section 2333 liability extends to claims of U.S. nationals and their families based on non-physical injuries, such as emotional distress and loss of consortium.[22] In fact, every court to construe § 2333 and the meaning of the phrase "injured in [their] person" has reached the same conclusion.[23] Thus, both direct and indirect victims of terror-

---

15. *See Bringing International Terrorist to Justice, supra* note 8, at 737.

16. Debra M. Strauss, *Enlisting the U.S. Courts in a New Front: Dismantling the International Business Holdings of Terrorist Groups Through Federal Statutory and Common–Law Suits,* 38 VAND. J. TRANSNAT'L L. 679, 682 (2005) [hereinafter *Dismantling the International Holdings of Terrorist Groups*].

17. Antiterrorism Act of 1991, 18 U.S.C. §§ 2331 *et seq.* "International terrorism" is a term of art under the ATA and is discussed more fully *infra.*

18. 18 U.S.C. § 2333(a) (2006).

19. 137 CONG. REC. S4511–04, S4511(1991) (statement of Sen. Grassley).

20. Boim v. Quranic Literacy Inst. & Holy Found. (*Boim I*), 291 F.3d 1000,

1010 (7th Cir. 2002). *See also* 137 CONG. REC. S4511–04, S4511 (1991) ("The [Antiterrorism Act] accords victims of terrorism the remedies of American tort law, including treble damages and attorney's fees.").

21. 18 U.S.C. § 2333(a) (2006).

22. *See* Linde v. Arab Bank (*Arab Bank I*), 384 F.Supp.2d 571, 589 (E.D.N.Y. 2005).

23. *See* Goldberg v. UBS AG, 660 F.Supp.2d 410, 425 (E.D.N.Y. 2009) ("The history and structure of the statute suggest that Congress intended to include non-physical injuries in the phrase 'injured in [their] person.' "); *Arab Bank I,* 384 F.Supp.2d at 589 ("In the absence of any limiting language in the statute, the court will not limit the scope of section 2333(a) to physical inju-

ism may sue under the statute. A successful plaintiff is entitled to triple his compensatory damages, and the losing party must pay legal fees and court costs. However, the recovery of punitive damages is not permitted. Finally, the ATA explicitly confers extraterritorial jurisdiction on federal courts for injuries and losses suffered from terrorist acts occurring abroad.

The ATA was enacted by Congress in direct response to the case of *Klinghoffer v. S.N.C. Achille Lauro*.[24] The *Klinghoffer* litigation involved the 1985 hijacking of the Achille Lauro cruise ship in which an American passenger, Leon Klinghoffer, was murdered and dumped into the Mediterranean Sea.[25] Klinghoffer's two daughters brought suit against the Palestine Liberation Organization (PLO) claiming that the killing was an act of terrorism carried out by members of the PLO.[26] The district court upheld the survivor's claims under federal admiralty jurisdiction and the Death on the High Seas Act because the tort occurred in navigable waters.[27] In enacting the ATA, Congress was cognizant that federal court jurisdiction existed in the *Klinghoffer* case only because the terrorist attack occurred aboard a ship in international waters and maritime law authorized jurisdiction.[28] However, a similar attack occurring in some other locale might not have been subject to civil action in the U.S. The ATA was intended to fill the jurisdictional gap. Further, the "[s]ponsors of the bill believed that victims who had previously encountered hesitant courts and jurisdictional hurdles in pursuing their tort actions or statutory claims should not be left without an adequate remedy."[29]

The ATA provides victims with an express right to recover damages for acts of international terrorism and enables them to seize the assets of terrorists which are within jurisdictional reach.

ries."); Biton v. Palestinian Interim Self–Gov't Auth., 310 F.Supp.2d 172, 182 (D.D.C. 2004) ("The [ATA] does not specifically require that a plaintiff suffer *physical* harm prior to filing suit."); Hurst v. Socialist People's Libyan Arab Jamahiriya, 474 F.Supp.2d 19 (D.D.C. 2007) (same).

24. Klinghoffer v. S.N.C. Achille Lauro, 739 F.Supp. 854 (S.D.N.Y. 1990), *vacated*, 937 F.2d 44 (2d Cir. 1991).

25. *Id.* at 856.

26. *Id.*

27. *Id.* at 858–59.

28. *See* H.R. REP. No. 102–1040, at 5 (1992) ("Only by virtue of the fact that the [Klinghoffer] attack violated certain Admiralty laws and the organization involved—the Palestine Liberation Organization—had assets and carried on activ-

ities in New York, was the court able to establish jurisdiction over the case. A similar attack occurring on an airplane or in some other locale might not have been subject to civil action in the U.S. In order to facilitate civil actions against such terrorists the Committee [on the Judiciary] recommends [this bill]."); 137 CONG. REC. S4511–04, S4511 (1991) (statement of Sen. Grassley) (section 2333 would "codify [the Klinghoffer] ruling and make the right of American victims definitive"); 136 CONG. REC. S4568–01 (1990). *See also* Boim v. Quranic Literacy Inst. & Holy Found. (*Boim I*), 291 F.3d 1000, 1010–11 (7th Cir. 2002) (discussing legislative history); Goldberg v. UBS AG, 660 F.Supp.2d 410, 421 (E.D.N.Y. 2009) (same).

29. *Bringing International Terrorists to Justice, supra* note 8, at 737.

However, the legislation imposes important limitations. First, the ATA is limited to U.S. nationals. Foreign nationals may not sue under the statute. Second, the ATA bars civil actions against state sponsors of terrorism. It codifies the act of state doctrine by barring claims arising from official acts of foreign governments. Section 2337 bars suits against a "foreign state, an agency of a foreign state, or an officer or employee of a foreign state or an agency thereof acting within his or her official capacity or under color of legal authority."[30] Also, the ATA excludes civil actions for injury or loss occurring in the context of war or armed conflict.[31]

Finally, the Attorney General may stay any civil action brought under § 2333, or limit or stay discovery, if the court finds that the civil action would unduly interfere with a criminal prosecution or national security operation. Section 2336(c) permits the Attorney General to intervene in any civil action brought under § 2333 for the purpose of seeking a stay of the civil action "if the continuation of the civil action would substantially interfere with a criminal prosecution which involves the same subject matter, in which an indictment has been returned, or interfere with national security operations related to the terrorist incident that is the subject of the civil action."[32] Further, § 2336(b) provides that if a party to an action under § 2333 seeks to discover the investigative files of the Department of Justice, the government "may object on the ground that compliance will interfere with a criminal investigation or prosecution of the incident, or a national security operation related to the incident, which is the subject of the civil litigation."[33] Despite these limitations, the ATA provides an important legal framework by which victims of international terrorism may seek civil redress and compensation.

b. "International Terrorism"

In order to sustain a claim under § 2333(a), plaintiffs must allege that they were injured "by reason of" an act of "international terrorism." The ATA, 18 U.S.C. § 2333(a), provides:

> Any national of the United States injured in his or her person, property, or business by reason of an act of international terrorism, or his or her estate, survivors, or heirs, may sue therefor in any appropriate district court of the United States

---

30. 18 U.S.C. § 2337(2) (2006). The statute further prohibits actions against "the United States, an agency of the United States, or an officer or employee of the United States or any agency thereof acting within his or her official capacity or under color of legal authority." *Id.* at § 2337(1).

31. 18 U.S.C. § 2336(a) (2006).

32. *Id.* at § 2336(c).

33. *Id.* at § 2336(b).

and shall recover threefold damages he or she sustains and the cost of the suit, including attorney's fees.[34]

In order to sustain a claim under § 2333(a), plaintiffs must allege that they were injured "by reason of" an act of "international terrorism."[35] Section 2331(1) defines "international terrorism" as activities that—

(A) involve violent acts or acts dangerous to human life that are a violation of the criminal laws of the United States or of any State, or that would be a criminal violation if committed within the jurisdiction of the United States or of any State;

(B) appear to be intended—

(i) to intimidate or coerce a civilian population;

(ii) to influence the policy of a government by intimidation or coercion; or

(iii) to affect the conduct of a government by mass destruction, assassination, or kidnaping; and

(C) occur primarily outside the territorial jurisdiction of the United States or transcend national boundaries in terms of the means by which they are accomplished, the persons they appear intended to intimidate or coerce, or the locale in which their perpetrators operate or seek asylum.[36]

Section 2331(1) sets forth a three-pronged definition of "international terrorism." First, the conduct condemned must "involve" the commission of "violent acts" or "acts dangerous to human life" that are a violation of the criminal laws of the United States or any State, or that would be a criminal violation if committed within the United States.[37] Second, the plaintiff must prove that the prohibited acts "appear to be intended" (i) to intimidate or coerce a civilian population, (ii) to influence the policy of a government by intimidation or coercion, or (iii) to affect the conduct of a government by mass destruction, assassination, or kidnaping.[38] Third, the prohibited conduct must have an extraterritorial nexus. The plaintiff must prove that the terrorist-related acts occurred "primarily outside the territorial jurisdiction of the United States," or "transcend[ed] national boundaries."[39] Under the statute, the plaintiff can prove that the terrorist acts transcended national boundaries in three ways: (1) the terrorist acts were accomplished by transcending national boundaries; (2) the persons the terrorist acts were intend-

---

34. *Id.* at § 2333(a).

35. *Id.*

36. 18 U.S.C. § 2331(1).

37. *Id.* at § 2331(1)(A).

38. *Id.* at § 2331(1)(B)(i)–(iii). The "appear to be intended" language does

not impose a state of mind requirement; "it is a matter of external appearance rather than a subjective intent." Boim v. Holy Land Found. (*Boim III*), 549 F.3d 685, 694 (7th Cir. 2008) (*en banc*).

39. 18 U.S.C. § 2331(1)(C).

ed to intimidate or coerce transcended national boundaries, or (3) the terrorist perpetrators conducted their operations abroad or after perpetrating their attack, they sought asylum or a safe haven in a foreign country.[40]

In *Smith ex rel Smith v. Islamic Emirate of Afghanistan,* the court determined that, although "the acts of September 11 clearly 'occurred primarily' in the United States," they were nevertheless acts of "international terrorism" in that they "transcend[ed] national boundaries in terms of the means by which they [were] accomplished . . . or the locale in which their perpetrators operate."[41] The plaintiffs, therefore, had stated a viable cause of action under the ATA. Moreover, under the statute, a terrorist attack against the United Nations headquarters in New York City perpetrated by homegrown terrorists would constitute an act of "international terrorism" if the persons the terrorists intended to intimidate or coerce were residents of multiple countries, thus transcending national boundaries.[42] Finally, if the terrorists sought refuge or asylum abroad after a terrorist attack on the U.S. homeland, the attack would also constitute an act of "international terrorism" under the statute.

c. Theories of Liability

A violation of § 2333 can be sustained under three different theories of liability. First, defendants can be held liable if they violated 18 U.S.C. §§ 2339A or 2339B, the criminal statutes prohibiting the provision of material support to terrorists or a foreign terrorist organization.[43] Second, civil liability may attach if the defendant violated 18 U.S.C. § 2339C, which makes it a crime to "unlawfully and willfully" "provide or collect" funds with the intention or knowledge that the funds are to be used in full or in part to carry out (1) an act which constitutes an offense within the scope of any of nine anti-terrorism treaties specified in the statute, or (2) any other act intended to cause death or serious bodily injury to a civilian, when the purpose of the deadly act was "to intimidate a population, or to compel a government or an international organization to do or abstain from doing any act."[44] Third, a civil action under § 2333 may be sustained for aiding and abetting an act of international terrorism.[45] However, merely giving money to a terrorist organization without knowledge of the donee's terrorist activ-

---

40. *Id.*

41. Smith ex rel. Smith v. Islamic Emirate of Afghanistan, 262 F.Supp.2d 217, 221 (S.D.N.Y. 2003) (citing 18 U.S.C. § 2331(1)(C)).

42. 18 U.S.C. § 2331(1)(C).

43. 18 U.S.C. §§ 2339A, 2339B.

44. 18 U.S.C. § 2339C.

45. Courts are divided on whether the ATA provides a civil cause of action for aiding and abetting international terrorism. *See* discussion *infra,* at 385–88.

ities does not violate the statute.[46] Merely providing funding to a terrorist organization is insufficient to support a violation of the ATA.

i. Providing Material Support to Terrorists

Although the ATA affords victims of international terrorism a private cause of action, it remained "virtually untested" for nearly a decade.[47] In 2001, however, plaintiffs brought a cause of action under § 2333 for the killing of their son David Boim, a Jewish teenager who was a United States and Israeli citizen living in Israel.[48] The complaint alleged that he was fatally shot by two Hamas gunmen while waiting at a bus stop near Jerusalem.[49] The Boim family filed suit not only against the terrorists themselves, but also against groups which they claimed were front organizations for Hamas in the United States. The complaint named as defendants the Holy Land Foundation for Relief and Development ("HLF") and the Quranic Literacy Institute ("QLI"), as well as other individuals and entities.[50] The complaint accused the defendants of providing financial support to Hamas, and in doing so,

46. Boim v. Quranic Literacy Inst. & Holy Land Found. (*Boim I*), 291 F.3d 1000, 1012 (7th Cir. 2002).

47. Seth Stratton, *Taking Terrorists to Court: A Practical Evaluation of Civil Suits Against Terrorists Under the Anti–Terrorism Act*, 9 SUFFOLK J. TRIAL & APP. ADVOC. 27, 32 (2004).

48. Boim v. Holy Land Found. (*Boim III*), 549 F.3d 685, 691 (7th Cir. 2008). The procedural history of the Boim case is lengthy and complex, spanning over seven years. In Boim v. Quranic Literacy Inst. (*Boim D.C. I*), 127 F.Supp.2d 1002 (N.D. Ill. 2001), the district court denied defendants' motion to dismiss for failure to state a claim. In *Boim I*, the Seventh Circuit affirmed the district court. The district court subsequently granted a summary judgment in favor of the plaintiffs with respect to the liability of three defendants other than the Quranic Literacy Institute. *See* Boim v. Quranic Literacy Inst. (*Boim D.C. II*), 340 F.Supp.2d 885 (N.D. Ill. 2004). A jury was convened and found the Quranic Literacy Institute liable. The jury then assessed damages of $52 million against all the defendants, jointly and severally. The amount was then trebled and attorneys' fees added.

The defendants appealed from a final judgment. In Boim v. Quranic Literacy Inst. (*Boim II*), 511 F.3d 707 (7th Cir.

2007), the Seventh Circuit vacated the judgment and remanded the case, directing the district court to establish causation and redetermine liability. The plaintiffs petitioned for rehearing *en banc*, and the full court granted the petition, primarily to consider the elements of 18 U.S.C. § 2333 against financial supporters of terrorism. *See Boim III*, 549 F.3d at 688.

49. *Boim III*, 549 F.3d at 687. David Boim's assailants were later identified as Amjad Hinawi and Khalil Tawfiq Al–Sharif. The Palestinian Authority arrested both Hinawi and Al–Sharif. They were released shortly thereafter, pending trial. Al–Sharif subsequently killed himself and five civilians and injured 192 other people in a suicide bombing in Jerusalem. Hinawi confessed to participating in the Boim killing and was eventually tried for his murder by a Palestinian Authority court and sentenced to ten years' imprisonment. *See Boim I*, 291 F.3d at 1002.

50. *Boim III*, 549 F.3d at 688. The complaint also named Mohammed Abdul Hamid Khalil Salah, the admitted U.S.-based leader of the military branch of Hamas. *See Boim I*, 291 F.3d at 1003. The American Muslim Society was also named as a defendant in the civil lawsuit. *See Boim III*, 549 F.3d at 687.

violating 18 U.S.C. § 2333(a).[51] More specifically, the Boims maintained that the seemingly humanitarian functions of these charitable organizations masked their core mission of raising and funneling funds to Hamas operatives to finance terrorist activities abroad.[52] Plaintiffs' central theory was that while two Hamas gunmen actually murdered their son, the assailants were financially supported by HLF, QLI, and other individuals and organizations.[53] Plaintiffs claimed that the provision of material support to terrorists, in violation of 18 U.S.C. §§ 2339A and 2339B, constitutes an act of "international terrorism," giving rise to civil liability under § 2333.[54]

In *Boim III*, the Seventh Circuit, sitting *en banc*, held that providing financial support to a terrorist group that targets Americans outside the United States may violate § 2333.[55] The court reached its conclusion based on a chain of explicit statutory incorporations by reference. The first link in the statutory chain is § 2333, which provides a civil cause of action for death or injuries suffered by reason of an act of "international terrorism."[56] The court next considered § 2331, which defines "international terrorism" as "activities that . . . involve violent acts or acts dangerous to human life that are a violation of the criminal laws of the United

---

51. *Boim III,* 549 F.3d at 688.

52. *Boim I,* 291 F.3d at 1003.

53. The Boims sought $100 million in compensatory damages and $100 million in punitive damages, plus court costs and attorney's fees, and requested treble damages under the ATA.

54. *Boim I,* 291 F.3d at 1003. In 1994, Congress passed 18 U.S.C. § 2339A, which criminalizes the provision of material support or resources to terrorists, "knowing or intending that they are to be used in preparation for, or in carrying out" an extensive list of violent crimes associated with terrorism, such as assassination, kidnaping, arson, and destruction of aircraft.

The term "material support or resources" means—

any property, tangible or intangible, or service, including currency or monetary instruments or financial securities, financial services, lodging, training, expert advice or assistance, safehouses, false documentation or identification, communications equipment, facilities, weapons, lethal substances, explosives, personnel (1 or more individuals who may be or include oneself), and transportation, except medicine or religious materials.

18 U.S.C. § 2339A(b)(1).

Two years later, Congress extended criminal liability to those providing material support to a foreign terrorist organization:

Whoever knowingly provides material support or resources to a foreign terrorist organization, or attempts or conspires to do so, shall be fined under this title or imprisoned not more than 15 years, or both.

18 U.S.C. § 2339B.

The Intelligence Reform and Terrorism Prevention Act of 2004 added the mens rea requirement that "a person must have knowledge that the organization is a designated terrorist organization . . . [or] that the organization has engaged in or engages in terrorist activity [or] . . . terrorism." Finally, the definition of "material support or resources" set forth in 18 U.S.C. § 2339A(b)(1) is incorporated by reference into § 2339B.

55. Boim v. Holy Land Found. (*Boim III*), 549 F.3d 685, 690 (7th Cir. 2008).

56. *Id.*

States," that "appear to be intended ... to intimidate or coerce a civilian population" or "affect the conduct of a government by ... assassination," and "transcend national boundaries in terms of the means by which they are accomplished" or "the persons they appear intended to intimidate or coerce."[57] The definition of "international terrorism" includes not only violent acts but also "acts dangerous to human life that are a violation of the criminal laws of the United States."[58]

The third statutory link involved the material support statute, 18 U.S.C. § 2339A.[59] Section 2339A punishes "whoever provides material support or resources ... knowing or intending that they are to be used in preparation for, or in carrying out, a violation of [18 U.S.C. § 2332]."[60] Finally, the court referenced § 2332. Section 2332 criminalizes the killing, conspiring to kill, or inflicting bodily injury on, any American citizen outside the United States.[61] By this chain of statutory incorporations by reference (§ 2333(a) to § 2331(1) to § 2339A to § 2332), the Seventh Circuit concluded that making donations to a terrorist organization that target Americans outside the United States constitutes "acts dangerous to human life" that may support a claim under § 2333.[62] The court posited that "[g]iving money to Hamas, like giving a loaded gun to a child (which also is not a violent act), is an 'act dangerous to human life.' "[63] Other courts that have decided the issue are uniform in holding that providing material support to a terrorist or foreign terrorist organization may give rise to liability under § 2333.[64]

ii. Terrorist Financing

The terrorist financing statute, 18 U.S.C. § 2339C can serve as a predicate crime giving rise to liability under the ATA. Section 2339C punishes whoever "unlawfully and willfully provides or collects funds with the intention that such funds be used, or with

57. *Id.* (*quoting* 18 U.S.C. § 2331(1)).

58. 18 U.S.C. § 2331(1).

59. 18 U.S.C. § 2339A.

60. *Id.*

61. 18 U.S.C. § 2332.

62. Boim v. Holy Land Found. (*Boim III*), 549 F.3d 685, 690 (7th Cir. 2008) (*en banc*). *See also* Boim v. Quranic Literacy Inst. & Holy Land Found. (*Boim I*), 291 F.3d 1000, 1014 (7th Cir. 2002) ("[I]t would be counterintuitive to conclude that Congress imposed criminal liability in sections 2339A and 2339B on those who financed terrorism, but did

not intend to impose civil liability on those same persons through section 2333.").

63. *Boim III*, 549 F.3d at 690.

64. *See* Linde v. Arab Bank (*Arab Bank I*), 384 F.Supp.2d 571, 580 (E.D.N.Y. 2005); Weiss v. National Westminster Bank, 453 F.Supp.2d 609, 622 (E.D.N.Y. 2006); Strauss v. Credit Lyonnais, 2006 WL 2862704, 10–14 (E.D.N.Y.); Goldberg v. UBS, 660 F.Supp.2d 410 (E.D.N.Y. 2009). *See also* Almog v. Arab Bank (*Arab Bank II*), 471 F.Supp.2d 257, 268 (E.D.N.Y. 2007) ("violations of sections 2339A, 2339B(a)(1), and 2339C can serve as predicate crimes giving rise to liability under the ATA"):

the knowledge that such funds are to be used, in full or in part," to carry out terrorist acts.[65] In *National Westminster Bank*, *Arab Bank I*, and *Credit Lyonnais*, the plaintiffs brought suit claiming that defendant banks were civilly liable for acts of international terrorism under § 2333.[66] The complaints alleged that the named banks administered accounts for various Islamic charities that allegedly operated as fundraising front organizations for terrorist groups. Defendants countered, arguing that for purposes of § 2339C, the terms "provide" and "collect" do not encompass the maintenance of bank accounts and processing of deposits, withdrawals, and transfers, but require active donations to, or active fundraising on behalf of, a terrorist organization.[67] As used in § 2339C, "the term 'provides' includes giving, donating, and transmitting," and "the term 'collects' includes raising and receiving" funds.[68] The courts have consistently rejected defendants' narrow construction of § 2339C, holding that "the banking activities of receiving deposits and transmitting funds between accounts" where "the accounts (and funds) belong to groups engaged in terrorist activity" or are "charity fronts that operate as agents of Hamas" may violate § 2339C.[69] The critical issue, discussed *infra*, is whether the bank employees acted with knowledge that the funds were to be used to carry out a terrorist-related crime.[70]

iii. Aiding and Abetting

Section 2333 is silent on whether liability extends to aiders and abettors of international terrorism. Moreover, the courts are divided on the issue. In *Boim III*, the Seventh Circuit, sitting *en banc*, held that § 2333 does not provide for aiding and abetting liability, reasoning that secondary liability is available only when a statute expressly provides for it.[71] In reaching its conclusion, the court

---

65. 18 U.S.C. § 2339C. Section 2339C makes it a crime to "unlawfully and willfully" "provide or collect" funds with the intention or knowledge that the funds are to be used to carry out (1) an act which constitutes an offense within the scope of any of nine anti-terrorism treaties enumerated in the statute, or (2) another act intended to cause death or serious bodily injury to a civilian, when the purpose of the deadly act was "to intimidate a population, or to compel a government or an international organization to do or to abstain from doing any act."

66. *See Arab Bank I*, 384 F.Supp.2d at 580; *Nat'l Westminster Bank*, 453 F.Supp.2d at 622; *Credit Lyonnais*, 2006 WL 2862704 at 10–14.

67. *See Nat'l Westminster Bank*, 453 F.Supp.2d at 628; *Arab Bank I*, at

384 F.Supp.2d at 588; *Credit Lyonnais*, 2006 WL 2862704 at 15.

68. 18 U.S.C. §§ 2339C(e)(4) & (5).

69. *See National Westminster Bank*, 453 F.Supp.2d at 629 (quoting *Arab Bank I*, 384 F.Supp.2d at 588). *Accord Credit Lyonnais*, 2006 WL 2862704 at 17 (E.D.N.Y.).

70. *See* Unfunding Terror, *supra* note 12 at 338 ("The courts found that plaintiffs' allegations that defendant banks knew that funds were received as deposits and transmitted to various terrorist front organizations to finance terrorist activities were sufficient to state a claim under § 2339C.").

71. Boim v. Holy Land Found. (*Boim III*), 549 F.3d 685, 689 (7th Cir. 2008) (*en banc*).

relied on *Central Bank of Denver v. First Interstate Bank of Denver*, where the Supreme Court held that a private plaintiff may not maintain an action for aiding and abetting under § 10(b) of the Securities and Exchange Act of 1934, which prohibits securities fraud.[72] The Supreme Court reasoned that when construing the meaning of a statute, the legal analysis must begin with an examination of the language of the statute. Because § 10(b) made no mention of secondary liability, the Supreme Court refused to allow civil liability for conduct not prohibited by the text of § 10(b).[73] The *Boim III* court agreed with the reasoning in *Central Bank of Denver*, concluding that "statutory silence [in section 2333] on the subject of secondary liability means there is none."[74]

Boim III reversed the first panel opinion, which held that § 2333 creates secondary liability. In *Boim I*, the first panel stated that while *Central Bank of Denver* provides guidance on whether § 2333 authorizes secondary liability, it is not determinative for a number of reasons:

> First, Central Bank addressed extending aiding and abetting liability to an implied right of action, not an express right of action as we have here in section 2333. Second, Congress expressed an intent in the terms and history of section 2333 to import general tort law principles, and those principles include aiding and abetting liability. Third, Congress expressed an intent in section 2333 to render civil liability at least as extensive as criminal liability in the context of terrorism cases, and criminal liability attaches to aiders and abettors of terrorism. Fourth, failing to extend section 2333 liability to aiders and abettors is contrary to Congress' stated purpose of cutting off the flow of money to terrorists at every point along the chain of causation.[75]

The *Boim III* court responded, arguing that the Supreme Court's holding was not limited to an implied private right of action, but encompassed suits by the SEC, which were expressly authorized by § 10(b).[76] However, the court failed to address the other reasons given in the panel opinion for distinguishing *Central Bank of Denver*. Instead, the court posited that to read secondary liability into § 2333 would enlarge the federal courts' extraterritorial jurisdiction.[77] While Congress has the power to impose liability for acts that occur abroad, it must make the extraterritorial scope

---

72. Central Bank of Denver v. First Interstate Bank of Denver, 511 U.S. 164, 177–78 (1994).

73. *Id.* at 174.

74. *Boim III*, 549 F.3d at 689.

75. Boim v. Quranic Literacy Inst. & Holy Land Found. (*Boim I*), 291 F.3d 1000, 1019 (7th Cir. 2002).

76. *Boim III*, 549 F.3d at 689.

77. *Id.* at 689–90.

of a statute clear. The *Boim III* court concluded that such legislative intent was not clearly manifest under the statute.[78]

In contrast, other courts have reached a different conclusion finding that § 2333 does support secondary liability. In *Arab Bank I*, which relied on the reasoning in *Boim I*, the court stated that "Congress expressed an intent in section 2333 to render civil liability at least as extensive as criminal liability in the context of terrorism cases, and criminal liability attaches to aiders and abettors of terrorism."[79] Also, in *National Westminster Bank* and *Credit Lyonnais*, the courts recognized aiding and abetting as a viable theory of liability under the ATA.[80] However, to support a claim of aiding and abetting under § 2333, plaintiffs must prove that the defendant provided "substantial assistance" to the perpetrators of the terrorist acts.[81] What constitutes "substantial assistance" depends on the facts of the case. For example, the mere receipt and transfer of funds to a terrorist front organization, without more, does not constitute "substantial assistance." In *Credit Lyonnais*, the court held that "[t]he maintenance of a bank account and the receipt or transfer of funds does not constitute [the] substantial assistance" necessary to sustain a claim of aiding and abetting liability.[82] In *Goldberg v. UBS*, the court reached a similar result, holding that defendant's actions in performing three wire transfers totaling approximately $25,000 to a designated terrorist organization failed to establish "substantial assistance" of the sort required to warrant aiding and abetting liability.[83]

In *Arab Bank I*, however, the court held that the financial services provided by Arab Bank amounted to substantial assistance to international terrorism.[84] The civil complaint alleged that Arab Bank administered accounts for several Islamic charities operating as front organizations for Hamas, raising and funneling funds to support terrorist activities. The most damaging allegations involved Arab Bank's involvement with the Saudi Committee for the Support of the Al Quds Intifada ("Saudi Committee"). Shortly after the commencement of the Second Intifada, the Saudi Committee was established as a private charity registered in Saudi Arabia.[85] The

78. *Id.*

79. Linde v. Arab Bank (*Arab Bank I*), 384 F.Supp.2d 571, 583 (E.D.N.Y. 2005) (citing *Boim I*, 291 F.3d at 1019).

80. *See Nat'l Westminster Bank*, 453 F.Supp.2d at 622; Strauss v. Credit Lyonnais, 2006 WL 2862704 (E.D.N.Y. 2006) (while aiding and abetting an act of international terrorism may violate section 2333, defendants' conduct did not constitute "substantial assistance" necessary to support such a claim).

81. *Arab Bank I*, 384 F.Supp.2d at 584 (quoting Restatement (Second) of Torts, § 876 (1979)).

82. *Credit Lyonnais*, 2006 WL 2862704 at 9; *see also Nat'l Westminster Bank*, 453 F.Supp.2d at 622.

83. Goldberg v. UBS, 660 F.Supp.2d 410, 425 (E.D.N.Y.2009).

84. *Arab Bank I,* 384 F.Supp.2d at 584.

85. *Id.* at 576.

plaintiffs alleged that the Saudi Committee was established for the purpose of raising money for the families of suicide bombers.[86] The Saudi Committee furnished a "comprehensive insurance death benefit" and "universal death and dismemberment plan" consisting of payments to the families of the "martyrs" killed or wounded in or imprisoned for committing terrorist attacks.[87] The Saudi Committee set up accounts at various financial institutions in the Middle East, including at Arab Bank, to raise funds for the families of so-called martyrs of Hamas and other terrorist groups.[88] Plaintiffs further alleged that Arab Bank administered the financial infrastructure by which the Saudi Committee distributed the death benefit payments to the families of the Hamas terrorists.[89] After the funds were transferred to designated accounts in Arab Bank branches, the Bank distributed the funds to families of suicide bombers.[90] Plaintiffs claimed that the payments by Arab Bank to the surviving family members of the suicide bombers facilitated the terrorist attacks, because the terrorists knew, that if they were killed in a terrorist bombing, their families would be financially supported.[91] The court in *Arab Bank I* held that by administering the terrorist death benefits program, which facilitated and created an incentive for the commission of terrorist attacks, Arab Bank substantially assisted in their commission.[92]

iv. Conspiracy

At least one court has sustained liability under the ATA on a theory of civil conspiracy. In *Arab Bank I*, the court stated that plaintiffs' allegations sufficiently supported an inference that

> Arab Bank and the terrorist organizations were participants in a common plan under which Arab Bank would supply necessary financial services to the organizations which would themselves perform the violent acts. Administering the death and dismemberment benefit plan further supports not only the existence of an agreement but Arab Bank's knowing and intentional participation in the agreement's illegal goals.[93]

The court's authority for extending liability under § 2333 to include conspiracy is unclear. The statutory text does not mention conspiracy. Further, the legislative history of the ATA is silent on the subject as well.

86. *Id.* at 576–77.

87. *Id.* at 577.

88. *Id.*

89. Linde v. Arab Bank (*Arab Bank I*), 384 F.Supp.2d 571, 577 (E.D.N.Y. 2005).

90. Almog v. Arab Bank, 471 F.Supp.2d 257, 263 (E.D.N.Y. 2007) ("*Arab Bank II*").

91. *Arab Bank I*, 384 F.Supp.2d at 582.

92. *Id.* at 584.

93. *Id.*

v. Funding Simpliciter

In *Boim I*, the court rejected plaintiffs' theory that the provision of funds to Hamas by HLF and QLI, without more, constitutes an act of "international terrorism" because it "involve[s] violent acts or acts dangerous to human life."[94] Plaintiffs compared payments to Hamas to murder for hire: "the person who pays for the murder does not himself commit a violent act, but the payment 'involves' acts in the sense that it brings about the violent act and provides an incentive for someone else to do it."[95] While the court agreed that Congress intended liability under the ATA to "reach beyond those persons who themselves commit the violent act that directly causes the injury," it held that merely giving money to a terrorist organization, without more, does not constitute an act of "international terrorism" under the ATA.[96] The court reasoned: "To hold the defendant's liable for donating money without knowledge of the donee's intended criminal use of the funds would impose strict liability."[97] Further, the court could find nothing in the statutory language or its structure or history to support that construction. Thus, a cause of action under § 2333 cannot be sustained on the theory that the defendants themselves committed an act of "international terrorism" when they donated money to a terrorist organization without knowledge or reason to suspect that the group would engage in terrorist acts.[98] At the very least, plaintiffs must show that the commission of terrorism was a reasonably foreseeable result of making a donation.[99] To date, no court has sustained an ATA claim based on a theory of "funding simpliciter."

d. Scienter

While § 2333(a) does not contain an explicit mens rea requirement, courts have interpreted the statute to require proof of some *deliberate wrongdoing* by the defendant, "in light of the fact that the statute contains a punitive element (i.e., treble damages)."[100] The *Boim III* court declared:

> Punitive damages are rarely if ever imposed unless the defendant is found to have engaged in deliberate wrongdoing. "Something more than the mere commission of a tort is always required for punitive damages. There must be circumstances of aggravation or outrage, such as spite or 'malice,' or a fraudulent or evil motive on the part of the defendant, or such

94. Boim v. Quranic Literacy Inst. & Holy Land Found., 291 F.3d 1000, 1005 (7th Cir. 2002).

95. *Id.*

96. *Id.* at 1012.

97. *Id.*

98. *Id.*

99. *Id.*

100. Goldberg v. UBS, 660 F.Supp.2d (E.D.N.Y. 2009).

conscious and deliberate disregard of the interests of others that the conduct may be called wilful or wanton."[101]

In *Boim III*, the Seventh Circuit held that the defendant must either know that the donee organization or the ultimate recipient of the funds engages in terrorist acts or the defendant is deliberately indifferent to whether it does or not.[102] Defendant is liable if he knows there is "a substantial probability that the organization engages in terrorism but ... does not care."[103] When the facts known to the defendant place him on notice of a risk, which he consciously disregards, that is recklessness. According to *Boim III*, recklessness satisfies the requirement of deliberate wrongdoing.[104] The court reasoned that if a donor to Hamas knows the aims and activities of the organization, it "would know that Hamas was gunning for Israelis."[105] It is therefore reasonably foreseeable that the donations to Hamas would augment its resources, enabling Hamas to kill or wound.[106] The donee would be aware of a substantial risk of death or seriously bodily injury. Further, by providing financial assistance to Hamas with such knowledge, he would knowingly disregard the risk. The donee's provision of financial assistance would be a reckless act, which would satisfy the requirement of deliberate wrongdoing. Ultimately, the *Boim III* court held that "[t]he mental element required to fix liability on a donor to Hamas is therefore present if the donor knows the character of that organization."[107]

Laundering donated funds through multiple intermediary organizations before reaching a terrorist group does not necessarily shield the defendant from civil liability. If the donor knows or is reckless in failing to discover that the donations were intended for a terrorist organization, the donor may violate § 2333. The *Boim III* court posited that if: "Donor A gives to innocent-appearing organization B which gives to innocent-appearing organization C which gives to Hamas. As long as A either knows or is reckless in failing to discover that donations to B end with Hamas, A is liable."[108] However, if this knowledge requirement is not satisfied, the donor is not liable.[109]

101. Boim v. Holy Land Found. (*Boim III*), 549 F.3d 685, 692 (7th Cir. 2008) (citing W. Page Keeton et al., PROSSER AND KEETON ON THE LAW OF TORTS § 2, pp. 9–10 (5th ed. 1984)).

102. *Boim III,* 549 F.3d at 693.

103. *Id.*

104. *Id.* at 692. *See also* Goldberg v. UBS, 660 F.Supp.2d 410 (E.D.N.Y. 2009) ("conscious and deliberate disre-gard of the interest of another, in the face of a known risk, can qualify as sufficiently deliberate wrongdoing" to support a violation of § 2333).

105. *Boim III,* 549 F.3d at 694.

106. *Id.*

107. *Id.* at 695.

108. *Id.* at 702.

109. *Id.*

Plaintiff is not required to prove that the defendant had the specific intent to aid or encourage the particular acts that injured plaintiff or defendant knew its actions would further terrorism.[110] In *Goldberg v. UBS*, the court upheld the complaint where plaintiffs alleged that defendant consciously disregarded the risk that it was supporting a terrorist organization, despite "strong probability that the bank's services would be used to further the organization's terrorist activities."[111] Plaintiff was not required to prove that UBS intended to further Hamas's terrorist agenda. Defendant's knowledge or reckless failure to learn that he is providing aid to an organization that engages in terrorism satisfies the mens rea requirement to support a violation of § 2333.

It is no defense that defendant intended that his contributions be used to support the terrorist organization's humanitarian activities. In *Boim III*, the court stated: "Anyone who knowingly contributes to the nonviolent wing of an organization that he knows to engage in terrorism is knowingly contributing to the organization's terrorist activities."[112] Such individual is liable whether or not he approves of the organization's violence.[113] Further, "[t]o require proof that the donor intended that his contributions be used for terrorism—to make a benign intent a defense—would as a practical matter eliminate donor liability except in cases in which the donor was foolish enough to admit his true intent."[114] Because money is fungible, there is nothing to prevent money earmarked for a humanitarian purposes from being used by the organization to fund its terrorist activities. Moreover, donations to the terrorist organization's humanitarian wing could indirectly aid its terrorism by freeing up funds for terrorist activities.[115] Finally, the ATA does not require proof that the victims were specifically targeted because of their United States' citizenship.[116]

---

110. *Id.* at 695.

111. *Id. See also Arab Bank I*, 384 F.Supp.2d at 586 n.9 (neither the material support or terrorist financing statutes require proof that the defendant provided financial services with the intent to carry out terrorist attacks to support a violation of § 2333); *accord Weiss v. National Westminster Bank*, 453 F.Supp.2d at 625–26; *Strauss v. Credit Lyonnais*, 2006 WL 2862704, at 13.

112. Boim v. Holy Land Found. (*Boim III*), 549 F.3d 685, 698–9 (7th Cir. 2008).

113. *Id.* at 700.

114. *Id.* at 698–99.

115. *Id.* at 698.

116. *See* Sokolow v. Palestine Liberation Organization, 583 F.Supp.2d 451, 455 (S.D.N.Y. 2008); Biton v. Palestinian Interim Self–Gov't Auth., 510 F.Supp.2d 144, 146 (D.D.C. 2007). *See also* Rubin v. Hamas–Islamic Resistance Movement, 2004 WL 2216489, at *2 (D.D.C. 2004) (the court had subject matter jurisdiction under the plain language of § 2333 of the ATA).

e. Causation

Section 2333 authorizes any national of the United States to sue where he was "injured in his or her person, property, or business by reason of an act of international terrorism." The words "by reason of" have been interpreted to require a showing that defendant's conduct proximately caused plaintiff's injury.[117] A showing of proximate causation requires proof that defendant's actions were "a substantial factor in the sequence of responsible causation," and that the injury was "reasonably foreseeable or anticipated as a natural consequence."[118] However, plaintiff is not required to establish a direct link between defendants' donations and the actual terrorist attack that harmed the plaintiff.[119] In other words, to establish liability plaintiffs are not required to trace the funds supplied by the defendants to the purchase of the actual weapons or explosives used to commit the terrorist attack. In *Goldberg v. UBS,* the court declared:

> Common sense requires a conclusion that Congress did not intend to limit recovery to those plaintiffs who could show that the very dollars sent to a terrorist organization were used to purchase the implements of violence that caused harm to the plaintiff. Such a burden would render the statute powerless to stop the flow of money to international terrorists, and would be incompatible with the legislative history of the ATA.[120]

In *Goldberg v. UBS,* the court found that plaintiffs had sufficiently plead that defendant's conduct was a "substantial cause" of their injuries where they alleged that defendant UBS had participated in three wire transfers totaling approximately $25,000 and the bank transferred those funds from a designated terrorist organization to an organization allegedly controlled by Hamas.[121] The court emphasized the fact that the wire transfers occurred proximate in time to the terrorist killing that constituted the basis of the complaint. The last wire transfer occurred a few weeks before the terrorist attack on a Jerusalem bus that killed the victim.[122] The allegations in the complaint sufficiently plead that defendant's conduct was a "substantial cause" of the death.[123] Further, the court held that the ultimate harm was "reasonably foreseeable." The court stated: "A fact finder could plausibly find that it was entirely foreseeable that transmitting money to a terrorist organi-

---

117. *See* Holmes v. Securities Investor Protection Corp., 503 U.S. 258, 265–68 (1992) (interpreting identical language in the civil RICO statute to require a showing of proximate causation).

118. Goldberg v. UBS, 660 F.Supp.2d (E.D.N.Y. 2009). (quoting Lerner v. Fleet Bank, N.A., 318 F.3d 113, 123 (2d Cir. 2003)).

119. *Goldberg,* 2009 WL 3077118, at 15.

120. *Id.*

121. *Id.* at 16.

122. *Id.*

123. *Id.*

zation would lead to violence and Congress had precisely that lethal connection in mind in passing the ATA."[124]

In *Boim III*, the Seventh Circuit applied a relaxed standard of causation. Proximate cause may be established by showing that defendant provided material support to, or collected funds for a terrorist organization that was responsible for the terrorist bombing which injured plaintiff.[125] According to the *Boim III* court, financial support to a terrorist organization enables its terrorism, regardless of whether the funds can be traced to the group's terrorist activities (let alone plaintiff's injury). The provision of a material support to a terrorist organization creates a dangerous situation and enhances the risk of harm, establishing a sufficient causal link between the defendant's conduct and the harm the plaintiff suffered. Under the majority's ruling, there is no requirement that the defendant's conduct was the "but for" cause of the death or injuries.[126] Further, plaintiff is not required to prove that defendant's actions would have been sufficient to support the primary actor's unlawful activities.[127] Finally, the *Boim III* court does not require proof that defendant's conduct was a "substantial factor" in the chain of causation. Instead, it is enough to make defendant liable that he helped create a danger. It is immaterial that "his acts could not be found to be either a necessary or a sufficient condition of the injury."[128] The court used the following hypothetical to explain its position:

> [C]onsider an organization solely involved in committing terrorist attacks and a hundred people all of whom know the character of the organization and each of whom contributes $1,000 to it, for a total of $100,000. The organization has additional resources from other, unknown contributors of $200,000 and it uses its total resources of $300,000 to recruit, train, and equip, and deploy terrorists who commit a variety of terrorist acts one of which kills an American citizen. His estate brings a suit under section 2333 against one of the knowing contributors of $1,000.[129]

For the Seventh Circuit, the fact that the death could not be traced to any of the contributors would be irrelevant.[130] Defendant would be liable because "[t]he knowing contributors as a whole would have significantly enhanced the risk of terrorist acts and thus the probability that the plaintiff's decedent would be a victim,

124. *Id.*

125. Boim v. Holy Land Found. (*Boim III*), 549 F.3d 685, 696 (7th Cir. 2008).

126. *Id. See also Arab Bank I*, 384 F.Supp.2d at 585 (plaintiffs are not re-quired to prove that Arab Bank was the "but for" cause of the terrorist attacks).

127. *Boim III*, 549 F.3d, at 698.

128. *Id.* at 697.

129. *Id.* at 698.

130. *Id.*

and this would be true even if Hamas had incurred a cost of more than $1,000 to kill the American, so that no defendant's contribution was a sufficient condition of his death."[131] Finally, the court stressed that primary and secondary actors are jointly and severally liable for any death and injuries resulting from the terrorist attack.[132]

If money is given to an organization that defendant knows to be engaged in terrorism, but the funds are earmarked for the organization's humanitarian activities, defendant's conduct may still support a violation of § 2333.[133] Any money given to a terrorist organization that engages in both terrorism and humanitarian activities, necessarily enables it to commit acts of terrorism, regardless of the purpose for which the money was given. The reasons given by the court are twofold. First, money is fungible: "If Hamas budgets $2 million for terrorism and $2 million for social services and receive a donation of $100,000 for those services, there is nothing to prevent its using that money for them while at the same time taking $100,000 out of its social services 'account' and depositing it in its terrorism 'account.' "[134] Second, Hamas's humanitarian activities reinforce its terrorist activities, for example, by providing economic assistance to the surviving family members of killed, wounded, and captured terrorists.[135] Also, the promise of financial assistance to the surviving families of suicide bombers is used to recruit new members. Finally, the court reasoned that social welfare activities serve to enhance Hamas's popularity and support in the Palestinian population.[136]

Liability for donors may extend for terrorist acts committed remote in time. The majority in *Boim III* suggested that a contribution to a terrorist organization in 1995 might render the donor civilly liable for the murder of an American citizen committed by members of that organization fifty years later.[137] Terrorism conflicts often last for many decades such as Ireland, Sri Lanka, the Philippines, Colombia, Kashmir, and Palestine, the court noted.[138] Ultimately, "[s]eed money for terrorism [could] sprout acts of violence long after the investment."[139]

131. *Id.*

132. *Id.*

133. *See* Boim v. Holy Land Found. (*Boim III*), 549 F.3d 685, 698 (7th Cir. 2008). *See also* Hussain v. Mukasey, 518 F.3d 534, 538–39 (7th Cir. 2008); Singh–Kaur v. Ashcroft, 385 F.3d 293, 301 (3d Cir. 2004).

134. *Boim III,* 549 F.3d at 698. *See also* Kilburn v. Socialist People's Libyan Arab Jamahiriya, 376 F.3d 1123, 1130 (D.C. Cir. 2004).

135. *Boim III*, 549 F.3d at 698.

136. *Id.*

137. *Id.* at 699–700.

138. *Id.* at 700.

139. *Id.* Judge Rovner, filed an opinion concurring in part and dissenting in part that was critical of the majority's ruling. Judge Rovner stated:

Liability under the majority's announced rule is sweeping: one who gives money to any Hamas entity,

Exception for Humanitarian Non–Governmental Organizations

According to the Seventh Circuit, humanitarian non-governmental organizations like the Red Cross and Doctors Without Borders who provide humanitarian medical assistance to members of a terrorist organization such as Hamas would not be liable under the ATA.[140] In *Boim III*, the court reasoned that while providing medical care to a Hamas terrorist would have the effect of aiding Hamas terrorism, such assistance would not satisfy the definition of "international terrorism" under § 2331. The rendering of such medical assistance would not "appear intended . . . to intimidate or coerce a civilian population" or "affect the conduct of a government by . . . assassination."[141] Without such appearance, the court stated, there is no act of "international terrorism" within the meaning of the statute.[142]

The court's ruling appears to contradict other statements in *Boim III* that donors who give money with knowledge that the organization engages in terrorist activities are liable under § 2333 regardless of the motive. The majority stated: "[I]f you give money to an organization that you know to be engaged in terrorism, the fact that you earmark it for the organization's nonterrorist activities does not get you off the liability hook."[143] Judge Rovner, concurring in part and dissenting in part, stated that the majority's exception was unprincipled and should extend to other situations where the donor providing aid to a terrorist organization with a humanitarian purpose. Judge Rovner stated:

> [F]or no apparent reason other than our own sense that organizations like the Red Cross and Doctors Without Borders are good and do good, the majority simply declares them exempt from the broad liability standard that it has announced. On the other hand, any other individual or organization that gives to a Hamas-controlled charity is deemed liable, regardless of whether the money is given with a humanitarian purpose and regardless of whether the money is, in fact, put to humanitarian use. So one cannot fund the construction of a Hamas hospital, buy the hospital an x-ray machine, or volunteer her medical services to the hospital because this is not providing direct aid to individuals in the manner of the Red Cross.[144]

even if it is a small donation to help buy an x-ray machine for at Hamas hospital, is liable from now until the end of time for any terrorist act that Hamas might thereafter commit against an American citizen outside of the United States. *Id.* at 710.

140. *Id.* at 699–700

141. *Id.* at 699.

142. *Id.*

143. *Id.* at 698.

144. *Id.* at 711. Ultimately, Judge Rovner would require proof that defendant intended to help Hamas's terrorist activities succeed. Persons who acted

It is unclear whether other courts will follow the majority's ruling in *Boim III* on civil liability for non-governmental organizations.

f. Sovereign Immunity

Under the ATA, 18 U.S.C. § 2337(2), an action may not be maintained against the United States or a foreign state, or the agencies, officers and employees thereof, acting within their official capacity or under color of legal authority.[145] The sovereign immunity doctrine "is premised upon the perfect equality and absolute independence of sovereigns," and "is designed to give foreign states and their instrumentalities some protection from the inconvenience of suit."[146] ATA's exclusion of foreign states, agencies and governmental actors from its coverage is to be applied in accordance with the sovereign immunity principles codified in the FSIA.[147] This position is supported by the legislative history of § 2337, which states:

> This provision maintains the status quo, in accordance with the Foreign Sovereign Immunities Act, with respect to sovereign states and their officials: there can be no cause of action for international terrorism against them.[148]

In other words, if a cause of action is barred under the FSIA, such claim cannot be maintained under § 2333. Further, because the ATA is to be construed in accordance with the FSIA, court decisions interpreting FSIA's scope of coverage would be highly relevant in construing § 2337(2) of the ATA.[149]

In *Lawton v. Republic of Iraq*, the district court granted the defendant's motion to dismiss for failure to state a claim, holding that a plain reading of § 2337 indicates that ATA bars § 2333 claims against foreign states, including the Republic of Iraq.[150]

---

with a humanitarian purpose would not be liable under § 2333, even if they had knowledge that the organization committed terrorist acts. *Id.* at 712.

145. 18 U.S.C. §§ 2337(1)–(2).

146. Republic of Philippines v. Pimentel, 553 U.S. 851, 863–65 (internal quotation marks and citations omitted).

147. *See* Sokolow v. Palestine Liberation Org., 583 F.Supp.2d 451, 458 (S.D.N.Y. 2008); Hurst v. Socialist People's Libyan Arab Jamahiriya, 474 F.Supp.2d 19, 29 n. 13 (D.D.C. 2007); Klieman v. Palestinian Auth., 424 F.Supp.2d 153, 158 (D.D.C. 2006); Estates of Ungar v. Palestinian Auth., 315 F.Supp.2d 164, 175 (D.R.I. 2004); Knox v. Palestine Liberation Org., 306 F.Supp.2d 424, 430–31 (S.D.N.Y. 2004) ("*Knox I*").

148. S.Rep. No. 102–342, 102d Cong., 2d Sess. (July 27, 1992), at 47.

149. The FSIA was recently amended creating an exception to sovereign immunity and authorizing a private cause of action by which a foreign state designated as a state-sponsor of terrorism can be held liable for damages arising from enumerated terrorist activities. *See* 28 U.S.C. §§ 1605A(a), discussed *infra*.

150. Lawton v. Republic of Iraq, 581 F.Supp.2d 43, 47 (D.D.C. 2008).

However, the courts have held that the sovereignty immunity provision does not extend to the Palestine Liberation Organization ("PLO") and Palestine Interim Self–Government Authority ("PA"). In *Sokolow v. Palestinian Liberation Organization,* United States citizens and the estates and family members of U.S. citizens killed or injured in terrorist attacks in Israel brought action under the ATA against the PLO and PA.[151] The defendants moved to dismiss the complaint for lack of jurisdiction, asserting that their sovereignty shielded them from suit under the ATA and FSIA[152] Their assertion of immunity purportedly derived from the claimed sovereignty of the State of Palestine.[153] The PLO and PA claimed that they are essential agencies of the State of Palestine, performing important government functions, entitling them to immunity.[154]

The *Sokolow* court rejected the defendants' argument, holding that since Palestine is not recognized, under United States law, as a "foreign state," the PLO and PA cannot derivatively secure sovereign immunity as agencies of Palestine.[155] Further, the court posited that Palestine does not meet the definition of a "state" under United States and international law.[156] Other courts that have decided the matter have uniformly reached the same conclusion.[157]

The definition of "state" is set forth in the Restatement (Third) of the Foreign Relations Law of the United States § 201, which provides:

> Under international law, a state is an entity that has a defined territory and a permanent population under the control of its own government, and that engages in, formal relations with other entities.[158]

The circuits are divided on whether the Restatement (Third) definition is the appropriate standard under the FSIA. In *Klinghoffer v. S.N.C. Achille Lauro,* the Second Circuit relied upon the definition of "state" set forth in the Restatement (Third) in determining statehood under the FSIA.[159] However, in *Ungar v. Palestine Liberation Org.,* the First Circuit stated that the Restatement

151. Sokolow v. Palestine Liberation Organization, 583 F.Supp.2d 451, 458 (S.D.N.Y. 2008).

152. *Id.* at 457.

153. *Id.* at 457.

154. *Id.*

155. *Id.* at 458.

156. *Id.* at 457–58.

157. *See e.g.,* Ungar v. Palestine Liberation Organization, 402 F.3d 274 (1st Cir. 2005) (*"Ungar IV"*); Biton v. Palestinian Interim Self–Government Auth., 510 F.Supp.2d 144, 147 (D.D.C. 2007) (*"Biton IV"*); Klieman I, 424 F.Supp.2d at 159–60; Biton v. Palestinian Self–Government Auth., 412 F.Supp.2d 1, 4–5 (D.D.C. 2005) (*"Biton II"*); Knox v. Palestine Liberation Organization, 306 F.Supp.2d 424 (S.D.N.Y. 2004).

158. Restatement (Third) of the Foreign Relations Law of the United States § 201.

159. Klinghoffer v. S.N.C. Achille Lauro, 937 F.2d 44, 47 (2d Cir. 1991).

(Third) standard may be misplaced.[160] The court opined that the appropriate standard may be "that a foreign state, for purposes of FSIA, is an entity that has been recognized as a sovereign by the United States government."[161] Because the United States does not recognize Palestine as a sovereign nation, the court held that it is not a foreign state under FSIA.[162] However, regardless of which standard is applied, the courts have consistently held that Palestine is not a foreign state for purposes of the FSIA and ATA. Thus, the PLO and PA are not entitled to sovereign immunity.

g. "Act of War" Exception

The ATA, 18 U.S.C. § 2336(a), excludes an action under § 2333 for injury or loss "by reason of" an "act of war."[163] The term "act of war" is defined in § 2331(4) to mean any act occurring in the course of "(A) declared war; (B) armed conflict, whether or not war has been declared between two or more nations; or (C) armed conflict between military forces of any origin."[164] Section 2336(a) is frequently raised as a defense in civil actions arising from the armed conflict between Israel and Palestine. Defendants argue that the Palestinian conflict constitutes an "armed conflict between military forces of any origin" under § 2331(4)(C).[165] The courts have consistently construed the term "act of war" to exclude deliberate attacks on innocent civilians. In *Sokolow v. Palestine Liberation Organization*, the district court rejected the defendants' argument that the "act of war" exception applied to the armed conflict between Israelis and Palestinians in the West Bank and Gaza Strip.[166] Plaintiffs alleged seven separate terrorist attacks that killed thirty-three civilians and wounded hundreds more.[167] In one shooting, the attacker fired at a civilian automobile traveling near Jerusalem. In the other, a civilian passerby in downtown Jerusalem was targeted.[168] The subject bombings all took place in Jerusalem, including at a crowded bus stop, a cafeteria on the Hebrew University campus, a passenger-filled civilian bus, and two bombings occurring in downtown Jerusalem.[169]

160. *Ungar IV,* 402 F.3d at 284 n. 6.

161. *Id.*

162. *Id. See also Knox I,* 306 F.Supp.2d at 438–40.

163. 18 U.S.C. § 2336(a). Section 2336(a) provides that "[n]o action shall be maintained under section 2333 of this title for injury or los by reason of an act of war."

164. 18 U.S.C. § 2331(4)(A)–(C).

165. Subsection (A) does not apply because there is no "declared war" be-

tween Israel and Palestine. Further, since Palestine is not a state, the armed conflict with Israel does not constitute an "armed conflict" between two or more nations under subsection (B). *See Biton II,* 412 F.Supp.2d at 10 n. 5.

166. Sokolow v. Palestine Liberation Organization, 583 F.Supp.2d 451, 459 (S.D.N.Y. 2008).

167. *Id.* at 454.

168. *Id.*

169. *Id.* at 454–55. These attacks resulted in killing thirty-three innocent persons and wounding hundreds of oth-

Defendants claimed that the Palestinian conflict constituted an "armed conflict between military forces of any origin" under § 2331(4)(C).[170] The district court rejected, defendants' argument, positing that the statutory exemption is limited to lawful acts of war. The court held that targeting noncombatant civilians outside of any combat or military zone did not constitute acts of war for purposes of the ATA.[171] Other courts have reached the same conclusion. In *Kleiman v. Palestinian Authority*, the estate and heirs of an American citizen killed in a terrorist attack on a public transport bus in Israel brought action against the Palestinian Interim Self–Government, Palestine Liberation Organization, several terrorist organization and individuals.[172] Defendants moved to dismiss the complaint, arguing that the acts alleged in the complaint constitute "acts of war" over which the ATA does not extend jurisdiction.[173] Defendants argued that the statutory definition of "act of war" in § 2331(4)(C) is broad, "cover[ing] 'any act' without limit or qualification and requires only that the act be one occurring in the course of an armed conflict between military forces of any origin."[174] Defendants maintained that even if the attack on a civilian bus violated the rules of war and armed conflict, the ATA still would bar this action:

> If illegal the attack may well be a war crime and subject to the sanctions as such. However, neither the heinous nor legality of acts of war occurring in the course of armed conflict is germane to the application of section 2336(a). Sec. 2336(a) when applicable bars civil actions under ATA sec. 2333 for "any act" without regard to its nature or seriousness, or whether the act if not barred by sec. 2336(a) would constitute international terrorism actionable under the ATA.[175]

The court rejected defendants' argument, reasoning that § 2331(4)(C)'s requirement that the act occur "in the course of" an "armed conflict between military forces of any origin" imposes limitations on what "acts" constitute "acts of war" under the statute. The court interpreted the phrase "in the course of" as a "gatekeeper" phrase that "exclude[s] from the scope of the statuto-

---

ers. Moreover, scores of American citizens were among those killed and wounded. *Id.* at 455.

170. *Id.* at 459.

171. *Id. See also* Klieman v. Palestinian Auth., 424 F.Supp.2d 153, 162 (D.D.C. 2006) (attack on public bus carrying noncombatant civilians did not occur during an armed conflict); Biton v. Palestinian Interim Self–Gov't Auth., 412 F.Supp.2d 1 (D.D.C. 2005) (attack on school bus carrying noncombatant students and teachers did not occur dur-

ing an armed conflict). *See also* Biton v. Palestinian Interim Self–Gov't Auth., 510 F.Supp.2d 144, 147 (D.D.C. 2007) ("[I]ntentionally bombing a bus load of school children[ ] is 'terrorism' by any measure, alleged ambiguities in international law notwithstanding.").

172. *Klieman v. Palestinian Auth.*, 424 F.Supp.2d 153.

173. *Id.* at 163.

174. *Id.*

175. *Id.*

ry provision a subset of conduct that, by it nature and substance, deviates from or is not sufficiently related to the general set of conduct otherwise governed by the provision."[176] An armed attack on a civilian bus, the court stated, violates established norms of international humanitarian law.[177] Violent attacks against civilians are recognized in international law as war crimes. The court reasoned that defendants' interpretation of the statute would create an impermissible conflict between § 2331 and § 2441, which criminalizes and punishes war crimes, "because it would single out and exclude § 2441 from the criminality component of the definition of 'international terrorism' in § 2331 which applies by its plain terms to any 'violation of the criminal laws of the United States'-including of course § 2441."[178] Such an interpretation "would create an absurd situation wherein persons guilty of War Crimes in which an American is killed would face the death penalty under § 2441, but would not face civil liability under § 2333," the court stated.[179] The court held that "[a]s a matter of law, an act that violates established norms of warfare and armed conflict under international law is not an act occurring in the course of an armed conflict."[180] Thus, because an attack on innocent civilians violates established norms of international law, it does not constitute an "act of war" under the ATA.[181]

Section 2336(a) should be construed to bar civil litigation only for lawful acts of war. If a person is immune from criminal prosecution under the laws and customs of war for killing members of the enemy forces, destroying the enemy's military facilities, or

176. *Id.* at 165 (string-citing cases).

177. *Id.* at 166. Attacks against innocent civilians during and armed conflict is prohibited by the laws and customs of war. The "principle of distinction," which requires parties to the conflict to distinguish between civilians and combatants, forbids the deliberate attacking of civilians. *See* 2 L. OPPENHEIM, INTERNATIONAL LAW § 214, at 524 (H. Lauterpacht ed., 7th ed. 1961); 1 JEAN–MARIE HENCKAERTS & LOUISE DOSWALD–BECK, CUSTOMARY INTERNATIONAL HUMANITARIAN LAW 3–4 (2005). This principle is also reflected in Common Article 3 of the Geneva Conventions of 1949, which provides in pertinent part:

In the case of armed conflict not of an international character occurring in the territory of one of the High Contracting Parties, each Party to the conflict shall be bound to apply, as a minimum, the following provisions:

(1) Persons taking no active part in the hostilities, including members of

armed forces who have laid down their arms and those placed in hors de combat by sickness, wounds, detention, or any other cause, shall in all circumstances be treated humanely....

To this end the following acts are and shall remain prohibited at any time and in any place whatsoever with respect to the above-mentioned persons:

(a) violence to life and person, in particular murder of all kinds, mutilation, cruel treatment and torture.

Geneva Convention Relative to the Protection of Civilian Persons in Time of War, art. III, Aug. 12, 1949, 6 U.S.T. 3316.

178. *Klieman v. Palestinian Auth.*, 424 F.Supp.2d at 165–66.

179. *Id.*

180. *Id.* at 166.

181. *Id.*

attacking other targets of military necessity, such person should also be immune from civil liability for the same conduct. However, it makes no sense to criminalize and punish persons for the wilful killing of civilians, which constitutes a "grave breach" of the Geneva Conventions of 1949, but immunize such individuals from civil liability under the ATA for their criminal acts.[182] Section 2336(a) should be construed in a manner consistent with principles of international humanitarian law. If a person is immune from prosecution for violent acts committed during time of war, he should be immune from civil liability as well. In contrast, if a person is criminally liable for violations of the laws and customs of war crimes, he should be subject to civil liability under § 2333, assuming his conduct constitutes an act of "international terrorism," as defined by § 2331.

2. ALIEN TORT CLAIMS ACT

a. Introduction

The Alien Tort Claims Act ("ATCA"), 28 U.S.C. § 1350, grants district courts "original jurisdiction of any civil action by an alien for a tort only, committed in violation of the law of nations or a treaty of the United States."[183] Under the statute, federal courts may entertain claims by foreign victims seeking damages for death and injuries resulting from acts of terrorism committed anywhere in the world. The statute confers federal subject-matter jurisdiction when the following requirements are satisfied: " '(1) an alien sues, (2) for a tort, (3) committed in violation of the law of nations.' "[184] The limitations period for filing civil claims under the ATCA is the 10–year period provided in the Torture Victim Protection Act.[185]

The ATCA was enacted by the nation's founders during the First Congress in 1789.[186] However, the statute remained virtually

---

182. See Geneva Convention Relative to the Treatment of Prisoners of War (Aug. 12, 1949), 75 U.N.T.S. 135, 6 U.S.T. 3316, T.I.A.S. No. 3364. The wilful killing of a protected person, including a civilian, is a "grave breach" of the Geneva Conventions. See Article 130.

183. 28 U.S.C. § 1350. The ATCA is also referred to as the Alien Tort Statute ("ATS").

184. Khulumani v. Barclay Nat. Bank Ltd., 504 F.3d 254, 267 (2d Cir. 2007) (quoting Kadic v. Karadzic, 70 F.3d 232, 238 (2d Cir. 1995)). See also Almog v. Arab Bank, 471 F. Supp.2d 257, 269 (E.D.N.Y. 2007) ("Arab Bank II").

185. See Van Tu v. Koster, 364 F.3d 1196 (10th Cir. 2004); Papa v. United States, 281 F.3d 1004 (9th Cir.

2002); Bowoto v. Chevron Corp., 557 F.Supp.2d 1080 (N.D. Cal. 2008); Doe v. Rafael Saravia, 348 F.Supp.2d 1112 (E.D. Cal. 2004); Doe v. Islamic Salvation Front, 257 F.Supp.2d 115 (D.D.C. 2003).

186. The legislative history of the ATCA is non-existent. See Sarei v. Rio Tinto, PLC, 487 F.3d 1193, 1215 (9th Cir. 2007) ("There is complete silence in the ATCA's legislative history."); IIT v. Vencap, Ltd., 519 F.2d 1001, 1015 (2d Cir. 1975) (characterizing the ATCA as "a kind of legal Lohengrin . . . no one seems to know whence it came"); In re Estate of Ferdinand E. Marcos Human Rights Litig., 978 F.2d 493, 498 (9th Cir. 1992) ("The debates that led to the Act's passage contain no reference to the Alien Tort Statute, and there is no di-

dormant for almost 200 years. In 1980, the ATCA was invoked in *Filartiga v. Pena–Irala,* by plaintiffs Dolly Filartiga and Joel Fillartiaga, citizens of Paraguay, against the Inspector General of Police in Asuncion, Parguay, for allegedly torturing and killing Joel Fillartiga's 17–year–old son.[187] The Second Circuit held that torture perpetrated under color of official authority violates the law of nations, and is thus actionable under the ATCA.[188] The *Filartiga* case is generally recognized as the "starting point" for the modern re-emergence of the ATCA.[189]

In *Sosa v. Alvarez–Machain,*[190] the Supreme Court settled an ongoing debate over whether § 1350 provides a private cause of action or is only a jurisdictional statute.[191] The Supreme Court rejected the argument that the First Congress passed the ATCA "as a jurisdictional convenience to be placed on the shelf for use by a future Congress or state legislature that might, some day, authorize the create of causes of action."[192] Instead, "the statute was intended to have practical effect the moment it became law."[193] Further, the immediate application of the statute would be realized by invoking the causes of action already available at common law. The Court posited that "[t]he jurisdictional grant is best read as having been enacted on the understanding that the common law would provide a cause of action for the modest number of international violations with a potential for personal liability at the time."[194] Because some torts in violation of the law of nations were understood to be within the common law of 1789, "the First Congress understood that the district courts would recognize private causes of action for certain

rect evidence of what the First Congress intended it to accomplish."); Tel–Oren v. Libyan Arab Republic, 726 F.2d 774, 789 (D.C. Cir. 1984) (Edwards, J., concurring) ("the legislative history offers no hint of congressional intent in passing the statute").

187. Filartiga v. Pena–Irala, 630 F.2d 876 (2d Cir. 1980).

188. *Id.* at 884–85.

189. *See* Anne–Marie Slaughter & David L. Bosco, *Alternative Justice,* GLOBAL POLICY FORUM, *available at* http://www.globalpolicy.org/intljustice/atca/2001/altfust.htm.

190. Sosa v. Alvarez–Machain, 542 U.S. 692 (2004). In *Sosa,* plaintiff-respondent Humberto Alvarez–Machain sought damages for injuries suffered resulting from an allegedly illegal arrest and detention by Mexican police officials acting as agents of the DEA. He was apprehended at his office in Guadalajara, Jalisco, Mexico, and forcibly trans-

ported to El Paso, Texas, where he was arrested on federal charges for his role in the kidnaping and murder of DEA Agent Enrique Camarena–Salazar. *Id.* at 697. The Supreme Court ultimately rejected Alavarez's claims under the ATCA, stating: "It is enough to hold that a single illegal detention of less than a day, followed by transfer of custody to lawful authorities and a prompt arraignment, violates no norm of customary international law so well defined as to support the creation of a federal remedy." *Id.* at 738.

191. *See* CIVIL LITIGATION AGAINST TERRORISM 129 (John Norton Moore ed., Carolina Academic Press 2004) ("[A] debate exists among legal scholars over whether § 1350 provides a cause of action or is only a jurisdictional statute.").

192. *Id.* at 719.

193. *Id.* at 724.

194. Sosa v. Alvarez–Machain, 542 U.S. 692, 724 (2004).

torts in violation of the law of nations.''[195] Thus, no additional substantive legislation was required.[196] Finally, the Court concluded that the ATCA does not limit jurisdiction to violations of international law considered judicially enforceable in 1789, but extends to a narrow class of international norms recognized today.[197] Moreover, these norms are enforceable not by creation of a statutory private cause of action, but through an exercise in "residual common law discretion" to create a right of action under federal common law to remedy the violation of these norms.[198]

The Court in *Sosa* cited five reasons for courts to exercise "great caution" before recognizing violations of international law that were not recognized in 1789:

> First, ... the [modern] understanding that the law is not so much found or discovered as it is either made or created[;] ... [s]econd, ... an equally significant rethinking of the role of the federal courts in making it[;] ... [t]hird, [the modern view that] a decision to create a private right of action is one better left to the legislative judgment in the great majority of cases[;] ... [f]ourth, ... risks of adverse foreign policy considerations[; and] ... [f]ifth[,] ... [the lack of a] congressional mandate to seek out and define new and debatable violations of the law of nations.[199]

The Supreme Court articulated the following standard for considering the kinds of claims that might implement the jurisdiction conferred by § 1350: "federal courts should not recognize private claims under federal common law for violations of any international law norm with less definite content and acceptance among civilized nations that the historical paradigms familiar when § 1350 was enacted.''[200] The Court's legal standard has two central component parts. First, the international norm serving as the basis for the tort claim must be as sufficiently definite as those recognized when the ATCA was enacted (that is, violations of safe conduct, assaults against ambassadors, and piracy). Second, the relevant international norm must have achieved general "acceptance among civilized nations.''[201] According to the Court in *Sosa*, "the determination whether a norm is sufficiently definite to support a cause of action should (and, indeed, inevitably must) involve an element of judgment about the practical consequences of making a new cause of action available to litigants in the federal courts.''[202]

195. *Id.* at 720, 724. Those primary tort offenses included violation of safe conduct, infringement of the rights of ambassadors, and piracy. *Id.* at 724.

196. *Id.* at 724.

197. *Id.* at 728–9.

198. *Id.* at 738.

199. *Sosa,* 542 U.S. at 725–28.

200. *Id.* at 732.

201. *Id.*

202. *Id.* at 732–33.

For example, recognizing a claim may have collateral consequences, such as implications on foreign relations. Thus, "federal courts should give serious weight to the Executive Branch's view of the case's impact on foreign policy."[203]

Finally, the Supreme Court suggested that it would be amenable to recognizing an exhaustion requirement as implicit in the ATCA.[204] However, the Court did not resolve the issue, but stated only that it "would certainly consider this [exhaustion] requirement in an appropriate case."[205] At least one circuit court has refused to incorporate an exhaustion requirement into the ATCA. In *Sarei v. Rio Tinto, PLC,* the Ninth Circuit held that legislative intent does not support importing an exhaustion requirement into the ATCA.[206] Further, the court declined to read an exhaustion requirement into the ATCA as an exercise of judicial discretion. The Ninth Circuit concluded that "it would be inappropriate, given the lack of clear direction from Congress (either in 1789 or when it revisited the issue in 1991), and with only an aside in a footnote on the issue from the Supreme Court, now to superimpose on our circuit's existing ATCA jurisprudence an exhaustion requirement where none has been required before."[207]

Violation of the Law of Nations

In deciding whether to recognize a claim under the ATCA, courts should consider the current state of international law.[208] As the *Filartiga* court stated, "courts must interpret international law not as it was in 1789, but as it has evolved and exists among the nations of the world today."[209] In discerning the current state of the law of nations, courts should consider the following sources of law:

> [W]here there is no treaty, and no controlling executive or legislative act, or judicial decision, resort must be had to the customs and usages of civilized nations; and, as evidence of these, to the works of jurists and commentators, who by years

---

203. *Id.* at 733 n. 21 ("Another possible limitation that we need not apply here is a policy of case-specific deference to the political branches.").

204. *Id.* The Court posited:

This requirement of clear definition is not meant to be the only principle limiting the availability of relief in the federal courts for violations of customary international law, though it disposes of this case. For example, the European Commission argues as amicus curiae that basic principles of international law require that before asserting a claim in a foreign forum, the claimant must have exhausted any remedies available in the domestic legal system, and perhaps in other fora such as international claims tribunals. We would certainly consider this requirement in an appropriate case.

Id. at 733 n. 21 (internal citations omitted).

205. *Id.* at 733 n. 21.

206. Sarei v. Rio Tinto, PLC, 487 F.3d 1193, 1218 (9th Cir. 2007).

207. *Id.* at 1223.

208. Sosa v. Alvarez–Machain, 542 U.S. 692, 733 (2004).

209. Filartiga v. Pena–Irala, 630 F.2d 876 (2d Cir. 1980).

of labor, research and experience, have made themselves peculiarly well acquainted with the subjects of which they treat. Such works are resorted to by judicial tribunals, not for the speculations of their authors concerning what the law ought to be, but for trustworthy evidence of what the law really is.[210]

This method of discerning the current state of international law is consistent with Article 38 of the Statute of the International Court of Justice, which provides:

1.   The Court, whose function is to decide in accordance with international law such disputes as are submitted to it, shall apply:

(a) international conventions, whether general or particular, establishing rules expressly recognized by the contesting states;

(b) international custom as evidence of a general practice accepted as law;

(c) the general principles of law recognized by civilized nations;

(d) subject to the provisions of Article 59, judicial decisions and the teachings of the most highly qualified publicists of the various nations, as subsidiary means for the determination of the rules of law.[211]

International treaties that impose legal obligations on States party constitute highly probative. evidence of the law of nations. Further, "[t]he more States that have ratified a treaty, especially those States with greater relative influence in international affairs, the greater the treaty's evidentiary value."[212]

b. Genocide

Plaintiffs who assert a claim under the ATCA must allege a violation of specific, universal, and obligatory international norms as part of such a claim.[213] In *Kadic v. Karadzic*, the Second Circuit held that acts of genocide are violations of the law of nations that may be the subject of ATCA claims against a private individual.[214] Other courts are in accord.[215] In concluding that genocide was actionable under the ATCA, the *Kadic* court relied on the Convention on the Prevention and Punishment of the Crime of Genocide

---

210. The Paquete Habana, 175 U.S. 677, 700 (1900); *see also Sosa*, 542 U.S. at 290; *Filartiga*, 630 F.2d at 880.

211. Statute of the International Court of Justice, article 38, June 26, 1945, 59 Stat. 1055, 1060, T.S. No. 933.

212. Almog v. Arab Bank, PLC, 471 F.Supp.2d 257, 273 (E.D.N.Y. 2007).

213. *Sosa*, 542 U.S. at 725; Papa v. United States, 281 F.3d 1004 (9th Cir. 2002).

214. Kadic v. Karadzic, 70 F.3d 232, 241–2 (2d Cir. 1995).

215. *See* Almog v. Arab Bank, PLC, 471 F.Supp.2d 257, 275 (E.D.N.Y. 2007) ("Applying the standards provided in the Genocide Convention and the Rome Statute to the facts alleged here, plaintiffs have successfully stated claims for genocide and crimes against humanity.").

("Genocide Convention"), which establishes that "genocide, whether committed in time of peace or in time of war, is a crime under international law."[216] The Genocide Convention has been ratified by more than 120 countries, including the United States.[217] Further, the international law norm proscribing genocide applies regardless of whether the defendant acted as a private individual or under color of law. Article IV makes clear that "[p]ersons committing genocide ... shall be punished, *whether they are constitutionally responsible rulers, public officials or private individuals.*"[218] Moreover, the Genocide Convention Implementation Act of 1987, 18 U.S.C. § 1091 (1988), provides that "[w]hoever" commits genocide shall be punished without regard to whether the offender was acting under color of law.[219] The court in *Kadic* embraced this view, holding that appellants' allegations "clearly state a violation of the international law norm proscribing genocide, regardless of whether Karadzi acted under color of law or as a private individual."[220]

c. War Crimes

Acts of murder, rape, torture, and arbitrary detention of civilians, committed during an armed conflict may support a claim under the ATCA. Such acts violate the law of war as codified by the Geneva Conventions of 1949.[221] The Geneva Conventions have been ratified by more than 180 nations, including the United States.[222] Common article 3 of the Conventions applies to "armed conflict[s] not of an international character" and binds "each Party to the conflict ... to apply, as a minimum, the following provisions":

> Persons taking no active part in the hostilities ... shall in all circumstances be treated humanely....

> To this end, the following acts are and shall remain prohibited at any time and in any place whatsoever with respect to the above-mentioned persons:

216. Convention on the Prevention and the Punishment of the Crime of Genocide, Dec. 9, 1948, 102 Stat. 3045, 78 U.N.T.S. 277, art. I; *see Kadic*, 70 F.3d at 241.

217. *Kadic*, 70 F.3d at 242. *See also* U.S. Dept. of State, *Treaties in Force* 345 (1994).

218. Genocide Convention, art. IV (emphasis added).

219. *Kadic*, 70 F.3d at 242. Genocide Convention Implementation Act of 1987, 18 U.S.C. § 1091 (1988) ("[w]hoever" commits genocide shall be punished, if the crime is committed within the United States or by a U.S. national).

220. *Kadic*, 70 F.3d at 242.

221. Convention for the Amelioration of the Condition of the Wounded and Sick in Armed Forces in the Field, 6 U.S.T. 3114, T.I.A.S. 3362, 75 U.N.T.S. 31[hereinafter *"Geneva Convention I"*]; Convention for the Amelioration of the Condition of the Wounded, Sick, and Shipwrecked Members of Armed Forces, 6 U.S.T. 3217, T.I.A.S. 3363, 75 U.N.T.S. 85; Convention Relative to the Treatment of Prisoners of War, 6 U.S.T. 3316, T.I.A.S. 3364, 75 U.N.T.S. 135; Convention Relative to the Protection of Civilian Persons in Time of War, 6 U.S.T. 3516, T.I.A.S. 3365, 75 U.N.T.S. 287.

222. *See* U.S. Department of State, *Treaties in Force*, at 398–99.

(a) violence to the life and person, in particular murder of all kinds, mutilation, cruel treatment and torture;

(b) taking of hostages;

(c) outrages upon personal dignity, in particular humiliating and degrading treatment;

(d) the passing of sentences and carrying out of executions without previous judgment pronounced by a regularly constituted court. . . .[223]

Under the Geneva Conventions, all "parties' to the conflict, which include insurgent groups, are obliged to adhere to these fundamental norms of the law of war."[224]

In *Kadic,* the plaintiffs alleged murder, rape, and other enumerated crimes committed against civilians in the course of armed hostilities.[225] The Second Circuit noted that such atrocities have long been recognized in international law as violations of the law of war.[226] The court held that the offenses alleged by plaintiffs, if proved, would violate "the most fundamental norms embodied in common article 3, which binds parties to internal conflicts."[227] Thus, the district court had jurisdiction pursuant to the ATCA over claims of war crimes and other violations of international humanitarian law.[228]

d. Crimes Against Humanity and Acts of Terrorism

In *Almog v. Arab Bank,* the court held that crimes against humanity violate the law of nations and these norms are of sufficient specificity and definiteness to be recognized under the ATS.[229] Crimes against humanity are part of jus cogens—the highest standing in international law norms.[230] Thus, the proscription of crimes against humanity constitutes a non-derogable rule of international law.[231] The *Almog* court cited numerous court decisions acknowledging that crimes against humanity are condemned by the civi-

---

223. *Geneva Convention I,* art. 3(1).

224. Kadic v. Karadzic, 70 F.3d 232, 242 (2d Cir. 1995).

225. *Id.*

226. *Id. See also* In re Yamashita, 327 U.S. 1 (1946).

227. *Id.* at 243.

228. *Id. See also* In re XE Services Alien Tort Litigation, 665 F.Supp.2d 569 (E.D. Va. 2009) (to state a valid claim for war crimes under the ATCA, plaintiffs must allege conduct constituting war crimes committed during an ongoing armed conflict).

229. Almog v. Arab Bank, PLC, 471 F.Supp.2d 257, 274 (E.D.N.Y. 2007). See also Kiobel v. Royal Dutch Petroleum Co., 456 F.Supp.2d 457 (S.D.N.Y. 2006) (Nigerian aliens stated claims for crimes against humanity under the ACTA); Doe v. Rafael Saravia, 348 F.Supp.2d 1112 (E.D. Cal. 2004) (assassination of El Salvadoran archbishop was crime against humanity actionable under the ATCA).

230. In re Agent Orange Prod. Liab. Litig., 373 F.Supp.2d 7, 136 (E.D.N.Y. 2005).

231. *Id.*

lized world.[232] Further, the court noted that Article 7 of the Rome Statute of the International Criminal Court ("Rome Statute"), punishes crimes against humanity.[233] The Rome Statute has been ratified by 110 nations, which establishes that the offense is a violation of international law.[234]

In *Almog*, the court held that suicide bombings and other murderous attacks on innocent civilians intended to intimidate or coerce a civilian population constitutes a violation of the law of nations.[235] The court observed that the prohibition against attacks on innocent civilians is reflected in the International Convention for the Suppression of Terrorist Bombings ("Terrorist Bombing Convention").[236] Article 2 provides in relevant part:

> Any person commits an offense within the meaning of this Convention if that person unlawfully and intentionally delivers, places, discharges or detonates an explosive or other lethal device in, into or against a place of public use, a State or government facility, a public transportation system or an infrastructure facility:
>
> (a) With the intent to cause death or serious bodily injury; or
>
> (b) With the intent to cause extensive destruction of such a place, facility or system, where such destruction results in or is likely to result in major economic loss.[237]

The Terrorist Bombing Convention makes it an offense to bomb public places or public transportation systems with the intent to cause death or serious bodily injury. Such acts are particularly condemned when intended to provoke a state of terror in the general public. In terms of its evidentiary weight, the Convention has been ratified by over 145 States, including the United States (June 26, 2002).[238] Further, United Nations Security Council Resolution 1566 condemns attacks against civilians intended to intimidate a civilian population, expressly providing that such attacks are under no circumstances justifiable by political, philosophical, ideological, racial, ethnic, or religious considerations.[239]

232. *Almog*, 471 F.Supp.2d at 274 (citing cases).

233. *Id.* at 275. Rome Statute of the International Criminal Court, July 17, 1998, 37 I.L.M. 999, 1004–05.

234. *See Treaties in Force, available at* http://state.gov/s/1treaty/tif/index. htm.

235. *Almog*, 471 F.Supp.2d at 279.

236. *Id.* at 276. International Convention for the Suppression of Terrorist Bombings, Jan. 12, 1998, G.A. Res. 52/164, 1, U.NH. Doc. A/RES/52/164.

237. Terrorist Bombing Convention, art. 2.

238. Convention for the Suppression of Terrorist Bombings, Jan. 12, 1998, art. 2, S. Treaty Doc. No. 106-6, 37 I.L.M. 249 available at http://treaties.un. org/.

239. S.C. Res. 1566, ¶ 3, U.N. Doc. S/RES/1566 (Oct. 8, 2004).

Two years after the Terrorist Bombing Convention was adopted by the United Nations General Assembly, the International Convention for the Suppression of the Financing of Terrorism ("Terrorist Financing Convention") was also adopted by the General Assembly.[240] The Terrorist Financing Convention has been ratified by 150 countries, including the United States (June 26, 2002).[241] The Convention makes it a crime to finance certain acts, including those proscribed by the Bombing Convention. Article 2 provides:

> Any person commits an offense within the meaning of the Convention if that person by any means, directly or indirectly, unlawfully and willfully provides or collects funds with the intention that they should be used or in the knowledge that they are to be used, in full or in part, in order to carry out:
>
> (a) An act which constitutes an offence within the scope of and as defined in [the Terrorist Bombing Convention]; or
>
> (b) Any other act intended to cause death or serious bodily injury to a civilian ... when the purpose of such act, by its nature and context, is to intimidate a population, or to compel a government or an international organization to do or abstain from doing any act.[242]

Further, Congress implemented the Terrorist Financing Convention by enacting the Suppression of the Financing of Terrorism Convention Implementation Act of 2002.[243]

After examining the Terrorist Bombing and Terrorist Financing Conventions, along with other authoritative sources, the *Almog* court held that "organized, systematic suicide bombings and other murderous attacks against innocent civilians for the purpose of intimidating a civilian population are a violation of the law of nations[for which this court ... recognize[s] a cause of action under the ATS."[244] Further the court posited that "the norm [terrorist bombing] is of sufficiently definite content and acceptance among

---

240. Almog v. Arab Bank, PLC, 471 F.Supp.2d 257, 277–8 (E.D.N.Y. 2007). International Convention for the Suppression of the Financing of Terrorism, Dec. 9, 1999, S. Treaty Doc. No. 106–49, 2178 U.N.T.S. 229.

241. Convention for the suppression of the Financing of Terrorism, 2175 U.N.T.S. 197, art. 6, U.N. Doc. A/RES/54/109 (Dec. 9, 1999) available at http://treaties.un.org/.

242. Terrorist Financing Convention, art. 2.

243. 18 U.S.C. § 2339C(a).

244. *Almog,* 471 F.Supp.2d at 285. The customary law of armed conflict, as reflected in the Geneva Conventions, also provided support for the court's conclusion. The court posited:

> While the principle of distinction and the Geneva Conventions apply expressly only in situations of armed conflict, their long-standing existence supports the conclusion, made explicit in the Bombing and Financing Conventions, that attacks against innocent civilians of the type alleged here are condemned by international law.

Id. at 279.

nations of the world as the historical paradigms familiar when § 1350 was enacted."[245]

Finally, hijacking constitutes a violation of the law of nations for purposes of the ATCA. In *Burnett v. Al Baraka Inv. and Development Corp.*, the district court upheld ATCA claims brought by foreign nationals who were victims of the September 11, 2001 terrorist attacks.[246] The court held that since aircraft hijacking was generally recognized as a violation of the law of nations, proof that defendants were accomplices, aiders and abettors, or co-conspirators would support a finding of liability under the ATCA.[247]

3. SECONDARY LIABILITY

a. Aiding and Abetting

A private cause of action may be sustained on a theory of aiding and abetting a violation of the law of nations. The Genocide, Terrorist Bombing and Terrorist Financing Conventions explicitly condemn acts of complicity or aiding and abetting by non-primary actors.[248] The concept of aiding and abetting liability is also recognized and enforced in international tribunals. The statutes creating the International Tribunals for the Former Yugoslavia and Rwanda impose individual criminal liability on any person "who planned, instigated, ordered, committed or otherwise aided and abetted in the planning, preparation or execution" of crimes within the jurisdiction of the tribunals.[249] The Rome Statute creating the International Criminal Court ("ICC") also authorizes criminal liability for aiding and abetting. Article 25(3)(c) provides that a person shall be criminally responsible for a crime within the jurisdiction of the Court if that person "aids, abets or otherwise assists in its commission."[250]

The courts consistently hold that plaintiffs may plead a theory of aiding and abetting liability under the ATCA.[251] In *Khulumani v.*

---

245. *Id.*

246. Burnett v. Al Baraka Inv. and Development Corp., 274 F.Supp.2d 86 (D.D.C. 2003).

247. *Id.*

248. *See* Genocide Convention, art. 3; Terrorist Bombing Convention, art. 2(3)(a); Terrorist Financing Convention, art. 2(5)(a).

249. Statute of the International Criminal Tribunal for Former Yugoslavia, U.N. S.C. Res. 827 (1993), art. 7; Statute of the International Tribunal for Rwanda, U.N. S.C. Res. 955 (Nov. 8, 1994), art. 6.

250. Rome Statute of the International Criminal Court (July 17, 1998), art. 25(3)(c).

251. *See* Presbyterian Church of Sudan v. Talisman Energy, Inc., 582 F.3d 244, 259 (2d Cir. 2009); In re South African Apartheid Litigation, 617 F.Supp.2d 228 (S.D.N.Y. 2009); Almog v. Arab Bank, PLC, 471 F.Supp.2d 257, 287 (E.D.N.Y. 2007) (noting the "vast body of law finding aiding and abetting liability available under the [ATCA]"); Kiobel v. Royal Dutch Petroleum Co., 456 F.Supp.2d 457, 463–64 (S.D.N.Y. 2006) (stating that "where a cause of action for violation of an international norm is viable under the ATS, claims for aiding and abetting that violation are viable as well"); Bowoto v. Chevron Corp., 2006 WL 2455752, *3–4 (N.D. Cal. 2006); In re Terrorist Attacks on September 11, 2001, 392 F.Supp.2d 539,

Barclay Nat. Bank, Ltd., the Second Circuit held that a defendant may be held liable for aiding and abetting in ATCA actions when such person "(1) provides practical assistance to the principal which has a *substantial effect* on the perpetration of the crime, and (2) does so with the *purpose* of facilitating the commission of that crime."[252] Thus, a defendant cannot be held liable under the ATCA absent proof that his conduct had a substantial effect upon the success of the criminal scheme and he acted with the purpose of aiding and abetting a violation of international law.[253] Further, the defendant's acts must have a "substantial effect" upon the success of the criminal venture. When so defined, aiding and abetting liability is sufficiently "well established[ ] [and] universally recognized" to be considered customary international law for the purposes of the ATCA.[254] Finally, applying the factors of Restatement (Second) of Torts § 867 for aiding and abetting, a defendant may further a violation of an international law in one of three ways: "(1) by knowingly ... assisting a principal tortfeasor ...; (2) by encouraging, advising ... a principal tortfeasor to commit an act while having actual or constructive knowledge that the principal tortfeasor will violate a clearly established customary international law norm ...; or (3) by facilitating the commission of human rights violations by providing the principal tortfeasor with the tools ... to commit those violations with actual or constructive knowledge that those tools ... will be (or could be) used in connection with that purpose."[255]

b. Conspiracy and Joint Criminal Enterprise

An ATCA claim may be based on a theory of conspiracy to violate the law of nations.[256] The Genocide Convention explicitly punishes conspiracy to commit acts of genocide.[257] However, conspiracy claims under the ATCA have been generally limited to conspiracy to commit genocide and wage aggressive war. In *Presbyterian Church of Sudan v. Talisman Energy, Inc.*, the Second

---

565 (S.D.N.Y. 2005); In re "Agent Orange" Prod. Liab. Litig., 373 F.Supp.2d 7, 52–54 (E.D.N.Y. 2005).

252. Khulumani v. Barclay Nat. Bank, Ltd., 504 F.3d 254, 277 (2d Cir. 2007). *See also* Presbyterian Church of Sudan v. Talisman Energy, Inc., 582 F.3d 244, 259 (2d Cir. 2009) ("[A]pplying international law, we hold that the mens rea standard for aiding and abetting liability in ATS actions is purpose rather than knowledge alone.").

253. *Khulumani*, 504 F.3d at 277.

254. *Id.*

255. *Lizarbe*, 642 F.Supp.2d at 491.

256. Cabello v. Fernandez–Larios, 402 F.3d 1148, 1157 (11th Cir. 2005) (affirming defendant's liability under the ATCA and TVPA for conspiring with members of the Chilean government to kill civilian prisoners in violation of international law); *Lizarbe*, 642 F.Supp.2d at 490 ("numerous U.S. and international bodies have recognized causes of action under the ATS/TVPA based on theories of conspiracy and aiding and abetting").

257. Genocide Convention, art. 3(B).

Circuit rejected plaintiffs claim that federal conspiracy law should apply to the ATCA.[258] The court held that while international law recognizes conspiracies to commit genocide and wage aggressive war, it does recognize liability encompassed by the *Pinkerton* doctrine.[259]

At lease one court has accepted the theory of joint criminal enterprise as an alternative basis for civil liability under the ATCA.[260] The concept of joint criminal enterprise provides for joint liability where there is a common design to pursue a course of conduct where: " '(i) the crime charged was a natural and foreseeable consequence of the execution of [the] enterprise, and (ii) the accused was aware that such a crime was a possible consequence of the execution of [the] enterprise, and, with that awareness, participated in [the] enterprise.' "[261] The Rome Statute of the International Criminal Court, as well as the Terrorist Bombing and Terrorist Financing Conventions, recognize criminal liability under the joint criminal enterprise doctrine.[262]

4.   TORTURE VICTIM PROTECTION ACT

a.   Introduction

The Torture Victim Protection Act ("TVPA"), enacted in 1992, creates a private cause of action for official torture and extrajudicial killing. The TVPA provides:

> An individual who, under actual or apparent authority, or color of law, of any foreign nation—
>
> (1) subjects an individual to torture shall, in a civil action, be liable for damages to that individual; or

258. Presbyterian Church of Sudan v. Talisman Energy, Inc., 582 F.3d 244, 260 (2d Cir. 2009).

259. *Id.* Under the *Pinkerton* doctrine a defendant is vicariously liable for criminal acts committed by (1) members of the conspiracy, (2) during the conspiracy, (3) in furtherance of the conspiracy, (4) while defendant was a member of the conspiracy, regardless of whether the defendant had the intent to commit the criminal acts. Pinkerton v. United States, 328 U.S. 640 (1946).

260. Bowoto v. Chevron Corp., et al., 2006 WL 2455752, at *8 n. 13 (N.D. Cal. 2006).

261. Lizarbe v. Rondon, 642 F.Supp.2d 473 (D. Md. 2009) (quoting Prosecutor v. Brdjanin, Case No. IT–99–36–T, Judgment, ¶ 265 (Sept. 1, 2004)).

262. Rome Statute, art. 25(3)(d); Terrorist Bombing Convention, art. 2(c); Terrorist Financing Convention, art.

5(c). Article 2 of the Rome Statute provides:

[A] person shall be criminally responsible . . . for a crime within the jurisdiction of the Court if that person:

(d) In any other way contributes to the commission or attempted commission of such a crime by a group of such persons acting with a common purpose. Such contribution shall be intentional and shall either:

(i) Be made with the aim of furthering the criminal activity or criminal purpose of the group, where such activity or purpose involves the commission of a crime within the jurisdiction of the Court; or

(ii) Be made in the knowledge of the intention of the group to commit the crime.

(2) subjects an individual to extrajudicial killing shall, in a civil action, be liable for damages to the individual's legal representative, or to any person who may be a claimant in an action for wrongful death.[263]

The TVPA creates a cause of action for official torture and extrajudicial killing. However, unlike the ATCA, this statute is not itself a jurisdictional statute.[264] Plaintiffs pursue their TVPA claims under the jurisdiction conferred by the ATCA and also under the general federal question jurisdiction of section 1331.[265]

"Torture," under the TVPA means "any act, directed against an individual in the offender's custody or physical control, by which severe pain or suffering . . . is intentionally inflicted."[266] The term "extrajudicial killing" means "a deliberated killing not authorized by a previous judgment pronounced by a regularly constituted court affording all the judicial guarantees which are recognized as indispensable by civilized peoples."[267]

The TVPA renders liable only those individuals who have committed torture or extrajudicial killing "under actual or apparent authority, or color of law, of any *foreign* nation."[268] To prove a claim, "the plaintiff must establish some [foreign] governmental involvement in the torture or killing."[269] Further, because the

263. 28 U.S.C. § 1350 note (a)(1).

264. *See* Kadic v. Karadzic, 70 F.3d 232, 246 (2d Cir. 1995).

265. *Id. But see* Arce v. Garcia, 434 F.3d 1254, 1257 n. 8 (11th Cir. 2006) (section 1331, not the ATCA, provides the jurisdictional basis for the TVPA).

266. 28 U.S.C. § 1350 note § (3)(b)(1). The TVPA defines "torture" as

any act, directed against an individual in the offenders' custody or physical control, by which severe pain or suffering (other than pain or suffering arising only from or inherent in, or incidental to lawful sanctions), whether physical or mental, is intentionally inflicted on that individual for such purposes as obtaining from that individual or a third person information or a confession, punishing that individual for an act that individual or a third person has committed or is suspected of having committed, intimidating or coercing that individual or a third person, or for any reason

based on discrimination of any kind.

267. *Id.* at § 3(a). *See* Estate of Bayani v. Islamic Republic of Iran, 530 F.Supp.2d 40 (D.D.C. 2007) (execution of naturalized American citizen by Islamic Republic of Iran was extrajudicial killing under the TVPA); Bakhtiar v. Islamic Republic of Iran, 571 F.Supp.2d 27 (D.D.C. 2008) (assassination of former Iranian prime minister constituted "extrajudicial killing").

268. *Id.* at § 2(a) (emphasis added). *See also* United States v. Arar, 585 F.3d 559 (2d Cir. 2009); *Kadic,* 70 F.3d at 245.

269. *Kadic,* 70 F.3d at 245 (quoting H.R.REP. NO. 367, 102d Cong., 2d Sess., at 5(1991), reprinted in 1992 U.S.C.C.A.N. 84, 87). *See also* Arar v. Ashcroft, 585 F.3d 559 (2d Cir. 2009) (*en banc*) ("[T]o state a claim under the TVPA, Arar must . . . allege that the defendants possessed power under Syrian law, and that the offending actions (i.e., Arar's removal to Syria and subsequent torture) derived from an exercise of that power, or that defendants could not have undertaken their culpable actions absent such power."); Harbury v.

statute does not extend to torture or killing by non-state actors, it would have no application to acts of torture or killing committed by members of private terrorist groups.[270] However, the state action requirement of the TVPA does not require that the particular government be officially recognized. Certain private groups, such as the Taliban, may constitute the *de facto* government which may be held liable under the TVPA.[271] In construing the term "color of law," courts are instructed to look to jurisprudence under 42 U.S.C. § 1983.[272] Under section 1983, "[t]he traditional definition of acting under color of state law requires that the defendant ... have exercised power 'possessed by virtue of state law and made possible only because the wrongdoer is clothed with the authority of state law.' "[273] The determination of whether a non-state party acts under color of state law requires a fact-specific judgment focusing on whether particular conduct may be attributed to the state.[274]

Under the TVPA, a cause of action may be brought by *any* individual.[275] Unlike the ATA, which is limited to claims brought by a U.S. citizen, and the ATCA, which restricts claims to those filed by an alien, the TVPA creates a cause of action for torture and extrajudicial killing committed against any "individual." Further, a private "individual" is liable under the TVPA if he commits torture or extrajudicial killing while acting under color of authority.[276] Only "individuals" are liable for damages under the statute. The term "individual" means human beings, and does not include organizations, such as the Palestinian Authority or Palestinian Liberation Organization,[277] or various Islamic charities and organizations that allegedly provided material support to foreign terrorists.[278] Further, the TVPA does not create a cause of action against foreign states, or their agencies or instrumentalities.[279] The text of the statute

Hayden, 444 F.Supp.2d 19 (D.D.C. 2006) (allegations that CIA agents tortured and murdered Guatemalan rebel leader did not raise a claim under the TVPA because agents were acting under color of federal law, not foreign law).

270. *See, e.g.*, Romero v. Drummond Co., Inc., 552 F.3d 1303 (11th Cir. 2008) (proof of general relationship between the Colombian government and paramilitary forces allegedly recruited by executives of U.S. corporation's Colombian subsidiary to torture and murder union leaders was insufficient to satisfy the "state action" requirement of the TVPA).

271. *See* Doe v. Islamic Salvation Front, 993 F.Supp. 3 (D.D.C. 1998).

272. Kadic v. Karadzic, 70 F.3d 232, 245 (2d Cir. 1995).

273. West v. Atkins, 487 U.S. 42, 49 (1988) (*quoting* United States v. Classic, 313 U.S. 299, 326 (1941)). *See also Arar v. Ashcroft*, 585 F.3d at 568.

274. *See* Brentwood Acad. v. Tenn. Secondary Sch. Athletic Ass'n, 531 U.S. 288, 295 (2001). *See also Arar v. Ashcroft*, 585 F.3d at 568.

275. 28 U.S.C. § 1350 note § (2)(a).

276. *Id.* at § 2(a)(1) & (2).

277. *See* Mohamad v. Rajoub, 664 F.Supp.2d 20, 22 (D.D.C. 2009).

278. *See* In re Terrorist Attacks on September 11, 2001, 538 F.3d 71 (2d Cir. 2008).

279. *See* Holland v. Islamic Republic of Iran, 496 F.Supp.2d 1, 18 (D.D.C. 2005) (based on the plain language of the statute and legislative history, the

(which specifies only individuals) and the legislative history establish Congress's intent "to confine liability for acts of torture and extrajudicial killing to private individuals," not foreign states.[280] However, the courts remain divided on whether the TVPA applies to corporations.[281]

The TVPA requires a plaintiff to exhaust available remedies in the place where the torture or extrajudicial killing occurred, to the extent that such remedies are "adequate and available," prior to suing in the U.S.[282] However, exhaustion of remedies is not required " 'when foreign remedies are unobtainable, ineffective, inadequate, or obviously futile.' "[283] Under the TVPA, the defendant bears the burden of proving that available and adequate remedies exist in the country where the tort was committed.[284] However, few cases under the TVPA have been dismissed for failure to exhaust domestic remedies.[285] Further, plaintiffs may not avoid the requirements of the TVPA by pursuing claims of torture and extrajudicial killing, as common law violations of the law of nations, under the ATCA generally. In *Enahoro v. Abubakar*, the Seventh Circuit held that

TVPA applies only to individuals, not foreign states); Collett v. Socialist Peoples' Libyan Arab Jamahiriya, 362 F.Supp.2d 230, 242 (D.D.C. 2005) (holding the TVPA does not apply to Libya or a Libyan intelligence agency).

280. Dammarell v. Islamic Republic of Iran, 2005 WL 756090 at *31; *see also* Mohamad v. Rajoub, 664 F.Supp.2d 20 (D.D.C.2009) (same); H.R. REP. NO. 102–367 (1991) (1992 U.S.CODE CONG. & ADMIN. NEWS 1991, pp. 84, 87 ("Only 'individuals,' not foreign states, can be sued under the bill."); S.REP. NO. 102–249, 1 (1991) ("The legislation uses the term 'individual' to make crystal clear that foreign states or their entities cannot be sued under this bill under any circumstances; only individuals may be sued.").

281. *See* Doe v. Exxon Mobil Corp., 393 F.Supp.2d 20, 28 (D.D.C. 2005) ("On balance, the plain reading of the statute strongly suggests that it only covers human beings, and not corporations."); Arndt v. UBS AG, 342 F.Supp.2d 132 (E.D.N.Y. 2004) (TVPA does not apply to Swiss corporation); Beanal v. Freeport–McMoRan, Inc., 969 F.Supp. 362 (E.D. La. 1997) (corporation is not an "individual" under the TVPA); *but see* Romero v. Drummond Co., Inc., 552 F.3d 1303 (11th Cir. 2008) (TVPA allows suits against corporate defendants); Aldana v. Del Monte Fresh Pro-

duce, N.A., Inc., 416 F.3d 1242, 1265 (11th Cir. 2005) (same).

282. 28 U.S.C. § 1350(2)(b). *See also* Enahoro v. Abubakar, 408 F.3d 877 (7th Cir. 2005); *Kadic*, 70 F.3d at 245 (the TVPA "requires that a plaintiff exhaust adequate and available local remedies"); Lizarbe v. Rondon, 642 F.Supp.2d 473, 483 (D.C. Md. 2009) (holding, remedy in Peru was ineffective and inadequate; plaintiff cannot obtain a civil remedy until the criminal charges against a defendant are adjudicated); Cabiri v. Assasie–Gyimah, 921 F.Supp. 1189 (S.D.N.Y. 1996) (exhaustion of remedies not required, where Ghana provided inadequate and unacceptable remedies for torture victim's claims).

283. *Lizarbe*, 642 F.Supp.2d at 484 (quoting S.Rep. No. 102–249, pt. 4, at 10 (1991)). It should be noted that the ATCA contains no exhaustion requirement. *See* Sarei v. Rio Tinto, PLC, 487 F.3d 1193, 1212–15 (9th Cir. 2007); Jean v. Dorelien, 431 F.3d 776, 781 (11th Cir. 2005); *Lizarbe*, 642 F.Supp.2d at 484.

284. *Lizarbe*, 642 F.Supp.2d at 484.

285. *Id.* at 485. *But see* Harbury v. Hayden, 444 F.Supp.2d 19 (D.D.C. 2006) (TVPA claim dismissed; victim's widow failed to exhaust her remedies in Guatemala); Corrie v. Caterpillar, Inc., 403 F.Supp.2d 1019 (W.D. Wash. 2005) (TVPA victim failed to exhaust remedies in Israel).

the TVPA essentially "occupied the field" as to claims of torture or extrajudicial killing, such that any common law claims were supplanted by the TVPA's provisions.[286] Further elaborating on the relationship between the ATCA and the TVPA, the court stated:

> It is hard to imagine that the *Sosa* Court would approve of common law claims based on torture and extrajudicial killing when Congress has specifically provided a cause of action for those violations and has set out how those claims must proceed. As relevant to this case, then, the ATS would provide jurisdiction over a suit against [the defendant] for violations of the Torture Victim Protection Act.[287]

Finally, the TVPA imposes a ten-year statute of limitations.[288] Subject to equitable tolling, the statute allows ten years from the time of the underlying offense for a plaintiff to bring a claim.[289] Equitable tolling delays the running of the statute of limitations in cases "where-due to circumstances external to the party's own conduct-it would be unconscionable to enforce the limitations period against the party and gross injustice would result."[290] The Supreme Court has stated that equitable tolling should be used sparingly and not applied when a claimant failed to preserve legal rights by exercising due diligence.[291] Courts have routinely applied the doctrine when it appears that "plaintiffs had no reasonable opportunity to pursue claims as a result of civil war, violence, imprisonment, and repressive and brutal acts against society."[292] Plaintiffs have the burden of proof on the issue of equitable tolling.[293]

B. SUING STATE SPONSORS OF TERRORISM

1. STATE–SPONSORED TERRORISM EXCEPTION TO FOREIGN STATE IMMUNITY

The Foreign Sovereign Immunities Act of 1976 ("FSIA") grants foreign states and their agencies and instrumentalities im-

286. *Enahoro,* 408 F.3d at 884–85.

287. *Id.* at 886.

288. 28 U.S.C. § 1350 note § 2(c).

289. *See Lizarbe,* 642 F.Supp.2d at 480; Doe v. Islamic Salvation Front, 257 F.Supp.2d 115, 119 (D.D.C. 2003).

290. Rouse v. Lee, 339 F.3d 238, 246 (4th Cir. 2003) (internal citations omitted).

291. *See* Irwin v. Department of Veterans Affairs, 498 U.S. 89, 96 (1990).

292. *Lizarbe,* 642 F.Supp.2d at 480. *See also* Arce v. Garcia, 434 F.3d 1254, 1263–64 (11th Cir. 2006) (equitable tolling from 1979 to 1992 based on "abductions, torture, and murder by the mili-

tary . . . [and] a judiciary too meek to stand against the [Salvadoran] regime"); Cabello v. Fernandez–Larios, 402 F.3d 1148, 1154–55 (11th Cir. 2005) (statute of limitations in TVPA case filed 26 years after the victim's death was properly tolled); Chavez v. Carranza, 407 F.Supp.2d 925, 929 (W.D.Tenn. 2004) (equitable tolling from 1979 to 1994 because the plaintiffs feared government reprisal if they complained about murder, torture and rape that occurred during the civil war in El Salvador).

293. *See Arce,* 434 F.3d at 1261, *Lizarbe,* 642 F.Supp.2d at 480.

munity from suit in the United States subject to enumerated exceptions.[294] The FSIA reflects a "restrictive" theory of sovereign immunity, under which immunity is confined to suits arising from the foreign state's public acts, and does not extend to acts that are private in nature, such as commercial activities.[295] Under the Act, a "foreign state" is presumptively immune from the jurisdiction of United States courts.[296] Unless a statutory exception applies, federal courts lack subject-matter jurisdiction over a claim against a foreign state.[297] Further, the FSIA provides the sole basis for obtaining

294. 28 U.S.C. §§ 1602–1611 (1976). Section 1604 provides: "Subject to existing international agreements to which the United States is a party at the time of enactment of this Act a foreign state shall be immune from the jurisdiction of the courts of the United States and of the States except as provided in sections 1605 to 1607 of this chapter."

295. 28 U.S.C. §§ 1602, 1603(d)–(e), 1605(a)(2). *See* Verlinden B.V. v. Central Bank of Nigeria, 461 U.S. 480, 488–89 (1983); *see also* H.R.Rep. No. 94–1487, at 7 (1976), *reprinted in* 1976 U.S.C.C.A.N. 6604, 6605 ("[T]he bill would codify the so-called 'restrictive' principle of sovereign immunity, as presently recognized in international law. Under this principle, the immunity of a foreign state is 'restricted' to suits involving a foreign state's public acts (jure imperii) and does not extend to suits based on its commercial or private acts (jure gestionis).").

296. The Act defines "foreign state" in § 1603 as follows:

(a) A "foreign state" . . . includes a political subdivision of a foreign state or an agency or instrumentality of a foreign state as defined in subsection (b).

(b) An "agency or instrumentality of a foreign state" means any entity—

(1) which is a separate legal person, corporate or otherwise, and

(2) which is an organ of a foreign state or political subdivision thereof, or a majority or whose shares or other ownership interest is owned by a foreign state or political subdivision thereof, and

(3) which is neither a citizen of a State of the United States as defined in section 1332(c) and

(e) of this title, nor created under the laws of any third country.

297. Saudi Arabia v. Nelson, 507 U.S. 349, 355 (1993). The FSIA recognizes exceptions to jurisdictional immunity of foreign states for commercial activities and torts. Section 1605(a)(2) provides that a foreign state shall not be immune from the jurisdiction of U.S. courts for actions based upon a "commercial activity" carried on in the United States by a foreign state. 28 U.S.C. § 1605(a)(2). Section 1605(a)(5), the torts exception, provides that a foreign state shall not be immune from the jurisdiction of the courts of the U.S. in any case

[I]n which money damages are sought against a foreign state for personal injury or death, or damage to or loss of property, occurring in the United States and caused by the tortious act or omission of that foreign state or of any official or employee of that foreign state while acting within the scope of his office or employment.

Subsection A then provides an exception to this exception:

[Section (a)(5) shall not apply to] any claim based upon the exercise or performance or the failure to exercise or perform a discretionary function regardless of whether the discretion be abused. 28 U.S.C. § 1605(a)(5)(A).

Courts have consistently denied terrorism-related claims based on the "commercial activity" and "noncommercial tort" exceptions, holding either that the foreign state was not engaged in commercial activity in the U.S. or "discretionary exception" to the noncommercial tort exception applied. *See, e.g.,* Burnett v. Al Baraka Inv. & Dev. Corp., 292 F.Supp.2d 9, 17–21 (D.D.C. 2003);

jurisdiction over a foreign state in U.S. courts.[298] Thus, the FSIA "must be applied by the District Courts in every action against a foreign sovereign, since subject matter jurisdiction in any such action depends on the existence of one of the specified exceptions to foreign sovereign immunity."[299]

Under the FSIA, immunity extends to "an agency or instrumentality" of a foreign state.[300] In *Samantar v. Yousuf*, the United States Supreme Court resolved a conflict in the federal circuits over whether a foreign official is entitled to immunity under the FSIA.[301] More specifically, the Supreme Court held that the term "agency or instrumentality" of a foreign state does not include a foreign official acting on behalf of the foreign state.[302] The Court concluded that based on the language and structure of the statute, corporations or other business entities, but not natural persons, may qualify as agencies or instrumentalities.[303] Focusing on section 1603(b), the Court stated that the statute specifies that "agency or instrumentality" means any "entity," and "entity" typically refers to an organization, rather than an individual.[304] Moreover, the Court observed that elsewhere in the FSIA Congress expressly mentioned officials when it intended to count their acts as equivalent to those of the foreign state, which suggests that officials are included within the term "foreign state." For example, under section 1605(a)(5), Congress provided an exception from the grant of immunity for cases in which "money damages are sought against a foreign state" for an injury in the United States "caused by the tortious act or omission of that foreign state or of any official or employee of that foreign state while acting within the scope of his office."[305] The Court opined: "If the term 'foreign state' by definition includes an individual acting within the scope of this office, the phrase 'or of any official or employee ...' in 28 U.S.C. § 1605(a)(5) would be unnecessary."[306]

In re Terrorist Attacks on Sept. 11, 2001, 349 F.Supp.2d 765 (S.D.N.Y. 2005).

298. Argentine Republic v. Amerada Hess Shipping Corp., 488 U.S. 428, 443 (1989) ("We hold that the FSIA provides the sole basis for obtaining jurisdiction over a foreign state in the courts of this country....").

299. Verlinden B.V. v. Central Bank of Nigeria, 461 U.S. 480, 493 (1983) (citing 28 U.S.C. § 1330(a)).

300. 28 U.S.C. § 1603(a).

301. Samantar v. Yousuf, 130 S.Ct. 2278 (2010).

302. *Id.* at 2292-3. The Court's decision abrogated In re Terrorist Attacks

on September 11, 2001, 538 F.3d 71, 83 (2d Cir. 2008); Keller v. Central Bank of Nigeria, 277 F.3d 811, 815-16 (6th Cir. 2002); Byrd v. Corporacion Forestal y Industrial de Olancho, 182 F.3d 380, 388-89 (5th Cir. 1999); El-Fadl v. Central Bank of Jordan, 75 F.3d 668, 671 (D.C. Cir. 1996); Chuidian v. Philippine Nat'l Bank, 912 F.2d 1095, 1103 (9th Cir. 1990).

303. *Samantar v. Yousuf*, 130 S.Ct. at 2286-88.

304. *Id.* at 2286.

305. 28 U.S.C. § 1605(a)(5).

306. *Samantar v. Yousuf*, 130 S.Ct. at 2288.

Finally, the Court rejected petitioner's argument that the FSIA codified the common law, which in petitioner's view was co-extensive with the law of state immunity and always immunized a foreign officials for acts taken on behalf of the foreign state.[307] The Court stated: "Although Congress clearly intended to supersede the common-law regime for claims against foreign states, we find nothing in the statute's origin or aims to indicate that Congress similarly wanted to codify the law of foreign official immunity."[308]

In 1996, Congress amended the FSIA to allow civil suits by U.S. victims of terrorism against a foreign state and their agencies and instrumentalities.[309] The Anti–Terrorism and Effective Death Penalty Act of 1996 ("AEDPA") amended the FSIA to provide that a foreign state is not immune from the jurisdiction of U.S. courts in any case—

> in which money damages are sought against a foreign state for personal injury or death that was caused by an act of torture, extrajudicial killing, aircraft sabotage, hostage taking, or the provision of material support or resources (as defined in section 2339A of title 18) for such an act if such act or provision of material support is engaged in by an official, employee, or agent of such foreign state while acting within the scope of his or her office, employment, or agency.[310]

The AEDPA, codified at 28 U.S.C. § 1605(a)(7), requires that the foreign state be designated as a state sponsor of terrorism at the time the act occurred or was later designated as such as a consequence of the act in question,[311] and that the foreign state be afforded an opportunity to arbitrate the claim if the terrorist act occurred in the territory of the defendant State.

After a court found that the waiver of sovereign immunity did not create a private right of action,[312] Congress enacted the Civil Liability for Acts of State–Sponsored Terrorism, also known as the *Flatow* Amendment.[313] The *Flatow* amendment gave parties injured

307. *Id.* at 2289.

308. *Id.* at 2292.

309. P.L. 104–132, Title II, § 221 (April 23, 1996); 110 Stat. 1241; 28 U.S.C. § 1605(a)(7) (repealed 2008).

310. 28 U.S.C. § 1605(a)(7) (repealed 2008).

311. The State Department designates state sponsors of terrorism pursuant to § 6(j) of the Export Administration Act of 1979 (50 App. U.S.C. § 2405(j)), § 620A of the Foreign Assistance Act (22 U.S.C. § 2371), and § 40(d) of the Arms Export Control Act

(22 U.S.C. § 2780(d)). Currently, the list of state sponsors of terrorism includes Cuba, Iran, Sudan, and Syria. *See infra* note 325.

312. *See* Flatow v. Islamic Republic of Iran, 999 F.Supp. 1 (D.D.C. 1998) (terrorism exception lifts foreign sovereign immunity, but does not create a private right of action).

313. Civil Liability for Acts of State–Sponsored Terrorism, P.L. 104–208, Title I, § 101(c) (September 30, 1996), 110 Stat. 3009–172; *codified at* 28 U.S.C. § 1605 note. This provision is known as the "Flatow Amendment," in

or killed by a terrorist act covered by the FSIA exception, or their legal representatives, a private cause of action for suits against "an official, employee, or agent of a foreign state designated as a state sponsor of terrorism" who commits the terrorist act "while acting within the scope of his or her office, employment, or agency."[314] Following the *Flatow* amendment, several suits were quickly filed against state sponsors of terrorism, including Iran, pursuant to the new provisions.[315] However, in 2004, civil litigation under the state terrorism exception was abruptly brought to a halt. In *Cicippio–Puleo v. Islamic Republic of Iran*, the D.C. Circuit Court of Appeals held that "neither 28 U.S.C. § 1605(a)(7) nor the Flatow Amendment, nor the two consolidated in tandem, creates a private right of action against a foreign government."[316] The court found that the *Flatow* Amendment creates a cause of action, but the liability imposed by the statute is limited to "an official, employee, or agent of a foreign state designated as a state sponsor of terrorism."[317] The D.C. Circuit further restricted the scope of liability stating that "insofar as the Flatow Amendment creates a private right of action against officials, employees, and agents of foreign states, the cause of action is limited to claims against those officials in their *individual*, as opposed to their official capacities."[318] According to the court, a claim against an individual acting in his official capacity is "in substance a claim against the government itself."[319] Thus, the

recognition of the family of Alisa Flatow, a college student studying abroad, who was killed in a terrorist in Israel. *See Flatow v. Islamic Republic of Iran*, 999 F.Supp.2d at 12.

The Flatow Amendment provides:

An official, employee, or agent of a foreign state designated as a state sponsor of terrorism ... while acting within the scope of his or her office, employment, or agency shall be liable to a United States national or the national's legal representative for personal injury or death caused by acts of that official, employee, or agent for which the courts of the United States may maintain jurisdiction under section 1605(a)(7) of title 28, United States Code ... for money damages which may include economic damages, solatium, pain and suffering, and punitive damages if the acts were among those described in section 1605(a)(7).

Omnibus Consolidated Appropriations Act, Pub. L. No. 104–208, § 589, 110 Stat. 3009–172 (1997), *codified in* 28 U.S.C. § 1605 note (2000).

314. 28 U.S.C. § 1605 note.

315. *See* Price v. Socialist People's Libyan Arab Jamahiriya, 274 F.Supp.2d 20, 32 (D.D.C. 2003); Smith v. Islamic Emirate of Afghanistan, 262 F.Supp.2d 217, 228 (S.D.N.Y. 2003); Cronin v. Islamic Republic of Iran, 238 F.Supp.2d 222, 231 (D.D.C. 2002).

316. Cicippio–Puleo v. Islamic Republic of Iran, 353 F.3d 1024, 1033 (D.C. Cir. 2004), *cert. denied,* 544 U.S. 1010 (2005). The Cicippio–Puleo case involved claims brought by relatives of Joseph Cicippio against Iran for financing the Hezbollah terrorists who kidnapped him in Beirut and held him hostage there for five years.

317. *Id.* at 1034 (quoting 28 U.S.C. § 1605 note).

318. *Id.* at 1034.

319. *Id. See also* In re Terrorist Attacks on September 11, 2001, 538 F.3d 71, 81 (2d Cir. 2008) ("We join our sister circuits in holding that an individual official of a foreign state acting in his official capacity is the 'agency or instrumentality' of the state, and is thereby protected by the FSIA."); Velasco v. Government of Indonesia, 370 F.3d 392, 399 (4th Cir. 2004) ("Claims

plaintiffs' only recourse is against foreign officials acting *ultra vires*.[320] Following *Cicippio–Puleo*, in *Acree v. Republic of Iraq*, the D.C. Circuit also held that FSIA plaintiffs cannot state a claim under the "generic common law" but must "identify a particular cause of action arising out of a specific source of law."[321] Following *Cicippio–Puleo* and *Acree,* courts uniformly held that the state common law or statutory laws of the state of the plaintiffs' domicile may be used to determine liability under the terrorism exception.[322] As a result, plaintiffs sued leaders of foreign states under the FSIA in their personal capacities, advancing claims based on state tort law of the domicile of the injured party or decedent.[323] However, the application of state tort law resulted in some disparity in the availability and amount of damages to which a successful plaintiff may be entitled.[324]

2. THE NATIONAL DEFENSE AUTHORIZATION ACT OF 2008

On January 28, 2008, the National Defense Authorization Act of 2008 ("NDAA") was enacted into law.[325] The NDAA, § 1083, revised the terrorism exception to foreign sovereign immunity by repealing § 1605(a)(7) of Title 28 and replaced it with a new provision, 28 U.S.C. § 1605A, which explicitly provides a private right of action against foreign state sponsors of terrorism.[326] The revised state-sponsored terrorism exception provides that a foreign state shall not be immune from suit in U.S. courts where plaintiffs seek money damages for personal injury or death caused by an act of "torture, extrajudicial killing, aircraft sabotage, hostage taking, or the provision of material support or resources," when conducted

---

against the individual in his official capacity are the practical equivalent of claims against the foreign state.").

320. *See Cicippio–Puleo*, 353 F.3d at 1034.

321. Acree v. Republic of Iraq, 370 F.3d 41, 59 (D.C. Cir. 2004), *cert. denied,* 544 U.S. 1010 (2005).

322. *See* Rux v. Republic of Sudan, 495 F.Supp.2d 541, 557 (E.D. Va. 2007) (citing cases). *See also* Dammarell v. Islamic Republic of Iran, 2005 WL 756090, at *14 (D.D.C. 2005) (After examining the text, structure, and legislative history of §§ 1605(a)(7) and 1606, the court concluded that "the causes of action that may be brought against the foreign state ... include any claims that could be brought against a private individual in like circumstances," including claims arising under "state common and statutory law, federal statutory law, and even the law of a foreign state.").

323. *See* Gates v. Syrian Arab Republic, 580 F.Supp.2d 53, 65 (D.D.C. 2008); *Rux v. Republic of Sudan*, 495 F.Supp.2d at 557; Blais v. Islamic Republic of Iran, 459 F.Supp.2d 40, 54–55 (D.D.C. 2006) (applying state laws of battery and intentional infliction of emotional distress); Reed v. Islamic Republic of Iran, 439 F.Supp.2d 53, 65–68 (D.D.C. 2006) (applying Massachusetts law); Price v. Socialist People's Libyan Arab Jamahiriya, 384 F.Supp. 2d 120, 132–34 (D.D.C. 2005) (applying state laws of assault, battery, and intentional infliction of emotional distress).

324. *See* Peterson v. Islamic Republic of Iran, 515 F.Supp.2d 25, 46 (D.D.C. 2007).

325. National Defense Authorization Act, Pub.L.No. 110–181, 122 Stat. 3, 338–44 (2008).

326. Section 1083(b)(1)(A)(iii) expressly repeals 28 U.S.C. § 1605(a)(7).

by "an official, employee, or agent of such foreign state while acting within the scope of his or her office, employment or agency."[327]

a. Private Right of Action

Most importantly, section 1605A(c) creates a private cause of action against a foreign state that is or was a state sponsor of terrorism for actions arising from the commission of five different crimes: (1) torture, (2) extrajudicial killing, (3) aircraft sabotage, (4) hostage taking, and (5) providing material support or resources to terrorists.[328] Section 1605A(c) provides:

> A foreign state that is or was a state sponsor of terrorism ... and any official, employee, or agent of that foreign state while acting within the scope of his or her office, employment, or agency, shall be liable ... for personal injury or death caused by acts described in subsections (a)(1) of that foreign state, or of an official, employee, or agent of that foreign state, for which the courts of the United States may maintain jurisdiction under this section for money damages.[329]

Liability extends to foreign terrorist states as well as their officials, employees, and agents, acting within the scope of their office, employment or agency.[330]

The terrorism exception only waives immunity of a foreign state that was "designated as a state sponsor of terrorism at the time the [terrorist] act ... occurred, or was so designated as a result of such act."[331] There are currently four states that have been designated by the Secretary of State as state sponsors of terrorism: Cuba, Iran, Sudan, and Syria.[332] All other states, such as

---

327. 28 U.S.C. § 1605A.

328. The terms "torture" and "extrajudicial killing" have "the meaning given those terms in section 3 of the Torture Victim Protection Act of 1991 (28 U.S.C. § 1350 note)." 28 U.S.C. § 1605A(h)(7). The term "aircraft sabotage has the meaning given that term in Article 1 of the Convention for the Suppression of Unlawful Acts Against the Safety of Civil Aviation,'" 974 U.N.T.S. 177, 24 U.S.T. 564, T.I.A.S. No. 7570 (1971). 28 U.S.C. § 1605A(h)(1). The term "hostage taking" has 'the meaning given that term in Article 1 of the International Convention Against the Taking of Hostages," 1316 U.N.T.S. 205 (1979). Id. at § 1605A(h)(2). Finally, the term "material support or resources" has "the meaning given that term in § 2339A of title 18." 28 U.S.C. § 1605A(h)(3).

329. 28 U.S.C. § 1605A(c).

330. Id.

331. 28 U.S.C. § 1605A(a)(2). The term "state sponsor of terrorism" means "a country the government of which the Secretary of State has determined, for purposes of section 6(j) of the Export Administration Act of 1979 (50 U.S.C. App. 2405(I)), section 620A of the Foreign Assistance Act of 1961 (22 U.S.C. 2371), section 40 of the Arms Export Control Act (22 U.S.C. 2780), or any other provision of law, is a government that has repeatedly provided support for acts of international terrorism." 28 U.S.C. § 1605A(h)(6).

332. See U.S. Dep't of State, State Sponsors of Terrorism, available at http://www.state.gov/s/ct/c14151htm. (last visited February 5, 2010). Iran has been designated a state sponsor of terrorism continuously since January 19, 1984. See 31 C.F.R. § 596.201 (2001);

Saudi Arabia, Somalia and Yemen, retain foreign sovereign immunity from prosecution under the FSIA.[333] Section 1605A(c) expands jurisdiction beyond claims brought by U.S. nationals as victim or claimant. Under the statute, a foreign state that is or was a state sponsor of terrorism shall to liable to "(1) a national of the United States,[334] (2) a member of the armed forces, (3) an employee of the Government of the United States, or of an individual performing a contract awarded by the United States Government, acting within the scope of the employer's employment, or (4) the legal representative of a person described in paragraph (1), (2), or (3)."[335] Section 1605A(a)(2)(A)(ii) requires only that either the claimant or the victim be a U.S. national, member of the armed forces, an employee of the United States Government, or an individual performing a contract awarded by the United States Government at the time of the act of terrorism.[336] Thus, relatives of a victim who was a United States national at the time of the terrorist attack have standing even though the relatives themselves were not U.S. nationals.[337]

Damages for proven acts of terrorism under section 1605A(c) may include economic damages, solatium, pain and suffering, and punitive damages.[338] Subsection (d) provides that actions may also be brought for reasonably foreseeable property loss, third party liability, and life and property insurance policy losses.[339] Further, if the act giving rise to a section 1605A(c) claim occurred in the foreign state being sued, the claimant must first "afford[ ] the foreign state a reasonable opportunity to arbitrate the claim in accordance with accepted international rules of arbitration."[340] Finally, the statute of limitations for claims under section 1605A requires the commencement of an action within 10 years after April

Flatow v. Islamic Republic of Iran, 999 F.Supp. 1, 11 (D.D.C. 1998). Since 1993, Sudan continuously has been designated as a state sponsor of terrorism. *See* 58 Fed.Reg. 52523–01 (Oct. 8, 1993); Rux v. Republic of Sudan, 495 F.Supp.2d 541, 548 (E.D. Va. 2007). Syria has been designated a state sponsor of terrorism since December 29, 1979. *See* Export Administration Act of 1979, Pub. L. No. 96–72, § 6, 93 Stat. 503, 513–515 (1979); 15 C.F.R. § 385.4(d) (1981). Finally, Cuba has been designated a state sponsor of terrorism since March 1, 1982. *See* 47 Fed. Reg. 16623–24 (April 19, 1982).

333. *See* In re Terrorist Attacks on Sept. 11, 2001, 538 F.3d 71, 89 (2d Cir. 2008) ("The State Department has never designated the Kingdom a state sponsor of terrorism. As a consequence, the Terrorism Exception is inapplicable here.").

334. The term "national of the United States" includes both U.S. citizens as well as someone, though not a citizen, who owes permanent allegiance to the United States. 8 U.S.C. § 1101(a)(22). *See* Acosta v. Islamic Republic of Iran, 574 F.Supp.2d 15, 26 (D.D.C. 2008) (cause of action under § 1605A does not extend to those persons who voluntarily and deliberately renounce American citizenship).

335. 28 U.S.C. § 1605A(c).

336. 28 U.S.C. § 1605A(a)(2)(A)(ii).

337. *Acosta v. Islamic Republic of Iran*, 574 F.Supp.2d at 26; Peterson v. Islamic Republic of Iran, 515 F.Supp.2d 25, 41 n.8 (D.D.C. 2007).

338. 28 U.S.C. § 1605A(c).

339. *Id.* at § 1605A(d).

340. *Id.* at § 1605A(a)(2)(A)(iii).

24, 1996, or 10 years from the date on which the cause of action arose.[341]

To establish liability against a foreign sovereign under section 1605A(c), plaintiffs must show that "(1) the foreign sovereign was designated by the State Department as a 'state sponsor of terrorism;' (2) the victim or plaintiff was either a U.S. national, a member of the armed forces, or a federal employee or contractor acting within the scope of employment at the time the acts took place; and (3) the foreign sovereign engaged in conduct that falls within the ambit of the statute."[342] Finally, if the act occurred within the designated foreign state, the claimant must have afforded the foreign state a reasonable opportunity to arbitrate the claim.[343]

Under section 1605A(c), state law no longer controls the nature of the liability and damages that can be sought when a foreign government is sued under the FSIA.[344] According to *Gates v. Syrian Arab Republic*, "[s]tate-law claims for damages are not available against a foreign state that has engaged in state-sponsored terrorism."[345] The only cause of action permissible against a state designated as a state sponsor of terror is a federal cause of action under the FSIA. Further, Congress should look to the Restatement (Second) of Torts, and not state law, for delineating the controlling substantive law.[346]

b. Pending Cases

Plaintiffs with "pending cases" brought under section 1605(a)(7) may be refiled under new section 1605A in certain circumstances. Section 1605A is more advantageous to plaintiffs than section 1605(A)(7). For example, in actions filed under section 1605A, plaintiffs may seek punitive damages against state sponsors of terrorism. Under section 1803(c)(2), an action filed under section 1605(a)(7), and any judgment in the action shall, on motion made by plaintiffs to the United States district court (where the action was initially brought, or judgment in the action initially entered) be given effect as if the action had originally been filed under section 1605A.[347] However, in order to refile a suit under new section

341. *Id.* at § 1605A(b).

342. *See* Acosta v. Islamic Republic of Iran, 574 F.Supp.2d 15, 25 (D.D.C. 2008) (setting forth the jurisdictional requirements for establishing liability the FSIA).

343. 28 U.S.C. § 1605A(a)(2)(A)(iii).

344. Gates v. Syrian Arab Republic, 580 F.Supp.2d 53, 66 (D.D.C. 2008) ("By providing for a private right of action and by precisely enumerating the types of damages recoverable, Congress has eliminated the inconsistencies that arise in these cases when they are decided under state law.") (citing cases).

345. *Id.*

346. *Id.* at 66 n.9.

347. NDAA, § 1083(c)(2). *See* Estate of Heiser v. Islamic Republic of Iran, 605 F.Supp.2d 248 (D.D.C. 2009) (granting plaintiffs' motion to convert

1605A(c), a plaintiff must satisfy four requirements set forth in section 1083(c)(2). Pursuant to section 1083(c)(2), the amendments to the FSIA shall apply to any action that "(1) was brought under § 1605(a)(7) before January 28, 2008; (2) [plaintiff] relied upon that provision as creating a cause of action; (3) [plaintiff] has been adversely affected on grounds that § 1605(a)(7) fails to create a cause of action against the foreign state; and (4) as of the date of enactment (January 28, 2008), is before the courts in any form, including on appeal or motion under rule 60(b) of the Federal Rules of Civil Procedure."[348]

The critical issue is whether the action originally filed under section 1605(a)(7) was "before the courts in any form" at the date of the enactment of the NDAA.[349] The mere possibility of filing an attachment or executing the judgment does not satisfy the requirement of section 1083(c)—that the action was "before the courts in any form."[350] Further, the courts hold that if a final judgment was entered in favor of the plaintiff, the judgement was not appealed, and there were no pending motions, the action was no longer "before the court" when the NDAA became law.[351]

c. Related Actions

Section 1083(c)(3) permits the filing of new cases involving incidents that are the subject of actions timely commenced under section 1605(a)(7). Pursuant to section 1083(c)(3) "any other action, arising out of the same act or incident may be brought under section 1605A."[352] The provision would appear to permit victims of State-supported terrorism to bring suit notwithstanding the expiration of the limitation time for filing, so long as another victim of the same terrorist incident had brought a timely action.[353] This provision would also allow claimants previously not covered by the terrorism exception, such as foreign nationals working for the U.S. government overseas who were injured or killed in a terrorist attack, to file a lawsuit.[354] However, such actions must be filed within sixty days after enactment of the NDAA or the date of the

---

their prior action under § 1605(a)(7) to a new action under § 1605A).

348. Blais v. Islamic Republic of Iran, 567 F.Supp.2d 143, 144 (D.D.C. 2008) (citing Pub.L. No. 110–181, 122 Stat. 3, § 1083(c)(2)(A)). *See also* Simon v. Republic of Iraq, 529 F.3d 1187, 1192 (D.C. Cir. 2008) (section 1083(c) sets forth the circumstances upon which plaintiffs with pending cases filed under § 1605(a)(7) may invoke § 1605A).

349. *See* Holland v. Islamic Republic of Iran, 545 F.Supp.2d 120, 122 (D.D.C. 2008).

350. *Id.*

351. *Blais v. Islamic Republic of Iran*, 567 F.Supp.2d at 144; Bodoff v. Islamic Republic of Iran, 567 F.Supp.2d 141, 142 (D.D.C. 2008).

352. NDAA, § 1083(c)(3).

353. JENNIFER K. ELSEA, SUITS AGAINST TERRORIST STATES BY VICTIMS OF TERRORISM, CONGRESSIONAL RESEARCH SERVICE REPORT FOR CONGRESS, CRS–60 (2008) [hereinafter "SUITS AGAINST TERRORIST STATES BY VICTIMS OF TERRORISM"].

354. *Id.*

entry of judgment in the original action.[355] Refiled actions and actions related to previous claims are permitted even if the foreign state is no longer designated as a state sponsor of terrorism, so long as the state was designated as a state sponsor of terrorism when the original action was filed.[356] Finally, in any action refiled under section 1083(c)(2)(A) the defenses of res judicata, collateral estoppel, and limitation period are waived.[357]

d. Applicability to Iraq

Section 1083(d) authorizes the President to "waive any provision of [section 1083 of the NDAA] with respect to Iraq," if he finds that "waiver is in the national security interest of the United States" and "will promote the reconstruction of, the consolidation of democracy in, and the relations with the United States and Iraq," and that "Iraq continues to be a reliable ally of the United States and partner in combating acts of international terrorism."[358] On the day the President signed the NDAA into law, he promptly exercised his authority under section 1083(d)(1) to waive "all provisions of section 1083 with respect to Iraq, and any agency or instrumentality thereof."[359] In *Simon v. Republic of Iraq*, the D.C. Circuit considered the effect of the President's waiver authority upon cases brought under § 1605(a)(7).[360] In *Simon*, Iraq argued that the repeal of section 1605(a)(7) by section 1083(c) of the NDAA eliminated the jurisdiction of U.S. courts over pending cases, while the presidential waiver prevented refiling such claims under new section 1605A.[361] The D.C. Circuit rejected Iraq's claims, interpreting section 1083(c) to repeal section 1605(a)(7) only as to future claims against state sponsors of terrorism. The court held that "courts retain jurisdiction pursuant to section 1605(a)(7) over cases that were pending under that section when the Congress enacted the NDAA."[362]

e. Providing Material Support and Resources

In *Gates v. Syrian Arab Republic*, the district court found that Syria was subject to suit under section 1605A, based on a claim that Syria, and its officials acting within the scope of their employment, provided material support and resources to terrorists and a foreign

355. NDAA, § 1083(c)(3).

356. *See* SUITS AGAINST TERRORIST STATES BY VICTIMS OF TERRORISM, *supra* note 246, at CRS–60–61.

357. NDAA § 1083(c)(2)(B).

358. *Id.* at § 1083(d)(1).

359. Presidential Determination No. 2008–9, 73 Fed.Reg. 6571 (Jan. 28, 2008).

360. Simon v. Republic of Iraq, 529 F.3d 1187 (D.C. Cir. 2008).

361. *Id.* at 1190.

362. *Id.* at 1192. The court also rejected Iraq's claim that the lawsuit should be dismissed as presenting a political question.

terrorist organization.[363] Relatives of two U.S. civilian contractors brutally murdered in Iraq brought suit against the Syrian Arab Republic, the President of Syria, the Syrian Military Intelligence, and the Director of the Syrian Military Intelligence.[364] Plaintiffs alleged that acting through these principals, Syria provided material support and resources to al Qaeda in Iraq and its leader, Abu Musab al-Zarqawi.[365] The court agreed, finding that Syria, a designated sponsor of terrorism,[366] provided material support and resources to al-Zarqawi and al Qaeda in Iraq, which contributed to hostage taking, torture, and extrajudicial killings.[367] The material support and resources provided by Syria consisted of serving as Zarqawi's organizational and logistical hub from 2002 to 2005, providing him a passport, and by providing munitions, training recruiting, and transportation to al-Zarqawi and his followers.[368]

Finally, civil conspiracy may provide a basis for liability under section 1605A(c).[369] The elements of civil conspiracy consist of: "(1) an agreement between two or more persons; (2) to participate in an unlawful act, or a lawful act in an unlawful manner; (2) an injury caused by an unlawful overt act performed by one of the parties of the agreement; (4) which overt act was done pursuant to and in furtherance of the common scheme."[370] In *Acosta v. Islamic Republic of Iran,* the court found that Iran's provision of material support in the form of funding, training, and safe haven to the Islamic Group for the purpose of committing terrorist attacks which resulted in death and injuries, satisfied the elements of civil conspiracy.[371]

363. Gates v. Syrian Arab Republic, 580 F.Supp.2d 53 (D.D.C. 2008).

364. *Id.* at 56.

365. *Id.*

366. Syria has been designated by the Department of State as a state sponsor of terrorism continuously since December 29, 1979, *see* http://www.state.gov/s/ct/c14151htm, and its continued designation was noted in 2004, 69 Fed. Reg. 28,098–28,100 (2004), and again in 2005, 31 C.F.R. § 596.201 (2005).

367. *Gates v. Syrian Arab Republic,* 580 F.Supp.2d at 67.

368. *Id.* at 68. Section 1605A(h)(3) defines "material support and resources" to have "the meaning given that term in section 2339A of title 18." Section 2339A provides:

"material support or resources" means any property, tangible or intangible, or service, including currency or monetary instruments or financial securities, financial services, lodging, training, expert advice or assistance, safehouses, false documentation or identification, communications equipment, facilities, weapons, lethal substances, explosives, personnel . . . and transportation, except medicine or religious materials.

18 U.S.C. § 2339A(b)(1).

369. *See Acosta v. Islamic Republic of Iran,* 574 F.Supp.2d at 26; Bodoff v. Islamic Republic of Iran, 424 F.Supp.2d 74, 84 (D.D.C. 2006) ("[s]ponsorship of terrorist activities inherently involves a conspiracy to commit terrorist attacks").

370. *Acosta v. Islamic Republic of Iran,* 574 F.Supp.2d at 27; *see also* Halberstam v. Welch, 705 F.2d 472, 477 (D.C. Cir. 1983).

371. *Acosta v. Islamic Republic of Iran,* 574 F.Supp.2d at 27.

f. Bringing Claims for Acts of Terrorism under the Torts and Commercial Activities Exceptions to the FSIA

In *In re Terrorist Attacks on September 11, 2001*, persons who incurred losses in the September 11, 2001 terrorist attacks brought tort claims under the FSIA against hundreds of parties, including the Kingdom of Saudi Arabia, four Saudi princes, a Saudi banker, and the Saudi High Commission for Relief to Bosnia and Herzegovina ("SHC").[372] Plaintiffs alleged that defendants played a critical role in the September 11 attacks by providing financial support and other resources to Muslim charities that, in turn, funneled millions of dollars to al Qaeda.[373] The Second Circuit Court of Appeals affirmed the district court's decision that it lacked jurisdiction over the claims against the Kingdom of Saudi Arabia, the four Saudi princes in their official capacities, and the SHC.[374] The court held that plaintiffs' claims against the Kingdom of Saudi Arabia did not fall within the statutory exception for state-sponsored terrorist acts, 28 U.S.C. § 1605A, because the Kingdom has not been designated a state sponsor of terrorism.[375] The court also declined to characterize plaintiffs' claims—expressly predicated on state-sponsored acts of terrorism—as sounding in tort.[376] Plaintiffs argued that defendants' tortious acts took the form of providing material support to terrorists.[377] The court noted that the terrorism exception to the FSIA governs those activities.[378] However, the terrorism exception applies only to designated state sponsors of terrorism. Because the State Department has never designated the Kingdom of Saudi Arabia a state sponsor of terrorism, the terrorism exception is inapplicable.[379] The Second Circuit reasoned that "to apply the Torts exception where the conduct alleged amounts to terrorism within the meaning of the Terrorism Exception would evade and frustrate that key limitation on the Terrorism Exception."[380] Thus, the court held that claims based on terrorism must be brought under the FSIA terrorism exception, and not under the torts exception.[381]

---

372. In re Terrorist Attacks on September 11, 2001, 538 F.3d 71 (2d Cir. 2008).

373. *Id.* at 76.

374. *Id.* at 75–6.

375. *Id.* at 75. The court also concluded that "the FSIA treats individual agents of the foreign state, when they undertake their official duties, as the 'foreign state' for purposes of the FSIA." Thus, because the Kingdom was entitled to immunity under the FSIA, the Saudi princes were immune for acts committed in their official capacity. *Id.* at 85.

376. *Id.* at 89. Congress enacted the Torts Exception "to eliminate a foreign state's immunity for traffic accidents and other torts committed in the United States, for which liability is imposed under domestic tort law." *Id.* at 87 (*quoting* Argentine Republic v. Amerada Hess Shipping Corp., 488 U.S. 428, 439–40 (1989)).

377. In re Terrorist Attacks on September 11, 2001, 538 F.3d 71, 85 (2d Cir. 2008).

378. *Id.* at 90.

379. *Id.* at 89.

380. *Id.*

381. *Id.* at 90.

Finally, the Second Circuit rejected plaintiffs' argument that the defendants' charitable contributions is a form of money laundering, which is commercial in nature, and therefore the commercial activities exception to the FSIA applies to defeat the defendants' immunity for harm caused by their charitable contributions.[382] The court held that plaintiffs' claims do not come within the statutory exception for a foreign sovereign's commercial activity, because defendants' alleged conduct—supporting Muslim charities that promote and finance terrorism—is not a commercial activity. Such conduct is not "part of the trade and commerce engaged in by a 'merchant in the marketplace.' "[383] Thus, the commercial activities exception of the FSIA does not apply.[384]

g. Enforcement of Civil Judgments

While courts have handed down large judgments against state sponsors of terrorism, generally in default, the U.S. government has regularly intervened to block the attachment of frozen assets to satisfy those judgments.[385] For example, in *Flatow* and *Alejandre v. Republic of Cuba,* plaintiffs sought to attach assets of Iran in the United States that had been blocked by the U.S. government pursuant to sanctions regulations.[386] Iranian assets located in the United States had been frozen under the International Emergency Economic Powers Act ("IEEPA")[387] at the time of the hostage crisis in 1979.[388] Cuba's assets were blocked pursuant to the Trading with

382. In re Terrorist Attacks on September 11, 2001, 538 F.3d 71, 90–1 (2d Cir. 2008).

383. *Id.* at 92.

384. *Id.*

385. See e.g., Weinstein v. Islamic Republic of Iran, 274 F.Supp.2d 53, 55 (D.D.C. 2003) (government intervened to quash writs of attachment against funds in four bank accounts and Iran Foreign Military Sales Program account to enforcement judgment); Hegna v. Islamic Republic of Iran, 2003 WL 25952462 (N.D.Ill. 2003) (government intervened to quash writs of attachment against two parcels of real estate owned by Iran to satisfy the award of damages).

386. Flatow v. Islamic Republic of Iran, 74 F.Supp. 2d 18 (D.D.C. 1999) (quashing a writ of attachment for funds frozen by the government); Flatow v. Islamic Republic of Iran, 76 F.Supp.2d 16 (D.D.C. 1999) (quashing writs of attachment for Iran's embassy and two

bank accounts holding proceeds from property rentals); Alejandre v. Republic of Cuba, 996 F.Supp. 1239 (S.D. Fla. 1997) ($50 million in compensatory damages and $137.7 million in punitive damages awarded to families of victims who were killed when Cuban aircraft shot down Brothers to the Rescue aircraft in 1996). *See also* Sean Murphy, *Satisfaction of U.S. Judgments Against State Sponsors of Terrorism,* 94 AM. J. INT'L L. 117 (2000).

387. 50 U.S.C. §§ 1701–1707. The IEEPA provides the President broad powers to regulate economic transactions with foreign countries and nationals to deal with "any unusual and extraordinary threat, which has its source in whole or substantial part outside the United States, to the national security, foreign policy, or economy of the United States, if he President declares a national emergency with respect to such threat." *Id.* at § 1701(a).

388. Executive Order 12170, 44 Fed.Reg. 65,729 (November 14, 1979).

the Enemy Act ("TWEA").[389] The Clinton Administration opposed efforts to attach those assets to enforce civil judgments to compensate victims of state-sponsored terrorism. The Administration maintained that such assets might be useful as leverage in resolving foreign policy disputes with Iran and Cuba.[390] Further, it was argued that numerous other U.S. nationals had legitimate claims against these countries that would be frustrated if the assets were used to compensate recent terrorism victims.[391] Attaching blocked assets would create a race to the courthouse benefitting one small deserving group of victims and complainants over a far larger group of deserving Americans. Finally, the Administration claimed that using frozen assets to compensate victims of state-sponsored terrorism could result in reciprocal action against U.S. assets by other States.[392]

In 1998, Congress amended the FSIA to provide that any property of a terrorist state frozen pursuant to IEEPA or TWEA, and any diplomatic property of such a State could be subject to attachment in aid of execution of a judgment under the terrorism exception to the FSIA.[393] Section 117 of the Treasury Department of Appropriations Act for Fiscal Year 1999 mandated that the State and Treasury Departments "fully, promptly, and effectively assist" any court issuing a judgment against a terrorist State "in identifying, locating, and executing against the property of that foreign state."[394] However, because of the Administration's continuing objections, Congress gave the President the authority to waive the requirements of the provision in the "interests of national security."[395] After the President signed the new legislation into law, he immediately executed the waiver.[396] For plaintiffs with default judg-

389. 50 U.S.C. App. § 5. The TWEA gives the President powers to regulate economic transactions with foreign countries and nationals in time of war.

390. *See* SUITS AGAINST TERRORIST STATES BY VICTIMS OF TERRORISM, *supra* note 346, at CRS 9.

391. *Id.*

392. *Id.*

393. P.L. 105–277, Div. A. Title I, § 117 (Oct. 21, 1998), 112 Stat. 2681–491, codified at 28 U.S.C. § 1610(f)(1)(A). This section was added to the FSIA by § 117 of the Treasury and General Government Appropriations Act of 1999, as contained in the Omnibus Consolidated and Emergency Supplemental Appropriations Act of 1999, P.L. 105–277 (1998), 112 Stat. 2681.

394. 28 U.S.C. § 1610(f)(2)(A).

395. *Id.* at § 1601(f)(3).

396. Presidential Determination 99–1 (Oct. 21, 1998), *reprinted in* 34 WEEKLY COMP. PRES. DOC. 2088 (Oct. 26, 1998). The White House Office of the Press Secretary issued the following explanatory statement:

[T]he struggle to defeat terrorism would be weakened, not strengthened, by putting into effect a provision of the Omnibus Appropriations Act for FY 1999. It would permit individuals who win court judgments against nations on the State Department's terrorist list to attach embassies and certain other properties of foreign nations, despite U.S. laws and treaty obligations barring such attachment.

The new law allows the President to waive the provision in the national

ments against Cuba and Iran, the President's waiver prevented the diplomatic property and frozen assets of those countries from attaching to satisfy those judgments.

In 2000, Congress enacted the Victims of Trafficking and Violence Protection Act of 2000 ("VTVPA").[397] Section 2002 of the VTVPA directed the Secretary of the Treasury to pay portions of any judgments against Cuba and Iran that had been ordered by July 20, 2002, or that would be handed down in any suits that had been filed on five specified dates on or before July 27, 2000.[398] To pay a portion of the judgment against Cuba in *Alejandre*, the President was directed to vest and liquidate Cuban properties that had been frozen under the TWEA.[399] For the designated cases against Iran, section 2002 provided for payment from the proceeds that had accrued from the rental of Iranian diplomatic and consular property in the U.S., and U.S. funds not otherwise obligated up to an amount specified in the statute.[400] Immediately after signing the new legislation into law, President Clinton exercised his waiver authority in the "interest of national security."[401] Thus, except to the extent that section 2002 allowed the blocked assets of Cuba to be used to satisfy a portion of the *Alejandre* judgment, the VTPA did not eliminate the bar to the attachment of diplomatic property and blocked assets to satisfy judgments against terrorist States.[402]

security interest of the United States.... If the U.S. permitted attachment of diplomatic properties, then other countries could retaliate, placing our embassies and citizens overseas at grave risk. Our ability to use foreign properties as leverage in foreign policy disputes would also be undermined.

Statement of the Press Secretary (Oct. 21, 1998).

397. Victims of Trafficking and Violence Protection Act of 2000 (VTVPA), P.L. 106–386, § 2002(f)(1) (October 28, 2000); 114 Stat. 1543. *See also* SUITS AGAINST TERRORIST STATES, at 15 (listing the cases and judgments effected by the VTVPA).

398. VTVPA, § 2002.

399. *Id.*

400. *Id.* Section 2002 gave the claimants in the designated suits against Cuba and Iran three options:

First, they could obtain from the Treasury Department 110 percent of the compensatory damages awarded in their judgments, plus interest, if they agreed to relinquish all rights to collect further compensatory and punitive damages;

Second, they could receive 100 percent of the compensatory damages awarded in their judgments, plus interest, if they agreed to relinquish (a) all rights to further compensatory damages awarded by U.S. courts and (b) all rights to attach certain categories of property in satisfaction of their judgments for punitive damages, including Iran's diplomatic and consular property as well as property that is at issue in claims against the United States before an international tribunal. The property in the latter category included Iran's Foreign Military Sales (FMS) trust fund, which remains at issue in a case before the Iran–U.S. Claims Tribunal.

Third, claimants could decline to obtain any payments from the Treasury Department and continue to pursue satisfaction of their judgments as best they could.

Sean Murphy, *Satisfaction of U.S. Judgments Against State Sponsors of Terrorism*, 94 AM. J. INT'L L. 117 (2000).

401. Presidential Determination No. 2001–03 (Oct. 28, 2000); 65 Fed. Reg. 66,483.

402. *See* SUITS AGAINST TERRORIST STATES, at 17–18.

In 2002, Congress enacted the Terrorism Risk Insurance Act ("TRIA").[403] Section 201 of the TRIA made frozen assets of state sponsors of terrorism available to satisfy judgments for compensatory damages against such States found liable for the commission of acts of terrorism. Section 201(a) of the TRIA provides:

> Notwithstanding any other provision of law, and except as provided in subsection (b), in every case in which a person has obtained a judgment against a terrorist party on a claim based upon an act of terrorism, or for which a terrorist party is not immune under section 1605(a)(7) of title 28, United States Code, the blocked assets of that terrorist party (including the blocked assets of any agency or instrumentality of that terrorist party) shall be subject to execution or attachment in aid of execution in order to satisfy such judgment to the extent of any compensatory damages for which such terrorist party has been adjudged liable.[404]

The TRIA defined "blocked assets" as "any asset seized or frozen by the United States under section 5(b) of the TWEA (50 U.S.C. App. 5(b)) or under sections 202 and 203 of the [IEEPA] (50 U.S.C. §§ 1701–1702)."[405] However, the term "blocked assets" does not include property that

> (i) is subject to a license issued by the United States Government for final payment, transfer, or disposition by or to a person subject to the jurisdiction of the United States in connection with a transaction for which the issuance of such license has been specifically required by statute other than [IEEPA] or the United Nations Participation Act of 1945 (22 U.S.C. 287 et seq.); or

> (ii) in the case of property subject to the Vienna Convention on Diplomatic Relations or the Vienna Convention on Consular Relations, or that enjoys equivalent privileges and immunities under the law of the United States, is being used exclusively for diplomatic and consular purposes.[406]

Thus, the term "blocked assets" excludes (1) property involved in certain transactions authorized by a license issued by the U.S. government pursuant to the IEEPA or the United Nations Participation Act of 1945, and (2) property subject to protection under the Vienna Convention on Diplomatic Relations or Vienna Convention

---

403. P.L. 107–297 (November 26, 2002), 116 Stat. 2322.

404. TRIA, § 201(a), 116 Stat. at 2337.

405. TRIA, § 201(d)(2)(A), 116 Stat. at 2339.

406. *Id.* at § 201(d)(2).

on Consular Relations that is "being used exclusively for diplomatic or consular purposes."[407]

To enforce a judgment for compensatory damages against the blocked assets of a foreign terrorist state, the plaintiff must satisfy the following requirements. First, the plaintiff must obtain a judgment under the FSIA against a "terrorist party."[408] Second, the judgment must be for a claim based on a terrorist act or a claim for which a terrorist party is not immune under the terrorism exception to the FSIA.[409] Third, the assets sought to be attached must be "blocked assets" within the meaning of the TRIA.[410] The TRIA allows the attachment of the blocked assets of any agency or instrumentality of a terrorist party even if the judgment is only against the terrorist party.[411] Finally, the assets sought to be attached are for compensatory damages, not punitive damages.[412]

The TRIA narrowed the authority previously afforded the President to waive the attachment of blocked assets. Section 201(b) authorizes the President to waive attachment of blocked assets upon determining on an asset-by-asset basis that waiver is necessary in the "interests of national security."[413] Prior to the TRIA,

---

407. *Id.* at § 201(d)(2)(B). Under the Vienna Convention on Diplomatic Relations, the U.S. is only obligated to protect "the premises of the mission," which is defined under Article 1 of the Convention as "the building or parts of buildings and land ancillary thereto, irrespective of ownership, used for the purposes of the mission including the residence of the head of mission." Vienna Convention on Diplomatic Relations, Apr. 18, 1961, 23 U.S.T. 3227, T.I.A.S. No. 7502. Article 1 of the Vienna Convention on Consular Relations imposes a similar duty with respect to "consular premises." Vienna Convention on Consular Relations, Apr. 24, 1963, 21 U.S.T. 77, T.I.A.S. No. 6820. Therefore, under the conventions, the U.S. is required to "respect and protect" the buildings, parts of buildings, and the land ancillary thereto, used exclusively for diplomatic and consular purposes.

408. The term "terrorist party" means a "terrorist, a terrorist organization (as defined in section 212(a)(3)(B)(vi) of the Immigration and Nationality Act (8 U.S.C. § 1182(a)(3)(B)(vi))), or a foreign state designated as a state sponsor of terrorism under section 6(j) of the Export Administration Act of 1979 (50 U.S.C. App. 2405(j)) or section 620A of the Foreign Assistance Act of 1961 (22 U.S.C. § 2371)." TRIA § 201(d)(4). *See also*

Weininger v. Castro, 462 F.Supp.2d 457, 479 (S.D.N.Y. 2006).

409. *Weininger,* 462 F.Supp.2d at 479.

410. *Id. See also* Ungar ex rel. Strachman v. Palestinian Auth., 304 F.Supp.2d 232, 241–42 (D.R.I. 2004) (ordering the attachment of "blocked assets" of the Holy Land Foundation for Relief and Development, blocked by the Treasury Department pursuant to Executive Orders 12947 and 13224).

411. TRIA, § 201.

412. *Id.*

413. *See* Hegna v. Islamic Republic of Iran, 2003 WL 25952462 (N.D. Ill. 2003) ("The TRIA removes barriers to the attachment of blocked assets by severely limiting the availability of the presidential waiver to protect blocked assets."). Section 201(b)(1) provides:

(b) Presidential Waiver—

(1) In General—Subject to paragraph (2), upon determining on an asset-by-asset basis that a waiver is necessary in the national security interest, the President may waive the requirements of subsection (a) in connection with (and prior to the enforcement of) any judicial order directing attachment in

legislation permitted the President to exercise a blanket waiver to protect blocked property. Under the TRIA, the President is required to make an "asset-by-asset" determination that waiver is warranted to protect national security. Further, under § 201(b)(2), a waiver shall not apply to "property subject to the Vienna Convention on Diplomatic Relations or the Vienna Convention on Consular Relations that has been used by the United States for any *nondiplomatic* purpose (including use as rental property), or the proceeds of such use."[414]

Finally, section 1083 of the NDAA made numerous changes to the FSIA terrorism exception, including provisions to facilitate plaintiffs' efforts to attach assets of a state sponsor of terrorism in satisfaction of a judgment.[415] Subsection (b)(3) of section 1083 amends 28 U.S.C. § 1610 to address the scope of property subject to attachment in execution of terrorism judgments against a state sponsor of terrorism. Section 1083(b)(3) creates a new subsection (g) to section 1610, which provides that the property of a foreign state against which a judgment has been entered under 28 U.S.C. § 1605A, or of an "agency or instrumentality" of such State, "including property that is a separate juridical entity or is an interest held directly or indirectly in a separate juridical entity," is subject to attachment in aid of execution upon a judgment.[416] Moreover, the statute renders subject to execution any property of the defendant foreign State regardless of—

(A) the level of economic control over the property by the government of the foreign state;

(B) whether the profits of the property go to that government;

(C) the degree to which officials of that government manage the property or otherwise control its daily affairs;

(D) whether that government is the sole beneficiary in interest of the property; or

(E) whether establishing the property as a separate entity would entitle the foreign state to benefits in United States courts while avoiding its obligations.[417]

Section 1610(g) "enable[s] any property in which the foreign state has a beneficial ownership to be subject to execution for terrorism judgments, except for diplomatic and consular proper-

aid of execution or execution against any property subject to the Vienna Convention on Diplomatic Relations or the Vienna Convention on Consular Relations.

414. TRIA, § 201(b)(2)(A) (emphasis added).

415. National Defense Authorization Act for Fiscal Year 2008, P.L. 110–181 (January 28, 2008).

416. 28 U.S.C. § 1610(g).

417. *Id.* at § 1610(g)(1).

ty."⁴¹⁸ The statute expressly authorizes the attachment of the assets of agencies or instrumentalities of a foreign State to satisfy a terrorism judgment. Arguably, section 1610(g) could be construed to make any entity in which a foreign State has any interest liable for terrorism judgments awarded against that State, even if the entity is not an agency or instrumentality of the State.⁴¹⁹

Subsection 1610(g)(2) authorizes the attachment of assets of a foreign State, or agency or instrumentality of a foreign State, "regulated" by the U.S. government pursuant to action taken under the TWEA or the IEEPA.⁴²⁰ Under the statute, such property is not immune from attachment for the purpose of executing a judgment under § 1605A. Unlike § 201 of the TRIA (28 U.S.C. § 1610 note), the new provision applies to "regulated" rather than "blocked" assets,⁴²¹ and it allows assets to be attached to enforce a judgment ordering punitive damages.⁴²² Finally, the 2008 amendments do not provide the President waiver authority except with respect to Iraq.⁴²³

h. Lis Pendens

Section 1083 of the NDAA creates a new provision, 28 U.S.C. § 1605A(g). The statute provides for the establishment of an automatic lien of *lis pendens* with respect to all real or tangible property located within the judicial district that is subject to attachment in aid of execution under § 1610(g) and is titled in the name of a defendant state sponsor of terrorism or any entities listed by plaintiff as "controlled by" that State.⁴²⁴ According to the court in

418. SUITS AGAINST TERRORIST STATES, at 55. *See also* H.R. 110–477, Conference Report to Accompany H.R. 1585, National Defense Authorization Act for Fiscal Year 2008, at 1001.

419. *See* SUITS AGAINST TERRORIST STATES, at 56.

420. Section 1610(g)(2), United States Sovereign Immunity Inapplicable, provides:

Any property of a foreign state, or agency or instrumentality of a foreign state, to which paragraph (1) applies shall not be immune from attachment in aid of execution, or execution, upon a judgment entered under section 1605A because the property is regulated by the United States Government by reasons of action taken against that foreign state under the Trading With the Enemy Act or the International Emergency Economic Powers Act.

421. TRIA, § 201(d)(2). Section 201(d)(2) of the TRIA defines "blocked

assets" to mean property seized or frozen pursuant the TWEA or the IEEPA, but excludes property subject to a license issued by the U.S. government or required by statute other than IEEPA or the United Nations Participation Act of 1945, or property subject to the Vienna Convention on Diplomatic Relations or Vienna Convention on Consular Relations.

422. Section 201 remains in force for use in efforts to attach blocked assets to satisfy judgments under 28 U.S.C. § 1605(a)(7).

423. NDAA, § 1083(d)(1).

424. Section 1605A(g) provides:

(1) In general.—In every action filed in a United States district court in which jurisdiction is alleged under this section, the filing of a notice of pending action pursuant to this section, to which is attached a copy of the complaint filed in the action, shall have the effect of establishing a lien of lis

Estate of Heiser v. Islamic Republic of Iran, "a notice of *lis pendens* is not a lien, but, assuming the proper procedures are adhered to, the legal effect of the notice is that any third-party purchaser who receives title to the property is bound by the outcome of the civil case, without any additional rights to the property."[425] Under the statute, plaintiffs are required to file a notice of pending action under § 1605A with the clerk of the district court "indexed by listing all named defendants and all entities listed as controlled by any defendant."[426] Finally, the statute expressly provides that liens of *lis pendens* are enforceable pursuant to 28 U.S.C. § 111.[427]

3. THE FUTURE OF CIVIL CAUSES OF ACTION FOR ACTS OF TERRORISM

Although Congress has enacted several statutes authorizing civil liability for personal injury or death caused by acts of international terrorism, those statutes have been largely ineffective in providing the victims of terrorism an adequate remedy for their losses. Civil actions are likely to be brought against three classes of defendants: the primary actors, state sponsors of terrorism, and the facilitators or aiders and abettors of terrorist acts. The primary actors are those persons who actually commit the terrorist act themselves. The difficulty that arises with respect to compensation from this class of offenders is that terrorists are highly unlikely to possess property in the United States. Thus, the victims of terror will be unable to attach any assets to enforce a civil judgment. Further, civil actions against defendants that fall within the second category, state sponsors of terrorism, are also unlikely to lead to unreasonable victim compensation. The primary reason revolves around the lack of foreign state assets located in the United States. Also, the U.S. government has only designated four states as state sponsors of terrorism: Cuba, Iran, Sudan, and Syria.[428] Thus, civil suits against Saudi Arabia, Somalia, and Yemen would be barred by the doctrine of foreign sovereign immunity. Further, sensitive diplomatic and foreign policy interests may cause the U.S. government to intervene and block the attachment of frozen assets to enforce a civil judgment.[429] In order to recover civil damages for

pendens upon any real property or tangible personal property that is—

(A) subject to attachment in aid of execution, or execution, under section 1610;

(B) located within that judicial district; and

(C) titled in the name of any defendant, or titled in the name of any entity controlled by any defendant if such notice contains a statement listing such controlled entity.

425. Estate of Heiser v. Islamic Republic of Iran, 605 F.Supp.2d 248, 250 (D.D.C. 2009).

426. 28 U.S.C. § 1605A(g)(2). The phrase "controlled by" is not defined by statute.

427. *Id.* at § 1605A(g)(3).

428. *See supra* note 327.

429. *See supra* note 385, discussing cases where the U.S. government intervened to quash writs of attachment

injuries caused by a terrorist attack, the victims of terrorism must prevail against the foreign government on the issue of civil liability and then overcome any legal obstacles raised by the U.S. government to prevent enforcement of the civil judgment against foreign assets located in the United States. Ultimately, civil causes of action will only be effective when brought against the third category of offenders, the facilitators of terrorist acts, such as corrupt charities and foreign banks.[430] Such entities are more likely to possess assets in the United States to support a civil judgment. Further, the U.S. government is unlikely to intervene in such cases to prevent enforcement of such judgments.

against Iranian assets located in the United States.

430. *See e.g.*, Boim v. Holy Land Found., 549 F.3d 685 (7th Cir. 2008) (en banc); Linde v. Arab Bank, 384 F.Supp.2d 571 (E.D.N.Y. 2005).

Table of Cases

431

Table of Statutes

Table of Law Review Articles and Other Legal Authorities

BOOKS:

1 Jean-Marie Henckaerts & Louise Doswald-Beck, Customary International Humanitarian Law (2005).

2 L. Oppenheim, International Law (H. Lauterpacht ed., 7th ed. 1961).

A.P.V. Rogers, Law on the Battlefield (2d ed. 2004).

Alistair Millar & Eric Rosand, Allied Against Terrorism (Century Foundation Press 2006).

Christopher L. Blakesley, Terrorism, Drugs, International Law, and the Protection of Human Liberty (1992).

Gary D. Solis, The Law of Armed Conflict: International Humanitarian Law in War (Cambridge Univ. Press 2010).

Geoffrey Best, Law & War Since 1945 (Oxford University Press, 1994) (quoting Max Huber in 'Die kriegsrechtlichen Vertage und die Kriegsraison' in Zeitschrift fur Volkerrecht (1913)).

Geoffrey S. Corn & Eric Talbot Jensen, War Crimes, in the War on Terror & the Law of War: A Military Perspective (Geoffrey S. Corn ed., Oxford Univ. Press, 2009).

James A. Schoettler, Jr., Detention of Combatants and the Global War on Terror, in THE WAR ON TERROR AND THE LAW OF WAR: A MILITARY PERSPECTIVE (Geoffrey S. Corn, ed., Oxford Univ. Press, 2009).

Jimmy Gurule & Jordan Paust & M.C. Bassiouni et. al, Human Rights Module: Crimes Against Humanity, Genocide, Other Crimes Against Human Rights, and War Crimes (2001).

Jimmy Gurulé, Complex Criminal Litigation: Prosecuting Drug Enterprises and Organized Crime (LEXIS, 2d ed. 2000).

Jimmy Gurulé, Sandra Guerra Thompson & Michael O'Hear, The Law of Asset Forfeiture 338 (LexisNexis, 2d ed. 2004).

Jimmy Gurulé, Unfunding Terror: The Legal Response to the Financing of Global Terrorism (Edward Elgar 2008).

451

JORDAN J. PAUST, M. CHERIF BASSIOUNI, ET AL., INTERNATIONAL CRIMINAL LAW, CASES AND MATERIALS (Carolina Academic Press, 3d ed. 2007).

LAWRENCE J. MORRIS, MILITARY JUSTICE: A GUIDE TO THE ISSUES (Santa Barbara, CA 2010).

LESLIE C. GREEN, THE CONTEMPORARY LAW OF ARMED CONFLICT (2d ed. 2000).

Leslie Green *What is—Why is There—the Law of War*, THE LAW OF ARMED CONFLICT: INTO THE NEXT MILLENNIUM Vol. 71 U.S. Naval War College International Studies, Naval War College, Newport, Rhode Island (1998).

MICHAEL N. SCHMITT, CHARLES H.B. GARRAWAY & YORAM DINSTEIN, THE MANUAL ON THE LAW OF NON-INTERNATIONAL ARMED CONFLICT WITH COMMENTARY (San Remo–International Institute of Humanitarian Law 2006).

U.K. Ministry of Defense, *The Manual for the Law of Armed Conflict,* Oxford University Press (2004).

W.   WINTHROP, MILITARY LAW AND PRECEDENTS (rev. 2d ed. 1920).

YORAM DINSTEIN, WAR, AGGRESSION, AND SELF-DEFENSE (3d ed. 2001).

LAW REVIEW AND JOURNAL ARTICLES:

Adam Roberts, *Counter Terrorism, Armed Forces and the Laws of War*, Survival (quarterly journal of IISS, London), vol.44, no.1, (Spring 2002).

Anne–Marie Slaughter & David L. Bosco, *Alternative Justice,* GLOBAL POLICY FORUM, *available at* http://www.globalpolicy.org/intljustice/atca/2001/altfust.htm.

Anthony C. Arend, *International Law and the Preemptive Use of Military Force*, 26 WASH. Q. 89 (2003).

Arsalan M. Suleman, *Recent Developments: Detainee Treatment Act of 2006*, 19 HARV. HUM. RTS. J. 260 (Spring 2006).

Beth Stephens, *Federalism and Foreign Affairs: Congress's Power to "Define and Punish . . . Offenses Against the Law of Nations,"* 42 WM. & MARY L. REV. 447 (2000).

Christopher Greenwood, *International Law and the Pre-emptive Use of Force: Afghanistan, Al–Qaeda, and Iraq,* SAN DIEGO INT'L L. J. 7 (2003).

Curtis Bradley & Jack Goldsmith, *Congressional Authorization and the War on Terrorism*, 118 HARV. L. REV. 2048 (2005).

David D. Coron & Jenny S. Martinez, *Availability of U.S. Courts to Review Decision to Hold U.S. Citizens as Enemy Combatants—Executive Power in War on Terror*, 98 A.J.I.L. 782 (2004).

Debra M. Strauss, *Enlisting the U.S. Courts in a New Front: Dismantling the International Business Holdings of Terrorist Groups Through Federal Statutory and Common–Law Suits*, 38 VAND. J. TRANSNAT'L L. 679 (2005).

Geoffrey Corn & Eric Jensen, *Untying the Gordian Knott: A Proposal for Determining Applicability of the Laws of War to the War on Terror*, 81 TEMP. L. REV. 787 (2008).

Geoffrey S. Corn & Eric T. Jensen, *Transnational Armed Conflict: A "Principled" Approach to the Regulation of Counter–Terror Combat Operations*, 42 ISRAEL L. REV. 45 (2009).

Geoffrey S. Corn, *Hamdan, Fundamental Fairness, and the Significance of Additional Protocol II*, THE ARMY LAWYER (Aug. 2006).

Geoffrey S. Corn, *Hamdan, Lebanon, and the Regulation of Armed Conflict: The Need to Recognize a Hybrid Category of Armed Conflict*, 40 VAND. J. TRANSNAT'L L. 295 (2006).

Geoffrey S. Corn, *Taking the Bitter with the Sweet: A Law of War Based Analysis of the Military Commission*, 35 STETSON L. REV. 811(2006).

Jan E. Aldykiewicz & Geoffrey S. Corn, Authority to Court Martial Non–U.S. Military Personnel for Serious Violations of International Humanitarian Law Committed during Internal Armed Conflicts, 167 MIL. L. REV. 74 (2001).

Jan Kittrich, *Can Self–Defense Serve as an Appropriate Tool Against International Terrorism?*, 61 ME. L. REV. 133 (2009).

John Bickers, *Military Commissions are Constitutionally Sound: A Response to Professors Katyal and Tribe*, 34 TEX. TECH. L. REV. 899 (2002–2003).

John D. Shipman, *Taking Terrorism to Court: A Legal Examination of the New Front in the War on Terrorism*, 86 N.C. L. REV. 526 (2008).

John F. Murphy, *The Future of Multilateralism and Efforts to Combat International Terrorism*, 25 COLUM J. TRANS. L. 35 (1986).

John P. McLoughlin et al., *Security Detention in Practice: Security Detention, Terrorism and the Prevention Imperative*, 40 CASE W. RES. J. INT'L L. 463 (2009).

Kenneth Watkin, *Controlling the Use of Force: A Role for Human Rights Norms in Contemporary Armed Conflict*, 98 AM.J.INT'L.L. 1 (2004).

LTC Paul Kantwill & Maj. Sean Watts, *Hostile Protected Persons or "Extra–Conventional Persons:" How Unlawful Combatants in the War on Terrorism Posed Extraordinary Challenges for Military Attorneys and Commanders*, 28 FORDHAM INT'L L.J. 681 (2005).

Major Geoffrey S. Corn & Major Michael L. Smidt, *"To Be Or Not To Be, That Is The Question"*, *Contemporary Military Operations and the Status of Captured Personnel,* 1999 ARMY LAWYER 1 (1999).

Mark L. Rockefeller, *The "Imminent Threat" Requirement for the Use of Preemptive Military Force: is it Time for a Non-temporal Standard?*, DENV. J. INT'L. L. & POL'Y (2004).

Mark R. Shulman et al., *The Legality and Constitutionality of the President's Authority to Initiate an Invasion of Iraq*, 41 Colum. J. Transnat'l L. 15 (2002).

Mary Ellen O'Connell, *When is War Not a War? The Myth of the Global War on Terror*, 12 ILSA J. OF INT'L & COMP. L. 2 (2005).

Mary Ellen O'Connell, *Defining Armed Conflict*, 13 J. CONFLICT & SEC. L. 393 (Winter 2008).

Matthew Lippman, *Conundrums of Armed Conflict: Criminal Defenses to Violations of the Humanitarian Law of War*, 15 DICK. J. INT'L L. 1 (1996).

Michael A. Newton, *Continuum Crimes: Military Jurisdiction over Foreign Nationals Who Commit International Crimes*, 153 MIL. L. REV. 1 (1996).

Michael J. Davidson, *War and the Doubtful Soldier*, 19 NOTRE DAME J.L. ETHICS & PUB. POL'Y 91 (2005).

Michael O. Lacey, *Military Commissions: A Historical Survey*, 2002 ARMY LAW. 41 (Mar. 2002).

Neal K. Katyal & Laurence H. Tribe, *Waging War, Deciding Guilt: Trying the Military Tribunals*, 111 YALE L.J. 1259 (2002).

Nina J. Crimm, *High Alert: The Government's War on the Financing of Terrorism and Its Implications for Donors, Domestic Charitable Organizations, and Global Philanthropy*, 45 WM. & MARY L. REV. 1341 (2004).

Olugbenga Shoyele, *Armed Conflicts and Canadian Refugee and Law Policy*, 16 INT'L J. REFUGEE L. 547 (2004).

Patricia L. Bellia, *The "Lone Wolf" Amendment and the Future of Foreign Intelligence Surveillance Law*, 50 VILL. L. REV. 424 (2005).

Robert Chesney & Jack Goldsmith, Terrorism and the Convergence of Criminal and Military Detention Models, 60 STAN. L. REV. 1079 (2008).

Ronald Reagan, *The U.S. Decision Not to Ratify Protocol I to the Geneva Conventions on the Protection of War Victims: Letter of Transmittal*, 81 A.J.I.L. 910 (Oct., 1987).

Rosa Brooks, *War Everywhere: Human Rights, National Security, and the Law of Armed Conflict in the Age of Terrorism,* 153 U. PA. L. REV. 675 (2004–2005).

Spencer J. Crona & Neil A. Richardson, *Justice for War Criminal of Invisible Armies: A New Legal and Military Approach to Terrorism,* 21 OKLA. CITY U.L. REV. 349 (1996).

Stephen I. Vladeck, *The Laws of War as a Constitutional Limit on Military Commission Jurisdiction,* 4 J. NAT'L SEC. L. & POL'Y (forthcoming 2010).

Terence Taylor, *The End of Imminence?,* 27 WASH. Q. 57 (2004).

The Antiterrorism Act of 1990: Bringing International Terrorists to Justice the American Way, 15 SUFFOLK TRANSNAT'L L.J. 726 (1992).

The Legality and Constitutionality of the President's Authority to Initiate an Invasion of Iraq, Report, 41 Colum. J. Transnat'l L. 15 (2002–2003).

Ulrika Ekman Ault, *The FBI's Library Awareness Program: Is Big Brother Reading Over Your Shoulder?,* 65 N.Y.U. L.Rev. 1532 (1990).

William C. Banks and M.E. Bowman, Executive Authority for National Security Surveillance, 50 Am. U. L. Rev. 1 (2000).

William Michael Reisman, *In Defense of World Public Order,* 95 AM. J. INT'L. L., 833 (2001).

William Michael Reisman, *International Legal Responses to Terrorism,* 22 Houston J. Int'l L. 3 (1999).

REPORTS:

ANNA C. HENNING & EDWARD C. LIU, CONG. RESEARCH SERV., R40138, AMENDMENTS TO THE FOREIGN INTELLIGENCE SURVEILLANCE ACT (FISA) SET TO EXPIRE FEBRUARY 28, 2010.

Bardo Fassbender, Targeted Sanctions and Due Process: The responsibility of the UN Security Council to ensure that fair and clear procedures are made available to individuals and entities targeted with sanctions under Chapter VII of the UN Charter (Study commissioned by the UN Office of Legal Affairs, Office of the Legal Counsel, Humboldt University of Berlin, Germany (March 2006)), *available at* http://www.un.org/law/counsle/Fassbender_study.pdf.

CHARLES DOYLE, CONG. RESEARCH SERV., RL33320, NATIONAL SECURITY LETTERS IN FOREIGN INTELLIGENCE INVESTIGATIONS: LEGAL BACKGROUND AND RECENT AMENDMENTS, CRS REPORT FOR CONGRESS 1 (2009).

Conference Report on H.R. 2338, Intelligence Authorization Act for Fiscal Year 2002 (which became P.L. 107–108), H.Rept. 107–328.

Daniel Benjamin, Coordinator, Office of the Coordinator for Counterterrorism, *Confronting 21st Century Terrorism: Challenges for U.S. Policy* (May 3rd, 2010) transcription available at http://www.state.gov/s/ct/rls/rm/2010/141443.htm.

DAVID ACKERMAN, CONG. RESEARCH SERV., Order Code RS21009, RESPONSE TO TERRORISM: LEGAL ASPECTS OF THE USE OF MILITARY FORCE (2001), *available at* http://www.au.af.mil/au/awc/awcgate/crs/rs 21009.pdf.

Financial Action Task Force, Terrorist Financing (Feb. 28, 2008), *available at* http://www.fatf-gafi.org/dataoecd/28/43/40285899.pdf.

Iain Cameron, European Convention on Human Rights, Due Process and United Nations Security Council Counter—Terrorism Sanctions (report prepared by Professor Iain Cameron for the European Council on Human Rights, Council of Europe, 6 February 2006).

JENNIFER ELSEA, CONG. RESEARCH SERV., Order Code RL31191, TERRORISM AND THE LAWS OF WAR: TRYING TERRORISTS AS WAR CRIMINALS BEFORE MILITARY COMMISSIONS (2001).

JENNIFER K. ELSEA & MICHAEL JOHN GARCIA, ENEMY COMBATANT DETAINEES: HABEAS CORPUS CHALLENGES IN FEDERAL COURTS DETENTIONS, CONG. RES. SERV., (Order Code No. RL33180) (last updated Jan. 29, 2009) *available at* http://www.fas.org/sgp/crs/natsec/RL33180.pdf (last visited Aug. 11, 2010).

JENNIFER K. ELSEA, CONG. RESEARCH SERV., RL33688, THE MILITARY COMMISSIONS ACT OF 2006: ANALYSIS OF PROCEDURAL RULES AND COMPARISON WITH PREVIOUS DOD RULES AND THE UNIFORM CODE OF MILITARY JUSTICE (2007).

JENNIFER K. ELSEA, SUITS AGAINST TERRORIST STATES BY VICTIMS OF TERRORISM, CONGRESSIONAL RESEARCH SERVICE REPORT FOR CONGRESS, CRS–60 (2008).

JEREMY M. SHARP, CONG. RESEARCH SERV., Order Code RS21324, CONGRESSIONAL ACTION ON IRAQ 1990–2002: A COMPILATION OF LEGISLATION (2002).

JOHN ROTH, ET AL, NATIONAL COMMISSION ON TERRORIST ATTACKS UPON THE UNITED STATES, MONOGRAPH ON TERRORIST FINANCING: STAFF REPORT TO THE COMMISSION 86 (Washington, D.C.: Gov't Printing Office 2004), *available at* http://www.govinfo.librarry.unt.edu/911/staff_statements911_TerrFin_Monograph.pdf.

National Commission on Terrorist Attacks upon the United States. (Philip Zelikow, Executive Director; Bonnie D. Jenkins, Counsel; Ernest R. May, Senior Advisor). *The 9/11 Commission Report.* New York: W.W. Norton & Company, 2004.

NATIONAL COMMISSION ON TERRORIST ATTACKS, THE 9/11 COMMISSION REPORT: FINAL REPORT OF THE NATIONAL COMMISSION ON TERRORIST ATTACKS UPON THE UNITED STATES 169 (W.W. Norton & Company 2004) *available at* http://www.9–11commission.gov/report/911 Report.pdf.

RAPHAEL PERL, CONG. RESEARCH SERV., Order Code IB10119, TERROR-ISM AND NATIONAL SECURITY: ISSUES AND TRENDS (2004), *available at* www.fas.org/irp/crs/IB10119.pdf.

RICHARD BARRETT, *Al-Qaeda and Taliban Sanctions Threatened,* The Washington Institute of Near East Policy (Oct. 6, 2008).

Tenth Report of the Analytical Support and Sanctions Monitoring Team, S/2009/502 (Oct. 2, 2009).

Terrorist Assets Report, Eighteenth Annual Report to Congress on Assets in the United States of Terrorist Countries and International Terrorism Program Designees 4, Office of Foreign Assets Control, U.S. Dep't of Treasury (2009).

UN General Assembly, Report of the Special Rapporteur [Martin Scheinin] on the Promotion and protection of human rights and fundamental freedoms while countering terrorism, A/61/267, New York, 16 August 2006.

U.N. SECURITY COUNCIL RESOLUTIONS:

S.C. Res. 1368, U.N. Doc. S/RES/1368 (Sept. 12th, 2001).

S.C. Res. 1214 , U.N. Doc. S/RES/1214 (Dec. 8th, 1998).

S.C. Res. 1267, U.N. Doc. S/RES/1267 (Oct. 15th, 1999).

S.C. Res. 1333, U.N. Doc. S/RES/1333 (Dec. 19th, 2000).

S.C. Res. 1526, U.N. Doc. S/RES/1526 (January 30th, 2004).

S.C. Res. 1566, U.N. Doc. S/RES/1566 (October 8th, 2004).

S.C. Res. 1617, U.N. Doc. S/RES/1617 (July 29th, 2005).

S.C. Res. 1904, U.N. Doc. S/RES/1904 (Dec. 19th 2009).

S.C. Res. 1696, U.N. Doc. S/RES/1696 (July 31th, 2006).

S.C. Res. 1737, U.N. Doc. S/RES/1737 (Dec. 27, 2006).

S.C. Res. 1747, U.N. Doc. S/RES/1747 (Mar. 24th, 2007).

GENERAL ASSEMBLY RESOLUTIONS:

Declaration on Measures to Eliminate International Terrorism, U.N. G.A. Res. 49/60, ¶ 1 (9 December, 1994).

Human Rights and Terrorism, U.N. G.A. Res. 59/195, ¶ 1 (20 December 2004).

Measures to eliminate international terrorism, U.N. G.A. Res. 46/51, U.N. Doc. A/46/654 (December 9th, 1991).

Protection of Human Rights and Fundamental Freedoms While Countering Terrorism, U.N. G.A. Res. 59/191, preamble (December 20th, 2004).

United Nations Global Counter–Terrorism Strategy ,G.A. Res. 60/288, U.N. Doc. A/RES/60/288 (Sept. 20th, 2006).

INTERNATIONAL CONVENTIONS:

Geneva Convention Relative to the Treatment of Prisoners of War (Aug. 12, 1949), 75 U.N.T.S. 135, 6 U.S.T. 3316, T.I.A.S. No. 3364.

International Convention for the Suppression of the Financing of Terrorism, Dec. 9, 1999, T.I.A.S. No. 13075, 2178 U.N.T.S. 229.

International Convention for the Suppression of Terrorist Bombings, G.A. Res. 52/164, U.N. Doc. A/RES/52/164 (Dec. 15th, 1997).

MISCELLANEOUS:

Al–Qaida and Taliban Sanctions Committee, Fact Sheet on Listing, *available at* http://ww.un.org/sc/committees/1267/fact_sheet_listing. shtml

An Attack on Us All: NATO's Response to Terrorism (Oct. 10, 2001), *available at* http://www.nato.int/cps/en/natolive/opinions.

Benjamin Wittes, Robert M. Chesney, and Rabea Benhalim, *The Emerging Law of Detention: The Guantánamo Habeas Cases as Lawmaking*, Brookings, January 22, 2010.

CENTER FOR LAW AND MILITARY OPERATIONS, THE JUDGE ADVOCATE GENERAL'S LEGAL CENTER & SCHOOL, U.S. ARMY, LEGAL LESSONS LEARNED FROM AFGHANISTAN AND IRAQ VOLUME I MAJOR COMBAT OPERATIONS (11 SEPT. 2001–1 MAY 2003).

Geoffrey S. Corn & Eric Talbot Jensen, *The Obama Administration's First Year and IHL: A Pragmatist Reclaims the High Ground,* Yearbook of International Humanitarian Law (forthcoming), *available at* http://papers.ssrn.com/sol3/papers.cfm?abstract_id =1596962.

Geoffrey S. Corn, *Making the Case for Conflict Bifurcation in Afghanistan: Transnational Armed Conflict, Al Qaida, and the Limits of the Associated Militia Concept,* International Law Studies (U.S. Naval War College), Vol. 85, 2009 (republished in the Israeli Yearbook of Human Rights).

INT'L & OPERATIONAL LAW DEP'T, THE JUDGE ADVOCATE GENERAL'S LEGAL CTR. & SCH., LAW OF WAR DESKBOOK (2010) *available at* http://www.loc. gov/rr/frd/Military_Law/pdf/LOW–Deskbook.pdf.

INT'L & OPERATIONAL LAW DEP'T, THE JUDGE ADVOCATE GENERAL'S LEGAL CTR. & SCH., THE LAW OF WAR DESKBOOK (2000).

INT'L & OPERATIONAL LAW DEP'T, THE JUDGE ADVOCATE GENERAL'S SCHOOL, U.S. ARMY, OPERATIONAL LAW HANDBOOK 86 (MAJ John Rawcliffe, ed., 2007).

International Committee of the Red Cross (ICRC), *Geneva Convention for the Amelioration of the Condition of the Wounded and Sick in Armed Forces in the Field (First Geneva Convention),* 12 August

1949, 75 UNTS 31, *available at* http://www.unhcr.org/refworld/docid/3ae6b3694.html (last visited August 11, 2010).

International Committee of the Red Cross (ICRC), *Geneva Convention for the Amelioration of the Condition of Wounded, Sick and Shipwrecked Members of Armed Forces at Sea (Second Geneva),* 12 August 1949, 75 U.N.T.S. 85, available at http://www.unhcr.org/refworld/docid/3ae6b37927.html (last visited Aug. 11, 2010).

International Committee of the Red Cross (ICRC), *Geneva Convention Relative to the Treatment of Prisoners of War (Third Geneva Convention),* 12 August 1949, 75 UNTS 135, *available at* http://www.unhcr.org/refworld/docid/3ae6b36c8.html (last visited Aug. 11, 2010).

International Committee of the Red Cross (ICRC), *Geneva Convention Relative to the Protection of Civilian Persons in Time of War (Fourth Geneva Convention),* 12 August 1949, 75 UNTS 287, *available at* http://www.unhcr.org/refworld/docid/3ae6b36d2.html (last visited Aug. 11, 2010).

International Committee of the Red Cross, INTERPRETIVE GUIDANCE ON THE NOTION OF DIRECT PARTICIPATION IN HOSTILITIES (May 2009).

International Committee of the Red Cross, *What is International Humanitarian Law,* Advisory Service on International Humanitarian Law, (07/2004), *available at http://www.icrc.org/Web/eng/siteeng 0.nsf/iwpList104/707D6551B17F0910C1256B66005B30B3.*

International Law Association, Use of Force Committee, Final Report on the Meaning of Armed Conflict in International Law, 25–28 (2010), *available at* http://www.ila-hq.org/en/committees/index.cfm/cid/1022.

Kirby Abott, *Terrorists: Combatants, Criminals, or ... ?,* published in THE MEASURES OF INTERNATIONAL LAW: EFFECTIVENESS, FAIRNESS, AND VALIDITY, Proceedings of the 31st Annual Conference of the Canadian Council on International Law, Ottawa, October 24–26, 2002.

NATIONAL STRATEGY FOR COMBATING TERRORISM 17 (2003) , *available at* http://www.cia.gov/news-information/cia-the-war-on-terrorism/counter_terrorism_strategy.pdf.

Nils Melzer, Legal Adviser, International Committee of the Red Cross, INTERPRETIVE GUIDANCE ON THE NOTION OF DIRECT PARTICIPATION IN HOSTILITIES UNDER INT'L HUMANITARIAN LAW (May 2009), *available at* http://www.icrc.org/Web/Eng/siteeng0.nsf/htmlall/p0990/$File/ICRC_002_0990.pdf.

Office of Foreign Assets Control list of specially designated global terrorists (SDGTs), *available at* http://www.treas.gov/offices/enforcement/ofac/programs/terror/terror.pdf (last visited May 30, 2010).

Operational Law Handbook (John Rawcliffe ed. The Judge Advocate General's Legal Center & School, U.S. Army) (2007) *available at* http://www.fas.org/irp/doddir/army/law2007.pdf.

RESTATEMENT (SECOND) OF FOREIGN RELATIONS LAW.

RESTATEMENT (THIRD) OF FOREIGN RELATIONS LAW.

Tenth Report of the Analytical Support and Sanctions Monitoring Team, S/2009/502, (OCT. 2, 2009).

Treaties in Force, available at http://treaties.un.org/pages/View Details.aspx?src=UNTSONLINE & tabid=1 & mtdsg_no=XVIII–10 & chapter=18 & lang=en#Participants.

U.S. CONST. amend. IV

U.S. CONST. amend. V

U.S. CONST. amend. I

U.S. DEP'T OF ARMY, FIELD MANUAL 27–10, THE LAW OF LAND WARFARE (July 1956).

U.S. Dep't of Treasury, National Money Laundering Strategy 7 (2003), *available at* http://www.treasury.gov/offices/enforcement/publications/ml2003.pdf.

US DEPARTMENT OF ARMY, FIELD MANUAL 6–20–10, TACTICS, TECHNIQUES AND PROCEDURES FOR THE TARGETING PROCESS (May 1996).

Index

461

✝